Neuropsychology of HIV Infection

Neuropsychology of HIV Infection

EDITED BY

Igor Grant, M.D., F.R.C.P. (C)
Professor of Psychiatry
Director, HIV Neurobehavioral Research Center
University of California, San Diego
La Jolla, California
Chief of Ambulatory Care for Psychiatry
Veterans Affairs Medical Center,
San Diego, California

Alex Martin, Ph.D.
Chief, Cognitive Studies Unit
Laboratory of Clinical Science
National Institute of Mental Health
Bethesda, Maryland

New York   Oxford
OXFORD UNIVERSITY PRESS
1994

Oxford University Press

Oxford   New York   Toronto
Delhi   Bombay   Calcutta   Madras   Karachi
Kuala Lumpur   Singapore   Hong Kong   Tokyo
Nairobi   Dar es Salaam   Cape Town
Melbourne   Auckland   Madrid

and associated companies in
Berlin   Ibadan

Library of Congress Cataloging-in-Publication Data
Neuropsychology of HIV Infection / edited by Igor Grant, Alex Martin,
p. cm.   Includes bibliographical references and index.
ISBN 0-19-507225-1
1. Nervous system—Infections—Complications.
2. Clinical neuropsychology.
3. HIV infections—Complications.
I. Grant, Igor, 1942–   . II. Martin, Alex, 1949–   .
[DNLM: 1. HIV Infections—psychology.
2. HIV Infections—complications.
3. Neurologic Manifestations.
4. Cognition Disorders—etiology.
WD 308 N4945 1994] RC347.N4825 1994   616.97′92—dc20
DNLM/DLC   93-26567

1 3 5 7 9 8 6 4 2

Printed in the United States of America
on acid-free paper

Preface

Acquired immune deficiency syndrome (AIDS) as we understand it today was first observed in 1981 when a few cases of unexplained diseases linked to collapse of cell-mediated immunity were described. At the time of this writing, there are estimated to be well over two million persons worldwide suffering with AIDS and over 12 million infected by human immunodeficiency virus type 1 (HIV-1).

Disorders in neurological functioning were being reported by 1982, but their causes remained obscure until HIV-1 was discovered and its presence was detected in the brains of persons dying with AIDS. Now we know that the majority of those dying with AIDS have HIV-1 present in the brain, and that perhaps 15% will suffer, in the advanced phase of their disease, from an incapacitating dementia.

Perhaps of greater importance, because far more individuals are affected, is the onset of mild neurocognitive disorders (minor cognitive-motor disorder) that can manifest themselves at the earliest stages after HIV infection. The signs include slowing of information processing, defects in attention, and disturbance in encoding and retrieval of information. These disorders can be subtle, and may require sophisticated neuropsychological assessments to reveal them. Although it is still unclear how early in the course of disease such disorders first become apparent, their presence in even a small minority of medically asymptomatic persons can translate into millions of young individuals becoming neuropsychologically impaired during the most productive periods of their lives. Seen in this light, the public health importance of these complications becomes apparent, as does the need to establish comprehensive, valid, reliable, and culturally relevant approaches to neuropsychological assessment of HIV-infected persons.

From a more academic standpoint, neuropsychology is playing an increasing role in efforts to understand the etiology and pathogenesis of HIV-associated brain disease. Neuropsychologists were among the first to point out that the pattern of cognitive impairment appeared to be "subcortical" in nature, an observation that was confirmed by neuropathological evidence and imaging studies suggesting early involvement of basal ganglia and other deep structures.

In the future, neuropsychological approaches will play an increasingly important role in linking early disturbances in behavior to results from dynamic brain imaging, electrophysiology, and ultimately, quantitated neuropathologic approaches to regional brain damage. As the pathogenesis of this retrovirally induced brain disease becomes clarified, there may be opportunities for pharmacological interventions that will require neuropsychological evidence of efficacy. For neuropsychology to play a decisive role in evaluating future treatments, it must first develop a firm foundation rooted in rigorous neurobehavioral observations of the many risk groups of HIV-infected persons. Such observations must be longitudinal in nature and must sample behaviors at different phases of infection.

The main purpose of this book is to summarize neuropsychological insights to date and to provide a basis for future research and development of theory. In keeping with our goals, we are fortunate to have secured contributions from most of the principal research groups working on the neuropsychology of HIV at the present time. The authors give us not only summaries of their own work and other research, but more importantly, insights into the meaning of the phenomena that we are all observing.

To conclude this preface, we want to express particular gratitude to Mary Beth Hiller in Igor Grant's office who assisted us with copy editing, tracking of manuscripts, communications among the authors, and interactions with our publisher. We want to thank also Jeffrey House, Vice President of Oxford University Press, for his encouragement of this work, and helpful critiques of the manuscript during its development. And, of course, we thank our distinguished group of authors for their thoughtful and timely contributions.

La Jolla, California   IGOR GRANT

Bethesda, Maryland   ALEX MARTIN

Contents

Contributors

JAMES T. BECKER, Ph.D.
Associate Professor of Psychiatry and
    Neurology
Neuropsychology Research Program
Department of Psychiatry
University of Pittsburgh Medical Center
Pittsburgh, Pennsylvania

ROBERT A. BORNSTEIN, Ph.D.
Professor and Associate Chairman
Department of Psychiatry
Neuropsychology Program
Ohio State University
Columbus, Ohio

PIM BROUWERS, Ph.D.
Head, Neuropsychology Unit
Clinical Oncology Program
Pediatric Branch
National Cancer Institute
Bethesda, Maryland

KAREN CASPER, B.A.
Department of Neurology
University of Texas Medical Branch
Galveston, Texas

LESLEY R. DICKSON, M.D.
Associate Professor of Psychiatry
Lexington Veterans Affairs and University of
    Kentucky Medical Center
Lexington, Kentucky

LEE E. EIDEN, Ph.D.
Section on Molecular Neuroscience
Laboratory of Cell Biology
National Institute of Mental Health
Bethesda, Maryland

FRANCISCO FERNANDEZ, M.D.
Associate Professor of Psychiatry
Baylor College of Medicine
Chief, Psychiatric Consultation Service
St. Luke's Episcopal Hospital
Houston, Texas

BENJAMIN B. GELMAN, M.D., Ph.D.
Department of Pathology/Neuropathology
The University of Texas Medical
    Branch
Galveston, Texas

IGOR GRANT, M.D., F.R.C.P.(C)
Chief, Ambulatory Psychiatry Service
San Diego Veterans Affairs Medical Center
Professor of Psychiatry
University of California, San Diego
La Jolla, California

ROBERT K. HEATON, Ph.D.
Professor of Psychiatry
University of California, San Diego
La Jolla, California

WILLIAM C. HEINDEL, Ph.D.
Department of Neurosciences
San Diego Veterans Affairs Medical Center
San Diego, California

JOHN R. HESSELINK, M.D.
Professor of Radiology and Neurosciences
Chief of Neuroradiology and Magnetic
  Resonance
University of California, San Diego
La Jolla, California

GILBERT R. HILLMAN, Ph.D.
Professor, Department of Pharmacology
The University of Texas Medical Branch
Galveston, Texas

TERRY L. JERNIGAN, Ph.D.
Staff Psychologist
San Diego Veterans Affairs Medical Center
Associate Professor of Psychiatry and
  Radiology
University of California, San Diego
La Jolla, California

THOMAS A. KENT, M.D.
Associate Professor
Departments of Neurology, Psychiatry, and
  Behavioral Sciences
The University of Texas Medical Branch
Galveston, Texas

DONALD KIRSON, Ph.D.
San Diego HIV Neurobehavioral Research
  Center
Department of Psychiatry
University of California, San Diego
La Jolla, California

HANS A. LANGSJOEN, M.D.
Assistant Professor
Departments of Neurology and Internal
  Medicine
The University of Texas Medical Branch
Galveston, Texas

HARVEY S. LEVIN, Ph.D.
Professor of Neurological Surgery
University of Maryland Medical System
Baltimore, Maryland

JOEL K. LEVY, Ph.D.
Assistant Professor of Psychiatry (Psychology)
Baylor College of Medicine

Director, Neurobehavioral Assessment and
  Rehabilitation Program
St. Luke's Episcopal Hospital
Houston, Texas

OSCAR L. LOPEZ, Ph.D.
Assistant Professor of Neurology
Alzheimer's Disease Research Center
University of Pittsburgh Medical
  Center
Pittsburgh, Pennsylvania

ALEX MARTIN, Ph.D.
Chief, Cognitive Studies Unit
Laboratory of Clinical Science
National Institute of Mental Health
Bethesda, Maryland

JUSTIN C. MCARTHUR M.B.,B.S.; M.P.H.
Associate Professor of Neurology and
  Epidemiology
Johns Hopkins University
Baltimore, Maryland

J. ALLEN MCCUTCHAN, M.D.
Professor of Medicine
Department of Medicine
University of California, San Diego
La Jolla, California

ERIC N. MILLER, Ph.D.
Assistant Professor of Psychiatry
Department of Psychiatry and Behavioral
  Sciences
Neuropsychiatric Institute and Hospitals
University of California, Los Angeles
Los Angeles, California

HOWARD MOSS, Ph.D.
Pediatric Branch
National Cancer Institute
Bethesda, Maryland and
Medical Illness Counseling Center
Chevy Chase, Maryland

ELISABETH A. MURRAY, Ph.D.
Laboratory of Neuropsychology
National Institute of Mental Health
Bethesda, Maryland

MADHAVAN P.N. NAIR, Ph.D.
Allergy and Immunology Division
SUNY–Buffalo
Buffalo General Hospital
Buffalo, New York

DIANE M. RAUSCH, Ph.D.
Section on Molecular Neuroscience
Laboratory of Cell Biology
National Institute of Mental Health
Bethesda, Maryland

PEDRO RUIZ, M.D.
Professor of Psychiatry
Baylor College of Medicine
Chief, Psychiatric Service
Ben Taub General Hospital
Houston, Texas

FREDERICK A. SCHMITT, Ph.D.
Associate Professor of Neurology, Psychiatry
    and Psychology
Sanders-Brown Center on Aging Associate
University of Kentucky Medical Center
Lexington, Kentucky

STANLEY A. SCHWARTZ, M.D., Ph.D.
Professor of Pediatrics, Epidemiology and
    Microbiology/Immunology
Allergy and Immunology Division
SUNY–Buffalo
Buffalo General Hospital
Buffalo, New York

OLA A. SELNES, Ph.D.
Assistant Professor
Cognitive Neurology
Johns Hopkins University School of Medicine
Baltimore, Maryland

YAAKOV STERN, Ph.D.
Associate Professor of Clinical
    Neuropsychology
Departments of Neurology and Psychiatry
College of Physicians and Surgeons of
    Columbia University
New York, New York

ROBERT A. VELIN, Ph.D.
Assistant Project Scientist and Manager
San Diego HIV Neurobehavioral Research
    Center
Department of Psychiatry
University of California, San Diego
La Jolla, California

FRANCES WILKIE, Ph.D.
Research Associate Professor
Department of Psychiatry
University of Miami School of Medicine
Miami, Florida

PAMELA WOLTERS, Ph.D.
Pediatric Branch
National Cancer Institute
Bethesda, Maryland and
Medical Illness Counseling Center
Chevy Chase, Maryland

Neuropsychology of HIV Infection

Introduction: Neurocognitive Disorders Associated with HIV-1 Infection

IGOR GRANT and ALEX MARTIN

Neurobehavioral complications occur commonly in persons infected with type 1 human immunodeficiency virus (HIV-1) (Grant, 1990). From an etiologic standpoint, it is convenient to think of these complications as either *neurobiologic* or *psychobiologic*. This division recognizes that the main sources of neurobehavioral morbidity are those that reflect disturbance in brain function and structure, on the one hand, and efforts to cope, on the other (Grant and Atkinson, 1990b).

Figure I–1 summarizes the main categories of etiology. Note that the neurobiologic disorders are divided into primary and secondary causes. *Primary* refers to those neurobiologic complications—mainly neurocognitive—that reflect the influence of HIV-1 on the central nervous system. It is these neurocognitive complications—and the contributions being made by neuropsychology to understanding them—that are the main focus of this book.

To set the stage for the following chapters, this Introduction provides a summary of our current understanding of the effects of infection with HIV-1 on the brain and behavior. To make sense of the neuropsychological features of HIV-1 infection, readers must have a basic grasp of the essential medical features of this condition.

HIV-1 Infection: Clinicopathological Features

There are two main forms of immunity: humoral and cell-mediated. Humoral immunity involves production of circulating proteins called *antibodies*. These attach to materials previously determined to be foreign and facilitate the neu-

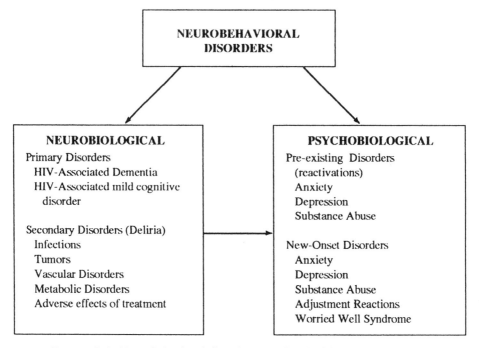

FIGURE I–1. Neurobehavioral disorders associated with HIV-1 infection.

tralization and elimination of such material. Humoral immunity, which is heavily dependent on the functioning of a type of immune cell termed the *B cell,* protects against common bacterial pathogens (e.g., pertussis) and toxins (e.g., diphtheria).

Cell-mediated immunity is important in protection against many viruses, fungi, and cancers. This form of immunity is orchestrated by a type of immune cell termed the *T cell.* Specifically, a T-cell subset termed *T4* (or *CD4+*) is critical in initiating and coordinating the activity of several other immune cells.

Acquired immunodeficiency syndrome (AIDS) is a clinical syndrome resulting from the collapse of cell-mediated immunity. The primary cause is infection with HIV-1. Infection with HIV-2 has been identified in parts of western and central Africa; while HIV-2 can also cause AIDS, the overwhelming majority of AIDS cases are linked to HIV-1.

Globally, two main patterns of spread have been identified. In Western countries, male homosexual intercourse and the sharing of contaminated paraphernalia among drug addicts remain the primary mechanisms, with smaller numbers of cases resulting from heterosexual intercourse and vertical (i.e., from mother to child during pregnancy) transmission. Medical transmission (e.g., via contaminated blood or instruments) is now extremely uncommon. In non-Western countries, heterosexual intercourse and vertical transfer account for the majority of cases of transmission; infections through contaminated blood products and medical instruments remain important risks as well.

The scope of HIV infection can be appreciated from Table I–1. It is esti-

TABLE I–1. Current and Projected HIV Infected and AIDS Cases by Geographic Area of Affinity[a]

Region	Infected with HIV		AIDS	
	All Adults 1992 (est.)	All Adults 1995 (proj.)	Adults 1992 (est.)	Adults 1995 (proj.)
North America	1,167	1,495	257.5	534.0
Western Europe	718	1,186	99.0	279.5
Australia/Oceania	28	40	4.5	11.5
Latin America	995	1,407	173.0	417.5
Sub-Saharan Africa	7,803	11,449	1,367.0	3,277.5
Caribbean	310	474	43.0	121.0
Eastern Europe	27	44	2.5	9.5
Southeast Mediterranian	35	59	3.5	12.5
Northeast Asia	41	80	3.5	14.5
Southeast Asia	675	1,220	65.0	240.5
Total	11,799	27,454	2,018.5	4.918.0

Source: Mann, J., Tarantola, D., and Netter, T.W. *AIDS in the World.* Cambridge, Mass., Harvard University Press, 1992.

[a]Estimates and projections of cumulative cases in thousands.

This table also appears in a chapter by Igor Grant and J. Hampton Atkinson, "Psychobiology of HIV Infection", to appear in the *Comprehensive Textbook of Psychiatry/VI* (Kaplan, H.I. and Sadock, B.J., Eds.), Baltimore: Williams and Wilkins, in press.

mated that approximately 2 million persons worldwide have AIDS, and close to 12 million may be infected with HIV-1. Those numbers are projected to rise dramatically in the next several years, to catastrophic proportions in sub-Saharan Africa and parts of Asia.

HIV-1 produces disease by progressively destroying the T4 lymphocyte subset that coordinates cell-mediated immunity, as well as other immune functions. The structure of HIV-1 and its mode of replication are described in Chapter 1. While the exact mechanisms are unclear, the effect of HIV-1 infection is to deplete the supply of T4 cells. Their number drops from $1000/mm^3$ of blood in the healthy individual to well below $200/mm^3$ in the typical patient with AIDS. The likelihood that a person will develop severe infections or cancers linked to immunodeficiency (such as Kaposi's sarcoma or lymphomas) increases markedly when the T4 count drops below $200/mm^3$.

As indicated in Chapter 1, we are in a period of transition regarding the system for classifying HIV-1 infection. At the time this book was written, the system in force was that proposed by the U.S. Centers for Disease Control (CDC) in 1986/87. Under this system there were four classes of infection. CDC I referred to signs and symptoms (usually self-limited and often resembling a flu-like illness) that developed in the period soon after infection. CDC II defined persons who were carriers of HIV-1 but were either totally asymptomatic from a medical standpoint or had only minor symptoms. CDC III identified individuals who had enlarged lymph nodes (generalized lymphadenopathy) but were otherwise asymptomatic, as in CDC II. CDC IV comprised persons who met the AIDS surveillance case definition and included those with major opportunistic infections, neoplasms, or severe systemic symptoms. The CDC (1987) system is described in more detail in Chapter 1.

In 1992, the CDC published new criteria termed the 1993 Revised Classification System for HIV Infection (CDC, 1992). This classification system permits assignment of HIV-infected individuals to clinical categories, as well as to levels based on their T4 counts. The 1993 system defines Category A as persons who are essentially asymptomatic, Category B as those with minor opportunistic infections (most of these were previously in CDC stage IVc2), and Category C as all of those who formerly would have been termed CDC IV (except for category IVc2). Once again, readers are referred to Chapter 1 for a further exposition of this topic. Note, however, that since the 1993 system was not available at the time this book was written, the CDC (1987) system remains in use throughout this volume.

Regardless of which classification system is employed, it is important to recognize that the vast majority of HIV-1-infected persons are medically asymptomatic or that, if they have symptoms, these symptoms do not meet the criteria for AIDS. For example, in the United States it is estimated that there are 10 asymptomatic carriers for every patient with AIDS. The length of the asymptomatic period is variable, though the median time from infection to an AIDS-defining diagnosis is estimated to be 10 years. Once AIDS is diagnosed, the typical length of survival is thought to be between 3 and 4 years, though again, there is great variability. The forms of treatment currently available are discussed in Chapter 1.

HIV-1 and the Brain

HIV-1 can invade the central nervous system (CNS) early in the course of infection. In approximately half of the individuals studied in the earlier phases of illness (old CDC II and III), HIV-1 is present in cultures of cerebrospinal fluid (CSF) (Sonnerborg et al., 1988; McArthur et al., 1989). Furthermore, indirect evidence of an inflammatory response in the CSF comes from elevations in CSF protein, white blood cells, and beta-2-microglobulin (Marshall et al., 1988; Brew et al., 1989).

Among persons dying with AIDS, particularly those who experience more severe CNS complications, HIV-1 has been detected in the brain by a variety of techniques (Ho et al., 1985). Interestingly, the cells that most often show evidence of viral infection are from the mononuclear-microglial lines and include multinucleated giant cells (Wiley et al., 1986). Occasionally, infection is detected in endothelial cells. Rarely has virus actually been demonstrated in neurons themselves. Despite this, there is evidence of neuronal loss among those dying with HIV encephalitis (Everall et al., 1991; Wiley et al., 1991).

These data raise interesting questions about the pathogenesis of neuronal damage in HIV-1 infection. If HIV-1 is unlikely to infect neurons directly, then it must be that the presence of HIV-1 in other cells surrounding neurons produces damage in an indirect manner. It has been speculated that activated mononuclear cells or astrocytes may be capable of producing cytokines (e.g., interleukin-1, interleukin-6, tumor necrosis factor) that may interfere with neuronal function (Merrill and Chen, 1991). It is also possible that such cells generate abnormal neurotransmitter metabolites (e.g., quinolinic acid) that are neurotoxic (Giulian et al., 1990; Heyes et al., 1991). Yet another explanation may lie in the capacity of certain viral fragments (e.g., the envelope protein GP 120) to interfere with neuronal function by docking at critical receptor sites (Kimes et al., 1991).

Regardless of the explanation, the fact that neurons are not themselves invaded by HIV-1 raises the possibility that, in early phases of CNS disease, neuronal dysfunction may be reversible. This possibility indicates the importance of seeking appropriate antiretroviral treatments that can influence positively the course of the central nervous system infection, and it emphasizes the necessity of establishing valid and reliable criteria for cognitive dysfunction. Neuropsychological testing can play a critical role in such diagnostic assessment.

Neurocognitive Disorders

The most severe form of neurocognitive disorder is HIV-1-associated dementia (HAD). HAD has been described mainly among patients in the later stages of AIDS (Navia et al., 1986), though there have been occasional reports of dementia as the initial presentation of HIV-1 infection (Navia and Price, 1987).

The dementia is characterized initially by disturbances in learning new information, attention, and speeded information processing. Psychomotor slowing is typically evident. Neuromotor signs can include ataxia and incoordination. As the dementia evolves, a severe dementing syndrome can occur. This may be characterized by amnesia, profound psychomotor retardation, occasional agitation, disorientation, naming difficulties, and dyscontrol of mood and behavior. There may be lability of affect, aggressive outbursts, or inappropriate behavior. Ultimately, the demented person becomes bedridden and may suffer from severe incoordination, weakness, and loss of bladder and bowel control.

The prevalence of HAD is poorly understood. Earlier reports suggested that two-thirds or more of patients with AIDS would suffer from this severe complication. Our own limited experience (which, however, may represent one of the few incidence studies in a previously zidovudine [AZT]-untreated group) indicates a yearly incidence of 14% or a cumulative incidence of 28% after 2 years of follow-up of patients with AIDS and AIDS-related complex (ARC) (Day et al., 1992). Data from the Multi-Center AIDS Cohort Study (MACS) suggest an annual incidence of about 7% in later-stage patients (McArthur et al., 1993).

There are probably two reasons why these estimates have varied. First, there was no commonly agreed-upon definition of dementia associated with HIV-1 until recently (see Chapter 5 for discussion of the term *dementia*). Therefore, it is possible that cases of mild neurocognitive disorder (see below) were inappropriately classified as dementia because of imprecise criteria. We have proposed that the criteria for dementia should include the presence of deficits in at least two areas of cognitive ability, that the deficits should be sufficiently severe to interfere with daily function, and that no other cause (beyond HIV-1 infection) can explain the deficits (Grant and Atkinson, in press). The Working Group of the American Academy of Neurology has also published recommended criteria for dementia (1991). These criteria are presented and discussed in Chapters 3 and 5 and in the Epilogue.

Second, there may be trends in the data reflecting the reality that most subjects who are currently being studied will have received AZT much earlier in the course of their infection than was true in the mid- and late-1980s. Because AZT does seem to benefit neurocognitive performance, both in adults and in children (Pizzo et al., 1988; Schmitt et al., 1988; Chapters 14 and 16), and because there are data indicating improvements on brain imaging, it is possible that the more severe cognitive disorder, dementia, is actually declining in incidence.

The more common though less well-characterized behavioral complication of HIV-1 is termed *mild neurocognitive disorder*. This condition is diagnosed when two or more cognitive functions are impaired (as documented by suitable neuropsychological assessment) but when the level of impairment is not so severe as to have a marked impact on a person's day-to-day functioning (see Chapter 5 and the Epilogue for criteria).

There is general agreement that mild neurocognitive disorder occurs commonly in CDC IV disease (Grant and Atkinson, 1990a). Our own early work indicated that 54–78% of AIDS/ARC patients had at least mild neuropsychological deficit (Grant et al., 1987). Data from the San Francisco Cohort suggest that the rate of neuropsychological impairment in ARC patients may be about 44% (Janssen et al., 1989). The MACS data give the lowest prevalence, approximately 15% for CDC IV (McArthur et al., 1989; Miller et al., 1990).

There is least agreement about the prevalence of mild neurocognitive disorder in earlier stages of HIV infection (i.e., CDC II and III). Early data from our group indicated a substantial prevalence (44%) (Grant et al., 1987), but results from much larger studies such as the MACS, the San Francisco Cohort, and the Air Force Cohort (Goethe et al., 1989) showed no impairment at earlier stages of infection. Very recent findings from a series of studies supported by the National Institute of Mental Health (NIMH) appear to be converging on the conclusion that there is some increase in the likelihood of detecting mild neurocognitive disorder among "medically asymptomatic or mildly symptomatic" HIV-infected persons (Wilkie et al., 1990; Stern et al., 1991; Bornstein et al., 1992; Martin et al., 1992).

Data from the San Diego HIV Neurobehavioral Research Center (HNRC) indicate that the rate of impairment may be lower than we previously reported but substantially higher than that suggested by the MACS and San Francisco Cohorts. For example, on the basis of data analysis from 400 subjects, we find that neuropsychological impairment, based on ratings from an extensive battery of tests, ranges from 16% in HIV-negative at-risk controls (i.e., homosexual/ bisexual men) to 33% in HIV-positive, asymptomatic persons (i.e., CDC II and III) to 49% in CDC IV (see Chapter 9). The most common areas of impairment are in the learning of new information and in measures of attention and speeded information processing.

The reasons for disagreements in studies of asymptomatic persons are probably two. The first involves differences in sampling, and the second different methods of testing and interpretation of results.

Regarding sampling, it is clear that early work, based on small series, might have oversampled accidently groups of asymptomatic persons who were in the later stages of the asymptomatic period, or who were impaired for some reason unrelated to HIV-1, despite efforts to screen out multiple substance abusers, persons with head injuries, and the like. Some of the larger series, for example the MACS, might not have been free of sampling difficulties either, despite very generous sample size (Grant et al., 1992). For example, most subjects in the MACS appear to be fairly highly educated homosexual/bisexual men who entered the MACS because they were sufficiently health-conscious to want to engage in a longitudinal medical monitoring exercise. It might be argued that such persons are selected against being cognitively impaired in the first instance. Some evidence that this may be true comes from preliminary subanalyses of the MACS data. These suggest that among those CDC II-III persons who had a high school education or below, there was a substantial increase in the rate of neu-ropsychological impairment (36%) compared to education-matched controls (17%) (Satz et al., 1993).

The second source of disagreement among studies has to do with the selec-tion of neuropsychological tests and the manner in which the test results have been analyzed and reported. Until recently, the smaller studies have tended to use more extensive protocols and more sensitive neuropsychological tests. Larger studies, such as the MACS, have tended to use restricted assessments (e.g., five to six neuropsychological tests, several of which were not particularly sensitive to early cerebral dysfunction). The comparison of rates of impairment from such asymmetric designs is problematic.

A related issue has been the manner in which groups have been compared. Some studies have used parametric statistics (analysis of variance, *t*-tests), whereas others have used cut points to classify groups as impaired or not impaired. Because cognitive disorders, if present among asymptomatic patients, tend to be fairly subtle, it is not surprising that univariate comparisons may have difficulty detecting early changes. Despite this, at least one NIMH-funded study that examined over 200 persons did find statistically significant neuropsycholog-ical differences between asymptomatic HIV+ homosexual/bisexual men and matched controls on tests of verbal memory, language, and executive function (Stern et al., 1991).

The studies using the cut point approach have differed in the settings. For example, some studies have adopted the criterion of scoring at least two standard deviations below the mean on two tests as a requirement to be classified as impaired. Other studies have used the criterion of 1.5 standard deviations, and others have used still more varied criteria. It is evident that estimates of rates of impairment will differ substantially, depending on the cut points used.

Despite all of these difficulties, the five NIMH-funded studies that are in progress seem to favor the conclusion that mild neurocognitive disorder is more prevalent among HIV+ asymptomatic/mildly symptomatic persons compared to suitably matched controls. But it appears that this impairment does not occur in most individuals at early stages of disease.

An important unanswered question is whether individuals who have mild neurocognitive disorder inevitably progress to a more severe form of impairment with time. Some preliminary information indicates slow progression. For example, our group followed a limited series for 1 year and observed a mild decline in neuropsychological performance in 24% of CDC IV and 15% of CDC II/III persons (Grant et al., 1993a). Others noted a considerable amount of stability; that is, it seems possible that there may be a mild, stable, nonprogressive cognitive impairment associated with HIV-1 infection (Robertson et al., 1990). The possibility that there may be fluctuations in the level of cognitive impairment must not be overlooked, either. For example, it seems possible that HIV-1 infection in some persons produces a low-grade encephalitis that waxes and wanes, somewhat akin to the fluctuating course of the cognitive disorder associated with demyelinating disease. While there are no concrete data to support this possibility, it is one that should not be excluded given the fragmentary state of our knowledge.

Correlates from Brain Imaging

Early imaging studies, employing both computed tomography (CT) and magnetic resonance imaging (MRI), focused on secondary CNS complications, such as toxoplasmosis and progressive multifocal leukoencephalopathy, and tumors such as lymphoma. These early reports did indicate, however, that persons with dementia associated with HIV-1 were likely to have evidence of brain shrinkage-ventricular enlargement and sulcal widening (Post et al., 1986).

Our own early studies indicated four types of MRI-determined abnormality associated with ARC and AIDS (Grant et al., 1987, 1988). The first type included multiple foci of high signal intensity, most evident in T_2-weighted images. The second type of abnormality involved more confluent areas of high signal intensity, usually bilateral, and frequently in the centrum semiovale. The third type was manifested by generalized reduction in the volume of brain parenchyma, as evidenced by enlargement of ventricles and sulci. This type of abnormality could also coexist with the first two types. The final group of abnormalities consisted of solitary lesions of unknown significance. Sometimes these represented opportunistic infections or tumors, while other cases could have been areas of vascular abnormality or infarction whose relationship to HIV-1 was unclear.

Most studies indicate that the various types of abnormalities described above occur mainly in patients with AIDS (Post et al., 1991). Patients with ARC are probably also more likely to have such abnormalities, although the exact prevalence is unknown. With respect to HIV+ asymptomatic persons, most studies have not shown appreciable increases compared to controls (McArthur et al., 1989; see Chapter 4).

Current research is beginning to concentrate on quantitative MRI analysis at various stages of HIV-1 infection (Jernigan et al., 1993). As these more sophisticated quantitative studies emerge, it will be possible to determine more clearly whether the HIV+ asymptomatic individuals are more likely to have volume loss in critical areas of the brain or evidence of subtle white matter abnormality compared to controls. Furthermore, whether any such changes are progressive or fluctuating will need to be established. An additional challenge will be to relate MRI changes, if found, to cognitive performance (see Chapter 13).

There is now limited work on "dynamic" imaging in HIV infection. Positron emission tomography (PET) studies indicate that the utilization of radiolabeled glucose may actually be increased in subcortical structures in the earliest phases of HAD, only to decline below control levels in later stages of dementia (Rottenberg et al., 1987).

Studies with single photon emission computed tomography have shown reductions in both cortical and subcortical cerebral blood flow at all stages of HIV-1 infection. The tracers used have included technetium 99m hexamethylpropyleneamine oxime (Schielke et al., 1990) and iodine 123 Iodoamphetamine (IMP) (Dupont et al., 1991). Recent data from San Diego indicate that both CDC II-III and CDC IV persons have flow reductions, suggesting the possibility of changes in underlying metabolism. Interestingly, preliminary comparisons between HIV+ persons who have been on intermediate-term AZT treatment (e.g., 2–12 months) and those who were untreated (or treated for brief periods of time) suggest that intermediate-term treatment is associated with IMP uptake closer to that of uninfected controls (Dupont et al., 1991). Whether these data are indicative of normalization of IMP uptake as a correlate of longer AZT treatment remains to be determined. However, data such as these, if confirmed, would suggest that either flow or metabolic abnormality in the brain may be reversible after treatment with AZT.

This possibility would be consistent with neuropsychological data from both children and adults treated with AZT. These studies indicate that AZT treatment is associated with improvement in developmental milestones in children (see Chapter 16), as well as with modest improvement in cognitive functioning in adults (see Chapter 14). Limited PET scan data also suggest that there may be normalization in metabolic abnormality after AZT (Yarchoan et al., 1988).

Are HIV-Associated Mood Disorders Related to Neuropsychological Impairment?

Persons with HIV-1 infection commonly report symptoms of stress, anxiety, and depression (Ostrow et al., 1988). Interestingly, sero*negative* homosexual/bisexual men and intravenous drug users also report symptoms of anxiety and depression, and the rates of syndromic depression (meeting criteria for major depression) do not distinguish at-risk seronegatives from asymptomatic seropositives or from persons with AIDS (Atkinson et al., 1988; Williams et al., 1991). Therefore, it would be an oversimplification to say that becoming infected or ill with HIV "causes" psychiatric disturbance. Rather, in the Western context at least, persons who become infected come from groups at higher risk for various forms of psychopathology, and this may be reactivated at various points in the natural history of HIV-1 disease (Atkinson et al., 1988).

Be that as it may, the possibility may be raised that subtle neuropsychological disturbances found among some seropositive individuals might be explained by mood disturbance. While some early research suggested that this might be so (Kocsis et al., 1989; Temoshok et al., 1989), the preponderance of research suggests that mood symptoms and neuropsychological performance are largely independent (Heinrichs, 1987; Poutiainen et al., 1988; Fitzgibbon et al., 1989; Grunberger et al., 1989; Kovner et al., 1989; Hinkin et al., 1992; Grant et al., 1993b; Mapou et al., 1993).

For example, Tables I–2 and I–3 illustrate some recently reported data from a mood measure and neuropsychological test results in a group of 139 seropositive and seronegative men. Table I–2 shows that subjects classified as neuropsychologically impaired on a commonly employed test of speeded information processing (PASAT) were no more likely to be depressed on a self-report measure of mood (POMS) than were neuropsychologically intact individuals. Table I–3 confirms this nonassociation. Results of this factor analytic study indicate that mood symptoms and neuropsychological test performance are largely orthogonal.

These results are important to bear in mind as readers evaluate the neuropsychological findings in Part II of this book. Specifically, we believe that readers can be reasonably confident that the neuropsychological observations made by our contributing authors can be viewed as true reflections of the underlying condition of the brain rather than epiphenomena related to depressed mood or stress.

TABLE I–2. Subjects Classified as Depressed on the POMS Depression-Dejection Subscale or as Impaired on the PASAT

	POMS Classification[a]	
PASAT Classification[b]	Not Depressed	Depressed
Unimpaired		
Group IV	13	11
Group II and III	47	12
HIV–	32	4
Impaired		
Group IV	10	5
Group II and III	2	1
HIV–	2	0

Note: Subjects were grouped according to the classification system of the Centers for Disease Control (1986, 1987). POMS = Profile of Mood States; PASAT = Paced Auditory Serial Addition Test.

[a]Subjects scoring 15 points or less were classified as not depressed, and subjects scoring more than 15 points were classified as depressed.

[b]Subjects scoring 3.95 or lower were classified as unimpaired, and subjects scoring higher than 3.95 were classified as impaired.

This table also appears in the referenced article by Grant et al. (1993b). In the public domain.

TABLE I–3.   Varimax Rotated Factor Matrix Showing Variable Loadings of
Neuropsychological Tests and the POMS Depression-Dejection Subscale

	Factor			
	1 *Verbal Ability*	*2* *Spatial Ability*	*3* *Speeded* *Problem Solving*	*4* *Mood*
WAIS-R Vocabulary subtest	**.53**	.21	.20	−.41
WMS Story Memory[a]				
Trial 1	**.93**	.02	−.08	.09
Learning	**.90**	.03	−.19	.12
% loss	−.30	−.47	−.04	.47
WMS Visual Memory Span[a]				
Trial 1	.04	**.95**	−.12	.08
Learning	−.09	**.95**	−.14	−.01
% loss	−.46	−.09	−.06	.22
Trail Making Test, Part B	−.01	−.17	**.79**	.06
Category Test	−.17	.19	**.72**	.05
PASAT	−.04	.12	**.79**	.20
POMS Depression-Dejection	.06	.12	.13	**.80**

Note: Variables loadings ≥.5 are in bold face. POMS = Profile of Mood States; WAIS-R = Wechsler Adult Intelligence Scale-Revised; WMS = Wechsler Memory Scale; PASAT = Paced Auditory Serial Addition Test.

[a]Administered in accordance with the procedures of Heaton et al. (1978) and Heaton et al. (1986).

This table also appears in the referenced article by Grant et al. (1993b). In the public domain.

Plan of the Book

Having set the scientific context for this volume, we will briefly orient readers to the plan of this book. The chapters are grouped into two parts. Part I provides some basic medical (Chapter 1), immunological (Chapter 2), neurological (Chapter 3), and neuroradiological (Chapter 4) information that may be important as background to the neuropsychological issues discussed in Part II. Part II begins with a discussion of the history and current usage of the concept of dementia, particularly in regard to the distinction between dementia and milder forms of cognitive change (Chapter 5; see also the Epilogue). This is followed by an analysis of conceptual and methodological issues specifically associated with neuropsychological investigation of HIV-infected individuals (Chapter 6). We turn next to assessment issues. Chapter 7 discusses the advantages and disadvantages of computerized testing, and Chapter 8 describes the development of a screening instrument for detecting HIV-related cognitive change. In contrast to the screening battery/psychometric approach, the usefulness of clinical ratings for determining the presence and degree of impairment is addressed in Chapter 9. This clinical approach is expanded in Chapter 10, which tackles the difficult yet extremely important issue of determining the real-world clinical significance of an observed impairment. In keeping with the theme of methodological concerns, Chapter 11 discusses the problems associated with neuropsychological assessment of intravenous drug abusers and presents current findings on HIV-infected members of this subpopulation. The next chapters are primarily concerned with neuropsychological/neuropathological correlations. Evidence suggestive of involvement of the basal ganglia is presented in Chapter 12, and neuroimaging data are discussed in Chapter 13. Having characterized the nature of HIV-related neurocognitive dysfunction, we turn next to attempts at treatment. Chapter 14 reviews the effects of antiretroviral drugs on neuropsychological functioning, and Chapter 15 explores the usefulness of psychostimulants in alleviating HIV-related depression and associated problems. Because the effects of HIV seem to be somewhat different in the developing as compared to the adult nervous system, the neuropsychological consequences of HIV in infants and children are reviewed in detail in Chapter 16. Finally, a monkey model for HIV infection of the CNS, using the simian immunodeficiency virus (SIV), is described in Chapter 17. The correspondence between the types of motor and cognitive deficits in monkey and in humans, and the relationship between these deficits and the level of an endogenous neurotoxin found in the cerebrospinal fluid of both species, may be particularly noteworthy (see also Chapter 12). Part II concludes with an epilogue that highlights some of the central themes articulated in this volume.

We believe that the contents of this book are as current as a published volume can reasonably be, and that the scientific coverage is reasonably complete, drawing as it does from contributions of most of the major clinical investigative groups that have been addressing themselves to the neuropsychology of HIV in recent years. Nevertheless, we must bear in mind that the entire area of research on CNS consequences of HIV is an extremely dynamic and rapidly evolving one. While the fact that HIV neuropsychology is a "moving target" may be frustrating and challenging, there is no doubt that those neuropsychologists who become interested in it will be rewarded by contributing to a better understanding of the pathogenesis and treatment of HIV-associated neurocognitive disorders.

Acknowledgment

Supported by the National Institute of Mental Health (NIMH) and the San Diego HIV Neurobehavioral Research Center (HNRC), which is affiliated with the University of California, San Diego, the Naval Hospital, San Diego, and the San Diego Veterans Affairs Medical Center. The principal support for the HNRC is provided by NIMH Center Grant 5 P50 MH294 (HIV Neurobehavioral Research Center). The views expressed in this introduction are those of the authors and do not reflect the official policy or positions of the Department of the Navy, the Department of the Defense, nor the U.S. government.

We express our sincere thanks to Mary Beth Hiller and Mary Eskes for their fine assistance in preparing this manuscript.

References

Atkinson, J.H., Grant, I., Kennedy, C.J., Richman, D.D., Spector, S.A., and McCutchan, J.A. (1988). Prevalence of psychiatric disorders among men infected with human immunodeficiency virus. *Archives of General Psychiatry, 45*, 859–864.

Bornstein, R.A., Nasrallah, H.A., Para, M.F., Whitacre, C.C., Rosenberger, P., Fass, R.J., and Rice, R., Jr. (1992). Neuropsychological performance in asymptomatic HIV infection. *Journal of Neuropsychiatry and Clinical Neurosciences, 4*, 386–394.

Brew, B.J., Bhalla, R.B., Fleisher, M., Paul, M., Khan, A., Schwartz, M.K., and Price, R.W. (1989). Cerebrospinal fluid beta-2-microglobulin in patients infected with human immunodeficiency virus. *Neurology, 39*, 830–834.

Centers for Disease Control. (1986). Classification system for human T-lymphotropic virus Type III/lymphadenopathy-associated virus infections. *Morbidity and Mortality Weekly Report, 35*, 334–339.

Centers for Disease Control. (1987). Revision of the CDC surveillance case definition for acquired immune deficiency syndrome. *Morbidity and Mortality Weekly Report, 36*(Suppl. 1), 3S–15S.

Centers for Disease Control. (1992). 1993 revised classification system for HIV infection and expanded surveillance case definition for AIDS among adolescents and adults. *Morbidity and Mortality Weekly Report, 41*(Suppl. 44-17), 1–19.

Day, J., Grant, I., Atkinson, J.H., Brysk, L., McCutchan, A., Hesselink, J., Spector, S., and Richman, D. (1992). Incidence of AIDS dementia in a two year follow-up of AIDS and ARC patients on an initial phase II AZT placebo-controlled study: San Diego Cohort. *Journal of Neuropsychiatry and Clinical Neurosciences, 4*, 15–20.

Dupont, R., Grant, I., Lehr, P., Lamoureux, G., Heaton, R., McCutchan, A., and Halpern, S. (1991). Effect of treatment of human immunodeficiency virus (HIV-1) infection on 123-I iodoamphetamine (IMG) images. *Journal of Nuclear Medicine, 32*, 992 (abst).

Everall, I., Luthert, P., and Lantos P. (1991). Neuronal loss in the frontal cortex in HIV infection. *The Lancet, 337*, 1119–1121.

Fitzgibbon, M.L., Cella, D.F., Humfleet, G., Griffin, E., and Sheridan, K. (1989). Motor slowing in asymptomatic HIV infection. *Perceptual and Motor Skills, 68*, 1331–1338.

Giulian, D., Vaca, K., and Moonan, C.A. (1990). Secretion of neurotoxins by mononuclear phagocytes infected with HIV-1. *Science, 250*, 1593–1596.

Goethe, K.E., Mitchell, J.E., Marshall, D.W., Brey, R.L., Cahill, W.T., Leger, D., Hoy, L.J., and Boswell, N. (1989). Neuropsychological and neurological function of human immunodeficiency virus seropositive asymptomatic individuals. *Archives of Neurology, 49*, 129–133.

Grant, I. (1990). The neuropsychiatry of human immunodeficiency virus. *Seminars in Neurology, 10*, 267–275.

Grant, I., and Atkinson, J.H. (1990a). The evolution of neurobehavioural complications of HIV infection. *Psychological Medicine, 20*, 747–754.

Grant, I., and Atkinson, J.H. (1990b). Neurogenic and psychogenic correlates of HIV infection. In B.H. Waksman, ed., *Immunological Mechanisms in Neurologic and Psychiatric Disease.* New York: Raven Press, pp. 291–304.

Grant, I., and Atkinson, J.H. (in press). Psychobiology of HIV infection. In H.I. Kaplan and B.J. Sadock, eds., *Comprehensive Textbook of Psychiatry/VI.* Baltimore: Williams and Wilkins.

Grant, I., Atkinson, J.H., Hesselink, R., Kennedy, C.J., Richman, D.D., Spector, S.A., and McCutchan, J.A. (1987). Evidence for early central nervous system involvement in the acquired immunodeficiency syndrome (AIDS) and other human immunodeficiency virus (HIV) infections. Studies with neuropsychologic testing and magnetic resonance imaging. *Annals of Internal Medicine, 107*, 828–836.

Grant, I., Atkinson, J.H., Hesselink, J.R., Kennedy, C.J., Richman, D.D., Spector, S.A., and McCutchan, J.A. (1988). Human immunodeficiency virus-associated neurobehavioural disorder. *Journal of the Royal College of Physicians of London, 22,* 148–157.

Grant, I., Caun, K., Kingsley, D., McDonald, W.I., Pinching, A.J., and Trimble, M.R. (1992). Neuropsychological and NMR abnormalities in HIV infection. The St. Mary's-Queen Square Study. *Neuropsychiatry, Neuropsychology and Behavioral Neurology, 5,* 185–193.

Grant, I., Heaton, R.K., Velin, R., Kirson, D., Atkinson, J.H., Mehta, P., McCutchan, J.A., and Chandler, J. (1993a). Rates of cognitive impairment and prediction of neuropsychological decline in HIV+ persons: A 2-year follow-up. Paper presented at the 9th International Conference on AIDS, Berlin, June 7–11.

Grant, I., Olshen, R.A., Atkinson, J.H., Heaton, R.K., Nelson, J., McCutchan, J.A., and Weinrich, J.D. (1993b). Depressed mood does not explain neuropsychological deficits in HIV-infected persons. *Neuropsychology, 7,* 53–61.

Grunberger, J., Linzmayer, L., Pakesch, G., Pfersmann, D., Guggenberger, K., and Loimer, N. (1989). Psychometric and psychophysiological studies in AIDS patients with reference to the "declining performance syndrome"—level reduction. *Wiener Medizinische Wochenschrift, 139,* 175–178.

Heaton, R.K., Chelune, G.J., and Lehman, R.A.W. (1978). Using neuropsychological and personality tests to assess the likelihood of patient employment. *Journal of Nervous and Mental Disease, 166,* 408–416.

Heaton, R.K., Nelson, L.M., Thompson, D.S., Burks, J.S., and Franklin, G.M. (1985). Neuropsychological findings in relapsing-remitting and chronic-progressive multiple sclerosis. *Journal of Consulting and Clinical Psychology, 53,* 103–110.

Heinrichs, R.W. (1987). Does depression in patients with known or suspected cerebral disease contribute to impairment on the Luria-Nebraska Neuropsychological Battery? *International Journal of Neuroscience, 32,* 895–899.

Heseltine, P., Eaton, E., Buchsbaum, M., Parker, E., McGrail, M., Leedom, J., and Bridge, P. (1991). Effect of Peptide T on AIDS dementia complex (ADC); Correlation of PET scans and cognitive domains. Vol. I, abstract book for VII International Conference AIDS, Florence, Italy, June 16–21, p. 183.

Heyes, M., Brew, B.J., Martin, A., Price, R.W., Salazar, A.M., Sidtis, J.J., Yergey, J.A., Mouradian, M.M., Sadler, A.E., Keilp, J., Rubinow, D., and Markey, S.P. (1991). Quinolinic acid in cerebrospinal fluid and serum in HIV-1 infection: Relationship to clinical and neurological status. *Annals of Neurology, 29,* 202–208.

Hinkin, C.H., van Gorp, W.G., Satz, P., Weisman, J.D., Thommes, J., and Buckingham, S. (1992). Depressed mood and its relationship to neuropsychological test performance in HIV-1 seropositive individuals. *Journal of Clinical and Experimental Neuropsychology, 14,* 289–297.

Ho, D.D., Rota, D.E., Schooley, R.T., Kaplan, J.C., Allan, J.F., Groopman, J.E., Resnick, L., Felsenstein, D., Andrews, C.A., and Hirsch, M.S. (1985). Isolation of HTLV-III from cerebrospinal fluid and neural tissues of patients with neurological syndromes related to the acquired immunodeficiency syndrome. *New England Journal of Medicine, 313,* 1493–1497.

Janssen, R.S., Saykin, A.J., Cannon, L., Campbell, J., Pinsky, P.F., Hessol, N.A., O'Malley, P.M., Lifson, A.R., Doll, L.S., Rutherford, G.W., and Kaplan, J.E. (1989). Neurological and neuropsychological manifestations of HIV-1 infection: Association with AIDS-related complex but not asymptomatic HIV-1 infection. *Annals of Neurology, 26,* 592–600.

Jernigan, T.L., Archibald, S., Hesselink, J.R., Velin, R.A., McCutchan, J.A., Chandler, J., Grant, I., and the HNRC Group. (1993). Magnetic resonance imaging morphometric analysis of cerebral volume loss in human immunodeficiency virus infection. *Archives of Neurology, 50*, 250–255.

Kimes, A.S., London, E.D., Szabo, G., Raymon, L., and Tabakoff, B. (1991). Reduction of cerebral glucose utilization by the HIV envelope glycoprotein Gp-120. *Experimental Neurology, 112*, 224–228.

Kocsis, A.E., Church, J., Vernals, S., and Green, J. (1989). Personality, behavior and cognitive changes in AIDS as rated by patients and as related to neuropsychological test results. Abstract book for V International Conference on AIDS, Montreal, Canada, June 6–9, p. 385.

Kovner, R., Perecman, E., Lazar, W., Hainline, B., Kaplan, M.H., Lesser, M., and Beresford, R. (1989). Relation of personality and attention factors to cognitive deficits in human immunodeficiency virus-infected subjects. *Archives of Neurology, 46*, 274–277.

Mapou, R.L., Law, W.A., Martin, A., Kampen, D.A., Salazar, A.M., and Rundell, J.R. (1993). Neuropsychological performance, mood, and complaints of cognitive and motor difficulties in individuals infected with the human immunodeficiency virus. *Journal of Neuropsychiatry and Clinical Neuroscience, 5*, 86–93.

Marshall, D.W., Brey, R.L., Cahill, W.T., Houk, R.W., Zajac, R.A., and Boswell, R.N. (1988). Spectrum of cerebrospinal fluid findings in various stages of human immunodeficiency virus infection. *Archives of Neurology, 45*, 954–958.

Martin, A., Heyes, M.P., Salazar, A.M., Kampen, M.S., Williams, J., Law, W.A., Coats, M.E., and Markey, S.P. (1992). Progressive slowing of reaction time and increasing cerebrospinal fluid concentrations of quinolinic acid in HIV-infected individuals. *Journal of Neuropsychiatry and Clinical Neuroscience, 4*, 270–279.

McArthur, J.C., Cohen, B.A., Selnes, O.A., Kumar, A.J., Cooper, K., McArthur, J.H., Soucy, G., Cornblath, D.R., Chmiel, J.S., Wang, M.C., Starkey, D.L., Ginzburg, H., Ostrow, D., Johnson, R.T., Phair, J.P., and Polk, B.F. (1989). Low prevalence of neurological and neuropsychological abnormalities in otherwise healthy HIV-1-infected individuals: Results from the Multicenter AIDS Cohort Study. *Annals of Neurology, 26*, 601–611.

McArthur, J.C., Hoover, D.R., Bacellar, H., Miller, E.N., Cohen, B.A., Becker, J.T., Graham, N.M.H., McArthur, J.H., Selnes, O.A., Jacobson, L.P., Visscher, B.R., Concha, M., Saah, A. (1993). Dementia in AIDS patients: incidence and risk factors. *Neurology, 43*, 2245–2253.

Merrill, J.E., and Chen, I.S. (1991). HIV-1, macrophages, glial cells, and cytokines in AIDS nervous system disease. *The FASEB Journal, 5*, 2391–2397.

Miller, E.N., Selnes, O.A., McArthur, J.C., Satz, P., Becker, J.T., Cohen, B.A., Sheridan, K., Machado, A.M., Van Gorp, W.G., and Visscher, B. (1990). Neuropsychological performance in HIV-1-infected homosexual men: The Multicenter AIDS Cohort Study (MACS). *Neurology, 40*, 197–203.

Navia, B.A., Jordan, B.D., and Price, R.W. (1986). The AIDS dementia complex: I. Clinical features. *Annals of Neurology, 19*, 517–524.

Navia, B.A., and Price, R.W. (1987). The acquired immunodeficiency syndrome dementia complex as the presenting or sole manifestation of human immunodeficiency virus infection. *Archives of Neurology, 44*, 65–69.

Ostrow, D., Grant, I., and Atkinson, H. (1988). Assessment and management of the AIDS patient with neuropsychiatric disturbances. *Journal of Clinical Psychiatry, 49*, 14–22.

Pizzo, P.A., Eddy, J., Falloon, J., Balis, F., Murphy, R., Moss, H., Wolters, P., Brouwers, P., Jarosinski, P., Rubin, M., Broder, S., Yarchoan, R., Burnetti, A., Maha, M., Nusinoff-Lehrman, S., and Poplack, D. (1988). Effect of continuous intravenous infusion of zidovudine (AZT) in children with asymptomatic HIV infection. *New England Journal of Medicine, 319*, 889–896.

Post, M.J., Berger, J.R., and Quencer, R.M. (1991). Asymptomatic and neurologically symptomatic HIV-seropositive individuals: Prospective evaluation with cranial MR imaging. *Radiology, 178*, 131–139.

Post, M.J., Sheldon, J.J., Hensley, G.T., Soila, K., Tobias, J.A., Chan, J.C., Quencer, R.M., and Moskowitz, L.B. (1986). Central nervous system disease in acquired immunodeficiency syndrome: Prospective correlation using CT, MR imaging and pathologic studies. *Radiology, 158*, 141–148.

Poutiainen, E., Iivanainen, M., Elovaara, I., Valle, S.L., and Lahdevirta, J. (1988). Cognitive changes as early signs of HIV infection. *Acta Neurologica Scandinavica, 78*, 49–52.

Robertson, K.R., Wilkins, J., Robertson, W., van der Horst, C., and Hall, C. (1990). Neuropsychological changes in HIV seropositive subjects over time. Paper presented at the AIDS Conference, Monterey, California, June 16–19.

Rottenberg, D.A., Moeller, J.R., Strother, S.C., Sidtis, J.J., Navia, B.A., Dhawan, V., Ginos, J.Z., and Price, R.W. (1987). The metabolic pathology of the AIDS dementia complex. *Annals of Neurology, 22*, 700–706.

Satz, P., Morgenstern, H., Miller, E., Selnes, O., McArthur, J., Cohen, B., Wesch, J., Becker, J., Jacobson, L., D'Elia, L.F., van Gorp, W., and Visscher, B. (1993). Low education as a possible risk factor for cognitive abnormalities in HIV-1: Findings from the Multicenter AIDS Cohort Study (MACS). *Journal of Acquired Immune Deficiency Syndromes, 6*, 503–511.

Schielke, E., Tatsch, K., Pfister, H., Trenkwalder, C., Leinsinger, G., Kirsch, C., Matuschke, A., and Einhaupl, K. (1990). Reduced cerebral blood flow in early stages of human immunodeficiency virus infection. *Archives of Neurology, 4*, 1342–1345.

Schmitt, F.A., Bigley, J.W., McKinnis, R., Logue, P.E., Evans, R.W., Deucker, J.L., and the AZT Collaborative Working Group. (1988). Neuropsychological outcome of zidovudine (AZT) treatment of patients with AIDS and AIDS-related complex. *New England Journal of Medicine, 319*, 1573–1578.

Sonnerborg, A.B., Ehrnst, A.C., Bergdahl, S.K., Pehrson, P.O., Skoldenberg, B.R., and Strannegard, O.O. (1988). HIV isolation from cerebrospinal fluid in relation to immunological deficiency and neurological symptoms. *AIDS, 2*, 89–93.

Stern, Y., Marder, K., Bell, K., Chen, J., Dooneief, G., Goldsten, M.A., Mindry, D., Richards, M., Sano, M., Williams, J., Gorman, J., Ehrhardt, A., and Mayeux, R. (1991). Multidisciplinary baseline assessment of homosexual men with and without human immunodeficiency virus infection: Neurologic and neuropsychological findings. *Archives of General Psychiatry, 48*, 131–138.

Temoshok, L., Drexler, M., Canick, J.P., Sweet, D.M., and Hollander, H. (1989). Neuropsychological change on longitudinal assessment: Prevalence and pattern in HIV spectrum disorders. Abstract book for the V International Conference on AIDS, Montreal, Canada, p. 210.

Wiley, C.A., Masliah, E., Morey, M., Lemere, C., DeTeresa, R., Grafe, M., Hansen, L., and Terry, R. (1991). Neocortical damage during HIV infection. *Annals of Neurology, 29*, 651–657.

Wiley, C.A., Schrier, R.D., Nelson, J.A., Lampert, P.W., and Oldstone, M.B.A. (1986). Cellular localization of human immunodeficiency virus infection within the brains of acquired immune deficiency syndrome patients. *Proceedings of the National Academy of Science, 83*, 7089–7093.

Wilkie, F.L., Eisdorfer, C.E., Morgan, R., Lowenstein, D.A., and Szapocznik, J. (1990). Cognition in early human immunodeficiency virus infection. *Archives of Neurology, 4*, 433–440.

Williams, J.B., Rabkin, J.G., Remien, R.H., Gorman, J.M., and Ehrhardt, A.A. (1991). Multidisciplinary baseline assessment of homosexual men with and without human immunodeficiency virus infection. *Archives of General Psychiatry, 48*, 124–130.

Yarchoan, R., Thomas, R.V., Grafman, J., Wichman, A., Dalakas, M., McAtee, N., Berg, G., Fischl, M., Perno, C.F., Klecker, R.N., Buchbinder, A., Tay, S., Larson, S.M., Myers, C.E., and Broder, S. (1988). Long-term administration of 3'-azido-2',3' dideoxythymidine to patients with AIDS-related neurological disease. *Annals of Neurology, 23*, S82–S87.

I

BACKGROUND: MEDICAL, IMMUNOLOGICAL, AND NEUROLOGICAL ASPECTS OF HIV

1

Virology, Immunology, and Clinical Course of HIV Infection

J. ALLEN McCUTCHAN

This chapter provides an overview of the virology, immunology, clinical course, and general management of human immunodeficiency virus (HIV) infection, as understood through late 1992. The epidemiology of HIV-1, which has been recently reviewed by Blattner (1991), will not be covered.

Like all retroviruses, HIV carries its genetic code as ribonucleic acid (RNA). In contrast to other RNA viruses, retroviruses reproduce by transcribing their genetic code into double-stranded deoxyribonucleic acid (DNA) and inserting this DNA copy (provirus) into the DNA genome of the host cell. Retroviruses cause cancers, immune deficiency, and slowly progressive neurologic disease in animals (Teich, 1985). Three pathogenic human retroviruses, human lymphotrophic virus-type 1 (HTLV-1), HIV-1, and HIV-2, have been identified in the past decade. Other important neurological diseases (e.g., multiple sclerosis) also may be caused by as yet unidentified retroviruses.

The first human retrovirus to be discovered, HTLV-1, is the cause of a distinctive, progressive myelopathy (spinal cord disease) described clinically as tropical spastic paraparesis and renamed HTLV-1-associated myelopathy (HAM) when its association with HTLV-1 was discovered (Osame et al., 1984; Johnson, 1987). HAM has a prolonged incubation period, is associated with a genetic predisposition, and has a slowly progressive course. HTLV-1 also causes a distinctive group of cutaneous T-cell lymphomas concentrated in geographically restricted areas such as the Caribbean basin and southern Japan (Blattner et al., 1983).

The second human retrovirus, human immunodeficiency virus-type 1 (HIV-1), causes immunosuppression, resulting in the opportunistic infections and tumors that define the acquired immunodeficiency syndrome (AIDS). Several neurological syndromes, including myelopathy, peripheral neuropathies, and progressive dementia, are thought to reflect direct effects of HIV on the nervous system (McArthur, 1987; Price et al., 1988; see also Chapter 3). The third human retrovirus, HIV-2, has a structure and clinical spectrum similar to that of HIV but has not been as widely distributed geographically. The potentially enormous social consequences of epidemic HIV-1 and HIV-2 (hereafter referred to collectively as HIV) infection have attracted intense attention from the international biomedical research community.

The clinical symptoms, course, and treatment of neurological syndromes associated with HIV infection are under study. Simultaneously, pathologists and virologists have described the pattern of tissue damage and the localization of HIV and other opportunistic viruses (e.g., cytomegalovirus [CMV], one of the family of human herpesviruses) that frequently reactivate in immunosuppressed patients. On the basis of these data and previous studies of neurotropic retroviruses in animals, hypotheses about the pathogenesis (mechanisms of damage) of HIV in the immune and nervous systems are being developed. Much of the pathogenesis of HIV in the brain remains unclear despite the impressively detailed understanding of HIV itself.

Virology of Human Immunodeficiency Virus-1

Structure

The core of HIV and related retroviruses consists of two single strands of RNA and an RNA-dependent DNA polymerase (reverse transcriptase) enclosed in a rigid protein coat consisting of polymers of structural protein (gag; Galberhorn et al., 1987) (Figure 1–1). A fragment of host cell (e.g., human lymphocyte) membrane into which viral proteins are inserted encloses the viral core as it exits the cell to produce an outer envelope (Figure 1–2). Because infectivity depends on an intact envelope, detergents and oxidants that damage this relatively fragile membrane rapidly inactivate HIV.

Genetics

In the past decade many primate retroviruses have been cultivated in vitro, an essential step in understanding their biology. Since its identification in 1983 by Montagnier and colleagues in Paris, HIV has become the best-characterized virus (Barre-Sinoussi et al., 1983; Gallo et al., 1984). In its relatively small RNA genome, HIV has the codes for (1) several structural proteins that provide the rod-shaped core of mature virus particles (p6, p9, p17, and p24); (2) enzymes to catalyze reverse transcription (reverse transcriptase = RT), protein cleavage (protease = PROT), digestion of RNA (RNAse = RH), and viral integration into host cell DNA (integrase = INT); and (3) a complex array of regulatory proteins (tat, rev, and nef, vif, vpt, vpu) and binding sites for regulatory proteins (long terminal repeats = LTR) that govern the rate of viral replication (Haseltine

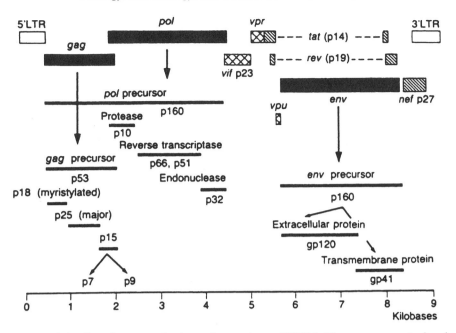

FIGURE 1–1. Genetic map and schematic structure of HIV-1. The arrangement of major structural genes (open boxes) and regulatory genes (shaped boxes) is illustrated above. The arrangement of the structural proteins in a mature, infectious virion is illustrated below. The proviral DNA is transcribed into long messenger RNA's which are further processed (cut and spliced) and translated into functional and regulatory proteins. Note that regulatory genes may overlap structural genes [nef overlaps the 3'LTR] or may be assembled from portions of two smaller, separate genes [e.g., tat]. LTR = long terminal repeat.

and Wong-Staal, 1988; Peterlin and Luciw, 1988). The genes for the major structural proteins (gag and env) and the reverse transcriptase (pol) are arranged in an order (gag-pol-env) common to other retroviruses (Figure 1–1). The genes overlap (e.g., gag and pol), requiring that RNA transcripts be cut and spliced to produce the messenger RNA coding for complete proteins. Enclosing the entire genome are two long terminal repeats (LTRs) that provide sites for integration of the DNA provirus formed by reverse transcription into the host cell genome and for regulator proteins (e.g., tat, rev, and nef) to control the rate of viral replication. Because HIV appears capable of prolonged periods of clinical latency characterized by low rates of replication, a knowledge of this complex system of control is important to understanding what "turns on and off" the virus.

Viral Replication

The life cycle of HIV consists of a series of steps (Figure 1–2) in which the genetic and synthetic functions of the host cell are subverted to reproduce enormous numbers of HIV (Peterlin and Luciw, 1988; Haseltine, 1991). In broad terms,

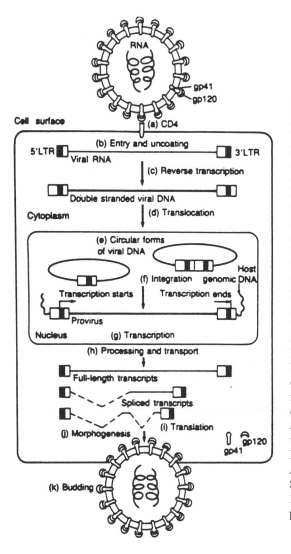

FIGURE 1–2. Life cycle of human immunodeficiency virus Type 1 (HIV-1). (The multiple steps involved from entry of a virus to reproduction of multiple copies of infectious HIV-1 provide many potential targets for antiviral therapy. Blocking of the attachment of gp120 to the CD$_4$ receptor on the viral surface (a) is currently the focus for vaccine development and treatment with soluble CD$_4$. The reverse transcription of RNA to DNA (c) is the target of antiviral chemotherapy with AZT and other analogues of the nucleic acid building blocks of DNA. CD = cluster determinant; RNA = ribonucleic acid; DNA = deoxyribonucleic acid; AZT = azidothymidine. From "Molecular Biology of HIV" by B.M. Peterlin and P.A. Luciw, 1988, *AIDS* 1988, 2 [Suppl.1], S29-S40. Copyright 1988 by *AIDS* 1988, 2[Suppl. 1]. Reprinted by permission.)

these steps consist of (1) attachment and (2) entry into host cells via a specific cell surface molecule; (3) reverse transcription of viral RNA into proviral DNA; (4) integration into host DNA; (5) transcription of the genome back into RNA with (6) processing to produce spliced RNA products; (7) translation and processing of messenger RNA to produce the structural and other proteins of the mature virus; (8) encapsulation of RNA into the viral core; and (9) budding and release of the virus through a modified portion of the host cell membrane. Several of these essential steps provide potential points of attack for therapy. Two steps deserve further attention because they are the basis for the initial approaches to treatment and immunization.

ATTACHMENT AND ENTRY.   The molecule of attachment on lymphocytes and possibly other cells is the CD4 membrane glycoprotein, which helps to define the *helper* subset of human T lymphocytes (Weber and Weiss, 1988). CD4 on lymphocytes (CD = cluster designation; previously called T4) normally serves as a binding site for cell surface proteins on macrophages (class II major histocompatibility complex [MHC] antigens) that are important during lymphocyte–macrophage interactions. During these interactions, foreign antigens are presented by macrophages to helper lymphocytes in a manner that causes the lymphocyte to promote vigorous antibody production and/or cell-mediated cytotoxicity (e.g., killing of virus-infected cells by lymphocytes). Thus, HIV uses a molecule crucial to the normal helper T-lymphocyte function in order to gain entry into cells.

The specific part of the virus that binds to CD4 is composed of four small, discontinuous portions of the envelope glycoprotein (GP-160) on the surface of the virus. A second step in attachment is cleavage of the tip of a loop structure (V_3 loop) of the GP-160 glycoprotein by cell surface proteases, a step enhanced by prior CD4 binding (Clements et al., 1991). The portions critical to function of both the CD4 binding site and the V_3 loop are conserved (i.e., do not vary), but adjacent areas of the glycoprotein vary greatly among HIV strains. HIV strains differ among patients, and the virus also evolves over time within a patient. This variation appears to interfere with production of cross-reactive, neutralizing antibody that might otherwise aid in terminating the infection. Thus, it may be difficult for an infected or vaccinated patient to produce antibodies that block the binding of all variants of the virus.

Strategies for both protective immunization and immunotherapy that are based on interference with attachment through immunization with envelope glycoproteins have been shown to be safe in human trials. For uninfected persons, immunization with envelope glycoprotein could produce antibodies that combine with the CD4 binding site or V_3 loop on the envelope glycoprotein to block HIV attachment to cells (Kang et al., 1991). Infected patients might benefit from immunization to improve both levels of neutralizing antibody and cell-mediated immunity (see the section on "Immunodeficiency in HIV Infection" below) directed at HIV. Trials of this immunotherapeutic approach have utilized HIV GP-160 expressed on the surface of live viruses (vaccinia); whole, killed (irradiated) HIV; or purified GP-160 (Redfield et al., 1991). The goal of such immunizations is to prolong the period during which HIV is subclinical, if not to eliminate the virus from the patient's body completely. A related approach to treating infected patients is infusion of soluble CD4 molecules (unattached to cells) to bind HIV, promote its removal, and prevent infection of new cells. Initial clinical trials of soluble CD4 have not produced clinical benefits, however.

REVERSE TRANSCRIPTION.   This crucial step in retroviral reproduction was targeted because transcription of RNA to DNA is not part of normal human physiology and precedes the establishment of permanent HIV infection of a cell. This step has been targeted by the antiviral nucleosides, such as azidothymidine (zidovudine or AZT; Richman et al., 1988). AZT probably acts by terminating the growing DNA chain because it resembles the nucleic acid thymidine, but it is chemically modified so that the next nucleic acid in the chain cannot be attached (Furman et al., 1986; Yarchoan et al., 1988). Other nucleic acid analogs, such as dideoxycytidine (ddC) and dideoxyinosine (ddI), probably act in a similar fashion. Resistance to AZT develops in a substantial proportion of patients within the first year of AZT treatment (Larder et al., 1989). Despite their similar mechanism of action, isolates from such patients remain susceptible to ddC and ddI, implying differences in the way that various nucleoside analogs interact with the RT of HIV.

Detection of HIV and Other Indicators of Infection

Growth of HIV in vitro required a solution to the problems of maintaining CD4 lymphocytes in long-term culture and of neutralizing their natural defenses against HIV (interferon production). Retroviruses are now grown in cell cultures in many research laboratories around the world but not in routine clinical laboratories. Other methods for direct detection of HIV based on antigens (e.g., p24) and nucleic acids (RNA or DNA) in blood and other tissues have contributed to studies of pathogenesis and treatment. Recently, a technique for multiplying small fragments of DNA or RNA by roughly a millionfold, called the *polymerase chain reaction (PCR)*, has dramatically improved the sensitivity of detection of HIV nucleic acids (Saiki et al., 1988). The sensitivity of PCR equals and may exceed that of viral culture. Except for p24 antigen detection, none of these methods are currently used for clinical management of most patients.

Methods to detect antibodies to HIV have become increasingly accurate, simple, and inexpensive since their introduction in mid-1985 for screening donated blood. A variety of techniques have been adopted, but the enzyme-linked immunosorbent assay (ELISA) remains the standard method for screening blood donors or determining whether patients are infected with HIV. Persons who have sexually transmitted diseases or who are in AIDS-risk groups should be tested to detect asymptomatic infection. For prisoners and military personnel in the United States and for persons seeking to immigrate to many countries, routine screening has been adopted.

Repeatedly positive ELISA tests are strong evidence of HIV infection for those in AIDS-risk groups. In persons at low risk of HIV infection, even repeatedly positive tests may be inaccurate (Schwartz et al., 1988). Confirmatory testing by one of a variety of techniques is recommended before patients are informed of positive results. Western blotting (also called *immunoblotting*) is a more complex and expensive, but also more sensitive and specific, technique than ELISA. It measures antibodies to each protein of the virus after they are separated in an electrified gel (Sarngadharan et al., 1984). Infected persons usually have antibodies to multiple HIV proteins (e.g., p24, p41, p55, and p160). Definitive interpretation of tests for HIV antibodies requires that a positive ELISA assay be followed by a positive confirmatory test such as immunoblotting.

Detection of antibody to HIV strongly suggests infection but does not indicate the severity of associated symptoms, which may range from none to severe. Antibodies do not develop immediately after infection, but they appear in the vast majority of infected persons within 3–6 months. Thus, a negative test for HIV antibody does not exclude recently acquired infection. On the other hand, children of infected mothers normally acquire antibody from their mother, whether or not they are infected. Because this antibody may persist for more than 1 year, antibody tests may not identify which infants are infected until they are 15–18 months of age.

Immunodeficiency in HIV Infection

Immunity to microorganisms and tumors depends on a complex, highly regulated, and very effective system of cells and circulating blood proteins (e.g., antibodies). The system recognizes the chemical constituents of microorganisms such as viruses and coordinates an attack that, when successful, kills and removes the invader with minimal damage to the host. The cells involved are of several types: (1) phagocytes that engulf and kill microorganisms (neutrophilic granulocytes and macrophages); (2) antibody-producing cells (B lymphocytes); and (3) memory cells (T lymphocytes) that store information and use it to regulate the activities of other cells and to kill abnormal cells. Cell-mediated immunity (CMI) is that branch of the immune system used to deal with microorganisms such as viruses that evade phagocytes and antibodies by living inside the cells of the host. A cell crucial to CMI, the helper or CD4 lymphocyte, is a major target cell for HIV (see the preceding section on "Viral Replication"). A second cell that HIV infects is the macrophage, a phagocytic cell, which is also important to CMI. Damage to these two populations of cells devastates CMI but leaves antibody-mediated immunity relatively intact, at least in adults. Another phagocytic cell, the neutrophilic granulocyte or "poly," is reduced in number, but the level in most patients is adequate for defense against bacteria and fungi.

The striking deficiency of CMI in AIDS resembles that of lymphatic tumors (lymphomas and Hodgkin's disease) and of the drug-induced immunosuppression necessary for the maintenance of organ transplants. Certain opportunistic infections (especially pneumocystis pneumonia, *Mycobacterium avium* bacteremia, and toxoplasmal encephalitis) and tumors (Kaposi's sarcoma and lymphomas of the brain) appear much more frequently than is expected from experience with other conditions that depress CMI. Thus, AIDS results from a profound and somewhat selective loss of CMI, which leads to vulnerability to certain specific infections and tumors.

During the evolution of HIV infection, a progressive loss of CD4 lymphocytes precedes the development of AIDS (Redfield and Burke, 1988). The numbers of CD4 lymphocytes in blood can be measured by flow cytometry after staining with monoclonal antibodies to the CD4 surface glycoprotein. Most patients have less than 15–20% ($<200/mm^3$) of the normal number of these cells at the time AIDS is diagnosed. In addition, the remaining CD4 cells are functionally impaired. The mechanisms of destruction and functional impairment of CD4 lymphocytes by HIV are not understood. Because only about 1/100 to 1/10,000 lymphocytes contain detectable HIV DNA or RNA, direct infection of the entire subset of lymphocytes does not seem likely (Harper et al., 1986).

Lymphocyte destruction by HIV occurs in three stages (Lang et al., 1989). First, at the time of seroconversion, a rapid decline by almost one-half (from

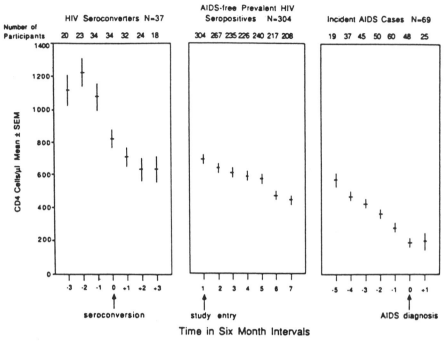

FIGURE 1–3. Pattern of depletion of CD_4 lymphocytes during human immunodeficiency virus Type 1 (HIV-1) infection. (The number of CD_4 lymphocytes [helper/inducer subset of thymus-derived lymphocytes] is shown during three stages of HIV infection. In the left panel, the rate of decline is greatest immediately before and after seroconversion [i.e., first visit at which ELISA was positive to antibody to HIV-1]. After a prolonged period of slower decline [middle panel], the rate again increases in the 2 years before diagnosis of acquired immunodeficiency syndrome [AIDS; right panel]. Numbers at the bottom of each panel refer to semiannual visits in relation to seroconversion, study entry, or AIDS diagnosis. From "Patterns of T-lymphocyte changes with human immunodeficiency virus infection: From seroconversion to the development of AIDS" by Lang et al., 1989, *Journal of Acquired Immunodeficiency Syndromes,* 2, pp. 63–69. Copyright 1989 by *Journal of Acquired Immunodeficiency Syndromes,* 2. Reprinted by permission.)

about 1200 cells/mm³ blood to about 600/mm³) occurs within 12 months (Figure 1–3, left panel). Second, during a prolonged period of HIV carriage, a slower rate of decline, averaging about 80 CD4 cells/mm³ per year ensues (center panel). Third, in the 2-year period before AIDS develops, a second accelerated period of CD4 destruction reduces average levels from 400–500/mm³ to <200/mm³ at the time of AIDS diagnosis (right panel). The smooth curves of mean CD4 counts in Figure 1–3 obscure the considerable variation in patterns of decline among individual patients. Nonetheless, the process of CD4 destruction proceeds at different rates during the evolution of disease, suggesting that natural or immune defenses are partially successful in slowing the process during the prolonged phase of asymptomatic carriage but ultimately lose control. The final reduction of CD4 number reaches a critical point when CMI can no longer control the opportunistic infections and tumors that define AIDS.

A hypothesis that may explain these stages is based on several observations of the changing growth rates and cytopathicity of viruses isolated at various stages of disease (Roos et al., 1992). Initially, HIV reproduces rapidly, causing high levels of viremia until HIV-specific, acquired immunity selects for slowly growing variants. This period of initial viremia corresponds to the first rapid drop in CD4 count. Slowly growing variants then gradually destroy the remaining CD4 cells over several years until CMI can no longer suppress the rapidly-growing, highly cytopathic variants of HIV. At this point a second period of rapid destruction of CD4 lymphocytes ensues, viremia increases, and clinical disease appears. In summary, following primary infection the highly cytopathic variants of HIV rapidly destroy CD4 lymphocytes, but they also signal their presence to an intact immune system that selects for less cytopathic variants. Only after CMI is suppressed below a critical threshold do the rapidly growing variants reemerge and accelerate the final destruction of CMI.

Despite the central importance of destruction of CD4 lymphocytes in HIV infection, cells of the monocyte/macrophage lineage in the brain, skin, and lymph nodes and endothelial cells of the brain are also infected (Ho et al., 1986; Wiley et al., 1986). Either migrating macrophages or infected endothelial cells in the brain may be responsible for the universal infection of the brain demonstrable in patients dying of AIDS. Most asymptomatic patients at all stages of clinical and immunological disease have low levels of virus culturable from acellular cerebrospinal fluid (CSF) (S.A. Spector et al., personal communication). Neuropsychological tests suggest that mild, clinically occult cognitive dysfunction is common in otherwise asymptomatic patients (Grant and Heaton, 1990). Thus, both low-level brain infection and cognitive dysfunction may occur before severe immunosuppression in some patients.

In addition to its impairment of T lymphocytes, HIV infection causes enlarged lymph nodes and hypersecretion of antibody by B lymphocytes, which are poorly responsive to further stimulation of antibody production (Lane et al., 1983; Jacobson et al., 1991). Infected patients often have high total levels of circulating antibodies (hypergammaglobulinemia) and may have elevated levels of antibodies to a variety of viruses. In general, adults with AIDS do not suffer the same bacterial and fungal infections that attack persons with antibody deficiency or low numbers of neutrophilic phagocytes. Their broad experience with multiple infectious agents continues to protect them because both antibodies and phagocytes continue to function. In contrast, children lack this experience and are more vulnerable to a variety of bacterial and viral infections to which HIV-infected adults remain immune. With advanced stages of infection (AIDS), protective levels of specific antibodies decline and vulnerability increases to some bacterial infections (e.g., pneumococcus or hemophilus) (Steinhoff et al., 1991).

Evolution of Clinical Disease

Within a few weeks of infection, many patients develop a self-limited (3- to 10-day), acute, mononucleosis-like illness with fever, sore throat, lymphadenopathy, malaise, skin rash, headache, and a variety of less frequent symptoms (Tindell et al., 1988). In most cases, this is followed by a prolonged period with minimal or no symptoms, during which variable combinations of diffuse lymphadenopathy (swelling of lymph glands), mild fatigue, recurrent fevers, and other nonspecific symptoms occur in a minority of patients. Infected persons may have no physical or laboratory abnormality during this period yet can infect others through sexual activity, blood donations, sharing needles, or pregnancy (Friedland and Klein, 1987). Virtually all have antibody to HIV proteins detectable by ELISA.

After a variable period, deterioration of CMI is heralded by the appearance of a variety of opportunistic infections, tumors, neurological illnesses, or nonspecific symptoms (fever, diarrhea, and wasting), which progress to death in a few years or less. Immune-mediated thrombocytopenia (low blood platelet level) and neurological syndromes may precede all other symptoms or may occur along with other manifestations of AIDS.

Two systems for classifying the progressive stages of HIV infection have been widely used (Centers for Disease Control [CDC], 1987) and Walter-Reed [Redfield et al., 1986]). Recently (1993), the CDC revised its classification substantially to include three strata of CD4 lymphocyte counts ($\geq$500/μL, 200–499/ μL, <200/μL) and three clinical levels (asymptomatic, minor symptoms, and AIDS-defining conditions) (Table 1–1) (CDC, 1992). The CDC also defined AIDS based on a CD4 cell count <200/mm^3, thus including groups A3, B3, and C1-3. The criteria for the conditions in the 1993 CDC classification that qualify patients for the B category are presented in Table 1–2. Minor infections and conditions listed in Table 1–2, such as oral candidiasis (thrush), reactivation of herpes zoster virus (shingles), or frequent recurrences of herpes simplex virus on the lips or genitals; nonspecific symptoms such as fever, weight loss, fatigue, diarrhea, or skin rashes; and laboratory abnormalities such as low red and white blood cell counts may precede AIDS by months or years. Occurrence of any of the AIDS-defining conditions listed in Table 1–3 establishes the diagnosis of AIDS and places patients in the C category of the CDC classification.

Kaposi's sarcoma is a tumor of the skin and internal organs that occurs much more frequently in homosexual men than in other risk groups. It may have a slightly better prognosis than other forms of AIDS because it often presents at a less advanced state of immunodeficiency (higher number of CD4 lymphocytes)

TABLE 1–1.   1993 Revised Classification System for HIV Infection and Expanded AIDS Surveillance Case Definition for Adolescents and Adults

CD4+ T-cell Categories	Clinical Categories		
	(A) Asymptomatic, Acute (Primary) HIV or PGL↑	(B) Symptomatic, Not (A) or (C) Conditions	(C) AIDS-Indicator Conditions
$\geq$500/μL	A1	B1	C1
200–499 μL	A2	B2	C2
<200 μL AIDS-indicator T-cell count	A3	B3	C3

TABLE 1–2.   Definition of Category B in the Revised (1993) CDC
Classification of HIV Infection

Category B consists of symptomatic conditions in an HIV-infected adolescent or adult that
are not included among conditions listed in clinical category C and that meet at least one
of the following criteria: (1) the conditions are attributed to HIV infection or are indicative
of a defect in CMI or (2) the conditions are considered by physicians to have a clinical
course or to require management that is complicated by HIV infection. *Examples* of conditions in clinical category B include *but are not limited to the following:*

- Bacillary angiomatosis
- Candidiasis, oropharyngeal (thrush)
- Candidiasis, vulvovaginal; persistent, frequent, or poorly responsive to therapy
- Cervical dysplasia (moderate or severe)/cervical carcinoma in situ
- Constitutional symptoms, such as fever (38.5°C) or diarrhea lasting >1 month
- Hairy leukoplakia, oral
- Herpes zoster (shingles) involving at least two distinct episodes or more than one
  dermatome
- Idiopathic thrombocytopenic purpura
- Listeriosis
- Pelvic inflammatory disease, particularly if complicated by tubo-ovarian abscess
- Peripheral neuropathy

For classification purposes, category B conditions take precedence over those in category
A. For example, someone previously treated for oral or persistent vaginal candidiasis (and
who has not developed a category C disease) but who is now asymptomatic should be
classified in clinical category B.

than do the AIDS-defining opportunistic infections, and it may progress slowly
at first. Occasionally, patients are debilitated by HIV-induced neurological symptoms such as dementia. Most patients die with multiple opportunistic infections
involving the lung, gastrointestinal tract, and brain (Niedt and Schinella, 1985).

The pace of progression of HIV infection varies widely. The observed period
between HIV infection and development of AIDS has been as short as 1 year
and as long as 13 years in adults, with an estimated average of 10 years or more
(Medley et al., 1987; Anderson and Medley, 1988; Lui et al., 1988). After an
initial 2-year period of lower risk, the annual risk of developing AIDS appears
to be about 5–7%. After 10 years, about one-half of a group of carriers will have
AIDS or be dead (Rothenburg et al., 1987). It is not yet clear if a fraction of
carriers will resist HIV-related illness indefinitely or if virtually all carriers will
develop AIDS within two decades.

Just as the period of asymptomatic carriage of HIV varies, so does survival
after AIDS is diagnosed (Glasner and Kaslow, 1990). Before the widespread use
of AZT, estimates of median survival were about 1 year (Rothenburg et al., 1987;
Anderson and Medley, 1988). A small percentage of patients (<15%) survive
longer than 4 years, but full recovery of immune function is extremely rare, if it
occurs. Treatment with AZT improves survival, but its full impact remains to be
clarified (Graham et al., 1992). Current data suggest that AZT delays both opportunistic infections and death in AIDS and AIDS-related complex (ARC)

TABLE 1–3. Conditions Included in the 1993 AIDS Surveillance Case
Definition

- Candidiasis of the bronchi, trachea, or lungs
- Candidiasis, esophageal
- Cervical cancer, invasive[a]
- Coccidioidomycosis, disseminated or extrapulmonary
- Cryptococcosis, extrapulmonary
- Cryptosporidiosis, chronic intestinal (>1 month's duration)
- Cytomegalovirus disease (other than of the liver, spleen, or nodes)
- Cytomegalovirus retinitis (with loss of vision)
- Encephalopathy, HIV-related
- Herpes simplex: chronic ulcer(s) (>1 month's duration); or bronchitis, pneumonitis, or esophagitis
- Histoplasmosis, disseminated or extrapulmonary
- Isosporiasis, chronic intestinal (>1 month's duration)
- Kaposi's sarcoma
- Lymphoma, Burkitt's (or equivalent term)
- Lymphoma, immunoblastic (or equivalent term)
- Lymphoma, primary, of brain
- *Mycobacterium-avium* complex or *M. kansasii,* disseminated or extrapulmonary
- *Mycobacterium tuberculosis,* any site (pulmonary[a] or extrapulmonary)
- *Mycobacterium,* other species or unidentified species, disseminated or extrapulmonary
- *Pneumocystis carinii* pneumonia
- Pneumonia, recurrent[a]
- Progressive multifocal leukoencephalopathy
- *Salmonella* septicemia, recurrent
- Toxoplasmosis of the brain
- Wasting syndrome due to HIV

---

[a]Added in the 1993 expansion of the AIDS surveillance case definition.

patients, but that after 6–12 months of treatment, deterioration of immunity continues in most patients (Richman et al., 1988). The failure of AZT to provide sustained benefit is probably a consequence of selection for AZT-resistant variants (Richman et al., 1992). The availability of other nucleoside analogs (ddC and ddI) should extend the period of benefit (Meng et al., 1990; Kahn et al., 1992).

Improvements in the quality and quantity of survival have resulted from both antiretroviral agents and drugs to prevent specific infectious diseases. Further progress in retarding the progression of HIV infection in the near future can be anticipated through serial or combined use of the nucleoside analogs (e.g. AZT, ddC, or ddI), use of antiretrovirals targeted at other viral proteins, and immunization to enhance CMI in the early stages of infection (Redfield et al., 1991). Given the integration of HIV DNA into apparently long-lived cells, complete cure remains a distant and difficult goal.

Patient Management

Organization of Medical and Psychosocial Support

Medical and psychosocial management of HIV-infected patients is a rapidly evolving, multidisciplinary process optimally involving a variety of physicians, nurses, mental health professionals, and other supportive specialists (Blanchet, 1988; Volberding, 1988). Because of the variety of previously rare conditions now seen commonly in AIDS patients, the primary physician should be a skilled generalist with experience in AIDS. Because the care of AIDS patients has not yet evolved into a medical subspecialty, a variety of generalists (internists, pediatricians, gynecologists, and family practitioners) and specialists in immunology, infectious diseases, oncology, or commonly affected organ systems (lung, gastrointestinal tract, skin, and nervous system) have provided care in major medical centers.

As an example, at the University of California, San Diego (UCSD) Medical Center, a clinic that emphasizes outpatient, primary care by intermediate-level providers (nurse practitioners) in collaboration with experienced physicians, pharmacists, psychologists, and nurses effectively manages a large case load (~700, mostly AIDS patients). The clinic population generates an inpatient census of about 20–25 patients who are managed by the internal medicine house staff and attending physicians. Excellent care is provided in San Diego in settings as variable as community and public health clinics, prepaid health maintenance organizations, a military hospital, and private practices. As the epidemic has increased and extended geographically, the need to integrate the care of HIV-infected patients into the practices of all physicians has become clear.

Supplementing medical care in many American cities has been a remarkable group of voluntary and professional health organizations providing nursing, social, psychological, legal, and informational services, as well as food and shelter. Started and supported initially by the gay and lesbian community, the voluntary support groups, assistance funds, residential facilities, hot lines, and patient organizations responded to an unanticipated and unaddressed need for services. Broad-based community support for these organizations is needed because the voluntary lay and professional leaders, workers, and supporters have been both exhausted by their effort and, in some cases, stricken by AIDS themselves.

Preexisting health organizations (hospitals, clinics, visiting and home nursing agencies, governmental medical programs, insurance companies, etc.) have also felt the impact of the epidemic. AIDS has revealed and exacerbated many weaknesses in the American health industry (Fineberg, 1988).

Goals of Patient Management at Various Stages of HIV Infection

Regardless of where the patient is cared for or the availability of adjunctive support services, the approach varies, depending on the clinical stage of the patient. The following discussion outlines the major issues to be addressed at each stage of the patient's illness. The outline is cumulative. Patients who are first seen at advanced stages need discussion of those issues usually dealt with at earlier stages.

For the asymptomatic HIV carrier, major issues are staging of disease for purposes of starting antiretroviral treatment, counseling to minimize the risk of transmission to others, and support for continuing as full and active a life as circumstances permit. Staging of patients requires some estimate of the extent of damage to the immune system. The most widely used single indicator is the CD4 lymphocyte blood count. Fewer than 200 CD4 lymphocytes is associated with a high risk for development of AIDS-defining infections. The CD4 lymphocyte count is used to decide when to give antiretroviral drugs. For example, AZT may be started at CD4 counts $<500/\mu L$ of blood (Fischl et al., 1990; Volberding et al., 1990; Hamilton et al., 1992). Prophylaxis against pneumocystis pneumonia with cotrimoxazole (Septra or Bactrim) or aerosolized pentamidine is started at CD4 counts $<200/\mu L$.

For the symptomatic patient, targeted investigation of symptoms seeks to identify specific treatable infections. For some constitutional symptoms (weight loss, fevers, fatigue, and diarrhea), either specific infections or HIV may be causal. For others, such as focal neurological signs, a definite cause other than HIV is nearly always found. Skillful treatment and prevention of opportunistic infections may provide both extended survival and a better quality of life. Prevention of recurrent pneumocystis pneumonia, toxoplasmal encephalitis, herpes skin infections, cytomegalovirus retinitis, or cryptococcal meningitis requires prolonged suppression with expensive and sometimes toxic drugs. Improved methods to prevent and suppress these infections are needed. Suppression of nonspecific constitutional symptoms with antipyretics, antidiarrheal agents, or supplemental nutrition may improve the quality of life.

For the preterminal patient, major issues are adjustment of goals and expectations of medical treatment, relief of pain and anxiety through reassurance and medications, marshaling emotional and physical support, completing a will, designating a power of attorney, and completing funeral and burial plans. Because most AIDS patients are relatively young, they may have little experience with death and dying. They need assurance that they will be physically cared for and emotionally supported, their pain relieved, their friends and relatives encouraged to be with them, and their spiritual needs addressed. For patients estranged from their families as a result of their sexual orientation, drug abuse, or fear of contagion, intervention by the care team can sometimes effect remarkable reconciliations.

In summary, a skillful, multifaceted approach to patient management by an experienced multidisciplinary team can prolong and improve the quality of life and can reduce the adverse effect of AIDS on patients, their families, friends, and communities.

Acknowledgment

Supported in part by the California Universitywide AIDS Research Program through the California Collaborative Treatment Group and the HIV Neurobehavioral Research Center of the University of California, San Diego (NIMH Center Grant 5 P50 MH45294).

References

Anderson, R.M., and Medley, G.F. (1988). Epidemiology of HIV infection and AIDS: Incubation and infectious periods, survival, and vertical transmission. *AIDS, 2*(Suppl. 1), 557–563.

Barre-Sinoussi, F., Chermann, J.C., Rey, F., Nugeyre, M.T., Chamaret, S., Guest, C., Dauguet, C., Axler-Blin, C., Brun-Vezinet, F., Rouz-Roux, C., Rozenbaum, W., and Montagnier, L. (1983). Isolation of a T-lymphocyte retrovirus from a patient at risk of acquired immune deficiency syndrome (AIDS). *Science, 220*, 868–870.

Blanchet, K.D. (1988). *AIDS: A Health Care Management Response.* Rockville, Md: Aspen Publications.

Blattner, W.A. (1991). HIV epidemiology: Past, present, and future. *The FASEB Journal, 5*, 2340–2348.

Blattner, W.A., Blayney, D.W., Robert-Guroff, M., Sarngadharan, M.G., Kalayanaman, V.S., Sarin, P.S., Jaffee, E.S., and Gallo, R.C. (1983). Epidemiology of human T cell leukemia/lymphoma virus. *Journal of Infectious Diseases, 147*, 406–415.

Centers for Disease Control. (1987). Revision of the CDC surveillance case definition for acquired immunodeficiency syndrome. *Morbidity and Mortality Weekly Report, 36*(Suppl. 1), 3S–15S.

Centers for Disease Control. (1992). 1993 revised classification system for HIV infection and expanded surveillance case definition for AIDS among adolescents and adults. *Morbidity and Mortality Weekly Report, 41*(Suppl. 44-17), 1–19.

Clements, G.J., Price-Jones, M.J., Stephens, P.E., Sutton, C., Schulz, T.F., Clapham, P.R., McKeating, J.A., McClure, M.O., Thompson, S., and Marsh, M. (1991). The V_3 loops of HIV-1 and HIV-2 surface glycoproteins contain protective sites: A possible function in viral fusion. *AIDS Research and Human Retroviruses, 7*, 1–15.

Fineberg, H. (1988). The social dimensions of AIDS. *Scientific American, 259*, 128–134.

Fischl, M.A., Richman, D.D., Hansen, N., Collier, A.C., Carey, J.T., Para, M.F., Hardy, W.D., Dolin, R., Powderly, W.G., and Allan, J.D. (1990). The safety and efficacy of zidovudine (AZT) in the treatment of subjects with mildly symptomatic human immunodeficiency virus type 1 (HIV) infection. A double-blind placebo-controlled trial. The AIDS Clinical Trial Group. *Annals of Internal Medicine, 112*, 727–737.

Friedland, G.H., and Klein, R.S. (1987). Transmission of the human immunodeficiency virus. *New England Journal of Medicine, 317*, 1125–1135.

Furman, P.A., Fyfe, J.A., St. Clair, M.H., Weinhold, K., Rideout, J.L., Freeman, G.A., Lehrman, S.N., Bolognesi, D.P., Broder, S., and Mitsuya, H. (1986). Phosphorylation of 3′azido 3′deoxythymidine and selective interaction of the 3′-triphosphate with human immunodeficiency virus reverse transcriptase. *Proceedings of the National Academy of Sciences, USA, 83*, 8333.

Gallo, R.C., Salahuddin, S., Popovic, M., Shearer, G.M., Kaplan, M., Haynes, B.F., Palker, T.J., Redfield, R., Oleske, J., Safai, B., Giber, W., Foster, P., and Maricham, P.D.

(1984). Frequent detection and isolation of cytopathic retroviruses (HTLV-III) from patients with AIDS and at risk of AIDS. *Science, 224,* 500–503.

Gelberhorn, H.R., Hausmann, E.H.S., Ozel, M., Pauli, G., and Koch, M.A. (1987). Fine structure of HIV and immunolocalization of structural proteins. *Virology, 156,* 171–176.

Glasner, P.D., and Kaslow, R.A. (1990). The epidemiology of human immunodeficiency virus infection. *Journal of Consulting and Clinical Psychology, 58,* 13–21.

Graham, N.M.H., Zeger, S.L., Park, L.P., Vermund, S.H., Detels, R., Rinaldo, C.R., and Phair, J.P. (1992). The effects on survival of early treatment of human immuno-deficiency virus infection. *New England Journal of Medicine, 326,* 1037–1042.

Grant, I., and Heaton, R.K. (1990). Human immunodeficiency virus-1 (HIV-1) and the brain. *Journal of Consulting and Clinical Psychology, 58,* 22–30.

Hamilton, J.D., Hartigan, P.M., Simberkoff, M.S., Day, P.L., Diamond, G.R., Dickinson, G.M., Drusano, G.L., Egorin, M.J., George, W.L., and Gordin, F.M. (1992). A controlled study of early versus late treatment with zidovudine in symptomatic HIV infection. *New England Journal of Medicine, 326,* 437–443.

Harper, M.E., Marselle, L.M., Gallo, R.C., and Wong-Staal, F. (1986). Detection of lym-phocytes expressing human T-lymphocyte virus type III in lymph nodes and periph-eral blood of infected individuals by *in situ* hybridization. *Proceedings of the National Academy of Sciences, USA, 83,* 772–776.

Haseltine, W.A. (1991). Molecular biology of the human immunodeficiency virus type 1. *The FASEB Journal, 5,* 2349–2360.

Haseltine, W.A., and Wong-Staal, F. (1988). The molecular biology of the AIDS virus. *Scientific American, 259,* 52–62.

Ho, D.D., Rota, R.T., and Hirsh, M.A. (1986). Infection of monocyte/macrophages by human lymphotropic virus type III. *Journal of Clinical Investigation, 77,* 1712–1716.

Jacobson, D., McCutchan, J.A., Spechko, P.L., Abramson, I., Smith, R.S., Bartok, A., Boss, G.R., Durand, D., Bozzette, S.A., Spector, S.A., and Richman, D.D. (1991). The evolution of lymphadenopathy and hypergammaglobulinemia are evidence for early and sustained polyclonal B lymphocyte activation during human immuno-deficiency virus infection. *Journal of Infectious Diseases, 163,* 240–247.

Johnson, R.T. (1987). Myelopathies and retroviral infection. *Annals of Neurology, 21,* 113–117.

Kahn, J.O., Lagakos, S.W., Richman, D.D., Cross, A., Pettinelli, C., Liou, S., Brown, M., Volberding, P.A., Crumpacker, C.S., Beall, G., Sacks, H.S., Merigan, T.C., Beltan-gady, M., Smaldone, L., Dolin, R., and the NIAID AIDS Clinical Trials Group. (1992). A controlled trial comparing continued zidovudine with didanosine in human immunodeficiency virus infection. *New England Journal of Medicine, 327,* 581–587.

Kang, C.Y., Nara, P., Chamat, S., Caralli, V., Ryskamp, T., Haigwood, N., Newman, R., and Kohler, H. (1991). Evidence for non-V_3 specific neutralizing antibodies that interfere with GP-120/CD4 binding in human immunodeficiency virus-1-infected humans. *Proceedings of the National Academy of Sciences, USA, 88,* 6171–6175.

Lane, H.C., Masur, H., Edgar, L.C., Whalen, G., Rook, A.H., and Fauci, A.S. (1983). Abnormalities of B-cell activation and immunoregulation in patients with acquired immunodeficiency syndrome. *New England Journal of Medicine, 309,* 453–458.

Lang, W., Perkins, H., Anderson, R.E., Royce, R., Jewell, N., and Winklestein, W., Jr. (1989). Patterns of T-lymphocyte changes with human immunodeficiency virus infection: From seroconversion to the development of AIDS. *Journal of Acquired Immunodeficiency Syndromes, 2,* 63–69.

Larder, B.A., Darby, G., and Richman, D.D. (1989). HIV with reduced sensitivity to zidovudine (AZT) isolated during prolonged therapy. *Science, 243*, 1731–1734.

Lui, K., Dallow, W.W., and Rutherford, G.W. (1988). A model-based estimate of the mean incubation period for AIDS in homosexual men. *Science, 240*, 1333–1335.

McArthur, J.C. (1987). Neurological manifestations of AIDS. *Medicine, 66*, 407–437.

Medley, G.F., Anderson, R.M., Cox, D.R., and Billard, L. (1987). Incubation period of AIDS in patients infected via blood transfusion. *Nature, 328*, 719–721.

Meng, T.C., Fischl, M.A., and Richman, D.D. (1990). AIDS Clinical Trials Group: Phase I/II study of combination 2',3'-dideoxycytidine and zidovudine in patients with acquired immunodeficiency syndrome (AIDS) and advanced AIDS-related complex. *American Journal of Medicine, 88* (Suppl. 5B), 27S–30S.

Niedt, G.W., and Schinella, R.A. (1985). Acquired immunodeficiency syndrome: Clinicopathologic study of 56 autopsies. *Archives of Pathology and Laboratory Medicine, 109*, 727–734.

Osame, M., Usuku, K., Izumo, S., Itichi, N., Amitani, H., Igata, A., Matsumoto, M., and Tata, M. (1984). HTLV-I associated myelopathy: A new clinical entity. *Lancet, 2*, 125–128.

Peterlin, B.M., and Luciw, P.A. (1988). Molecular biology of HIV. *AIDS, 2*(Suppl. 1), S29–S40.

Price, R.W., Brew, B., Sidtis, J., Rosenblum, M., Scheck, A.C., and Cleary, P. (1988). The brain in AIDS. *Science, 239*, 586–592.

Redfield, R.R., and Burke, D.S. (1988). HIV infection: The clinical picture. *Scientific American, 259*, 90–98.

Redfield, R.R., Birx, D.L., Ketter, N., Tramont, E., Polonis, V., Davis, C., Brundage, J.F., Smith, G., Johnson, S., and Fowler, A. (1991). A phase I evaluation of the safety and immunogenicity of vaccination with recombinant gp 160 in patients with early human immunodeficiency virus infection. *New England Journal of Medicine, 324*, 1677–1684.

Redfield, R.R., Wright, D.G., and Tramont, E.C. (1986). The Walter Reed staging classification for HTLV III/LAV infection. *New England Journal of Medicine, 314*, 131–132.

Richman, D.D., Andrews, J., and the AZT Collaborative Working Group. (1988). Results of continued monitoring of participants in the placebo-controlled trial of zidovudine for serious human immunodeficiency virus infection. *American Journal of Medicine, 89*(Suppl. 24), 208–213.

Richman, D.D., Guatelli, J.C., Grimes, J., Tsiatis, A., and Gingeras, T. (1992). Detection of mutations associated with zidovudine resistance in human immunodeficiency virus by use of the polymerase chain reaction. *Journal of Infectious Diseases, 164*, 1075–1081.

Roos, M.T.L., Lange, J.M.A., DeGoede, R.E.Y., Coutinho, R.A., Schellekens, P.T., Miedema, F., and Tersmette, M. (1992). Viral phenotype and immune response in primary human immunodeficiency virus type 1 infection. *Journal of Infectious Diseases, 165*, 427–432.

Rothenburg, R., Waifel, M., Stoneburner, R., Milberg, J., Parker, R., and Truman, B. (1987). Survival with the acquired immunodeficiency syndrome. *New England Journal of Medicine, 317*, 1297–1302.

Saiki, R.K., Gelfand, D.H., Stoffel, S., Scharf, S.T., Higughi, R., Horn, G.T., Moulis, K.B., and Erlich, H.A. (1988). Primer-directed enzymatic amplification of DNA with thermostable DNA polymerase. *Science, 239*, 487–491.

Sarngadharan, M.G., Popovic, M., Bruch, L., Schüpbach, J., and Gallo, R.C. (1984). Antibodies reactive with human T-lymphotrophic retroviruses (HTLV-III) in the serum of patients with AIDS. *Science, 224*, 506–508.

Schwartz, J.S., Dans, P.E., and Kinosian, B.P. (1988). Human immunodeficiency virus test evaluation, performance, and use. *Journal of the American Medical Association, 259*, 2574–2579.

Steinhoff, M.C., Auerbach, B.S., Nelson, K.E., Vlahov, D., Becker, R.L., Graham, N.M., Schwartz, D.H., Lucas, A.H., and Chaisson, R.E. (1991). Antibody responses to *Haemophilus influenzae* type B vaccines in men with human immunodeficiency virus infection. *New England Journal of Medicine, 325*, 1837–1842.

Teich, N. (1985). Taxonomy of retroviruses. In R. Weiss, N. Teich, H. Varmus, and J. Coffer, eds., *RNA Tumor Viruses* (2nd ed.). New York: Cold Spring Harbor Laboratory, pp. 1–16.

Tindell, B., Barker, S., Donovan, B., Barnes, T., Roberts, J., Kronenberg, C., Gold, J., Penny, R., Cooper, D., and the Sydney AIDS Study Group. (1988). Characterization of the acute illness associated with human immunodeficiency virus infection. *Archives of Internal Medicine, 148*, 945–949.

Volberding, P.A. (1988). Caring for the patient with AIDS in medical management of AIDS. *Infectious Diseases Clinics of North America, 2*, 543–550.

Volberding, P.A., Lagakos, S.W., Koch, M.A., Pettinelli, C., Myers, M.W., Booth, D.K., Balfour, H.H., Jr., Reichman, R.C., Bartlett, J.A., and Hirsch, M.S. (1990). Zidovudine in asymptomatic human immunodeficiency virus infection. A controlled trial in persons with fewer than 500 CD4-positive cells per cubic millimeter. *New England Journal of Medicine, 322*, 941–949.

Weber, J., and Weiss, R.A. (1988). HIV infection: The cellular picture. *Scientific American, 259*, 101–109.

Wiley, C.A., Schrier, R.D., Nelson, J.A., Lampert, P.W., and Oldstone, M.B. (1986). Cellular localization of human immunodeficiency virus infection within brains of acquired immunodeficiency syndrome patients. *Proceedings of the National Academy of Sciences, USA, 83*, 7089–7093.

Yarchoan, R., Mitsuya, H., and Broder, S. (1988). AIDS therapies. *Scientific American, 259*, 110–119.

2

Immunopathogenesis of HIV Infections: CNS-Immune Interactions

MADHAVAN P.N. NAIR and STANLEY A. SCHWARTZ

Since the discovery of the acquired immunodeficiency syndrome (AIDS) in 1981, the intense efforts to study its biological and molecular aspects and its etiological agent, the human immunodeficiency virus (HIV), have also advanced our understanding of the immune system, its regulatory circuits, and its interactions with other tissues and organs such as the central nervous system (CNS). The epidemiology of HIV infections is frequently compared to an iceberg, in which the small visible part represents patients with AIDS while the unobserved lower portion comprises the vast majority of HIV-infected patients, including those who are asymptomatic or have other disease manifestations, such as lymphadenopathy. Despite all the progress in our understanding of the molecular biology of HIV, the precise mechanisms of pathogenesis of the infection are not yet clearly understood. This has been extensively reviewed elsewhere (Fauci, 1988; Ioachim, 1990). The natural history and clinical course of HIV infection are marked by different phases: (1) the acute phase, which involves several weeks of nonspecific symptoms often similar to those of mononucleosis; (2) a prolonged chronic phase characterized by few if any symptoms and having an average duration of about 7 years; and (3) the full-blown disease stage, which is marked by distinct symptoms of AIDS, resulting in various opportunistic infections and neoplasia.

The hallmark of the immunopathogenesis of HIV infection is the progressive depletion of the CD4$^+$, helper T-lymphocyte subpopulation throughout the various phases of infection. Although HIV has a selective tropism for CD4$^+$ cells, it has been shown that other types of cells can also be infected with HIV (Bedinger et al., 1988; Hammarskjold and Rekosh, 1989). A report from the Seventh International Conference on AIDS held in Florence, Italy, indicated that dendritic cells are at least 10-fold more susceptible to infection by HIV than either CD4[+] lymphocytes or monocytes/macrophages (Cohen, 1991). Since CD4[+] lymphocytes are involved in almost every type of immune response and in many nonimmunological biological functions, a decrease in CD4[+] cell function or numbers can affect other components of the immune system including macrophages, cytotoxic T lymphocytes, natural killer (NK) cells, suppressor cells, and B cells.

As HIV infection has a relatively prolonged course, it is reasonable to suggest that HIV replication may be inhibited by host immune responses. However, several factors described below may be associated with activation of the virus and subsequent clinical manifestation of the disease.

Neuropsychological Factors

There is a communication network between the CNS and the immune system that is primarily mediated through shared neuropeptide signals produced in response to the hypothalamic-pituitary-adrenal (HPA) axis (Dunn, 1988; Stein et al., 1988; Bateman et al., 1989; Kiecolt-Glaser and Glaser, 1989; Biondi and Kotzalidis, 1990). Lymphocytes also possess receptors for corticosteroids, insulin, testosterone, estrogens, beta-adrenergic agents, histamine, growth hormones, acetylcholine, and methionine-enkephalin (Solomon, 1985). Cell differentiation antigens such as Ia and CD3 are shared by neural and hematopoietic cells (Garson et al., 1982; Fontana et al., 1984; Wong et al., 1984; Sun and Wekerle, 1986). The CD4 antigen, which is a specific receptor for HIV, is also found on both neuronal and glial cells (Maddon et al., 1986; Pert et al., 1986; Funke et al., 1987). Monoclonal antibodies to the Leu 7 surface marker that specifically recognize NK and antibody-dependent cellular cytotoxic (ADCC) cells, important early host defense mechanisms against virus infections and cancer, also bind to myelin sheath cells and cells in the peripheral nervous system (Lipinski et al., 1983; Schuller-Petrovic et al., 1983). All of these observations support the concept of shared recognition molecules between the cells of the nervous and immune systems.

Further evidence for the linkage of immune and nervous systems comes from work on stress and immunity. Psychological stress and depression can activate the HPA axis (Dunn, 1989; Biondi and Kotzalidis, 1990). Stress can alter many of the immune responses of the host, including the activities and number of NK cells, lymphocyte proliferative responses to various mitogens and recall antigens, and the production of gamma interferon by lymphocytes (Schleifer et al., 1983; Glaser et al., 1986; Teshima et al., 1987). Stress has also been shown to reduce cytotoxic T lymphocyte functions and interleukin-2 (IL-2) production, which has been associated with increased tumor growth (Borysenko, 1984). Moreover, the phagocytic and cytotoxic functions of monocytes and macrophages may be reduced by stress (Pavlidis and Chrigos, 1980; Teshima et al., 1987).

Cellular immune responses play an important role in the maintenance of latent infections with type 1 herpes simplex virus, Epstein-Barr virus, and cytomegalovirus (Oakes et al., 1980; Klein et al., 1981; Openshaw et al., 1981; Rickinson et al., 1981; Harada et al., 1982). Glaser et al. (1985, 1987) showed that psychological stress, associated with the reactivation of latent viral infections, can have profound deleterious effects on cellular immune responses. In a prospective study they found that stress induced in medical students by taking examinations significantly correlated with a reduction in gene expression for the IL-2 receptor.

Besides attacking cells of the immune system, HIV affects the nervous system, leading to a number of neuropsychological disorders that may even become manifest before any immunological abnormalities appear (Grant et al., 1987). It is estimated that about 60% of adult AIDS patients and more than 80% of HIV-infected children experience neurological abnormalities during the course of their illness (Nielsen et al., 1984; Navia et al., 1986; Fauci, 1988; Wiley et al., 1990), and productive infection of the brain with HIV can be detected in up to 80% of AIDS patients (Wiley et al., 1990). Direct signs of cellular pathology in the brain are apparently restricted to macrophages, capillary endothelial cells, and microglial cells (which may be brain-resident macrophages). A recent study indicated that pediatric AIDS patients can show intellectual improvement after treatment with AZT (Pizzo, 1990), suggesting that the observed neurotoxicity is reversible. Other studies, however, have shown a direct pathological effect of virus on non-hematogenous CNS cells in the fetal brain (Lyman et al., 1990). Once infected, the resident macrophages of the brain can produce altered levels of immunotransmitters, causing further dysfunction of the immune system. Since neurological impairment is disproportionate to the relatively small numbers of virus-infected CD4$^+$ lymphocytes or macrophages, it has been proposed that noninfectious mechanisms may also play an important role in the neuropathogenesis of HIV infections, supporting the hypothesis that products of the immune system may affect the nervous system.

Although the term *neuropsychoimmunology* was first coined by Solomon and Moos in 1964, the concept of the neuropsychoimmunology of AIDS has become more prominent recently, possibly because increasing numbers of patients are experiencing a devastating terminal disease with major social and psychological ramifications for which there is no effective therapy at present (Solomon and Moos, 1964). A relationship between altered CNS-associated neuropeptides and modulation of monocyte-macrophage function in the immunopathogenesis of HIV infections has been proposed (Hassan and Douglas, 1990). Depression is commonly associated with HIV infection (Loewenstein and Sharfstein, 1984; Perry and Jacobsen, 1986). It has been suggested that stress may exacerbate the clinical symptoms and progression of disease in HIV patients (Glaser et al., 1987) or may facilitate the activation of latent HIV infection (Sodroski et al., 1984). Folks et al. (1986) demonstrated that stress-induced impairment of immune responses can activate viral gene expression.

Glucocorticosteroids are the end products of HPA activation and are considered to be the primary mediators of endocrine–immune interactions. Stress has been shown to increase serum corticosteroid levels. Thus, one mechanism by which the nervous system might adversely influence the immune system is via increasing circulating corticosteroids.

To examine this notion, we studied the effect of prednisolone (PRD) (a corticosteroid) on the NK cell activities of normal lymphocytes in vitro (Nair and Schwartz, 1984, 1988). Data presented in Table 2–1 show the effect of prolonged

TABLE 2–1. Effect of PRD on the Cytotoxic Activities of HNK-1[+] Cells[a]

PRD Concentration (mol/L)	Cytotoxicity[b] (LU)	Suppression (%)
0	100.6 ± 8.0^c	—
10^{-6}	67.8 ± 3.9 (p < 0.005)[d]	32.6[e]
10^{-7}	71.0 ± 3.4 (p < 0.005)	29.4
10^{-8}	74.6 ± 6.3 (p < 0.01)	25.8
10^{-9}	88.3 ± 4.5 (p < 0.1)	12.2

[a]Two $\times$ 10^6 HNK-1[+] cells per milliliter were preincubated with varying concentrations of PRD for 72 hours, washed, and tested for NK activity against K562 target cells. The purity of the HNK-1[+] subpopulation was always >85%, as assessed by immunofluorescence with fluorescein isothiocyanate (FITC)-labeled HNK-1 monoclonal antibody. The HNK-1[-] subpopulation contained >2% HNK-1[+] cells (>98% purity).

[b]Cytotoxicity was calculated at Lytic units (LU) per 10^7 effector cells.

[c]Values represent the mean $\pm$ SD of four experiments performed in triplicate.

[d]The significance of the difference in mean values was determined with a single-tailed Student's t test.

[e]Percentage of suppression was calculated on the basis of the cytotoxic activity of lymphocytes precultured in media alone.

exposure to PRD on the cytotoxic potential of peripheral blood lymphocytes (PBL) from healthy donors. Preincubation of HNK-1[+] lymphocytes with PRD at concentrations of 10^{-6} to 10^{-9} mol/L for 72 hours resulted in a significant reduction of cytotoxic function. When PBL were first precultured with PRD and then separated into HNK-1[+] and HNK-1[-] subpopulations, both suppressed the target-binding and lytic activities of fresh, allogoneic large granular lymphocytes (LGL) with the PRD-treated HNK-1[+] cells demonstrating greater suppression than the PRD-treated HNK-1[-] cells (Table 2–2). We further investigated the effect of α-interferon (IFN), an agent known to enhance NK activity on PRD-

TABLE 2–2. Suppression of Target Binding and NK Activity of LGL by PRD-Treated Lymphocytes[a]

Suppressor Cells	% Binding	% Cytotoxicity
None	21.4 ± 3.2^b	6.2 ± 0.9
PRD control HNK-1[+]	17.2 ± 2.8 (p = NS)[c]	5.1 ± 1.1 (p = NS)
PRD-treated HNK-1[+]	7.8 ± 1.2 (p < 0.0025)	2.5 ± 0.4 (p < 0.005)
PRD control HNK 1[-]	16.7 ± 2.1 (p = NS)	4.9 ± 0.5 (p = NS)
PRD-treated HNK 1[-]	12.8 ± 2.7 (p < 0.05)	2.9 ± 0.3 (p < 0.01)

NS = nonsignificant.

[a]HNK-1[+] and HNK-1[-] lymphocyte subpopulations were isolated by panning from PBL precultured with or without 10^{-6} mol/L PRD for 72 hours. Fresh allogeneic effector LGLs were separated on a Percoll gradient, labeled with FITC, and mixed with suppressor cells at a 1:1 effector:suppressor ratio for 1 hour at 37°C before use in the suppressor assay.

[b]Values represent the mean $\pm$ SD of three experiments performed in triplicate. A minimum of 300 lymphocytes were scored on each slide.

[c]The statistical significance of differences was calculated with a single-tailed Student's t test.

induced suppression of NK functions. Lymphocytes were preincubated alone or with PRD or IFN individually or together for 1 hour, washed, and tested for their cytotoxic potential. Table 2–3 shows that PBL preincubated with 250 and 500 U of IFN for 1 hour demonstrate enhanced NK activity compared to lymphocytes precultured in media alone. Lymphocytes preincubated with PRD alone for 1 hour manifested a 30% suppression of NK activity, which was significantly reversed to only 5.9% and 9.5% suppression by treatment with 250 U and 500 U of IFN, respectively. These results show that culture of PBL with IFN for 1 hour can reverse the inhibitory effect of PRD. An interesting report with regard to the effect of corticosteroids and the host response to virus infections is that of Markham et al. (1986), which showed that the ability of HIV-1 to productively infect normal human PBL was significantly enhanced by supplementing the culture medium with steroids including hydrocortisone. Klein et al. (1987) showed that lymphocytes from HIV-infected subjects demonstrated increased levels of cortisol-induced cell death.

Of course the influence of nervous system activity on the immune system cannot be unidirectional. Whereas some psychological states and some transmitters are immunosuppressive, others may be immunoenhancing. Recent studies suggest that coping with stress modifies stress-induced effects on the clinical symptoms and immunological responses of the host, including HIV-infected subjects (Locke et al., 1984; Lovejoy et al., 1988). It has been recently reported that AIDS-related conditions may respond to treatment with neuroendocrine products. Enkephalin (EK) derived from leukocytes has slowed the progression of HIV infection, increased T-cell counts, and diminished symptoms of the disease (Plotnikoff and Wybran, 1989). Use of thymostimulin and methionine-EK has improved both clinical and laboratory parameters in HIV disease (Wybran and Plotnikoff, 1988). These studies suggest that neuroendocrine axis mediators can function as a link between the CNS and the immune system. Thus, immunological, neurological, and endocrine transmitters may exert a significant immunomodulatory effect on the pathogenesis of various infections, including HIV.

TABLE 2–3. Reversal of PRD-Induced Suppression of NK Cell Activity by an IFN[a]

Treatment of Effector Cells	% Cytotoxicity[b]	% Suppression[c]
None	51.0 ± 3.8	—
IFN (250 U)	62.2 ± 2.8	−26.3[d]
IFN (500 U)	61.6 ± 0.3	−19.3
PRD	36.0 ± 0.3	30.2
PRD + IFN (250 U)	58.5 ± 0.4	5.9
PRD + IFN (500 U)	55.7 ± 0.7	9.5

[a]Lymphocytes were cultured alone or with either 1×10^{-4} M PRD or IFN or PRD + IFN for 1 hour, washed, and tested for NK activity against K562 targets at an effector:target (E:T) cell ratio of 50:1.

[b]Results are the mean of three experiments, each done in triplicate, and expressed as the percentage of mean cytotoxicity ± SEM.

[c]A negative sign ("−") indicates enhancement.

HIV-Derived Soluble Products

Infection with HIV often results in severe dysfunction of NK cells despite normal numbers, as identified by several monoclonal antibodies (CDC, 1982; Wong-Staal and Gallo, 1985; Aiuti et al., 1989; Sirianni et al., 1990). This suggests that either the virus or soluble factors derived therefrom may be responsible for the effect. Data presented in Table 2–4 show that a 270 amino acid recombinant fusion product consisting of an 80 amino acid sequence from HIV gp 41 (env 560–639) and a 190 amino acid sequence from the HIV p24 gene (gag 87–276) that includes 21 amino acids derived from the *Escherichia coli* expression vector can induce de novo immunoglobulin synthesis and can suppress pokeweed mitogen (PWM)-induced immunoglobulin production by normal lymphocytes in vitro. Further, we showed that the recombinant HIV protein, env-gag and other HIV envelope gene-derived recombinant and synthetic peptides such as env 80-DHFR, env 487-511, and env 578-608 could stimulate the proliferation of peripheral blood mononuclear cells from normal donors (Figure 2–1). Previous studies have shown that CD3$^-$, CD16$^+$ LGL can be infected with HIV (Ruscetti et al., 1986; Robinson et al., 1988) and that uninfected CD3$^-$, CD16$^+$ LGL could lyse the HIV-infected cells in a non–major histocompatibility complex (MHC)-restricted fashion (Sirianni et al., 1988). Earlier we showed that direct addition of HIV peptides to cultures of normal donor lymphocytes and NK target cells did not cause any observable effects on cytotoxicity. However, by contrast, direct addition of HIV peptides to lymphocytes from AIDS patients suppressed the NK activities of approximately 60% of the patients studied (Nair et al., 1993). This suggests that synthesis and shedding of such peptides into the circulation during HIV infections may result in subsequent suppression of NK cell activity, as observed in patients

TABLE 2–4.   HIV-1 env-gag Peptide Suppression of Polyclonal Immunoglobulin Synthesis by Lymphocytes with a Recombinant HIV-1 Fusion Protein[a]

Additions to Culture	IgG Concentration (ng/ml)	
Media control	200 ± 81	
env-gag (5 ng/ml)	320 ± 63	NS
env-gag (10 ng/ml)	670 ± 127	p < .025
env-gag (50 ng/ml)	692 ± 130	p < .025
PWM (5 μg/ml)	4725 ± 275	p < .0005
PWM + env-gag (5 ng/ml)	929 ± 192	p < .0005
PWM + env-gag (10 ng/ml)	1832 ± 149	p < .0005
PWM + env-gag (50 ng/ml)	3726 ± 329	p < .025

[a]Peripheral blood mononuclear cells (1×10^5) from healthy, HIV negative individuals were cultured in RPMI 1640 medium containing 5% fetal calf serum to which various concentrations (5, 10, or 50 ng/ml) of the HIV fusion peptide env-gag ± PWM (5 μg/ml) were added. Cultures were incubated at 37°C for 9 days, and supernatants were assayed for IgG by ELISA. Values are the mean ± SD of triplicate determinations from a single experiment. Three other experiments produced similar results. Statistical values were determined by a single-tailed Student's *t* test.

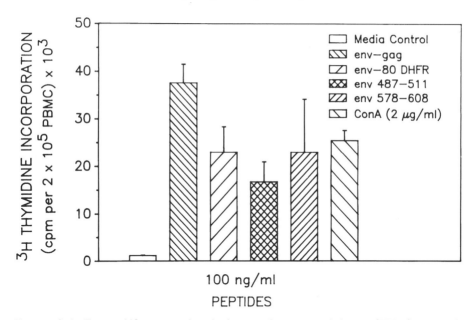

FIGURE 2–1. Two × 10⁵ mononuclear leukocytes from normal donors (HIV⁻) were cultured with 100 ng/ml of different HIV peptides or Con-A (2μg/ml) or media alone for 72 hr and proliferative responses were measured as a function of incorporation of ³H thymidine. Values represent the mean ± SEM of three separate experiments performed in triplicate.

with active HIV infections. One explanation for the CD4⁺ cell depletion seen in AIDS is the specific lysis of HIV-infected CD4 cells expressing viral antigens by autologous lymphocytes via an ADCC reaction. Figure 2–2 shows that normal lymphocytes can mediate cytotoxicity in vitro against env-gag-coated CEM target cells in the presence of sera from HIV-infected patients compared to negligible cytotoxicity manifested with normal donor sera. These results suggest that circulating HIV-derived gene products may enhance cytotoxicity against HIV antigen-bearing CD4 cells in vivo, causing loss of these cells and progression of disease.

Evidence for the presence of HIV antigens in brain tissues has been reported (Kure et al., 1990; Lyman et al., 1990; Wiley et al., 1990). However, the potential mechanism of brain pathology and progressive CNS dysfunction in HIV disease is not clearly understood. In AIDS dementia, macrophages and microglial cells constitute the majority of HIV-infected cells of the CNS. However, whether the manifestation of CNS disease is solely due to the direct infection of these cells with HIV remains a point of controversy. It is also possible that the neurological effects of HIV infection may be a secondary effect mediated by the release of various cytokines such as IL-1 or IL-6, tumor necrosis factor, and/or granulocyte-monocyte colony-stimulating factor (Merrill and Chen, 1991; Sundar et al., 1991).

Earlier studies showed that the CD4 molecule present on the surface membranes of helper T lymphocytes and macrophages is a major receptor for HIV, and it was subsequently demonstrated that a similar if not identical molecule is

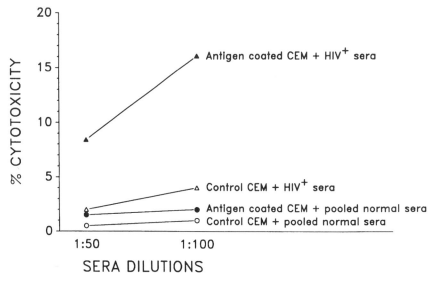

FIGURE 2–2. Prelabeled ^{51}Cr CEM target cells (1×10^5 cell/ml) were treated in media alone or with 100 ng/ml of env-gag peptides at room temperature for 1 hr, washed and used as target in ADCC assays using HIV$^+$ or normal pooled sera. Total mononuclear leukocytes were used as effector cells at 100:1 E:T cell ratio.

present on some human brain cells (Maddon et al., 1986; Dewhurst et al., 1987; Funke et al., 1987). Pert and associates (1988) have shown that the expression of CD4 surface molecules can be modulated by vasoactive intestinal peptide (VIP). Moreover, it was reported that peptide T, a pentapeptide whose sequence was derived from the HIV envelope glycoprotein, gp 120, also could modulate the binding of VIP and HIV to CD4 receptor. Further, gp 120 has been shown to induce N-methyl-D-aspartate (NMDA) receptor-mediated neuronal cytotoxicity, as well as stimulate the release of endogenous glutamate by neurons (Giulian et al., 1990; Lipton et al., 1990). It has recently been shown that quinolinic acid, an agonist of the NMDA receptor and an excitotoxic metabolite, is significantly elevated in the CSF of patients with AIDS dementia complex, suggesting that it plays a role in the pathogenesis of brain dysfunction associated with HIV-1 infection (Heyes et al., 1990, 1991). Others, however, have reported that quinolinic acid did not produce any neurotoxicity in rats with an intact, mature blood-brain barrier (Vezzani et al., 1989). These disparate observations remain to be resolved.

Environmental or Exogenous Factors

Earlier studies have shown that a significant proportion of people exposed to HIV do not become immunodeficient or contract AIDS immediately, suggesting that some cofactors may also influence disease progression. It is well known that intravenous drug users are at increased risk for developing AIDS and subsequent neuropsychiatric abnormalities (Perry and Jacobsen, 1986; Grant et al., 1987). Various recreational drugs such as marijuana, heroin, cocaine, amyl nitrite, ethyl chloride, and alcohol, alone or in combination with neuropsychiatric effects including depression, may contribute in part to the downward course of HIV infections. Cocaine use in particular has been associated with AIDS (Donahoe and Falek, 1988). There may be an association between the duration of heroin addiction, the presence of autoantibodies to brain peptides, and evidence of HIV dementia (Jankovic et al., 1991). Other studies also suggest a potential relationship between AIDS and alcohol abuse (Siegel, 1986; Lake-Bakaar et al., 1988; Bagasra et al., 1989). These drug-using behaviors may have an important impact, either directly or through the neuroendocrine axis, on the immune system of the host and its ability to inhibit various infections, including HIV. We previously demonstrated that PBL from patients with a history of intravenous drug use (IVDU) and alcohol abuse demonstrated decreased levels of NK and ADCC activity, two important host defense mechanisms operating against various infectious diseases and cancer (Table 2–5). It has also been shown that moderate alcohol ingestion increased the in vitro susceptibility of normal peripheral blood mononuclear cells to infection with HIV (Bagasra et al., 1989). Further, a high rate of alcohol consumption has been correlated with more advanced HIV disease (Lake-Bakaar et al., 1988). Watson et al. (1988), using a murine AIDS model, showed that ethanol ingestion in vivo significantly reduced monocyte numbers and decreased immune responses to retrovirus infection.

Cigarette smoking has been shown to have a number of deleterious effects

TABLE 2–5. Comparison of the NK and ADCC Activities of Lymphocytes from Healthy Donors and IVDU at Varying E:T Cell Ratios[a]

		E:T Cell Ratios			
		ADCC		NK	
Expt	Lymphocyte Source	100:1	50:1	100:1	50:1
1	Controls	38.2 ± 8.2	36.7 ± 6.7	42.8 ± 3.8	36.9 ± 5.6
	IVDU	21.1 ± 10.8	19.6 ± 7.6	35.1 ± 8.2	26.5 ± 9.8
2	Controls	51.2 ± 6.2	47.2 ± 7.1	53.4 ± 8.2	43.3 ± 7.2
	IVDU	24.9 ± 3.0	21.3 ± 2.1	29.6 ± 5.9	25.3 ± 6.3
3	Controls	49.2 ± 3.7	45.2 ± 4.8	48.1 ± 5.6	32.1 ± 4.1
	IVDU	32.0 ± 10.9	29.0 ± 11.1	25.5 ± 7.8	23.1 ± 8.2
4	Controls	51.4 ± 4.8	47.6 ± 5.6	52.4 ± 7.1	47.8 ± 4.9
	IVDU	20.6 ± 1.2	17.7 ± 5.3	18.6 ± 1.0	14.3 ± 1.2
		$p < 0.005$	$p < 0.01$	$p < 0.005$[b]	$p < 0.004$

[a]Effector cells were depleted of phagocytic cells, and SB and K562 target cells were labeled with ^{51}Cr. Values represent the mean percentage of cytotoxicity $\pm$ SD. A total of 7 controls and 14 IVDU samples were examined in four separate experiments with triplicate determinations. Each experiment employed two to four IVDU patients and one to two controls samples.

[b]Statistical significance was determined by a two-way analysis of variance, using an F test to account for day-to-day experimental variations in cytotoxicity.

on the immune response of human lymphocytes, such as decreased immuno-globulin production, alteration in the T4:T8 lymphocyte ratio (Gerard et al., 1980), reduced NK activity (Ferson et al., 1979), and depressed mitogen-induced lymphocyte transformation responses (Peterson et al., 1983). We showed that nicotine and alcohol at noninhibitory concentrations, when added separately, caused significant suppression of NK when used in combination (Nair et al., 1990). Nicotine also significantly suppressed PWM-induced immunoglobulin synthesis in vitro by lymphocytes from healthy donors (unpublished observations). Recently we reported that alcohol selectively inhibits the NK activities of lymphocytes from AIDS patients (Nair et al. 1992). Thus, the synergistic suppressive effects of nicotine and alcohol combined on immune responses may play a role in increasing susceptibility to AIDS in HIV-infected subjects, especially since cigarette smoking and alcohol consumption are frequently associated with other risk behaviors for HIV infection.

Concluding Remarks

Behavioral conditions associated with HPA activation release messenger chemicals such as neuroendocrine mediators and neurotransmitters that directly or indirectly may have subsequent immunoregulatory activities. Stress, depression, and viral infections are known to activate the HPA axis. Thus, a close bidirectional communication network exists between the CNS and the immune system. In HIV infection, where retroviral infection, depression, and brain pathology can occur concomitantly, HPA activation may subsequently cause immune perturbations, leading to progression of the disease. Since neurological damage in AIDS is disproportionate to the number of virus-infected target cells in the host, noninfectious mechanisms may also play an important role in the immunopathogenesis of the immunological and neurological dysfunction associated with HIV infections. Both in vitro and in vivo studies have yielded evidence of immune perturbations of normal and HIV-infected subjects in response to a variety of agents cited above, including neuroendocrine factors, neurotransmitters, HIV-derived gene products, and various drugs of abuse. Thus, these factors, working alone or in synergy with one another, may cause a more rapid progression of HIV infection, leading to full-blown AIDS. By elucidating these mechanisms, we may be able to develop new therapeutic and prophylactic interventions.

Acknowledgments

This work was supported in part by NIH Grants 1 RO1 MH42988, 2 RO1 CA35922, 1 RO1 MH47225, 1 P50 AA07378, and 1 P50 MH43564 and by a grant from Hoffman LaRoche, Inc., of Nutley, New Jersey.

We wish to express our appreciation to Denise DuPrie for her excellent secretarial assistance.

References

Aiuti, F., Sirianni, C., Mezzaroma, I., D'Offizi, G.P., Pesce, A.M., Papetti, C., Ensoli, F., and Luzi, G. (1989). HIV-1 infection: Epidemiological features and immunological alterations during the natural history of the disease. *Clinical Immunology and Immunopathology, 50*, S157–S165.

Bagasra, O., Kajdacsy-Balla, A.K., and Lischner, H.W. (1989). Effects of alcohol ingestion on in vitro susceptibility of peripheral blood mononuclear cells to infection with HIV and of selected T-cell functions. *Alcoholism: Clinical and Experimental Research, 13*, 636–643.

Bateman, A., Singh, A., Kral, T., and Solomon, S. (1989). The immune-hypothalamic-pituitary-adrenal axis. *Endocrine Reviews, 10*, 92–112.

Bedinger, P., Moriarty, A., von Borstel, R.C., 2nd, Donovan, N.J., Steimer, K.S., and Littman, D.R. (1988). Internationalization of the human immunodeficiency virus does not require the cytoplasmic domain of CD4. *Nature, 334*, 162–165.

Biondi, M., and Kotzalidis, G.D. (1990). Human psychoneuroimmunology today. *Journal of Clinical Laboratory Analysis, 4*, 22–38.

Borysenko, T. (1984). Stress, coping and immune system. In J.D. Matarazzo, S.M. Weiss, J.A. Herd, and N.E. Miller, eds., *Behavioral Health.* New York: Wiley, pp. 248–260.

Centers for Disease Control Task Force on AIDS. (1982). Update on acquired immune deficiency syndrome (AIDS)—United States. *Morbidity and Mortality Weekly Report, 31*, 507–514.

Cohen, J. (1991). Seventh AIDS conference: Mostly "fine tuning" [news]. *Science, 252*, 1779.

Dewhurst, S., Stevenson, M., and Volvsky, D.J. (1987). Expression of the T4 molecules (AIDS virus receptor) by human brain-derived cells. *FEBS Letters, 213*, 133–137.

Donahoe, R.M., and Falek, A. (1988). Neuroimmunomodulation by opiates and other drugs of abuse: Relationship to HIV infection and AIDS. In T.P. Bridge, ed., *Psychological Neuropsychiatric, and Substance Abuse Aspects of AIDS.* New York: Raven Press, pp. 145–158.

Dunn, A.J. (1988). Nervous system–immune system interactions: An overview. *Journal of Receptor Research, 8*, 559–607.

Dunn, A.J. (1989). Psychoimmunology for the psychoneuroendocrinologist: A review of animal studies of nervous system–immune system interactions. *Psychoneuroendocrinology, 14*, 251–274.

Fauci, A.S. (1988). The human immunodeficiency virus: Infectivity and mechanisms of pathogenesis. *Science, 239*, 617–622.

Ferson, M., Edwards, A., Lind, A., Milton, G.W., and Hersey, P. (1979). Low natural killer cell activity and immunoglobulin levels associated with smoking in human subjects. *International Journal of Cancer, 23*, 603–609.

Folks, T., Powell, D.M., Lightfoote, M., Benn, S., Martin, M.A., and Fauci, A.S. (1986). Induction of HTLV-III/LAV from a nonvirus-producing T cell line. Implications for latency. *Science, 231*, 600–602.

Fontana, A., Fierz, W., and Wekerle, H. (1984). Astrocytes present myelin basic protein to encephalitogenic T cell lines. *Nature, 307*, 273–276.

Funke, I., Hahn, A., Reiber, E.P., Weiss, E., and Reithmuller, G. (1987). The cellular receptor (CD4) of the human immunodeficiency virus is expressed on neurons and glial cells in human brain. *Journal of Experimental Medicine, 165*, 1230–1235.

Garson, J.A., Beverly, B.C.L., Coakham, H.B., and Harper, E.I. (1982). Monoclonal antibodies against human T lymphocytes label Purkinje neurones of many species. *Nature, 298,* 375–377.

Gerard, J.W., Heiner, P.C., Mink, J., Meyers, A., and Dosman, J.A. (1980). Immunoglobulin levels in smokers and non-smokers. *Annals of Allergy, 44,* 261–262.

Giulian, D., Vaca, K., and Noonan, C.A. (1990). Secretion of neurotoxins by mononuclear phagocytes infected with HIV-1. *Science, 250,* 1593–1596.

Glaser, R., Kiecolt-Glaser, J.K., Speicher, C.E., and Holiday, J.E. (1985). Stress, loneliness, and changes in herpes virus latency. *Journal of Behavioral Medicine, 8,* 249–260.

Glaser, R., Rice, J., Sheridan, J., Fertel, R., Stout, J., Speicher, C., Pinsky, D., Kotur, M., Post, A., Beck, M., and Kiecolt-Glaser, J. (1987). Stress-related immune suppression health implications. *Brain, Behavior, and Immunity, 1,* 7–20.

Glaser, R., Rice, J., Speicher, C.E., Stout, J.C., and Kiecolt-Glaser, J.K. (1986). Stress depresses interferon production by leucocytes concomitant with a decrease in natural killer cell activity. *Behavioral Neuroscience, 100,* 675–678.

Grant, I., Atkinson, J., Hesselink, J.R., Kennedy, C.J., Richman, D.D., Spector, S.A., and McCutchan, J.A. (1987). Evidence for early central nervous system involvement in the acquired immunodeficiency syndrome (AIDS) and other human immunodeficiency virus (HIV) infections. Studies with neuropsychologic testing and magnetic resonance imaging. *Annals of Internal Medicine, 107,* 828–836.

Hammarskjold, M.L., and Rekosh, D. (1980). The molecular biology of the human immunodeficiency virus. *Biochimica et Biophysica Acta, 989,* 269–280.

Harada, S., Bechtold, T., Seeley, J.K., and Purtilo, D.T. (1982). Cell-mediated immunity to Epstein-Barr virus (EBV) and natural killer (NK) cell activity in the X-linked lymphoproliferative syndrome. *International Journal of Cancer, 30,* 739–744.

Hassan, N.F., and Douglas, S.D. (1990). Stress-related neuroimmunomodulation of monocyte-macrophage functions in HIV-1 infection. *Clinical Immunology and Immunopathology, 54,* 220–227.

Heyes, M.P., Brew, B.J., Martin, A., Price, R.W., Salazar, A.M., Sidtis, J.J., Yergey, J.A., Mouradian, M.M., Sadler, A.E., Keilp, J., Rubinow, D., and Markey, S. (1991). Quinolinic acid in cerebrospinal fluid and serum in HIV-1 infection: Relationship to clinical and neurologic status. *Annals of Neurology, 29,* 202–209.

Heyes, M.P., Mefford, I.N., Quearry, B.J., Dedhia, M., and Lackner, A. (1990). Increased ratio of quinolinic acid to kynurenic acid in cerebrospinal fluid of D retrovirus–infected rhesus macaques: Relationship to clinical and viral status. *Annals of Neurology, 27,* 666–675.

Ioachim, H.L. (1990). Immunopathogenesis of human immunodeficiency virus infection. *Cancer Research, 50*(Suppl), 5612S–5617S.

Jankovic, B.D., Horvat, J., Djordjijevic, D., Ramah, A., Fridman, V., and Spahic, O. (1991). Brain-associated autoimmune features in heroin addicts: Correlation to HIV infection and dementia. *International Journal of Neuroscience, 58,* 113–126.

Kiecolt-Glaser, J.K., and Glaser, R. (1989). Psychoneuroimmunology: Past, present, and future. *Health Psychology, 8,* 677–682.

Klein, A., Bruser, B., Robinson, J.B., Pinkerton, P.H., and Malkin, A. (1987). Effect of a non-viral fraction of acquired immunodeficiency syndrome plasma on the vulnerability of lymphocytes to cortisol. *Journal of Endocrinology, 112,* 259–264.

Klein, E., Ernberg, I., Masucci, M.G., Szigeti, R., Wu, Y.T., Masucci, G., and Svedmyr, E. (1981). T-cell response to B-cells and Epstein-Barr virus antigens in infectious mononucleosis. *Cancer Research, 41,* 4210–4215.

Kure, K., Lyman, W.D., Weidenheim, W.M., and Dickson, D.W. (1990). Cellular localization of an HIV-1 antigen in subacute AIDS encephalitis using an improved double labeling immunohistochemical method. *American Journal of Pathology, 136*, 1085–1092.

Lake-Bakaar, G., Gupta, N., Beidas, S., and Straus, E.W. (1988). Alcohol and the acquired immunodeficiency syndrome in intravenous drug addicts. In *Abstracts of the 4th International Congress on AIDS.* Stockholm, Sweden, p. 459.

Lipinski, M., Braham, K., Cailland, J.M., Carlu, C., and Twiz, T. (1983). HNK-I antibody detects an antigen expressed on neuroectodermal cells. *Journal of Experimental Medicine, 158*, 1775–1780.

Lipton, S.A., Kaiser, P.K., Sucher, N.J., Dreyer, E.B., and Offermann, J.T. (1990). AIDS virus coat protein sensitized neurons to NMDA receptor mediated cytotoxicity. *Society of Neuroscience Abstracts, 16*, 268 (abst).

Locke, S.E., Kraus, L., Lesserman, J., Hurst, M.W., Heisel, J.S., and Williams, R.M. (1984). Life change stress, psychiatric symptoms and natural killer cell activity. *Psychosomatic Medicine, 46*, 441–453.

Loewenstein, R.J., and Sharfstein, S.S. (1984) Neuropsychiatric aspects of acquired immune deficiency syndrome. *International Journal of Psychiatry in Medicine, 13*, 255–260.

Lovejoy, N.C., Moran, T.A., and Paul, S. (1988). Self-care behaviors and informational needs of seropositive homosexual/bisexual men. *Journal of Acquired Immune Deficiency Syndromes, 1*, 155–161.

Lyman, W.D., Kress, Y., Kure, K., Rashbaum, W.K., Rubinstein, A., and Soeiro, R. (1990). Detection of HIV in fetal central nervous system tissue. *AIDS, 4*, 917–920.

Maddon, P.J., Dalgleish, A.G., McDougal, J.S., Clapham, P.R., Weiss, R.A., and Axel, R. (1986). The T4 gene encodes the AIDS virus receptor and is expressed in the immune system and the brain. *Cell, 47*, 333–348.

Markham, P.D., Salahuddin, S.Z., Veren, K., Orndorff, S., and Gallo, R.C. (1986). Hydrocortisone and some other hormones enhance the expression of HTLV-III. *International Journal of Cancer, 37*, 67–72.

Merrill, J.E., and Chen, I.S.Y. (1991). HIV-1, macrophages, glial cells, and cytokines in AIDS nervous system disease. *FASEB Journal, 5*, 2391–2397.

Nair, M.P.N., Kronfol, Z.A., and Schwartz, S.A. (1990). Effect of alcohol and nicotine on cytotoxic response of human lymphocytes. *Clinical Immunology and Immunopathology, 54*, 395–409.

Nair, M.P.N., and Schwartz, S.A. (1984). Immunoregulatory effects of corticosteroids on natural killer and antibody dependent cellular cytotoxic activities of human lymphocytes. *Journal of Immunology, 132*, 2876–2882.

Nair, M.P.N., and Schwartz, S.A. (1988). Immunoregulation of human natural killer cells (NK) by corticosteroids: Inhibitory effect of culture supernatants. *Journal of Allergy and Clinical Immunology, 82*, 1089–1098.

Nair, M.P.N., Schwartz, S.A., Kronfol, Z.A., Saravolatz, L.A., Heimer, E.P., Pottahil, R., and Greden, J.F. (1992). Selective inhibition of natural killer cell activity of lymphocytes from AIDS patients by alcohol. *Immunology and Infectious Diseases, 2*, 229–232.

Navia, B.A., Jordan, B.D., and Price, R.W. (1986). The AIDS dementia complex: I. Clinical features. *Annals of Neurology, 19*, 517–524.

Nielsen, B.L., Petito, C.K., Urmacher, C.D., and Posner, J.B. (1984). Subacute encephalitis in acquired immune deficiency syndrome: A postmortem study. *American Journal of Clinical Pathology, 82*, 678–682.

Oakes, J.E., Davis, W.E., Taylor, J.A., and Weppner, W.A. (1980). Lymphocyte reactivity contributes to protection conferred by specific antibody passively transferred to herpes simplex virus–induced mice. *Infection and Immunity, 29*, 642–649.

Openshaw, H., Sekizawa, T., Wohlenberg, C., and Notkins, A.L. (1981). The role of immunity in latency and reactivation of herpes simplex viruses. In A.J. Nahmias, W.R. Dowdle, and R.F. Schlanzi, eds., *The Human Herpes Viruses: An Interdisciplinary Perspective.* New York: Elsevier/North Holland, pp. 289–296.

Pavlidis, N., and Chrigos, M. (1980). Stress-induced impairment of macrophage tumoricidal function. *Psychosomatic Medicine, 42*, 47–54.

Perry, S., and Jacobsen, P. (1986). Neuropsychiatric manifestations of AIDS-spectrum disorders. *Hospital and Community Psychiatry, 37*, 135–142.

Pert, C.B., Hill, J.M., Ruff, M.R., Berman, R.M., Robey, W.A., Arthur, L.O., Ruscetti, F.W., and Farrar, W.L. (1986). Octapeptides deduced from the neuropeptide receptor-like pattern of antigen T4 in brain potently inhibit human immunodeficiency virus receptor binding and T-cell infectivity. *Proceedings of the National Academy of Sciences, USA, 83*, 9254–9258.

Pert, C.B., Smith, C.C., Ruff, M.R., and Hill, J.M. (1988). AIDS and its dementia as a neuropeptide disorder: Role of VIP receptor blockade by human immunodeficiency envelope. *Annals of Neurology, 23*, S71–S73.

Peterson, B.H., Steimul, L.F., and Callaghan, J.T. (1983). Suppression of mitogen-induced lymphocyte transformation in cigarette smoking. *Clinical Immunology and Immunopathology, 27*, 135–140.

Pizzo, P.A. (1990). Pediatric AIDS: Problems within problems. *Journal of Infectious Diseases, 161*, 316–325.

Plotnikoff, N.P., and Wybran, J. (1989). Methionine-enkephalin shows promise in reducing HIV in blood [news]. *American Family Physician, 40*, 234.

Rickinson, A.B., Moss, D.J., Wallace, L.E., Rowe, M., Misko, I.S., Epstein, M.A., and Pope, J.H. (1981). Long-term T-cell mediated immunity to Epstein-Barr virus. *Cancer Research, 41*, 4216–4221.

Robinson, W.E. Jr., Mitchell, W.M., Chambers, W.H., Schuffman, S.S., and Montefiori, D.C. (1988). Natural killer cell infection and inactivation in vitro by the human immunodeficiency virus. *Human Pathology, 19*, 535–540.

Ruscetti, F.W., Mikovits, J.A., Kalyanaraman, U.S., Overton, R., Stevenson, H., Stromberg, K., Herberman, R.B., Farrer, W.L., and Ortaldo, J.R. (1986). Analysis of effector mechanisms against HTLV-I and HTLK-III/LAV-infected lymphoid cells. *Journal of Immunology, 136*, 3619–3624.

Schleifer, S.J., Keller, S.E., Camerino, M., Thornton, J.C., and Stein, M. (1983). Suppression of lymphocyte stimulation following bereavement. *Journal of the American Medical Association, 250*, 374–377.

Schuller-Petrovic, S., Gebhart, W., Lassmann, H., Rumpold, H., and Kraft, D. (1983). A shared antigenic determinant between natural killer cells and nervous tissue. *Nature, 306*, 179–181.

Siegel, L. (1986). AIDS: Relationship to alcohol and other drugs. *Journal of Substance Abuse Treatment, 3*, 271–274.

Sirianni, M.C., DeSanctis, G., Maachi, B., Soddu, S., Ensoli, F., Aiuti, F., and Fontana, L. (1988). Natural killer activity from peripheral blood lymphocytes against a human T lymphotrophic retrovirus type III (HTLV-III)-infected cell line. *Diagnostic and Clinical Immunology, 5*, 297–303.

Sirianni, M.C., Taglia-Ferri, F., and Aiuti, F. (1990). Pathogenesis of natural killer cell deficiencies in AIDS. *Immunology Today, 11*, 81–82.

Sodroski, J.G., Rosen, C.A., and Haseltine, W.A. (1984). Transacting transcription of the long terminal repeat of human T lymphotropic viruses in infected cells. *Science, 225*, 381–385.

Solomon, G.F. (1985). The emerging field of psychoneuroimmunology. *Advances, 2*, 6–19.

Solomon, G.F., and Moos, R.H. (1964). Emotions, immunity and disease: A speculative theoretical investigation. *Archives of General Psychiatry, 11*, 657–674.

Stein, M., Keller, S.E., and Schleifer, S.J. (1988). Immune system. Relationship to anxiety disorders. *Psychiatric Clinics of North America, 11*, 349–360.

Sun, D., and Wekerle, H. (1986). Ia-restricted encephalitogenic T lymphocytes mediating EAE lyse autoantigen-presenting astrocytes. *Nature, 320*, 70–72.

Sundar, S.K., Cierpial, M.A., Kamaraju, L.S., Long, S., Hsieh, S., Lorenz, C., Aaron, M., Ritchie, J.C., and Weiss, J.M. (1991). Human immunodeficiency virus glycoprotein (gp120) infused into rat brain induces interleukin I to elevate pituitary-adrenal activity and decrease peripheral cellular immune response. *Proceedings of the National Academy of Science, USA, 88*, 11246–11250.

Teshima, H., Sogawa, H., Kihara, H., Nagata, S., Ago, Y., and Nakagawa, T. (1987). Changes in populations of T cell subsets due to stress. *Annals of the New York Academy of Science, 496*, 459–466.

Vezzani, A., Stasi, M.A., Wu, H.Q., Castiglioni, M., Weckermann, B., and Samanin, R. (1989). Studies on the potential neurotoxic and convulsant effects of increased blood levels of quinolinic acid in rats with altered blood-brain barrier permeability. *Experimental Neurology, 106*, 90–98.

Watson, R.R., Prabhala, R.H., Darban, H.R., Yahya, M.D., and Smith, T.L. (1988). Changes in lymphocyte and macrophage subset due to morphine and ethanol treatment during retrovirus infection causing murine AIDS. *Life Science, 43*, 5–11.

Wiley, C.A., Belman, A.L., Dickson, D.W., Rubinstein, A., and Nelson, J.A. (1990). Human immunodeficiency virus within the brains of children with AIDS. *Clinical Immunopathology, 9*, 1–6.

Wong, G.H., Bartlett, P.F., Clark-Lewis, I., Battye, F., and Schrader, J.W. (1984). Inducible expression of H-2 and Ia antigens on brain cells. *Nature 310*, 688–691.

Wong-Staal, F., and Gallo, R.C. (1985). Human T-lymphotropic retroviruses. *Nature 317*, 395–403.

Wybran, J., and Plotnikoff, N.P. (1988) An open trial with methionin enkephalin (Met Enk). Immunological and clinical results. *Fourth International Conference on AIDS*. Stockholm, Sweden, Abstract No. 3044.

3

Neurological and Neuropathological Manifestations of HIV Infection

JUSTIN C. MCARTHUR

The acquired immunodeficiency syndrome (AIDS) appeared in 1981 with the recognition of clusters of a previously unusual form of pneumonia caused by *Pneumocystis carinii.* Described initially among previously healthy young homosexual men, the new syndrome included opportunistic infections, depletion of T helper (CD4) lymphocytes, and a previously rare skin cancer—Kaposi's sarcoma. Within a few months, the syndrome was also recognized among users of intravenous drugs and their heterosexual contacts, recipients of blood transfusions, hemophiliacs, and children.

In the early years of the epidemic, before the retrovirus human immunodeficiency virus-1 (HIV-1) was identified in 1984 as the cause of AIDS, a variety of opportunistic infections involving the central nervous system (CNS) were described. The severe disruption of cellular immunity permitted reactivation of latent infections and the emergence of truly opportunistic infections (Pitlik et al., 1983). As experience grew with the clinical manifestations of AIDS, it became obvious that neurological disorders were common in patients with HIV infection and that some could not be ascribed to opportunistic processes but appeared to represent novel conditions (Table 3–1). These disorders probably represent the direct or indirect effects of HIV infection on the CNS.

There are important parallels between these human conditions and the animal lentivirus infections, since all lentiviruses cause a degree of neurological damage (Johnson et al., 1988). The lentiviruses or "slow viruses," of which HIV-1 is a member, share certain pathogenic similarities, including mechanisms by which they evade host defenses and immune clearance and cause persistent infection. They typically have long incubation periods and are associated with chronic dis-

TABLE 3–1.   Major Neurological Complications of HIV-1 Infection and Approximate Frequency in the United States

HIV-1 Related	Frequency (%)	Opportunistic Infections	Frequency (%)
Acute aseptic meningitis	1–2	Cryptococcal meningitis[a]	8
Chronic meningitis	25–50	Toxoplasmosis[a]	5–10
HIV-1 dementia[a]	15–30	Cytomegalovirus retinitis/encephalitis[a]	15
Vacuolar myelopathy[a]	10	Other CNS opportunistic infections[a]	5
Sensory neuropathy	30	Herpes zoster radiculitis	10
Inflammatory demyelinating polyneuropathy	<1	Progressive multifocal leukoencephalopathy[a]	4
Mononeuritis multiplex	<1	Primary CNS lymphoma[a]	5
Myopathy	5–10	Systemic lymphoma[a]	5
Toxic neuropathies from antiretrovirals	10	Neurosyphilis	5

[a]AIDS-defining illnesses (CDC, 1987)

eases occurring in nature: visna virus with which HIV-1 shares morphological and genomic characteristics; caprine arthritis encephalitis virus; equine infectious anemia virus; and feline immunodeficiency virus (Figure 3–1). Human infection with HIV-2 and simian disease with simian immunodeficiency virus type 1 (SIV-1), which produces an AIDS-like syndrome after experimental inoculation in macaques, complete the currently recognized list. HIV is a nontransforming retrovirus that produces a cytopathic or lytic effect on T cells, although the precise mechanisms of T-cell depletion are uncertain. The CD4 receptor is the principal target site for HIV; however, there may be other cellular receptors. The replicative cycle of HIV produces an opportunity for rapid mutation, and differences among HIV strains may account for biological differences in tropism or cytopathic effect. Initially, it was thought that after infection and integration of HIV into the host cell genome (producing a provirus), a long period of latency followed. Recent work suggests that this is not a true latent infection and that even during the long incubation period of HIV infection, there may be viral transcription with production of new active virions (Michael et al., 1992).

A type of retrovirus distinct from HIV-1 is prevalent in parts of western Africa and has been termed HIV-2 (de-The et al., 1989). Although there have been some reports of neurological disease associated with HIV-2, it does not appear to be frequent in the United States.

Neuroepidemiology of HIV-1 Infection: Introduction

The Centers for Disease Control (CDC) report that from the beginning of the AIDS epidemic through June 1992, approximately 225,000 cases of AIDS had been diagnosed in the United States and approximately 150,000 of those patients

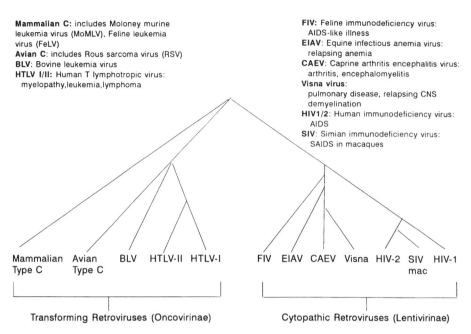

Mammalian C: includes Moloney murine leukemia virus (MoMLV), Feline leukemia virus (FeLV)
Avian C: includes Rous sarcoma virus (RSV)
BLV: Bovine leukemia virus
HTLV I/II: Human T lymphotropic virus: myelopathy, leukemia, lymphoma

FIV: Feline immunodeficiency virus: AIDS-like illness
EIAV: Equine infectious anemia virus: relapsing anemia
CAEV: Caprine arthritis encephalitis virus: arthritis, encephalomyelitis
Visna virus: pulmonary disease, relapsing CNS demyelination
HIV1/2: Human immunodeficiency virus: AIDS
SIV: Simian immunodeficiency virus: SAIDS in macaques

FIGURE 3–1. Evolutionary relationships of retroviruses and associated diseases. The closer the "branches," the greater the genomic similarity. (Adapted from Ho et al., 1987; Olmsted et al., 1989.)

had died (CDC, 1992). The CDC also estimates that 1 million individuals in the United States are infected with the AIDS virus. On a worldwide scale, the WHO estimates that approximately 8–10 million people are infected with HIV and that 5–6 million cases of AIDS will be reported in the decade 1990–2000. Though the disease was originally recognized in homosexual men and intravenous drug users, spread by heterosexual contact and in utero transmission from mother to infant are now recognized as important contributors to the growing number of cases (Figure 3–2).

Epidemiological Features

Surveillance data from the CDC indicate that CNS complications (excluding HIV-1 encephalopathy) made up 7% of all AIDS-defining diseases in the first 23,307 patients with AIDS (Levy et al., 1988b). A retrospective series from the University of California at San Francisco found that 39% of patients with AIDS or AIDS-related complex (ARC) had neurological symptoms and estimated that 10% of all AIDS patients presented with complaints referable to the nervous system (Levy et al., 1985). A similar proportion was reported from New York (Snider et al., 1983b), and other investigators have confirmed the frequency and diversity of neurological disorders associated with HIV-1 infection (McArthur, 1987). Table 3–1 shows the neurological disorders that are considered as "AIDS-indicator" diseases (CDC, 1987).

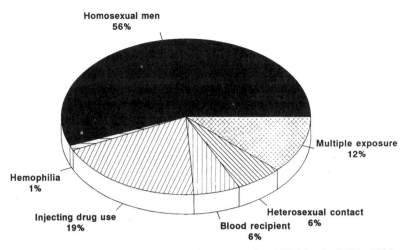

FIGURE 3–2. Risk behavior groups for AIDS in the USA, 1992.

The frequency of the different disorders varies with the geographic, racial, and age characteristics of the population and for some differs, depending on the risk group for HIV-1 acquisition. For example, cryptococcal meningitis occurs significantly more frequently in intravenous drug users than in other risk groups. Racial factors appear to be important too; for example, the prevalence of cryptococcal meningitis is highest among blacks and lowest among whites, with Hispanics being at intermediate risk. Because of increased exposure to *Toxoplasma gondii* organisms, toxoplasmosis is more common in Florida and Europe than in northern states in the United States. Both progressive multifocal leukoencephalopathy (PML) and primary CNS lymphoma may be underreported because they are difficult to diagnose reliably without a brain biopsy, but they appear to have a uniform distribution across the United States (Levy et al., 1988b).

Worldwide, tuberculosis is probably the most common systemic infection associated with HIV-1 infection, and cryptococcal meningitis constitutes the most prevalent neurological disorder.

Spectrum of Primary HIV-1 Related Neurological Disorders

Some of the primary neurological disorders that have been associated with HIV-1 occur at an early stage of infection in the absence of any constitutional symptoms (Figure 3–3). For example, inflammatory demyelinating neuropathies have been described in otherwise asymptomatic individuals. Other disorders, such as HIV-related myelopathy, occur typically in patients with symptomatic HIV disease, ARC, or AIDS. The differences in the timing of these disorders, in their courses and natural history, and among their pathological features suggest that there are different underlying pathogenetic mechanisms.

HIV RELATED NEUROLOGICAL DISEASES

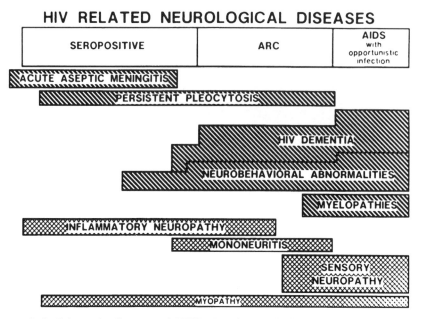

FIGURE 3–3. Schematic diagram of HIV-related neurological diseases. Diseases that affect central (diagonal lines) and peripheral (cross-hatched) nervous systems evolve at different times in relation to stage of infection, and occur at different frequencies (vertical width). (From Johnson et al., 1988.)

HIV-Related Meningitis

A small proportion of individuals undergoing primary HIV-1 infection develop symptoms similar to those of infectious mononucleosis, including fever, myalgias, and rash (Cooper et al., 1985). This acute, usually self-limited illness coincides with the development of antibodies against HIV-1 (seroconversion) and appears to represent the initial response of the nervous system to primary HIV-1 infection. About 1–2% of recently infected individuals will develop acute aseptic meningitis with headache, meningismus, cranial neuropathies, and occasionally transient encephalopathy (Cooper et al., 1985; Ho et al., 1985b) or myelopathy (Denning et al., 1987). Typically, the acute symptoms of HIV-1-related meningitis are self-limited, require only symptomatic treatment with analgesics and antipyretics, and resolve within a few weeks. Up to 60% of HIV-1 carriers will develop a more indolent variant of HIV-1-related meningitis, with chronic pleocytosis and other spinal fluid abnormalities, that is either clinically silent or associated only with headaches (Hollander and Stringari, 1987; McArthur, 1987). Serological testing for HIV-1—and for human T-cell lymphotropic virus type 1 (HTLV-1) should be added to the evaluation of patients with aseptic meningitis or chronic pleocytosis.

HIV-1 Dementia

Within the first year or two of clinical experience with AIDS, it became apparent that many patients developed cognitive impairment (Snider et al., 1983b; Levy et al., 1985). At first, the psychomotor slowing and mental dulling was mistakenly attributed to "depression" or "delirium" or was confused with opportunistic infections of the nervous system. It became obvious, however, that a definable dementia develops in association with infection with HIV-1 (Snider et al., 1983b; Navia et al., 1986a). This is known as *HIV-1-associated dementia complex* (Janssen et al., 1991). It has also been termed *HIV encephalopathy* (CDC, 1987), *subacute encephalitis* (Snider et al., 1983b), *AIDS encephalopathy,* and *AIDS dementia complex* (Navia et al., 1986a,b). The prevalence of HIV dementia has been estimated from CDC surveillance figures at 7% (Janssen et al., 1992). In adults it increases progressively with age, from 6% in the age range 15–34 to 19% in those older than 75 years. McArthur et al. (1993) found an annual incidence of dementia of 7% in homosexual men with AIDS. Risk factors included anemia, constitutional symptoms, and low weight before developing AIDS, suggesting that the sickest patients developed dementia. Cognitive impairment is evident in about one-third of patients with late-stage AIDS. In adults, HIV dementia rarely develops before constitutional symptoms, immune deficiency, and systemic opportunistic processes (McArthur, 1987; Navia and Price, 1987). More commonly, HIV dementia develops after other AIDS-defining illnesses and progresses in the late stages of AIDS. Although several groups have described high rates of neuropsychological test abnormalities in otherwise healthy HIV-1-infected homosexual men (Grant et al., 1987; Janssen et al., 1988; Stern et al., 1991) and in intravenous drug users (Silberstein et al., 1987), the clinical significance of these findings is uncertain (see Chapter 8). These neuropsychological abnormalities are not necessarily progressive and may reflect the confounding effects of low education, age, and substance use rather than HIV-1 infection. Among several hundred HIV-1 seropositive men without AIDS or constitutional symptoms in the Multi-Center AIDS Cohort Study (MACS), the prevalence of HIV dementia was less than 1%, and the overall frequency of neuropsychological impairment was not significantly higher than in HIV-1 seronegative controls (McArthur et al., 1989a; Miller et al., 1990). These findings have been confirmed by other groups (Goethe et al., 1989; Janssen et al., 1989; Clifford et al., 1990; Koralnik et al., 1990; Franzblau et al., 1991; Collier et al., 1992; McAllister et al., 1992). From longitudinal neuropsychological evaluation among AIDS-free HIV seropositives in separate cohorts of homosexual men and intravenous drug users, no evidence of cognitive decline was found during the asymptomatic phase of infection (Selnes et al., 1990, 1992; Saykin et al., 1991).

In children, progressive encephalopathy occurs more commonly than opportunistic infections (Epstein et al., 1985; Mintz et al., 1989). Belman et al. (1988) estimate that 62% of HIV-infected children will dement, with a typical survival of 6–24 months. Clinical features in children include microcephaly, progressive motor dysfunction, and developmental delay, leading to loss of developmental milestones, with death occurring within the first few years of life.

TABLE 3–2. Clinical Staging of HIV-Associated Dementia

Stage	Clinical Description
Stage 0 (normal)	Normal mental and motor function
Stage 0.5 (equivocal/ subclinical)	Absent, minimal, or equivocal symptoms without impairment of work or capacity to perform activities of daily life (ADL). Mild signs (snout response, slowed ocular or extremity movements) may be present. Gait and strength are normal.
Stage 1 (mild)	Able to perform all but the more demanding aspects of work or ADL, but with unequivocal evidence (signs or symptoms that may include performance on neuropsychological testing) of functional intellectual or motor impairment. Can walk without assistance.
Stage 2 (moderate)	Able to perform basic activities of self-care, but cannot work or maintain the more demanding aspects of daily life. Ambulatory, but may require a single prop.
Stage 3 (severe)	Major intellectual incapacity (cannot follow news or personal events, cannot sustain a complex conversation, considerable slowing of all outputs) or motor disability (cannot walk unassisted, requiring a walker or personal support, usually with slowing and clumsiness of the arms as well).
Stage 4 (end stage)	Nearly vegetative. Intellectual and social comprehension and output are at a rudimentary level. Nearly or absolutely mute. Paraparetic or paraplegic, with urinary and fecal incontinence.

Source: Developed at Memorial Sloan Kettering Center (Price and Brew, 1988).

The clinical manifestations of HIV dementia suggest predominantly subcortical involvement, at least initially (Navia et al., 1986a). A typical presentation includes apathy and inertia, memory loss and cognitive slowing, depressive symptoms, and withdrawal from usual activities. The early symptoms are often subtle and may be confused with psychiatric complaints or even overlooked. With advancing dementia, new learning and memory deteriorate, there is a further slowing of mental processing, and language impairment becomes more obvious. The terminal phases of the syndrome are characterized by global impairment, with severe psychomotor retardation and mutism. A staging scheme has been developed that is useful both in clinical practice and for research studies (Price and Brew, 1988) (Table 3–2). The dementia may progress rapidly over a few weeks or months, with a mean survival of about 6 months.

Neuropsychological testing (see Chapter 8) shows a typical pattern of deficits (Figure 3–4), with most impairment in timed tasks measuring psychomotor speed and mental flexibility. Verbal memory is affected early, with a discrepancy between recall and recognition memory. Frontal lobe or executive function is also abnormal early, but language, simple attention, and concentration frequently remain normal until more advanced stages of HIV dementia.

Neurological examination is often normal in the early stages of HIV dementia, although there may be demonstrable impairments of rapid eye and limb movements and diffuse hyperreflexia. Widely used tests other than mental status

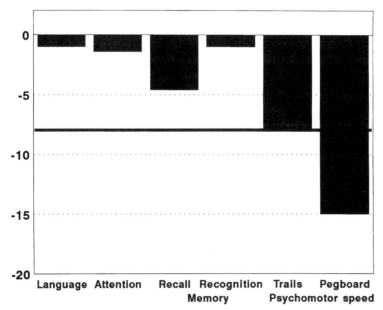

FIGURE 3–4. Typical neuropsychological test profile from a 53-year-old homosexual man with moderate HIV dementia (12 years education). Each bar represents performance in a particular cognitive domain, relative to population norm. Thus a z-score of -5 reflects performance 5 S.D. below the population mean. Note the dramatic impairments in measures of psychomotor speed and memory recall, with better preservation of recognition, memory, language, and attention. (Provided by Dr. Ola Selnes.)

tests, such as the Mini-Mental State Exam, are insensitive in HIV dementia. As HIV dementia progresses, increased muscle tone develops, particularly in the lower extremities, and is usually accompanied by psychomotor slowing, tremor, clonus, diffuse release signs, and hyperactive reflexes. The examination may reflect the effects of concurrent HIV-related myelopathy or a peripheral neuropathy. Retinal "cotton-wool" spots occur in 60% of patients with AIDS; however, these are not pathognomonic for HIV dementia (Pomerantz et al., 1987).

In the early stages of HIV dementia, differential diagnosis is particularly difficult because the initial symptoms can be confused with depression, anxiety disorders, or the effects of psychoactive substances. Often detailed historical information from friends, family members, or coworkers is helpful, and psychiatric consultation may be indicated. Differentiation from CNS opportunistic infections such as cytomegalovirus (CMV) encephalitis, cerebral toxoplasmosis, neurosyphilis, and cryptococcal or tuberculous meningitis is critical. Table 3–3 lists features that may be helpful in establishing this diagnosis, and Table 3–4 provides the recent definitions of HIV-associated dementia complex and minor cognitive and motor disorder developed by the American Academy of Neurology Task Force on AIDS (Janssen et al., 1991).

TABLE 3–3.   Clinical Features Useful for Diagnosis of HIV-Associated Dementia

---

HIV-1 seropositivity (Western blot confirmation)

History of *progressive* cognitive/behavioral decline with apathy, memory loss, slowed mental processing

Neurological exam: diffuse CNS signs including slowed or rapid eye/limb movements, hyperreflexia, hypertonia, and release signs

Neuropsychological assessment: progressive deterioration on serial testing in at least two areas, including frontal lobe, motor speed, and nonverbal memory

CSF analysis: nonspecific abnormalities of IgG and protein, elevated CSF beta-2-microglobulin, exclusion of neurosyphilis and cryptococcal meningitis

Imaging studies: diffuse cerebral atrophy with ill-defined white matter hyperintensities on magnetic resonance imaging in the absence of opportunistic processes

Absence of major psychiatric disorder or active substance abuse

Absence of metabolic derangement (e.g., hypoxia, sepsis)

Laboratory Findings

Lumbar puncture is important to exclude opportunistic infections in the patient with suspected HIV dementia. The majority of patients with HIV dementia will have cerebrospinal fluid (CSF) abnormalities; however, similar patterns of CSF abnormalities are frequently found in neurologically normal HIV carriers. At present, no single CSF test or combination of tests can reliably diagnose HIV dementia; however, a completely normal CSF profile, with no abnormalities of protein or IgG, points away from the diagnosis. Elevated total protein is found in up to 65% of cases and increased total immunoglobulin (IgG) fraction in up to 80% (see Figure 3–5) (McArthur, 1987). Markers of immune activation in the CSF such as neopterin and beta-2-microglobulin are frequently elevated (Brew et al., 1989, 1992). In the absence of opportunistic infections, beta-2-microglobulin has a specificity of 95% and a positive predictive value of 75% for HIV dementia (McArthur et al., 1992). Oligoclonal bands are found in up to 35%, but myelin basic protein is usually not elevated, although it has been found to be elevated by one group of investigators (Grimaldi et al., 1991). Intrathecal synthesis (ITS) of anti-HIV-1 IgG is a nonspecific finding since ITS can be detected in up to 45% of neurologically normal HIV carriers (Van Wielink et al., 1990). The CSF is usually acellular, but it may show a mild lymphocytic pleocytosis with proportions of CD4+ and CD8+ lymphocytes that parallel those found in peripheral blood (McArthur et al., 1989b). Quinolinic acid, a metabolite of tryptophan, is also elevated during HIV dementia and may reflect macrophage activation within the CNS (Heyes et al., 1989); it is elevated with opportunistic processes and thus is a nonspecific marker.

Imaging studies are critical in the evaluation of suspected HIV dementia to exclude mass lesions. Computed tomographic (CT) features include both central and cortical atrophy (Gelman and Guinto, 1992; Raininko et al., 1992) and white matter rarefaction. In children, calcifications of the basal ganglia are commonly seen on CT scan. Virtually all patients with cognitive impairment show atrophy,

TABLE 3–4. Nomenclature for HIV-Associated CNS Disorders

Severe Manifestations	
Terminology	*Diagnostic Criteria*
A. HIV-1-associated dementia complex	1. Acquired cognitive abnormality in two or more domains, causing functional impairment.
	2. Acquired abnormality in motor performance or behavioral change.
	3. No clouding of consciousness or other confounding etiology, including active CNS opportunistic infection, psychiatric disorder, or active substance abuse.
B. HIV-1-associated myelopathy	1. Symptoms of weakness, incoordination, or urinary incontinence and signs of paraparesis, spasticity, and hyperreflexia.
	2. Myelopathic disturbance severe enough to require support for walking.
	3. No HIV dementia.
	4. Other causes of myelopathy excluded.
Mild Manifestations	
Terminology	*Diagnostic Criteria*
A. HIV-1-associated minor cognitive/motor disorder	1. At least two symptoms: impaired attention/concentration, mental slowing, impaired memory, slowed movements, incoordination, personality change, and acquired cognitive/motor abnormality on neurological or neuropsychological testing.
	2. No evidence of another etiology.

Source: Janssen et al. (1991).

and up to 70% of all patients with AIDS will also show atrophy (Raininko et al., 1992). Generalized atrophy is more frequent in the later stages of HIV infection with lower CD4 counts (Dal Pan et al., 1992b; Raininko et al., 1992). However, with HIV dementia, it appears that there may be specific regional atrophy in basal ganglia structures (Dal Pan et al., 1992b). Both central and cortical atrophy often progress in parallel with clinical deterioration (Figure 3–6a,b).

Magnetic resonance imaging (MRI) more readily demonstrates white matter abnormalities in HIV dementia that appear as ill-defined areas of increased signal intensity on T_2-weighted images (Levy et al., 1986b; Price and Navia, 1987; Olsen et al., 1988; Post et al., 1988). These often evolve from small, ill-defined areas of hyperintensities seen in deep white matter in patients with early HIV dementia to more diffuse abnormalities in severely demented individuals (Figure 3–7).

Both single-photon emission computed tomography (SPECT) and positron emission tomography (PET) have been used in small numbers of individuals with HIV dementia. Using PET, Rottenberg and colleagues (1987) demonstrated subcortical hypermetabolism in the early stages of HIV dementia, with later pro-

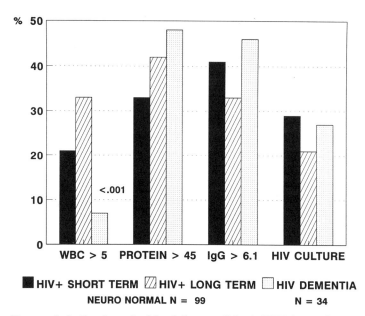

FIGURE 3–5. Cerebrospinal fluid abnormalities in HIV dementia. Note the relatively high frequency of CSF pleocytosis, protein elevation, elevated IgG and positive HIV isolation from neurologically *normal* individuals. CSF pleocytosis is significantly *less* frequent in HIV dementia.

gression to cortical and subcortical hypometabolism. Normalization of PET abnormalities has also been shown with administration of antiviral medications (Yarchoan et al., 1987). With SPECT, abnormalities in cerebral blood flow have been identified in most individuals with HIV dementia and in neurologically normal HIV-1 carriers, suggesting that SPECT may be a useful predictive tool (LaFrance et al., 1988). Neither of these techniques is widely available, however, and their interpretation and quantitation are difficult, particularly in the setting of cocaine abuse, which can cause similar perfusion defects (Holman et al., 1992). Their usefulness in detecting HIV dementia or in assessing treatment effects remains to be determined. MR spectroscopy has been used to assess brain energy and phospholipid metabolism. One study has shown lower adenosine triphosphate (ATP) concentrations in white matter, suggesting that impaired brain metabolism may occur with dementia (Deicken et al., 1991).

An increased rate of electroencephalographic (EEG) abnormalities was reported in one study of asymptomatic seropositives (Koralnik et al., 1990), but this was not confirmed in larger prospective studies (Nuwer et al., 1992). EEG has not been systematically studied in either the diagnosis or staging of HIV dementia. In the late stages of HIV dementia, a diffuse slowing is frequently noted (Navia et al., 1986a); however, in less advanced stages of dementia the EEG can be normal in up to 50% of patients (McArthur, 1987). The specificity of EEG in differentiating psychiatric disorders from early dementia is uncertain; in general, neither standard EEG nor computerized spectral analysis adds significantly to the diagnostic evaluation of HIV dementia.

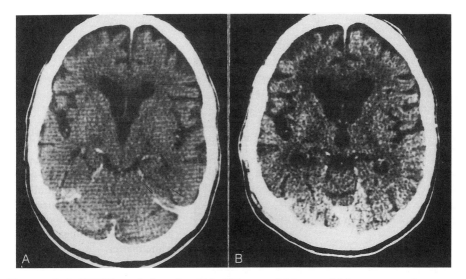

FIGURE 3–6. HIV Encephalopathy. (A). CT scan of 36-year-old intravenous drug user with AIDS-related complex and early HIV dementia. Mild fronto-temporal atrophy and ventricular enlargement are seen. (B). CT scan of same patient 3 months later with far advanced HIV dementia. Severe fronto-temporal atrophy and ventriculomegaly are noted with attentuation of the periventricular white matter.

Pathological Features

Cerebral atrophy is common in patients with HIV dementia, often occurring in a frontotemporal distribution with ventricular enlargement. In a quantitative postmortem analysis, expansion of CSF spaces was found in 37/64 consecutively autopsied patients with AIDS (Gelman and Guinto, 1992), with maximum expansion in the frontal and temporal lobes and more central atrophy than cortical atrophy. While clinical details were lacking, patients with postmortem atrophy were more likely to have multinucleated giant cells (28% vs. 7%), microglial nodules (53% to 25%), leptofibrosis (64% vs. 30%), and vacuolar myelopathy (40% vs. 13%), but not white matter injury (66% vs. 54%). Any HIV-related pathological change was found in 91% of those with atrophy compared with 59% of those without it. Antemortem cranial CT scans were available in 47 of the autopsied AIDS patients, and planimetry was used to quantify the extent of atrophy that correlated well with the presence of pathological atrophy but not with its severity.

The microscopic hallmark of HIV dementia is the presence of multinucleated giant cells (Figure 3–8b) (Sharer et al., 1985; Budka, 1986; Rhodes, 1987). Their presence correlates with both the degree of dementia and the detection of HIV-1 DNA (Price et al., 1988). Multinucleated giant cells are thought to reflect HIV-1 replication and fusion of infected macrophages, since giant multinucleated cells form in HIV-1 macrophage cultures (Gartner et al., 1986) and the giant cells contain HIV nucleic acid (Wiley et al., 1986). The combination of multinucleated

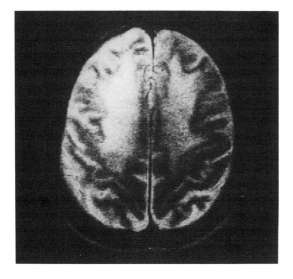

FIGURE 3–7. HIV Encephalopathy. MRI scan (T2 weighted image) of 38-year-old bisexual male with late HIV dementia demonstrating enlargement of the ventricles, cerebral atrophy and diffuse abnormalities throughout the white matter.

giant cells, microglial nodules, and perivenular inflammation was originally termed *subacute encephalitis* (Snider et al., 1983b; Sharer and Kapila, 1985; Navia et al., 1986b) but is now designated *HIV encephalitis* (Budka et al., 1991). It has been identified in 30–90% of patients dying with AIDS, depending on the series (de la Monte et al., 1987). *HIV encephalitis* is a pathological term that is synonymous with *subacute encephalitis, multinucleated cell encephalitis,* and other terms (Budka et al., 1991). One unresolved paradox is the discordance between the clinical severity of dementia and the sometimes bland neuropathology. Not all demented patients have multinucleated giant cells, although evidence of productive HIV infection in the brain may be detectable by immunocytochemistry. In fact, in a recent series, only 25% of clinically demented patients had multinucleated giant cells (Glass et al., 1992).

Multiple small nodules containing macrophages, lymphocytes, and microglia (termed *microglial nodules*) (Figure 3–8a) are scattered throughout both the gray and white matter of the brain, appearing more commonly in white matter and in the subcortical gray matter of the thalamus, basal ganglia, and brain stem (de la Monte et al., 1987). These inflammatory nodules are not specific for HIV-1 infection and occur in other infections, including toxoplasmosis and CMV encephalitis. The number of nodules does not correlate with the severity of the dementia (Navia et al., 1986b). Perivascular infiltrations of lymphocytes and monocyte-macrophages are also frequently seen (Navia et al., 1986b; Wiley et al., 1986; de la Monte et al., 1987; Rhodes, 1987) and contain viral nucleic acid sequences (Wiley et al., 1986).

In addition to the pathological features of multinucleated giant cell formation (HIV encephalitis), a diffuse pallor of the white matter with astrocytosis is frequently observed. This has recently been termed *HIV leukoencephalopathy* (Table 3–5) and probably underlies the white matter changes seen on MRI.

It had been uncertain whether the atrophy reflected loss of gray matter or the leukoencephalopathy. Recently, several investigators have used morpho-

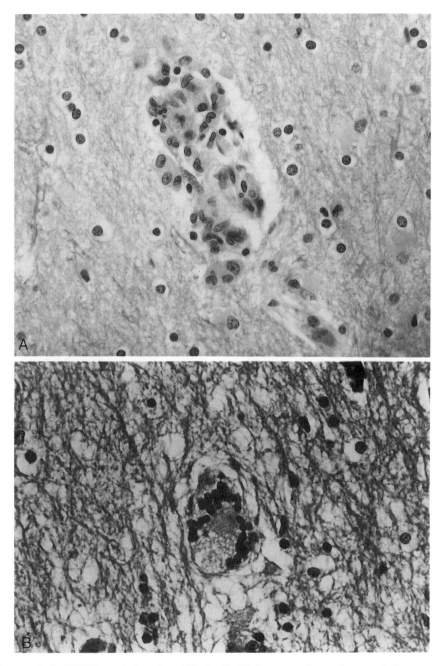

FIGURE 3–8. HIV Encephalopathy. (A) *(Left)*. High-power photomicrograph from centrum semiovale (hematoxylin and eosin) of a patient dying with advanced HIV dementia demonstrating a microglial nodule. Mag. 800 ×. (B) *(Right)* High-power photomicrograph from centrum semiovale of same patient (hematoxylin and eosin) showing a multinucleated giant cell. Mag. 800 ×.

TABLE 3–5. Recommended Neuropathy Terminology for HIV-Associated CNS Disease

New Terminology	Old Terminology	Definition
HIV encephalitis	Giant cell encephalitis, multinucleated cell encephalitis, subacute encephalitis	Multiple disseminated foci of microglia, macrophages, and multinucleated giant cells (MNGCs). If MNGCs are not present, HIV antigen or nucleic acids are demonstrated by immunocytochemistry or in situ hybridization.
HIV leukoencephalopathy	Diffuse myelin pallor, progressive diffuse leukoencephalopathy	Diffuse damage to white matter with myelin loss, reactive astrogliosis, macrophages, and MNGCs or detectable HIV antigen or nucleic acids.
Diffuse poliodystrophy	Subacute encephalitis	Diffuse reactive astrogliosis and microglial activation involving cerebral gray matter. Note: This term designates diffuse pathology of cortical and subcortical gray matter structures that may underlie neuronal loss or changes in synaptic or dendritic anatomy.
Vacuolar myelopathy	Vacuolar myelopathy	Multiple areas of spinal cord involved by vacuolar myelin changes, with macrophages identifiable in at least some vacuoles.

Source: Budka et al. (1991).

metric techniques to document neuronal loss in cortical areas (Ketzler et al., 1990; Everall et al., 1991; Wiley et al., 1991). This has been confirmed by in vivo work using quantitative MRI showing atrophy in basal ganglia structures in HIV dementia (Dal Pan et al., 1992b; Aylward et al., 1993). There are also changes in synaptic density or dendritic arborization (Masliah et al., 1992) in advanced HIV infection. Such changes in gray matter may be accompanied by astrocytosis and have been termed *diffuse poliodystrophy* (Table 3–5).

The neuropathological features of HIV dementia in children differ from those in adults. Vascular mineralization of the basal ganglia and white matter is common (Belman et al., 1986). Perivenular infiltrates and multinucleated giant cells are seen in both adults and children, but white matter pallor is difficult to identify in the developing brain.

It is important to note that clinicopathological correlations between the pattern and severity of dementia and the presence of HIV encephalitis, leukoencephalopathy, or poliodystrophy are incomplete. It is uncertain whether different clinical presentations are associated with different pathological expressions; more detailed clinicopathological correlation will be needed to explore this issue.

Evidence for HIV-1 as the Causative Agent

Initially, CMV was suspected to be the cause of the progressive dementia (Snider et al., 1983b). The evidence for HIV-1 as the causative agent rests on morphological identification of the virus (Epstein et al., 1984; Gyorkey et al., 1987), intrathecal synthesis of antibody (Resnick et al., 1985; Elovaara et al., 1987; Van Wielink et al., 1990), virus isolation (Ho et al., 1985a; J.A. Levy et al., 1985; Stoler et al., 1986; de la Monte et al., 1987), immunocytochemical staining for viral antigens (Gabuzda et al., 1986; Wiley et al., 1986; de la Monte et al., 1987; Gyorkey et al., 1987; Pumarola-Sune et al., 1987; Vazeux et al., 1987; Price et al., 1988), and in situ hybridization (Shaw et al., 1985; Koenig et al., 1986; Wiley et al., 1986).

Localization and Neurotropism of HIV-1

The majority of studies have consistently shown that HIV-1 infection is more frequent in macrophages and multinucleated giant cells, and that the deep white matter and basal ganglia are more commonly involved than the cortical gray matter. A detailed study of gp41 immunoreactivity showed regional variations in the distribution of HIV-1 antigens. The highest concentrations of gp41 staining were seen in the medial globus pallidus, corpus striatum, thalamus, ventral midbrain, and dentate nuclei (Kure et al., 1990). Parenchymal cells such as oligodendrocytes or neurons rarely, if ever, contain replicating virus.

HIV-1 probably gains access to the CNS from the bloodstream, either by direct infection of capillary endothelial cells (Johnson et al., 1988) or, more likely, by ingress of infected macrophages. Despite numerous studies demonstrating that both astrocytes (Dewhurst et al., 1987) and oligodendrocytes (Gyorkey et al., 1987) can act in vitro as targets for HIV-1 infection, these cells are unlikely primary targets. It is possible that certain strains of HIV-1 with specific sequence changes in envelope have an increased propensity to invade and cause damage in the CNS. Most attention has focused on variations in the V3 loop portion of the envelope region. Several investigators have demonstrated that sequence differences in a site adjacent to the CD4 receptor binding site may be important determinants of in vitro tropism (Cann et al., 1990, 1992; O'Brien et al., 1991).

Pathogenetic Mechanisms

The pathogenetic mechanisms involved in the production of HIV dementia remain obscure since even with severe dementia there may only be relatively mild neuropathological changes (de la Monte et al., 1987; Price et al., 1988; Glass et al., 1992). Only a small fraction of cells within inflammatory nodules or perivenular infiltrates contain viral antigens (Gabuzda et al., 1986), and the overall burden of actively replicating HIV may be low. This discrepancy between the small amounts of replicating HIV-1 present and the severity of the dementia suggests that factors other than direct cellular damage by HIV-1 may be important in pathogenesis (Johnson et al., 1988). Other lentiviral infections have been used as animal models of HIV encephalitis. SIV induces an encephalitis in macaques with pathological changes similar to those of HIV encephalitis (Lackner et al., 1991). In cats with natural feline immunodeficiency virus (FIV) infection, neurological signs develop in 5%, including dementia, behavioral change, and seizures (Pedersen et al., 1989). Neuropathological features include perivascular infiltration, microglial nodules, and generalized astrocytosis, but multinucleated giant cells are notably absent (Dow et al., 1990). Unfortunately, available animal models have not advanced our understanding of the pathogenesis in human disease.

One plausible pathogenetic mechanism is that the local release of cytokines or other soluble factors from infected or activated macrophages in the brain impairs the function of neural cells or modifies neurotransmitter function (Navia et al., 1986b; Johnson et al., 1988). Alternatively, the release of these soluble factors might cause the leukoencephalopathy. The precise mechanisms underlying these changes in vivo have not yet been defined, but the similarities to the lesions of postinfectious encephalomyelitis or visna infection suggest that it may result from immune-mediated mechanisms or that it may be a form of "bystander demyelination" mediated by proteases and other products of activated macrophages (Johnson et al., 1988). Immunocytochemistry has demonstrated high levels of cytokines including tumor necrosis factor-α (TNFα) and interleukin-6 (IL-6) in the brains of AIDS patients (Tyor et al., 1992b). Levels of messenger RNA (mRNA) for TNFα are elevated in demented brains (Wesselingh et al., 1993). TNFα has a number of actions, including increasing blood-brain barrier permeability and stimulating microglial and astrocytic proliferation; it can also damage oligodendrocytes in vitro (Robbins et al., 1987; Merrill, 1991). Thus TNFα has become an important suspect in the pathogenesis of HIV dementia.

Other possible mechanisms include direct neural cell infection with HIV or a neurotoxic effect from HIV proteins. However, there is little evidence for *productive HIV infection* in neurons, oligodendroglia, or astroglia. The question of whether there might be viral latency or proviral DNA in neural cells is unanswered. It has been proposed that gp120 is neurotoxic from experiments demonstrating that gp120 in vitro leads to neuronal death (Brenneman et al., 1988) and increases the amount of free calcium within neurons (Dreyer et al., 1990). The increase in free intracellular calcium might damage neurons in the same manner that calcium is thought to be neurotoxic in other neurological disorders. Several reports describe drops in neuronal density (Ketzler et al., 1990; Everall et al., 1991; Wiley et al., 1991) or in dendritic synaptic density (Masliah et al., 1992). Interestingly, dystrophic changes similar to those observed by Masliah et al. were found in rats exposed to gp120 (Hill et al., 1993). Calcium channel antagonists such as nimodipine block the in vitro neurotoxicity of gp120, and their use in the clinical setting is currently under trial. Tardieu et al. (1992) have shown in vitro that human neurons and astrocytes are resistant to HIV infection but can be destroyed by HIV-infected monocytic cells adherent to their membranes. In their experiments, a cytopathic effect could not be induced by cytokines and was not dependent on release of free radicals, suggesting that local release of viral antigens or other unidentified neurotoxic substances is important for the neurotoxic effect. No cytopathic effect was noted when the cultured neural cells were exposed to TNF, IL-1, or interferon-gamma, except for very high doses of TNF-α (1000 U/ml).

Last, the role of toxins in inducing neural dysfunction has been explored. The CSF of demented individuals contains greatly elevated levels of quinolinic acid, an excitatory neurotoxic metabolite of tryptophan, which acts at NMDA receptors (Heyes et al., 1989, 1990). Giulian et al. (1990) showed that HIV-infected macrophages release an unidentified small molecular weight substance that kills neurons in vitro and can be blocked by NMDA antagonists. Pulliam et al. (1991) showed similar toxicity on human fetal brain cell aggregates with HIV-infected macrophages. The nature of these released toxic factors, whether they are cytokines or fragments of viral proteins, is unknown. It is possible that glutamate activation of NMDA receptors is a critical step in HIV-related pathogenesis (Lipton, 1992a) and that NMDA antagonists, like memantine, may be useful in reversing HIV dementia (Lipton, 1992b).

In summary, the clinical, radiological, and pathological features of HIV dementia suggest predominantly subcortical involvement with multinucleated giant cell encephalitis and prominent leukoencephalopathy but relatively low amounts of productive HIV infection. Because of the absence of multinucleated giant cells or leukoencephalopathy in some severely demented individuals, neurotoxic effects from products of infected or activated macrophages may be relevant. The frequency of CSF abnormalities in the early stages of infection and of neuropathological abnormalities suggests that viral invasion of the nervous system occurs in the majority of HIV-1-infected patients, yet not all develop progressive dementia. Differences in neurovirulence or in rates of replication among strains of HIV-1 may be of great importance in explaining this discrepancy.

Treatment of HIV Dementia

Despite the unresolved questions about pathogenesis, antiretroviral agents are used in the treatment of HIV dementia. Open-label studies with azidothymidine (Retrovir, AZT, ZDV) in demented individuals showed promising improvements in clinical functioning, neuropsychological performance, and normalization of PET scans (Yarchoan et al., 1987). More widespread and earlier use of AZT may have reduced the incidence of HIV dementia; a drop in the semiannual incidence of HIV dementia from 53% before AZT was available to 10% has been reported (Portegies et al., 1989).

Evidence from the original licensing trial (Fischl et al., 1987) of AZT in patients with AIDS or ARC suggests that AZT improves neuropsychological function (Schmitt et al., 1988). Children treated with intravenous AZT showed improvement in neuropsychological performance, although no clear dose-response correlation was seen (Pizzo et al., 1988).

The only placebo-controlled trial of AZT in HIV dementia suggests that there is a dose-response correlation, with more neurocognitive improvement seen with AZT doses of about 2000 mg/day (Sidtis et al., 1993). This is substantially higher than the currently recommended dose for systemic use of 500 mg/day. Hematological toxicity is the major toxicity of AZT and is dose dependent. Because of this counterplay between hematological toxicity and adequate CNS penetrance, the optimal dose of AZT for treatment of HIV dementia has not been determined. Current practice for HIV dementia is to start AZT at 1000 mg/day, checking blood counts regularly. Erythropoietin (Epogen) or granulocyte colony-stimulating factor (Neupogen) can be used to counter anemia or leukopenia. An alternative antiretroviral didanosine (Videx), can be initiated if dementia progresses on AZT, if there is hematological toxicity, or if there is a high likelihood of AZT resistance (e.g., after more than 18 months of prior AZT use) (Yarchoan et al., 1990). As research progresses on the pathogenetic mechanisms underlying HIV dementia, other therapeutic advances will be made, including perhaps the use of cytokine blockers such as pentoxifylline (Dezube et al., 1992), calcium channel antagonists such as nimodipine (Dreyer et al., 1990), and NMDA antagonists such as memantine (Lipton, 1992b). A novel approach using a synthetic peptide (peptide T) that is purported to block gp120 neurotoxicity in vitro has shown some promise in early clinical trials (Bridge et al., 1991). As with other CNS viral infections, early initiation of antimicrobial therapy is likely to be essential in stabilizing or restoring brain function.

Symptomatic treatment is an important adjunct to antiviral treatment. Patients with HIV dementia are extremely susceptible to the adverse effects of psychoactive drugs, so hypnotics and anxiolytics should be avoided. Small doses of neuroleptics, such as haloperidol (Haldol), 0.5 mg, may be needed in the agitated or combative patient. If marked depressive symptoms are present, tricyclic antidepressants or fluoxetine (Prozac) can be tried in doses 25–50% of the usual dose. Full doses of tricyclics may precipitate delirium, and serum levels should be monitored frequently. In patients with progressive dementia, medicolegal issues should be discussed at an early stage before the dementia becomes too severe: establishing a durable power of attorney, completion of a living will, and arrangement for the disposal of assets.

HIV-1-Associated Myelopathies

The most common myelopathy associated with HIV-1 infection, termed *vacuolar myelopathy,* clinically affects up to 20% of adult patients with AIDS, although evidence of this condition can be found in up to 50% of adult autopsies but in only 10% of pediatric cases (Mintz et al., 1989). It presents with a progressive, spastic paraparesis and sensory ataxia, and in about 60% of those with myelopathy, cognitive impairment develops concurrently. Occasionally, the myelopathy develops before dementia and even with HIV seroconversion (Denning et al., 1987) or as the first AIDS-defining illness, but usually the two develop and progress in parallel in the later stages of HIV disease (see Figure 3–3). Often a peripheral neuropathy coexists; thus, the combined clinical picture can include cognitive deficits as well as myeloneuropathy, typically with ankle areflexia and hypotonia. Table 3–5 indicates the recently developed criteria for the clinical diagnosis of HIV-associated myelopathy (Janssen et al., 1991). Subclinical myelopathy may in fact be more common than was originally anticipated. Using somatosensory evoked potentials, Jakobsen et al. (1989) detected delayed conduction times in asymptomatic HIV carriers. The abnormalities progressed over 2 years of follow-up, pointing to dysfunction in lumbar cord or roots.

The major pathological finding is a patchy vacuolation in the spinal white matter, particularly in the lateral and posterior columns of the thoracic spinal cord (Figure 3–9a,b). In 80% of cases, the myelopathy is unrecognized before death (Dal Pan et al., 1992a). The vacuoles develop from splitting of the myelin lamellae by intramyelinic edema. There appears to be a gradation of severity of lesions, perhaps reflecting their temporal development. Early lesions have small numbers of vacuoles with intramyelinic macrophages. The macrophages are activated and appear to produce cytokines (Tyor et al., 1992b). Later or more severe lesions show complete demyelination with astrocytic gliosis and some evidence of remyelination. The final or most severe stage includes necrosis and replacement by foamy macrophages and astrocytic processes.

HIV-1 has been isolated from both the spinal cord and CSF of individuals with progressive myelopathy (Ho et al., 1985a), but it is not certain whether HIV-1 is directly pathogenic to the spinal cord. A similar type of vacuolar change develops in other conditions not associated with HIV-1 infection, including vitamin B_{12} deficiency with subacute combined degeneration of the cord, and in other immune deficiency states (Kamin and Petito, 1988). The frequency of identification of HIV in vacuolar myelopathy is variable and seems dependent on the presence of multinucleated giant cells. Maier et al. (1989) found abundant HIV and giant cells, while Rosenblum et al. (1989) found evidence of productive HIV infection in only 15% of cords. Given the variable presence of HIV, CMV has been implicated in pathogenesis, but Grafe and Wiley (1989) found no evidence of CMV using immunocytochemical staining of spinal cord in eight patients with vacuolar myelopathy. As with HIV dementia, products of activated macrophages may be critical in inducing cord damage (Tyor et al., 1992b).

The approach to the HIV-infected patient with spastic paraparesis should be to exclude HTLV infection, structural lesions, and vitamin B_{12} deficiency. A sensory level is unusual with vacuolar myelopathy, so if one is present, particularly in the presence of back pain, MRI of the spine or myelography should be performed to exclude extrinsic cord compression. Spinal MRI is usually normal, and CSF analysis is not diagnostic. AZT is not usually effective in reversing the myelopathy, which generally progresses inexorably. Antispasticity agents such as baclofen (Lioresal) may relieve some of the spasticity.

Peripheral Nerve Disorders Associated with HIV-1

Although the CNS complications of HIV-1 infection constitute the most significant neurological disorders with respect to morbidity and mortality, the peripheral nervous system can be involved in diverse ways. Not only do novel and distinct clinical syndromes exist, but the frequency and timing of onset vary (see

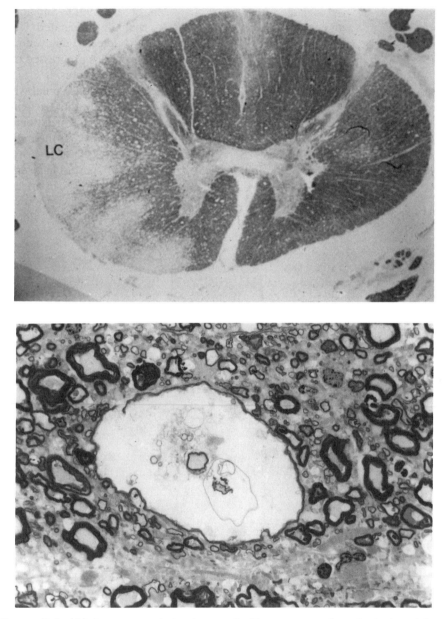

FIGURE 3–9. (A). Low power photomicrograph of transverse section of spinal cord demonstrating asymmetric vacuolar myelopathy with spongiform change, particularly evident in the lateral columns (LC) (luxol fast blue 11 ×). (B). High power photomicrograph showing a macrophage within a vacuole in spinal cord (mag. approximately 400 ×).

Figure 3–1), suggesting that diverse pathogenetic mechanisms may produce different peripheral neuropathies (Cornblath et al., 1987; Parry, 1988).

The incidence of neuropathy increases with advancing immunosuppression and onset of symptomatic HIV disease. Rarely, peripheral or cranial neuropathies develop with HIV-1 seroconversion, usually together with an acute aseptic meningitis (Vendrell et al., 1987; Belec et al., 1989; Wechsler and Ho, 1989). The incidence of symptomatic peripheral neuropathy is very low among HIV carriers; however, up to 10% may have electrophysiological abnormalities suggesting early involvement of peripheral nerves (Chavanet et al., 1988). Careful examination and electrophysiological testing have documented evidence of neuropathy in the majority of patients with AIDS (So et al., 1988; Gastaut et al., 1989). The neuropathy is usually sensory and can be silent. Morphometric analysis of nerve biopsy or autopsy specimens has shown reductions in both large myelinated fibers and unmyelinated fibers (Fuller et al., 1989; Griffin et al., 1992).

Sensory Neuropathy

Up to 30% of patients with AIDS develop a neuropathy characterized by painful sensory symptoms in the feet (Snider et al., 1983b; Cornblath and McArthur, 1988), usually late in the course of HIV-1 infection and in association with systemic opportunistic infections and profound immunodeficiency (see Figure 3–3). This disorder can be recognized by characteristic complaints of paresthesias, dysesthesias, and contact hypersensitivity in the feet with reduced or absent ankle reflexes and elevated vibratory thresholds. Weakness, if present, is usually confined to the foot intrinsics and is minor. Electrophysiological studies usually reveal a neuropathy affecting both sensory and motor fibers suggestive of a dying back axonopathy. In some patients, a striking selective degeneration of the gracile tract has been observed (Rance et al., 1988) and nerve biopsy specimens typically show a mixed picture of axonal loss with patchy demyelination.

Dorsal root ganglia infection with CMV has also been proposed as a cause of this type of painful neuropathy. Fuller et al. (1989) found active systemic CMV infection in 75% of 12 patients with sensory neuropathy and in only 23% of 30 AIDS patients without neuropathy and suggested that CMV infection of dorsal root ganglia might induce the neuropathy. However, Griffin et al. (1992) found no evidence of CMV in dorsal root ganglia using immunocytochemistry, and it seems plausible that sensory neuropathy develops with central-peripheral axonal degeneration through the effects of activated macrophages within peripheral nerves. As with dementia and myelopathy, local cytokine release may be an important step in inducing the nerve damage.

In evaluating patients with sensory neuropathy, consideration should be given to nutritional and toxic causes of sensory neuropathy, such as alcohol, diabetes, pyridoxine excess, and vitamin B_{12} deficiency. Antiretroviral agents, such as dideoxycytidine (ddC) and dideoxyinosine (ddI), have been linked to the development of a similar sensory neuropathy after several weeks of high-dose treatment (Dubinsky et al., 1989; Lambert et al., 1990). The symptoms are similar to those of HIV-associated sensory neuropathy and have the classical features of a toxic neuropathy: related to dosage and duration of use, worse in individuals with preexisting neuropathies, and improvement with discontinuation after a period of "coasting." The pathogenesis is unknown but may involve the unmasking of HIV sensory neuropathy by these agents. At current doses of ddI and ddC, the incidence of toxic neuropathy is low, probably around 15% (Kahn et al., 1992).

Occasionally, symptoms of peripheral neuropathy will improve with zidovudine; however, more often there is no dramatic response. Symptomatic relief with pain-modifying agents, such as amitriptyline (Elavil) or mexilitene (Mexitil), may be useful. Topical capsaicin creams (Axsain, Zostrix), which deplete C fibers of substance P, or lidocaine may also provide symptomatic relief.

Inflammatory Demyelinating Polyneuropathies

Besides the relatively well-characterized opportunistic infections and neoplastic involvement of the nervous system, a number of possible immune-mediated phenomena have been described in association with HIV infection, including inflammatory demyelinating polyneuropathies (IDPs) (Cornblath et al., 1987; Miller et al., 1989) and thrombocytopenia. Both disorders often occur at a relatively early stage of HIV infection, before profound immunoincompetence develops, and probably result from immune dysregulation.

Clinically recognized IDP is uncommon, and the majority of reported cases have presented in the early stages of HIV infection without constitutional symptoms. Sometimes the neuropathy is a manifestation of the acute seroconversion illness (Cornblath et al., 1987). The presentations of IDP take two forms: either an acute demyelinating neuropathy (Guillain-Barré syndrome) or a more chronic, sometimes relapsing course with predominantly motor weakness (CIDP). Among the CSF changes that distinguish HIV-1-related IDP from IDP unrelated to HIV infection is the presence of a CSF pleocytosis (Cornblath et al., 1987). The CSF total protein is usually markedly elevated (mean, 178 mg/dl), as in IDPs occurring in uninfected individuals. Nerve biopsy specimens disclose mononuclear-macrophage infiltration and internodal demyelination—typical of IDP (Cornblath et al., 1987; Chaunu et al., 1989).

The pathogenesis of the demyelinating process is unclear even though circulating antiperipheral nerve antibodies have been identified in some patients (Kiprov et al., 1986; Miller et al., 1989). These may represent an epiphenomenon rather than being the primary cause of the neuropathy.

At present, plasmapheresis is the treatment of choice. This technique may remove circulating antibodies or modulate the immune mechanisms that trigger IPDs. In Guillain-Barré syndrome, a course of five plasma exchanges is given (Cornblath et al., 1987). With CIDP, an induction course is followed by maintenance exchanges as needed. Where plasmapheresis is impractical or unavailable, short courses of intravenous gamma globulin are generally tolerated well, without triggering opportunistic infections even in patients with advanced immunodeficiency.

Mononeuropathies

Mononeuritis multiplex is another type of peripheral neuropathy that has been recognized in HIV-1 infection. It typically affects patients with symptomatic HIV-1 disease (see Figure 3–3) (Cornblath et al., 1987). Lipkin et al. (1985) described 11 ARC patients with mononeuritis multiplex who had occasional CNS findings, mixed axonal-demyelinating conduction study results, and nerve biopsy specimens showing a spectrum of pathological changes ranging from axonal degeneration to mixed axonal degeneration and demyelination. One-third of these patients later progressed to AIDS, and several appeared to develop a more widespread peripheral neuropahty with features of CIDP. It is unclear, therefore, whether mononeuritis multiplex represents a variant of HIV-related CIDP or is a separate entity. Because some cases have marked vasculitic changes and centrofascicular degeneration, circulating immune complexes may play a causative role.

Cranial Neuropathies

Cranial neuropathies are relatively uncommon, affecting 2–3% of patients with AIDS. Occasionally, cranial neuropathies occur with HIV seroconversion and HIV-related meningitis (Ho et al., 1985a; Levy et al., 1985). HIV infection should be considered with any patient presenting with "Bell's palsy." Multiple cranial neuropathies may be a manifestation of CIPD or of mononeuritis multiplex and can develop rapidly with fulminant cryptococcal meningitis. Rarely will lymphomatous meningitis present with cranial neuropathies.

Nutritional Deficiency and Antimicrobial-induced Neuropathies

Nutritional deficiencies, particularly of B-group vitamins and vitamin E, should be considered in any patient presenting with a neuropathy. In patients with AIDS, malnutrition, weight loss, and diarrhea are common and may lead to deficiencies of vitamins B_{12} or E. Excessive dose of pyridoxine (vitamin B_6) can produce a sensory neuropathy, so daily doses should be limited to less than 200 mg.

   Some of the neuropathic symptoms seen in AIDS may result from antimicrobial use. Neuropathies have been linked to a number of antimicrobials including isoniazid, metronidazole (Flagyl), nitrofurantoin, and sulfonamides (Goldstick et al., 1985), as well as dapsone and vincristine.

Entrapment Neuropathies

The patient with AIDS and wasting syndrome who is bed-bound is susceptible to nerve compression. The most common symptom complexes are (1) ulnar nerve compression at the elbow, producing pain and paresthesias in the forearm and in the fourth and fifth digits, sometimes with weakness in the intrinsic hand muscles; (2) common peroneal nerve compression at the fibula head, resulting in a foot drop with numbness over the lateral lower extremity and dorsum of the foot; and (3) posterior tibial nerve compression in the tarsal tunnel at the ankle, producing foot pain and abnormal sensation on the sole of the foot. These neuropathies are recognizable clinically and can be confirmed with electrophysiological testing. Treatment consists of appropriate padding and limb positioning to avoid further trauma.

Autonomic Neuropathies

An early study of five patients with AIDS proposed that autonomic neuropathies could occur in HIV disease (Lin-Greenberg and Taneja-Uppal, 1987). In patients with advanced HIV infection, severe cachexia, and systemic infections, it is extremely difficult to determine whether there is concurrent autonomic dysfunction. Several studies have suggested, however, that autonomic dysfunction can be identified with a variety of autonomic function tests even in asymptomatic HIV carriers (Cohen and Laudenslager, 1989; Freeman et al., 1990). Further study is needed to identify the frequency of clinically significant autonomic abnormalities and whether they are caused directly by HIV-1 or by the numerous medications used in patients with AIDS, or whether they represent adrenal involvement by CMV (Klatt and Shilbata, 1988).

Myopathies

Two types of myopathy occur in patients with HIV-1 infection. The first, HIV-1-associated myopathy, is uncommon and has been described at all stages of systemic disease (see Figure 3–3) (Simpson and Bender, 1988). It may be immune-mediated, like IDP, and presents like polymyositis with myalgias, proximal weakness, and elevated serum creatine phosphokinase (CPK) levels. There is usually electromyographic (EMG) evidence of an irritative myopathy, and muscle biopsy specimens show inflammation and necrosis.

The second type of myopathy, toxic myopathy, has been associated with the long-term use of AZT (cumulative doses >400 g) and is being increasingly recognized as more patients remain on AZT for months or years. The range of clinical features is not yet completely defined, but this has been reviewed by Simpson and Wolfe (1991). Some patients present with marked myopathy that is clinically indistinguishable from the HIV-1-associated myopathy. Others simply have mild proximal weakness and myalgias with a moderately elevated CPK level (two to four times normal). Neither EMG findings nor biopsy can reliably distinguish between the two conditions, although the presence of abnormal mitochondria—"ragged red fibers"—has been proposed as an indicator of toxic myopathy (Dalakas et al., 1990).

In practice, for a patient with myopathy that develops while using AZT, a "drug holiday," stopping AZT for 2–4 weeks, should result in some clinical improvement in myalgias and a drop in CPK if the myopathy is a toxic effect of AZT. If there is severe and function-limiting myopathy with biopsy evidence of inflammatory necrosis, immunomodulatory agents such as corticosteroids or intravenous immunoglobulin can be used (Simpson and Bender, 1988; Simpson and Wolfe, 1991). In the patient with advanced immunodeficiency, the use of corticosteroids can lead to a variety of infectious complications, including worsening of oropharyngeal candidiasis and listeria meningitis. Their use should, therefore, be restricted to patients with severe, life-threatening muscle weakness with greatly elevated CPK levels and biopsy documentation of fiber necrosis and inflammation.

Opportunistic Infections

Equally common as the HIV-related neurological disorders are the opportunistic infections. In the setting of HIV-1 infection, opportunistic infections of the nervous system reflect the underlying immunoincompetence produced by infection and lysis of CD4 lymphocytes. It is unusual for CNS opportunistic processes to develop before the peripheral blood CD4 count has dropped below 200/mm³. These disorders are important because they are common—about 15% of patients with AIDS develop CNS opportunistic infection—and, if correctly diagnosed, treatment is effective. Treatment often needs to be maintained throughout life after an opportunistic infection. Individual with AIDS may have multiple concurrent opportunistic infections with a wide range of organisms (see Table 3–1).

The organisms that cause opportunistic infections in AIDS are somewhat different from those associated with other immunodeficiency states. For example, among transplant recipients, *Listeria* is a frequent cause of CNS infection, yet it is rare in AIDS. *Aspergillus* brain infection is common in patients with hematological malignancies or following bone marrow transplantation; by contrast, *Cryptococcus* is the predominant fungal infection in HIV infection. The reason for this variability is unclear, but presumably it reflects the broader disruption of cellular immune processes in transplant recipients or patients receiving immunosuppressive medications as opposed to the more selective effect of HIV-1 infection on a specific subpopulation of immune cells, the CD4$^+$ lymphocytes. A final point of contrast between AIDS and other immunodeficiency states is the need in patients with HIV infection for lifelong secondary prophylaxis after an opportunistic infection. Table 3–6 lists the most frequent causes of CNS opportunistic infections, with particular clinical presentations.

In the United States, the most frequent CNS opportunistic infections are toxoplasmosis, cryptococcal meningitis, progressive multifocal leukoencephalopathy, and CMV encephalitis. Table 3–1 indicates the prevalence and autopsy frequency of these infections.

Cryptococcal Meningitis

Cryptococcus neoformans, a ubiquitous yeast, produces CNS infection in about 10% of patients with AIDS, and in 5% of these patients it may be the first

TABLE 3–6.   Common Organisms Associated with
Specific Syndromes

Syndrome	Organism
Acute meningitis	*Cryptococcus neoformans*
Subacute/chronic meningitis	*C. neoformans*
	HIV-1
	Mycobacterium tuberculosis
	Treponema pallidum
Encephalitis	HIV-1
	Cytomegalovirus
Abscess	*Toxoplasma gondii*

recognized opportunistic infection. In the United States it is the most common CNS opportunistic infection, and it is also one of the most common AIDS-defining illnesses in Africa. The most common presentation is as meningitis, with headache, meningismus, altered mentation, fever, and nausea (Zuger et al., 1986; Dismukes, 1988; Chuck and Sande, 1989). From 10% to 20% of patients develop papilledema from elevated intracranial pressure (Plate IB) and in these patients, neuropathies from cranial nerve infiltration with cryptococci can occur. Cryptococcomas can develop in these fulminant cases, typically in the basal ganglia, where the yeasts invade the brain along penetrating arteries in the Vichow-Robin space to form perivascular clumps of organisms that can coalesce into mass lesions (Fig. 3–12ci–ii).

In contrast to sporadic cryptococcal meningitis unrelated to AIDS, in AIDS-related cryptococcal meningitis the CSF may have normal cellular and protein constituents. In one series (Kovacs et al., 1985), two-thirds of patients had no pleocytosis and one-third had normal protein levels. Assay of cryptococcal antigen is highly specific and sensitive and should be performed on all samples from HIV-seropositive individuals with suspected meningitis, irrespective of the normalcy of other CSF constituents. Contrast-enhanced MRI and CT scans may demonstrate meningeal enhancement or nonenhancing cryptococcomas, which are typically in the basal ganglia (Figure 3–10a). Factors associated with successful therapy include a normal mental state at presentation, an initial CSF cryptococcal antigen titer less than 1:1024, and a CSF white blood cell count above 20 cells/mm^3 (Saag et al., 1992). Factors associated with treatment failure include a positive India ink stain, the presence of visual abnormalities, age less than 35 years, and the lack of previous AZT treatment.

Antifungal therapy is less effective in AIDS-related cryptococcal meningitis than in sporadic cryptococcal meningitis. Regimens consisting of either amphotericin B alone (0.6 mg/kg/day) or, in fulminant cases, a combination of amphotericin B (0.7 mg/kg/day) and flucytosine (Ancobon) (150 mg/kg/day) have been used for 6 weeks, with response rates of about 60% (Kovacs et al., 1985; Zuger et al., 1986). Flucytosine may improve the initial response and long-term survival but can cause limiting side effects, including diarrhea and bone marrow suppression. Amphotericin B is often poorly tolerated because of renal impairment, chills, and fevers, and must be given intravenously, usually via an indwelling Hickman catheter. During successful treatment, both the serum and CSF cryptococcal antigen titers can be expected to fall by at least four dilutions and the CSF fungal culture should become negative. Persistently positive cultures implies failure or relapse. Complete clearance of the organism is unusual, and CSF cryptococcal antigen may remain positive. The median survival after diagnosis of cryptococcal meningitis is 9 months (Schuster et al., 1986). Suppressive treatment must be continued for life with an oral antifungal, fluconazole (Diflucan), which is more effective and better tolerated than amphotericin for maintenance.When given in an oral dose of 200 mg/day, 2 of 106 patients relapsed compared with 13 of 77 receiving amphotericin (Sugar and Saunders, 1988). Retreatment in those who relapse is often unsuccessful, and ultimately cryptococcal meningitis is directly fatal in about 30%. Fulminant cryptococcal meningitis, with elevated intracranial pressure, cranial neuropathies, and formation of cryptococcomas, may require additional surgical intervention with ventricular shunting procedures.

Cerebral Toxoplasmosis

CNS infection with *Toxoplasma gondii,* an obligate intracellular protozoan, causes necrotic abscesses that are often multifocal and scattered throughout the cerebral hemispheres, with a predilection for the basal ganglia (Plate IC). The infection is caused by the *reactivation* of latent organisms encysted within the brain as opposed to the true opportunistic infection of cryptococcosis. Frequently, the abscesses contain both tissue cysts (bradyzoites) and the active organisms (tachyzoites) in an area with prominent macrophage infiltration (see Figure 3–12a). Antibodies to *T. gondii* are found in 10 to 90% of patients with AIDS, with wide regional variation. The estimated probability of developing cerebral toxoplasmosis is 28% for antibody-positive individuals (Grant et al., 1990). Toxoplasmosis represents the most common cause of intracranial mass lesions in patients with AIDS. Surveillance data from the CDC show that toxoplasmosis occurred in 2.68% of the first 23,307 patients with AIDS in the United States (Levy et al., 1988b). However, in some regions, toxoplasmosis is seen much more frequently (in up to 20% of patients), possibly because of referral patterns or geographical differences in primary exposure to *T. gondii.*

Toxoplasmosis typically presents with the development of fever (about 30–40%), altered mentation, seizures, and focal neurological signs developing over a few days (Navia et al., 1986c). Despite the propensity for toxoplasmosis to develop subacutely and to cause focal neurological deficits, the clinical features are not sufficiently specific to allow distinction from primary CNS lymphoma, the other major process associated with intracranial mass lesions in AIDS. In both conditions, imaging studies demonstrate multiple contrast-enhancing mass lesions. Areas of edema usually surround toxoplasma lesions, sometimes producing mass effect and shift of surrounding structures. Toxoplasma abscesses are more typically small "ring" lesions, whereas lymphoma lesions are larger, with more heterogeneous enhancement (see Figure 3–10b,d). The abscesses show an

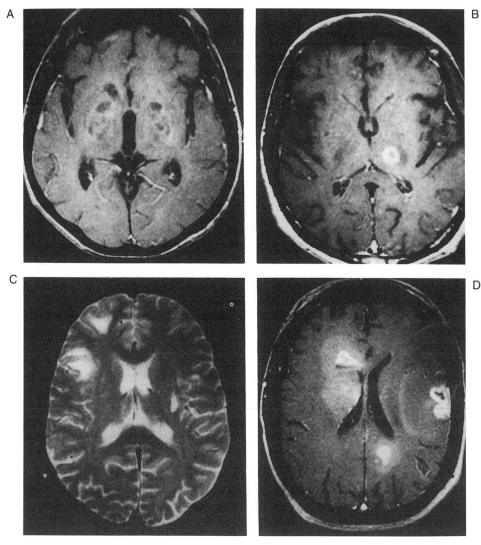

FIGURE 3–10. (A). Cryptococcoma. MRI of a patient with fulminant cryptococcal meningitis. Numerous punctate areas of low density are seen in the basal ganglia on T1
weighted images. Some have coalesced to form a mass lesion. (B). Cerebral toxoplasmosis.
MRI scan with gadolinium of patient presenting with aphasia and hemiparesis showing
enhancement in basal ganglion and mass effect. (C). Progressive multifocal leukoencephalopathy. MRI scan showing multiple areas of hyperintensity confined to white matter.
There is no mass effect and no enhancement with contrast. (D). Primary CNS lymphoma.
CT scan of a patient with autopsy-proven primary CNS lymphoma. There is a multicentric
contrast-enhancing lesion in the frontal lobes with massive surrounding edema and posterior displacement of the middle cerebral arteries.

A

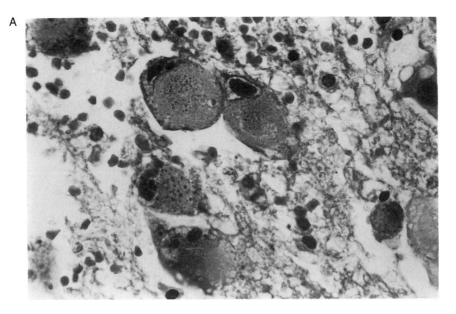

B

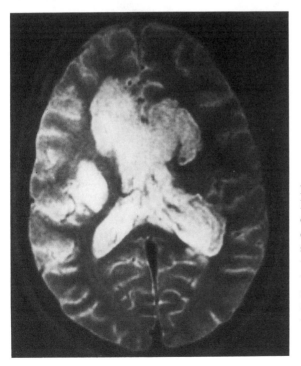

FIGURE 3–11. (A). *(Top.)* High power photomicrograph of several typical cytomegalic cells containing typical inclusions within a microglial nodule in an area of necrosis in the subependymal region (hematoxylin and eosin) (mag. 800 ×). (B). *(Bottom.)* T2 weighted axial MRI in CMV encephalitis. Severe periventricular inflammation.

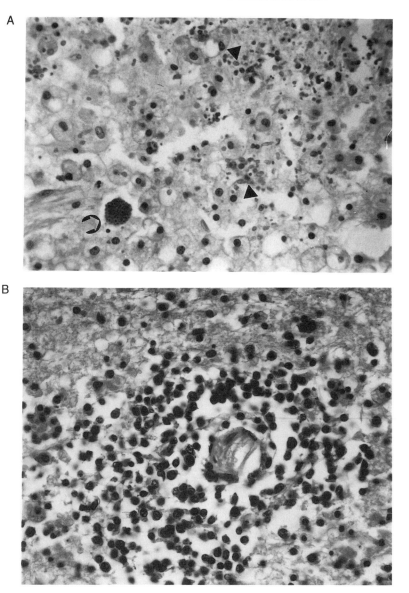

FIGURE 3–12. (A). High power photomicrograph of an autopsy specimen of toxoplasmosis showing a tissue cyst (arrow) and clusters of tachyzoites (arrowheads) within a
necrotic abscess (hematoxylin and eosin) (mag. 350 ×). (B). High power photomicrograph
of an autopsy specimen in primary CNS lymphoma. There is a characteristic dense con-
centric perivascular cuffing with a mixed population of plasmacytoid lymphocytes in atypical lymphoblasts (hematoxylin and eosin) (mag. 800 ×). (C). Cryptococcus. (i). High
power photomicrograph of numerous yeast forms within cerebrospinal fluid space (mag.
approximately 300 ×). (ii). Gross autopsy photograph of section through caudate nucleus
showing multiple coalescent cryptococcomas. (D). Progressive multifocal leukoencephalopathy. (i). Low power photomicrograph of superior frontal gyrus showing numerous
coalescent areas of demyelination in white matter (luxol fast blue mag 12 ×). (ii). High
power photomicrograph of an area of demyelination showing numerous bizarre astrocytes
transformed by JC virus (mag. approximately 400 ×).

Ci
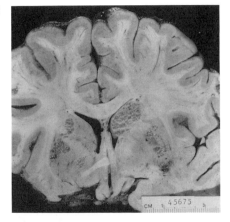

Cii
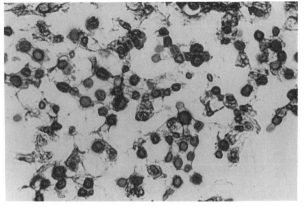

Di
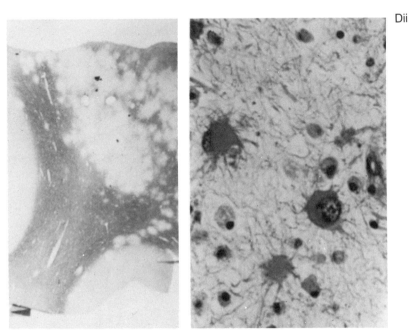
Dii

unexplained predilection for the basal ganglia regions. Other areas affected, in order of frequency, include the frontal, parietal, and occipital lobes and occasionally the cerebellum. Contrast MRI is more sensitive than CT, frequently showing lesions that are not identifiable even on contrast CT (Levy et al., 1985, 1986b). Unfortunately, neither the number of discrete CT or MRI lesions, nor their location, nor their radiological characteristics allow reliable differentiation of toxoplasmosis from lymphoma or other causes of brain abscess. CSF is usually abnormal, with elevated protein and pleocytosis; however, because of the mass effect associated with toxoplasma abscesses, lumbar puncture often has to be deferred to avoid herniation.

Serological testing is not diagnostic; however, because this is a reactivated infection, 85% or more of patients with toxoplasmosis have detectable anti-toxoplasma IgG, and a negative serological titer should suggest an alternative diagnosis. Measurement of intrathecal synthesis of toxoplasma antibody has been suggested as a useful diagnostic test, but in practice CSF cannot always be safely obtained.

Prompt initiation of treatment with pyrimethamine and sulfadiazine will lead to clinical improvement in 80% of cases within 1–4 weeks (Navia et al., 1986a; McArthur, 1987). Pyrimethamine (Daraprim) is administered orally in a loading dose of 150 mg and is continued at 75 mg/day with 5 mg folinic acid (Leucovorin) to prevent anemia. Sulfadiazine is given orally in a dose of 1.5 g every 6 hours. About 40% of patients develop a reaction to the sulfa component, usually within 7–10 days, with development of fever, rash, and chemical hepatitis. Clindamycin (Cleocin) can be substituted at a dose of 900 mg every 6 hours, either orally or intravenously, and appears to have equivalent efficacy (Rolston and Hoy, 1987). After 6 weeks of induction therapy, maintenance therapy of pyrimethamine at 25 mg/day with folinic acid and a second agent, either sulfadiazine or clindamycin, 300 mg every 6 hours, needs to be continued lifelong. Alternative agents that are currently under study include trimetrexate and spiramycin. Corticosteroids should be avoided for at least two reasons. First they cause additional immunosuppression. Second, any mass lesion may show nonspecific improvement after steroid use, thus masking any effect of the antimicrobial drugs. In patients with large mass lesions with a prominent shift and potential for herniation, dexamethasone (Decadron) should be used in doses of 10 mg every 6 hours.

The role of brain biopsy in the management of patients with AIDS and intracranial mass lesions has changed over the past few years as experience has accumulated with empiric toxoplasma therapy. Presently, empiric therapy for toxoplasmosis is started for patients with AIDS presenting with contrast-enhancing intracranial mass lesions. Biopsy can be reserved for individuals who (1) fail a 2-week trial of empiric toxoplasmosis therapy; (2) have atypical presentations (e.g., single large lesions developing over several months); and (3) can tolerate biopsy and radiation therapy. Stereotactic CT-guided biopsy is, in general, preferable to open biopsy and allows for precise biopsy of deep-seated lesions with minimal morbidity. In cerebral toxoplasmosis, biopsies can fail to provide a definitive pathological diagnosis for several reasons. First, the biopsy may miss the lesion or sample only the necrotic core of the abscess. Second, therapy has often been started at the time of biopsy, making it difficult to recognize the tachyzoites histologically. Last, routine hematoxylin and eosin staining is insensitive, and immunoperoxidase staining should be used (Luft et al., 1984; Moskowitz et al., 1984b).

Primary prophylactic therapy can be instituted in toxoplasma-seropositive individuals with peripheral blood CD4 counts below 200/mm³. The optimal regimen has not been determined, and a community-based trial of pyrimethamine and clindamycin is underway. In a retrospective study comparing trimethaprim-sulfamethoxazole (TMP-SMX) to aerosolized pentamidine, a secondary prophylaxis for *Pneumocystis carinii* pneumonia, no patient in the TMP-SMX group developed toxoplasmosis after 3 years of follow-up, while one-third of those in the aerosolized pentamidine group developed toxoplasmosis after a mean period of 15 months (Carr et al., 1992).

CMV Encephalitis/Retinitis

CMV also causes an opportunistic infection leading to encephalitis (Snider et al., 1983b; Moskowtiz et al., 1984a; Levy et al., 1985; Vinters et al., 1989). CMV encephalitis is probably underrecognized because of difficulty in premortem diagnosis and because the presentation can be confused with HIV-1 dementia (Holland et al., in press). The course is often rapidly progressive, with prominent periventriculitis and encephalitis in the setting of CMV retinitis or disseminated CMV infection. CMV adrenalitis, with hyponatremia or a frank addisonian state, is common. Radiological studies show periventricular white matter abnormalities and contrast-enhancing lesions in subependymal and cortical regions (Post et al., 1986) (Figure 3–11b). CSF analysis is not diagnostic because cultures are usually negative (Power et al., 1992). Neuropathological findings are variable, ranging from rare isolated CMV inclusions to severe necrotizing ependymitis and meningoencephalitis (Vinters et al., 1989) (Figure 3–11a). An acyclovir analog, gangiclovir (Cytovene), is licensed for treatment of CMV retinitis and, in the setting of suspected CMV encephalitis, could be initiated. Controlled clinical trials are lacking, although open-label use has suggested some efficacy (Peters et al., 1992).

CMV retinitis is the most common ocular infection in patients with AIDS and causes a hemorrhagic retinitis in up to 20% (Jabs et al., 1989). CMV retinitis is recognized by its characteristic appearance of retinal necrosis mixed with hemorrhage on ophthalmoscopy (see Fig. Plate IA). In up to 60% of patients it becomes bilateral. Untreated, CMV retinitis is a progressive disease that can lead to blindness. It is important but sometimes difficult to distinguish CMV retinitis from "cotton-wool" spots, microinfarcts of the nerve fiber layer of the retina that do not interfere with vision. They occur in 40–92% of patients with AIDS (Newsome et al., 1984), are noninfectious in origin, and may be related to immune complex deposition. It is generally possible to culture CMV from either the blood or urine of patients with active CMV retinitis.

The only currently available form of treatment for CMV retinitis is ganciclovir. Several open-labeled studies have demonstrated the efficacy of ganciclovir in suppressing CMV infection, with a clinical response observed in about 80% (Collaborative DHPG Treatment Study Group, 1986). Treatment consists of an initial induction phase for about 2 weeks, with the drug being given intravenously twice daily. Subsequently, maintenance therapy, using a once-daily intravenous infusion, must be continued lifelong because interruption of ganciclovir almost universally results in the reactivation of active CMV retinitis (Jabs et al., 1989). The most significant side effect of ganciclovir is reversible leukopenia, which occurs to a mild degree in most patients. In an open-label study comparing ganciclovir to phosphonoformate (Foscarnet), a pyrophosphate analog with in vitro activity against CMV and HIV in CMV retinitis, no difference in the progression of retinitis was found. However, mean survival in the ganciclovir group was significantly shorter than for those receiving phosphonoformate. The patients in the ganciclovir group received less antiretroviral therapy on average than those in the phosphonoformate group, although other unidentified factors may be involved in the survival differences (Studies of Ocular Complications of AIDS Research Group, 1992).

CMV can also cause a progressive radiculopathy involving lumbar and sacral roots (Miller et al., 1990). Typically occurring in patients with advanced immunodeficiency with CD4 peripheral blood levels less than $100/mm^3$, there is usually subacute onset of flaccid paralysis of the lower extremities with sacral pain, paresthesias, and sphincter dysfunction. CSF analysis is helpful in diagnosis, showing a polymorphonuclear pleocytosis (often several hundred), hypoglycorrhachia, and elevated protein. CMV can be isolated in about 50% of cases. Necrosis and inflammation with cytomegalic cells and CMV immunoreactivity have been demonstrated in lumbosacral roots (Eidelberg et al., 1986; Miller et al., 1990). Disseminated CMV infection with viremia and CMV retinitis are frequent concomitants. An acyclovir analog, ganciclovir (Cytovene, DHPG), if initiated early, can produce stabilization or even improvement, particularly in patients whose course is more indolent. Persistent CSF pleocytosis predicts a poor response to treatment and may reflect ganciclovir resistance (Cohen et al., 1992).

Herpes Zoster Radiculitis

From 5% to 10% of patients with HIV-1 infection will develop herpes zoster radiculitis representing reactivation of latent herpes zoster infection. Dermatomal herpes zoster does not require antiviral treatment unless cervical or lumbar dermatomes are involved (see Plate 1D). In this setting, a severe myeloradiculitis can develop, leading to permanent motor deficits; therefore, intravenous acyclovir (Zovirax) (30 mg/kg/day) should be used. The development of postherpetic neuralgia may require the use of pain-modifying agents such as amitriptyline (Elavil) or carbamazepine (Tegretol). After the vesicles have completely healed, topical capsaicin (Zostrix) can reduce the neuralgic pains.

Progressive Multifocal Leukoencephalopathy

Reactivation of papovavirus (usually the JC strain) under conditions of immune deficiency leads to the demyelinating disorder progressive multifocal leukoencephalopathy (PML) (Narayan et al., 1973). Serological studies have shown that about 70% of all adults have antibodies to JC virus, implying that the infection is common in humans, although the primary infection is usually silent. The condition has been reported most frequently in patients with lymphoma or leukemia, and in those receiving immunosuppressive drugs for the treatment of rheumatoid arthritis, sarcoidosis, or following organ transplantation.

AIDS is now the most common cause of PML, and about 2% of patients with AIDS will develop this disease (Gillespie et al., 1991). The reactivated papovavirus affects the hemispheric white matter and causes patchy foci of demyelination, which may become confluent (Figure 3–10c). The subcortical areas are usually the first sites of involvement, but the gray matter or periventricular areas may be affected, occasionally even before the typical subcortical lesions are recognized. Giant atypical astrocytes and oligodendroglia with viral inclusions are seen (see Figure 3–12di–ii). Electron microscopy may reveal intranuclear papovavirions within the oligodendroglia, and inflammatory infiltrates may be seen. The lesions of PML in AIDS are often more destructive than those of PML not associated with HIV infection (Rhodes et al., 1988).

PML typically presents with focal neurological deficits that progress inexorably over weeks or a few months to death (Snider et al., 1983b; Levy et al., 1985; Berger et al., 1987). The median survival in one series was 16 weeks (Berger et al., 1987); however, spontaneous improvements in patients with AIDS have been documented (Berger and Mucke, 1988). Typical presentations include aphasia, ataxia, and hemiparesis. The diagnosis is usually made by recognition of a typical indolent clinical course, with imaging studies demonstrating multiple abnormal areas within the subcortical white matter. Typically, the lesions cause no mass effect, are confined to the subcortical white matter, and fail to enhance with contrast (see Figure 3–10c). CSF analysis and electroencephalography show nonspecific abnormalities or may be normal. Biopsy may be necessary to differentiate PML from cerebral toxoplasmosis, other opportunistic infections, or CNS lymphoma. Immunostaining with antibody to the related papovavirus SV40 or electron microscopic identification of inclusions is necessary for definitive pathological diagnosis.

There is no effective treatment, and the neurological disorder usually progresses inexorably to death over weeks or a few months. A variety of antivirals, including amantadine, adenosine arabinoside, and cytosine arabinoside, have been tried, with little success.

Other Infections

CNS infection with other opportunistic organisms occurs but is much less frequent than infection with *T. gondii* or *C. neoformans* (Pitlik et al., 1983; Levy et al., 1985; Rhodes, 1987). Isolates have included *Candida albicans, Coccidioides immitis, Treponema pallidum, Aspergillus fumigatus,* and *Mycobacteria* (Levy et al., 1986a). Experience with the spectrum of pathological findings in AIDS indicates that multiple intracranial infections are not uncommon (Levy et al., 1985). Bacterial infections, either cerebral abscesses or meningitis are uncommon in this population (Snider et al., 1983b; Levy et al., 1985), unlike other immunodeficiency disorders. Herpes zoster and herpes simplex viruses can both cause encephalitis, which responds to acyclovir (Levy et al., 1985).

Opportunistic Neoplasms

Primary CNS Lymphoma

Prior to the advent of AIDS, primary CNS lymphoma was a very rare tumor developing in immunosuppressed hosts such as transplant recipients. Up to 2% of patients with AIDS will develop primary CNS lymphoma, making AIDS the most common associated disease. About half of all primary CNS lymphomas are clinically silent and are detected only at autopsy. The tumors are multicentric and of B-cell origin, and are similar in histological appearance to those observed in immunosuppressed renal allograft recipients (see Figure 3–12b) (Snider et al., 1983b). Epstein-Barr virus has been linked with its development and can be detected in the majority of tissue specimens (MacMahon et al., 1991). The typical presentation is with slowly progressive neurological deterioration leading to death within 3 months (Rosenblum et al., 1988). Focal neurological signs can develop in about 40% of cases, but neither clinical nor radiological presentations are specific enough to differentiate lymphoma from toxoplasmosis (see Figure 3–10d). Patients receiving radiation therapy usually die of opportunistic infections rather than tumor progression, suggesting that the tumor itself is radiosensitive; however, the median survival even after whole brain irradiation is only 4 months (Baumgartner et al., 1990).

Metastatic Systemic Lymphoma

Most lymphomas are extranodal, diffuse, high-grade non-Hodgkin's malignant lymphomas of B-cell origin. CNS involvement occurs in over 50% of patients with systemic lymphoma, with cranial neuropathies, meningeal involvement, cerebral metastasis, and spinal cord compression.

Metabolic Encephalopathies

These occur frequently in patients with AIDS, particularly when opportunistic pulmonary infections with *P. carinii* cause hypoxia or when multiorgan failure develops (Snider et al., 1983b; Levy et al., 1985). A number of therapeutic agents, including AZT and ganciclovir, have been linked to reversible delirium (Collaborative DHPG Treatment Study Group, 1986). Patients with HIV dementia are particularly predisposed to develop delirium with psychoactive medications, infection, or metabolic derangements.

Cerebrovascular Disease

Cerebrovascular accidents were noted in 9 of 124 (7%) of AIDS patients in one series (Levy et al., 1985), including examples of both cerebral infarction and hemorrhage. Pathological series have documented cerebrovascular lesions in one-third of patients with AIDS (Mizusawa et al., 1988), but the causes are varied. Overall, there is no clear evidence that HIV infection per se increases the rate of cerebrovascular disease, although there are several conditions associated with HIV infection, including intravenous drug use, which may do so. Circulating antiphospholipid antibodies occur in HIV infection, but their role in inducing stroke is unclear. The thrombocytopenia that sometimes accompanies HIV infection may contribute to an increased incidence of intracranial hemorrhage. Other causes of intraparenchymal or subarachnoid hemorrhage include ruptured mycotic aneurysms or hemorrhage into toxoplasma abscesses, lymphoma, and rarely into intracerebral Kaposi's sarcoma lesions. Cerebral infarctions can occur as a result of nonbacterial thrombotic endocarditis (Levy et al., 1985) or as a consequence of bacterial endocarditis in intravenous drug users. There are scattered case reports of cerebral granulomatous angiitis developing in association with HIV infection (Levy et al., 1985; Yankner et al., 1986). The exact role of HIV in causing this disorder remains uncertain.

Neurosyphilis

Nationwide, the rate of syphilis has increased in the United States since 1986. While it is not strictly an opportunistic infection, it has been suggested that the course of syphilis may be accelerated by the disturbance in cellular immunity accompanying HIV-1 infection (Hook, 1989). The clinical features of neurosyphilis may be modified and the time course from primary to tertiary syphilis shortened (Johns et al., 1987; Passo and Rosenblum, 1988; Musher et al., 1990). There are several case reports (Hicks et al., 1987) of false-negative syphilis serology in individuals with biopsy-proven syphilis; however, in general, standard syphilis serology is reliable. In studies from Seattle, Lukehart et al. (1988) documented isolation of *T. pallidum* by rabbit inoculation from 12 (30%) of 40 patients with primary or secondary syphilis. CSF Venereal Disease Reference Laboratory (VDRL) was reactive in 4 (14%) and protein elevated in 6 (21%). Isolation of *T. pallidum* was no more frequent in HIV-1 positive individuals. Despite this, there was evidence of treatment failure in three of four HIV-1-seropositive patients treated with benzathine penicillin. In two, there was persistence of viable *T. pallidum;* in one, rising serum and CSF VDRL titers.

In a neurologically normal HIV-1 carrier with a history of *treated* syphilis who is serofast (blood rapid plasma reagin [RPR] is 1:8 or less consistently), there is probably no indication for additional syphilis therapy or for CSF analysis (CDC, 1988). In fact, the CSF is quite likely to be abnormal, with pleocytosis and protein elevation, because of the frequency of early HIV-1 infection of the CNS (McArthur et al., 1988). When neurological symptoms are present, the CSF should be examined. If CSF VDRL is positive or serum RPR is high or rising (above 1:16) and clinical features are suggestive of neurosyphilis, treatment with intravenous penicillin (24 mU for 10 days) should be given. An alternative untested regimen is procaine penicillin, 2.4 mU with probenecid, or ceftriaxone, 2 g intravenously or intramuscularly, for 10 days. Reexamination of the CSF should be performed at 3–6 months. Benzathine penicillin should not be used for treatment of neurosyphilis because of poor CSF penetrance.

Neurological Projections

The World Health Organization estimates that there are at least 10 million individuals already infected with HIV worldwide. While there is some uncertainty over the ultimate number who will develop AIDS, it is clear that large numbers of relatively young individuals are already infected with HIV-1 and are thus at risk for subsequent development of a wide variety of neurological problems. The incidence of HIV dementia makes HIV infection the most common cause of dementia under the age of 50 (Janssen et al., 1992). Extrapolating from the current CDC estimates for 1993 and from current prevalence figures for the different neurological disorders, the following numbers of neurological cases might be expected during 1993 in the United States:

Living AIDS cases	145,000	Cryptococcosis	30,000
Dementia	30,000	CNS lymphoma	1,500
Sensory		CNS	
neuropathy	30,000	toxoplasmosis	7,000

Acknowledgments

The pathological figures were supplied by Drs. P.S. Becker and J. Glass (Department of Neurology) and Dr. S. Silver (Department of Pathology) and the radiological figures by Dr. V. Mathews (Department of Neuroradiology). Supported by NIAID Contract AI-72634 and NINDS Grant 1 PO1 NS 26643 and by the GCRC Outpatient Center RR0072.

References

Aylward, E.H., Henderer, J.D., McArthur, J.C., Brettschneider, P.D., Barta, P.E., and Pearlson, G.D. (1993). Reduced basal ganglia atrophy in HIV-1 associated dementia complex: Results from quantitative neuroimaging. *Neurology, 43,* 2099–2104.

Baumgartner, J.E., Rachlin, J.R., Beckstead, J.H., Meeker, T.C., Levy, R.M., Wara, W.M., and Rosenblum, M.L. (1990). Primary central nervous system lymphomas: Natural history and response to radiation therapy in 55 patients with acquired immunodeficiency syndrome. *Journal of Neurosurgery, 73,* 206–211.

Belec, L., Bherardi, R., Georges, A.J., Schuller, E., Vuillecard, E., DiCostanzo, B., and

Martin, P.M.V. (1989). Peripheral facial paralysis and HIV infection: Report of four African cases and review of the literature. *Journal of Neurology, 236*, 411–414.

Belman, A.L., Diamond, G., Dickson, D., Horoupian, D., Llena, J., Lantos, G., and Rubinstein, A. (1988). Pediatric acquired immunodeficiency syndrome. Neurologic syndromes [published erratum appears in Am J Dis Child 1988 May;142(5):507]. *American Journal of Diseases of Children, 142*, 29–35.

Belman, A.L., Lantos, G., Horoupian, D., Novick, B.E., Ultmann, M.H., Dickson, D.W., and Rubinstein, A. (1986). AIDS: Calcification of the basal ganglia in infants and children. *Neurology, 36*, 1192–1199.

Berger, J.R., Kaszovitz, B., Post, M.J., and Dickinson, G. (1987). Progressive multifocal leukoencephalopathy associated with human immunodeficiency virus infection. A review of the literature with a report of sixteen cases. *Annals of Internal Medicine, 107*, 78–87.

Berger, J.R., and Mucke, L. (1988). Prolonged survival and partial recovery in AIDS-associated progressive multifocal leukoencephalopathy. *Neurology, 38*, 1060–1065.

Brenneman, D., Buzy, J., and Ruff, M. (1988). Peptide T sequences prevent neuronal cell death produced by the protein gp120 of the human immunodeficiency virus. *Drug Development and Research, 15*, 361–369.

Brew, B.J., Ghalla, R., Paul, M., Schwartz, M., and Price, R.W. (1989). CSF β2 microglobulin as a marker of the presence and severity of AIDS dementia complex. Presented at the Fifth International Conference on AIDS, Montreal, 1989.

Brew, B.J., Ghalla, R.B., Paul, M., Sidtis, J.J., Keilp, J.J., Sadler, A.E., Gallardo, H., McArthur, J.C., and Price, R.W. (1992). Cerebrospinal fluid β2 microglobulin in patients with AIDS dementia complex: An expanded series including response to zidovudine treatment. *AIDS, 6*, 461–465.

Bridge, T.P., Heseltine, P.N.R., Parker, E.S., Eaton, E.M., Ingraham, L.J., McGrail, M.L., and Goodwin, F.K. (1991). Results of extended peptide T administration in AIDS and ARC patients. *Psychopharmacological Bulletins, 27*, 237–245.

Budkac, H. (1986). Multinucleated giant cells in brain: A hallmark of the acquired immune deficiency syndrome (AIDS). *Acta Neuropathologica, 69*, 253–258.

Budka, H., Wiley, C.A., Kleihues, P., Artigas, J., Asbury, A.K., Cho, E.-S., Cornblath, D.R., Dal Canto, M.C., DeGirolami, U., Dickson, D., Epstein, L.G., Esiri, M.M., Giangaspero, F., Gosztonyi, G., Gray, F., Griffin, J.W., Henin, D., Iwasaki, Y., Janssen, R.S., Johnson, R.T., Lantos, P.L., Lyman, W.D., McArthur, J.C., Nagashima, K., Peress, N., Petito, C.K., Price, R.W., Rhodes, R.H., Rosenblum, M., Said, G., Scaravilli, F., Sharer, L.R., and Vinters, H.V. (1991). HIV-associated disease of the nervous system: Review of nomenclature and proposal for neuropathology-based terminology. *Brain Pathology, 1*, 143–152.

Cann, A.J., Churcher, M.J., Boyd, M., O'Brien, W., Zhao, J.-Q., Zack, J., and Chen, I.S.Y. (1992). The region of the envelope gene of human immunodeficiency virus type 1 responsible for determination of cell tropism. *Journal of Virology, 66*, 305–309.

Cann, A.J., Zack, J.A., Go, A.S., Arrigo, S.J., Koyanagi, Y., Green, P.L., Pang, S., and Chen, I.S.Y. (1990). Human immunodeficiency virus type 1 T-cell tropism is determined by events prior to pro-virus formation. *Journal of Virology, 64*, 4735–4742.

Carr, A., Tindall, B., Brew, B.J., Marriott, D.J., Harkness, J.L., Penny, R., and Cooper, D.A. (1992). Low-dose trimethoprim-sulfamethoxazole prophylaxis for toxoplasmic encephalitis in patients with AIDS. *Annals of Internal Medicine, 117*, 106–111.

Centers for Disease Control. (1987). Revision of the CDC surveillance case definition for acquired immunodeficiency syndrome. *Morbidity and Mortality Weekly Report, 36(Suppl. 1S)*, 3S–15S.

Centers for Disease Control. (1988). Leads from the MMWR. Recommendations for diagnosing and treating syphilis in HIV-infected patients. *Journal of the American Medical Association, 260*, 2488–2489.

Centers for Disease Control. (1992). 1993 revised classification system for HIV infection and expanded surveillance case definition for AIDS among adolescents and adults. *Morbidity and Mortality Weekly Reports, 41*, 1–19.

Chaunu, M.P., Ratinahirana, H., Raphael, M., Henin, D., Leport, C., Brun-Vezinet, F., Leger, J.M., Brunet, P., and Hauw, J.J. (1989). The spectrum of changes on 20 nerve biopsies in patients with HIV infection. *Muscle and Nerve, 12*, 452–459.

Chavanet, P.Y., Giroud, M., Lancon, J.P., Borsotti, J.P., Waldner-Combernoux, A.C., Pillon, D., Maringe, E., Caillot, D., and Portier, H. (1988). Altered peripheral nerve conduction in HIV-patients. *Cancer Detection and Prevention, 12*, 249–255.

Chuck, S.L., and Sande, M.A. (1989). Infections with *Cryptococcus neoformans* in acquired immunodeficiency syndrome. *New England Journal of Medicine, 321*, 794–799.

Clifford, D.B., Jacoby, R.G., Miller, J.P., Seyfried, W.R., and Glicksman, M. (1990). Neuropsychometric performance of asymptomatic HIV-infected subjects. *AIDS, 4*, 767–774.

Cohen, B.A., McArthur, J.C., Grohman, S., Patterson, B., and Glass, J.D. (1993). Neurologic prognosis in CMV polyradiculomyelopathy in AIDS. *Neurology 43*: 493–499.

Cohen, J.A., and Laudenslager, M. (1989). Autonomic nervous system involvement in patients with human immunodeficiency virus infection. *Neurology, 39*, 1111–1112.

Collaborative DHPG Treatment Study Group. (1986). Treatment of serious cytomegalovirus with 9-(1,2-dihydroxy-2-propoxymethyl) guanine in patients with AIDS and other immunodeficiencies. *New England Journal of Medicine, 314*, 801–805.

Collier, A.C., Marra, C., Coombs, R.W., Claypoole, K., Cohen, W., Longstreth, W.T., Townes, B.D., Maravilla, K.R., Critchlow, C., Murphy, V.L., and Handsfield, H.H. (1992). Central nervous system manifestations of human immunodeficiency virus infection without AIDS. *Journal of Acquired Immune Deficiency Syndromes, 5*, 229–241.

Cooper, D.A., Gold, J., Maclean, P., Donovan, B., Finlayson, R., Barnes, T.G., Michelmore, H.M., Brooke, P., and Penny, R. (1985). Acute AIDS retrovirus infection: Definition of a clinical illness associated with seroconversion. *Lancet, 1*, 537–540.

Cornblath, D.R., and McArthur, J.C. (1988). Predominantly sensory neuropathy in patients with AIDS and AIDS-related complex. *Neurology, 38*, 794–796.

Cornblath, D.R., McArthur, J.C., Kennedy, P.G., Witte, A.S., and Griffin, J.W. (1987). Inflammatory demyelinating peripheral neuropathies associated with human T-cell lymphotropic virus type III infection. *Annals of Neurology, 21*, 32–40.

Dalakas, M.C., Illa, I., Pezeshkpour, G.H., Laukaitis, J.P., Cohen, B., and Griffin, J.L. (1990). Mitochondrial myopathy caused by long-term zidovudine therapy. *New England Journal of Medicine, 322*, 1098–1105.

Dal Pan, G.J., Glass, J., Zeidman, S., and McArthur, J. (1992a). Atypical HIV-associated myelopathy: Diagnosis by cord biopsy. *Neurology, 42*, 257.

Dal Pan, G.J., McArthur, J.H., Aylward, E., Selnes, O.A., Nance-Sproson, T.E., Kumar, A.J., Mellits, E.D., and McArthur, J.C. (1992b). Patterns of cerebral atrophy in HIV-1 infected individuals: Results of a quantitative MRI analysis. *Neurology 42*, 2125–2130.

Deicken, R.F., Hubesch, B., Jensen, P.C., Sappey-Marinier, D., Krell, P., Wisniewski, A., Vanderburg, D., Parks, R., Fein, G., and Weiner, M.W. (1991). Alterations in brain phosphate metabolite concentrations in patients with human immunodeficiency virus infection. *Archives of Neurology, 48*, 203–209.

de la Monte, S.M., Ho, D.D., Schooley, R.T., Hirsch, M.S., and Richardson, E.P., Jr. (1987). Subacute encephalomyelitis of AIDS and its relation to HTLV-III infection. *Neurology, 37*, 562–569.

de-The, G., Giordano, C., Gessain, A., Howlett, W., Sonan, T., Akani, F., Rosling, H., Carton, H., Mouanga, Y., Caudie, C., Stenger, F., and Malone, G. (1989). Human retroviruses HTLV-I, HIV-1 and HIV-2 and neurological diseases in some equatorial areas of Africa. *Journal of Acquired Immune Deficiency Syndromes, 2*, 550–556.

Denning, D.W., Anderson, J., Rudge, P., and Smith, H. (1987). Acute myelopathy associated with primary infection with human immunodeficiency virus. *British Medical Journal, 294*, 143–144.

Dewhurst, S., Bresser, J., Stevenson, M., Sakai, K., Evinger-Hodges, M.J., and Volsky, D.J. (1987). Susceptibility of human glial cells to infection with human immunodeficiency virus (HIV). *FEBS Letters, 213*, 138–143.

Dezube, B.J., Pardee, A.B., Chapman, B., Beckett, L.A., Korvick, J.A., Novick, W.J., Chiurco, J., Kasdan, P., Ahlers, C.M., Ecto, L.T., and Crumpacker, C.S. (1993). Pentoxifylline decreases tumor necrosis factor expression and serum triglycerides in people with AIDS. *J.AIDS, 6*, 787–794.

Dismukes, W.E. (1988). Cryptococcal meningitis in patients with AIDS. *Journal of Infectious Diseases, 157*, 624–628.

Dow, S.W., Poss, M.L., and Hoover, E.A. (1990). Feline immunodeficiency virus: A neurotropic lentivirus. *Journal of Acquired Immune Deficiency Syndromes, 3*, 658–668.

Dreyer, E.B., Kaiser, P.K., Offermann, J.T., and Lipton, S.A. (1990). HIV-1 coat protein neurotoxicity prevented by calcium channel antagonists. *Science, 248*, 364–367.

Dubinsky, R.M., Yarchoan, R., Dalakas, M., and Broder, S. (1989). Reversible axonal neuropathy from the treatment of AIDS and related disorders with 2′,3′-dideoxycytidine (ddC). *Muscle and Nerve, 12*, 856–860.

Eidelberg, D., Sotrel, A., Vogel, H., Walker, P., Kleefield, J., and Crumpacker, C.S., 3rd. (1986). Progressive polyradiculopathy in acquired immune deficiency syndrome. *Neurology, 36*, 912–916.

Elovaara, I., Iivanainen, M., Valle, S.L., Suni, J., Tervo, T., and Lahdevirta, J. (1987). CSF protein and cellular profiles in various stages of HIV infection related to neurological manifestations. *Journal of Neurological Science, 78*, 331–342.

Epstein, L.G., Sharer, L.R., Cho, E.S., Myenhofer, M., Navia, B., and Price, R.W. (1984). HTLV-III/LAV-like retrovirus particles in the brains of patients with AIDS encephalopathy. *AIDS Research, 1*, 447–454.

Epstein, L.G., Sharer, L.R., Joshi, V.V., Fojas, M.M., Koenigsberger, M.R., and Oleske, J.M. (1985). Progressive encephalopathy in children with acquired immune deficiency syndrome. *Annals of Neurology, 17*, 488–496.

Everall, I.P., Luthert, P.J., and Lantos, P.L. (1991). Neuronal loss in the frontal cortex in HIV infection. *Lancet, 337*, 1119–1121.

Fischl, M.A., Richman, D.D., Grieco, M.H., Gottlieb, M.S., Volberding, P.A., Laskin, O.L., Leedom, J.M., Groopman, J.E., Mildvan, D., Schooley, R.T., Jackson, G.G., Durack, D.T., King, D., and the AZT Collaborative Working Group. (1987). The efficacy of azidothymidine (AZT) in the treatment of patients with AIDS and AIDS-related complex. *New England Journal of Medicine, 317*, 185–191.

Franzblau, A., Letz, R., Hershman, D., Mason, P., Wallace, J.I., and Bekesi, J.G. (1991). Quantitative neurologic and neurobehavioral testing of persons infected with human immunodeficiency virus type 1. *Archives of Neurology, 48*, 263–268.

Freeman, R., Roberts, M.S., Friedman, L.S., and Broadbridge, C. (1990). Autonomic function and human immunodeficiency virus infection. *Neurology, 40*, 575–580.

Fuller, G.N., Jacobs, J.M., and Guiloff, R.J. (1989). Association of painful peripheral neuropathy in AIDS with cytomegalovirus infection. *Lancet, 2,* 937–941.

Gabuzda, D.H., Ho, D.D., de la Monte, S.M., Hirsch, M.S., Rota, T.R., and Sobel, R.A. (1986). Immunohistochemical identification of HTLV-III antigen in brains of patients with AIDS. *Annals of Neurology, 20,* 289–295.

Gartner, S., Markovits, P., Markovitz, D.M., Kaplan, M.H., Gallo, R.C., and Popovic, M. (1986). The role of mononuclear phagocytes in HTLV-III/LAV infection. *Science, 233,* 215–219.

Gastaut, J.L., Gastaut, J.A., Pellissier, J.F., Tapko, J.B., and Weill, O. (1989). Neuropathies with HIV infection. Prospective study of 56 cases. *Revue Neurologique, 145,* 451–459.

Gelman, B.B., and Guinto, F.C. (1992). Morphometry, histopathology, and tomography of cerebral atrophy in the acquired immunodeficiency syndrome. *Annals of Neurology, 32,* 31–40.

Gillespie, S.M., Chang, Y., Lemp, G., Arthur, R., Buchbinder, S., Steimle, A., Baumgartner, J., Rando, T., Neal, D., Rutherford, G., Schonberger, L., and Janssen, R. (1991). Progressive multifocal leukoencephalopathy in persons infected with human immunodeficiency virus, San Francisco, 1981–1989. *Annals of Neurology, 30,* 597–604.

Giulian, D., Vaca, K., and Noonan, C.A. (1990). Secretion of neurotoxins in mononuclear phagocytes infected with HIV-1. *Science, 250,* 1593–1596.

Glass, J.D., Wesselingh, S.L., Selnes, O.A., McArthur, J.C. Clinical-pathological correlation in HIV-associated dementia. *Neurology* (in press).

Goethe, K.E., Mitchell, J.E., Marshall, D.W., Brey, R.L., Cahill, W.T., Leger, G.D., Hoy, L.J., and Boswell, R.N. (1989). Neuropsychological and neurological function of human immunodeficiency virus seropositive asymptomatic individuals. *Archives of Neurology, 46,* 129–133.

Goldstick, L., Mandybur, T.I., and Bode, R. (1985). Spinal cord degeneration in AIDS. *Neurology, 35,* 103–106.

Grafe, M.R., and Wiley, C.A. (1989). Spinal cord and peripheral nerve pathology in AIDS: The roles of cytomegalovirus and human immunodeficiency virus. *Annals of Neurology, 25,* 561–566.

Grant, I., Atkinson, J.H., Hesselink, J.R., Kennedy, C.J., Richman, D.D., Spector, S.A., and McCutchan, J.A. (1987). Evidence for early central nervous system involvement in the acquired immunodeficiency syndrome (AIDS) and other human immunodeficiency virus (HIV) infections. Studies with neuropsychologic testing and magnetic resonance imaging [published erratum appears in Ann Intern Med 1988 Mar;108(3):496]. *Annals of Internal Medicine, 107,* 828–836.

Grant, I.H., Gold, J.W.M., Rosenblum, M., Niedzwiecki, D., and Armstrong, D. (1990). *Toxoplasma gondii* serology in HIV-infected patients: The development of central nervous system toxoplasmosis in AIDS. *AIDS, 4,* 519–521.

Griffin, J.W., Crawford, T.O., Glass, J.D., Price, D.L., Cornblath, D.R., and McArthur, J.C. (1992). Sensory neuropathy in AIDS: I. Neuropathology. *Brain,* in press.

Grimaldi, L.M.E., Martino, G.V., Franciotta, D.M., Brustia, R., Castagna, A., Pristera, R., and Lazzarin, A. (1991). Elevated alpha-tumor necrosis factor levels in spinal fluid from HIV-1-infected patients with central nervous system involvement. *Annals of Neurology, 29,* 21–25.

Gyorkey, F., Melnick, J.L., and Gyorkey, P. (1987). Human immunodeficiency virus in brain biopsies of patients with AIDS and progressive encephalopathy. *Journal of Infectious Diseases, 155,* 870–876.

Heyes, M.P., Brew, B.J., Markey, S.P., Martin, A., Price, R.W., and Rubinow, D. (1989).

Quinolinic acid concentrations are increased in plasma and cerebrospinal fluid in AIDS and correlates with AIDS dementia. Presented at the Fifth International Conference on AIDS. Montreal.

Heyes, M.P., Mefford, I.N., Quearry, B.J., Dedhia, M., and Lackner, A. (1990). Increased ratio of quinolinic acid to kynurenic acid in cerebrospinal fluid of D retrovirus-infected Rhesus macaques: Relationship to clinical and viral status. *Annals of Neurology, 27*, 666–675.

Hicks, C.B., Benson, P.M., Lupton, G.P., and Tramont, E.C. (1987). Seronegative secondary syphilis in a patient infected with the human immunodeficiency virus (HIV) Kapasi sarcoma. *Annals of Internal Medicine, 107*, 492–495.

Hill, J.M., Mervis, R.F., Avidor, R., Moody, T.W., and Brenneman, D.E. (1993). HIV envelope protein-induced neuronal damage and retardation of behavioral development in rat neonates. *Brain Research, 603*, 222–233.

Ho, D.D., Rota, T.R., Schooley, R.T., Kaplan, J.C., Allan, J.D., Groopman, J.E., Resnick, L., Felsenstein, D., Andrews, C.A., and Hirsch, M.S. (1985a). Isolation of HTLV-III from cerebrospinal fluid and neural tissues of patients with neurologic syndromes related to the acquired immunodeficiency syndrome. *New England Journal of Medicine, 313*, 1493–1497.

Ho, D.D., Pomerantz, R.J., and Kaplan, J.C. (1987). Pathogenesis of infection with human immunodeficiency virus. *New England Journal of Medicine, 317*, 278–286.

Ho, D.D., Sarngadharan, M.G., Resnick, L., diMarzo-Veronese, F., Rota, T.R., and Hirsch, M.S. (1985b). Primary human T-lymphotropic virus type III infection. *Annals of Internal Medicine, 103*, 880–883.

Holland, N.R., Power, C., Mathews, V.P., Glass, J.D., Forman, M., and McArthur, J.C. (in press). CMV encephalitis in acquired immunodeficiency syndrome (AIDS): clinical features and course: *Neurology*.

Hollander, H., and Stringari, S. (1987). Human immunodeficiency virus–associated meningitis. Clinical course and correlations. *American Journal of Medicine, 83*, 813–816.

Holman, B.L., Barada, B., Johnson, K.A., Mendelson, J., Hallgring, E., Teoh, S.K., Worth, J., and Navia, B. (1992). A comparison of brain perfusion SPECT in cocaine abuse and AIDS dementia complex. *Journal of Nuclear Medicine, 33*, 1312–1315.

Hook, E.W. (1989). Syphilis and HIV infection. *Journal of Infectious Diseases, 160*, 530–534.

Jabs, D.A., Enger, C., and Bartlett, J.G. (1989). Cytomegalovirus retinitis and acquired immunodeficiency syndrome. *Archives of Ophthalmology, 107*, 75–80.

Jakobsen, J., Smith, T., Gaub, J., Helweg-Larsen, S., and Trojaborg, W. (1989). Progressive neurological dysfunction during latent HIV infection. *British Medical Journal, 299*, 225–228.

Janssen, R.S., Cornblath, D.R., Epstein, L.G., Foa, R.P., McArthur, J.C., Price, R.W., Asbury, A.K., Beckett, A., Benson, D.F., Bridge, T.P., Leventhal, C.M., Satz, P., Saykin, A.J., Sidtis, J.J., and Tross, S. (1991). Nomenclature and research case definitions for neurological manifestations of human immunodeficiency virus type-1 (HIV-1) infection. Report of a Working Group of the American Academy of Neurology AIDS Task Force. *Neurology, 41*, 778–785.

Janssen, R.S., Nwanyanwu, O.C., Selik, R.M., and Stehr-Green, J.K. (1992). Epidemiology of human immunodeficiency virus encephalopathy in the United States. *Neurology, 42*, 1472–1476.

Janssen, R.S., Saykin, A.J., Cannon, L., Campbell, J., Pinsky, P.F., Hessol, N.A., O'Malley, P.M., Lifson, A.R., Doll, L.S., Rutherford, G.W., and Kaplan, J.E. (1989). Neurological and neuropsychological manifestations of HIV-1 infection: Association with AIDS-related complex but not asymptomatic HIV-1 infection. *Annals of Neurology, 26*, 592–600.

Janssen, R.S., Saykin, A.J., Kaplan, J.E., Spira, T.J., Pinsky, P.F., Sprehn, G.C., Hoffman, J.C., Mayer, W.B., Jr., and Schonberger, L.B. (1988). Neurological complications of human immunodeficiency virus infection in patients with lymphadenopathy syndrome. *Annals of Neurology, 23*, 49–55.

Johns, D.R., Tierney, M., and Felsenstein, D. (1987). Alteration in the natural history of neurosyphilis by concurrent infection with the human immunodeficiency virus. *New England Journal of Medicine, 316*, 1569–1572.

Johnson, R.T., McArthur, J.C., and Narayan, O. (1988). The neurobiology of human immunodeficiency virus infections. *FASEB Journal, 2*, 2970–2981.

Kahn, J.O., Lagakos, S.W., Richman, D.D., Cross, A., Pettinelli, C., Brown, M., Volberding, P.A., Crumpacker, C.S., Beall, G., Sacks, H.S., Beltangady, M., Smaldone, L., and Dolin, R. (1992). A controlled trial comparing continued zidovudine with didanosine in human immunodeficiency virus infection. *New England Journal of Medicine, 327*, 581–587.

Kamin, S.S., and Petito, C.K. (1988). Vacuolar myelopathy in immunocompromised non-AIDS patients. *Journal of Neuropathology and Experimental Neurology, 47*, 385.

Katzler, S., Weis, S., Haug, H., and Budka, H. (1990). Loss of neurons in the frontal cortex in AIDS brains. *Acta Neuropathologica, 80*, 92–94.

Kiprov, D.D., Abrams, D., Pfaeffl, W., Jones, F., and Miller, R. (1986). ARC/AIDS-related autoimmune syndromes and their treatment. Presented at the second International Conference on AIDS, Paris.

Klatt, E.C., and Shilbata, D. (1988). Cytomegalovirus infection in the acquired immunodeficiency syndrome. *Archives of Pathology and Laboratory Medicine, 112*, 540–544.

Koenig, S., Gendelman, H.E., Orenstein, J.M., Dal Canto, M.C., Pezeshkpour, G.H., Yungbluth, M., Janotta, F., Aksamit, A., Martin, M.A., and Fauci, A.S. (1986). Detection of AIDS virus in macrophages in brain tissue from AIDS patients with encephalopathy. *Science, 233*, 1089–1093.

Koralnik, I.J., Beaumanoir, A., Hausler, R., Kohler, A., Safran, A.B., Delacoux, R., Vibert, D., Mayer, E., Burkhard, P., and Nahory, A. (1990). A controlled study of early neurologic abnormalities in men with asymptomatic human immunodeficiency virus infection. *New England Journal of Medicine, 323*, 864–870.

Kovacs, J.A., Kovacs, A.A., Polis, M., Wright, W.C., Gill, V.J., Tuazon, C.U., Gelmann, E.P., Lane, H.C., Longfield, R., Overturf, G., Macher, A.M., Fauci, A.S., Parrillo, J.E., Bennett, J.E., and Masur, H. (1985). Cryptococcosis in the acquired immunodeficiency syndrome. *Annals of Internal Medicine, 103*, 533–538.

Kure, K., Weidenheim, K.M., Lyman, W.D., and Dickson, D.W. (1990). Morphology and distribution of HIV-1 gp41-positive microglia in subacute AIDS encephalitis. Pattern of involvement resembling a multisystem degeneration. *Acta Neuropathologica, 80*, 393–400.

Lackner, A.A., Dandekar, S., and Gardner, M.B. (1991). Neurobiology of simian and feline immunodeficiency virus infections. *Brain Pathology, 1*, 201–212.

LaFrance, N., Pearlson, G.D., Schaerf, F.W., McArthur, J.C., Polk, B.F., Links, J.M., Bascom, M.J., Knowles, M.D., and Galen, S.S. (1988). I-123 IMP-SPECT in HIV-related dementia. *Advances in Functional Imaging, 1*, 9–15.

Lambert, J.S., Seidlin, M., Reichman, R.C., Plank, C.S., Laverty, M., Morse, G.D., Knupp, C., McLaren, C., Pettinelli, C., Valentine, F.T., and Dolin, R. (1990). 2′,3′-Dideoxyinosine (ddI) in patients with the acquired immunodeficiency syndrome or AIDS-related complex. A phase I trial. *New England Journal of Medicine, 322*, 1333–1340.

Levy, J.A., Shimabukuro, J., Hollander, H., Mills, J., and Kaminsky, L. (1985). Isolation of AIDS-associated retroviruses from cerebrospinal fluid and brain of patients with neurological symptoms. *Lancet, 2*, 586–588.

Levy, R.M., Bredesen, D.E., Davis, R.L., and Rosenblum, M.L. (1986a). Multiple intracranial pathologies in the acquired immunodeficiency syndrome (AIDS): A report of 20 cases. Presented at the second International Conference on AIDS, Paris.

Levy, R.M., Bredesen, D.E., and Rosenblum, M.L. (1985). Neurological manifestations of the acquired immunodeficiency syndrome (AIDS): Experience at UCSF and review of the literature. *Journal of Neurosurgery, 62*, 475–495.

Levy, R.M., Janssen, R.S., Bush, T.J., and Rosenblum, M.L. (1988a). Neuroepidemiology of acquired immunodeficiency syndrome. In M.L. Rosenblum, R.M. Levy, and D.E. Bredesen, eds., *AIDS and the Nervous System.* New York: Raven Press, pp. 13–27.

Levy, R.M., Janssen, R.S., Bush, T.J., and Rosenblum, M.L. (1988b). Neuroepidemiology of acquired immunodeficiency syndrome. *Journal of Acquired Immune Deficiency Syndromes, 1*, 31–40.

Levy, R.M., Rosenbloom, S., and Perrett, L.V. (1986b). Neuroradiologic findings in AIDS: A review of 200 cases. *American Journal of Roentgenology, 147*, 977–983.

Lin-Greenberg, A., and Taneja-Uppal, N. (1987). Dysautonomia and infection with the human immunodeficiency virus [letter]. *Annals of Internal Medicine, 106*, 167.

Lipkin, W.I., Parry, G., Kiprov, D., and Abrams, D. (1985). Inflammatory neuropathy in homosexual men with lymphadenopathy. *Neurology, 35*, 1479–1483.

Lipton, S.A. (1992a). Models of neuronal injury in AIDS: Another role for the NMDA receptor? *Trends in Neuroscience, 15*, 75–79.

Lipton, S.A. (1992b). Memantine prevents HIV coat protein-induced neuronal injury in vitro. *Neurology 42*, 1403–1405.

Luft, B.J., Brooks, R.G., Conley, F.K., McCabe, R.E., and Remington, J.S. (1984). Toxoplasmic encephalitis in patients with acquired immune deficiency syndrome. *Journal of the American Medical Association, 252*, 913–917.

Lukehart, S.A., Hook, E.W., 3rd., Baker-Zander, S.A., Collier, A.C., Critchlow, C.W., and Handsfield, H.H. (1988). Invasion of the central nervous system by *Treponema pallidum:* Implications for diagnosis and treatment. *Annals of Internal Medicine, 109*, 855–862.

MacMahon, E., Glass, J.D., Hayward, S.D., Mann, R.B., Becker, P.S., Charache, P., McArthur, J.C., and Ambinder, R.F. (1991). Epstein-Barr virus in AIDS-related primary central nervous system lymphoma. *Lancet, 338*, 969–973.

Maier, H., Budka, H., Lassmann, H., and Pohl, P. (1989). Vacuolar myelopathy with multinucleated giant cells in the acquired immune deficiency syndrome (AIDS). Light and electron microscopic distribution of human immunodeficiency virus (HIV) antigens. *Acta Neuropathologica, 78*, 497–503.

Masliah, E., Ge, N., Morey, M., De Teresa, R., Terry, R.D., and Wiley, C.A. (1992). Cortical dendritic pathology in human immunodeficiency virus encephalitis. *Laboratory Investigation, 66*, 285–291.

McAllister, R.H., Herns, M.V., Harrison, M.J.G., Newman, S.P., Connolly, S., Fowler, C.J., Fell, M., Durrance, P., Manji, H., Kendall, B.E., and Valentine, A.R. (1992). Neurological and neuropsychological performance in HIV seropositive men without symptoms. *Journal of Neurology, Neurosurgery, and Psychiatry, 55*, 143–148.

McArthur, J.C. (1987). Neurologic manifestations of AIDS. *Medicine (Baltimore), 66*, 407–437.

McArthur, J.C., Cohen, B.A., Farzedegan, H., Cornblath, D.R., Selnes, O.A., Ostrow, D., Johnson, R.T., Phair, J., and Polk, B.F. (1988). Cerebrospinal fluid abnormalities in homosexual men with and without neuropsychiatric findings. *Annals of Neurology, 23*, S34–S37.

McArthur, J.C., Cohen, B.A., Selnes, O.A., Kumar, A.J., Cooper, K., McArthur, J.H., Soucy, G., Cornblath, D.R., Chmiel, J.S., Wang, M.C., Starkey, D.L., Ginzburg, H., Ostrow, D.G., Johnson, R.T., Phair, J.P., and Polk, B.F. (1989a). Low prevalence of neurological and neuropsychological abnormalities in otherwise healthy HIV-1-infected individuals: Results from the Multicenter AIDS Cohort Study. *Annals of Neurology, 26*, 601–611.

McArthur, J.C., Hoover, D.R., Bacellar, H., Miller, E.N., Cohen, B.A., Becker, J.T., Graham, N.M.H., McArthur, J.H., Selnes, O.A., Jacobson, L.P., Visscher, B.R., Concha, M., Saah, A. (1993). Dementia in AIDS patients: incidence and risk factors. *Neurology, 43*, 2245–2253.

McArthur, J.C., Nance-Sproson, T.E., Griffin, D.E., Hoover, D., Selnes, O.A., Miller, E.N., Margolick, J.B., Cohen, B.A., Farzadegan, H., and Saah, A. (1992). The diagnostic utility of elevation in cerebrospinal fluid β2 microglobulin in HIV-1 dementia. *Neurology, 42*, 1707–1712.

McArthur, J.C., Sipos, E., Cornblath, D.R., Welch, D., Chupp, M., Griffin, D.E., and Johnson, R.T. (1989b). Identification of mononuclear cells in CSF of patients with HIV infection. *Neurology, 39*, 66–70.

Merrill, J.E. (1991). Effects of interleukin-1 and tumor necrosis factor-α on astrocytes, microglia, oligodendrocytes, and glial precursors in vitro. *Developmental Neuroscience, 13*, 130–137.

Michael, N.L., Vahey, M., Burke, D.S., and Redfield, R.R. (1992). Viral DNA and mRNA expression correlate with the stage of human immunodeficiency virus (HIV) type 1 infection in humans: Evidence for viral replication in all stages of HIV disease. *Journal of Virology, 66*, 310–316.

Miller, E.N., Selnes, O.A., McArthur, J.C., Satz, P., Becker, J.T., Cohen, B.A., Sheridan, K., Machado, A.M., Van Gorp, W.G., and Visscher, B. (1990). Neuropsychological performance in HIV-1 infected homosexual men: The Multicenter AIDS Cohort Study (MACS). *Neurology, 40*, 197–203.

Miller, R.G., Storey, J., and Greco, C. (1989). Successful treatment of progressive polyradiculopathy in AIDS patients. *Neurology, 39*(Suppl.), 271.

Miller, R.G., Storey, J.R., and Greco, C.M. (1990). Ganciclovir in the treatment of progressive AIDS-related polyradiculopathy. *Neurology, 40*, 569–574.

Mintz, M., Epstein, L.G., and Koenigsberger, M.R. (1989). Neurological manifestations of acquired immunodeficiency syndrome in children. *International Pediatrics, 4*, 161–171.

Mizusawa, H., Hirano, A., Llena, J.F., and Shintaku, M. (1988). Cerebrovascular lesions in acquired immune deficiency syndrome (AIDS). *Acta Neuropathologica, 76*, 451–457.

Moskowitz, L.B., Gregorios, J.B., Hensley, G.T., and Berger, J.R. (1984a). Cytomegalovirus. Induced demyelination associated with acquired immune deficiency syndrome. *Archives of Pathology and Laboratory Medicine, 108*, 873–877.

Moskowitz, L.B., Hensley, G.T., Chan, J.C., Conley, F.K., Post, M.J., and Gonzalez-Arias, S.M. (1984b). Brain biopsies in patients with acquired immune deficiency syndrome. *Archives of Pathology and Laboratory Medicine, 108*, 368–371.

Musher, D.M., Hamill, R.J., and Baughn, R.D. (1990). Effect of human immunodeficiency virus (HIV) infection on the course of syphilis and on the response to treatment. *Annals of Internal Medicine, 113*, 872–881.

Narayan, O., Penney, J.B., Johnson, R.T., Herndon, R.M., and Weiner, L.P. (1973). Etiology of progressive multifocal leukoencephalopathy. Identification of papovavirus. *New England Journal of Medicine, 289*, 1278–1282.

Navia, B.A., Cho, E.S., Petito, C.K., and Price, R.W. (1986b). The AIDS dementia complex: II. Neuropathology. *Annals of Neurology, 19*, 525–535.

Navia, B.A., Jordan, B.D., and Price, R.W. (1986a). The AIDS dementia complex: I. Clinical features. *Annals of Neurology, 19*, 517–524.

Navia, B.A., Petito, C.K., Gold, J.W., Cho, E.S., Jordan, B.D., and Price, R.W. (1986c). Cerebral toxoplasmosis complicating the acquired immune deficiency syndrome: Clinical and neuropathological findings in 27 patients. *Annals of Neurology, 19*, 224–238.

Navia, B.A., and Price, R.W. (1987). The acquired immunodeficiency syndrome dementia complex as the presenting or sole manifestation of human immunodeficiency virus infection. *Archives of Neurology, 44*, 65–69.

Newsome, D.A., Green, W.R., Miller, E.D., Kiessling, L.A., Morgan, B., Jabs, D.A., and Polk, B.F. (1984). Microvascular aspects of acquired immune deficiency syndrome retinopathy. *American Journal of Ophthalmology, 98*, 590–601.

Nuwer, M.R., Miller, E.N., Visscher, B.R., Niedermeyer, E., Packwood, J.W., Carlson, L.G., Satz, P., Jankel, W., and McArthur, J.C. (1992). Asymptomatic HIV infection does not cause EEG abnormalities: Results from the Multicenter AIDS Cohort Study (MACS). *Neurology, 42*, 1214–1219.

O'Brien, W.A., Koyanagi, Y., Namazie, A., Zhao, J., Diagne, A., Idler, K., Zack, J.A., and Chen, I.S.Y. (1991). HIV-1 tropism for mononuclear phagocytes can be determined by regions of gp120 outside the CD4-binding domain. *Nature, 349*, 69–73.

Olmsted, R.A., Hirsch, V.M., Purcell, R.H., and Johnson, P.R. (1989). Nucleotide sequence analysis of feline immunodeficiency virus: Genome organization and relationship to other lentiviruses. *Proceedings of the National Academy of Sciences, USA, 86*, 8088–8092.

Olsen, W.L., Longo, F.M., Mills, C.M., and Norman, D. (1988). White matter disease in AIDS: Findings at MR imaging. *Radiology, 169*, 445–448.

Parry, G.J. (1988). Peripheral neuropathies associated with human immunodeficiency virus infection. *Annals of Neurology, 23*, S49–S53.

Passo, M.S., and Rosenblum, J.T. (1988). Ocular syphilis in patients with human immunodeficiency virus infection. *American Journal of Ophthalmology, 106*, 1–6.

Pedersen, N.C., Yamamoto, J.K., Ishida, T., and Hansen, H. (1989). Feline immunodeficiency virus infection. *Veterinary Immunology and Immunopathology, 21*, 111–129.

Peters, M., Timm, U., Schurmann, D., Pohle, H.D., and Ruf, B. (1992). Combined and alternating ganciclovir and Foscarnet in acute and maintenance therapy of human immunodeficiency virus–related cytomegalovirus encephalitis refractory to ganciclovir alone. *Clinical Investigation, 70*, 456–458.

Pitlik, S.D., Fainstein, V., Bolivar, R., Guarda, L., Rios, A., Mansell, P.A., and Gyorkey, F. (1983). Spectrum of central nervous system complications in homosexual men with acquired immune deficiency syndrome [letter]. *Journal of Infectious Diseases, 148*, 771–772.

Pizzo, P.A., Eddy, J., Falloon, J., Balis, F.M., Murphy, R.F., Moss, H., Wolters, P., Brouwers, P., Jarosinski, P., and Rubin, M. (1988). Effect of continuous intravenous infusion of zidovudine (AZT) in children with symptomatic HIV infection. *New England Journal of Medicine, 319*, 889–896.

Pomerantz, R.J., Kuritzkes, D.R., de la Monte, S.M., Rota, T.R., Baker, A.S., Albert, D., Bor, D.H., Feldman, E.L., Schooley, R.T., and Hirsch, M.S. (1987). Infection of the retina by human immunodeficiency virus type 1. *New England Journal of Medicine, 317*, 1643–1647.

Portegies, P., de Gans, J., Lange, J.M., Derix, M.M., Speelman, H., Bakker, M., Danner,

S.A., and Goudsmit, J. (1989). Declining incidence of AIDS dementia complex after introduction of zidovudine treatment [published erratum appears in BMJ 1989 Nov 2;299(6708):1141]. *British Medical Journal, 299*, 819–821.

Post, M.J., Hensley, G.T., Moskowitz, L.B., and Fischl, M. (1986). Cytomegalic inclusion virus encephalitis in patients with AIDS: CT, clinical, and pathologic correlation. *American Journal of Roentgenology, 146*, 1229–1234.

Post, M.J., Tate, L.G., Quencer, R.M., Hensley, G.T., Berger, J.R., Sheremata, W.A., and Maul, G. (1988). CT, MR, and pathology in HIV encephalitis and meningitis. *American Journal of Roentgenology, 151*, 373–380.

Power, C., Holland, N.R., Mathews, V.P., Glass, J.D., and McArthur, J.C. (1992). CMV encephalitis in AIDS: Distinction from HIV dementia. *Neurology, 42*, 211.

Price, R.W., and Brew, B.J. (1988). The AIDS dementia complex. *Journal of Infectious Diseases, 158*, 1079–1083.

Price, R.W., and Navia, B.A. (1987). Infections in AIDS and in other immunosuppressed patients. In P.G.E. Kennedy and R.T. Johnson, eds., *Infections of the Nervous System.* London: Butterworths, pp. 247–273.

Price, R.W., Sidtis, J., and Rosenblum, M. (1988). AIDS dementia complex: Some current questions. *Annals of Neurology, 23*(Suppl.), S27–S33.

Pulliam, L., Herndier, B.G., Tang, N.M., and McGrath, M.S. (1991). Human immunodeficiency virus–infected macrophages produce soluble factors that cause histological and neurochemical alterations in cultured human brains. *Journal of Clinical Investigation, 87*, 503–512.

Pumarola-Sune, T., Navia, B.A., Cordon-Cardo, C., Cho, E.-S., and Price, R.W. (1987). HIV antigen in the brains of patients with the AIDS dementia complex. *Annals of Neurology, 21*, 490–496.

Raininko, R., Elovaara, I., Virta, A., Valanne, L., Haltia, M., and Valle, S.-L. (1992). Radiological study of the brain at various stages of human immunodeficiency virus infection: early development of brain atrophy. *Neuroradiology, 34*, 190–196.

Rance, N.E., McArthur, J.C., Cornblath, D.R., Landstrom, D.L., Griffin, J.W., and Price, D.L. (1988). Gracile tract degeneration in patients with sensory neuropathy and AIDS. *Neurology, 38*, 265–271.

Resnick, L., DiMarzo-Veronese, F., Schupbach, J., Tourtellotte, W.W., Ho, D.D., Muller, F., Shapshak, P., Vogt, M., Groopman, J.E., Markham, P.D., and Gallo, R.C. (1985). Intra-blood-brain-barrier synthesis of HTLV-III-specific IgG in patients with neurologic symptoms associated with AIDS or AIDS-related complex. *New England Journal of Medicine, 313*, 1498–1504.

Rhodes, R.H. (1987). Histopathology of the central nervous system in the acquired immunodeficiency syndrome. *Human Pathology, 18*, 636–643.

Rhodes, R.H., Ward, J.M., Walker, D.L., and Ross, A.A. (1988). Progressive multifocal leukoencephalopathy and retroviral encephalitis in acquired immunodeficiency syndrome. *Archives of Pathology and Laboratory Medicine, 112*, 1207–1213.

Robbins, D.S., Shirazi, Y., Drysdale, B.E., Lieberman, A., Shin, H.S., and Shin, M.L. (1987). Production of cytotoxic factor for oligodendrocytes by stimulated astrocytes. *Journal of Immunology, 139*, 2593–2597.

Rolston, K.V. and Hoy, J. (1987). Role of clindamycin in the treatment of central nervous system toxoplasmosis. *American Journal of Medicine, 83*, 551–554.

Rosenblum, M.L., Scheck, A.C., Cronin, K., Brew, B.J., Khan, A., Paul, M., and Price, R.W. (1989). Dissociation of AIDS-related vacuolar myelopathy and productive HIV-1 infection of the spinal cord. *Neurology, 39*, 892–896.

Rosenblum, M.L., Levy, R.M., Bredesen, D.E., So, Y.T., Wara, W., and Ziegler, J.L.

(1988). Primary central nervous system lymphomas in patients with AIDS. *Annals of Neurology, 23*, S13–S16.

Rottenberg, D.A., Moeller, J.R., Strother, S.C., Sidtis, J.J., Navia, B.A., Dhawan, V., Ginos, J.Z., and Price, R.W. (1987). The metabolic pathology of the AIDS dementia complex. *Annals of Neurology, 22*, 700–706.

Saag, M.S., Powderly, W.G., Cloud, G.A., Robinson, P., Grieco, M.H., Sharkey, P.K., Thompson, S.E., Sugar, A.M., Tuazon, C.U., Fisher, J.F., Hyslop, M., Jacobson, J.M., Hafner, R., and Dismukes, W.E. (1992). Comparison of amphotericin B with fluconazole in the treatment of acute AIDS-associated cryptococcal meningitis. *New England Journal of Medicine, 326*, 83–89.

Saykin, A.J., Janssen, R.S., Sprehn, G.C., Kaplan, J.E., Spira, T.J., and O'Connor, B. (1991). Longitudinal evaluation of neuropsychological function in homosexual men with HIV infection: 18-month follow-up. *Journal of Neuropsychiatry, 3*, 286–298.

Schmitt, F.A., Bigley, J.W., McKinnis, R., Logue, P.E., Evans, R.W., Drucker, J.L., and the AZT Collaborative Working Group. (1988). Neuropsychological outcome of zidovudine (AZT) treatment of patients with AIDS and AIDS-related complex. *New England Journal of Medicine, 319*, 1573–1578.

Schuster, M., Zuger, A., Simberkoff, M.S., Rahal, J.J., and Holzman, R.S. (1986). Maintenance therapy of cryptococcal meningitis in patients with AIDS. Presented at the Second International Conference on AIDS, Paris.

Selnes, O.A., McArthur, J.C., Royal, W., 3rd, Updike, M.L., Nance-Sproson, T., Concha, M., Gordon, B., Solomon, L., and Vlahov, D. (1992). HIV-1 infection and intravenous drug use: Longitudinal neuropsychological evaluation of asymptomatic subjects. *Neurology, 42*, 1924–1930.

Selnes, O.A., Miller, E., McArthur, J.C., Gordon, B., Munoz, A., Sheridan, K., Fox, R., and Saah, A.J. (1990). HIV-1 infection: No evidence of cognitive decline during the asymptomatic stages. *Neurology, 40*, 204–208.

Sharer, L.R., Cho, E.-S., and Epstein, L.G. (1985). Multinucleated giant cells and HTLV-III in AIDS encephalopathy. *Human Pathology, 16*, 760.

Sharer, L.R., and Kapila, R. (1985). Neuropathologic observations in acquired immunodeficiency syndrome (AIDS). *Acta Neuropathologica, 66*, 188–198.

Shaw, G.M., Harper, M.E., Hahn, B.H., Epstein, L.G., Gajdusek, D.C., Price, R.W., Navia, B.A., Petito, C.K., O'Hara, C.J., Groopman, J.E., Cho, E.-S., Oleske, J.M., Wong-Staal, F. and Gallo, R.C. (1985). HTLV-III infection in brains of children and adults with AIDS encephalopathy. *Science, 227*, 177–182.

Sidtis, J.J., Gatsonis, C., Price, R.W., Singer, E.J., Collier, A.C., Richman, D.D., Hirsch, M.S., Schaerf, F., Fischl, M.A., Keiburtz, K., Simpson, D., Koch, M.A., Feinberg, J., Dafni, U., and the AIDS Clinical Trials Group. (1993). Zidovudine treatment of the AIDS dementia complex: Results of a placebo-controlled trial. *Annals of Neurology, 33*, 343–349.

Silberstein, C.H., McKegney, F.P., O'Dowd, M.A., Selwyn, P.A., Schoenbaum, E., Drucker, E., Feiner, C., Cox, C.P., and Freidland, G. (1987). A prospective longitudinal study of neuropsychological and psychosocial factors in asymptomatic individuals at risk of HTLV-III/LAV infection in a methadone program: Preliminary findings. *International Journal of Neuroscience, 32*, 669–676.

Simpson, D.M., and Bender, A.N. (1988). Human immunodeficiency virus–associated myopathy: Analysis of 11 patients. *Annals of Neurology, 24*, 79–84.

Simpson, D.M., and Wolfe, D.E. (1991). Neuromuscular complications of HIV infection and its treatment. *AIDS, 5*, 917–926.

Snider, W.D., Simpson, D.M., Aronyk, K.E., and Nielsen, S.L. (1983a). Primary lymphoma of the nervous system associated with acquired immune-deficiency syndrome [letter]. *New England Journal of Medicine, 308*, 45.

Snider, W.D., Simpson, D.M., Nielsen, S., Gold, J.W., Metroka, C.E., and Posner, J.B. (1983b). Neurological complications of acquired immune deficiency syndrome: Analysis of 50 patients. *Annals of Neurology, 14*, 403–418.

So, Y.T., Holtzman, D.M., Abrams, D.I., and Olney, R.K. (1988). Peripheral neuropathy associated with acquired immunodeficiency syndrome. Prevalence and clinical features from a population-based survey. *Archives of Neurology, 45*, 945–948.

Stern, Y., Marder, K., Bell, K., Chen, J., Dooneief, G., Golstein, S., Mindry, D., Richards, M., Sano, M., Williams, J., Gorman, J., Ehrhardt, A., and Mayeux, R. (1991). Multidisciplinary baseline assessment of homosexual men with and without human immunodeficiency virus infection. III. Neurologic and neuropsychological findings. *Archives of General Psychiatry, 48*, 131–138.

Stoler, M.H., Eskin, T.A., Benn, S., Angerer, R.C., and Angerer, L.M. (1986). Human T-cell lymphotropic virus type III infection of the central nervous system. A preliminary in situ analysis. *Journal of the American Medical Association, 256*, 2360–2364.

Studies of Ocular Complications of AIDS Research Group and AIDS Clinical Trials Group. (1992). Mortality in patients with the acquired immunodeficiency syndrome treated with either Foscarnet or ganciclovir for cytomegalovirus retinitis. *New England Journal of Medicine, 326*, 213–220.

Sugar, A.M., and Saunders, C. (1988). Oral fluconazole as suppressive therapy of disseminated cryptococcosis in patients with acquired immunodeficiency syndrome. *American Journal of Medicine, 85*, 481–489.

Tardieu, M., Hery, C., Peudenier, S., Boespflug, O., and Montagnier, L. (1992). Human immunodeficiency virus type 1-infected monocytic cells can destroy human neural cells after cell-to-cell adhesion. *Annals of Neurology, 32*, 11–17.

Tyor, W.R., Glass, J.D., Baumrind, N., McArthur, J.C., Griffin, J.W., Becker, P.S., and Griffin, D.E. (1993). Cytokine expression of macrophages in HIV-1 associated vacuolar myelopathy. *Neurology, 43*:1002–1009.

Tyor, W.R., Glass, J.D., Griffin, J.W., Becker, P.S., McArthur, J.C., Bezman, L., and Griffin, D.E. (1992b). Cytokine expression in the brain during AIDS. *Annals of Neurology, 31*, 349–360.

Van Wielink, G., McArthur, J.C., Moench, T., Farzadegan, H., Johnson, R.T., and Saah, A. (1990). Intrathecal synthesis of anti-HIV-IgG: Correlation with increasing duration of HIV-1 infection. *Neurology, 40*, 816–819.

Vazeux, R., Brousse, N., Jarry, A., Henin, D., Marche, C., Vedrenne, C., Mikol, J., Wolff, M., Michon, C., Rosenblum, W., Bureau, J.-F., Montagnier, L., and Brahic, M. (1987). AIDS subacute encephalitis. Identification of HIV-infected cells. *American Journal of Pathology, 126*, 403–410.

Vendrell, J., Heredia, C., Pujol, M., Vidal, J., Blesa, R., and Graus, F. (1987). Guillain-Barré syndrome associated with seroconversion for anti-HTLV-III [letter]. *Neurology, 37*, 544.

Vinters, H.V., Kwok, M.K., Ho, H.W., Anders, K.H., Tomiyasu, U., Wolfson, W.L., and Robert, F. (1989). Cytomegalovirus in the nervous system of patients with the acquired immune deficiency syndrome. *Brain, 112*, 245–268.

Wechsler, A.F., and Ho, D.D. (1989). Bilateral Bell's palsy at the time of HIV seroconversion. *Neurology, 39*, 747–748.

Wesselingh, S.L., Power, C., Glass, J.D., Tyor, W.R., McArthur, J.C., Farber, J.M., Griffin, J.W., and Griffin, D.E. (1993). Intracerebral cytokine messenger RNA expression in acquired immunodeficiency syndrome dementia. *Annals of Neurology. 33*:576–582.

Wiley, C.A., Masliah, E., Morey, M., Lemere, C., Deteresa, R., Grafe, M., Hansen, L., and Terry, R. (1991). Neocortical damage during HIV infection. *Annals of Neurology, 29*, 651–657.

Wiley, C.A., Schrier, R.D., Nelson, J.A., Lampert, P.W., and Oldstone, M.B. (1986). Cellular localization of human immunodeficiency virus infection within the brains of acquired immune deficiency syndrome patients. *Proceedings of the National Academy of Sciences, USA, 83*, 7089–7093.

Yankner, B.A., Skolnik, P.R., Shoukimas, G.M., Gabuzda, D.H., Sobel, R.A., and Ho, D.D. (1986). Cerebral granulomatous angiitis associated with isolation of human T-lymphotropic virus type III from the central nervous syste ı. *Annals of Neurology, 20*, 362–364.

Yarchoan, R., Berg, G., Brouwers, P., Fischl, M.A., Spitzer, A.R., Wichman, A., Grafman, J., Thomas, R.V., Safai, B., Brunetti, A., Perno, C.F., Schmidt, R.J., Larson, S.M., Myers, C.E., and Broder, S. (1987). Response of human immunodeficiency virus-associated neurological disease to 3'-azido-3'-deoxythymidine. *Lancet, 1*, 132–135.

Yarchoan, R., Pluda, J.M., Thomas, R.V., Mitsuya, H., Brouwers, P., Wyvill, K.M., Hartman, N., Johns, D.G., and Broder, S. (1990). Long-term toxicity/activity profile of 2',3'-dideoxyinosine in AIDS and AIDS-related complex. *Lancet, 336*, 526–529.

Zuger, A., Louie, E., Holzman, R.S., Simberkoff, M.S., and Rahal, J.J. (1986). Cryptococcal disease in patients with the acquired immunodeficiency syndrome. Diagnostic features and outcome of treatment. *Annals of Internal Medicine, 104*, 234–

4

Structural Brain Imaging of HIV Infection

JOHN R. HESSELINK, TERRY L. JERNIGAN, and
WILLIAM C. HEINDEL

Central nervous system (CNS) involvement has been reported in 30–73% of patients with acquired immunodeficiency syndrome (AIDS), and up to 87% of patients show CNS pathology at autopsy (Belman et al., 1985; Levy et al., 1985). Many of the neurological complications involve opportunistic infections, such as toxoplasmosis, cryptococcosis and progressive multifocal leukoencephalopathy (PML), or neoplasia such as lymphoma. However, the most common pathogen of the neuraxis appears to be human immunodeficiency virus (HIV) itself (Shaw et al., 1985), which can produce aseptic meningitis, subacute white matter encephalitis, and vacuolar myelopathy. Imaging studies in HIV-infected individuals have revealed brain atrophy (dilated cortical sulci and ventricles), parenchymal mass lesions secondary to opportunistic infection or lymphoma, diffuse white matter abnormality related to subacute encephalitis, and focal white matter lesions of uncertain etiology (Post et al., 1985; Jarvik et al., 1988).

Since pathological tissue is not easily obtained and not always available from clinical patients, it is important to develop imaging techniques and elucidate criteria for diagnosing HIV infection of the brain and its associated opportunistic infections and neoplastic diseases. Magnetic resonance imaging (MRI) offers several advantages over previous in vivo methods for visualizing the human brain. No ionizing radiation is used. This permits multiple examinations over the course of an illness without known risk to the patient. Moreover, images can be acquired in the axial, coronal, and sagittal planes with identical spatial resolution. This may be helpful when a particular brain structure (e.g., hippocampus, cerebellum) is difficult to resolve in one plane but relatively easy to delimit and measure in another. Finally, by changing the operator-controlled variables (repetition time [TR] and echo time [TE]), the relative weighting of the relaxation parameters (longitudinal relaxation, T_1, and transverse relaxation, T_2) may be altered to increase the sensitivity of MRI to specific tissue abnormalities.

Studies of AIDS patients have shown MRI to be superior to high-resolution computed tomography (CT) for detecting white matter lesions and pathology associated with surrounding edema but without breakdown of the blood-brain barrier (BBB) (Post et al., 1986). Although CT is very useful in evaluating enhancing parenchymal masses (Kelly and Brant-Zawadzki, 1983; Whelan et al., 1983), more diffuse processes without mass effect and an intact BBB, such as PML and subacute encephalitis secondary to HIV or cytomegalovirus (CMV) infection, are more elusive (Post et al., 1985). Correlative studies indicate that MRI is more sensitive in detecting the viral infections, but MRI of the microscopic glial nodules and multinucleated giant cells seen histologically in HIV infection of the brain is still difficult (Post et al., 1988). Also, MRI is better for assessing the secondary nonspecific changes of cortical atrophy and HIV-induced foci of demyelination and infarction. In this chapter, we will first review the use of MRI and, to a lesser extent, CT imaging in the investigation of HIV infection and its associated opportunistic infections and lymphomas. We will then describe in greater detail our recent studies from the HIV Neurobehavioral Research Center (HNRC) at the University of California, San Diego, involving both the qualitative and quantitative analysis of cranial MR images.

CNS Effects of HIV Infection

In recent years, much interest has centered on a subacute encephalitis involving the white matter seen in HIV-seropositive patients because of both its association with HIV infection of the brain (Wiley et al., 1986) and its correlation with a primary AIDS dementia complex (Holland and Tross, 1985; Navia et al., 1986a,b). Subacute encephalitis is seen in up to 30% of patients with AIDS; CMV may be the causal agent in some cases. Levy et al. (1985) reported that 54 (17%) of 315 patients in their clinical series had subacute encephalitis. In another series (Anders et al., 1986), 31.4% had microglial nodular encephalitis suggesting HIV, whereas CMV was found in only 14.4% of those cases. The two viruses often coexist in brain specimens taken from AIDS patients (Wiley and Nelson, 1988). Additional studies have confirmed a predominant HIV etiology for the microglial nodules and the subacute white matter encephalitis (Shaw et al., 1985; Gabuzda and Hirsch, 1987).

In a study of 21 patients with HIV encephalitis (Post et al., 1988), both CT and MRI were found to be relatively insensitive to the early stages of involvement, manifested pathologically by widespread microscopic microglial nodules with multinucleated giant cells. The secondary changes of atrophy were well seen by both modalities in the majority of patients, and parenchymal lesions consistent with demyelination were noted in three of seven patients studied by MRI. In this same study, CT was superior to nonenhanced MRI in detecting one case of HIV encephalitis.

A study by Chrysikopoulos et al. (1990) of 24 patients with biopsy-proven HIV encephalitis produced similar results. Neither MRI nor CT could detect the microglial nodules or multinucleated giant cells, the hallmark of HIV encephalitis. Atrophy, the most common finding, was found in 18. White matter abnormality was imaged in only four patients. The white matter changes on MRI and CT correlated pathologically with the demyelination and vacuolation associated with severe HIV infection.

Correlative radiological-pathological studies were conducted in our laboratory on 10 formalin-fixed brains of AIDS patients that came to autopsy (Grafe et al., 1990). Postmortem MRI did not detect microglial nodules unless they occurred in relatively large clusters. The difficulty of detecting microglial nodules is probably due to their small size (50–100 μm). The "in-plane" resolution of MR images is about 0.7 mm (700 μm), and the 5-mm-thick sections are subject to partial volume effects; for example, one-half of a 6-mm lesion may be included in each of adjacent sections. This is supported by the fact that the microglial nodules detected by MRI in our series were clusters greater than 3 mm in size.

In the same study, severe ventriculitis and gliosis were also visible by MRI. Brain infarcts and areas of necrosis secondary to CMV infection and toxoplasmosis demonstrated the best correlation between MRI and pathology. Infarcts are readily seen on proton density and T_2-weighted images because of the central region of necrosis surrounded by astrocytic reaction and partial demyelination. The astrocytes become swollen from absorption of proteinaceous edema fluid and are highly visible on histological examination with glial fibrillary acidic protein (GFAP) staining (Marshall et al., 1988).

Opportunistic Infections and Lymphoma

The more commonly reported secondary CNS complications of AIDS include opportunistic fungal, viral, and protozoan infections and lymphoma. In one of the largest reviews of the neurological manifestations of AIDS (Levy et al., 1986), out of a total of 315 patients with CNS complications, viral syndromes were seen in 94. These consisted of subacute encephalitis (54),[1] aseptic meningitis (21), herpes simplex encephalitis (9), PML (6), viral myelitis (3), and varicella-zoster encephalitis (1). Nonviral infections included *Toxoplasma gondii* (103), *Cryptococcus neoformans* (41), *Candida albicans* (6), atypical mycobacteria (6), *Treponema pallidum* (2), and *Mycobacterium tuberculosis, Aspergillus,* and *Escherichia coli* (1 each). Neoplasms included primary CNS lymphoma (15), systemic lymphoma with CNS involvement (12), and metastatic Kaposi's sarcoma (3). Cranial and peripheral nerve complications were seen in 51 patients. Many of these neuropathies, as well as the cases of subacute encephalitis and atypical aseptic meningitis, may have been due to direct infection with HIV.

---

[1]Note: the diagnosis of subacute encephalitis is based on the presence of definite histopathological changes and should not be equated to HIV-1 infection of the brain, which probably occurs in 80% or more of AIDS cases.

Toxoplasmosis

T. gondii, a protozoan, is the most common opportunistic infection in AIDS patients, accounting for 13.4–33% of all CNS complications. Haitian AIDS patients appear to be particularly susceptible to this infection. The characteristic MRI appearance consists of multiple ring-enhancing lesions located at the cortical–medullary junction, but the basal ganglia and white matter are also frequently involved (Figure 4–1). The amount of peripheral edema is variable. Earlier in the evolution of the abscesses, the nodule may exhibit more homogeneous enhancement, with little mass effect or edema. In general, fungal abscesses evolve more slowly than bacterial ones, but in immunocompromised individuals the fungal lesions can be quite aggressive. Dual infections are common in AIDS patients. In such cases, invariably one of the pathogens is *T. gondii.* Toxoplasmosis may also coexist with lymphoma. Another confounding fact is that the inflammatory reaction to toxoplasmosis may mimic lymphoma on biopsy or CSF cytology.

Cryptococcosis

Cryptococcosis is the most common CNS fungal infection in AIDS, occurring in 8.7–13% of patients. *C. neoformans* has a peculiar propensity to affect individuals with cell-mediated immunity, and it usually produces a meningitis. Cerebrospinal fluid (CSF) antibody titers are not always reliable for diagnosis because the immune response in AIDS patients is so variable. Imaging studies may be negative or may show only mild ventricular dilatation. Since cerebral atrophy is common in AIDS patients, distinguishing central atrophy from hydrocephalus is not always easy, and sometimes repeated scanning to correlate with the clinical picture is necessary. Meningeal enhancement is not often present unless a chronic inflammation has developed. A chronic relapsing infection can result in cryptococcal brain abscesses.

Progressive Multifocal Leukoencephalopathy

PML is a disorder characterized by widespread foci of demyelination caused by reactivation of a latent papovavirus. Most cases occur in the setting of an immunocompromised host secondary to neoplasia, chemotherapy, and, increasingly, AIDS. The lesions are initially round or oval, becoming larger and more confluent with time. Subcortical white matter may be the first area of involvement with later spread to the deeper white matter. The pattern is often asymmetric (Figure 4–2). MRI appearance reflects the long T_1 and long T_2 relaxation times of the lesions, typically without mass effect. The high T_2 signal is related to both demyelination and edema. These lesions do not usually enhance on CT, and preliminary experience with MRI suggests that most do not enhance with gadolinium (Gd-DTPA) (Mark and Atlas, 1989).

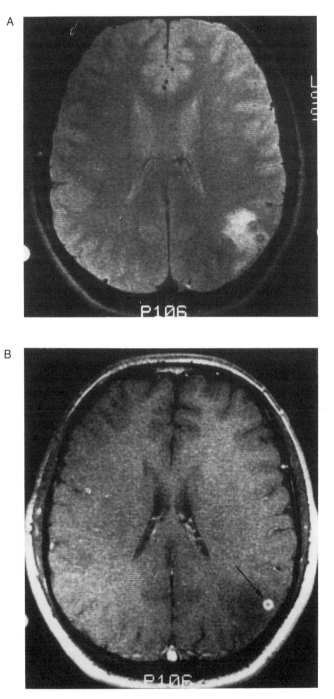

FIGURE 4–1. Toxoplasmosis. A proton-density weighted image (A) shows an area of hyperintensity in the left posterior parietal lobe. Following gadolinium infusion a T1-weighted scan (B) reveals a small enhancing nodule (arrow) with surrounding edema. The punctate central area that does not enhance probably represents necrosis.

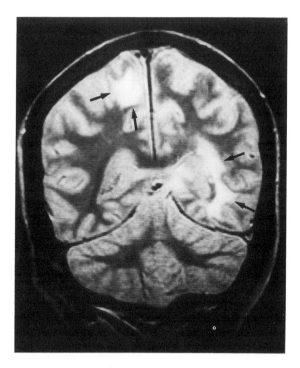

FIGURE 4–2. Progressive multifocal leukoencephalopathy (PML). A coronal T2-weighted image discloses two areas of hyperintensity within the cerebral white matter (arrows)—one in the left occipital lobe, and another in the right medial parietal lobe. The peripheral location and outer scalloped margins are features of PML.

Lymphoma

Primary malignant lymphoma, formerly called *reticulum cell sarcoma, histiocytic lymphoma,* and *microglioma,* is a non-Hodgkin's lymphoma that occurs in the brain in the absence of systemic involvement. These tumors are highly cellular and grow rapidly. About 70% represent large-cell variants of the B-cell type. Favorite sites include the deeper parts of the frontal and parietal lobes, basal ganglia, and hypothalamus. While cerebral lymphomas are very radiosensitive and respond dramatically to steroid therapy, the prognosis remains poor (see Chapter 3).

Lymphomas typically appear as homogeneous, slightly high-signal to isointense masses deep within the brain on T_2-weighted images. The observed mild T_2 prolongation is probably related to dense cell packing within these tumors, leaving relatively little interstitial space for accumulation of water. Lymphomas are frequently found in close proximity to the corpus callosum and have a propensity to extend across it into the opposite hemisphere, a feature that mimics glioblastoma. Multiple lesions are present in as many as 50% of cases (Figure 4–3) (Schwaighofer et al., 1989).

In the non-AIDS patient, CNS lymphomas are associated with only a mild or moderate amount of peritumoral edema. They are infiltrative tumors. At presentation they can be quite large and yet can produce relatively little mass effect. Despite their rapid growth, central necrosis is uncommon. Intratumoral cysts and hemorrhage are unusual. Most lymphomas show bright, homogeneous contrast

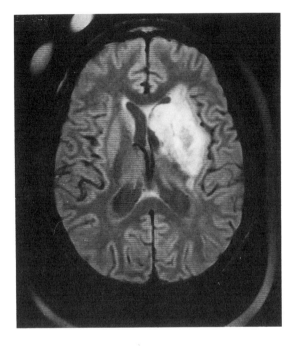

FIGURE 4–3. Lymphoma. An axial proton-density weighted scan demonstrates a large mass deep within the left cerebral hemisphere. The mass involves the caudate nucleus, the internal capsule, and the lentiform nucleus. It compresses the frontal horn of the left lateral ventricle, and the sylvian fissure is displaced laterally.

enhancement. This pattern is modified somewhat in AIDS patients. Multiplicity is more common. Moreover, lymphomas exhibit more aggressive behavior and readily outgrow their blood supply. As a result, central necrosis and ring enhancement are often seen in lymphomatous masses in AIDS patients, making lymphoma indistinguishable from toxoplasmosis.

HNRC Imaging Studies

Subject Imaging Protocol

Although standard imaging protocols may be sufficient for many clinical purposes, research into the neuroradiology of HIV requires approaches that both yield reliable qualitative research ratings and permit the evolution of quantitative image analytic strategies. In this section we describe the techniques that have been developed as part of the HNRC. There longitudinal imaging studies are performed to determine the effects of HIV infection on the brain at various stages of the disease. All subjects entering the study are imaged by MRI at baseline and at 6- to 12-month intervals to assess brain structure. The MRI studies are performed on a 1.5 Tesla MRI system (General Electric, Milwaukee). Three consecutive spin-echo pulse sequences are used to obtain images in each of three orthogonal planes. Using a T_1-weighted (T_1W: TR = 600 milliseconds, TE = 20 milliseconds) sequence, sagittal images centered at the midsagittal plane are acquired to visualize the corpus callosum, brain stem, and other medial hemispheric surface landmarks. Subsequently, proton-density-weighted (PDW) and T_2-weighted (T_2W) images are obtained in axial and coronal planes using multiple-echo sequences (TR = 2000 milliseconds, TE = 25, 70 milliseconds and TR = 3000 milliseconds, TE = 30, 80 milliseconds, respectively). Slice thickness is 5 mm, with a 2.5-mm gap between successive slices for the axial, and 5 mm contiguous (no gap) for the coronal. A 256 × 256 matrix and a 24-cm field of view, corresponding to a 0.9375 × 0.9375 mm pixel size, are used for all three acquisitions. All studies undergo a qualitative analysis (i.e., clinical ratings), and quantitative analyses are then performed on sampled subgroups of subjects based on the results of the qualitative evaluation and neuropsychological ratings.

Qualitative Analyses

The MR images are reviewed by three neuroradiologists in a blinded manner to assess brain volume and any parenchymal abnormalities. A brain rating booklet was designed, with sample images for each category and grade of disease. Cortical sulci and ventricular size are graded separately as normal, mild, moderate, or severely enlarged (Figures 4–4 and 4–5). Parenchymal abnormalities are graded according to the size and number of parenchymal hyperintensities. Grades include normal, borderline, mild, moderate, and severe disease (Figures 4–6 and 4–7). The parenchymal abnormalities are further classified as punctate, patchy, or confluent-diffuse. Follow-up scans are also given a change rating: better, no change, or worse.

Preliminary imaging data were reviewed on 409 subjects, including 282 in Centers for Disease Control (CDC) classes II, III, and IV-C2 (intermediate group), 50 in CDC class IV (advanced group), and 77 control subjects. The intermediate and advanced groups had significantly more cortical ($p = .05$) and central ($p = .009$) volume loss compared to the control group. There was a slightly higher incidence of parenchymal lesions in the advanced group, but the difference was not statistically significant. As part of the longitudinal study, 168 subjects had two or more MRI studies. A change on the follow-up images was noted in 40, all showing worsening (Figure 4–8). Increased volume loss was noted in 13 and increased parenchymal disease in 15. A significantly higher percentage of the studies in the advanced group worsened (46%) compared to 17% in the intermediate group and 11% in the control subjects.

Our controlled, prospective study shows that parenchymal brain abnormalities may be relatively subtle on MRI until HIV-positive subjects advanced to CDC class IV. Also, longitudinal studies reveal accelerated brain atrophy and parenchymal disease in CDC class IV.

Most reports of brain involvement in HIV-infected individuals have been retrospective analyses of patients presenting with neurological symptoms. In a Miami study of 51 patients (Post et al., 1985), CT scans of the brain were abnormal in 76%. An earlier pilot study by our own group (Grant et al., 1987) disclosed a relatively high percentage of abnormal MR images. Abnormalities were noted in the brains of 69% of AIDS patients and 50% of ARC patients. Analysis of the specific MRI patterns disclosed that focal lesions were equally distributed

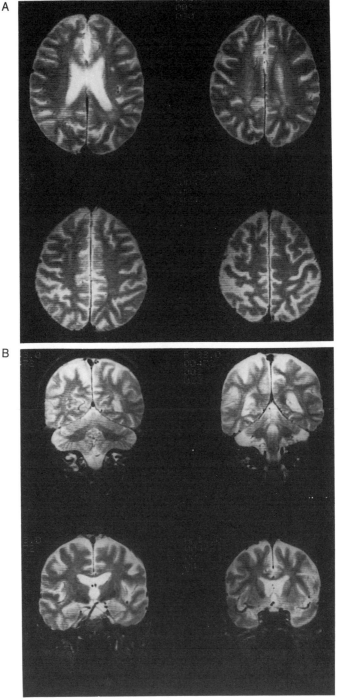

FIGURE 4–4. Moderate cortical volume loss. Axial (A) and coronal (B) scans show moderate enlargement of the cortical sulci over both cerebral hemispheres. The ventricles are normal in size. A single hyperintensity is present in the left frontal lobe.

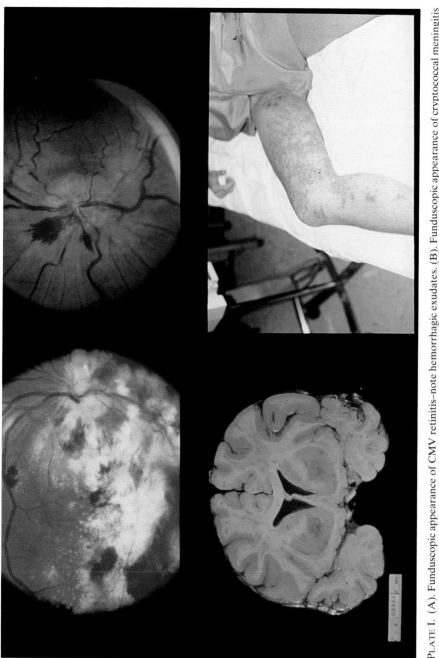

PLATE I. (A). Funduscopic appearance of CMV retinitis–note hemorrhagic exudates. (B). Funduscopic appearance of cryptococcal meningitis with papilledema and small hemorrhage. (C). Symmetrical involvement of basal ganglia with toxoplasmosis. (D). Severe involvement of several lumbar dermatomes by *H. zoster* radiculitis.

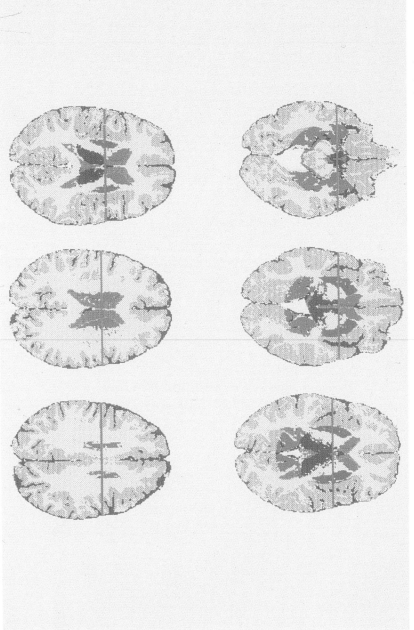

PLATE II. Representative, fully-processed images. Pixels are classified and regions have been designated using anatomical and some stereotactic criteria. The pixels have been color-coded to display the region designations: cerebral cortex = grey, temporal limbic structures = green, caudate = blue, lenticular nucleus = magenta, diencephalon = purple. Ventricular CSF is coded in red, sulcal CSF in black, and white matter pixels are displayed here in white. The red line shown within the sections indicates the position of the coronal dividing plane.

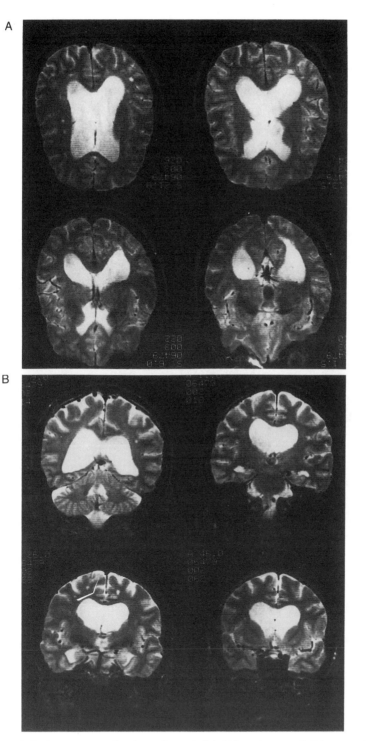

FIGURE 4–5. Severe central volume loss. Axial (A) and coronal (B) scans demonstrate marked dilatation of the lateral ventricles. The cortical volume is within normal limits. A few punctate hyperintensities are noted within the subcortical white matter of both cerebral hemispheres.

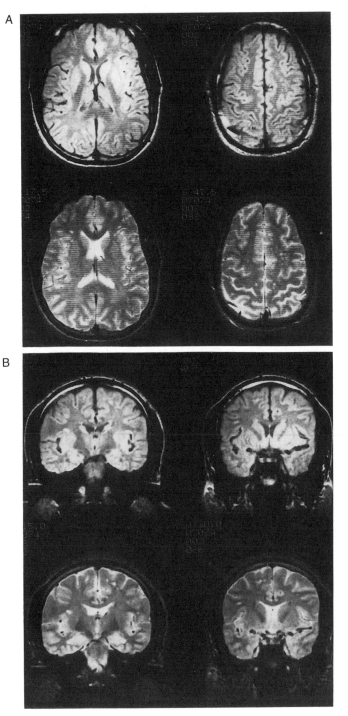

FIGURE 4–6. Mild-moderate parenchymal disease. Axial (A) and coronal (B) scans show multiple punctate subcortical hyperintensities scattered throughout both cerebral hemispheres. The cortical sulci over the occipital lobes are slightly enlarged; the ventricles are normal.

118

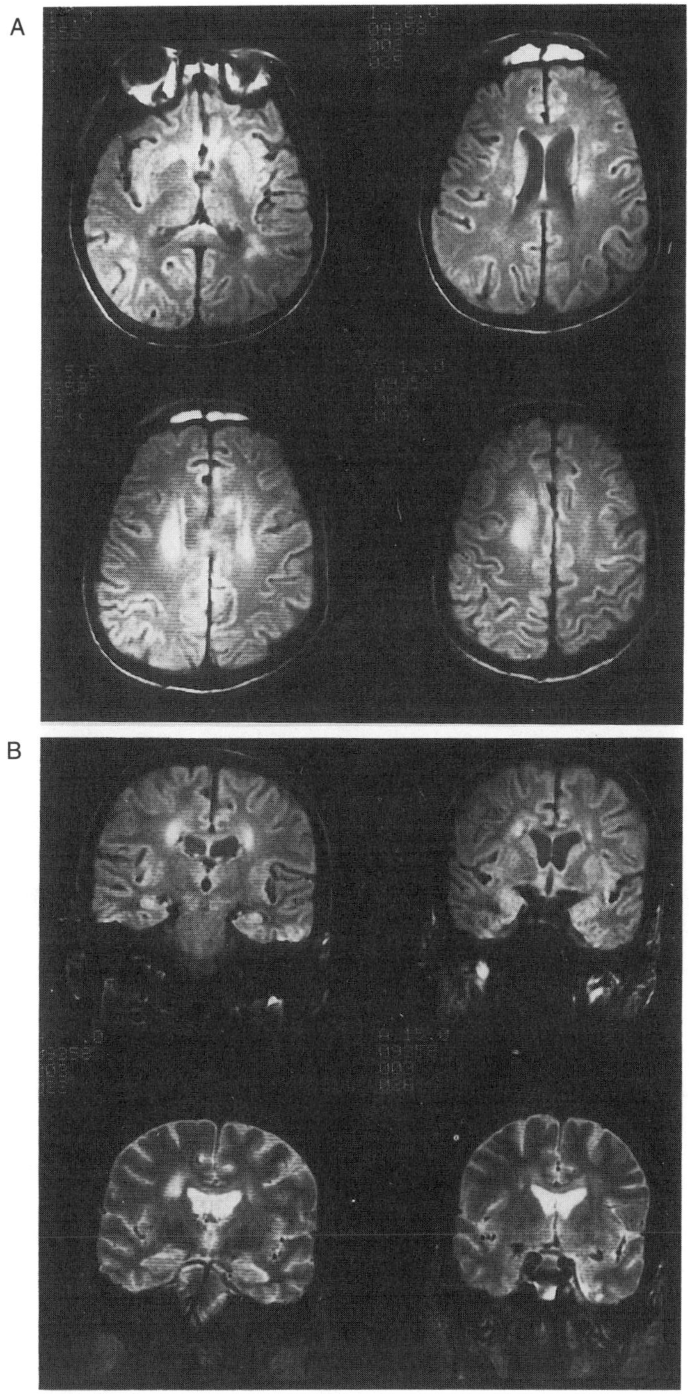

FIGURE 4–7. Moderate parenchymal disease. Axial (A) and coronal (B) scans reveal a confluent pattern of abnormality within the periventricular white matter bilaterally in a patient with HIV encephalitis. The cortical sulci are borderline in size, but the ventricles are normal.

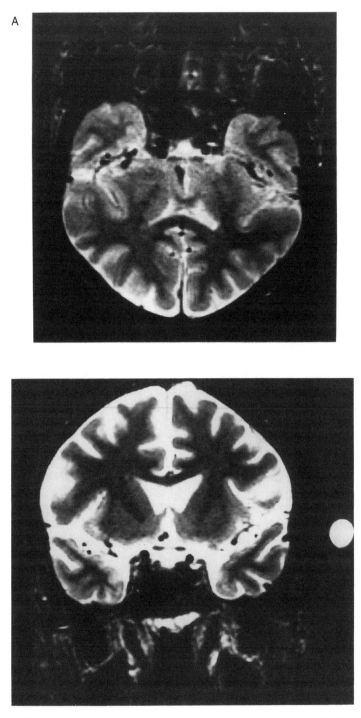

FIGURE 4–8. Longitudinal study showing progressive cortical atrophy. A. Coronal scan obtained at baseline is normal. B. A follow-up scan at 12 months discloses moderate cortical volume loss.

between the two subgroups, whereas all four patients with diffuse parenchymal abnormality were from the subgroup with AIDS.

In a recent study by Post et al. (1991) of 119 HIV-positive patients, MRI abnormalities were found in 13% of the asymptomatic ones and 46% of the symptomatic ones. Also, in the neurologically symptomatic group, the white matter lesions were usually larger and more numerous, and atrophy was more often present. No correlation was found between the brain abnormalities and patients' age, history of intravenous drug usage, head injury, or hypertension. A correlation was found between depressed CD4 lymphocyte counts (<400 cells/mm³) and cortical atrophy but not with white matter lesions.

The incidence of abnormalities in our present study may be lower because many of the subjects enrolled in the HNRC are entering earlier in the course of their disease, some shortly after seroconversion. Also, virtually all late-stage patients receive antiretroviral treatment. Ongoing longitudinal studies at our San Diego center provide an opportunity to investigate the time course of structural alterations in the brain and to compare the sensitivity of MRI in detecting these early changes compared to clinical parameters, neuropsychological findings, and pathologic findings.

Quantitative Analyses

A subgroup of subjects followed in the HNRC, free of opportunistic infections of the nervous system and without clinical dementia at their entry into the study, have been examined using semiautomated morphometric analysis of MRI (Jernigan et al., 1993). Quantitative image-analytic techniques were used to estimate volumes of ventricular and cortical CSF in order to assess the degree of brain volume loss. Then separate volumes of cerebral white matter, and of cortical and subcortical grey matter structures, were obtained to attempt to localize the observed losses.

Four groups of subjects were compared in this study. One group consisted of HIV+ subjects, either having symptoms and signs that met criteria for frank AIDS defined by the CDC—that is, CDC class IV, excluding IV-C2 ($N = 22$), or having an absolute T4 cell count of 200 per microliter (μl) or less ($N = 9$) (CDC, 1987). There were 31 men in this group, which we term "HIV+ symptomatic." A second group ($N = 63$) consisted of men classified as CDC classes II, III, and IV-C2 who were not significantly immunosuppressed (i.e., T4 cell counts were greater than 200 per microliter). While these men could have lymphadenopathy and certain other relatively minor medical symptoms, as a shorthand reference we shall term them "HIV+ asymptomatic" to distinguish them from the seropositive, symptomatic group with more advanced disease. HIV infection was established in these two groups of subjects by a repeatedly positive enzyme-linked immunosorbent assay and a confirmatory immunoblot for HIV-1 antibody. The third group consisted of 39 men from a high-risk population who were seronegative for HIV. They were comparable in age, education, alcohol or drug abuse histories, and behaviors that might place them at risk for HIV infection to the two seropositive groups (we term these the "HIV− high-risk controls"). A second control group ($N = 26$) consisted of men recruited for other neuropsychiatric studies within the Department of Psychiatry at the University of California at San Diego (termed "HIV− low-risk controls"). The four groups were very closely matched for age and education.

Detailed descriptions of the image-analytic approach used in our studies are contained in several articles (Jernigan et al., 1990, 1991a,b). Image data sets are assigned (random) numeric codes, and all analyses are conducted blind to any subject characteristics. Briefly, each pixel location within a section of the imaged brain is classified on the basis of its signal values in both original images (TE = 25 milliseconds, TE = 70 milliseconds) as most resembling CSF, gray matter, white matter, or signal hyperintensity (tissue abnormality). Consistently identifiable landmark points and structural boundaries are then designated on the pixel-classified images by trained image analysts. The processed image data are transformed spatially so that all locations within the brain images may be identified relative to a common anatomical coordinate system. Some regional boundaries are then defined relative to this coordinate scheme (i.e., stereotactially).

To delineate specific gray matter and CSF structures, the operators circumscribed pixels classified as gray matter or CSF that were visually determined to be in the ventricles, cortical sulci, caudate nuclei, lenticular nuclei, diencephalic gray matter structures (which included but did not separately delineate mamillary bodies, hypothalamic gray, septal nuclei, and thalamus), and cerebral cortex (including the contiguous amygdala).

The cortical and diencephalic regions were then further subdivided. The mesial temporal lobe (temporal limbic) structures were separated from the remaining cortex, and the functionally distinct hypothalamic and septal structures within the diencephalic region were separated from the bulk of the thalamus on the basis of a stereotactically defined coronal dividing plane. The fully processed images are illustrated in Plate II. The different regions are color-coded as follows: Diencephalic areas are purple, caudate nuclei are blue, and lenticular nuclei are magenta. The red line running through each section indicates the position of the coronal dividing plane. This plane divides the hypothalamic and septal structures (lying anteriorly) from the bulk of the thalamus (lying posteriorly). The region designated as temporal limbic structures (uncus, amygdala, hippocampus, and parahippocampal gyrus) are green, and the remaining cerebral cortex is gray. Note that areas within the lenticular nucleus containing significant iron deposits, particularly in the globus pallidus, do not meet the signal criteria for gray matter and are thus not included in this region. Ventricular fluid is shown in red, sulcal fluid in black, and white matter in white.

The volume of the supratentorial cranium was estimated by summing the supratentorial voxels (including CSF, signal hyperintensities, gray matter, and white matter) over all sections. The voxels within each of the regions were summed over all sections in which the designated structures appeared. The sum of all supratentorial white matter voxels was also computed. In addition, the total number of subcortical white matter voxels with increased T_2 values and the total number with frankly hyperintense signal values (a more stringent criterion) were computed.

The MRI measures used in the comparisons of the four groups were subjected to additional analyses to remove irrelevant variability due to cranium size and age. These adjustments were based on analyses conducted earlier on a larger group of 107 normal controls. Normal age-related changes and effects of supratentorial cranium size were estimated for each measure with multiple regression analyses. On the basis of these analyses, new measures were computed for each subject that expressed the original values as deviations from the values predicted from the subjects' ages and cranium sizes in age-appropriate standard deviation units.

In order to establish the clinical validity of these quantitative MRI measures, we have examined the relationship between these measures and the clinical MRI ratings (i.e., qualitative measures) that have also been developed for this project. To date, a total of 160 subjects have undergone both quantitative and qualitative evaluations. Clinical ratings of cortical volume loss were found to be highly significantly correlated with quantitative estimates of cortical CSF volume, whereas clinical ratings of central volume loss were highly correlated with estimated ventricular CSF volume. Volume estimates of the caudate nucleus, diencephalon, and abnormal white matter were also, although to a lesser degree, correlated with central volume loss. Clinical ratings of parenchymal abnormalities were found to be significantly correlated with quantitative estimates of both abnormal white matter and subcortical hyperintensities. Interestingly, multiple linear regression analyses revealed that these two quantitative white matter measures made independent significant contributions to the predicted (qualitative) parenchymal abnormality measure.

The four subject groups (HIV+ symptomatic, HIV+ asymptomatic, HIV− high-risk controls, HIV− low-risk controls) were then compared on volumes of ventricular CSF, cortical sulcal CSF, and cerebral white matter using one-way analyses of variance, followed, when significant group differences were detected, by post hoc t-tests. Then additional comparions were made for the volumes of subcortical structures, temporal lobe limbic structures, and cerebral cortex.

Significant group differences were observed on both CSF measures and the white matter z-scores. The CSF group differences were primarily due to significant increases in both cortical sulcal and ventricular CSF in the asymptomatic HIV+ group relative to all other groups. Unexpectedly, post hoc comparisons also revealed a significant increase in cortical sulcal CSF in the HIV− high-risk controls relative to both the asymptomatic HIV+ group and the low-risk controls. No CSF increases were observed in asymptomatic HIV+ patients relative to controls. Thus, there was definite evidence of brain volume loss in the medically symptomatic patients relative to all other groups, but there was also unexpected evidence of a modest degree of volume loss in the HIV− high-risk controls as well, as reflected in increased subarachnoid CSF.

Post hoc group comparisons of the white matter volumes suggest that a substantial amount of the volume loss observed in the symptomatic seropositive subjects was due to white matter loss. This group had significant white matter volume reduction relative to all other groups. No other two-group comparisons reached significance.

The comparisons of the gray matter volume z-scores yielded a significant group difference only on the temporal limbic measure. Although they did not meet our criterion for significance ($p < 0.01$), there were also trends for differences in caudate ($p < .05$), anterior diencephalon ($p < 0.10$), and overall cerebral cortex ($p < .10$). The observed pattern of group differences was similar for the temporal limbic, caudate, and cerebral cortex measures. Reductions were observed in HIV+ symptomatic subjects *and* HIV− high-risk controls relative to *both* low-risk controls and asymptomatic HIV+ subjects. These results are presented in more detail in Jernigan et al. (1993).

The results of this study confirmed and extended earlier reports of brain volume loss in HIV+ subjects. We observed definite evidence of volume loss only in the medically symptomatic subjects. The degree of atrophy was impressive, given that *none* of these subjects demonstrated clinical evidence of HIV-associated dementia. The results of secondary analyses suggested that this HIV-related volume loss was at least partly attributable to loss of white matter volume. It seems possible that previously described neuropathological changes in frank HIV encephalopathy, that is, neuronal loss, loss of dendritic spines, axonal and dendritic vacuolation, loss of synaptosomes (Wiley et al., 1991), may be occurring to a lesser degree in these patients, even though they are neurologically asymptomatic. Longitudinal observations using MRI, and follow-up autopsy studies, will be necessary to determine if the volume losses we have observed in these neurologically asymptomatic persons progress and become associated with frank neurological signs.

The comparisons of HIV+ symptomatic subjects with HIV+ asymptomatic subjects and low-risk controls suggest that, among the gray matter structures examined, limbic cortical structures of the temporal lobe and caudate nuclei might also be particularly affected by the virus. However, the presence of similar abnormalities in the seronegative high-risk controls complicates the interpretation of the gray matter losses in the symptomatic subjects.

One critical methodological question is which of the groups is the most appropriate control for determining the nature and extent of HIV-related pathology. Although gray matter reductions were present in HIV− high-risk controls, they are unlikely to be related to risk behaviors per se, since they were not present in the asymptomatic HIV+ group drawn from the same population. The fact that the white matter volume reductions were specific to the HIV+ symptomatic group suggests that the process by which gray matter losses occurred in this group is probably different than that in the high-risk controls.

Others have also reported abnormal findings in HIV− controls (McArthur et al., 1989; Sönnerborg et al., 1990; Dooneief et al., 1992). While we attempted to exclude subjects (both HIV− high-risk and HIV+) who might have had sources of subclinical neurological insults unrelated to HIV, it is possible that we were not fully successful in this regard. For example, some of the volume changes (e.g., more CSF) might reflect acute effects of heavier alcohol consumption that was not so intense as to qualify for alcohol dependence (a definite exclusion). It is also possible that differences in use of substances that were not specific exclusions (e.g., inhalational nitrites) could contribute to subtle MRI abnormalities in high-risk controls. The fact that HIV+ subjects in the asymptomatic phase had fewer abnormalities than did the high-risk controls suggests that significant self-selection factors operating in these groups may be playing a role.

Unfortunately, attempts to identify any such factors have so far been unsuccessful.

Whatever the source of MRI abnormality in high-risk controls, we would expect it to be static in nature or even likely to improve (if related to acute alcohol or other drug effects). In contrast, if data from the neurologically intact but medically symptomatic subjects are reliable, the possibility exists that such changes will gradually progress in the symptomatic group and might also begin to appear in the later stages of the asymptomatic period. The longitudinal investigation in which we are engaged should help sort out some of these possibilities and, hopefully, yield more definitive information about the nature and location of early HIV-related processes within the CNS.

In short, our MRI morphometric analyses revealed that HIV+ persons who are medically symptomatic or immunosuppressed, but who are free of clinical neurological signs, nevertheless manifest a significant increase in cortical sulcal and ventricular CSF, as well as volume loss in white matter and cerebral gray matter structures. Such changes were not observed in HIV+ asymptomatic persons. It remains to be determined whether such MRI changes progress in those CDC IV subjects who develop frank neurological complications, and whether similar subtle changes will be revealed in the later stages of CDC II/III illness.

Summary and Future Directions

HIV infection has been associated with a variety of neurological complications, including a constellation of cognitive, motor, and behavioral deficits termed the *AIDS dementia complex*. Although the CNS of AIDS patients is susceptible to a wide variety of opportunistic infections and neoplasms, the AIDS dementia complex has been particularly associated with a subacute encephalitis that affects primarily the deep white matter and basal ganglia and that may be caused by primary HIV infection of the brain. However, the extent of clinical symptoms and pathology is often greater than expected by the amount of virus detected, suggesting the possible influence of indirect mechanisms (e.g., cytotoxicity of retroviral proteins, disruption of the BBB, immune system–mediated damage), as well as in vivo interactions between HIV and other viral infections such as CMV in their pathogenesis.

MRI is assuming an increasingly important role is the diagnostic workup of HIV-infected patients. T_2-weighted images are most sensitive in detecting the brain abnormalities associated with HIV. Compared to CT, MRI is better especially for assessing white matter diseases and other abnormalities with an intact BBB. Contrast enhancement is helpful for differentiating lesions from surrounding edema, discriminating between lesions in close proximity, judging lesion activity, and defining small cortical lesions with minimal edema.

The major problems in interpreting MR images in AIDS patients have been the lack of specificity of the findings, the frequent coexistence of different pathologies, and the relatively infrequent pathological proof. Jarvik et al. (1988) describe four patterns of signal abnormality with corresponding pathology. The best correlation was between a pattern of multiple small, discrete foci of high signal intensity with toxoplasmosis and PML. Toxoplasmosis lesions tended to be heterogeneous with discrete margins, and PML lesions were homogeneous with indistinct margins. Also, PML involves the subcortical white matter and rarely enhances. An additional differentiating feature is the lack of mass effect with PML. Lymphoma can mimic toxoplasmosis in AIDS patients. Less common infections, such as aspergillosis and tuberculosis, are occasionally encountered. Other patterns described had more limited pathological proof. Large, bilateral, patchy to confluent lesions in white matter were seen with subacute encephalitis secondary to HIV. Solitary high T_2 signal lesions were due to nonviral opportunistic infections. The final pattern of generalized atrophy was associated with chronic HIV infections, as described above.

Olsen et al. (1988) found white matter abnormalities in 31% of the AIDS patients that they studied. Clinical findings and disease course were used to determine the exact etiology in most instances, as pathological material was available in a minority of cases. They reported patterns of signal abnormality and clinical correlations similar to those described above. Diffuse, widespread involvement correlated with AIDS dementia complex. Rarely, punctate or patchy lesions were noted with AIDS dementia complex. Focal white matter lesions were noted in all six patients with PML, in two patients with lymphoma, and in one patient with toxoplasmosis. Focal white matter lesions were not seen with AIDS dementia complex. The clinical presentation may also be a differentiating feature in that only 2 of 33 patients with AIDS dementia complex had focal neurological findings.

Because of the cross-sectional design of most studies, little is known about the evolution and development of MRI abnormalities in HIV-infected patients, or about the relationship between changes in these abnormalities and changes in the patients' clinical status. The white matter abnormalities detected by MRI are thought to reflect secondary demyelination and gliosis that develop slowly and progressively from small, unilateral lesions to (in some cases) large, bilateral, confluent areas. However, some very preliminary results from the HNRC involving the quantitative analysis of serial MR images taken at 6-month intervals suggest that at least some AIDS patients also demonstrate large longitudinal fluctuations in the extent of their white matter and other structural abnormalities. These fluctuations could reflect the dynamic interactions between coexistent viral infections and the multiple indirect mechanisms that may underlie HIV-mediated CNS damage.

These preliminary results suggest that models of change in MRI measures over time that assume monotonic, linear deterioration may not be appropriate and that different cross-sectional studies could yield very different results, depending on the time point at which the population was sampled. Given these implications, future studies should emphasize the longitudinal progression of MRI brain abnormalities in HIV-infected patients, with MRI studies obtained both at relatively short (e.g., 6-month) intervals and time-locked to specific changes in clinical status (e.g., a precipitous drop in T4 cell count, onset of a major opportunistic infection). The use of quantitative morphometric techniques may prove to be particularly useful for such longitudinal studies, since quantitative analyses would help to minimize variability in measurements over repeated studies and would help to detect subtle changes in white matter signal intensity that may not be considered clinically abnormal. Finally, in addition to volumetric measures, changes in the molecular properties of neural tissue in HIV-infected subjects should be assessed by deriving estimates of both spin-lattice (i.e., T_1) and spin-spin (i.e., T_2) relaxation times from various gray and white structures. That is, the brain changes associated with HIV encephalitis may prove to be reflected not only in actual volume changes within particular structures, but also in changes in the distribution of the MRI signal values within the brain.

Acknowledgments

This work was supported by the HNRC and by the Medical Research Service of the Department of Veterans Affairs. The principal support for the HNRC is provided by NIMH Center Grant 5 P50 MH45294 (HIV Neurobehavioral Research Center). The views expressed in this chapter are those of the authors and do not reflect the official policy or position of the Department of the Navy, the Department of Defense, or the U.S. government. In the public domain.

References

Anders, K.H., Guerra, W.F., Tomiyasu, U., Verity, M.A., and Vinters, H.V. (1986). The neuropathology of AIDS: UCLA experience and review. *American Journal of Pathology, 124*, 537–558.

Belman, A.L., Ultmann, M.H., Horoupian, D., Novick, B., Sprio, A.J., Rubinstein, A., Kurtzberg D., and Cone-Wesson, B. (1985). Neurological complications in infants and children with acquired immune deficiency syndrome. *Annals of Neurology, 18*, 560–566.

Center for Disease Control. (1987). Revision of the CDC surveillance case definition for acquired immunodeficiency syndrome. *Morbidity and Mortality Weekly Report, 36*(Suppl. 1S), 3S–15S.

Chrysikopoulos, H.S., Press, G.A., Grafe, M.R., Hesselink, J.R., and Wiley, C.A. (1990). Encephalitis caused by human immunodeficiency virus: CT and MR imaging manifestations with clinical and pathologic correlation. *Radiology, 175*, 185–191.

Dooneief, G., Bello, J., Todak, G., Mun, I.K., Marder, K., Malouf, R., Gorman, J., Hilal, S., Stern, Y., and Mayeux, R. (1992). A prospective controlled study of magnetic resonance imaging of the brain in gay men and parenteral drug users with human immunodeficiency virus infection. *Archives of Neurology, 49*, 38–43.

Gabuzda, D.H., and Hirsch, M.S. (1987). Neurologic manifestations of infection with human immunodeficiency virus. Clinical features and pathogenesis. *Annals of Internal Medicine, 107*, 383–391.

Grafe, M.R., Press, G.A., Berthoty, D.P., Hesselink, J.R., and Wiley, C.A. (1990). Abnormalities of the brain in AIDS patients: Correlation of postmortem MR findings with neuropathology. *American Journal of Neuroradiology, 11*(5), 905–911.

Grant, I., Atkinson, J.H., Hesselink, J.R., Kennedy, C.J., Richman, D.D., Spector, S.A., and McCutchan, J.A. (1987). Evidence for early central nervous system involvement in the acquired immunodeficiency syndrome (AIDS) and other human immunodeficiency virus (HIV) infections. Studies with neuropsychologic testing and magnetic resonance imaging. *Annals of Internal Medicine, 107*, 828–836.

Holland, J.C., and Tross, S. (1985). The psychosocial and neuropsychiatric sequelae of the acquired immunodeficiency syndrome and related disorders. *Annals of Internal Medicine, 103*, 760–764.

Jarvik, J.G., Hesselink, J.R., Kennedy, C., Teschke, R., Wiley, C., Spector, S., Richman, D., and McCutchan, A. (1988). Acquired immunodeficiency syndrome. Magnetic resonance patterns of brain involvement with pathological correlation. *Archives of Neurology, 45*, 731–736.

Jernigan, T.L., Archibald, S.L., Berhow, M.T., Sowell, E.R., Foster, D.S., and Hesselink, J.R. (1991a). Cerebral structure on MRI, Part I: Localization of age-related changes. *Biological Psychiatry, 29*(1), 55–67.

Jernigan, T.L., Archibald, S., Hesselink, J.R., Atkinson, J.H., Velin, R.A., McCutchan, J.A., Chandler, J., and Grant, I. (1993). MRI morphometric analysis of cerebral volume loss in HIV infection. *Archives of Neurology, 50*:250–255.

Jernigan, T.L., Press, G.A., and Hesselink, J.R. (1990). Methods for measuring brain morphologic features on magnetic resonance images: Validation and normal aging. *Archives of Neurology, 47*, 27–32.

Jernigan, T.L., Salmon, D.P., Butters, N., and Hesselink, J.R. (1991b). Cerebral structure on MRI, Part II: Specific changes in Alzheimer's and Huntington's diseases. *Biological Psychiatry, 29*(1), 68–81.

Kelly, W.M., and Brant-Zawadzki, M. (1983). Acquired immunodeficiency syndrome: Neuroradiologic findings. *Radiology, 149*, 485–491.

Levy, R.M., Bredesen, D.E., and Rosenblum, M.L. (1985). Neurological manifestations of the acquired immunodeficiency syndrome (AIDS): Experience at UCSF and review of the literature. *Journal of Neurosurgery, 62*, 475–495.

Levy, R.M., Rosenbloom, S., and Perrett, L.V. (1986). Neuroradiologic findings in AIDS: A review of 200 cases. *American Journal of Roentgenology, 147*(5), 977–983.

Mark, A.S., and Atlas, S.W. (1989). Progressive multifocal leukoencephalopathy in patients with AIDS: Appearance on MR images. *Radiology, 173*, 517–520.

Marshall, V.G., Bradley, W.G., Marshall, C.E., Bhoopat, T., and Rhodes, R.H. (1988). Deep white matter infarction: Correlation of MR imaging and histopathologic findings. *Radiology, 167*, 517–522.

McArthur, J.C., Cohen, B.A., Selnes, O.A., Kumar, A.J., Cooper, K., McArthur, J.H., Soucy, G., Cornblath, D.R., Chmiel, J.S., Wang, M.-C., Starkey, D.L., Ginzburg, H., Ostrow, D.G., Johnson, R.T., Phair, J.P., and Polk, B.F. (1989). Low prevalence of neurological and neuropsychological abnormalities in otherwise healthy HIV-1 infected individuals. Results from the multicenter AIDS cohort study. *Annals of Neurology, 26*, 601–611.

Navia, B.A., Cho, E.-S., Petito, C.K., and Price, R.W. (1986b). The AIDS dementia complex: II. Neuropathology. *Annals of Neurology, 19*, 525–535.

Navia, B.A., Jordan, B.D., and Price, R.W. (1986a). The AIDS dementia complex: I. Clinical features. *Annals of Neurology, 19*, 517–524.

Olsen, W.L., Longo, F.M., Mills, C.M., and Norman, D. (1988). White matter disease in AIDS: Findings at MR imaging. *Radiology, 169*, 445–448.

Post, M.J.D., Berger, J.R., and Quencer, R.M. (1991). Asymptomatic and neurologically symptomatic HIV seropositive individuals: Prospective evaluation with cranial MR imaging. *Radiology, 178*, 131–139.

Post, M.J.D., Kursunolglu, S.J., Hensley, G.T., Chan, J.C., Moskowitz, L.B., and Hoffman, T.A. (1985). Cranial CT in acquired immunodeficiency syndrome: Spectrum of diseases and optimal contrast enhancement technique. *American Journal of Roentgenology, 145*(5), 929–940.

Post, M.J.D., Sheldon, J.J., Hensley, G.T., Soila, K., Tobias, J.A., Chan, J.C., Quencer, R.M., and Moskowitz, L.B. (1986). Central nervous system disease in acquired immunodeficiency syndrome: Prospective correlation using CT, MR imaging and pathologic studies. *Radiology, 158*(1), 141–148.

Post, M.J.D., Tate, L.G., Quencer, R.M., Hensley, G.T., Berger, J.R., Sheremata, W.A., and Maul, G. (1988). CT, MR, and pathology in HIV encephalitis and meningitis. *American Journal of Roentgenology, 151*, 373–380.

Schwaighofer, B.W., Hesselink, J.R., Press, G.A., Wolf, R.L., Healy, M.E., and Berthoty, D.P. (1989). Primary intracranial CNS lymphoma: MR manifestations. *American Journal of Neuroradiology, 10*, 725–729.

Shaw, G.M., Harper, M.E., Hahn, B.H., Epstein, L.G., Gajdusek, D.C., Price, R.W., Navia, B.A., Petito, C.K., O'Hara, C.J., Groopman, J.E., Cho, E.-S., Oleske, J.M., Wong-Staal, F., and Gallo, R.C. (1985). HTLV-III infection in brains of children and adults with AIDS encephalopathy. *Science, 227*, 177–182.

Sönnerborg, A., Sääf, J., Alexius, B., Strannegård, Ö., Wahlund, L.O., and Wetterberg, L. (1990). Quantitative detection of brain aberrations in human immunodeficiency virus type 1–infected individuals by magnetic resonance imaging. *Journal of Infectious Diseases, 162*, 1245–1251.

Whelan, M.A., Kricheff, I.I., Handler, M., Ho, V., Crystal, K., Gopinathan, G., and Laubenstein, L. (1983). Acquired immunodeficiency syndrome: Cerebral computed tomographic manifestations. *Radiology, 149*, 477–484.

Wiley, C.A., Masliah, E., Morey, M., Lemere, C., DeTeresa, R., Grafe, M., Hansen, L., and Terry, R. (1991). Neocortical damage during HIV infection. *Annals of Neurology, 29*, 651–657.

Wiley, C.A., and Nelson, J.A. (1988). Role of human immunodeficiency virus and cytomegalovirus in AIDS encephalitis. *American Journal of Pathology, 133*, 73–81.

Wiley, C.A., Schrier, R.D., Nelson, J.A., Lampert, P.W., and Oldstone, M.B.A. (1986). Cellular localization of human immunodeficiency virus infection within the brains of acquired immune deficiency syndrome patients. *Proceedings of the National Academy of Sciences of the United States of America, 83*, 7089–7093.

II

NEUROPSYCHOLOGICAL ASPECTS OF HIV: ISSUES, APPROACHES, AND FINDINGS

5

The Dementias and AIDS

JAMES T. BECKER, ALEX MARTIN, and OSCAR L. LOPEZ

> When his memory is impaired, his feelings quenched, his intelligence enfeebled or extinct, he is said to be suffering from dementia.
>
> H. MAUDSLEY (1895)

Although dementia has a long history, only during the past 20 years have there been attempts to develop highly specific diagnostic criteria for the different dementia syndromes. In particular, a great deal of attention has been paid to the dementia often seen in patients with the acquired immunodeficiency syndrome (AIDS). In this chapter we will present a brief historical overview of the concept of dementia. We will then argue that current systems for classifying the dementias suffer from having combined two independent problems: determining whether a dementia syndrome exists and determining the condition responsible for that particular syndrome. We will suggest that many of the problems of diagnosis and classification of the dementias in general, and of human immunodeficiency virus (HIV)- and AIDS-related dementia in particular, might be avoided if these two questions were dealt with separately.

Historical Considerations

In the Beginning

The concept of dementia has appeared in medical writings for centuries, and was noted by Lucretius as 'being out of one's mind' (McMenemy, 1970, cited by Berrios and Freeman, 1991). However, the conceptualization of this disorder, including its symptoms and presumed etiology (e.g., toxins, infections, age), has evolved during the past 200 years as a function of progress in medical knowledge and the prevailing social context. The notion of dementia as primarily a cognitive disorder, and the prominent role that has been assigned to memory impairment in comparison to other types of cognitive deficits, arose within a specific historical context. The interaction between medical knowledge and social context is, in our view, important in understanding the current concept of dementia and may be critical in developing a rational approach to dementia classification and diagnosis.

The *Oxford English Dictionary* notes that the term *dement* is from the Latin *dementare,* meaning "to deprive of mind, drive mad," in contrast to the term *encephalopathy,* which refers simply to "a disease of the brain." In the French Encyclopedia of 1778, dementia was described as being "difficult to cure as it is probably related to damage of brain fibers or of nervous fluids" (Berrios and Freeman, 1991). At that time, dementia was distinguished from acute confusional states and was regarded as a chronic condition, although irreversibility was not considered a core feature of the syndrome. The term *dementia* first appeared in English in Davis' translation of Pinel's *A Treatise on Insanity* (Pinel, 1806), where it was defined as "a species of insanity characterized by failure or loss of mental power" (p. 252). Copland's *Dictionary of Medicine* (1858) noted that "Maniacs and monomaniacs are carried away ... by illusions and hallucinations ... [in contrast] ... the demented person neither imagines or supposes anything." Pinel viewed the syndrome as progressive: "To cause periodical and curable mania to degenerate into dementia or idiotism" (Pinel, 1806). Pinel bridged the 18th and 19th centuries and it was due to his work that "the term and concept became well established to include all states of psychosocial incompetence due to impairment of intellectual function. These could be reversible or irreversible, congenital or acquired, and caused by brain disorder or by insanity" (Berrios and Freeman, 1991, p. 12f).

By the time that Alzheimer began reporting his cases, dementia of the elderly had been described as including psychotic and other noncognitive symptoms. After World War I, however, this definition changed, and cognitive or neuropsychological deficits became the central feature of the dementia syndromes. Although there were probably many reasons for this shift in emphasis, an important factor was the notion that subjective experiences such as hallucinations and delusions, which could be well described by psychotic patients, were difficult to elicit or verify in demented patients (Berrios and Freeman, 1991). As a result, psychiatric symptoms became a neglected component of diagnostic schemes and programs of research. Having focused attention primarily on cognition, psychologists and physicians of the late nineteenth century were then faced with the problem of how to measure what was admittedly still an ill-defined concept. Because memory was then the focus of much research and because it was the only cognitive function that clinicians felt they could adequately measure, "deficits in memory became, de facto, if not de jure, the central feature of the state of dementia" (Berrios and Freeman, 1991, p. 27).

Dementia Since 1975

In the second edition of their textbook of neurology, Adams and Victor (1981) noted that "the term dementia usually denotes a clinical syndrome composed of failing memory and loss of other intellectual functions due to a chronic progressive degenerative disease of the brain" (p. 311). However, they emphasized that "there are several states of dementia of multiple causation and mechanism and that a diffuse degeneration of neurons (usually chronic) is only one of the many causes" (p. 311). As a result, Adams and Victor suggested that it was more correct to speak of "the dementias or of the dementing diseases." Similarly, DSM-III (APA, 1987) described the dementias as a "wide variety of diseases which more often than not involve many areas of the nervous system" (p. 1).

Although he took no specific position with regard to whether dementia per se is progressive, Karp (1978) did describe Alzheimer's disease as one of the "progressive dementias." But he also observed a dementia syndrome associated with metabolic and toxic encephalopathies, thus suggesting that progression was not a requirement for diagnosis. However, Karp stressed that the onset of the dementia must occur at a sufficiently slow rate so as not to be confused with an acute event or a delirium. In his first volume on the dementing disorders, Wells (1977) presented the psychiatric viewpoint of the mid-1970s. He emphasized that the term *dementia* was useful for describing "those clinical states resulting from diffuse or disseminated disease of the cerebral hemispheres" (p. 1) and that dementia must be distinguished from diseases resulting in focused neurobehavioral abnormalities (e.g., aphasia, apraxia). The term *dementia* could refer to a change in or deterioration of mental status, but "clearly, irreversibility will not be considered the *sine qua non* for the diagnosis of dementia" (p. 2). Nor was progression considered critical since the neurobehavioral consequences of carbon monoxide poisoning were called a dementia syndrome. Wells also stressed the importance of noncognitive factors. For example, consider his description of the patient early in the course of a dementing illness:

> In the incipient phases of cerebral degeneration the individual experiences diminished energy and enthusiasm. He has less interest and concern for vocational, family, and social activities. Lability of affect is common often with considerable increase in overall anxiety level, particularly as the individual becomes aware of his failing powers. He has less interest in goals and achievements, diminished creativity, less incentive to stick to a task, trouble concentrating, and difficulty screening out disturbing environmental stimuli. Failures, frustrations, changes, postponements, and troublesome decisions produce more annoyance and internal upheaval than usual, and it is harder to recover equilibrium after such disturbances. The individual's characteristic defense mechanisms are utilized more frequently and more blatantly, often with less than normal effectiveness. (p. 5)

In addition to these behavioral changes, Wells (1977) emphasized that dementia could be associated with a broad range of impairment, "from a barely discernible deviation from normal to virtual cerebral death" (p. 11). Here we see the importance of keeping separate the notions of cognitive deficit, dementia, and presumed etiology. For example, at some point in time, every individual with Alzheimer's disease must have had very mild cognitive deficits, or perhaps only a single deficit, as a direct consequence of the neuropathological changes associated with Alzheimer's disease. Thus, with the benefit of hindsight, we could claim that, at that particular point in time, the patient had Alzheimer's disease. However, we would be equally correct to insist that, at that same point in time, the patient was not demented. In the current social and health care policy climate, the notion of classifying a patient as having dementia (in Wells' sense of having mild cognitive impairment that would invariably progress) would present many difficulties, even if we knew for certain that the patient's condition would eventually progress to a frank dementia. In particular, in the context of HIV infection and AIDS, where the patients are often young and gainfully employed, there are potentially profound health and social policy consequences. However, it is important to note that context is critical. If there was a treatment available for HIV-related cognitive dysfunction, as there is for depression or other neuropsychiatric disorders, then the failure to diagnosis these patients properly would certainly be unethical. The fact that currently there are no known treatments, coupled with the fear of adding another stigma to an already stigmatized individual, may serve to bias us against classifying HIV-infected individuals as cognitively impaired.

DSM-III and Afterward

> The essential feature is a loss of intellectual abilities of sufficient severity to interfere with social or occupational functioning. (APA, 1980, p. 107)

> Dementia is a deterioration or loss of intellectual ability characterized by impairment of memory and of other cognitive functions to a level below a person's previous mental capacity. (Karp and Mirra, 1990, p. 1)

> When the Dementia is the result of some clearly defined episode of neurological disease, . . . it may begin quite suddenly, but then remain stationary for a long period of time. Primary Degenerative Dementia . . . is usually insidious in onset and slowly, but relentlessly, progresses to death over a period of several years. (APA, 1980, p. 110)

According to DSM-III (APA, 1980), the dementias may be treatable and reversible, although it was recognized that full recovery may not be possible with widespread damage to the brain. Differential diagnoses included delirium, schizophrenia, and major depressive disorder. The criteria for diagnosis specified that a memory impairment must exist, as well as impairment in at least one additional area of cognitive function. By the time the DSM-III was revised (APA, 1987), the extent of intellectual impairment necessary for a diagnosis of dementia remained the same (p. 105), but the assumptions about clinical course were now specified:

> In the past, Dementia often implied a progressive or irreversible course. The definition of Dementia in this manual . . . carries no connotation concerning prognosis. Dementia may be progressive, static, or remitting. The reversibility of a Dementia is a function of the underlying pathology and of the availability and timely application of effective treatment (p. 104).

From the neurologist's perspective, the thinking on dementia was changing as well. In the revision of their textbook, Adams and Victor (1985), while not modifying their concept of dementia, did suggest that the dementing disorders could be classified into three groups: (1) those with associated signs of medical disease (e.g., hypothyroidism, nutritional deficiency), (2) those associated with neurological signs but not obvious medical disease (e.g., Huntington's disease, progressive supranuclear palsy), and (3) those in which the dementia is the only evidence of neurological or medical disease (e.g., Alzheimer's disease). In 1984, the report of a National Institute of Neurological, Communicative Disease and Stroke/Alzheimer's Disease and Related Disorders Association (NINCDS-ADRDA)-sponsored work group was published to establish clinical criteria for the diagnosis of Alzheimer's disease (McKhann et al., 1984). The work group noted that their criteria should be regarded as tentative and subject to change due to uncertainty about the disease at that time.

> Dementia is the decline of memory and other cognitive functions in comparison with the patient's previous level of function as determined by a history of decline in performance and by abnormalities noted from clinical examinations and neuropsychological tests. (p. 939)

Because the NINCDS-ADRDA work group was concerned with Alzheimer's disease specifically, "a progressive worsening of memory and other cognitive function" was assumed. They also developed criteria that were appropriate for both research and clinical applications and that allowed for a grading of the confidence in the diagnosis. These very useful and powerful ideas were adapted for use with HIV-related conditions by a group established by the American Academy of Neurology (AAN).

DSM-IV: A Look Forward

The APA has recently approved a revision of the Diagnostic and Statistical Manual (DSM-IV), which contains revisions of the section on dementia and other "organic" mental disorders that are relevant to this discussion. First, there is now a classification of dementia "due to other conditions," which includes HIV-related dementia as a category. The criteria for this diagnosis are shown in Table 5–1. Of particular relevance is the continued adherence to the concept that memory *must* be impaired before a diagnosis of dementia can be made. It remains to be seen, of course, to what extent this has an effect on patterns of diagnosis and classification, but it is important to note that memory loss, at least verbal memory loss, is not the primary presenting symptom of HIV-related dementia, as it is in many other dementing disorders.

However, that having been said, it is also important to note that the DSM-IV criteria are more specific with regard to delirium, the presence of which is a specific exclusion for the diagnosis of *any* dementia syndrome. Delirium can be caused by a medical condition and includes disturbed consciousness, changing cognitive function, onset in hours to days, and fluctuating course during the day.

TABLE 5–1. Diagnostic Criteria for Dementia

A. The development of multiple cognitive deficits manifested by both:

   (1) memory impairment (inability to learn new information and to recall previously learned information)

   (2) at least one of the following cognitive disturbances:

      (a) aphasia (language disturbance)

      (b) apraxia (inability to carry out motor activities despite intact motor function)

      (c) agnosia (failure to recognize or identify objects despite intact sensory function)

      (d) disturbance in executive functioning (i.e., planning, organizing, sequencing, abstracting)

B. The cognitive deficits cause a significant impairment in social or occupational functioning and represent a significant decline from a previous level of functioning.

C. The deficits do not occur exclusively during the course of Delirium.

D. There is evidence from the history, physical examination, or laboratory findings of one of the following conditions judged to be etiologically related to the disturbance.

   F02.4   Dementia Due to HIV Disease

   F02.8   Dementia Due to Head Trauma

   F02.3   Dementia Due to Parkinson's Disease

   F02.2   Dementia Due to Huntington's Disease

   F02.0   Dementia Due to Pick's Disease

   F02.1   Dementia Due to Jakob-Creutzfeldt Disease

   F02.8   Dementia Due to Other Cognition (e.g., normal pressure hydrocephalus, hypothyroidism, brain tumor, vitamin B_{12} deficiency)

Source: DSM-IV (APA, in press).

This additional exclusion criterion may be important in the context of HIV-related dementia in that it might decrease the extent to which a dementia diagnosis is applied, in our opinion often inappropriately, in the terminal phase of HIV-related illness(es) (Table 5–2).

Finally, the addendum to the DSM-IV contains a discussion of the concept of the *mild neurocognitive disorder* that the authors (Gutierrez et al., 1993) believe should be added to the nosology of cognitive disorders (Table 5–3). This diagnosis includes disturbances of cognition related to a physical disorder but not sufficiently severe to be diagnosed as a delirium, dementia, or other "cognitive impairment disorder." This concept, that of an unequivocal impairment in cognitive function that does not meet the criteria for dementia, may be very important in the context of the natural history of central nervous system (CNS) disorders in HIV infection and AIDS. While delirium and dementia are well recognized in medically ill individuals, including those with AIDS, they represent only the extremes of a continuum. According to the DSM-IV model, the milder cognitive dysfunction would not have had an applicable DSM-III diagnosis, but nevertheless it is of sufficient severity to have significant implications for activities of daily living (Heaton and Pendelton, 1981; Gutierrez et al., 1993). To the extent that these disorders of cognition (e.g., delirium and dementia) become more apparent to treating clinicians, the use of a specific diagnosis will increase the reliability of classification.

In the context of HIV infection and AIDS, the relationship between these

TABLE 5–2. Criteria for Diagnosis: Delirium Due to a General Medical Condition

A. Disturbance of consciousness (i.e., reduced clarity of awareness of the environment) with reduced ability to focus, sustain, or shift attention.

B. Change in cognition (such as memory deficit, disorientation, language disturbance, perceptual disturbance) that is not better accounted for by preexisting, established, or evolving dementia.

C. The disturbance develops over a short period of time (usually hours to days) and tends to fluctuate during the course of the day.

D. There is evidence from the history, physical examination, or laboratory findings of a general medical condition judged to be etiologically related to the disturbance.

Source: DSM-IV (APA, in press).

milder disorders, and frank delirium and dementia, will need to be carefully evaluated. In particular, treatment that may alter the risk of dementia (i.e., decreasing) may also alter the risk of developing the mild neurocognitive disorder (i.e., increasing). These two diagnoses also may have different prognostic significance for an individual patient, and the relationships between these disorders (i.e., one as the milder form of the other) is not yet clear.

Nosology of HIV-Related Dementia

Once it was recognized that significant cognitive dysfunction could occur in association with HIV infection and AIDS, an attempt was made to specifically codify criteria for the diagnosis and staging of an HIV-related dementia syndrome (AAN, 1989, 1991). The dementia syndrome associated with AIDS was originally described in detail by Navia and colleagues (1986) and was later presented in a more systematic way by Price and Brew (1988). In the later report, a staging system was suggested to determine the severity of the syndrome. Notable among the symptoms described was the presence of motor system dysfunction as well as an emphasis on cognitive, but not specifically memory, dysfunction.

More recently, however, the AAN Task Force on AIDS has worked to develop nomenclature on HIV-associated neurological diseases in general and the dementia syndrome in particular. This was the result of consultation among behavioral neurologists and neuropsychologists, and attempts to provide consensus nomenclature and case definitions for research purposes (p. 778). The criteria proposed by the AAN Task Force for HIV-1-associated cognitive/motor complex are presented in Chapter 3. Note that these criteria are not identical to those of AIDS dementia complex (Price and Brew, 1988) but are consistent with them. The AAN criteria make no assumptons about whether the cognitive manifestations of HIV infection and AIDS are due to a single factor, or whether the spectrum of severity, from mild to severe, even represents the same underlying etiology. Noted also that although impaired memory is not required, a subject must have either a motor deficit, or a decline in motivation or emotional control, or a change in social behavior in order to be classified as demented.

TABLE 5–3. Criteria for Diagnosis of a Mild Neurocognitive Disorder

---

A. The presence of two of the following impairments in cognitive functioning, lasting most of the time for a period of at least two weeks (as reported by the individual or a reliable informant);

   (1) memory impairment as identified by a reduced ability to learn or recall information.

   (2) disturbance in executive functioning (i.e., planning, organizing, sequencing, abstracting)

   (3) diminished concentration

   (4) impairment in perceptual motor abilities

   (5) impairment in language (e.g., comprehension, word finding)

B. Objective evidence of a systemic illness or central nervous system dysfunction from physical examination or laboratory findings (including neuroimaging techniques) that is judged to be etiologically related to the cognitive disturbance.

C. Evidence of an abnormality or decline in performance from neuropsychological testing or quantified cognitive assessment.

D. The cognitive deficits cause a mild impairment in social or occupational functioning and represent a decline from a previous level of functioning.

E. The cognitive disturbance does not meet criteria for any specific Cognitive Impairment Disorder and is not better accounted for by another mental disorder.

Source: Gutierrez et al. (1993).

Proposed Guidelines

In contrast to the detailed HIV-specific diagnostic and classification system proposed by the AAN, we suggest that general rules can be formulated to serve as guidelines for the diagnosis of *all* dementia syndromes, including that associated with HIV infection and AIDS. In our view, the concept of dementia is well delineated and thus is amenable to an internally consistent and easily understood diagnostic system. Central to our proposal is the notion that the diagnostician must address two distinct and independent questions. First, is the patient demented? Second, with what disease, disorder, or condition is the dementia associated? We will address each of these questions in turn.

Definition of Dementia

In our view, dementia should be defined in its broadest sense, that is, as a decline in behavioral and/or cognitive, but not motor, functions. Cognition should be broadly defined to subsume all of the major domains, including attention, language, perception, spatial abilities, memory, abstract thinking, problem solving, judgment, and others. No assumptions need be made, or should be made, concerning the type or nature of the impairments or whether these impairments reflect a specific pattern of CNS dysfunction (e.g., cortical vs. subcortical dementia). The only restriction is that more than one domain must be compromised. Thus, this formulation allows for marked individual variation in the pattern of cognitive deficits and their progression over time (i.e., qualitatively distinct subgroups of patients as defined by their cognitive performance (Capitani et al., 1985;

Becker et al., 1988; Martin, 1990). The possibility of a single, domain-specific abnormality is also recognized, but it would not be classified as dementia unless or until either impairment developed within an additional cognitive domain or there was evidence of significant behavioral disturbances (e.g., delusions, aggression). Thus, at the heart of the issue, this position is more closely aligned with the neurological conceptions of dementia than with the continuing insistence on a core memory defect, as espoused in the DSM.

Further, consistent with the older views on the dementias, and in keeping with the increasing interest in psychiatric symptoms (Lopez et al., 1990, 1991), we believe that behavioral manifestations such as hallucinations, delusions, aggression, and personality change should be considered part of the diagnostic picture of a dementia. These subjective symptoms, in fact, can be reliably elicited from demented patients even though the qualitative features of the symptoms may not be as well described as they are by patients with non-dementia-related psychotic disorders. In addition, the observed impairments must be severe enough to interfere with activities of daily living, including work, social activities, and/or personal relationships (Berg et al., 1988). Therefore, the relatively subtle cognitive impairments that may be found during the earlier stages of any dementia syndrome, including that of HIV infection, are not considered dementia but may be usefully described as a mild neurocognitive impairment. Further, the possibility remains that these early changes may be predictive of the eventual development of dementia, although evidence in support of this possibility is lacking at this time. Further, regardless of the impact of the decline in real-world functioning, it is assumed that neuropsychological test impairment is operationally defined as performance below the fifth percentile of the age-, education-, and culture-appropriate normative sample.

Finally, although motor dysfunction may be a common and perhaps even a universal impairment in cases of HIV-related dementia, motor deficits themselves play no role in the definition or diagnosis of dementia. Thus, the critical impairments must be either cognitive or psychiatric. We recognize that it may often be difficult to disentangle the effects of motor dysfunction from those of cognitive impairment on activities of daily living. We also recognize that motor deficits can have substantial impact on cognitive test performance. Yet, these problems are neither insurmountable nor unique to HIV-related conditions. Indeed, the impact of motor impairment on cognitive test performance in patients with Parkinson's disease has been a long-standing concern, and specific recommendations for avoiding the confounding effects of motor deficits have been offered (Sagar, 1991).

The general guidelines for the diagnosis of dementia that we are proposing are offered in Table 5–4. We believe that they can be applied to any dementia syndrome in adults, and with only minor modification could be applied to children as well. These guidelines are derived from our understanding of the development of the concept of dementia, as well as its current usage. They are independent of the underlying cause or putative causes of the condition (e.g., toxins, viruses, neuronal degeneration) and are directed solely at the syndrome of behavioral and/or cognitive change.

TABLE 5–4. Criteria for the Clinical Diagnosis of Dementia

---

1. Evidence of decline in intellectual function. This may include:

   a. Evidence from mental status examination, confirmed by neuropsychological evaluation, of a decline in cognitive function from previous level of functioning.

   b. Change in personality and/or behavior, including the development of violent or aggressive behavior, hallucinations, delusions, or other signs of neuropsychiatric disturbance.

   There must be either changes in two or more cognitive functions (i.e., 1a) or, if only one cognitive domain is affected, then evidence of behavior change (i.e., 1b) must be present.

2. Evidence from clinical history, confirmed by collaborative information, of marked change in activities of daily living including, for example, impaired work or social functioning, withdrawal from activities, or obvious impairment in functional capacity.

3. Clinical features that are consistent with a dementia syndrome include:

   a. Remission or stabilization of decline in functions

   b. The development of additional cognitive or behavioral manifestations of dementia, including depression, insomnia, incontinence, delusions, illusions, hallucinations, catastrophic outbursts (verbal, emotional, or physical), sexual disorders, and weight change.

Definition of the Associated Disease

The second question that must be addressed—the nature of the disease associated with the dementia—requires a second set of guidelines or criteria. The AAN Task Force scheme for AIDS-related dementia adopted the view that the specificity of the diagnosis can be stratified. This notion, initially developed in the NINCDS/ADRDA framework for the diagnosis of Alzheimer's disease, is quite useful. By classifying a disease (e.g., Parkinson's disease) or factor (e.g., carbon monoxide poisoning) as the probable or possible causative agent, it allows the clinician and researcher to group patients reliably according to presumed etiology. In the case where a specific neuropathological feature may be the defining characteristic of the disease, it may also be possible to include a category of definite (McKhann et al., 1984; Khachaturian, 1985).

In Table 5–5 we present the general scheme for the use of the terms *probable* and *possible* in the context of disease classification. The guidelines are drawn directly from the NINCDS/ADRDA criteria but lack some of the details that were included there since the focus was on a single disease state. In terms of HIV-related dementia, however, certain specific conditions do come to mind. It is, of course, necessary to exclude the possibility of CNS infections, both viral and bacterial, and malignancies. Further, age-related disorders cannot be excluded simply because of the presence of HIV infection. Thus, among individuals over the age of 45, the development of parkinsonian features or of a progressive cognitive impairment should be viewed as new clinical states until demonstrated to be otherwise. At the present time, there is not enough information about the presentation and progression of HIV-related dementia among older individuals to allow us to make strong statements about neuropsychiatric comorbidities.

TABLE 5–5.   Schema for Classifying Underlying Nature of Dementia

---

1. The criteria for the clinical classification of a PROBABLE underlying cause for the dementia syndrome include:

   a. Dementia syndrome established by clinical criteria (see Table 5–3)

   b. Absence of systemic or neuropsychiatric disorders, other than the one(s) under primary consideration, that could in themselves account for the dementia syndrome.

2. The classification of the underlying cause of the dementia as PROBABLE must be supported by factors specifically related to the disease in question. These include the results of specific laboratory tests such as electroencephalograms, cerebrospinal fluid analysis, static imaging studies (i.e., computed tomography scan and magnetic resonance imaging), and functional neuroimaging (i.e., single photon emission computed tomography, positron emission tomography scans, xenon-enhanced computed tomography scans).

3. Clinical classification of the POSSIBLE underlying etiology of the dementia can be made in the presence of the dementia syndrome,

   a. In the absence of other neuropsychiatric or systemic disorders sufficient to cause the dementia, but with variations in the presentation and/or course of the dementia in the context of the presumed disorder,

   b. May be made in the presence of a second disorder that is sufficient to cause the dementia but is not considered to be the sole cause of the dementia.

Concluding Comments

Dementia is a syndrome of acquired dysfunction that includes cognitive and behavioral manifestations. It can be progressive or static, or it may remit. It can have a variety of causes, but the underlying supposition is that the dementia is always the direct result of an alteration in CNS function, either permanent or temporary. The diagnosis and classification of any dementia syndrome must proceed in two steps; first, establish that sufficient intellectual change has occurred to warrant a diagnosis of dementia; second, establish, with various levels of confidence, the disease(s) or causal factor(s) associated with the development of the dementia. We view this two-step process to be general in that it may be applied to any dementia syndrome. Further, it should be stressed that we view these guidelines as nothing particularly new, but simply a codification of how we view the process as proceeding. Much can be gained by keeping guidelines simple, easy to apply, and yet theoretically and intellectually sound. Indeed, a review of the DSM-IV criteria for delirium, and for dementia and amnestic disorders, suggests that the APA has adopted a similar position, although with certain structural/organizational differences.

In closing, it is worthwhile to consider other comments by Berrios and Freeman (1991). With specific reference to Alzheimer's disease, they noted that "The fundamental problem is that in spite of the large amount of completed research, not enough is known on any one specific feature of the disease to develop a valid [clinical] marker" (p. 6). Surely this conclusion applies equally well to the dementia syndromes associated with Parkinson's disease (Sagar, 1991), AIDS dementia, and a variety of other conditions. They continue:

So paradoxically, the more that scientific detail has accumulated on Alzheimer's disease, the more elusive the 'illness' has become. In an effort to make it a separate entity, the creators of the disease may have narrowed its clinical boundaries unduly, so that current research workers are trapped in the vicious circle of only finding what they themselves put there in the first place. (p. 7)

Clearly, the current interest in noncognitive disorders in Alzheimer's disease suggests that we have begun to heed this warning. We hope that investigators of HIV-related cognitive and behavioral disorders and dementia will maintain a broad, unbiased focus as well.

Acknowledgments

The preparation of this chapter was supported in part by funds from the National Institutes of Mental Health to J.T.B. (1RO1-MH-45311), by a contract from the National Institute of Allergy and Infectious Diseases (NO1-AI-72632), and by the National Institute on Aging (AGO5133).

References

Adams, R.D., and Victor, M. (1981). Dementia and the amnesic (Korsakoff) syndrome. In R.D. Adams and M. Victor, eds., *Principles of Neurology*. New York: McGraw-Hill, pp. 285ff.

Adams, R.D., and Victor, M. (1985). Dementia and the amnesic (Korsakoff) syndrome. In R.D. Adams and M. Victor, eds., *Principles of Neurology*. New York: McGraw-Hill, pp. 311ff.

American Academy of Neurology (AAN). (1989). Human immunodeficiency virus (HIV) infection and the nervous system: Report from the American Academy of Neurology Task Force. *Neurology, 39*, 119–122.

American Academy of Neurology (AAN). (1991). Nomenclature and research case definitions for neurologic manifestations of human immunodeficiency virus-type 1 (HIV-1) infection. *Neurology, 41*, 778–785.

American Psychiatric Association (APA). (1980). *Diagnostic and Statistical Manual of Mental Disorders* (3rd ed.). Washington, D.C.: American Psychiatric Association Press.

American Psychiatric Association (APA). (1987). *Diagnostic and Statistical Manual of Mental Disorders (DSM-III)* (3rd rev. ed.). Washington, D.C.: American Psychiatric Association Press.

Becker, J.T., Huff, F.J., Nebes, R.D., Holland, A., and Boller, F. (1988). Neuropsychological functioning in Alzheimer's disease: Patterns of impairment and rates of progression. *Archives of Neurology, 45*, 263–268.

Berg, L., Miller, J.P., and Sorandt, M. (1988). Mild senile dementia of the Alzheimer type: 2. Longitudinal assessment. *Annals of Neurology, 23*, 477–484.

Berrios, G.E., and Freeman, H.L. (1991). *Alzheimer and the Dementias (Eponymists in Medicine)*. London: Royal Society of Medicine Services, Ltd.

Capitani, E., Della Sala, S., and Spinnler, H. (1985). Neuropsychological approach to dementia. In K. Poeck, H.J. Freund, and H.J. Gaensehirt, eds., *Neurology.* Heidelberg: Springer-Verlag, pp. 61–69.

Copland, J. (1858). *A dictionary of practical medicine: Comprising general pathology, the nature and treatment of diseases . . . with numerous prescriptions . . . a classification of diseases . . . a copious bibliography with references, and an appendix of approved formulary.* London: Longmans, Brown, Green, Longmans & Roberts.

Gutierrez, R., Atkinson, J.H., and Grant, I. (1993). Mild neurocognitive disorder: A needed addition to the nosology of cognitive impairment (organic mental) disorders. *Journal of Neuropsychiatry and Clinical Neurosciences, 5,* 161–177.

Heaton, R.K., and Pendelton, M.G. (1981). Use of neuropsychological tests to predict adult patients' everyday functioning. *Journal of Consulting and Clinical Psychology, 49,* 307–321.

Karp, H.R. (1978). Dementia in adults. In A.B. Baker and L.H Baker, eds., *Clinical Neurology,* Vol. 2. (2nd ed.). Hagerstown, Md.: Harper and Row, pp. 1–29.

Karp, H.R., and Mirra, S.S. (1990). Dementia in adults. In R. Joynt, ed., *Clinical Neurology,* Vol. 3. (3rd ed.). Philadelphia: J.B. Lippincott, pp. 1–29.

Khachaturian, Z. (1985). Diagnosis of Alzheimer's disease. *Archives of Neurology, 42,* 1097–1105.

Lopez, O.L., Becker, J.T., Brenner, R.P., Rosen, J., Bajulaiye, O.I., and Reynolds, C.F. (1991). Alzheimer's disease and delusions and hallucinations: Neuropsychological and electroencephalographic correlates. *Neurology, 41,* 906–912.

Lopez, O.L., Boller, F., Becker, J.T., Miller, M., and Reynolds, C.F. (1990). Alzheimer's disease amd depression: Neuropsychological impairment and progression of the illness. *American Journal of Psychiatry, 147,* 855–860.

Martin, A. (1990). Neuropsychology of Alzheimer's disease: The case for subgroups. In M.F. Schwartz, ed., *Modular Deficits in Alzheimer's-Type Dementia.* Cambridge, Mass.: Bradford/MIT, pp. 143–175.

Maudsley, H. (1895). *The Pathology of Mind.* London: Macmillan.

McKhann G., Drachman, D.A., Folstein, M.F., Katzman, R., Price, D.L., and Stadlan, E. (1984). Clinical diagnosis of Alzheimer's disease: Report of the NINCDS-ADRDA Work Group under the auspices of the Department of Health and Human Services Task Force on Alzheimer's disease. *Neurology, 34,* 939–944.

Navia, B.A., Jordan, B.D., and Price, R.W. (1986). The AIDS dementia complex: I. Clinical features. *Annals of Neurology, 19,* 517–524.

Pinel, P.H. (1806). *A Treatise on Insanity.* Sheffield, England: Cadell and Davies.

Price, R.W., and Brew, B.J. (1988). The AIDS dementia complex. *Journal of Infectious Diseases, 158,* 1079–1083.

Sagar, H. (1991). Specificity of cognitive impairment in neurological disease: A methodological critique of Parkinson's disease. *Behavioral Neurology, 4,* 89–102.

Wells, C.E. (1977). Dementia: Definition and description. In C.E. Wells, ed., *Dementia* (2nd ed.). New York: F.A. Davis, pp. 1–14.

6

Methodological and Conceptual Issues in the Study of Cognitive Change in HIV Infection

ROBERT A. BORNSTEIN

Very early in the human immunodeficiency virus (HIV) epidemic, it was observed that a variety of neurological, psychiatric, and neuropsychological symptoms may appear in association with the primary immunological compromise. Although a number of mechanisms have been proposed (see Chapters 2 and 3), the pathophysiology underlying the neurological and neuropsychological concomitants of HIV infection has yet to be precisely defined. After it was recognized that neuropathological changes occurred in a large proportion of patients with acquired immunodeficiency virus (AIDS) (Snider et al., 1983; Neilson et al., 1984; Navia et al., 1986a), Navia and Price (1987) reported that cognitive changes could be the initial sign of progression to AIDS in approximately 20% of patients. Initial estimates suggested that as many as two-thirds of patients with AIDS would ultimately develop a constellation of cognitive and motor deficits that has been described as the AIDS Dementia Complex. These proved high, but there is now general agreement that a substantial proportion of AIDS patients will develop significant neurobehavioral deficits. What remains unclear, and extremely controversial, is the extent to which these neurobehavioral changes can be observed in patients at early stages of HIV infection. As reviewed elsewhere in this volume, there have been more than 30 published studies, as well as numerous abstracts, addressing the question of neuropsychological deficits in patients with asymptomatic HIV infection. These studies are almost equally divided in reporting neuropsychological differences between HIV-seropositive, asymptomatic individuals and control subjects. The differences between these studies can be traced largely to conceptual and methodological issues that are the focus of this chapter.

Conceptual Issues

As in all areas of scientific investigation, the methodology and experimental design of studies are ultimately linked to the conceptualization of the issue under examination. It is crucial, therefore, that conceptualizations be as specific and unambiguous as possible to facilitate the comparison of results among studies of the same question. It is also important to recognize that these conceptualizations essentially represent hypothetical constructs that must remain flexible as new data emerge. The avoidance of premature closure is particularly important for new concepts in which a broad general consensus has not yet evolved.

Early in the course of the HIV epidemic, Navia et al. (1986b) identified a syndrome of neurobehavioral deficit that they termed the *AIDS dementia complex*. This syndrome was appropriately named because it was identified among patients meeting diagnostic criteria for AIDS and consisted of a severe cognitive deficit. Subsequent studies, however (see Chapters 10–14), have demonstrated that subtle forms of neuropsychological impairment may be observed in an undetermined proportion of asymptomatic, HIV-infected patients. The finding in numerous studies (Grant et al., 1987a; Saykin et al., 1988; Carne et al., 1989; Field et al., 1989; Perry et al., 1989; McKegney et al., 1990; Naber et al., 1990; Wilkie et al., 1990; Lunn et al., 1991; Skorazewski et al., 1991; Stern et al., 1991) that some asymptomatic patients may exhibit subtle cognitive deficit suggests that the concept of AIDS dementia complex is in need of modification.

There is little argument that HIV infection can produce neuropathological changes that become increasingly evident in the later stages of disease progression. It is also clear that HIV can be demonstrated in cerebrospinal fluid soon after seroconversion (McArthur et al., 1988). Therefore, it is not unreasonable to hypothesize that this process may begin to manifest itself in some patients at a relatively early stage of infection. This may be analogous to the situation in Alzheimer's dementia. In general, this is a disorder of later adult life, but it is well known that some patients may begin to demonstrate symptoms in their sixties or even earlier.

There are at least two aspects of the term *AIDS dementia complex* that require modification. At least 12 published studies have now reported significant differences between asymptomatic, HIV-infected men and control subjects on various neuropsychological measures. In addition, some studies, which conclude that there are no differences in group means, nevertheless identify a proportion of asymptomatic patients with neuropsychological deficit (Goethe et al., 1989; Swanson et al., 1991). Thus, it is clear from the available data that some asymptomatic patients do in fact have mild forms of neuropsychological impairment. Therefore, use of the term *AIDS* in the description of the syndrome incorrectly implies that these changes are observed only in later stages of HIV infection.

The second component of the definition of AIDS Dementia Complex that requires modification relates to the word *dementia.* Incorporation of this term may have been appropriate for the patients initially reported (Navia et al., 1986b; Navia and Price, 1987), but *dementia* has the connotation of a very severe deficit that does not appear to be characteristic of the neurobehavioral impairment in earlier stages of HIV infection.

Although some patients may experience broad cognitive decline, others have more circumscribed areas of cognitive dysfunction. Such patients would not meet criteria for dementia, but it does not necessarily follow that their neuropsychological function is normal. In fact, it might be argued that the examination of patients who already meet criteria for dementia is unlikely to shed light on the fundamental character of the dysfunction. Rather, careful evaluation and identification of patients at the very earliest stages of symptom onset may provide the best opportunity for characterizing and understanding HIV-associated cognitive impairment because of the lack of potential confound with opportunistic infections.

The AIDS Dementia Complex has been used both to define a specific clinical syndrome and to refer to the neuropsychological, psychiatric, and neurological deficits associated with HIV infection. It may well be necessary to dissociate these two uses of the term. The term *AIDS dementia complex* may continue to be useful in defining a specific clinical syndrome that, in association with a positive test for HIV antigen, will satisfy diagnostic criteria for AIDS. On the other hand, this term no longer appears to adequately meet the needs of a construct that encompasses all the phenomena under investigation. Based on currently available data, it appears that a broader term, such as *HIV-related neurobehavioral dysfunction,* might be more accurate in delineating the scope of the problem. This, however, is simply another transitional term that may require further modification as new data become available. A number of fundamental issues remain to be resolved, not the least of which is how infection with HIV produces neurological deficit. These conceptualizations will continue to evolve, but a recognition of their current status is critical to understanding the many differences in approaches and findings in the investigations reported thus far. The recent nomenclature and research case definitions (Janssen et al., 1991) represent a clear step forward that will help clarify clinical and research questions.

Methodological Issues

The nature of the question posed in any scientific study is defined on conceptual grounds. However, there are a host of methodological variables that determine how adequately those questions can be addressed. The following sections will review a number of the methodological issues that have contributed to the divergence of experimental results. Among the specific topics to be addressed are the method of subject recruitment, the nature of the study groups, the type and extent of the neuropsychological examinations, the timing of these examinations, and the methods of statistical analysis.

HIV-Infected Subjects

Several questions can be raised about the selection of HIV-infected patients for research purposes. The central issue relates to the nature of the subjects themselves. Most published data have been based on white homosexual or bisexual men. There have been some recent studies of intravenous drug users (Stern et al., 1991), but the interpretation of data from these subjects requires consideration of several subgroup-specific issues (see Chapter 12). The focus on homosexual or bisexual men is appropriate in view of the fact that this represents the largest subgroup of infected patients in North America.

In the specific context of infection, the duration of illness or the degree of immune suppression may be important. There has been some variability in the structure of studies that influences the recruitment of subjects. Some studies recruit subjects in relation to an HIV testing clinic and may obtain subjects at very early stages of immunosuppression. Other studies recruit asymptomatic subjects with a greater degree of immune decline (e.g., CD4 counts of 400–500/mm^3 of blood). If the degree of neurobehavioral dysfunction is related to the extent of immune decline, this may contribute to differences among studies. Medication factors may also be important since several studies (Schmitt et al., 1988; Yarochan et al., 1988) have shown that treatment with azidothymidine (AZT) may improve performance on neuropsychological measures. In view of current recommendations for the treatment of asymptomatic patients with CD4 counts below 500/mm^3 of blood, longitudinal studies will have to examine medication effects. Furthermore, ideally, initial studies will be restricted to unmedicated patients.

The effects of potentially important subject characteristics such as age, race, and gender have not been extensively explored. The variations among major areas of HIV concentration (e.g., San Francisco, New York, Miami) in regard to racial and sociodemographic factors suggests that consideration of these issues may be important in regard to interpretation of data and generalization to specific local situations. The increasing number of infected women (Ellerbrock et al., 1991) would also seem to mandate specific examination of this subgroup. In addition to these subject characteristics, one particularly important issue with respect to neuropsychological performance is educational and intellectual level. Although there have been some exceptions (Goethe et al., 1989; Kovner et al., 1989), the mean educational level in most reported subgroups has been approximately 16 years. Most studies have not reported mean IQ levels, although the relationship between IQ and neuropsychological performance per se is well known and requires careful control. It is not known, however, whether intellectual level has any influence on the expression of HIV-related neurobehavioral dysfunction (see subsequent sections of this chapter).

Selection Site

There has been considerable variation in the nature of the setting in which studies of HIV-related neurobehavioral dysfunction have been performed. Many of these investigations have been reported from university hospital- or clinic-based research groups with subjects recruited specifically for participation in the research project. Other studies are based on patients referred for clinical care to specialized HIV or sexually transmitted disorder clinics. Still other studies are based on subjects referred for neuropsychiatric symptoms. It is obvious that the proportion of subjects with neurobehavioral dysfunction will be directly related to the base rates in the sample under study. In addition, there may be systematic differences in the nature of patients who receive treatment in these different facilities.

Exclusion Criteria

It is necessary to exclude some subjects because of factors that can influence the variable under study. In the examination of the neurobehavioral sequelae of HIV infection, patients with head injuries have typically (but not always) been excluded. Most studies of homosexual or bisexual men have also excluded subjects with histories of intravenous drug use. In addition, some studies have excluded patients with lifetime histories of affective disorder. The rationale for this exclusion is based on the presumed effect of depression on neuropsychological performance. However, most studies that have examined the influence of depression on neuropsychological performance in patients with HIV infection have failed to identify any significant effects. There is no clear rationale for excluding patients who may have had a depressive episode many years prior to their neuropsychological examination. Furthermore, there is considerable evidence of an increased rate of affective disorder in the homosexual population in general that may not be significantly elevated among HIV-infected individuals (Atkinson et al., 1988; Williams et al., 1991). Broad application of exclusionary criteria may produce subject groups that are experimentally relatively homogeneous but unrepresentative of the target population of interest.

Control Subjects

The selection of an appropriate control group is always important, and in view of the complex issues associated with neurobehavioral dysfunction in HIV infection, more than one control group may be necessary. The best group would be one that differs only in regard to HIV seropositivity. In addition to controlling for such obvious factors as age, education, and socioeconomic level, it is advisable to control for lifestyle variables. For example, there appears to be a considerable prevalence of drug and alcohol use (Atkinson et al., 1988; Williams et al., 1991) in the homosexual population. Rather than excluding subjects on the basis of drug or alcohol use, it would be desirable to recruit a control group with the same drug use characteristics as the HIV-infected subgroup. Another potentially relevant lifestyle issue that may require control are the situational stresses associated with living with a chronic, potentially life-threatening illness. Most HIV-negative homosexual or bisexual men have had close associations with individuals who have died from AIDS-related disorders. It might be argued that such individuals share some of the same stresses associated with HIV infection. The stresses related to acquiring HIV infection may be similar in some ways to those experienced by infected individuals concerned about progression to symptomatic levels. In studies of neuropsychiatric aspects of HIV infection, it may be useful to include a control group (matched on demographic variables) that suffers from a non-HIV-related chronic and debilitating medical condition. This will be important in the attempt to determine whether the observed findings are specific to HIV infection.

Use of control groups that are not matched on potentially important demographic or lifestyle characteristics (e.g., sexual preference) may fail to account adequately for the currently poorly understood effects of these variables. It is important, however, that the control group be as carefully selected as the experimental group in regard to elimination of potentially confounding variables. One recent study (Goethe et al., 1989) used a control group composed of individuals who had a history of significant head injury (mean loss of consciousness, 1.6 hours). Although the mean duration from head injury was approximately 7 years, this control group consists of individuals who might be expected to have subtle neurobehavioral deficits. The finding that a group of asymptomatic, HIV-infected men does not differ from such a control group is open to a number of interpretations. Although this study concluded that the results provided no evidence of neurobehavioral dysfunction among the HIV-infected subjects, it is impossible to draw this conclusion from this particular control group.

Sample Size

Many early studies of HIV-related neurobehavioral dysfunction were based on small groups of subjects (Miller et al., 1990). The statistical unreliability of means based on small samples is a fundamental notion of experimental investigation and needs no amplification here. More recent investigations have employed samples of 50 subjects or more, which are adequate for data interpretation. Some large studies (in terms of sample size) have also been reported. Most notable is the Multi-Center AIDS Cohort Study (MACS), which has recruited thousands of subjects (Miller et al., 1990). Although only a subgroup of the total MACS sample participates in the neuropsychological screening, such large numbers are nearly unprecedented in neuropsychological studies. These large sample sizes could potentially offer definitive answers to many of the basic questions regarding HIV-related neurobehavioral dysfunction. However, as will be discussed later, the nature of the examination employed by the MACS, as well as the conceptual model underlying the MACS study, denies this potential.

Multicenter studies have the distinct advantage of being able to accumulate large sample sizes rapidly, but they also have a number of inherent methodological problems. It is necessary that all centers employ the same battery of tests and that those tests be administered in exactly the same way. Simply using well-known and accepted neuropsychological measures is insufficient because of the wide variation in administration procedures used with so-called standardized tests. Extensive common training procedures for technicians or others used in the administration of these tests is critical (Grant et al., 1987b). Recruitment of subjects from geographically diverse regions also raises the question of center effects. It is critical that the performance of the subjects from various centers (within disease subgroups) be shown to be equivalent. Similarly, control subjects should be recruited from all centers involved in the study, and should be shown to be equivalent to each other as well as to the experimental groups in regard to important demographic characteristics (see above).

Neuropsychological Measures

There has been considerable debate about the appropriate measures to be used in the investigation of HIV-related neurobehavioral dysfunction. Some studies (McArthur et al., 1989; Miller et al., 1990) use a 25- to 30-minute screening battery, whereas other studies (e.g., Saykin et al., 1988) employ test batteries requiring many hours. It will come as no surprise that the likelihood of identifying a problem is related to the time spent in examination of that problem. Conversely, studies employing large test batteries must protect against spurious findings associated with the administration of a large number of tests. The latter was probably an issue in the high proportion of asymptomatic subjects reported to be impaired by Grant et al. (1987a). It is almost always the case that a balance must be struck between the breadth and depth of examination, on the one hand, and the amount of time before which the patience and good will of research subjects are exhausted, on the other. Studies in which neurobehavioral issues are not paramount (e.g., the MACS) often face severe constraints in regard to the time allocated for neuropsychological examination.

Much of the debate regarding neuropsychological dysfunction in patients with asymptomatic HIV infection has centered on the methods of examination. Several consensus conferences led to a recommended battery of tests which requires 7–9 hours of examination. It was further recommended that all test protocols be reviewed by two neuropsychologists (Butters et al., 1990). Butters et al. recognized that this extensive test battery is likely to be impractical. Therefore, a 1- to 2-hour screening battery was proposed, which may be more feasible in terms of patient tolerance and requirements for examination of other areas (e.g., psychosocial and psychiatric) of inquiry. Butters et al. proposed 10 areas of examination, including premorbid intelligence, attention, speed of processing, memory, abstraction, language, visuoperception, constructional abilities, motor abilities, and psychiatric assessment. The battery incorporates both traditional and experimental measures and emphasizes divided and sustained attention, speed of processing, and retrieval from working and long-term memory. This proposed emphasis of investigation differs substantially from the emphasis in the screening battery employed by the MACS, which focuses on psychomotor and visual constructional skills (Selnes et al., 1990).

Both the MACS (McArthur et al., 1989; Miller et al., 1990; Selnes et al., 1990) and the NIMH working group (Butters et al., 1990) suggest that their screening batteries are composed of measures likely to be sensitive to early HIV-related neurobehavioral dysfunction based on the commonly reported neuropathological changes seen in patients at later stages of infection. It is unclear, therefore, why the two screening batteries have such a different focus. The focus on speed of information processing and attentional skills advocated by Butters et al. (1990) appears to be consistent with the idea of a subcortical dementia. This concentration appears reasonable in view of the reportedly predominant subcortical neuropathology observed in association with AIDS (Navia et al., 1986a). The specific rationale for the measures included in the MACS screening battery is not as readily apparent, and there is some inconsistency in the reports from that study as to whether the measures employed would in fact be expected to be sensitive to HIV-associated neurobehavioral dysfunction (see Miller et al., 1990, p. 198). The limited examination time, combined with selection of measures that do not appear to conform to conceptualizations about the nature of the presumed dysfunction (McArthur et al., 1989; Selnes et al., 1990), would appear to increase the risk of type I error (i.e., the failure to detect a difference when one exists). These difficulties with respect to the nature and extent of the MACS neuropsychological examination appear to represent problems for which even extremely large sample size cannot compensate.

Breadth of Examination

It is necessary that the neuropsychological examination of HIV-infected subjects be broadly structured. The current conceptualizations about the nature of HIV-related neurobehavioral dysfunction has not generated a clear consensus about which functions are impaired. Furthermore, there is no necessary reason to assume homogeneity in the areas of brain preferentially involved and, therefore, the specific nature of the neuropsychological dysfunction. It may well be that there are different patterns of neurobehavioral dysfunction, and that a prematurely focused test battery will fail to elicit the range of problems that may be associated with this disease. Adoption of a broad neuropsychological battery that includes measures of function that are expected to be abnormal, in addition to measures of a broad range of functions not yet implicated in HIV infection, would appear to be effective in defining the scope and nature of HIV-related neurobehavioral dysfunction.

Repeated Examinations

Many currently ongoing studies are designed to examine the natural history of HIV-related neurobehavioral dysfunction. Typically, this involves sequential examination of subjects over varying time intervals. These repeated measures designs require careful consideration of appropriate time intervals that balance practice effects and the hypothesized rate of change. With respect to test selection, it may be advantageous to use measures with alternative forms or to employ measures that in previous studies have been found relatively resistant to the effects of repeated administration.

The sensitivity of some measures (e.g., the Halstead Category Test) depends to a considerable extent on the novelty of the task. This factor also increases the vulnerability of these measures to practice effects. Incorporation of such tests in a repeated measures design may engender a convoluted logic in which improvement to a lesser extent than that shown in controls is interpreted as declining performance. It would be preferable to avoid such tests and the attendant logical gymnastics that may be required in interpreting changes in performance. The problem of practice effects may be compounded in studies based on well-educated and highly intelligent subjects.

Finally, in regard to selection of measures, the pertinence of neuropsychological test findings to daily life requires consideration. In some studies reporting mean differences between asymptomatic infected subjects and controls, the means of the HIV-infected group are still within normal limits. The interpretation of mean differences may depend to some extent on the demonstration that such differences are reflected in compromise of daily skills and functions. It is therefore particularly advisable for studies of neurobehavioral dysfunction in association with HIV infection (or other disorders) to include ratings by patients and/ or others of daily functioning. One such measure is the Sickness Impact Profile (Bergner et al., 1976), which provides subjective ratings of the impact of symptoms on various aspects of daily life. Demonstration of a relationship between these ratings and neurobehavioral dysfunction tends to suggest that deficits identified on neuropsychological tests do in fact have an impact on an individual's daily functioning.

Statistical Issues

A number of data-analytic procedures have been used to evaluate the question of neurobehavioral dysfunction in patients with asymptomatic HIV infection. Most studies have involved conventional parametric analyses of group means, although some (McArthur et al., 1989) have analyzed group medians. In addition, it has been observed (Butters et al., 1990) that there is considerable variability in the neuropsychological performance of asymptomatic, HIV-infected patients. It is therefore necessary that homogeneity of variance be specifically examined before parametric analyses are employed. In the case of unequal variance, nonparametric procedures are indicated and may demonstrate differences not readily apparent by the misapplication of parametric procedures.

In addition to the analysis of measures of central tendency, it is becoming increasingly important to determine the extent to which those means are reflective of the individuals who compose those groups. Because of the likely heterogeneity in the nature and pattern of neurobehavioral dysfunction, analysis of group means should be accompanied by analyses of the proportion of groups (HIV-infected and controls) who exceed some defined criterion level for impairment. Such analyses will help define the frequency of dysfunction in these various areas and provide a better characterization of the patterns of neurobehavioral dysfunction associated with HIV infection. In addition to analyzing individual tests, it may be of interest to compute a summary neuropsychological impairment rating that reflects overall performance on the test battery. Often this is defined as the proportion of tests that meet criteria for impaired performance.

Criteria for Impairment

The criteria used to define impaired performance are a central issue in the interpretation of neuropsychological performance and have been the topic of extensive debate. A wide range of criteria have been employed that differ markedly in their threshold for identification of impairment. Most studies have defined impairment in terms of deviations from some standard mean, whereas others (e.g., Grant et al., 1987a) have been based on clinical ratings by experienced clinicians. To a considerable extent, the criteria for impairment used in a particular study are related to the conceptual model of neurobehavioral dysfunction that underlies the investigation. Studies that conceptualize the problem as a true dementia appropriately require more severe levels of impairment to satisfy the criterion. In contrast, studies with inherent conceptualizations of subtle neurobehavioral dysfunction may appropriately require less severe levels of dysfunction. There are three principal factors for the definition of criteria for impairment: (1) the reference base against which the subjects are compared, (2) the extent of deviation from that reference base, and (3) the proportion of measures with appropriate levels of deviation that are required.

REFERENCE BASE.   In most cases, it is preferable to base definitions of normal performance on a group of control subjects that is sufficiently large and as well matched as possible to the experimental sample of interest. The issues regarding control group characteristics have been discussed previously. Some studies, including those that base impairments on ratings by clinicians, are founded either implicitly or explicitly on normal samples whose concordance with HIV-infected subjects on important characteristics is typically not completely known. In addition, the normative data on the various tests in a test battery are typically based on different subject groups, which raises the significant problem of cohort effects. The use of a well-matched control group that is used to define normal performance on the complete range of neuropsychological measures avoids these difficulties and is unquestionably the ideal procedure for defining the normal range of performance.

EXTENT OF DEVIATION FROM NORMAL.   As suggested previously, the extent of deviation from normative standards required to meet criteria for impairment is intimately linked to the conceptual model underlying the study. Models that hypothesize a subtle degree of neurobehavioral impairment tend to use deviations of 1 standard deviation from the control mean as the definition of abnormality, whereas models that hypothesize a more severe dementia have used 1.5 or 2 standard deviations from the control mean as the criterion for impairment. It is evident that the proportion of subjects identified as abnormal on a given test will decrease with increasingly stringent criteria for impairment. In the context of HIV infection, this phenomenon has been explicitly demonstrated by Janssen et al. (1989) and Miller et al. (1990).

EXTENT OF IMPAIRMENT. Virtually all studies have required evidence of impairment (albeit to different degrees) on more than one measure for an individual's neuropsychological performance to be considered abnormal. Some studies have grouped the various neuropsychological measures according to domains of function and require impairment in two or more areas to meet criteria for overall impairment. Other studies focus on individual test measures and require a certain number of tests to be abnormal by various criteria in order for an individual to be identified as impaired. It is also possible to base criteria for impairment on a summary neuropsychological rating measure. A critical level of impairment based on clinical or empirical considerations could be set, and impairment would be determined for individuals who exceed this level. Two problems with impairment criteria that focus on individual measures are the considerable overlap among various tests and the number of variables that may be derived from an individual test. It is therefore necessary to combine measures from particular tests or groups of tests to avoid undue influence of any particular test or area of dysfunction in regard to estimates of impairment.

Future Directions

There is little doubt that neurobehavioral dysfunction can be associated with HIV infection, particularly at later stages of disease progression. Furthermore, there is no evidence to suggest that such severe cognitive impairment is observed in patients with asymptomatic HIV infection. However, there is sufficient evidence from many studies to conclude that subtle forms of neurobehavioral dysfunction are observed in a subgroup of asymptomatic patients. To some extent, the current controversy regarding this issue can be attributed to different conceptualizations of the problems and to the resulting methodologies derived from those models. To a large degree, the disagreement is due to the fact that these studies are asking fundamentally different questions (prevalence of dementia vs. subtle impairment). It is no surprise that different answers are obtained. The MACS is undoubtedly correct in concluding that the prevalence of a true dementia is not increased in asymptomatic HIV infection. That data, however, cannot be used to address the different question of the prevalence of more subtle forms of neurobehavioral dysfunction. Although the MACS studies purport to study neuropsychological abnormalities rather than dementia per se, the restricted range of tests, criteria of impairment, and the choice of insensitive measures in these studies seem likely to de facto identify only the most impaired individuals. This may account for the very low rates of abnormality reported in the MACS studies (McArthur et al., 1989; Miller et al., 1990).

Continued arguments about which battery of tests is best or what proportion of asymptomatic patients are impaired would appear to be counterproductive. Answers to more interesting and important questions will improve our understanding of the nature and course of HIV-associated neurobehavioral dysfunction. For example, it is clear that only a subgroup of HIV-infected patients will develop significant neurobehavioral deficits. It would be of considerable scientific and clinical value to identify the characteristics of patients who are at risk for development of this problem. Similarly, it would be of value to identify factors that influence the rate of neuropsychological deterioration. There have been no reported examinations of different patterns of initial deficit, nor have there been studies of the potential prognostic significance of those different patterns.

In addition to these studies, which focus on the nature or pattern of neuropsychological dysfunction, studies are needed that examine how the effects of HIV infection interact with other potentially significant factors such as drug use or previous neurological injury. Price et al. (1988) propose a model of AIDS-related neurological dysfunction that is based on the interaction of a compromised immune system and the brain. It is possible that the threshold for manifestation of neurobehavioral dysfunction implicit in that model might be significantly altered in patients with a nervous system that had been previously compromised (e.g., mild head injury or alcohol abuse). Chapter 2 discusses brain–immune system interactions. Finally, it is also possible that certain patient characteristics may influence the onset, nature, or course of neurobehavioral dysfunction. One possibility, for example, is that patients with above-average premorbid abilities may be less likely to demonstrate HIV-related neurobehavioral dysfunction than patients with below-average premorbid abilities. This hypothesis is not without precedent (Gronwall, 1989) and may be related to greater cerebral flexibility or reserves in patients with higher premorbid abilities. Various other subject characteristics, such as age at seroconversion and specific strain of the virus with which patients are infected, require formal investigation.

In summary, there are a number of conceptual and methodological factors that have defined and fueled the controversy regarding the prevalence of neurobehavioral dysfunction in patients at early stages of HIV infection. There is now sufficient evidence to conclude that a subgroup, but by no means the majority, of these patients appear to have subtle forms of neurobehavioral impairment. It is no longer productive to continue bickering about the precise proportion who are so affected. Further studies directed to more essential questions will increase the understanding of a disease that has already become a major public health problem.

Acknowledgment

The preparation of this manuscript was supported in part by a grant (MH 45649) from the National Institutes of Mental Health.

References

Atkinson, J.H., Grant, I., Kennedy, C.J., Richman, D.D., Spector, S.A., and McCutchan, J.A. (1988). Prevalence of psychiatric disorders among men infected with human immunodeficiency virus: A controlled study. *Archives of General Psychiatry, 45,* 859–864.

Bergner, M., Bobbit, R.A., Pollard, W.E., Martin, D.P., and Gilson, B.S. (1976). The sickness impact profile: Validation of a health status measure. *Medical Care, 14,* 57–67.

Butters, N., Grant, I., Haxby, J., Judd, L.L., Martin, A., McClelland, J., Pequegnat, W., Schacter, D., and Stover, E. (1990). Assessment of AIDS related cognitive changes: Recommendations of the NIMH workshop on neuropsychological assessment approaches. *Journal of Clinical and Experimental Neuropsychology, 12,* 963–978.

Carne, C.A., Stibe, C., Bronkhurst, A., Newman, S.P., Weller, I.V.D., Kendall, B.E., and Harrison, M.J.G. (1989). Subclinical neurological and neuropsychological effect of infection with HIV. *Genitourinary Medicine, 65,* 151–156.

Ellerbrock, T.V., Bush, T.J., Chamberland, M.R., and Oxtoby, M.J. (1991). Epidemiology of women with AIDS in the United States, 1981 through 1990. *Journal of the American Medical Association, 265,* 2971–2975.

Field, M., Tate, J., Kunze, H., and Grazer, I.H. (1989). Cerebral dysfunction with evidence of cerebral HIV infection amongst asymptomatic HIV seropositive subjects. *Australian and New Zealand Journal of Medicine, 19,* 694–698.

Goethe, K.E., Mitchell, J.E., Marshall, D.W., Brey, R.L., Cahill, W.T., Leger, D., Hoy, L.J., and Boswell, N. (1989). Neuropsychological and neurological function of human immunodeficiency virus seropositive asymptomatic individuals. *Archives of Neurology, 46,* 129–133.

Grant, I., Atkinson, J.H., Hesselink, J.R., Kennedy, C.J., Richman, D.D., Spector, S.A., and McCutchan, J.A. (1987a). Evidence for early central nervous system involvement in the acquired immunodeficiency syndrome (AIDS) and other human immunodeficiency virus (HIV) infections. *Annals of Internal Medicine, 107,* 828–836.

Grant, I., Prigatano, G.P., Heaton, R.K., McSweeny, A.J., Wright, E.C., and Adams, K.M. (1987b). Progressive neuropsychologic impairment and hypoxemia. *Archives of General Psychiatry, 44,* 999–1006.

Gronwall, D. (1989). Cumulative and persistent effects of concussion on attention and cognition. Neuropsychological. In H.S. Levin, H.M. Eisenberg, and A.L. Benton, eds., *Mild Head Injury.* New York: Oxford University Press, pp. 153–162.

Janssen, R.S., and the American Academy of Neurology AIDS Task Force. (1991). Nomenclature and research case definitions for neurologic manifestations of human immunodeficiency virus-type 1 (HIV-1) infection. *Neurology, 41,* 778–785.

Janssen, R.S., Saykin, A.J., Cannon, L., Campbell, J., Pinsky, P.F., Hessol, N.A., O'Malley, P.M., Lifson, A.R., Doll, L.S., Rutherford, G.W., and Kaplan, J.E. (1989). Neurological and neuropsychological manifestations of HIV-1 infection: Association with AIDS-related complex but not asymptomatic HIV-1 infection. *Annals of Neurology, 26,* 592–600.

Kovner, R., Perecman, E., Lazar, W., Hainline, B., Kaplan, M.H., Lesser, M., and Beresford, R. (1989). Relation of personality and attentional factors to cognitive deficits in human immunodeficiency virus-infected subjects. *Archives of Neurology, 46,* 274–277.

Lunn, S., Skydsbjerg, M., Schulsinger, H., Parnas, J., Pedersen, C., and Mathiesen, L. (1991). A preliminary report on the neuropsychologic sequelae of human immunodeficiency virus. *Archives of General Psychiatry, 48,* 139–142.

McArthur, J.C., Cohen, B.A., Farzedegan, H., Cornblath, D.R., Selnes, O.A., Ostrow, D., Johnson, R.T., Phair, J., and Polk, B.F. (1988). Cerebrospinal fluid abnormalities in homosexual men with and without neuropsychiatric findings. *Annals of Neurology, 23*(Suppl), S34–S37.

McArthur, J.C., Cohen, B.A., Selnes, O.A., Kumar, A.J., Cooper, K., McArthur, J.H., Soucy, G., Cornblath, D.R., Chmiel, J.S., Wang, M.C., Starkey, D.I., Ginzburg, H., Ostrow, D.G., Johnson, R.T., Phair, J.P., and Polk, B.F. (1989). Low prevalence of neurological and neuropsychological abnormalities in otherwise healthy HIV-1 infected individuals: Results from the Multicenter AIDS Cohort Study. *Annals of Neurology, 26,* 601–611.

McKegney, F.P., O'Dowd, M.A., Feiner, C., Selwyn, P., Drucker, E., and Friedland, G.H. (1990). A prospective comparison of neuropsychologic function in HIV-seroposi-tive and seronegative methadone-maintained patients. *AIDS, 4,* 565–569.

Miller, E.N., Selnes, O.A., McArthur, J.C., Satz, P., Becker, J.T., Cohen, B.A., Sheridan, K., Machado, A.M., Van Gorp, W.G., and Visscher, B. (1990). Neuropsychological performance in HIV-1-infected homosexual men: The Multicenter AIDS Cohort Study (MACS). *Neurology, 40,* 197–203.

Naber, D., Perro, C., Schick, U., Schmauss, M., Erfurth, A., Bove, D., Goebel, F.D., and Hippmus, H. (1990). Psychiatric symptoms and neuropsychological deficit in HIV infection. *Neuropsychopharmacology, 2,* 745–755.

Navia, B.A., Eun-Sook, C., Petito, C.K., and Price, R.W. (1986a). The AIDS dementia complex: II. Neuropathology. *Annals of Neurology, 19,* 525–535.

Navia, B.A., Jordan, B.D., and Price, R.W. (1986b). The AIDS dementia complex: I. Clinical features. *Annals of Neurology, 19,* 517–524.

Navia, B.A., and Price, R.W. (1987). The acquired immunodeficiency syndrome dementia complex as the presenting or sole manifestation of human immunodeficiency virus infection. *Archives of Neurology, 44,* 65–69.

Nielson, S.E., Petito, C.K., Urmacher, C.D., and Posner, J.B. (1984). Subacute encephalitis in acquired immune deficiency syndrome: A postmortem study. *American Journal of Clinical Pathology, 82,* 678–682.

Perry, S., Belsky-Barr, D., Barr, W.B., and Jacobsberg, L. (1989). Neuropsychological function in physically asymptomatic HIV-seropositive men. *Journal of Neuropsy-chiatry and Clinical Neuroscience, 1,* 296–302.

Price, R.W., Brew, B., Sidtis, J., Rosenblum, M., Scheck, A.C., and Cleary, P. (1988). The brain in AIDS: Central nervous system HIV-1 infection and AIDS dementia com-plex. *Science, 239,* 586–592.

Saykin, A.J., Janssen, R.S., Sprehn, G.C., Kaplan, J.E., Spira, T.J., and Weller, P. (1988). Neuropsychological dysfunction in HIV infection: Characterization in a lymphad-enopathy cohort. *International Journal of Clinical Neuropsychology, 10,* 81–95.

Schmitt, F.A., Bigley, J.W., McKinnis, R., Logue, P.E., Evans, R.W., Drucker, J.L., and the AZT Collaborative Working Group. (1988). Neuropsychological outcome of zidovudine (AZT) treatment of patients with AIDS and AIDS-related complex. *New England Journal of Medicine, 319,* 1573–1578.

Selnes, O.A., Miller, E., McArthur, J., Gordon, B., Munoz, A., Sheridan, K., and Fox, R. (1990). Multicenter AIDS Cohort Study. HIV-2 infection: No evidence of cognitive decline during the asymptomatic stages. *Neurology, 40,* 204–208.

Skoraszewski, M.J., Ball, J.D., and Mikulka, P. (1991). Neuropsychological functioning of HIV-infected males. *Journal of Clinical and Experimental Neuropsychology, 13,* 278–290.

Snider, W.D., Simpson, D.M., Nielson, S., Gold, J.W., Metroka, C.E., and Posner, J.B. (1983). Neurological complications of acquired immune deficiency syndrome: Analysis of 50 patients. *Annals of Neurology, 14,* 403–418.

Stern, Y., Marder, K., Bell, K., Chen, J., Dooneief, G., Goldstein, S., Mindry, R.D., Rich-ards, M., Sano, M., Williams, J., Gorman, J., Ehrhardt, A., and Mayeux, R. (1991).

Multidisciplinary baseline assessment of homosexual men with and without human immunodeficiency virus infection. *Archives of General Psychiatry, 48,* 131–138.

Swanson, B., Kessler, H.A., Cronin-Stubbs, D., Bieliauskas, L.A., and Zeller, J.M. (1991). Infrequent neuropsychological impairment in asymptomatic persons infected with the human immunodeficiency virus. *Clinical Neuropsychologist, 5,* 183–189.

Wilkie, F.L., Eisdorfer, C., Morgan, R., Loewenstein, D.A., and Szapocznik, J. (1990). Cognition in early human immunodeficiency virus infection. *Archives of Neurology, 47,* 433–440.

Williams, J.B., Rabkin, J.G., Remien, R.H., Gorman, J.M., and Ehrhardt, A.A. (1991). Multidisciplinary baseline assessment of homosexual men with and without human immunodeficiency virus infection. II. Standardized clinical assessment of current and lifetime psychopathology. *Archives of General Psychiatry, 48,* 124–130.

Yarchoan, R., Thomas, R.V., Grafman, J., Wichman, A., Dalakas, M., McAtee, N., Berg, G., Fischl, M., Perno, C.F., Klecker, R.W., Buchbinder, A., Tay, S., Larson, S.M., Myers, C.E., and Broder, S. (1988). Long-term administration of 3'-azido-2',3'-dideoxythymidine to patients with AIDS related neurological disease. *Annals of Neurology, 23*(Suppl), S82–S87.

7

Computerized Testing to Assess Cognition in HIV-Positive Individuals

ERIC N. MILLER and FRANCES L. WILKIE

A critical issue in the study of human brain function is the accurate assessment of pathological cognitive decline. This is of particular relevance to human immunodeficiency virus (HIV) infection since the natural progression of HIV-1-related encephalopathic conditions is poorly understood. Therefore, reliable and valid indicators of cognitive functioning are crucial for identifying early stages of potentially serious brain compromise, as well as for monitoring and characterizing the progression of HIV-1 disease in the nervous system.

While traditional neuropsychological tasks are commonly viewed as the gold standard for characterizing cognitive dysfunction, these procedures are labor-intensive, time-consuming, and expensive, and they require the skills of experienced clinicians. This discourages the routine neuropsychiatric screening of large risk groups such as HIV-1-positive individuals. Further, while conventional neuropsychological procedures are extremely useful for characterizing many kinds of brain dysfunction, they are not necessarily sensitive to the subtle cognitive changes that may occur due to HIV-1 infection. The development of measures sensitive to subtle changes in information processing holds great promise for early identification of at-risk individuals. Early identification may provide a unique opportunity for researchers and clinicians to study and treat reversible conditions or to attempt various interventions that may slow or alter the disease process.

Advantages of Computerized Assessment

One method for addressing many of these issues is the use of computerized assessment procedures. Computerized measures have several advantages over traditional neuropsychological tools. While the theoretical and applied knowledge of highly trained professionals provides the basis of test development, the actual test can be administered by technical personnel. A computer can control the presentation of complex stimuli to the patient, thus reducing variability in test administration. It can automatically record subject performance and produce a report of this performance in minutes. Additionally, such tasks are well suited to study designs that require serial assessments since the computer can be relied on to present and score stimuli uniformly across multiple visits.

Such procedures, if well designed, adequately normed, and appropriately validated against existing neuropsychological measures and other indices of functional status, can assess a variety of cognitive domains in a short time and can provide instantaneous feedback on any patterns of impairment that might suggest the need for more comprehensive neuropsychological evaluation. The current availability of powerful, low-cost microcomputers means that such procedures have the potential for being installed in a broad range of research, hospital, and private practice settings.

Use of Computerized Assessment for Studying the Effects of HIV-1

Some investigators have suggested that, for several reasons, computerized assessment might be particularly well suited to studying HIV-1-associated cognitive impairment (Perdices and Cooper, 1989; Wilkie et al., 1990; Miller et al., 1991). First, computerized measures should have less error variance associated with task administration, scoring, and examiner bias. Second, computerized assessment of fine motor functioning such as tremor and reaction time is considerably more precise (e.g., to the nearest millisecond) than can be achieved by a human examiner. Third, currently available measures of reaction time, based on tenets of cognitive psychology, can be applied to assess extremely subtle differences in speed of information processing. Finally, the kinds of cognitive changes most often associated with HIV-1 infection of the nervous system (motor and psychomotor slowing, impaired vigilance) are precisely the types of functions that are measured best with computer technology.

The high level of precision available in computerized assessment means that, potentially, computerized tasks could be used to measure subtle changes in normal information processing that might otherwise go undetected. Even if such cognitive changes are not associated directly with functional impairment in normal activities, they might predict the onset of a treatable brain disease or dementing process. In addition, computerized procedures are well suited for tracking known cognitive impairments across multiple visits, for assessing changes over time due to medication and other drug effects, and perhaps even for disentangling confounding conditions that frustrate skilled neuropsychologists. For example, some reaction time measures are designed specifically to separate the effects of motor slowing from changes in speed of decision making (Wilkie et al., 1990; Miller et al., 1991; A. Martin et al., 1992; E.M. Martin et al., 1992b).

Current Applications of Computer Technology

To date, most research in the area of computerized assessment has focused either on computer adaptations of existing neuropsychological measures (computerized versions of the Halstead-Reitan battery, the Wisconsin Card Sorting Task, the Finger-Tapping Test, etc.) or on simple and choice reaction time measures. While computer-administered versions of traditional neuropsychological measures provide uniform stimulus presentation and scoring and help minimize expensive examiner time, there is little savings in time for the subject who is taking the tests. Reaction time measures, on the other hand, have the advantage of brevity and sensitivity but have less well-defined psychometric properties, although several investigators are beginning to address these limitations (Miller et al., 1991). In addition to reaction time, currently available computerized procedures assess such functions as visual scanning, brief attention, vigilance, and speed of different kinds of decision making, memory scanning, and other information processing.

In the area of HIV-1, most investigators have used computerized procedures for assessing simple and choice reaction time. To date, each laboratory has used a different set of computerized procedures, making comparisons across studies difficult. In one of the first of these studies, Perdices and Cooper (1989) examined 36 homosexual men with symptomatic HIV-1 disease (Centers for Disease Control [CDC] class IV); 20 medically asymptomatic, HIV-1 seropositive men; and 23 HIV-1-seronegative controls, using measures of simple and choice reaction time. In their choice reaction time measure, subjects were asked to decide whether or not a trio of letters of the alphabet were in consecutive order. They found no differences between their seropositive and seronegative groups on measures of simple reaction time, but found significant slowing in choice reaction time for the symptomatic group relative to the seronegative controls. The asymptomatic seropositive group did not differ significantly from the seronegative controls on any of the measures.

A. Martin and colleagues (1992) studied simple and choice visual reaction time (a go–no go paradigm) for 52 HIV-1-seropositive individuals (both symptomatic and asymptomatic), 15 seronegative psychiatric patients with adjustment disorders, and 18 seronegative controls with no medical or psychiatric illness. They found that the HIV-1-positive subjects were significantly slower on measures of reaction time than both of the seronegative groups. Forty-two of the seropositive subjects were seen at 6-month follow-up and were found, on average, to be significantly slower on all of the reaction time measures than they had been at baseline. These researchers further reported that there was a significant correlation between change in reaction time over time and cerebrospinal fluid levels of an endogenous neurotoxin, quinolinic acid.

E.M. Martin and colleagues (1992b) examined simple and choice reaction times for 9 medically symptomatic, HIV-1-seropositive patients (CDC class IV); 10 clinically asymptomatic, HIV-1-seropositive subjects; and 13 controls. Their choice reaction time measure required simple red-green color discrimination. They found that both groups of HIV-1-seropositive subjects were significantly slower than the controls in speed of choice reaction time but not in simple reaction time.

More recently, E.M. Martin and colleagues have studied the effects of HIV serostatus and symptom status using a variety of reaction time procedures, including measures of spatial attention (E.M. Martin et al., 1992c), Stroop Color-Word interference (E.M. Martin et al., 1992a), and speed of memory scanning (E.M. Martin et al., 1993). Depending on the specific procedure used, subject group sizes ranged from 11 to 17 for symptomatic, HIV-1-seropositive subjects; from 19 to 20 for asymptomatic, HIV-1-seropositive subjects; and from 14 to 17 for HIV-controls. Despite considerable overlap in subjects across the three studies, the three procedures yielded very different results. Using the reaction time Stroop task, these researchers found significant slowing in both symptomatic and asymptomatic, seropositive subjects relative to seronegative controls (E.M. Martin et al., 1992a). By contrast, reaction time slowing was observed only in the symptomatic, seropositive group using a measure of covert visual orienting (E.M. Martin et al., 1992c), and no differences were observed among any of the seronegative and seropositive groups when using the Sternberg speed of memory scanning task (E.M. Martin et al., 1993). Based on these results, E.M. Martin and colleagues suggest that the motor slowing and attentional deficits associated with HIV may be more selective than the commonly used description "cognitive slowing" may imply. They propose that psychomotor deficits are more likely to be seen in controlled processing tasks such as the Stroop, perhaps because these tasks place greater cognitive demands on the subject than automatic tasks such as rote motor movements and brief attention.

In a study that included computerized reaction time, conventional neuropsychological procedures, and magnetic resonance imaging (MRI), Levin et al. (1990) tested 5 medically symptomatic, HIV-1-seropositive subjects; 11 seropositive subjects with lymphadenopathy (CDC class III); 9 asymptomatic, seropositive subjects; and 7 control subjects with unknown serostatus. They found significantly slower simple and choice reaction times for the symptomatic seropositive group relative to controls, as well as a trend toward slower choice reaction times for the seropositive group with lymphadenopathy relative to controls. These results may have been confounded to some extent since six of the seropositive subjects had focal brain lesions and five of the seropositive subjects had histories of intravenous drug use. The IV drug users and the subjects with focal brain lesions performed slower on simple and choice reaction time measures relative to nondrug users and subjects without focal brain lesions, though these differences were not statistically significant.

Wilkie et al. (1990) included two information processing measures in a battery of neuropsychological tests administered to a sample of 46 asymptomatic, seropositive homosexual men and 13 seronegative controls. In addition to the simple and choice reaction time tests used in the studies described above, these investigators used two measures to assess speed of manipulating information in memory. To study long-term memory access for overlearned materials, they used the Posner Letter Matching task (Posner and Mitchell, 1967), in which the subject must decide whether or not pairs of letters are physically identical (AA) or have the same name (Aa). To assess short-term memory search speeds, they used the Sternberg paradigm (Sternberg, 1966, 1975), in which subjects must decide whether or not a target number is included in a set of from one to four digits.

Wilkie et al. found that their medically asymptomatic, seropositive sample was significantly slower in processing information on both the long-term (Posner Letter Matching) and short-term (Sternberg) memory search tasks. They found no differences between their subject groups using other reaction time measures.

In the largest study to date, Miller et al. (1991) administered a battery of computerized and conventional neuropsychological measures to a group of 507 HIV-1 seronegative; 439 medically asymptomatic, HIV-1 seropositive; and 47 symptomatic, HIV-1-seropositive (CDC class IV) homosexual men enrolled in the Multicenter AIDS Cohort Study (MACS). They adapted the Continuous Performance Test by expanding the stimulus materials to include both verbal and nonverbal targets, by increasing the decision difficulty of choice reaction time measures, and by incorporating memory components into the task. By adding these features, they hoped to assess a broader range of cognitive domains than is normally assessed using these techniques. Tasks included measures of brief attention, lexical discrimination, serial pattern matching, simultaneous pattern matching, rapid visual scanning, and response reversal. Comparison of group means revealed significant differences in performance between HIV-1 seronegative and symptomatic HIV-1-seropositives on one measure of simple reaction time and on a serial pattern-matching measure of choice reaction time. Using a composite index of impairment, they found a significantly higher percentage of abnormal results in the symptomatic group (28%) compared with the seronegative controls (14%). Asymptomatic, seropositive men, on the other hand, did not differ significantly from seronegative subjects on any of the measures of reaction time. Further, the asymptomatic, seropositive men were no more likely to be impaired on the composite index of impairment than were the seronegative controls (13% vs. 14%).

Miller and colleagues (1989) have reported considerable agreement between their computerized and conventional neuropsychological screening measures, with the two sets of measures agreeing on "impaired" status 84–87% of the time across multiple assessments. Their factor analyses of the computerized and conventional procedures have shown independent clustering of the different procedures, indicating that, despite considerable overlap among computerized and conventional measures, each type of procedure contributes unique information. These investigators have also reported that their computerized assessment procedures are more sensitive than conventional neuropsychological screening tasks for detecting HIV-1-related cognitive impairment when used both cross-sectionally and longitudinally. Recently, Miller (1992) reported that the reaction time slowing observed in a group of 41 subjects who had been tested both before and after developing HIV-1-Associated Cognitive Motor Disorder was comparable to or greater than the motor slowing observed using conventional neuropsychological procedures.

Most of the investigations described above used measures of simple and choice reaction time drawn from the area of cognitive psychology to assess psychomotor speed and information processing. Other laboratories have focused on alternative procedures such as using computerized versions of standard neuropsychological procedures. Franzblau et al. (1991) studied 13 HIV-1-negative men; 30 asymptomatic, HIV-1-positive men; and 17 patients with symptomatic HIV-1 disease (CDC class IV). Instead of the simple and choice reaction time measures used by most of the investigators above, Franzblau et al. used computerized versions of several common neuropsychological tasks, including Grooved Pegboard, Finger Tapping, Symbol Digit Substitution, and vocabulary. They also included a version of the Continuous Performance Test and some novel tasks to assess addition, hand–eye coordination, and serial digit learning. They found no statistically significant differences among their three groups, but they did find that their medically symptomatic group performed worse on 12 of 13 individual performance tests.

K. Syndulko (personal communication) has used a novel (and expensive) computerized memory assessment package developed by Glen Larrabee and Thomas Crook (1988). This computerized procedure uses sophisticated laser disk technology to present ecologically valid tests of memory such as recalling names and faces, attending to a news report while simulating driving a car, finding objects in a room, and so on. Syndulko administered this battery along with traditional neuropsychological tests to a group of symptomatic and asymptomatic, HIV-1-infected subjects. Surprisingly, the traditional neuropsychological measures showed significant differences between the groups, while the computerized memory battery did not. Although many factors could account for this discrepancy, one possibility is that in the earliest stages of central nervous system infection, subjects who are presented with everyday tasks do not yet show impairment since these tasks are highly overlearned and do not have the novel, albeit artificial, quality that the traditional cognitive measures do. Thus it may be that tasks that present novel demands yield more sensitivity in the early stage of disease than tasks more representative of everyday functioning.

Interpretation of Reaction Time and Speed of Information Processing Findings

Reaction time is considered a composite measure of motor speed and the time required for mental events such as perception, stimulus processing, and decision making. In most studies, simple reaction time reflects the time required for perception and motor speed, with little additional overhead for stimulus processing or decision making. Choice reaction time, on the other hand, requires that the individual make a decision about whether or not the current stimulus can be classified as a target. The difference between simple and choice reaction times for any individual represents the speed of information processing for a particular choice decision.

At a theoretical level, indices of different types of information processing can be derived by varying the types of decision processes. For example, in the assessment battery developed by Miller and colleagues (1991), six different types of decision processes are assessed (lexical discrimination, simple pattern matching, serial pattern matching, pattern matching with distraction, pattern matching coupled with rapid visual scanning, and matching of nonnameable forms).

At a practical level, there are many varied approaches to the measurement of reaction time and information processing. Stimuli may include visual, auditory, olfactory, or kinesthetic signals (Schmidt, 1982), while responses may include measures of finger or body movements, vocal responses, eye blinks, galvanic skin response, and so on. Each of these methods for assessing reaction time yields different hypotheses about the underlying cognitive constructs that are being assessed. The questions asked about the integrity of the information processing system guide the selection of the tasks, test stimuli, and dependent measures.

There is an extensive literature focusing on the numerous paradigms and variables that may influence reaction time (Posner, 1978; Schmidt, 1982; Vernon, 1987); on age differences (Welford, 1980); on reaction time slowing in diseases other than HIV-1 infection that affect subcortical structures such as Parkinson's and Huntington's diseases (Cummings, 1986); and on the relationship between intelligence and the speed of processing information (Vernon, 1987). Welford (1980) provides a thorough review of the history, models, and results of reaction time studies. Crabtree and Antrim (1988) present guidelines on instrumentation; subject controls; design issues for measuring reaction time, including recommendations on the number of trials per condition; and interpretation of results.

The interpretation of response latencies depends on whether simple or choice reaction time paradigms are utilized. *Simple reaction time* is the individual's response latency to the onset of a single stimulus. Between the stimulus and the movement output, at least three stages of information processing may occur: stimulus identification, response selection, and response programming. In studies in which the electrical activity of muscles has been monitored during a simple reaction time procedure, a *premotor* period of 40–60 milliseconds may elapse before the *motor* period, when the musculature is activated. The premotor reaction time is thought to reflect central processes such as the perception and recognition of the signal and decisions that are made in response to a simple stimulus. Although this latter approach is not widely used, it could be useful for determining whether the slowing in HIV-1 infection is due to either peripheral (motor) or central (decision-processing) functions. Neuropathy and myelopathy associated with HIV-1 infection may influence response latency, although this has not been demonstrated.

Choice reaction time is the response latency to one of two or more distinct stimuli that may occur, each requiring a different response. As early as 1868, Donders (1969) noted, choice reaction time was found to be greater than simple reaction time, and he postulated that the difference between these two reaction times was a measure of the central processing time required to discriminate and make decisions. In many studies, a linear increase in choice reaction time has been observed as the number of possible stimulus-response alternatives increases (e.g., Hick, 1952). The zero intercept of this linear function is viewed as a measure of the overall speed of the perceptual and motor systems independent of the time required to decide which response to make. The slope is viewed as the amount of time required to process one additional bit of information, or the speed of decision making during the response-selection stage of processing.

A number of different tasks have been designed to measure the speed of manipulating different types of information in short-term memory, including the Sternberg (1966, 1975) task that measures the speed of searching short-term memory; the Carpenter and Just (1975) sentence-picture verification task that measures the coordination of linguistic and visual information, using simple sentences and pictures; and the test battery developed by Miller and colleagues (1991). For these tasks, reaction time increases as a function of task complexity. For the Sternberg short-term memory search paradigm, task complexity varies as a function of the number of digits (or letters) in the memory set. For the sentence verification task, complexity is varied according to whether the sentences are affirmatively or negatively worded (e.g., STAR IS ABOVE PLUS; PLUS IS NOT BELOW STAR) and whether the sentences are true or false descriptions of a simple picture of a star and a plus sign. For these tasks, an intercept and slope would be obtained from reaction time examined as a function of task complexity. In the computerized assessment package developed by Miller and colleagues, task difficulty is manipulated by varying the reaction time paradigm (simple vs. choice), as well as the types of decision processes (lexical discrimination, serial pattern matching, rapid visual scanning), although all of these measures are highly intercorrelated.

These paradigms, which have been used in several studies involving HIV-1-infected individuals (Wilkie et al., 1990; Miller et al., 1991; A. Martin et al., 1992; E.M. Martin et al., 1992b; E.M. Martin et al., 1993), have the advantage of attempting to disentangle the motor reaction time from the central decision-making reaction time. Seen this way, the slope and intercept represent two different underlying processes involved in performance. If this is true, then different experimental variables may affect the intercept and the slope.

An evaluation of within-subject variability in reaction time provides information on the ability to maintain a consistent level of selective attention and vigilance (Bruhn and Parsons, 1971; Wilkinson and Allison, 1989). In tasks involving many trials, fatigue can be examined by determining whether response latency increases within a task or over repetition of tasks (Bruhn and Parsons, 1971; Wilkie et al., 1990). The ability to be vigilant and to attend selectively to signals can also be evaluated in situations where a response to infrequent signals is required. In addition, the interpretation of practice effects on reaction time and information processing speeds is important in the longitudinal studies involving HIV-1-infected individuals. In general, practice results in improvement in reaction time (Mowbray and Rhoades, 1959; Norrie, 1967; Clarkson and Kroll, 1978), and the learning effect may well interact with other parameters (Welford, 1986) such as HIV-1 progression, as reflected in changes in CD4 cell counts and nutritional status (Wilkie et al., 1991; Beach et al., 1992).

Simple reaction time has also been used as a secondary task in studies evaluating the attention (mental effort, resources) required to perform a primary task such as a memory task (Kerr, 1973; Lansman and Hunt, 1982). When two tasks that compete for the same attentional resource are performed concurrently, with one designated as primary and the other as secondary, the resource demands of the primary task should be fulfilled first. Therefore, secondary task performance should provide a measure of the spare capacity not required by the primary task. The probe reaction time when utilized as a secondary task can be contrasted with a control probe reaction time condition, since both the secondary and primary tasks are performed alone and then concurrently. Wilkie and colleagues (1990, 1991) have used a probe reaction time task as the secondary task to evaluate indirectly the attention (mental effort) required to update and remember continuous paired associates in HIV-1-infected individuals. Increased mental effort may be required to perform a task when there are subtle decrements in memory.

Hypothetical Mechanisms Underlying Slowed Information Processing

Although HIV-1 infection is frequently accompanied by alterations in attention and memory, along with a slowing in motor and information processing speeds, relatively little is known about the underlying physiological mechanisms, nutritional factors, and mood changes that may be related to these cognitive changes.

The slowing in processing speed and the clinical presentation of the HIV-1-Associated Cognitive/Motor Complex is best described as a subcortical dementia (Navia et al., 1986; Price et al., 1990) that may be similar to that seen in Parkinson's and Huntington's diseases. Neuropathological studies indicate that the brain areas affected by HIV-1 infection are primarily the white matter and deep gray subcortical structures, with the cerebral cortex generally spared. Subcortical structures affected in HIV-1 infection include the basal ganglia, thalamus, pons, and brain stem areas (Navia et al., 1986; Levy and Bredesen, 1988). In studies of Parkinson's disease, a slowing in choice, but not simple, reaction times has been reversed by dopamine treatment. This finding suggests that dopaminergic functions may contribute to the psychomotor slowing observed in these patients (Rafal and Grimm, 1981). In a similar study, Stern and Langston (1985) reported that abnormalities in cerebrospinal fluid (CSF) levels of norepinephrine were associated with changes in reaction time in patients with Parkinson's disease. Thus it is possible that the psychomotor retardation observed in late-stage HIV-1 infection may be related to changes in normal levels of neurotransmitters. In support of this hypothesis, Levin and colleagues (1991) recently reported that CSF levels of dopamine were significantly correlated with the progression of HIV-1 infection, with depressive symptoms, and with 13 measures of neuropsychological functions covering a wide range of processes. Unfortunately, they did not include indices of simple or choice reaction times in their study.

In addition to these studies of neurotransmitters, there have been reports of a relationship between altered cognition and endogenous neurotoxins. A. Martin and colleagues (1992) observed in both asymptomatic and symptomatic, HIV-1-infected individuals that high CSF levels of quinolinic acid, a neurotoxin and convulsant, were associated with poor neuropsychological status and slow reaction times (Heyes et al., 1991). During a 6-month follow-up interval, these investigators also reported that increases in CSF quinolinic acid were accompanied by increased slowing in reaction time (A. Martin et al., 1992). Quinolinic acid is an abnormal by-product of the catabolism of tryptophan, a precursor in the synthesis of serotonin, which is decreased in AIDS dementia complex (Singer et al., 1990; Heyes et al., 1991). Quinolinic acid also acts as an agonist of N-methyl-D-aspartate receptors, which have a role in memory processes (Morris et al., 1986). The precise mechanisms responsible for increases in quinolinic acid in HIV-1 infection are not yet known.

Changes in cognitive functioning have also been associated with nutritional factors. In an 18-month follow-up of asymptomatic (CDC classes II and III) and mildly symptomatic (CDC classes IVa and IVc2) subjects, Wilkie and colleagues (1991) found that lower plasma vitamin B_6 levels were associated with the degree of change in reaction time and in memory on tasks involving a motor component. Vitamin B_6 is a cofactor in the rate-limiting decarboxylation step in the synthesis of serotonin from tryptophan, suggesting a possible link between the findings on quinolinic acid (Heyes et al., 1991; A. Martin et al., 1992) and vitamin B_6 deficiency (Wilkie et al., 1991). Several investigators (Baum et al., 1990; Mantero-Atienza et al., 1991; Beach et al., 1992) have reported that vitamin B_{12} deficiency was associated with a slowing in the speed of retrieving highly overlearned name codes, as measured by the Posner Letter Matching task, paired associates response times, and speed of visual scanning and discrimination. In a study consisting primarily of AIDS patients, Kieburtz and colleagues (1991) found that vitamin B_{12} deficiency was associated with both myelopathy and neuropathy, with the latter reversed by vitamin B_{12} supplementation.

Since depression and anxiety are symptoms frequently experienced by HIV-1-infected individuals, it is important to determine their effects on the speed of processing information. In other diseases involving subcortical structures (e.g., Parkinson's and Huntington's diseases), depression has been observed in many patients. Many investigators believe that the depression seen in subcortical dementias is biologically associated with the underlying neuropathological changes rather than a psychological response to the physical disability (Cummings, 1986). Some investigators (Perdices and Cooper, 1989; Law et al., 1990; Wilkie et al., 1990; Miller et al., 1991; Wilkie et al., 1991) have reported slowing in processing speeds in HIV-1-infected individuals that did not appear to be due to differences between their groups in anxious or depressive symptoms. In other studies, it was not clear whether mood changes had been examined in relation to the reaction time measures (Levin et al., 1990). However, at this time, little is known about the mechanisms causing depression in HIV-1 infection.

In studies evaluating reaction times and central processing speeds in HIV-1 infection, variables that may possibly alter performance should be examined, including mood state and the history and current use of alcohol and drugs. In addition, many recent studies suggest that neurotoxins, neurotransmitters, and nutritional changes in HIV-1 infection may be important factors contributing to the neuropsychological changes and slowing in simple reaction time and central processing speeds observed in some HIV-1-infected individuals.

Limitations of Current Research Using Computerized Techniques

Except for the work by Larrabee and Crook (1988) and by Franzblau et al. (1991), most of the computerized procedures used in these studies are similar in that they are all variations on simple and choice reaction time paradigms. There are, however, many differences that prevent direct comparisons across studies. Most of these studies included a simple reaction time procedure and a basic go–no go choice reaction time procedure. Although these procedures appear superficially similar, they differ in their methods of presentation, numbers of trials and practice trials, use of warning signals, and so on. More complicated procedures, such as the Posner Letter-Matching test and the Sternberg task used by Wilkie et al. (1990) and E.M. Martin et al. (1993), and the sequential and serial pattern matching tasks developed by Miller et al. (1991), bear even less superficial resemblance to each other, although these procedures are designed to assess similar underlying constructs such as speed of information processing and memory scanning.

In addition to problems of comparison across studies, there are several pitfalls associated with the implementation of computerized measures. Like any new assessment tool, a computerized testing battery must be shown to be reliable, valid, and practical. Although many researchers are now experimenting with computerized neuropsychological assessment techniques, surprisingly few have attempted to address these critical psychometric concerns. Miller et al. (1991) established the feasibility of using computerized assessment for wide-scale screening in settings such as the MACS. These investigators have also shown that such a test battery can be used to identify many of the same people who would be identified by a conventional neuropsychological screening battery. However, their factor-analytic work also indicates that their computerized test battery complements rather than replaces conventional neuropsychological procedures.

Given current implementations, it is unlikely that any computerized assessment battery can totally replace conventional neuropsychological procedures. While the computerized procedures described above are often more sensitive than conventional neuropsychological screening measures, they are not very specific. Consequently, such computerized procedures probably are better suited for use as screening instruments in a "successive hurdles" approach to risk detection (Meehl and Rosen, 1955). For example, subjects identified as being at risk for early functional decline by the computerized screening measure could subsequently be assessed using more comprehensive neuropsychological and medical procedures. The goal of this successive hurdles approach is to minimize the cost of screening large groups of at-risk individuals while improving the likelihood (beyond population base rates) of detecting and treating early stages of cognitive decline.

Future Directions for Computerized Assessment

The studies described above illustrate the potential for computerized techniques. These procedures are rapid, efficient, and inexpensive tools for detecting cognitive changes in HIV-1-infected individuals. When used longitudinally, computerized measures appear to have slightly greater sensitivity for identifying individuals at risk for HIV-1 encephalopathy than do conventional neuropsychological procedures.

Despite the promise of current technology, these studies also suggest that computerized techniques work best in conjunction with traditional neuropsychological measures. No computerized battery yet developed adequately assesses all areas of cognitive functioning, and it is unlikely that current technology can replace the subtle clinical judgments often necessary for understanding the significance of complex patterns of strengths and weaknesses seen on conventional neuropsychological exams. At present, computerized procedures seem most appropriate as screening measures and adjuncts to normal clinical practice.

The technology for incorporating computerized assessments into existing clinical and research settings already exists. As the demand for assessment of higher cognitive functioning increases, it is likely that computerized procedures will eventually become common as screening tools in the study of both HIV-1-positive individuals and other high-risk groups.

Acknowledgments

Dr. Wilkie's work was supported in part by Grant 1 PH50 MH/DA42455 from the National Institutes of Mental Health. Dr. Miller's work was supported in part by National Institutes of Health Contract N01 AI 72631.

References

Baum, M.K., Beach, R., Morgan, R., Mantero-Atienza, E., Wilkie, F., and Eisdorfer, C. (1990). Vitamin B_{12} and cognitive function in HIV infection. *Neurological and Neuropsychological Complications of HIV Infection, 1*, 55 (abst.).

Beach, R.S., Morgan, R., Wilkie, F., Mantero-Atienza, E., Blaney, N., Shor-Posner, G., Lu, Y., Eisdorfer, C., and Baum, M.K. (1992). Plasma vitamin B_{12} level as a potential cofactor in studies of human immunodeficiency virus type 1–related cognitive changes. *Archives of Neurology, 49*, 501–506.

Bruhn, P., and Parsons, O.A. (1971). Continuous reaction time in brain damage. *Cortex, 7*, 278–291.

Carpenter, P.A., and Just, M.A. (1975). Sentence comprehension: A psycholinguistic processing model of verification. *Psychological Review, 82*, 45–73.

Clarkson, P.M., and Kroll, W. (1978). Practice effects on fractionated response time related to age and activity level. *Journal of Motor Behavior, 10*, 275–286.

Crabtree, D.A., and Antrim, L.R. (1988). Guidelines for measuring reaction time. *Perceptual and Motor Skills, 66*, 363–370.

Cummings, J.L. (1986). Subcortical dementia: Neuropsychology, neuropsychiatry and pathophysiology. *British Journal of Psychiatry, 149*, 682–697.

Donders, F.C. (1969). On the speed of mental processes. *Acta Psychologica (Amsterdam), 30*, 412–431.

Franzblau, A., Letz, R., Hershman, D., Mason, P., Wallace, J.I., and Bekesi, J.G. (1991). Quantitative neurologic and neurobehavioral testing of persons infected with human immunodeficiency virus type 1. *Archives of Neurology, 48*, 263–268.

Heyes, M.P., Brew, B.J., Martin, A., Price, R.W., Salazar, A.M., Sidtis, J.J., Yergey, J.A., Mouradian, M.M., Sadler, A.E., Keilp, J., Rubinow, D., and Markey, S.P. (1991). Quinolinic acid in cerebrospinal fluid and serum in HIV-1 infection: Relationship to clinical and neurological status. *Annals of Neurology, 29*, 202–209.

Hick, W.E. (1952). On the rate of gain of information. *Quarterly Journal of Experimental Psychology, 4*, 11–26.

Kerr, B. (1973). Processing demands during mental operations. *Memory and Cognition, 1*, 401–412.

Kieburtz, K.D., Giang, D.W., Schiffer, R.B., and Vakil, N. (1991). Abnormal vitamin B_{12} metabolism in human immunodeficiency virus infection. *Archives of Neurology, 48*, 312–314.

Lansman, M., and Hunt, E. (1982). Individual differences in secondary task performance. *Memory and Cognition, 10*, 10–24.

Larrabee, G.J., and Crook, T. (1988). A computerized everyday memory battery for assessing treatment effects. *Psychopharmacology Bulletin, 24*, 695–697.

Law, W.A., Martin, A., Williams, J., Roller, T., Kampen, D., and Salazar, A.M. (1990). The Beck Depression Inventory in HIV infection: Independence of cognitive slowing from psychiatric symptoms. *Neurological and Neuropsychological Complications of HIV Infection, 1*, 52 (abst.).

Levin, B., Kumar, M., Fernandez, B., and Duncan, R. (1991). Cerebrospinal fluid dopamine levels in HIV-1 infection: Correlations with immune function and neuropsychological profile. *Neurological and Neuropsychological Complications of HIV Infection, 2*, 122 (abst.).

Levin, H.S., Williams, D.H., Borucki, M.J., Hillman, G.R., Williams, J.B., Guinto, F.C., Amparo, E.G., Crow, W.N., and Pollard, R.B. (1990). Magnetic resonance imaging and neuropsychological findings in human immunodeficiency virus infection. *Journal of Acquired Immune Deficiency Syndromes, 3*, 757–762

Levy, R.M., and Bredesen, D.E. (1988). Central nervous system dysfunction in acquired immunodeficiency syndrome. *Journal of Acquired Immune Deficiency Syndromes, 1*, 41–64.

Mantero-Atienza, E., Baum, M.K., Morgan, R., Wilkie, F., Shor-Posner, G., Fletcher, M.A., Eisdorfer, C., and Beach, R.S. (1991). Vitamin B_{12} in early human immunodeficiency virus-1 infection [letter]. *Archives of Internal Medicine, 151*, 1019–1020.

Martin, A., Heyes, M.P., Salazar, A.M., Kampen, D.L., Williams, J., Law, W.A., Coats, M.E., and Markey, S.P. (1992). Progressive slowing of reaction time and increasing cerebrospinal fluid concentrations of quinolinic acid in HIV-infected individuals. *Journal of Neuropsychiatry and Clinical Neurosciences, 4*, 270–279.

Martin, E.M., Robertson, L.C., Edelstein, H.E., Jagust, W.J., Sorensen, D.J., San Giovanni, D., and Chirurgi, V.A. (1992a). Performance of patients with early HIV-1 infection on the Stroop task. *Journal of Clinical and Experimental Neuropsychology, 14*, 840–851.

Martin, E.M., Robertson, L.C., Sorensen, D.J., Jagust, W.J., Mallon, K.F., and Chirurgi, V.A. (1993). Speed of memory scanning is not affected in early HIV-1 infection. *Journal of Clinical and Experimental Neuropsychology, 15*, 311–320.

Martin, E.M., Sorensen, D.J., Edelstein, H.E., and Robertson, L.C. (1992b). Decision-making speed in HIV-1 infection: A preliminary report. *AIDS, 6*, 109–113.

Martin, E.M., Sorensen, D.J., Robertson, L.C., Edelstein, H.E., and Chirurgi, V.A. (1992c). Spatial attention in HIV-1 infection: A preliminary report. *Journal of Neuropsychiatry and Clinical Neurosciences, 4*, 288–293.

Meehl, P.E., and Rosen, A. (1955). Antecedent probability and the efficiency of psychometric signs, patterns, or cutting scores. *Psychological Bulletin, 52*, 194–216.

Miller, E.N. (1992). Use of computerized reaction time in the assessment of dementia. *Neurology, 42*, 220 (abst.).

Miller, E.N., Satz, P., Van Gorp, W., Visscher, B., and Dudley, J. (1989). Computerized screening for HIV-related cognitive decline in gay men: Cross-sectional analyses and one-year follow-up. *International Conference on AIDS, 5*, 465 (abst.).

Miller, E.N., Satz, P., and Visscher, B.V. (1991). Computerized and conventional neuropsychological assessment of HIV-1 infected homosexual men. *Neurology, 41*, 1608–1616.

Morris, R.G., Anderson, E., Lynch, G.S., and Baudry, M. (1986). Selective impairment of learning and blockade of long-term potentiation by an *N*-methyl-D-aspartate receptor antagonist, AP5. *Nature, 319*, 774–776.

Mowbray, G.H., and Rhoades, M.V. (1959). On the reduction of choice reaction times with practice. *Quarterly Journal of Experimental Psychology, 11*, 16–23.

Navia, B.A., Cho, E-S., Petito, C.K., and Price, R.W. (1986). The AIDS dementia complex: II. Neuropathology. *Annals of Neurology, 19*, 525–535.

Norrie, M.L. (1967). Practice effects on reaction latency for simple and complex movements. *Research Quarterly: The American Association for Health and Physical Education, 38*, 79–85.

Perdices, M.A., and Cooper, D.A. (1989). Simple and choice reaction time in patients with human immunodeficiency virus infection. *Annals of Neurology, 25*, 460–467.

Posner, M.I. (1978). *Chronometric Explorations of Mind.* Hillsdale, N.J.: Erlbaum.

Posner, M.I., and Mitchell, R.F. (1967). Chronometric analysis of classification. *Psychological Review, 74*, 392–409.

Price, R.W., Brew, B.J., and Rosenblum, M. (1990). The AIDS dementia complex and HIV-1 brain infection: A pathogenetic model of virus-immune interaction. *Research Publications—Association for Research in Nervous and Mental Disease, 68*, 269–290.

Rafal, R.D., and Grimm, R.J. (1981). Progressive supranuclear palsy: Functional analysis of the response to methysergide and antiparkinsonian agents. *Neurology, 31*, 1507–1518.

Schmidt, R.A. (1982). *Motor Control and Learning: A Behavioral Emphasis.* Champaign, Ill.: Human Kinetics.

Singer, E.J., Wilkins, J., Syndulko, K., Mitsuyasu, R., Setoda, D., Fahy-Chandon, B., Singer, P., Tuico, E., Gaffield, J., and Tourtellotte, W.W. (1990). Cerebrospinal fluid (CSF) biogenic amines increase, and cortisol levels decrease, after zidovudine (AZT) therapy in subjects with the AIDS dementia complex (ADC). *Neurological and Neuropsychological Complications of HIV Infection, 1*, 145 (abst.).

Stern, Y., and Langston, J.W. (1985). Intellectual changes in patients with MPTP-induced parkinsonism. *Neurology, 35*, 1506–1509.

Sternberg, S. (1966). High-speed scanning in human memory. *Science, 153*, 652–654.

Sternberg, S. (1975). Memory scanning: New findings and current controversies. *Quarterly Journal of Experimental Psychology, 27*, 1–32.

Vernon, P.A. (1987). New developments in reaction time research. In P.A. Vernon, ed., *Speed of Information Processing and Intelligence.* Norwood, N.J.: Ablex, pp. 1–20.

Welford, A.T. (1980). *Reaction Times.* New York: Academic Press.

Welford, A.T. (1986). Note on the effects of practice on reaction times. *Journal of Motor Behavior, 18*, 343–345.

Wilkie, F.L., Eisdorfer, C., Morgan, R., Loewenstein, D.A., and Szapocznik, J. (1990).

Cognition in early human immunodeficiency virus infection. *Archives of Neurology, 47*, 433–440.

Wilkie, F., Shor-Posner, G., Mantero-Atienza, E., Beach, R.S., Ayala, M., Morgan, R., Eisdorfer, C., and Baum, M.K. (1991). Association of vitamin B_6 status and reaction time in early HIV-1 infection. *Neurological and Neuropsychological Complications of HIV Infection, 2*, 67 (abst.).

Wilkinson, R.T., and Allison, S. (1989). Age and simple reaction time: Decade differences for 5,325 subjects. *Journal of Gerontology, 44*, 29–36.

8

Development of a Screening Battery for HIV-Related Cognitive Impairment: The MACS Experience

OLA A. SELNES and ERIC N. MILLER

Many efforts have been made to characterize the frequency, severity, and pattern of neurocognitive deficits during different stages of human immunodeficiency virus (HIV) infection. Early studies were primarily cross-sectional and were directed largely to assessing the frequency of cognitive impairment during the symptomatic stages of the infection (Joffe et al., 1986; Ayers et al., 1987; Bruhn, 1987; Bocellari et al., 1988; Morgan et al., 1988; Derix et al., 1989; Perdices and Cooper, 1990). A number of subsequent investigators have reported cross-sectional results suggesting that the frequency and severity of cognitive symptoms increase with the onset of constitutional symptoms or opportunistic infections (Grant et al., 1987; Tross et al., 1988; Janssen et al., 1989; Van Gorp et al., 1989). A significant effort also has been made to answer the question of whether cognitive impairment attributable to HIV occurs during the presymptomatic phase of the infection. Although no consensus has been reached, most studies with smaller groups have concluded that there is an increase in neuropsychological abnormalities during the presymptomatic period (Grant et al., 1987; Perry et al., 1989; Wilkie et al., 1990; Lunn et al., 1991), while studies with larger groups have reached the opposite conclusion (Janssen et al., 1989; McArthur et al., 1989; Miller et al., 1990).

Many attempts have been made to characterize the *patterns* of cognitive impairment in HIV-associated dementia (Morgan et al., 1988; Poutiainen et al., 1990). There is now converging evidence from several studies that the constellation of deficits in late acquired immunodeficiency syndrome (AIDS) or HIV-associated dementia includes many of the characteristics of subcortical dementias (Cummings, 1990). It is unclear, however, whether there are subtypes of HIV-associated dementia that may differ either in rate of progression or pattern and severity of cognitive deficits. Several recent studies have focused on the rate of progression of cognitive deficits associated with HIV (Selnes et al., 1990; Gastaut et al., 1990; Robertson et al., 1990), while others have evaluated the efficacy of various types of antiviral treatment in alleviating the cognitive symptoms associated with HIV infection (Tozzi et al., 1991; Routy et al., 1991; Grunseit et al., 1991).

Whereas the cross-sectional approach to neuropsychological assessment may accommodate comprehensive testing, large-scale longitudinal assessment of HIV-related cognitive impairment is, of necessity, more constrained. In designing a test battery for longitudinal assessment of cognitive impairment in HIV, a number of factors need to be taken into consideration. The choice of the specific screening measures used in the Multicenter AIDS Cohort Study was motivated by several concerns: (1) the tests should be sensitive to a wide range of impairments, (2) the tests should be robust to the effect of serial repetition, (3) the test battery should include tests already demonstrated to be sensitive to HIV-related changes in cognition, and (4) the overall testing period should be relatively brief. In this chapter, we describe the development and rationale for such a test battery.

The MACS Neuropsychological Study

The Multicenter AIDS Cohort Study (MACS) is an epidemiological study initiated in 1984 to assess the natural history of HIV infection. The neuropsychological component of the study was started in the fall of 1986 in Baltimore and Chicago and the following spring in Pittsburgh and Los Angeles. Due to the high cost of administering the neuropsychological battery, only a subset of the cohorts in Baltimore, Chicago, and Pittsburgh were recruited for neuropsychological assessment, whereas in Los Angeles all subjects were invited to participate. More detailed descriptions of the MACS neuropsychology study are provided elsewhere (McArthur et al., 1989; Miller et al., 1990; Selnes et al., 1990). The full cohort included 84 medically symptomatic, HIV-1-positive subjects; 727 medially asymptomatic, HIV-1-positive subjects; and 769 HIV-1-negative controls.

Neuropsychological Screening Battery: Phase I

The original MACS neuropsychological test battery, developed in 1986, consisted of a two-stage approach of screening and comprehensive follow-up for participants who met criteria for possible neuropsychological impairment on the screening exam. The screening exam was designed to be sensitive to a wide spectrum of brain impairment and was consequently heavily weighted toward measures of psychomotor functioning and memory. This battery consisted of the Symbol Digit

Modalities test (Smith, 1982), the Trail-Making test (Parts A and B) (Reitan, 1979), the Rey Auditory Verbal Learning Test, the Grooved Pegboard test (Kløve, 1963), the Controlled Oral Word Association Test (Verbal Fluency) (Benton et al., 1983), and the CES Depression scale (Radloff, 1977). In addition, each of the four MACS centers introduced one or more measures that were administered to their full neuropsychological cohorts, but only at their center: California Computerized Assessment Package (CalCAP); Halstead Booklet Categories Test (DeFilippis and McCampbell, 1979); Wisconsin Card Sorting Test (Heaton, 1981). The CalCAP is a computerized reaction time test battery that was developed specifically for this study (Miller et al., 1991).

Comprehensive Neuropsychological Assessment: Phase II

The Phase II comprehensive follow-up, administered to selective controls and those who met criteria for impairment on the Phase I screening, included additional measures of general intelligence (Shipley-Hartford or Satz-Mogel short form of the Wechsler Adult Intelligence Scale-Revised) [WAIS-R] [Shipley, 1946; Satz and Mogel, 1962]); language (Warrington Word Recognition [Warrington, 1984]; Wechsler Memory Scale-Revised (WMS-R) Logical Prose; Boston Naming Test [Kaplan et al., 1983]), verbal memory (Warrington Word Recognition; Rey Auditory Verbal Memory test), visual memory (Warrington Face Recognition; Rey-Osterieth Complex Figure recall), visuoconstructional skills (Warrington Face Recognition; Rey-Osterreith Complex Figure; WAIS-R Block Design [Wechsler, 1981]; WMS-R Visual Reproductions), divided attention (Paced Auditory Serial Addition [Gronwall and Sampson, 1974]; Visual Search [Lewis and Rennick, 1979]; Stroop Color Interference [Stroop, 1935]), and mood (Hamilton Depression and Anxiety scales [Hamilton, 1959, 1960]; MMPI [Hathaway and McKinley, 1966]; Beck Depression Inventory [Beck, 1987]; State-Trait Anxiety Inventory [Speilberger et al., 1970]).

Over the past 4 years, we have had an opportunity to collect an extensive set of data on neuropsychological performance in the MACS cohort of homosexual and bisexual men. The Phase I (neuropsychological screening exam) and Phase II (comprehensive neuropsychological exam) measures have sampled the full range of cognitive domains as traditionally assessed by neuropsychological testing. This approach has provided very detailed information about which measures may be most sensitive to HIV-related changes in cognitive functions, at least among subjects in the MACS.

Principles Used to Develop a Brief Neuropsychological Test Battery

We used a multistage approach to derive a brief neuropsychological assessment battery that would be sensitive to HIV infection. First, we used analysis of variance to identify those measures that best discriminated the performance of patients with late-stage disease (AIDS) from the performance of seronegative

TABLE 8–1.   Neuropsychological Measures Used to Assess
Cognitive Functions in the MACS

Neuropsychological Test	Number of Subjects		
	SN[a]	*ASX SP*[b]	*SX SP*[c]
Grooved Pegboard Symbol Digit Modalities Verbal Fluency (F,A,S) Digit Span (WAIS-R)	769	727	84
Simple and Choice Reaction Time Trail Making A and B	452	402	39
Paced Auditory Serial Addition Warrington Recognition Memory Rey-Osterreith Complex Figure Block Design (WAIS-R) Rey Auditory Verbal Learning	268	257	116
WAIS-R (Satz-Mogel Short Form) WMS-R Subtests[d] Boston Naming Test	121	87	39
Shipley Hartford Visual Search	147	171	76
Stroop Color Interference	236	209	16
CES-D Depression	769	727	84
Beck Depression Inventory State-Trait Anxiety	268	257	116
MMPI Hamilton Depression Scale Hamilton Anxiety Scale	121	87	29

[a]Seronegative

[b]Asymptomatic seropositive

[c]Symptomatic seropositive

[d]The following subtests were included: Logical Prose, Visual Reproductions, Paired Associates, and Mental Control

controls. Second, we identified major areas of cognitive functioning by performing factor analyses using data from the available neuropsychological measures. Finally, we eliminated redundancies among the different neuropsychological measures by selecting the one measure from each cognitive domain derived in the factor analysis that showed the greatest power for discriminating AIDS patients from seronegative controls.

Because of time constraints and other concerns, several of the neuropsychological tests included in the MACS assessment were administered only to subsets of the cohort (Table 8–1). Since none of the subjects received all of the neuropsychological measures, it was not possible to perform omnibus factor analyses or analyses of covariance. Instead, we performed analyses of covariance (using age and education as covariates) separately for each task. Because there were many tests ($n = 24$) and even more individual variables ($n = 56$), it is important to keep in mind that some results may have occurred by chance alone. However, since there is considerable shared variance among the measures, and since the power of each analysis varied in part as a function of the number of subject who completed the test, a simple Bonferroni correction would not be appropriate. Instead, as discussed below, we evaluated the overall trends observed in the data sets across functional domains.

Identification of Tasks Sensitive to HIV-1 Disease

The three groups of subjects (seronegative, asymptomatic seropositive, and symptomatic seropositive) did not differ from each other on measures of pre-morbid intelligence (Satz-Mogel short form of the WAIS-R, Shipley Hartford) or attentional skills (Digit Span, Rey Auditory Verbal Learning Test Trial 1, Symbol Digit Modalities). The groups also did not differ on any of four measures of langauge-related functions or on any of three measures of visuoconstructional abilities. On measures of memory, only two marginal differences were found out of a total of 15 variables assessing verbal and nonverbal memory: (1) symptomatic, seropositive subjects performed worse than seronegative controls on Immediate Recall of the Rey-Osterreith Complex Figure (but not on Delayed Recall of the same figure), and (2) asymptomatic, seropositive subjects performed better than seronegative controls on the Recognition memory subtest of the Rey Auditory Verbal Learning Test.

On measures of speed of processing, symptomatic, seropositive subjects performed significantly slower than seronegative controls on measures of Simple Reaction Time (Trial 3) and Choice Reaction Time (serial pattern matching procedure) but not on any other measures of simple or choice reaction time or on the Paced Auditory Serial Addition Test (PASAT). There was a general trend across all of the reaction time measures for the symptomatic, seropositive group to perform more slowly than the seronegative controls and the asymptomatic, seropositive group.

Measures of divided attention and abstraction were more consistent, with symptomatic, seropositive subjects performing worse than seronegative controls on five out of six measures (Trail-Making Test, Part B, Stroop Color Card, Stroop Word Card, Stroop Interference Card and Symbol Digit Substitution). Some of these differences may be due to generalized motor slowing, since symptomatic seropositive subjects were consistently slower on all three measures of motor skills (Trail Making Test, Part A, Grooved Pegboard Dominant hand, Grooved Pegboard Non-dominant hand).

On measures of mood, symptomatic subjects were consistently more dis-tressed than seronegative controls on measures of depression and anxiety (CES Depression Scale, Beck Depression Inventory, Hamilton Depression Scale, Hamilton Anxiety Scale, MMPI Depression Scale). There were no differences among the groups on the State Trait Anxiety Scale.

These results agree in large part with those of other investigators in identifying motor performance, speed of processing, and abstraction as the main areas of early cognitive deficits in patients with symptomatic HIV disease (AIDS) (e.g., Van Gorp et al., 1989; Perry, 1990). We also found that depression was the area in which the most pronounced differences were found between our symptomatic, seropositive subjects and seronegative controls. More marginal differences in performance were observed for measures of verbal and nonverbal memory.

Identification of Principal Cognitive Domains

We performed two types of factor analysis to identify redundancies among the neuropsychological measures: (1) a single factor analysis looking at those measures completed by most of the study cohort, and (2) a set of eight factor analyses with tasks grouped by functional domains (Memory, Language, Attention, Executive Functions, Motor Functions, Visuoconstructional Functions, Speed of Processing, and Personality). The first factor analysis confirmed that our tests measure at least seven major functional domains: Brief Attention (Digit Span), Verbal Memory (Rey Auditory Verbal Learning Test), Motor Speed (Grooved Pegboard Test), Visuoconstructional Skills (Rey-Osterreith Complex Figure, Wais-R Block Design), Simple Reaction Time, Choice Reaction Time, and Affect (CES Depression Scale, Beck Depression Scale).

In the second set of factor analyses, we combined all of the measures that theoretically measure a specific cognitive function to determine if they would form a single factor or multiple factors. For example, we performed a factor analysis on five measures of language functioning (Rey Auditory Verbal Learning test Trial 1, Trial 5, Recognition Memory, Controlled Oral Word Association—FAS, and Animal Naming) and found that all of these measures loaded on a single factor. We also found single-factor structures for measures of Attention (Digit Span Forward and Backward, Rey Auditory Verbal Learning Test Trial 1, Symbol Digit Modalities); Motor Skills (Grooved Pegboard, dominant and nondominant hands; Trail Making Part A; Symbol Digit Modalities); Visuoconstructional Skills (WAIS-R Block Design, Rey-Osterreith Complex Figure, Warrington Recognition Memory for Faces); and Personality (State-Trait Anxiety Scale, Beck Depression Inventory, CES Depression Scale).

Our measures of Executive functions separated into two factors, with Paced Auditory Serial Addition forming a separate factor from Symbol Digit Modalities, Verbal Fluency, and Trail Making Part B. A similar division was found on our measures of speed of processing, with all simple reaction time measures forming one factor and all choice reaction time measures forming a second factor. The measures of Memory separated into three factors: (1) Verbal Memory (Rey Auditory Verbal Learning Test, Trials 1–5, Trial 1, Recognition Memory); (2) Nonverbal Memory (Rey Complex Immediate and Delayed Recall); and (3) Brief Memory (Digit Span Forward and Backward).

The MACS Brief Neuropsychological Test Battery

These data essentially confirmed that the 24 different neuropsychological measures used in the MACS were measuring a small number of functional domains. Thus, we could legitimately reduce the number of tasks, provided that all of these functional cognitive domains were represented in our final neuropsychological test battery. The final form of this test battery includes the tests shown in Table 8–2.

The brief test battery developed for longitudinal evaluation of cognitive functioning in the MACS includes all of the tests used in this study that have been shown to discriminate the performance of patients with AIDS from the performance of seronegative controls. It includes measures of Verbal (Rey Auditory Verbal Learning Test) and Nonverbal Memory (Rey-Osterreith Complex Figure Recall), Attention (Rey Auditory Verbal Learning Test, Trial 1, Symbol Digit), Visuoconstructional Skills (Rey-Osterreith Complex Figure, Copy), Motor Speed (Trails A, Symbol Digit, Grooved Pegboard), Executive Functions (Trails B, Symbol Digit), Simple and Choice Reaction Time (California Computerized Assessment package), and Mood (CES Depression).

Thus, through detailed analysis of the data collected over the first 4 years of the neuropsychological component of the MACS, we have been able to develop a neuropsychological test battery that is both brief (taking approximately 45 minutes to complete) and sensitive to the earliest symptoms of HIV-induced cognitive impairment. This modification in the neuropsychological study design helps resolve issues of sensitivity and specificity with our two-stage testing design while at the same time greatly increasing the number of subjects involved in the full neuropsychological study.

Implications of a Brief Neuropsychological Test Battery

The development of a brief neuropsychological test battery is important not only for conservation of resources, but also because medically symptomatic, HIV-infected patients may tire easily. In fact, in our studies of reaction time (Miller et al., 1991), we have found statistically significant declines in reaction time performance among symptomatic, HIV-infected subjects over a period of only 20–25 minutes. This implies that the use of neuropsychological test batteries for more than 4–5 hours may suffer from artifacts due solely to constitutionally induced fatigue rather than true cognitive impairment.

The question of which group of tests works best for the assessment of early HIV-related cognitive changes has been the subject of extensive discussion. In a recent review of organic mental disorders associated with HIV, Perry (1990) concluded that there may be "no shortcuts for an extensive (albeit time-consuming and burdensome) one-on-one neuropsychological battery that assesses multiple functions with an emphasis on timed rather than open-ended tasks and requirements for concentration, attention and precise and rapid motor performance" (p. 699). A similar point of view was advanced in a recent publication of recommendations from the National Institutes of Mental Health (NIMH) workshop for neuropsychological assessment approaches to AIDS-related cognitive changes (Butters et al., 1990). The proposed battery includes 25 different neuropsychological tests that cover 10 separate cognitive domains. It requires an estimated 7–9 hours for administration. The NIMH battery is clearly well suited for documenting the full range of neuropsychological deficits associated with HIV infection, although it is, of course, impractical for longitudinal assessment. In the

TABLE 8–2.   Revised MACS Neuropsychological Screening Battery

1. Trail Making Test
   Parts A and B

2. Grooved Pegboard
   Dominant and nondominant hands

3. Symbol Digit Modalities
   Raw score
   Paired recall

4. Rey Auditory Verbal Learning Test
   Trials 1–5
   Interference
   Recall after interference
   Delayed recall
   Delayed recognition

5. Rey-Osterreith Complex Figure Test
   Copy
   Immediate recll
   Delayed recall

6. Stroop Color Interference test

7. California Computerized Assessment Package (CalCAP)
   Simple reaction time
   Choice reaction time
   Serial pattern matching (sequential reaction time)

event that practical considerations preclude administration of the full NIMH battery, a brief (1- to 2-hour) battery of highly sensitive tests is recommended. Surprisingly, the recommendation for the abbreviated battery does not include any tests of motor speed or abstraction, areas of cognitive functioning that are commonly impaired in HIV-associated dementia.

As emphasized by Ingraham et al. (1990), only longitudinal studies will be able to describe accurately the natural history of the cognitive symptoms associated with HIV infection. It remains to be documented whether the various types of cognitive abnormalities found in asymptomatic individuals on cross-sectional assessment are early precursors of an insidious dementia or sporadic or transient abnormalities not specifically related to the effect of the virus on the central nervous system. Similarly, there is a need to determine which of the neuropsychological deficits associated with symptomatic disease (AIDS-related complex and AIDS) are related specifically to the effect of the virus and which ones are secondary to nonspecific factors associated with disease progression (reduced stamina and fatigue, metabolic changes, medication side effects, etc.). The fact that a much greater frequency of neuropsychological abnormalities has been reported among patients with AIDS than current estimates of the incidence of actual dementia cases (15–20%) suggests that not all cases of abnormal neuropsychological functioning will necessarily progress to a clinically significant dementia.

Finally, although the choice of specific test instruments is obviously of considerable importance, there is an equally important need to interpret the findings from the tests in the context of appropriate age- and education-adjusted normative data, as well as to consider other premorbid factors that may influence the outcome of neuropsychological testing. It is also important to consider that one of the most consistent predictors of performance on neuropsychological tests is overall IQ. Although years of education correlates reasonably well with this variable, in most situations greater precision will be achieved in the interpretation of the neuropsychological test findings if a measure of IQ (e.g., the Shipley-Hartford Test or the Satz-Mogel short form of the WAIS-R) is used as a covariate rather than just years of completed education.

The debate concerning the composition of an optimal test battery for assessment of early HIV-associated cognitive changes is likely to go on for some time. It is important to keep in mind that one specific battery is not likely to be optimal for all of the different situations in which assessment of cognitive functioning is indicated. For example, more detailed cross-sectional workup of individual cases may require a comprehensive assessment approach along the lines of the NIMH recommendations. On the other hand, in longitudinal studies of treatment effects in symptomatic patients, a brief, well-focused battery with emphasis on psychomotor speed, memory, and visuoconstructional abilities similar to the battery discussed in this chapter would be more appropriate.

Acknowledgments

With special thanks to all of the loyal participants and the MACS advisory boards in Baltimore, Chicago, Los Angeles, and Pittsburgh. The authors also would like to thank Helena Bacellar, Lisa Jacobson, and others who contributed to the analysis of the data for this report. Supported by Grants NINDS NS 26643, RR 00722, and NAIDA DA 04334.

References

Ayers, M.R., Abrams, D.I., Newell, T.G., and Friedrich, F. (1987). Performance of individuals with AIDS on the Luria Nebraska Neuropsychological Battery. *International Journal of Clinical Neuropsychology, 9*, 101–105.

Beck, A.T. (1987). *Beck Depression Inventory: Manual.* San Antonio, Tex.: Psychological Corporation.

Benton, A.L., Hamsher, K. deS., Varney, N.R., and Spreen, O. (1983). *Contributions to Neuropsychological Assessment.* New York: Oxford University Press.

Bocellari, A., Dilley, J.W., and Shore, M.D. (1988). Neuropsychiatric aspects of AIDS dementia complex: A report on a clinical series. *Neurotoxicology, 9*, 381–390.

Bruhn, P. (1987). AIDS and dementia: A quantitative neuropsychological study of unselected Danish patients. *Acta Neurologica Scandinavica, 76*, 443–447.

Butters, N., Grant, I., Haxby, J., Judd, L.L., Martin, A., McClelland, J., Pequegnat, W., Schachter, D., and Stover, E. (1990). Assessment of AIDS-related cognitive changes: Recommendations of the NIMH Workshop on Neuropsychological Assessment Approaches. *Journal of Clinical and Experimental Neuropsychology, 12*, 963–978.

Cummings, J.L. (1990). *Subcortical Dementia.* New York: Oxford University Press.

DeFilippis, N.A., and McCampbell, E. (1979). *The Booklet Category Test.* Odessa, Fla.: Psychological Assessment Resources.

Derix, M.M.A., de Gans, J., Stam, J., and Portegies, P. (1989). Mental changes in patients with AIDS. *Clinical Neurology and Neurosurgery, 92*, 215–222.

Gastaut, J.L., Bolgert, F., Brunet, D., Cances, A.M., Chave, B., Chieze, F., Dhiver, C., Gastaut, J.A., Gentilini, M., Katlama, C., Pierrot-Desselligny, C., and Signoret, J.L. (1990). Early intellectual impairment in HIV seropositive patients. A longitudinal study (Abst. NPS-33). Paper presented at the meeting Neurological and Neuropsychological Complications of HIV Infection, Monterey, Calif.

Grant, I., Atkinson, J.H., Hesselink, J.R., Kennedy, C.J., Richman, D.D., Spector, S.A., and McCutchan, J.A. (1987). Evidence for early central nervous system involvement in the acquired immunodeficiency syndrome (AIDS) and other human immunodeficiency virus (HIV) infections. *Annals of Internal Medicine, 107*, 828–836.

Gronwall, D.M.A., and Sampson, H. (1974). *The Psychological Effects of Concussion.* Auckland, N.Z.: Auckland University Press.

Grunseit, A., Perdices, M., Dunbar, N., Craven, A., and Cooper, D.A. (1991). The effect of zidovudine on neuropsychological performance in patients with asymptomatic HIV infection (Abst. MB 2060). Paper presented at the VIIth International Conference on AIDS, Florence, Italy.

Hamilton, M. (1959). The assessment of anxiety states by rating. *British Journal of Medical Psychology, 32*, 50–55.

Hamilton, M. (1960). A rating scale for depression. *Journal of Neurology, Neurosurgery and Psychiatry, 23*, 56–62.

Hathaway, S.R., and McKinley, J.C. (1966). *Minnesota Multiphasic Personality Inventory.* New York: Psychological Corporation.

Heaton, R.K. (1981). *Wisconsin Card Sorting Test Manual.* Odessa, Fla.: Psychological Assessment Resources.

Ingraham, L.J., Bridge, T.P., Janssen, R.S., Stover, E., and Mirsky, A.F. (1990). Neuropsychological effects of early HIV-1 infection: Assessment and methodology. *Journal of Neuropsychiatry and Clinical Neurosciences, 2*, 174–182.

Janssen, R.S., Cornblath, D.R., Epstein, L.G., McArthur, J., and Price, R.W. (1989). Human immunodeficiency virus (HIV) infection and the nervous system: Report from the American Academy of Neurology AIDS Task Force. *Neurology, 39*, 119–122.

Joffe, R.T., Rubinow, D.R., Squillace, K., Lane, C.H., Duncan, C.C., and Fauci, A.S. (1986). Neuropsychiatric manifestations of the acquired immune deficiency syndrome (AIDS). *Psychopharmacology Bulletin, 22*, 684–688.

Kaplan, E.F., Goodglass, H., and Weintraub, S. (1983). *The Boston Naming Test.* Philadelphia: Lea & Febiger.

Kløve, H. (1963). Clinical neuropsychology. In F.M. Forster, ed., *The Medical Clinics of North America.* New York: W.B. Saunders, pp. 1647–1658.

Lewis, R.F., and Rinnick, P.M. (1979). *Manual for the Repeatable Cognitive-Perceptual-Motor Battery.* Grosse Point Park, Michigan: Axon.

Lunn, S., Skydsbjerg, M., Schulsinger, H., Parnas, J., Pedersen, C., and Mathiesen, L. (1991). A preliminary report on the neuropsychologic sequelae of human immunodeficiency virus. *Archives of General Psychiatry, 48*, 139–142.

McArthur, J.C., Cohen, B.A., Selnes, O.A., Kumar, A.J., Cooper,. K., McArthur, J.H., Soucy, G., Cornblath, D.R., Chmiel, J.S., Wang, M.C., Starkey, D.L., Ginzburg, H., Ostrow, D.G., Johnson, R.T., Phair, J.P., and Polk, B.F. (1989). Low prevalence of neurological and neuropsychological abnormalities in otherwise healthy HIV-1-

infected individuals: Results from the Multicenter AIDS Cohort Study. *Annals of Neurology, 26*, 601–611.

Miller, E.N., Satz, P., and Visscher, B. (1991). Computerized and conventional neuropsychological assessment of HIV-1 infected homosexual men. *Neurology, 41*, 1608–1616.

Miller, E.N., Selnes, O.A., McArthur, J.C., Satz, P., Becker, J.T., Cohen, B.A., Sheridan, K., Machado, A.M., Van Gorp, W.G., and Visscher, B. (1990). Neuropsychological performance in HIV-1 infected homosexual men: The Multicenter AIDS Cohort Study (MACS). *Neurology, 40*, 197–203.

Morgan, M.K., Clark, M.E., and Hartman, W.L. (1988). AIDS-related dementia: A case report of rapid cognitive decline. *Journal of Clinical Psychology, 44*, 1025–1028.

Perdices, M., and Cooper, D.A. (1990). Neuropsychological investigation of patients with AIDS and ARC. *Journal of Acquired Immune Deficiency Syndrome, 3*, 555–564.

Perry, S.W. (1990). Organic mental disorders caused by HIV: Update on early diagnosis and treatment. *American Journal of Psychiatry, 147*, 696–710.

Perry, S.W., Blesky-Barr, D., Barr, W.B., and Jacobsberg, L. (1989). Neuropsychological function in physically asymptomatic, HIV-seropositive men. *Journal of Neuropsychiatry, 1*, 296–302.

Poutianinen, E., Haltia, M., Elovaara, I., Lahdevirta, J., and Livanainen, M. (1990). Dementia associated with human immunodeficiency virus: Subcortical or cortical? *Acta Psychiatrica Scandinavica, 83*, 297–301.

Radloff, L.S. (1977). The CES-D scale: A self-report depression scale for research in the general population. *Applied Psychological Measurement, 1*, 385–401.

Reitan, R. (1979). *Manual for Administration of Neuropsychological Test Batteries for Adults and Children.* Tucson, Ariz.: Neuropsychology Laboratory.

Robertson, K.R., Wilkins, J., Robertson, W., Van der Horst, C., and Hall, C. (1990). Neuropsychological changes in HIV seropositive subjects over time (Abst. NPS27). Paper presented at the meeting Neurological and Neuropsychological Complications of HIV infection, Monterey, Calif.

Routy, J.P., Allegre, T., Blanc, A.P., Rodriguez, E., Kiegel, P., Vialley, P., and Lagier, E. (1991). Intrathecal zidovudine for AIDS dementia complex (Abst. MB 2050). Paper presented at the VIIth International Conference on AIDS, Florence, Italy.

Satz, P., and Mogel, S. (1962). An abbreviation of the WAIS for clinical use. *Journal of Clinical Psychology, 18*, 77–79.

Selnes, O.A., Miller, E., McArthur, J.C., Gordon, B., Munoz, A., Sheridan, K., Fox, R., and Saah, A.J. (1990). HIV-1 infection: No evidence of cognitive decline during the asymptomatic stages. *Neurology, 40*, 204–208.

Shipley, W.C. (1946). *Institute of Living Scale.* Los Angeles: Western Psychological Services.

Smith, A. (1982). *Symbol digit modalities test. Manual.* Los Angeles: Western Psychological Services.

Speilberger, C.D., Gorsuch, R.L., and Lushene, R.E. (1970). *Manual for the State-Trait Anxiety Inventory.* Palo Alto, Calif.: Consulting Psychologists Press.

Stroop, J.R. (1935). Studies of interference in serial verbal reaction. *Journal of Experimental Psychology, 18*, 643–662.

Tozzi, V., Galagni, S., Gerace, C., Narciso, P., Balestra, P., Sette, P., Meccia, A., Pau, F., and Visco, G. (1991). An open study on zidovudine therapy for ADC: One year follow-up (Abst. MB 2011). Paper presented at the VIIth International Conference on AIDS, Florence, Italy.

Tross, S., Price, R.W., Navia, B., Thaler, H.T., Gold, J., and Sidtis, J.J. (1988). Neuropsychological characterization of the AIDS dementia complex: A preliminary report. *AIDS, 2,* 81–88.

Van Gorp, W.G., Miller, E.N., Satz, P., and Visscher, B. (1989). Neuropsychological performance in HIV-1 immunocompromised patients: A preliminary report. *Journal of Clinical and Experimental Neuropsychology, 11,* 763–773.

Warrington, E.K. (1984). *Recognition Memory Test.* Berkshire, England: Windsor: NFER-Nelson.

Wechsler, D. (1981). *WAIS-R Manual.* New York: Psychological Corporation.

Wilkie, F.L., Eisdorfer, C., Morgan, R., Loewenstein, D.A., and Szapocznik, J. (1990). Cognition in early human immunodeficiency virus infection. *Archives of Neurology, 46,* 433–440.

9

The Utility of Clinical Ratings for Detecting Cognitive Change in HIV Infection

ROBERT K. HEATON, DONALD KIRSON, ROBERT A. VELIN,
IGOR GRANT, and the HNRC GROUP

Central nervous system (CNS) dysfunction is a well-recognized and common complication of human immunodeficiency virus (HIV) infection (Price and Brew, 1988; Price et al., 1988). It has been estimated that two-thirds of acquired immunodeficiency syndrome (AIDS) patients will eventually develop clinically apparent signs of CNS involvement before death (Price and Brew, 1988). AIDS dementia is a particularly disabling neurological complication that typically occurs late in the course of HIV infection, within the context of severe immunosuppression and other medical symptoms (Price et al., 1988). In addition, however, both the 1987 and 1993 Centers for Disease Control (CDC) classification systems for HIV infection indicate that patients can have HIV-associated frank neurological disease before they develop other AIDS-defining medical conditions (CDC, 1987, 1992). There have also been reports of milder HIV-associated neurocognitive impairments even in patients who are not medically symptomatic or seriously immunocompromised, although continuing controversy remains about this phenomenon (World Health Organization, 1988; Grant and Heaton, 1990; Grant et al., 1992).

The neuropsychological literature contains numerous reports of conflicting findings regarding the prevalence of subclinical brain dysfunction in medically asymptomatic, HIV-infected individuals. Recent reviews of this work identified a number of methodological factors that may account for this diversity of results (Grant and Heaton, 1990; Grant et al., 1992; Chapter 6). These factors include differences in (1) subject inclusion and exclusion criteria, (2) the presence and adequacy of control groups, and (3) the nature and comprehensiveness of the neuropsychological testing. In addition, the existing studies differed considerably in the methods they used to analyze and interpret the available neuropsychological test data.

Although most neuropsychological studies have compared HIV-infected groups' and control groups' mean scores on the various tests, in some investigations additional analyses have been directed at determining whether a higher percentage of *individuals* in the infected groups show impairment on various test batteries. This is an important way to look at the data because there are reasons to suspect that group mean comparisons on the tests may fail to detect real group differences in the prevalence of neurocognitive deficits.

Especially in the early stages of HIV infection, only a significant minority (e.g., 25–40%) of individuals may have neurobehavioral impairment. Moreover, such impairment, if present, may affect different patterns of abilities in different people (Heaton et al., in press). If either or both of these conditions apply in the early stages of infection, any existing neuropsychological impairment is likely to be poorly represented in the group means on individual tests; that is, on any given test measure, the good scores of the many subjects who do not have deficits in the ability affected will tend to "wash out" or overshadow the poor scores of the few individuals who are impaired on that measure.

The question to be addressed in this chapter is: What is the best way to establish and compare the prevalence of neurocognitive impairment in HIV-positive and HIV-negative subject groups?

Identifying Cognitive Impairment in Individual Subjects

Some studies have rather arbitrarily classified a subject as impaired if a specified number of neuropsychological test scores were more than one or two standard deviations below the means of some reference group (or groups). In some cases, the reference groups came from other studies and were not comparable to each other or to the HIV-positive group with respect to demographic characteristics that can affect neuropsychological test performance (Grant and Heaton, 1990). Moreover, since no previous studies have established the validity of these test score cutoffs for detecting independently verified cerebral lesions, the sensitivity and clinical significance of these diagnostic classifications are unknown.

Clinical Ratings

Another approach to diagnostic classification in neuropsychological research employs blind clinical ratings of the test data. A major advantage of clinical ratings is that they can give appropriate weight to diverse patterns of mild deficits that together implicate important neurocognitive abilities and/or cerebral systems and therefore suggest an acquired brain disorder. On the other hand, patterns of test results that are more likely to reflect developmental disabilities or educational/cultural disadvantages are given less weight in clinical ratings.

The clinical ratings approach has been used in many large-scale neuropsychological studies of neurological and other medical conditions not associated with HIV. Thus, studies have used this method to classify neurobehavioral impairment associated with structural brain lesions of diverse etiologies (Reitan, 1964; Heaton et al., 1991), multiple sclerosis (Heaton et al., 1985; Filley et al., 1990), chronic alcohol abuse (Grant et al., 1979), polydrug abuse (Grant et al., 1978), chronic obstructive pulmonary disease (Grant et al., 1982, 1987; Heaton et al., 1983), and diabetes mellitus (Ryan et al., 1991). Typically, the clinician raters in these studies have been provided only test data and demographic characteristics of the subjects, and have made a decision as to whether each subject's data suggest a cerebral disorder. Separate ratings may address levels of overall neuropsychological functioning and functioning in several major ability areas (e.g., verbal skills, abstraction, memory) and may classify the dysfunction as being relatively diffuse or as involving one cerebral hemisphere more than the other. Finally, in longitudinal studies, ratings consider whether the subjects' neurobehavioral functioning has remained stable or has gotten significantly better or worse over the test-retest interval (Grant et al., 1978; Heaton et al., 1983; Grant et al., 1987).

The research just cited has demonstrated the reliability and validity of clinical ratings in neuropsychology, both for diagnostic purposes and for detecting even relatively subtle changes in patients' functioning. For example, in a study comparing clinical and automated neuropsychological test interpretations, two experienced clinicians performed independent blind ratings of Halstead-Reitan Battery (HRB) data from 100 normal controls and 150 patients with verified cerebral lesions (Heaton et al., 1981). The clinicians' ratings regarding global levels of neuropsychological functioning were highly correlated ($r = .95$), and in 93% of the cases they agreed on the presence or absence of cerebral dysfunction. Furthermore, the respective raters' diagnostic judgments agreed with the neuroradiological criteria in 91% and 88% of the cases.

In a large-scale longitudinal study of supplemental oxygen treatment in hypoxemic chronic obstructive pulmonary disease, these same independent raters obtained excellent agreement on the presence and degree of baseline neurobehavioral impairment (Grant et al., 1982), as well as the presence and degree of change over successive neuropsychological examinations (Heaton et al., 1983). Also, the clinical change ratings demonstrated significant and predicted differences between treatment conditions, whereas group mean comparisons on the individual test measures were inconclusive.

In a study of recovering alcoholics, Grant et al. (1987) found that the rate of improvement, using blinded clinical ratings, was associated with the length of abstinence. Similarly, polydrug users who discontinued or sharply reduced drug taking improved on clinical ratings of change after a 3-month follow-up, whereas matched controls did not (Grant et al., 1978).

Recently, neuropsychological approaches for assessing HIV-related cognitive changes were considered in a detailed report by a National Institute of

Mental Health (NIMH)-sponsored work group (Butters et al., 1990). Several important recommendations were included in this report. It was noted that sensitivity and comprehensiveness are essential characteristics of test batteries to be employed for early detection of neurocognitive impairment, and that such assessments necessarily involve an extensive set of tests requiring 7–9 hours to administer. Specific tests covering several major ability areas were recommended. Furthermore, based on the available neuroimaging and neuropsychological findings with HIV-positive subjects, it was recognized that neurobehavioral impairment is likely to be quite variable in the early, medically asymptomatic or minimally symptomatic stages of infection (i.e., CDC stages II and III). Therefore, the report also recommended that future neuropsychological studies use blind clinical ratings to establish sensitively the prevalence of clinically significant impairment, in addition to employing group mean comparisons on individual test measures.

The NIMH work group recommendations represent a consensus of several experts regarding the best methods for detecting neuropsychological impairment in HIV-positive groups. Nevertheless, to date there have been no studies demonstrating the superiority of clinical ratings over more direct statistical approaches to identifying neurocognitive impairment in this disease. In this chapter we will explore the relative sensitivities of clinical versus statistical approaches, using baseline neuropsychological data from an ongoing longitudinal study of CNS involvement in HIV infection.

The HIV Neurobehavioral Research Center (HNRC)

The HNRC is an NIMH-funded research center created to examine the etiology, pathogenesis, natural history, and features of neurobehavioral disorders associated with HIV infection. The research program is conducted by investigators from several departments of the School of Medicine of the University of California at San Diego, in collaboration with the Veterans Affairs Medical Center and the U.S. Naval Hospital, San Diego.

Briefly, the HNRC research plan involves multidisciplinary longitudinal assessments of 500 HIV antibody-positive (HIV+) and -negative (HIV−) men over a period of at least 5 years. The core assessments conducted on all subjects include those by medicine, virology, neurology, neuropsychology, neuroradiology, and psychiatry; for subjects who die during the course of the research, postmortem neuropathologic studies also are performed.

For the present analyses, we will focus on the baseline neuropsychological test results of the first 400 subjects entered into the HNRC.

Subject Samples

Our 400 male subjects include 89 HIV− controls, 272 HIV+ subjects in CDC stages II/III and IVc2 (called medically asymptomatic/mildly symptomatic), and

TABLE 9–1. Group Demographic and Immune Status Comparisons

	Controls (n = 89)	HIV + Asymptomatics (n = 272)	HIV + Symptomatics (n = 39)	Pairwise Comparisons[a]
Age				
Mean	34.2	31.2	34.7	A < S, C
(SD)	(8.5)	(6.5)	(4.7)	
Education				
Mean	15.1	13.8	15.0	A < C, S
(SD)	(2.2)	(2.1)	(2.1)	
Race				
% white	84.7	74.1	88.9	N.S.
Absolute T4 cells				
Mean	856.7	481.6	175.4	C > A > S
(SD)	(327.7)	(239.0)	(231.1)	

[a]Significant differences by Tukey-HSD or by chi square with Bonferroni alpha correction (race).
C = controls, A = asymptomatic HIV+, S = symptomatic HIV+.

39 HIV+ subjects in CDC stage IV (called symptomatic).[1] The preponderance of asymptomatic, HIV+ subjects reflects the study's goal of identifying the first appearance of neurobehavioral changes associated with this disease. We wanted to begin following most of our subjects in the earlier, asymptomatic stages of infection, when the expectation was that CNS involvement is either not present or is relatively subtle and of recent onset.

The HIV serological status of all subjects was established by repeatedly positive enzyme-linked immunosorbent assays (ELISA) plus a confirmatory test.

Potential subjects were not entered into the study if they met any of the following exclusion criteria: (1) age greater than 50 or less than 18 years; (2) education less than 10 years; (3) a history of learning disability or attention deficit disorder/hyperkinesis requiring treatment; (4) English as a secondary language and reading skills in English testing below the 10th grade level; (5) any neurological illness predating HIV infection; (6) any history of an event causing loss of consciousness for more than 30 minutes or requiring hospitalization for more than 24 hours due to neurological complications; (7) met DSM-III-R criteria for alcohol or other psychoactive drug use disorder in the preceding year; and (8) past or present intravenous drug abuse. In addition, because a goal of the study was to detect and longitudinally follow the earliest neurobehavioral abnormalities associated with HIV infection, potential HIV+ subjects were excluded if they showed evidence of frank neurological disease related to AIDS at baseline.

The three subject groups' basic demographic and immunocompetence data are summarized in Table 9–1. On average, all groups are in their fourth decade of life and have completed some college. The asymptomatic group is a little younger and averages 1 less year of education than the other two groups, but the

[1]The symptomatic group excluded stage IVc2 subjects because their baseline immune status and health status were much more similar to those of the CDC II/III subjects.

effect of these differences is minimized by the use of demographically corrected neuropsychological scores in all our analyses (see below). Although the HIV+ asymptomatic group had a slightly higher percentage of nonwhite subjects, group differences in race distributions were not statistically significant. The highly significant group differences in T4 lymphocyte counts reflects the known progression of immunodeficiencies in successive stages of HIV infection.

Neuropsychological Testing

All neuropsychological assessments were conducted by trained technicians according to the standard instructions contained in the various test manuals. The extensive test battery takes more than 8 hours to administer to most subjects and was given over at least a 2-day period. Multiple test sessions and rest breaks within sessions were arranged to accommodate the needs of the participants, with the goals being to minimize stress and obtain the best performances of which each subject was capable. Symptomatic subjects were not tested during acute exacerbations of illness.

The comprehensive test battery consists of the Wechsler Adult Intelligence Scale-Revised (Wechsler, 1981), as well as an expanded Halstead-Reitan Battery (HRB) that includes all core Halstead-Reitan tests and the Digit Vigilance Test, the Story Memory Test, the Figure Memory Test, the Boston Naming Test, the Thurstone Word Fluency Test, the Complex Ideational Material subtest of the Boston Diagnostic Aphasia Exam, the Hand Dynamometer Test, and the Grooved Pegboard Test (see test descriptions and additional references in Heaton et al., 1991). Also administered were the Paced Auditory Serial Addition Test (PASAT; Gronwall, 1977) and the oral letter and category fluency tests from the Multilingual Aphasia Examination (Benton and Hamsher, 1976). Table 9–2 lists all 52 test variables that are derived from this battery, grouped into a set of five summary scores and sets of measures covering the eight major ability areas.[2]

For all but 3 test measures in the 52-variable battery, raw scores were converted to age-, education-, and sex-corrected *T*-scores based on results of large samples of normal subjects collected in previous normative studies; these subject samples and the *T*-score conversions are described in detail elsewhere (Thompson and Heaton, 1989; Heaton et al., 1991). Similar procedures were used with data from the present normal control group to convert raw scores to age- and education-corrected *T*-scores on the remaining three tests: the PASAT and the letter and category fluency measures. All *T*-scores are scaled so that higher scores reflect better performance. In large neurologically normal groups, *T*-scores should be normally distributed and should have a mean of 50 and a standard deviation of 10 (Heaton et al., 1991).

---

[2]The first 97 subjects in the study were given a somewhat abbreviated baseline battery, as indicated in Table 9–2. When these subjects were first given the additional tests as part of their longitudinal assessments, their scores did not differ significantly from those of the 303 subjects who completed the full battery at baseline. Thus, the results of the restricted sample given the added tests at baseline are considered representative of those of the total subject group.

TABLE 9–2. Neuropsychological Test Measures

Summary Scores	Psychomotor Skills	Verbal Skills
WAIS-R Verbal IQ[a]	Tactual Performance Test	Aphasia Screening Test[a]
Performance IQ[a]	(four Time scores)	Boston Naming Test[a]
Full Scale IQ[a]	Spatial Relations[a]	Thurstone Word Fluency Test[a]
Halstead Impairment Index	Trails A	Controlled Oral Word Association
Average Impairment Rating[a]	WAIS-R Picture Completion[a]	Category Fluency (animals)[a]
	Picture Arrangement[a]	Complex Ideational Material[a]
	Block Design[a]	WAIS-R Vocabulary
	Object Assembly[a]	Information[a]
	Digit Symbol[a]	Comprehension[a]
		Similarities[a]

Attention/Speed of Information Processing	Abstraction/Flexibility of Thinking	Learning and Incidental Memory
Digit Vigilance (Time and Errors)[a]	Category Test	Story Memory Test—Learning
PASAT (Total Correct)	Trails B	Figure Memory Test—Learning
Seashore Rhythm Test	*Memory*	Tactual Performance Test
Speech Sounds Perception Test	Story Memory Test—Memory[a]	Memory
WAIS-R Digit Span	Figure Memory Test— Memory[a]	Location
Arithmetic[a]	*Sensory Skills*	
	Sensory-Perceptual Exam (Left, Right, Total)	
	Tactile Form Recognition (Left, Right)[a]	
	Motor Skills	
	Finger Tapping Test (Dominant, Nondominant)	
	Hand Dynamometer (Dominant, Nondominant)	
	Grooved Pegboard (Dominant, Nondominant)[a]	

[a]$N = 303$. The first 97 subjects in the study were administered an abbreviated test battery that did not include these measures.

Comparisons of Group Mean T-scores

Group comparisons on the 52 measures in the test battery were performed using analyses of variance followed by post hoc group contrasts with the Tukey-HSD procedure. Table 9–3 presents these results for the five neuropsychological summary scores, which are quite representative of the findings for the entire test battery. On all five measures, the symptomatic HIV+ group was significantly impaired relative to the controls. While the asymptomatic HIV+ group tended to obtain scores that are intermediate between those of the other two groups, their results were much more similar to those of the normal controls than of the symptomatic group.

Similarly, the symptomatic HIV+ group was impaired relative to the controls on 28 of the 52 measures in the full test battery. In addition to the symp-

TABLE 9–3. Group Mean Comparisons of Controls and HIV+ Asymptomatic and Symptomatic Groups on the WAIS-R and HRB Summary *T*-Scores

Summary Score	HIV − Controls Mean (SD)	HIV+ Asymptomatic Mean (SD)	HIV+ Symptomatic Mean (SD)	Pairwise Comparisons[a]
Verbal IQ	49.2 (7.4)	45.8 (9.3)	44.0 (9.5)	S < C
Performance IQ	52.6 (9.1)	51.2 (9.2)	45.1 (13.8)	S < C, A
Full-scale IQ	51.2 (8.1)	48.1 (9.4)	43.1 (11.0)	S < C, A
Halstead imp. index	49.2 (8.6)	47.6 (10.1)	43.5 (10.8)	S < C, A
Average imp. rating	52.6 (11.3)	48.7 (11.5)	39.5 (13.5)	S < C, A

[a]Significant differences by Tukey-HSD procedure, following significant overall analysis of variance.
C = controls, A = asymptomatic HIV+, S = HIV+ symptomatic.

tomatic groups' significantly worse summary scores, they showed deficits on measures of verbal functioning (Boston Naming Test, Thurstone Word Fluency Test, WAIS-R Comprehension and Similarities), abstraction (Category Test), psychomotor skills (Tactual Performance Test-Time, Spatial Relations, and WAIS-R Digit Symbol, Block Design, and Object Assembly), attention and speed of information processing (PASAT, Digit Vigilance Test), learning and incidental memory (Learning component of Story Memory Test, Memory component of the Tactual Performance Test), sensory skills (Tactile Form Recognition Test), and motor skills (Finger Tapping Test, Hand Dynamometer, Grooved Pegboard).

On the other hand, the asymptomatic HIV+ group performed significantly worse than the controls on only 3 of the 52 test measures. This number of "significant" results could well represent chance-level findings, as 2.6 comparisons out of 52 would be expected to be different at the .05 level. The apparent differences occurred only on measures of word retrieval and semantic knowledge (Boston Naming Test, WAIS-R Vocabulary and Information). In the absence of supporting evidence from other tests in the battery, these few relative deficits clearly are insufficient to suggest any acquired CNS impairment in the HIV+ asymptomatic group.

In sum, the results of the group mean comparisons on the neuropsychological test battery reveal impaired neurobehavioral functioning in the symptomatic HIV+ group but not in the asymptomatic HIV+ group. What remains to be determined is whether this reflects a true absence of difference between HIV+ asymptomatics and normal controls or a limitation of the group mean comparison method for detecting neurocognitive impairment in this stage of HIV infection.

Clinical Ratings: Reliability and Group Differences

The HNRC ratings of neuropsychological data are performed using the following 9-point scale: 1 = above-average functioning, 2 = average, 3 = below average, 4 = borderline/atypical, 5 = definite mild impairment, 6 = mild to moderate impairment, 7 = moderate impairment, 8 = moderate to severe impairment, 9

= severe impairment. After rating each of the eight major ability areas listed in Table 9–2, a separate rating is made for global neuropsychological functioning using the same 9-point scale. A score of 5 or higher on the global rating indicates significant neurocognitive impairment that would predict a cerebral disorder in any clinical context. To be rated as definitely impaired globally, the subject must receive an impaired rating on at least two of the eight ability areas; that is, even a severe deficit in a single ability area would not qualify.

The principal investigator of the HNRC neuropsychology core (R.K.H.) performs the clinical ratings, blind to the HIV serostatus and to the CDC stage of the subjects. However, to assess the interrater reliability of these ratings, a random sample of 50 subjects was rated independently by a second experienced neuropsychologist (I.G.). The reliability estimates are listed in Table 9–4. Since the results of the clinical ratings focus on the dichotomous classification of the subject as impaired or not (a clinical rating of 5 or above vs. less than 5), the first two columns in Table 9–4 list the two raters' agreement percentages and Cohen's kappas (Cohen, 1960). These are followed by the Spearman rank order correlations and gamma (Goodman and Kruskal, 1954) estimates of reliability for the ordinal (9-point scale) ratings. Consistent with the results of previous studies of this type, the two clinicians showed a high degree of interrater reliability in both their impairment classifications and their ordinal ratings.

Table 9–5 presents and compares the percentages of subjects in the three groups who were classified as impaired by clinical ratings. In general, the symptomatic HIV+ group showed the highest prevalence of impairment, followed by successively lower prevalence rates in the HIV+ asymptomatic group and the HIV− controls. Impairment rates were significantly higher for symptomatics than for controls in only three of the eight individual ability areas (Attention/Speed of Information Processing, Sensory, Motor) and were significantly higher for asymptomatics than for controls in only one area (Verbal). However, on the *global* rating, both HIV+ groups showed significantly more impairment than did the controls. In fact, the prevalence of impairment in even the HIV+ asymptomatic group was more than twice that in the control group (34.6% vs. 15.7%).

Why was the neuropsychological impairment of the HIV+ symptomatic group detected with both the group mean comparison and clinical rating approaches, whereas only the clinical ratings revealed an increased prevalence of deficits in the HIV+ asymptomatic group? The data in Table 9–5 reveal one reason: A significantly higher percentage of symptomatic than asymptomatic HIV+ subjects were impaired. Other possible reasons might be that the impairment in the HIV+ symptomatic group was more severe and/or affected more abilities than did the impairment in the asymptomatics. To explore these possibilities, additional analyses were performed on the results of the subjects in both HIV+ groups who were classified as impaired on their global ratings.

Considering the global ratings of only the impaired HIV+ subjects, three times as many symptomatics as asymptomatics were rated as having more than mild overall impairment (16% vs. 47%; χ^2 $(df = 1) = 9.3, p = .002$). Thus, when deficits existed in the symptomatic group, they tended to be more severe than those in the asymptomatic group. Furthermore, there was a nonsignificant trend for impaired symptomatic subjects to have more abilities affected: 78% of these

TABLE 9–4. Interrater Reliability of Dichotomous (Impaired vs. Unimpaired) and Ordinal (9-Point Scale) Clinical Ratings ($N = 50$)

Ability Area	Impairment Classification		Ordinal Ratings	
	% Agreement	Kappa	Rho	Gamma
Verbal	90	.70	.89	.94
Abstraction	94	.81	.91	.96
Psychomotor	96	.90	.91	.95
Attention	94	.85	.85	.86
Learning	92	.83	.92	.94
Memory	92	.70	.92	.95
Sensory	96	.88	.92	.94
Motor	90	.73	.82	.87
Global	92	.84	.91	.94

subjects had three or more deficient ability areas compared to 57% of the impaired asymptomatic subjects (χ^2 ($df = 1$) = 3.2, $p = .07$).

Table 9–6 shows the distributions of ability deficits in the two impaired HIV+ subgroups. In both subgroups the two most prevalent cognitive deficits are in the areas of attention/speed of information processing and learning efficiency, which would be consistent with relatively greater subcortical than cortical involvement. Of more interest in the present context, however, is the variable pattern of deficits that is particularly apparent in the asymptomatic subjects. Even in the minority of subjects who were classified as impaired on their global ratings, there is little consistency in which of their abilities are affected. In the impaired asymptomatic subgroup, no more than 62% of subjects had any single ability affected, and most abilities were deficient in fewer than one-half of the subjects.

To summarize the results of the clinical ratings, they suggest a significantly increased risk of neurocognitive impairment in both the medically symptomatic and the asymptomatic stages of HIV infection. It is important to note, however, that only a minority of our subjects in both stages of infection gave evidence of CNS dysfunction, and that neuropsychological impairment was significantly less prevalent in the asymptomatic group. Furthermore, when HIV+ asymptomatic subjects did show neuropsychological impairment it tended to be milder, to affect fewer abilities, and to be especially variable in terms of which abilities were involved. All of these characteristics would be expected to reduce the impacts of existing deficits on the results of group mean comparisons on individual neuropsychological test measures.

Statistical Approaches to Establishing the Prevalence of Impairment

The above results strongly suggest that the group mean comparison approach has significant limitations in its ability to detect the relatively subtle and variable

TABLE 9–5. Percentage of Subjects Classified as Impaired by Clinical Ratings

Ability Area	HIV− Controls (n = 89)	HIV+ Asymptomatics (n = 272)	HIV+ Symptomatics (n = 39)	Pairwise Comparisons[a]
Verbal	7.9	20.0	18.0	A > C
Abstraction	5.6	9.2	20.5	N.S.
Psychomotor	9.0	14.3	20.5	N.S.
Attention	15.7	23.6	43.6	S > A, C
Learning	16.9	26.6	30.8	N.S.
Memory	16.9	15.8	23.1	N.S.
Sensory	6.7	11.0	23.1	S > A, C
Motor	7.9	15.4	41.0	S > A, C
Global	15.7	34.6	48.7	S > A > C

[a]Groups significantly different by chi square with Bonferroni alpha corrections.
C = controls, A = HIV+ asymptomatics, S = HIV+ symptomatics.

types of neurobehavioral deficits that exist in some HIV+ asymptomatic subjects. Nevertheless, it remains possible that the clinical ratings method is not the only approach that can detect such impairment.

In this section, we will explore the performance of three statistical approaches to classifying subjects as impaired or unimpaired. To establish the cut points that define impairment for these approaches, we will identify those points that yield prevalence estimates in the control group that are approximately equal to those established by the clinical ratings. Thus, for comparison purposes, we will force all four methods to have equal specificity and then explore possible differences in sensitivity to HIV-related neurobehavioral impairment. Implicit in this approach are the assumptions that (1) at the outset, the clinical ratings provide the best available estimates of actual impairment but that (2) the method that provides the best group separation while maintaining a clinically relevant specificity rate is to be preferred.

Two of the statistical methods employed here are similar to those used in previous studies of neuropsychological deficits associated with HIV infection: that is, impairment is defined according to the number of scores in the total test battery that are either one or two standard deviations below the means of some reference group or groups. However, there are two potential improvements in the present use of this approach. First, it will be applied to the results of a more comprehensive test battery that has already been shown (by clinical ratings) capable of detecting differences between HIV− controls and both symptomatic and asymptomatic HIV+ groups. Second, the one and two standard deviation cutoffs used in the present study are demographically corrected and are based upon large normative subject samples (Thompson and Heaton, 1989; Heaton et al., 1991).

The third statistical approach is a little more complex. Instead of simply counting the number of impaired scores in the battery, it considers both the number and the severity of deficits detected. In this approach, all demographically corrected T-scores on individual test measures are converted to impairment

TABLE 9–6. Group Comparisons on Percentage of Impaired Subjects with Deficits in Each Ability Area

Ability Area	HIV+ Asymptomatics (n = 94)	HIV+ Symptomatics (n = 19)	p^a
Verbal	48.9	36.8	N.S.
Abstraction	22.6	42.1	.08
Psychomotor	34.0	42.1	N.S.
Attention	50.0	84.2	.006
Learning	61.7	52.6	N.S.
Memory	34.0	42.1	N.S.
Sensory	26.6	42.1	N.S.
Motor	33.0	57.9	0.04

[a]Significance level by chi square.

ratings ranging from 0 (no impairment) to 5 (severe impairment) and then are averaged to create a "deficit score."[3] The resulting global deficit score measure is similar to the well-known Average Impairment Rating from the HRB interpretation system that was developed by Russell et al. (1970). Again, however, our summary measure is based on a much more comprehensive battery, and the component scores are all demographically corrected.

For present purposes, we will focus on classifications of *overall* impairment, using all of the test measures available on each subject (exclusive of summary scores).[4] As noted above, the first 97 subjects were administered a somewhat abbreviated test battery at baseline, although most subjects ($n = 303$) were given the full test battery described in Table 9–2. In all cases, both the clinical ratings and the statistical approaches were applied to the same test measures (i.e., the abbreviated battery for 97 subjects and the full battery for the rest).

Figure 9–1 displays the results achieved by the four classification approaches. All four approaches revealed a significantly greater prevalence of neurobehavioral impairment in the HIV+ symptomatic group than in the HIV− controls. In addition, the clinical ratings and the deficit score method both showed highly significant differences ($p < .01$) between the controls and the HIV+ asymptomatic group.

Neither the one standard deviation nor the two standard deviation cutoff approach significantly discriminated between the HIV+ asymptomatics and the HIV− controls. However, the former (one standard deviation) approach almost reached significance, with impairment prevalence estimates of 15.7% for controls and 25.4% for HIV+ asymptomatics (χ^2 ($df = 1$) = 3.5, $p = .06$).

Of the three statistical approaches to classifying impairment in individuals, the deficit scores yielded group prevalence estimates that are closest to those

[3]The conversions from *T*-scores to impairment ratings are as follows: >39 $T = 0$; 35–39 $T = 1$; 30–34 $T = 2$; 25–29 $T = 3$; 20–24 $T = 4$; <20 $T = 5$. These *T*-score ranges correspond to the levels of impairment described in Heaton et al. (1991).

[4]Classifications also can be made regarding the presence or absence of impairment in the specific ability areas defined in Table 9–2, although these will not be presented in this chapter.

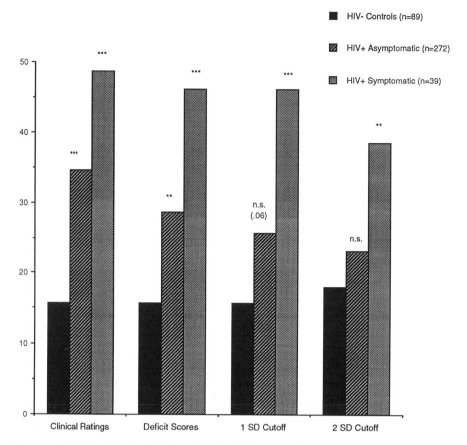

FIGURE 9–1. Results of clinical and statistical approaches for estimating prevalence of neurobehavioral impairment for HIV− and HIV+ subject groups.

achieved by the clinical ratings. Figure 9–2 also shows that the deficit scores and clinical ratings agreed on the presence or absence of neuropsychological impairment in 89% of HIV+ subjects. This high agreement rate for the two different methods approaches that of the two clinical raters using the same method (89–92%). If the clinical ratings are considered the gold standard in classifying neuropsychological impairment, the results in Figure 9–2 further estimate that deficit scores have a sensitivity of 0.77 and a specificity of 0.96 in this population. Thus, the deficit scores are quite accurate in predicting the outcomes of the more complex and time-consuming clinical ratings and appear to represent a useful, completely objective approach to identifying clinically significant neurobehavioral impairment in HIV+ individuals.

In summary, while all classification approaches easily demonstrate an increased rate of impairment among symptomatic HIV+ subjects, they differ in their sensitivity to the subtler impairments among asymptomatic HIV+ subjects. Of the three statistical approaches, the deficit scores provide the best discrimination between HIV− controls and HIV+ asymptomatics. On the other hand,

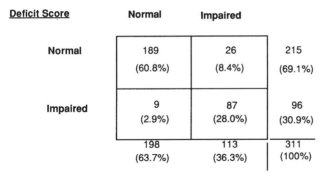

FIGURE 9–2. Comparison of clinical and deficit score impairment classifications for HIV+ subjects.

the statistical approach that uses a two standard deviation cutoff appears to be the least adequate method for detecting neurobehavioral impairment associated with HIV infection; its sensitivity to impairment in the symptomatic group was less than that of the other approaches, and it was the only neuropsychological classification procedure that did not even come close to separating the HIV− controls from the HIV+ asymptomatic subjects.

Summary and Conclusions

The goal of this chapter was to explore the effectiveness of clinical and statistical methods for analyzing neurobehavioral data in studies of HIV infection. Especially if one wants to detect subclinical CNS involvement that may occur in the early stages of infection, it is assumed that a comprehensive test battery is needed (Butters et al., 1990). However, once an adequate test battery has been administered, the question remains of how best to analyze the results to establish whether or not there are increased risks for impairment in various HIV+ groups.

The methods we considered include group mean comparisons on the test scores, as well as both clinical and statistical approaches to classifying individual subjects as being impaired or unimpaired. All of these methods have been used in previous studies of neurobehavioral impairment in HIV infection, and it has been proposed that differences in the sensitivity of the methods may at least partly account for differences in study outcome (especially in studies of subjects in the earlier stages of infection).

To compare the effectiveness of the different data-analytic methods, we used test results from the first 400 subjects of a large, multidisciplinary study of CNS involvement in HIV infection. The subjects consisted of HIV− controls, HIV+ subjects who were relatively free of medical symptomatology, and symptomatic HIV+ subjects. The middle group was the largest, and was of greatest interest because of the conflicting conclusions in the literature about the possibility of

CNS dysfunction in some medically asymptomatic HIV+ subjects. As expected, the symptomatic HIV+ group was seriously immunocompromised, whereas the immune status of the asymptomatic group was intermediate between that of the controls and the symptomatics.

The results of group mean comparisons on the various test measures revealed significant widespread neurobehavioral impairment in the symptomatic HIV+ group. This impairment was observed on all summary scores in our expanded HRB, as well as on individual tests of verbal skills, psychomotor skills, abstraction and flexibility of thinking, attention and speed of information processing, learning and incidental memory, and sensory-perceptual and motor skills. However, group mean comparisons showed no difference between HIV+ asymptomatic subjects and HIV− controls. If this were the only data analytic approach used in the study, the clear (but erroneous) conclusion would be that there is no increased risk of neurobehavioral impairment among HIV+ subjects who are not seriously immunocompromised and medically symptomatic.

Our suspicion about the relative insensitivity of the group mean comparison approach was confirmed by the results of blind clinical ratings of individual subjects' neurobehavioral test data. Consistent with the results of previous neuropsychological studies of other diseases, the clinical ratings were found to be highly reliable and sensitive to even fairly subtle and "spotty" deficits. The clinical ratings revealed more than a threefold increase in impairment among medically symptomatic HIV+ subjects (49% vs. 16% for controls) but also more than a twofold increase among asymptomatic HIV+ subjects (35% vs. 16%); both of these group differences are highly significant ($p < .001$). Thus, the correct conclusion from our results is that there *is* some increased risk of neurobehavioral impairment even in medically asymptomatic HIV+ persons, but that this impairment is unlikely to be detected in studies that rely solely on group mean comparisons on individual test measures.

Why are clinical ratings so much more sensitive to neuropsychological deficits in medically asymptomatic HIV+ subjects? Further analyses of the clinical rating results provide several reasons for this finding. First, only a minority of asymptomatic subjects show significant impairment (35% vs. 49% in symptomatic subjects). In addition, the impairment that exists in asymptomatics is milder and involves fewer abilities than the impairment in symptomatics. Finally, in asymptomatics there is less consistency regarding *which* abilities are affected. In those HIV+ subgroups that showed neuropsychological impairment, 84% of symptomatics had deficits in the area of attention and speed of information processing, whereas substantially fewer impaired asymptomatics had deficits in any single ability area (see Table 9–6). It is not surprising that group mean comparisons are insensitive to mild, spotty deficits that occur in only about one-third of our asymptomatic HIV+ subjects; on each individual test measure, the good performances of the large majority of asymptomatic subjects overshadow the mild deficits of the few. On the other hand, clinicians are able to detect varying patterns of mild deficits in individual subjects. Also, even mild deficits can have important effects on everyday functioning and therefore are of considerable clinical significance (Heaton and Pendleton, 1981).

Although the use of clinician ratings of neuropsychological test data has advantages of sensitivity and flexibility, this approach is quite time-consuming and requires the availability of raters with considerable training and experience in test interpretation. Also, despite repeated demonstrations of the reliability of this method, to some it may appear rather subjective, and therefore less rigorous and convincing than strictly statistical methods. For this reason, it is noteworthy that the global deficit score from our test battery proved sensitive to neuropsychological impairment in both the symptomatic and asymptomatic HIV+ subject groups. In fact, this entirely objective summary score had adequate sensitivity and excellent specificity in replicating the diagnostic classifications made through clinical ratings (see Figures 9–1 and 9–2).

Like the clinician ratings, the deficit score approach considered the full range of test scores generated by the neuropsychological battery. The later scores are demographically corrected and have the same distributional properties in normals, so that standard cutoffs for defining impairment yield consistent diagnostic specificity for all test measures (Heaton et al., 1991). Also, both the clinical ratings and the deficit scores give increasing weight to deficits of increasing severity.

The clinician rating process does have additional complexities, such as the use of test score pattern analyses and consideration of pathognomonic signs of cerebral dysfunction (e.g., Reitan, 1966). Future research might investigate whether algorithms for considering pattern and pathognomonic features of test data add significantly to the current deficit score approach in detecting early CNS involvement associated with HIV infection.[5] However, such algorithms are likely to be most helpful with neurological conditions that cause more focal CNS damage than is usually seen with HIV infection (especially in its early stages). In any case, it would be difficult to improve substantially on the success achieved by deficit scores in predicting clinician diagnostic classifications in the current study.

Finally, in future research, it would be interesting to compare different approaches to neuropsychological test interpretation in association with other aspects of HIV-related CNS disease. Studies should determine whether the different neuropsychological methods vary in their abilities to predict *nonbehavioral* evidence of CNS involvement, such as abnormalities on magnetic resonance imaging and dynamic brain imaging, or increases in neurotoxins and beta-2-microglobulin in the cerebrospinal fluid of infected individuals (Brew et al., 1989; Heyes et al., 1991; McCutchan et al., 1991). Also, neuropsychological approaches should be used to predict important aspects of HIV infected persons' everyday functioning, such as changes in employment status and job functioning. Longitudinal studies should determine whether baseline evidence of subclinical CNS dysfunction predicts future development of the clinically apparent syndromes of minor cognitive motor disorders and HIV-associated dementias (American Academy of Neurology AIDS Task Force, 1991). Results of such studies would provide further information about which neuropsychological methods are best for studying HIV-related CNS disorders, and would answer substantive questions about the causes and clinical significance of neurobehavioral impairment in the earlier stages of HIV infection. As we have seen, such impairment can be detected with some neuropsychological analytic approaches but not with others.

---

[5]Examples of such algorithms can be seen in Russell et al. (1970) and Reitan and Wolfson (1988).

Acknowledgments

The principal support for this work was provided by NIMH Center Grant 5P50 MH45294 (HIV Neurobehavioral Research Center). The views expressed in this chapter are those of the authors and do not reflect the official policy or position of the Department of the Navy, the Department of Defense, or the U.S. government. In the public domain.

References

American Academy of Neurology AIDS Task Force. (1991). Nomenclature and research case definitions for neurologic manifestations of human immunodeficiency virus-type 1 (HIV-1) infection. *Neurology, 41*, 778–785.

Benton, A.L., and Hamsher, K. deS. (1976). *Multilingual Aphasia Examination.* Iowa City: University of Iowa.

Brew, B.J., Bhalla, R.B., Fleisher, M., Paul, M., Khan, A., Schwartz, M.K., and Price, R.W. (1989). Cerebrospinal fluid beta-2-microglobulin in patients infected with human immunodeficiency virus. *Neurology, 39*, 830–834.

Butters, N., Grant, I., Haxby, J., Judd, L.L., Martin, A., McClelland, J., Pequegnat, W., Schacter, D., and Stover, E. (1990). Assessment of AIDS-related cognitive changes: Recommendations of the NIMH Workshop on Neuropsychological Assessment Approaches. *Journal of Clinical and Experimental Neuropsychology, 12*, 963–978.

Centers for Disease Control. (1987). Revision of the CDC surveillance case definition for acquired immunodeficiency syndrome. *Morbidity and Mortality Weekly Report, 36*(Suppl. 1S), 3S–15S.

Centers for Disease Control. (1992). 1993 revised classification system for HIV infection and expanded surveillance case definition for AIDS among adolescents and adults. *Morbidity and Mortality Weekly Report, 41*, 1–19.

Cohen, J. (1960). C coefficient of agreement for nominal scales. *Educational and Psychological Measurement, 20*, 37–46.

Filley, C.M., Heaton, R.K., Thompson, L.L., Franklin, G.M., and Nelson, L.M. (1990). Effects of disease course on neuropsychological functioning in multiple sclerosis. In S.M. Rao, ed., *Multiple Sclerosis: A Neuropsychological Perspective.* New York: Oxford University Press, pp. 135–148.

Goodman, L.A., and Kruskal, W.H. (1954). Measures of association for cross classifications. *Journal of the American Statistical Association, 49*, 732–764.

Grant, I., Adams, K.M., Carlin, A.S., Rennick, P., Judd, L.L., and Schoof, K. (1978). The collaborative neuropsychological study of polydrug users. *Archives of General Psychiatry, 35*, 1063–1074.

Grant, I., Adams, K.M., and Reed, R. (1979). Normal neuropsychological abilities of alcoholic men in their late 30's. *American Journal of Psychiatry, 136*, 1263–1269.

Grant, I., Caun, K., Kingsley, D.P.E., Winer, J., Trimble, M.R., and Pinching, A.J. (1992). Neuropsychological and NMR abnormalities in HIV infection. The St. Mary's-Queen Square study. *Neuropsychiatry, Neuropsychology, and Behavioral Neurology, 5*, 185–193.

Grant, I., and Heaton, R.K. (1990). Human immunodeficiency virus-type 1 (HIV-1) and the brain. *Journal of Consulting and Clinical Psychology, 58*(1), 22–30.

Grant, I., Heaton, R.K., McSweeny, A.J., Adams, K.M., and Timms, R.M. (1982). Neuropsychological findings in hypoxemic chronic obstructive pulmonary disease. *Archives of Internal Medicine, 142*, 1470–1476.

Grant, I., Prigatano, G.P., Heaton, R.K., McSweeny, A.M., Wright, E.C., and Adams, K.M. (1987). Progressive neuropsychological impairment in relation to hypoxemia in chronic obstructive pulmonary disease. *Archives of General Psychiatry, 44*, 999–1006.

Gronwall, D.M.A. (1977). Paced auditory serial-addition task: A measure of recovery from concussion. *Perceptual and Motor Skills, 44*, 367–375.

Heaton, R.K., and Pendleton, M.G. (1981). Use of neuropsychological tests to predict adult patients' everyday functioning. *Journal of Consulting and Clinical Psychology, 49*, 807–821.

Heaton, R.K., Grant, I., Anthony, W.Z., and Lehman, R.A.W. (1981). A comparison of clinical and automated interpretation of the Halstead-Reitan Battery. *Journal of Clinical Neuropsychology, 3*, 121–141.

Heaton, R.K., Grant, I., and Matthews, C.G. (1991). *Comprehensive Norms for an Expanded Halstead-Reitan Battery: Demographic Corrections, Research Findings, and Clinical Applications.* Odessa, Fla.: Psychological Assessment Resources.

Heaton, R.K., McSweeny, A.J., Grant, I., Adams, K.M., and Petty, T.L. (1983). Psychological effects of continuous and nocturnal oxygen therapy in hypoxemic chronic obstructive pulmonary disease. *Archives of Internal Medicine, 143*, 1941–1947.

Heaton, R.K., Nelson, L.M., Thompson, D.S., Burks, J.S., and Franklin, G.M. (1985). Neuropsychological findings in relapsing-remitting and chronic-progressive multiple sclerosis. *Journal of Consulting and Clinical Psychology, 53*, 103–110.

Heaton, R.K., Velin, R.A., Atkinson, H.J., Gulevich, S.J., McCutchan, J.A., Hesselink, J.R., Chandler, J.L., Grant, I., and the HNRC Group (in press). Neuropsychological impairment in an HIV-positive male cohort. In A. Baum and M. Stein, eds., *Perspectives on Behavioral Medicine.* East Sussex, England: Erlbaum.

Heyes, M.P., Brew, B.J., Martin, A., Price, R.W., Salazar, A.M., Sidtis, J.J., Yergey, J.A., Mouradian, M.M., Sadler, A.E., Keilp, J., Rubinow, D., and Markey, S.P. (1991). Quinolinic acid in cerebrospinal fluid and serum in HIV-1 infection: Relationship to clinical and neurological status. *Annals of Neurology, 29*, 202–209.

McCutchan, J.A., Gulevich, S., Durand, D., Velin, R., Heaton, R., Thal, L., Villasana, D., Kaplanski, M., Malone, J., Chandler, J., Atkinson, J., and Grant, I. (1991). Cerebrospinal fluid (CSF) beta-2 microglobulin (B2M) is increased in non-demented neurocognitively-impaired men with HIV-1 infection. Paper presented at the Seventh International Conference on AIDS, Florence, Italy.

Price, R.W., and Brew, B.J. (1988). The AIDS dementia complex. *Journal of Infectious Diseases, 158*, 1079–1083.

Price, R.W., Brew, B., Sidtis, J., Rosenblum, M., Scheck, A.C., and Cleary, P. (1988). The brain and AIDS: Central nervous system HIV-1 infection and AIDS dementia complex. *Science, 239*, 586–592.

Reitan, R.M. (1964). Psychological deficits resulting from cerebral lesions in man. In J.M. Warren and K.A. Akert, eds., *The Frontal Granular Cortex and Behavior.* New York: McGraw-Hill, pp. 295–312.

Reitan, R.M. (1966). A research program on the psychological effects of brain lesions in human beings. In N.R. Ellis, ed., *International Review of Research in Mental Retardation,* Vol. I. New York: Academic Press, pp. 153–218.

Reitan, R.M., and Wolfson, D. (1988). *Traumatic Brain Injury,* Vol. II, *Recovery and Rehabilitation.* Tucson, Ariz.: Neuropsychology Press.

Russell, E.W., Neuringer, C., and Goldstein, G. (1970). *Assessment of Brain Damage: A Neuropsychological Key Approach.* New York: Wiley.

Ryan, C.M., Adams, K.M., Heaton, R.K., Grant, I., Jacobson, A.M., and the DCCT Research Group. (1991). Neurobehavioral assessment of medical patients in clinical trials: The DCCT experience. In E. Mohr and P. Brouwers, eds., *Handbook of Clinical Trials: The Neurobehavioral Approach.* Amsterdam: Swets and Zeitlinger, pp. 215–241.

Thompson, L.L., and Heaton, R.K. (1989). A comparison of the WAIS and WAIS-R using T-score conversions that correct for age, education and sex. *Journal of Clinical and Experimental Neuropsychology, 11*, 478–488.

Wechsler, D. (1981). *WAIS-R Manual.* New York: Psychological Corporation.

World Health Organization (1988, March). Report of the Consultation on the Neuropsychiatric Aspects on HIV Infection. Paper presented at the Global Programme on AIDS, Geneva, Switzerland.

10

Everyday Functioning and Its Relationship to Cognitive Impairment in HIV Disease

ROBERT A. VELIN, ROBERT K. HEATON,
IGOR GRANT, and the HNRC GROUP

Infection with Human Immunodeficiency Virus type-1 (HIV-1) can have a wide variety of effects on the individual patient, as well as on society at large. While HIV on the individual level has an obviously deleterious effect on the immune system and general medical well-being of the infected person (an effect that generally occurs over the course of several years), it also has consequences in other important areas of life. For example, a recent study indicated that movement into the symptomatic stages of HIV disease was associated with a significant decrease in rate of employment and, for those patients who remained employed, in level of income (Ganz et al., in press). Not only does this lead to possible financial hardship for the individual, but society also suffers from the loss of a productive worker. In addition, recent changes in legislation mean that more energy must now be devoted to keeping individuals with medical disabilities on the job. Understanding what real-life difficulties might arise from specific disease processes is the first step in attempting to deal with potential changes in workers' abilities. Thus, in addition to the obvious medical aspects, there are many other HIV-related effects on both the individual and society that should not be overlooked.

It has been well established that HIV can have a significant impact on the central nervous system (CNS), especially during the later, symptomatic stages of infection (Janssen et al., 1989; Grant and Atkinson, 1990; Grant and Heaton, 1990; Miller, et al., 1990; Lunn et al., 1991; Heaton et al., in press-a). Often this is manifested by a mild level of CNS dysfunction that may not be obvious on a routine examination. In addition to evidence regarding late-stage CNS effects, there is mounting evidence that HIV can have a negative impact on the CNS even during the early, asymptomatic or mildly symptomatic stages of disease (Grant et al., 1987; Perry et al., 1989; Koralnik et al., 1990; McKegney et al., 1990; Wilkie et al., 1990; Bornstein et al., 1991; Lunn et al., 1991; Stern et al., 1991), long before the infected person begins to show signs of serious immunological compromise. An important question that remains largely unanswered is whether this usually mild neuropsychological impairment is clinically significant. That is, does the impairment have any real-life implication or is it simply a subtle phenomenon that can be appreciated only as the result of a neuropsychological laboratory evaluation, with no important relationship to health status, disease progression, or the ability to carry out essential everyday tasks and activities?

Neuropsychological Findings and Disease Progression

Whether and how neuropsychological functioning may relate to disease progression are important questions, and although they are not yet fully answered, there is evidence that the development of frank dementia during the course of HIV infection is related to rapid physical deterioration (Day et al., 1992). In addition, a recent study has suggested that cognitive impairment is associated with increased mortality in HIV-infected men. Mayeux and his colleagues (1993) found that in their sample of 111 homosexual, seropositive men, those with neuropsychological impairment had a significantly higher risk of death over a 3-year follow-up period than neuropsychologically normal individuals. Using Cox proportional-hazard models, they demonstrated that the mortality risk ratio for neuropsychologically impaired subjects was 2.9. Stated in different terms, neuropsychologically impaired subjects were almost three times more likely to die than were nonimpaired subjects over the 3-year follow-up period. The mortality risk ratio increased to 4.1 when the model was adjusted for the impact of other baseline variables, including CD4 and red blood cell counts, age, HIV-related motor symptoms, and azidothymidine (AZT) use. When time-dependent variables (eg., change in CD4 count) were included in the model, the risk ratio increased to 4.7.

The findings from the Day and Mayeux studies suggest that neuropsychological status as a potential marker for disease progression warrants further exploration. Several long-term longitudinal studies are currently underway that can further address these issues.

Neuropsychology and Everyday Functioning

Although definitive conclusions regarding the clinical relevance of neurocognitive impairment in predicting disease progression cannot yet be drawn, there is evidence that the impairment is clinically relevant because it affects the ability to carry out essential everyday tasks and activities. Examining how and when neurocognitive impairment may affect everyday functioning, however, requires a movement away from using neuropsychological data simply for diagnostic purposes and toward relating performance on specific tests to the ability to function in the real world in specific environments. This change in direction reflects the role that neuropsychologists are increasingly being asked to play. That is, consumers frequently want to know not only whether neurocognitive impairment is present and what abilities are affected, but also what this impairment means in terms of a person's ability to carry out everyday tasks and activities. We will begin addressing this issue by presenting an overview of our current knowledge of the relationship between neuropsychological findings and everyday functioning in general. Then we will focus specifically on what is known about this relationship in the context of HIV infection.

Historical Background

Attempting to relate neuropsychological performance to measures of everyday functioning is not a new endeavor. Over the years, numerous investigators have acknowledged that the prediction of real-life functioning from neuropsychological data is both feasible and worthwhile. Since the concept of everyday functioning covers a wide variety of potential activities, however, it is necessary to define the concept operationally in a manner that lends itself to measurement and research. Frequently this has been accomplished by defining it in terms of academic success, rehabilitational progress, employment status, or vocational functioning.

Early research showed that even the most general measures of neurocognitive functioning (intelligence tests) are related to important measures of everyday functioning. Matarazzo (1972), for example, provided several illustrations of the relationships between general intelligence and measures of academic achievement, vocational attainment, and socioeconomic status. Thus, the fact that more precise measures of specific cognitive abilities can relate to everyday functioning should not be surprising.

Along these lines, data emerging from studies of several neuropsychiatric patient groups indicate that the results of comprehensive neuropsychological examinations accurately predict employment and other aspects of everyday functioning. For example, Heaton and his colleagues (1978) demonstrated that they could use data from an extended Halstead-Reitan Neuropsychological Battery (HRB) to predict accurately the employment status of 85% of the patients referred to them for evaluation. This high level of predictive accuracy was replicated in a separate study of patients with stable neurological conditions when they used a single HRB summary score to classify correctly 78% of patients as either employed or unemployed over a 6-month follow-up period (Newnan et al., 1978).

Rao and his colleagues (1991) had similar success in predicting employment status in their study of patients with multiple sclerosis. They found that neuropsychological functioning was significantly related to employment status independent of the patients' physical and psychiatric symptoms. Furthermore, they demonstrated that patients with neuropsychological impairment experienced greater difficulty in performing even routine household tasks.

Another group of researchers found that in their sample of patients with closed head injury, neuropsychological performance on a modified version of the Lezak Tinker Toy test (Lezak, 1982) was clearly related to employment status over a 2-year period (Bayless et al., 1989). More specifically, in a group of 50 adult patients who had experienced a closed-head injury (and who had no resultant physical disabilities), they found that nearly one-half of the 25 patients who were unable to work or sustain competitive employment scored below the worst control subject on this neuropsychological test. In stark contrast, of the 25 patients who had returned to work, all but one scored normally on the test.

As this abbreviated review shows (for more detailed discussion, see Heaton and Pendleton, 1981; Chelune and Moehle, 1986), neuropsychological tests can indeed be useful in predicting some aspects of everyday functioning. Given that mild neurocognitive impairment is common in persons with acquired immunodeficiency syndrome (AIDS), and may also occur in medically symptomatic HIV+ persons, it is important to determine whether such subclinical cognitive disorders have measurable effects on the ability to work and perform day-to-day tasks.

Neuropsychology, Everyday Functioning, and HIV Infection

Determining the everyday implications of neurocognitive defects in AIDS is particularly difficult because of the nature of the disease and the deficits. That is, the accompanying physical symptoms, emotional distress, and progressive nature of the disease can make it difficult to determine why someone is unemployed or having vocational difficulties. In addition, an HIV-infected person who is not diagnosed as having AIDS may be experiencing significant fatigue and as a result may be unable to function effectively in the vocational arena. On the other hand, a person who has experienced and fully recovered from an episode of *Pneumocystis carinii* pneumonia may be fully able to continue functioning at a very high vocational level despite an AIDS diagnosis. This issue is further complicated by the fact that the neurocognitive impairment accompanying HIV infection is often mild and patchy in its presentation. For example, Heaton and colleagues (in press-a) have shown that of the HIV+ subjects in their sample who evidenced *any* neuropsychological impairment, no more than 60% showed impairment in any one particular ability area. This finding remained consistent through later analyses on a larger number of subjects (see Chapter 9).

Despite these inherent difficulties, if the various extraneous factors that might have a significant impact on one's ability to carry out everyday tasks are controlled for (such as medical symptoms), it should be possible to determine whether and to what extent neurocognitive impairment is playing a role. Initial efforts in exploring this area have shown promising results. For this discussion, we will borrow heavily from a recently published work focusing on employment, neuropsychological functioning, and HIV infection (Heaton et al., in press-b), which represents one of the first large-scale attempts to explore this relationship.

The reader is referred to that work for a more specific presentation of the data presented here.

Recent Findings

We have been following a sample of HIV+ men over the past few years as part of a longitudinal neurobehavioral study, and recently we began to explore the relationships between neuropsychological functioning and employment status in a more specific manner (taking into account both medical and psychiatric factors). Analyses of these data indicate that the generally mild neuropsychological impairment evident in a subset of the HIV+ subjects is related to both employment status and self-perception of occupational functioning.

More specifically, in order to investigate whether the neuropsychological impairment seen in the sample was clinically significant, we chose to explore how it related to employment status (employed vs. unemployed), as well as self-perceptions of change in vocational abilities (for those subjects who were still employed). A subject was classified as employed if he reported being gainfully employed more than half of the time. Those subjects employed half of the time or less were classified as unemployed.

We began by comparing unemployment rates for 289 neuropsychologically normal and neuropsychologically impaired HIV+ subjects on whom we have employment data (for method of ascertaining neuropsychological impairment, see Chapter 9). A chi-square analysis indicated that significantly more neuropsychologically impaired subjects were unemployed relative to neuropsychologically normal (unimpaired) subjects ($p < .001$; Figure 10–1). Almost 27% of the impaired subjects were classified as unemployed compared to approximately 10% of the unimpaired subjects. Importantly, of the 26 unemployed, HIV+ sub-

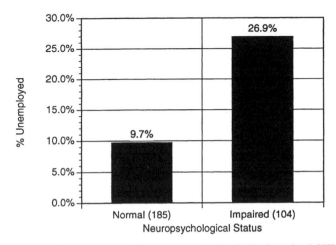

FIGURE 10–1. Unemployment rates for neuropsychologically impaired HIV+ subjects were almost three times higher than for unimpaired HIV+ subjects.

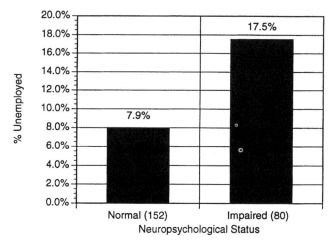

FIGURE 10–2. When HIV+ subjects with medical symptoms believed sufficient to inter-fere with work were excluded from the analysis, over two times as many neuropsycho-logically impaired subjects were unemployed relative to unimpaired subjects.

jects, the majority (69%) were in the medically asymptomatic or mildly symp-tomatic stages of disease (CDC II/III or IVc2), making it unlikely that medical symptoms was the major factor leading to unemployment.

To address this issue further, however, we removed from the sample all subjects who reported that they were currently experiencing medical symptoms that were considered potentially disabling ($n = 57$). For example, subjects report-ing temperatures above 102°F, fatigue at a level sufficient to interfere with work, diarrhea more than five times per day, severe anorexia with minimal food intake, or sensory symptoms believed by the subject to be severe enough to interfere with normal work were excluded from the sample. When the analyses were repeated on this "medically restricted" sample of 232 subjects, only 7.9% of the neuropsychologically unimpaired subjects reported being unemployed, relative to roughly twice as many (17.5%) of the neuropsychologically impaired subjects ($p < .05$; Figure 10–2).

In addition to the differential rates of unemployment, we examined reports of self-perceived decreases in the ability to perform occupational tasks among the neuropsychologically intact and neuropsychologically impaired HIV+ sub-jects *who were still employed*. The neuropsychologically impaired subjects reported that they were "less able to perform their job over the last month" five times more frequently than the neuropsychologically intact subjects ($p < .001$; Figure 10–3).

Again, to help control for medical symptoms, when the analysis was repeated on the medically restricted sample, the difference between the neuropsycholog-ically normal and impaired subject groups remained significant ($p < .0001$). In this case, only 4% of the neuropsychologically normal, employed subjects reported a decrease in functioning relative to almost 30% of the neuropsycho-logically impaired subjects (Figure 10–4).

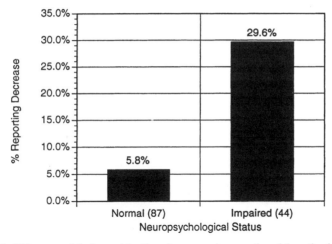

FIGURE 10–3. When considering subjective decreases in vocational functioning, the percent of neuropsychologically impaired HIV+ subjects reporting a decrease in their ability to "perform their job over the last month" was five times greater than for neuropsychologically normal subjects.

After focusing on potential medical confounds, we explored the possible impact of psychiatric factors. Specifically, we were interested in whether syndromic depression (based on the Structured Clinical Interview for DSM-III-R [SCID] or the Diagnostic Interview Schedule [DIS]) might be accounting for the differences in vocational variables. A subsample of 219 subjects for whom neuropsychological, employment, and psychiatric data were available was examined. Of these subjects, only a small minority (5%) reported having a current depressive disorder. When only medically restricted subjects were considered, again only 5% (7 out of 156) met criteria for a current depressive episode. Based on these data, we believe that current episodes of syndromic depression were sufficiently rare in our cohort to conclude that clinical depression would be an unlikely confounding factor.

Taking our analysis of possible psychiatric confounds one step further, a comparison of Beck Depression Inventory (BDI) and Depression/Dejection subscale scores from the Profile of Mood States (POMS) indicated that there were no significant differences between employed and unemployed, medically clean subject groups (Table 10–1).

Furthermore, if all subjects reporting symptoms of depression at a moderate level or above were removed from the analysis (defined as a score above 18 on the BDI [Beck et al., 1988]), neuropsychologically impaired subjects continued to demonstrate higher rates of unemployment (19.2% vs. 8.8%, $N = 177$; $p = .05$) and complaints regarding vocational functioning (28.6% vs. 4.6%, $N = 93$; $p = .001$). Based on these data, we concluded that neither syndromic depression nor depression symptoms could account for the differences in unemployment rates for the neuropsychologically normal and impaired subjects.

Our finding of a significant relationship between neuropsychological status

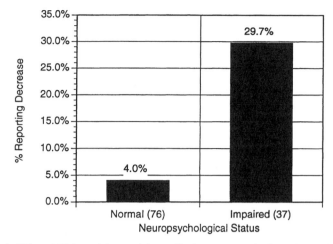

FIGURE 10–4. When HIV+ subjects with medical symptoms believed sufficient to inter-fere with work were excluded, subjects with neuropsychological impairment reported a subjective decrease in vocational functioning over seven times more frequently than unim-paired subjects.

and employment/vocational factors is strengthened by the fact that several aspects of the above study may have biased us toward underestimating the impact that HIV and neurocognitive dysfunction can have on vocational functioning. For example, our population of HIV+ men was only in their early to mid-thirties, and most (87%) were in the relatively early stages of HIV disease. In addition, subjects who had changed to less stressful or demanding work were still classified as employed as long as they were working at least half the time, irrespective of whether they had experienced deterioration in vocational functioning. Finally, subjects presenting with obvious neurological disease at the time of entry into the study were excluded, effectively reducing the prevalence and degree of sever-ity of neurocognitive impairment in our symptomatic subjects. Thus, with these factors in mind, there appears to be an important link between the HIV-related neuropsychological deficits and measures of real-world functioning.

The conclusion that the neuropsychological impairment in HIV infection can impact vocational functioning is consistent not only with research findings but also with clinical experience. For example, over the past several years we have completed neuropsychological evaluations on a number of HIV-infected

TABLE 10–1.   Scores on Mood Inventories for Medically Restricted, HIV+, Employed and Unemployed Subjects

Inventory (No. Employed/No. Unemployed)	Avg. Score (SD) Employed	Avg. Score (SD) Unemployed	t	p
BDI (161/22)	5.9 (5.6)	8.1 (6.1)	1.70	N.S.
POMS dep/dej. (163/20)	8.3 (10.1)	8.7 (8.2)	0.17	N.S.

individuals at various stages of disease who were referred because of vocational difficulties. One of these cases, which was published along with the above study, is also presented here for illustrative purposes.

This patient was in the relatively early stages of HIV infection (he had not progressed to AIDS-related complex or AIDS) at the time of his neuropsychological testing, and he was not showing frank signs of dementia. In addition, according to a DIS interview, he was not experiencing a DSM III-R, Axis I disorder. In this case, the work supervisor had reported significant changes in vocational performance prior to the referral for a neuropsychological evaluation.

Case

This patient was a Navy enlisted man who was 31 years of age at the time of his neuropsychological evaluation. He reported to the examiner that he had completed 2 years of college courses, for a total of 14 years of formal education. He was classified as a yeoman, performing various administrative and secretarial duties. The patient reported that he was having considerable difficulty remembering things, which was interfering with his ability to function vocationally. This change in his level of functioning was noted by a supervisor. The patient stated that he had been having memory difficulties for the last 1.5 years. He denied any significant risk factors, such as a learning disability, substance abuse, head trauma, or other neurological insult or injury that might account for his altered level of neurocognitive functioning. His medical history was significant only for testing positive for HIV 3 years before his neuropsychological evaluation when his CD4+ lymphocyte count was $469/mm^3$ of blood.

The patient's various scores on the neuropsychological battery suggested mild neurocognitive impairment overall. Table 10–2 lists the demographically corrected *T*-scores and corresponding percentiles on the various tests in the battery. A *T*-score below 40 represents an impaired performance and reflects a score more than one standard deviation below the normative mean. As one can see, this patient not only has numerous scores (16) below the *T*-score cutoff of 40, but also six scores more than two standard deviations below the mean (*T*-score below 30). A score at this level is very rare in neurologically normal individuals (Heaton et al., 1991). Importantly, although this patient's memory appears intact (as reflected by *T*-scores above 40 and thus not shown in the table), both verbal and figural (nonverbal) learning are impaired. His ability to learn new verbal material is almost two standard deviations below average, and his ability to learn nonverbal material is more than two standard deviations below average. Even though he did not demonstrate rapid forgetting of learned information, any serious inefficiency in learning new material is often subjectively experienced by patients as a memory impairment. In addition to his learning impairment, he demonstrated difficulty in following new sequential procedures (Trail Making B), poor auditory comprehension (BDAE), reduced verbal fluency (Thurstone Word Fluency Test), and decreased concentration and attention (WAIS-R Digit Span and Arithmetic, Rhythm and Speech Sounds Perception Test), all of which could be expected to interfere with his vocational functioning.

In this case, then, a young and otherwise healthy HIV+ administrative

TABLE 10–2. Impaired Neuropsychological Scores of a Healthy, HIV+ Patient Who Has Work Performance Difficulty

Variable	T-Score	Percentile
WAIS-R Verbal IQ	39	13.6
WAIS-R Performance IQ		
Halstead Impairment Index	35	6.7
Average Impairment Rating	26	0.8
Category Test		
Trail Making A		
Trail Making B	29	1.8
Wisconsin Card Sort (Perseverative Resp.)		
Tactual Performance Test Total Time		
Tactual Performance Test Memory	33	4.5
Tactual Performance Test Location		
Seashore Rhythm Test	33	4.5
Speech Sounds Perception Test	35	6.7
Digit Vigilance—Time		
Digit Vigilance—Errors		
Story Learning	31	2.9
Story Memory		
Figure Learning	26	0.8
Figure Memory		
Aphasia Screening Test	38	11.5
Boston Naming Test		
Thurstone Word Fluency	39	13.6
BDAE Complex Material	18	<0.1
Spatial Relations		
Sensory Errors—Right	28	1.4
Sensory Errors—Left	23	0.4
Grip Strength—Dominant Hand	33	4.5
Grip Strength—NonDominant Hand	39	13.6
Grooved Pegboard Dominant Hand		
Grooved Pegboard NonDominant Hand		

Note: T-scores from 35 to 39 reflect mild impairment; 30–34 = mild to moderate impairment; 25–29 = moderate impairment; 20–24 = moderate to severe impairment; <20 = severe impairment. T - scores in the normal range (>39) are not reported.

worker experienced vocational difficulties that were verified by his supervisor. This change in vocational functioning was associated with mild neurocognitive impairment and could not be accounted for by any other obvious factors.

Summary

Although we now have some empirical evidence of a significant relationship between mild HIV-associated neuropsychological impairment and real-world measures of functioning, there is a clear need for additional research in this area. In particular, for HIV+ people who are able to continue working, there is a need for further research focusing specifically on objective work performance, and efforts should be made to explore what types of occupational tasks are particularly affected by the types of deficits most frequently seen in HIV. That is, we must determine what job-specific tasks (e.g., filing, typing, monitoring radar screens) are adversely affected by specific ability area deficits (e.g., attention, learning, memory, etc), and what level of impairment is necessary for a detrimental functional impact. In general, it seems likely that job performance in high-level vocations is probably more sensitive to mild neuropsychological changes and impairment than in lower-level positions, and complex tasks are probably more vulnerable to disruption than simple tasks. Thus, when using neuropsychological results to guide predictions regarding vocational functioning, the specific job demands as well as the specific disabilities must be considered.

It must be emphasized that, based on the evidence presented here, we *are not* suggesting that HIV-infected individuals generally are unable or less able to function in a competitive vocational arena. In fact, our data indicate that most HIV-infected individuals do not even show mild neuropsychological impairment (especially during the asymptomatic or mildly symptomatic stages), and of those who do, only a subset report vocational difficulties. Instead, the conclusion we reach from these data is that patients *who do evidence* mild impairment *may* indeed experience the effects of this impairment in their everyday lives. As such, the impairment should not be ignored. For example, vocational counseling or changes in job-specific demands, when possible, may allow those experiencing vocational disruption as a result of their neurocognitive status to continue working for a longer period of time. Given that many HIV+ individuals attempt to limit the impact of HIV on their daily routine as much as possible, this could be a positive and important outcome. On the other hand, and just as important, these data also suggest that disability or medical retirement claims may be warranted in some cases, even if the person is still *physically* capable of performing his/her job.

In closing, the interaction between neuropsychological impairment and everyday functioning is very complex and requires much more exploration. However, we now have evidence that the generally mild neurocognitive impairment that not infrequently occurs in HIV disease can be clinically significant, since it appears to be related to important aspects of everyday functioning.

Acknowledgments

The principal support for the HNRC is provided by NIMH Center Grant 5 P50 MH45294 (HIV Neurobehavioral Research Center). The views expressed in this chapter are those of the authors and do not reflect the official policy or position of the Department of the Navy, the Department of Defense, or the U.S. government.

References

Bayless, J.D., Varney, N.R., and Roberts, R.J. (1989). Tinker toy test performance and vocational outcome in patients with closed-head injuries. *Journal of Clinical and Experimental Neuropsychology, 11*, 913–917.

Beck, A., Steer, R., and Garbin, M. (1988). Psychometric properties of the Beck Depression Inventory. *Clinical Psychology Review, 8,* 77–100.

Bornstein, R.A., Nasrallah, H.A., Para, M.F., Fass, R.J., Whitacre, C.C., and Rice, R.R. (1991). Rate of CD4 decline and neuropsychological performance in HIV infection. *Archives of Neurology, 48,* 704–707.

Chelune, G., and Moehle, K. (1986). Neuropsychological assessment and everyday functioning. In D. Wedding, A. Horton, Jr., and J. Webster, eds.,*The Neuropsychology Handbook: Behavioral and Clinical Perspectives.* New York: Springer, pp. 489–525.

Day, J., Grant, I., Atkinson, J.H., Brysk, L., McCutchan, J.A., Hesselink, J., Spector, S., and Richman, D. (1992). Incidence of AIDS dementia in a two year follow-up of AIDS and ARC patients on an initial Phase II AZT placebo-controlled study: San Diego cohort. *Journal of Neuropsychiatry and Clinical Neurosciences, 4,* 15–20.

Ganz, P.A., Schag, A.C., Kahn, B., and Petersen, L. (in press). Assessing the quality of life of HIV infected persons: Clinical and descriptive information and studies with the HOPES. *Psychology and Health.*

Grant, I., and Atkinson, J.H. (1990). The evolution of neurobehavioral complications of HIV infection. *Psychological Medicine, 20,* 747–750.

Grant, I., Atkinson, H., Hesselink, J., Kennedy, C., Richmond, D., Spector, S.A., and McCutchan, J.A. (1987). Evidence for early central nervous system involvement in the acquired immunodeficiency syndrome (AIDS) and other human immunodeficiency virus (HIV) infections. *Annals of Internal Medicine, 107,* 828–836.

Grant, I., and Heaton, R.K. (1990). Human immunodeficiency virus-type 1 (HIV-1) and the brain. *Journal of Consulting and Clinical Psychology, 58,* 22–30.

Heaton, R.K., and Pendleton, M. (1981). Use of neuropsychological tests to predict adult patients' everyday functioning. *Journal of Consulting and Clinical Psychology, 49,* 807–821.

Heaton, R.K., Chelune, G., and Lehman, R. (1978). Using neuropsychological and personality tests to assess likelihood of patient employment. *Journal of Nervous and Mental Disorders, 166,* 408–416.

Heaton, R.K., Grant, I., and Matthews, C. (1991). *Comprehensive Norms for an Expanded Halstead-Reitan Battery: Demographic Corrections, Research Findings, and Clinical Applications.* Odessa, Fla.: Psychological Assessment Resources.

Heaton, R.K., Velin, R.A., Atkinson, J.H., Gulevich, S.J., McCutchan, J.A., Hesselink, J.A., Chandler, J.R., and Grant, I. (in press-a). Neuropsychological impairment in an HIV-positive male cohort. In G.M. Stein and A. Baum, eds. *Perspectives on Behavioral Medicine.* Key West, Fla.: Erlbaum.

Heaton, R.K., Velin, R.A., McCutchan, J.A., Gulevich, S.J., Atkinson, J.H., Wallace, M.R., Godfrey, H.P.D., Kirson, D.A., Grant, I., and the HNRC Group. (in press-b). Neuropsychological impairment in HIV-infection: Implications for employment. *Psychosomatic Medicine.*

Janssen, R.S., Saykin, A.J., Cannon, L., Campbell, J., Pinsky, P., Hessol, N., O'Malley, P., Lifson, A., Doll, L., Rutherford, G., and Kaplan, J. (1989). Neurological and neuropsychological manifestations of HIV-1 infection: Association with AIDS-related complex but not asymptomatic HIV-1 infection. *Annals of Neurology, 26,* 592–600.

Koralnik, I.J., Beaumanoir, A., Hausler, R., Kohler, A., Safran, A., Delacoux, R., Vibert, D., Mayer, E., Burkhard, P., Nahory, A., Magistris, M.R., Sanches, J., Myers, P., Paccolat, F., Quoex, F., Gabriel, V., Perrin, L., Mermillod, B., Gauthier, G., Waldvogel, F.A., and Hirschel, B. (1990). A controlled study of early neurologic abnormalities in men with asymptomatic human immunodeficiency virus infection. *New England Journal of Medicine, 323,* 864–870.

Lezak, M.D. (1982). The problem of assessing executive functions. *International Journal of Psychology, 17,* 281–297.

Lunn, S., Skydsbjerg, M., Schulsinger, H., Parnas, J., Pedersen, C., and Mathiesen, L. (1991). A preliminary report on the neuropsychological sequelae of human immunodeficiency virus. *Archives of General Psychiatry, 48,* 139–142.

Matarazzo, J.D. (1972). *Wechsler's Measurement and Appraisal of Intelligence* (5th ed.). Baltimore, Md.: Williams and Wilkins.

Mayeux, R., Stern, Y., Tang, M.-X., Todak, G., Marder, K., Sano, M., Richards, M., Stein, Z., Ehrhardt, A.A., and Gorman, J.M. (1993). Mortality risks in gay men with human immunodeficiency virus infection and cognitive impairment. *Neurology, 43,* 176–182.

McKegney, F.P., O'Dowd, M.A., Feiner, C., Selwyn, P., Drucker, E., and Friedland, G.H. (1990). A prospective comparison of neuropsychological function in HIV-seropositive and seronegative methadone-maintained patients. *AIDS, 4,* 565–569.

Miller, E., Selnes, O., McArthur, J., Satz, P., Becher, J., Cohen, B., Sheridan, K., Machado, A., VanGorp, W., and Visscher, B. (1990). Neuropsychological performance in HIV-1 infected homosexual men: The Multicenter AIDS Cohort Study (MACS). *Neurology, 40,* 197–203.

Newnan, O., Heaton, R.K., and Lehman, R. (1978). Neuropsychological and MMPI correlates of patients' future employment characteristics. *Perceptual Motor Skills, 46,* 635–642.

Perry, S., Belsky-Barr, D., Barr, W., and Jacobsberg, L. (1989). Neuropsychological function in physically asymptomatic, HIV-seropositive men. *Journal of Neuropsychiatry, 1,* 296–302.

Rao, S.M., Leo, G.J., Ellington, L., Nauertz, T., Bernardin, L., and Unverzagt, F. (1991). Cognitive dysfunction in multiple sclerosis. II. Impact on employment and social functioning. *Neurology, 41,* 692–696.

Stern, Y., Marder, K., Bell, K., Chen, J., Dooneief, G., Goldstein, S., Mindry, D., Richards, M., Sano, M., Williams, J., Gorman, J., Ehrhardt, A., and Mayeux, R. (1991). Multidisciplinary baseline assessment of homosexual men with and without human immunodeficiency virus infection: III. Neurologic and neuropsychological findings. *Archives of General Psychiatry, 48,* 131–138.

Wilkie, F., Eisdorfer, C., Morgan, R., Loewenstein, D., and Szapocznik, J. (1990). Cognition in early human immunodeficiency virus infection. *Archives of Neurology, 47,* 433–440.

11

Neuropsychological Assessment of Seropositive Intravenous Drug Users

Yaakov Stern

Intravenous drug users (IVDUs) are the fastest-growing population in the human immunodeficiency virus (HIV) epidemic. While the rate of HIV seroconversion in the homosexual population has stabilized, the rate of seroconversion among IVDUs has continued to increase 14% annually (Hahn et al., 1989). Still, relatively little attention has been paid to potential neuropsychological changes in this group. Studies of IVDUs are more complex since they must carefully control for potential covariates such as lower education and socioeconomic status. However, they may be more likely to detect subtle neuropsychological changes since these individuals' lower education and socioeconomic status might provide a lower threshold for the effects of the virus on the central nervous system (CNS). In addition, they allow the opportunity to evaluate the effects of alternative modes of HIV transmission, as well as the potential effects on another understudied group—women.

This chapter reviews some of the issues that must be taken into account when assessing neuropsychological performance in the IVDU population. These issues are weighed against the various benefits of studying this population. In addition, specific methodological considerations are discussed. Finally, the results of several studies of neuropsychological changes in the HIV+ IVDU population are presented.

Issues Specific to the IVDU Population

Results of neuropsychological testing of IVDUs must be interpreted cautiously. The long-term usage of IV drugs may have permanent effects on physiology that influence test performance. The various factors that contribute to the initiation of IV drug use, including socioeconomic conditions and psychiatric illness, may also influence performance on testing. Increased concurrent illness and poor access to medical treatment can play a role as well. In addition, one must consider the potential acute effects of drug use, including methadone. All of this underlines the point that the interpretation of neuropsychological testing in IVDUs must be done with few preconceptions about normative performance and with careful consideration of other potential influences on performance.

Effect of Drugs on Neuropsychological Performance

One major issue to be considered when assessing the influence of HIV on cognitive function in IVDUs is the effect of the drugs on their performance. The literature on neuropsychological performance of IVDUs is sparse. However, it does suggest that some drugs, particularly opiates, can affect performance on neuropsychological testing (Grant et al., 1977). The issue is complicated by the many variations in patterns of drug use. Factors such as duration of drug abuse, the actual drugs chosen, or whether the patient is currently intoxicated or not can have a direct impact on neuropsychological test performance. They are strong potential founding factors.

IVDUs might be divided into three tiers. First is the recovered IVDU, who no longer uses drugs. Performance in this case is potentially influenced by the lasting physiological effect of drug use on the CNS. Second is the methadone patient, who ostensibly receives a consistent dose of narcotic. Third is the active IVDU, who experiences acute effects of drug use. A systematic approach to investigating the neuropsychological effects of drug use might begin with the simplest case, the recovered IVDU.

A separate practical problem is the potential difference between active IVDUs and those in treatment programs. Clearly, it is not safe to assume that a patient currently in a methadone treatment program is not also using drugs. Beyond this, there may be a host of factors that differentiate these two groups. While patients in treatment programs may include those who desire to reenter society, they also include individuals who were unable to cope on the street and sought the relative security of a methadone maintenance program.

Sociodemographic Considerations

In most published studies of HIV in homosexual men, the subject pool has been drawn from well-educated individuals of high socioeconomic status. When studying IVDUs, the picture becomes much more complicated. There are many specific issues.

RACE/ETHNICITY. The IVDU population has a large percentage of minorities, and there is a paucity of normative data for most neuropsychological tests in these populations. Although this area is underinvestigated and somewhat controversial, it is fair to say that the psychometric and performance characteristics of most neuropsychological tests are not well understood by minority populations. At a minimum, careful attention must be given to establishing appropriate normative data or control groups for minority population subjects.

EDUCATION.   Similarly, the IVDU population has a wide variation in educational attainment. Some tests are inappropriate for individuals in lower educational ranges because their performance relies on information or skills obtained in school. Even when tests can be administered, it is a truism that performance on almost all neuropsychological tests correlates with education.

Adjusting for education is complicated since it is not simply an interval-level variable that can be covaried in a statistical analysis. The implications of attaining a particular number of years of education may differ across ethnic groups because of the limits that socioeconomic status might place on the ability to obtain education. In addition, the quality of education varies widely from place to place, so that a specific level of educational attainment might not be comparable. In our experience, many subjects report completing high school equivalency examinations, but this may not be comparable to completing high school.

In subjects with very low educational levels, two possibilities must be strongly considered. The first is learning disability since most educational systems pass students from grade to grade unless there is a serious problem. A second consideration is illiteracy. While the illiterate subject might report completing several years of education, the potential impact on test performance is even more severe than this would suggest. Careful investigation and control of these two issues is warranted in studies of IVDUs.

CULTURE/EXPOSURE.   The IVDU population can contain people for whom English is not a first language, as well as people with widely divergent cultural exposures. Again, the content of tests can be biased against these people, and careful item-by-item analysis of commonly used tests might be necessary to avoid this problem.

SEX.   In contrast to the homosexual male population, the IVDU population includes both men and women. The potential contribution of gender to neuropsychological performance is an area that has been well studied, so it does not bear repetition here. Another issue that must be considered in the IVDU population is that the pattern of drug use may differ in IVDU men and women. Finally, the potential differential effects of HIV on men and women has not been well investigated.

Medical Issues

The potential contribution of medical cofactors is much more pronounced in the IVDU population since this group often does not have good access to appropriate medical care.

PERINATAL STATUS. The contribution of medical issues probably begins even before birth since the mothers of many IVDUs do not receive appropriate perinatal care. This may not be an issue particular to IVDUs, but rather to the socioeconomic groups from which they are often drawn.

ILLNESS. Recent epidemiological studies suggest that residents of inner-city areas are less likely to receive appropriate basic medical care, are more likely to suffer from many potentially treatable medical conditions, and have a higher risk of mortality (McCord and Freeman, 1990). Potential sources of influence include direct effects, such as action on the CNS, as well as constitutional effects on performance. In addition, the use of IV drugs provides an avenue for infection. Medical complications that occur in heroin addicts, for example, include thrombophlebitis and pulmonary embolism; chronic abdominal pain and intestinal pseudo-obstruction; heroin nephropathy, which can cause symptomatic uremia, malignant hypertension, hypertensive encephalopathy, or hemorrhagic stroke; renal damage; and altered pulmonary function (Brust, 1990).

In the IVDU cohort followed at our center, over 50% of the subjects reported a history of head trauma with loss of consciousness (Marder et al., 1992). A review of selected cases suggests that often this constituted severe head trauma resulting from car accidents, falls, and head injuries from blunt objects. In addition, seizures were common. Conditions such as these can have clear effects on neuropsychological function and may eliminate any chance to detect the effect of HIV.

PSYCHIATRIC ILLNESS. As in any population, psychiatric illness must be considered as a possible contributor to cognitive performance. This issue is complicated in the IVDU population since depression is common, as are other psychiatric illnesses (Rounsaville et al., 1979; Kosten and Kleber, 1988). Another potential complication is the possible relation between affective problems and drug abuse. For example, some theorize that drug abuse can be a form of "self-treatment" for a psychiatric condition.

PERCEIVED BARRIERS. One of the most potent issues discouraging research in IVDUs are the perceived barriers in working with this population. A major concern has been the extent to which good cooperation with testing can be obtained from this group. Neuropsychological testing is dependent on the optimal performance of the subject, and there has been concern that IVDUs would not fully attend to tasks. Complicating this situation is the potential for subject intoxication. On a practical level, studies of IVDUs must be designed so that they enlist the cooperation of the subjects and involve them in the issues. In addition, testers must be trained to be sensitive to potential signs of drug use, and a threshold for discontinuing testing must be carefully established. Still, our experience at the HIV Center in New York City has been encouraging. The tests have good face validity since subjects perceive them as tapping areas of concern such as poor memory.

Another perceived barrier to testing IVDUs is potential difficulty with follow-up. However, with careful attention to issues of subject tracking, subject involvement, and compensation, good follow-up can be maintained.

Reasons for Interest in Studying IVDUs

Given all of the potential difficulties in assessing neuropsychological function in IVDUs, the reasons for the importance of studying the effect of HIV on this population should be stressed.

IVDUS AS PART OF AN EPIDEMIC. One major reason is that IVDUs represent the fastest-growing group in the HIV epidemic. Only by focusing specifically on this population can the extent of the effects of this epidemic be assessed.

UNDERSTANDING COFACTORS. Many of the features discussed above are potential cofactors that can influence the course and expression of HIV's effects.

Since the mode of transmission in the IVDU population is different, it is not immediately clear whether the medical and cognitive manifestations of the HIV virus will be similar to those better described in homosexual men. In addition, injection offers multiple opportunities for reinfection with different strains of the virus.

Since IVDUs often have other concomitant medical conditions, it is important to determine whether these exacerbate the variance of the HIV virus or the speed of its expression. In addition, the act of injecting drugs provides a route for multiple exposures to the virus that may introduce a multitude of strains or cause a more virulent infection.

PUBLIC HEALTH CONSIDERATIONS. The study of IVDUs is an important adjunct for the initiation of drug trials in this undertreated population. Only with an accurate picture of the cognitive and neurological effects of HIV in this population can rational drug trials be planned. In addition, including IVDUs in long-term cohort studies is an effective way of introducing various prevention efforts, including the teaching of safe sex practices, needle cleaning, and prevention of needle sharing.

An associated issue is that most prevention strategies require the active cooperation and comprehension of the IVDU. For example, prevention of needle sharing requires that the person comprehend the risks involved. It is crucial to understand the interaction between risky behavior and cognitive capacity for effective planning of intervention strategies.

THRESHOLD FOR COGNITIVE EFFECTS. Despite the myriad potential influences on neuropsychological test performance that are present in IVDUs, they may represent a better population for understanding the effects of the HIV virus on cognition. Many of the homosexual male cohorts studied to date are well educated and have high socioeconomic status. It is possible that subtle effects of HIV on cognition might be missed in this group because of potential reserves or coping mechanisms that might be provided by this relatively above-average baseline attainment. In contrast, the effects of HIV in the IVDU population may be more directly observable since other factors have already depleted any potential cognitive reserve. Supporting this concept is a recent report from the Multicenter Aids Cohort Study, which did not note differences in the neuropsychological performance of HIV− and HIV+ asymptomatic homosexual men. However, when comparisons were restricted to men with below-high-school education, effects of seropositivity were noted (Satz, 1993).

OPPORTUNITY TO STUDY DRUG USE ISSUES.   A more prosaic consideration is that the IVDU population has been understudied in general since it has not received a high priority for funding. Studies of HIV in this population, besides giving us more information about the virus, will yield important information about the effects of drug usage on cognitive function.

Design Issues

This review of the potential pitfalls and benefits of the study of IVDUs suggests several design issues that might be considered when planning a study with this population.

ADEQUATE CONTROLS.   The inclusion of adequate HIV− IVDU controls cannot be overstressed. Only by including a strong sampling of individuals with the same potential confounds and risk factors can the potential effect of HIV be isolated. It would probably not be wise to rely on any published norms when dealing with the IVDU population, so the use of internally generated norms is required. Again, this requires that an adequate number of controls be tested. Any judgment of normal or abnormal performance can then be based on the distribution of test performance within the HIV+ and HIV− IVDUs assessed.

MEDICAL/PSYCHIATRIC EVALUATION.   Clearly, the neuropsychological function of IVDUs cannot be studied in isolation. Without excellent medical, neurological, and psychiatric evaluations, the relative contributions of these factors cannot be assessed.

INTOXICATION/FATIGUE.   In studies of active IVDUs, it is a relative certainty that subjects will occasionally arrive for testing in an intoxicated state. Grant et al. (1977) described an observational scale intended to detect the clinical signs of intoxication, but its effectiveness was not established. A first step in dealing with this issue is careful training of examiners so that they can recognize signs of intoxication. A decision must then be made about criteria for terminating or postponing testing. At our center, if a subject is nodding out, or appears to have difficulty comprehending or following task demands, testing is terminated. If the examiner merely has the impression that the subject is intoxicated, this is not grounds for terminating testing.

A related issue is fatigue, which can be seen more commonly in the IVDU population for reasons not always related to drug use. Again, the use of consistent criteria for canceling a test session is recommended.

In either circumstance, a form filled out by the examiner that estimates the subject's level of attention, arousal, and comprehension is useful for addressing the potential effects of these conditions.

Test Selection Issues

FLOOR EFFECTS.   As in any population with the possibility of relatively poor performance on neuropsychological tests, careful attention should be given to potential floor effects. The selection process often must rely on experience more than logic. For example, an abstract reasoning task specifically designed for subjects with limited reading ability (the Conceptual Levels Analogies Test) proved to be difficult for the majority of our IVDU cohort, while performance on the Wechsler Adult Intelligence Scale-Revised (WAIS-R) Similarities was at acceptable levels.

RELIABILITY.   The psychometric characteristics of most standard neuropsychological tests have not been established in IVDU and minority populations. One concern in prospective studies is the extent to which variations in performance are due to the confounding factors discussed above rather than to an HIV-related cognitive change.

VALIDITY.   Again, the ability of tests to assess what they intend to assess is not well established in the IVDU population. Sensitivity to obvious cultural confounds is encouraged. In addition, consideration should be given to the mode of response since this may influence levels of performance. In planning our battery, for example, we avoided tests that required written responses.

ADJUNCT SERVICES.   Since a study of an IVDU population is likely to detect medical, psychiatric, or cognitive problems that have not been previously diagnosed or treated, it is important to have appropriate referral resources to address these problems adequately.

DRUG HISTORY.   Accurate information about past and present drug use is crucial for examining the contribution of drug use to test performance. Different standardized approaches for eliciting a drug history exist (e.g., Grant et al., 1977). More important in this regard is the subject's knowledge of and trust in assurances of confidentiality.

A useful adjunct to a drug history is laboratory measures of current drug use, such as urine toxicology screens.

SUBJECT TRACKING.   Provisions must be made for tracking patients. In our experience at the HIV Center in New York City, payment for visits encourages good follow-up.

Analytic Issues

There is still some variation in approaches to data analysis in studies of HIV. Only issues specific to IVDUs are discussed here.

STAGE VS. CD4. Subjects in HIV-related studies are often grouped in rough approximation of Centers for Disease Control (CDC) stages, with typical divisions made between those who are asymptomatic, have mild symptoms, AIDS-related complex (ARC), or AIDS. These divisions are somewhat more problematic in IVDUs since the differentiation between HIV-related symptoms and symptoms due to coexisting conditions is not always clear. For this reason, markers of immunological status may have more utility in stratifying subjects for analysis. As our understanding of the mechanism of HIV's effect on neuronal function improves, it will be important to reference neuropsychological performance to indices that are related to or measure the CNS effect of HIV. Examples are attempts to correlate neuropsychological performance with cerebrospinal fluid concentrations of neopterin and quinolinic acid, two compounds that may partially reflect HIV's effect on neuronal function (Griffin et al., 1991; Martin et al., 1992).

CONTROLLING FOR EDUCATION. As discussed above, variability in education presents a complex problem that cannot be solved completely by statistical adjustment. Another possible approach is to rely on other measures, such as level of employment or socioeconomic status, in order to help adjust for these variables. The use of the National Adult Reading Test has also been recommended to provide an estimate of premorbid intelligence and educational attainment (Grober et al., 1990).

Another approach is to utilize a measure of "crystallized intelligence" as a covariate. Since this would presumably tap native intelligence that is independent of whether opportunities for educational advancement existed, it would correct for some of the difficulties with measuring education that have been discussed.

Current Findings

HIV-related neurological and neuropsychological signs and symptoms in IVDUs have received less attention than in other populations. In a retrospective study of HIV infection done prior to the advent of HIV antibody testing in a population with AIDS, 64% of whom were IVDUs, 23% had neurological disease (Koppel et al., 1985). In a prospective survey completed at Harlem Hospital Center of 190 inpatients with AIDS or ARC, of whom 80% were IVDUs, 91% had neurological symptoms or signs, the most common of which was altered mental status, followed by focal cerebral signs (Malouf et al., 1990). No difference was seen between IVDUs and non-IVDUs in the prevalence of neurological findings, nor was there a difference in neurological findings between AIDS and LA/ARC patients.

Several studies are discussed below. First, our experience in assessing the reliability of neuropsychological tests in IVDUs is reviewed. The use of a brief dementia screen in seropositive IVDUs was explored by Kovner et al. (1992), with good success. Two groups have reported more in-depth studies of IVDUs, the Montefiore Hospital group in the Bronx and the Edinburgh group, and their findings are briefly reviewed. Finally, our preliminary findings at the HIV Center in New York are described.

Test-Retest Reliability

In preparation for initiating a large-scale natural history study of HIV in IVDUs, we felt it was important to address the issue of test-retest reliability in this group (Richards et al., 1992). This was motivated by concern about potential effects of acute intoxication at individual visits, as well as variability in the compliance of the subjects.

Sixteen patients who were currently IVDUs or who were in methadone maintenance were recruited for this study from an outpatient drug treatment unit. Each patient was tested twice; the second test session was approximately 2 weeks later than the first.

The following battery of neuropsychological tests was administered at each session in a standard order: Modified Mini-Mental State Examination, Conceptual Levels Analogies Tests (CLAT), Selective Reminding Test (12-item, 6-trial with 15-minute delayed recall and recognition), Boston Naming Test (30 items), Controlled Word Association (CFL), Animal Naming, Odd-Man Out, Benton Judgment of Line Orientation, Cancellation Tests (shape and letter triad), WAIS-R Digit Symbol, Trail Making Test (Parts A and B), and the Purdue Pegboard.

Fourteen individuals admitted to drug use within 24 hours before one of the testing sessions. Eight of these admitted to drug use prior to both sessions. Only two individuals denied drug usage prior to both test sessions.

Intraclass correlations were calculated between performance on each test at time 1 and time 2. For all but two tests, correlation coefficients exceeded .5, and in most cases they were substantially higher. For the Selective Reminding Test and the Purdue Pegboard, reliability was poor.

These results suggest that, in general, test-retest reliability in the assessed population is quite good. This applied to tests of general intelligence, reasoning, visuospatial ability, sustained attention, language, speeded performance, and set switching.

There was more variability in performance on the Selective Reminding Test. There are several possible explanations for this finding. First, memory functions may simply be more vulnerable to intercurrent drug use or to subtle shifts in attention and concentration. Another possibility is that this test is more challenging than some of the others and is therefore more vulnerable to disruption.

The variability in Purdue Pegboard performance may be due in part to the important role played by subject motivation on this test. In addition, in the present administration, the dominant hand was always tested first. This afforded some practice with the task that might have served to increase reliability on the subsequent nondominant-hand and both-hand sequences.

In summary, for most tests administered, test-retest reliability in this population of IVDUs was good. These findings help support the validity of neuropsychological studies in these populations and suggest that prospective studies with these patients can yield fruitful results.

Use of a Dementia Screen

Kovner et al. (1992) administered the Mattis Dementia Rating Scale (DRS) to 43 IVDUs. Twenty-two were HIV- and 21 HIV+ (11 with AIDS). Subjects with obvious learning disabilities were excluded, using a cut score for performance on the Wide Range Achievement Test-Revised reading decoding subtest. The HIV- subjects had significantly higher DRS scores than the HIV+ subjects; the performance of HIV+ subjects with and without AIDS did not differ significantly. Using a cut score of 138 on the DRS to differentiate normal from abnormal performance, all HIV- subjects were classified as normal. In contrast, 57% of the HIV+ subjects scored below this cut point. While the trend is not significant, 45% of the non-AIDS, HIV+ subjects scored in the abnormal range compared to 70% of those with AIDS.

These findings suggest that neuropsychological dysfunction is common in HIV+ IVDUs and can be detected with a brief screening instrument. In clinical settings, the DRS might be used to screen patients for further, more in-depth neuropsychological evaluation.

Findings of the Montefiore Group

Silberstein et al. (1987) studied 211 IVDUs, all without overt symptoms of AIDS-related illness. They reported data on only black and Hispanic subjects; 66 were HIV+ and 91 HIV-. In two separate analyses of these ethnic groups, seropositive subjects were more impaired than seronegative subjects on finger tapping (dominant hand) and WAIS Similarities. Multivariate analyses that adjusted for age, sex, and patterns of drug use found poorer performance in the seronegative subjects on conceptual learning ability, a combination of scores on the Similarities and the Wechsler Memory Scale Associate Learning subtest.

A follow-up study of 91 patients from this cohort was conducted after a mean interval of 7.4 months from baseline testing (McKegney et al., 1990). At follow-up, seropositives continued to be more cognitively impaired than seronegatives, but there was no deterioration in the performance of the initial seropositives over the time interval. After a mean follow-up of 47 months, 128 of the subjects were again evaluated. Neuropsychological performance declined more rapidly in the seropositive than in the seronegative subjects (Silberstein et al., 1991).

The Edinburgh Study

Egan et al. (1990) compared the performance of 80 HIV+ and 12 HIV-IVDUs and found no significant differences between the two groups. In addition, cognitive function did not deteriorate with increasing severity of illness. The authors concluded that AIDS dementia was a late finding in HIV infection and that any intellectual impairment was probably due more to drug use. They suggest the use of the National Adult Reading Test (NART) as an index of premorbid intelligence that is relatively unaffected by the effects of drug use.

Baseline Studies at the HIV Center in New York

Our group is conducting a multidisciplinary prospective study of HIV− and HIV+ IVDUs (Marder et al., 1992). Subjects consist of 221 men and women who had had used IV drugs at least 10 times since 1982. Subjects who met criteria for AIDS according to the CDC National Surveillance Criteria (1985) upon entry were excluded (CDC, 1987).

There were 145 men and 76 women: 99 HIV− subjects (62 men, 37 women) and 122 HIV+ subjects (83 men, 39 women). Of the HIV+ subjects, 33 (24 men, 9 women) were completely asymptomatic, 28 (22 men, 6 women) had mild medical symptoms such as lymphadenopathy, and 61 (37 men, 24 women) had significant medical symptoms but did not meet criteria for AIDS.

Standardized neurological examinations were performed blind to HIV status. Examinations were performed prior to the elicitation of pertinent medical symptoms in order to be certain that the examiner did not know the HIV status of the subject or the medications being taken.

The neuropsychological examination, performed with testers blind to HIV status, was a truncated version of the exam used to assess homosexual men (Stern et al., 1991), and lasted for approximately 75 minutes. Besides evaluating individual test scores, the neuropsychological test performance was summarized in two ways. For one set of summary measures we calculated the mean and standard deviation for each subject score on each neuropsychological test, expressed in terms of z-scores. Performance on each test was considered defective if it was two or more standard deviations below the mean. Overall performance was considered defective if two or more areas were impaired. The mean of z-scores for all tests in each area was calculated as a summary score. In addition, two neuropsychologists who were blind to HIV status reviewed each test protocol and classified it as normal, borderline, or abnormal.

There were no differences seen in the percentage of HIV− and HIV+ subjects who had any impairment in cranial nerves, fine alternating movements, or sensory perception. Significantly more HIV+ subjects than HIV− subjects had extrapyramidal signs ($p < .02$) or frontal release signs ($p < .002$).

Rigidity was the only extrapyramidal sign present more often in the HIV+ subjects (7.4%) than the HIV− subjects (0%). Tremor, bradykinesia, postural instability, or hypomimia were rare but similar in HIV+ and HIV− subjects.

Neuropsychological indices were contrasted in HIV+ and HIV− subjects using multiple analysis of variance. The following main effects were examined: serostatus, sex, first language, and head injury. A serostatus by head injury interaction was also included in the model based on preliminary observations of a relation between these two variables. Rated depression and anxiety, as well as years of education and age, were included as covariates.

HIV+ and HIV− patients were compared. Neither serostatus nor serostatus × head injury reached significance. When univariate F tests were inspected, there were significant serostatus and serostatus × head injury interactions for several tests, suggesting that performance was more impaired in HIV+ patients who had head injury.

When only HIV− and HIV+ asymptomatic subjects were contrasted, the univariate F tests revealed significant serostatus × head injury interactions for the Selective Reminding Test (intrusions) and Cancellations (time and commission errors).

In summary, the HIV+ group performed more poorly on tests of memory (verbal and nonverbal), naming, visuospatial function, abstract reasoning, speeded attentional processing, and speeded motor function. In the asymptomatic HIV+ patients, relative performance deficits in memory and speeded attentional processing were noted.

The significant interactions between serostatus and head injury is an intriguing finding. It suggests that the effect of HIV on performance may be more pronounced in individuals with a history of head injury.

Conclusions

Research on the neuropsychological effects of HIV in the IVDU population presents unique challenges and opportunities. The need for these studies is clear, since this group represents an ever-growing segment of the HIV epidemic. Preliminary evidence suggests that it is possible to surmount many of the methodological difficulties in studying this population and to document HIV-related cognitive changes. Follow-up work in already established cohorts, as well as new studies of broader scope, will be required in order to understand the neuropsychological impact of HIV in the drug-using population.

Acknowledgment

This work was supported in part by Center Grant MH43520 from the National Institute of Mental Health/National Institute on Drug Abuse.

References

Brust, J.C.M. (1990). Drug dependence. In Joynt, R.J., ed., *Clinical Neurology,* Vol. 2. Philadelphia: Lippincott, pp. 1–92.
Centers for Disease Control. (1987). Revision of the CDC surveillance case definition for

acquired immunodeficiency syndrome. *Morbidity and Mortality Weekly Report, 36*(Suppl), 1S–15S.

Egan, V.G., Crawford, J.R., Brettle, R.P., and Goodwin, G.M. (1990). The Edinburgh cohort of HIV-positive drug users: Current intellectual function is impaired, but not due to early AIDS dementia complex. *AIDS, 4*, 651–656.

Grant, I., Adams, K.M., Carlin, A.S., and Rennick, P.M. (1977). Neuropsychological deficit in polydrug users. A preliminary report of the findings of the collaborative neuropsychological study of polydrug users. *Drug and Alcohol Dependence, 2*, 91–108.

Griffin, D.E., McArthur, J.C., and Cornblath, D.R. (1991). Neopterin and interferon-gamma in serum and cerebrospinal fluid of patients with HIV-associated neurologic disease. *Neurology, 41*, 69–74.

Grober, E., Sliwinski, M., and Buschke, H. (1990). Premorbid intelligence in the elderly. (Abst). *Journal of Clinical and Experimental Neuropsychology, 12*, 30.

Hahn, R.A., Onorato, I.M., Jones, T.S., and Dougherty, J. (1989). Prevalence of HIV infection among intravenous drug users in the United States. *Journal of the American Medical Association, 251*, 2677–2683.

Koppel, B.S., Wormser, G.P., Tuchman, A.J., Maayan, S., Hewlett, D., and Daras, M. (1985). Central nervous system involvement in patients with acquired immune deficiency syndrome. *Acta Neurologica Scandinavica, 71*, 337–353.

Kosten, T.R., and Kleber, H.D. (1988). Differential diagnosis of psychiatric comorbidity in substance abusers. *Journal of Substance Abuse and Treatment, 5*, 102–206.

Kovner, R., Sazar, J.W., Lesser, M., Perecman, E., Kaplan, M.H., Hainline, B., and Napolitano, B. (1992). Use of the dementia rating scale as a test for neuropsychological dysfunction in HIV positive IV drug abusers. *Journal of Substance Abuse Treatment, 9*, 133–137.

Malouf, R., Jacquette, G., Dobkin, J., and Brust, J.C.M. (1990). Neurologic disease in human immunodeficiency virus-infected drug abusers. *Archives of Neurology, 47*, 1002–1007.

Marder, K., Stern, Y., Malouf, R., Tang, M., Bell, K., Dooneief, G., El Sadr, W., Goldstein, S., Gorman, J., Richards, M., Sano, M., Sorrell, S., Todak, G., Williams, J., Ehrhardt, A., and Mayeux, R. (1992). Neurological and neuropsychological manifestations of human immunodeficiency virus infection in intravenous drug users without AIDS: Relationship to head injury. *Archives of Neurology, 49*, 1169–1175.

Martin, A., Heyes, M.P., Salazar, A.M., Kampen, M.S., Williams, J., Law, W.A., Coats, M.E., and Markey, S.P. (1992). Progressive slowing of reaction time and increasing cerebrospinal fluid concentrations of quinolinic acid in HIV-infected individuals. *Journal of Neuropsychiatry and Clinical Neuroscience, 4*, 270–279.

McCord, C., and Freeman, H.P. (1990). Excess mortality in Harlem. *New England Journal of Medicine, 322*, 173–177.

McKegney, F.P., O'Dowd, M.A., Feiner, C., Selwyn, P., Drucker, E., and Friedland, G.H. (1990). A prospective comparison of neuropsychologic function in HIV-positive and seronegative methadone-maintained patients. *AIDS, 4*, 565–569.

Richards, M., Sano, M., Goldstein, S., Mindry, D., Todak, G., and Stern, Y. (1992). The stability of neuropsychological test performance in a group of parenteral drug users. *Journal of Substance Abuse and Treatment, 9*, 371–377.

Rounsaville, B.J., Weissman, M.M., Rosenberger, P.H., Wilber, C.H., and Kleber, H.D. (1979). Detecting depressive disorders in drug abusers: A comparison of screening instruments. *Journal of Affective Disorders, 1*, 255–267.

Satz, P. (1993). Brain reserve capacity on symptom onset after brain injury: A formulation and review of evidence for threshold theory. *Neuropsychology, 7*, 273–295.

Silberstein, C.H., McKegney, F.P., O'Dowd, M.A., Selwyn, P.A., Schoenbaum, E., Drucker, E., Feiner, C., Cox, C.P., and Friedland, G. (1987). A prospective longitudinal study of neuropsychological and psychosocial factors in asymptomatic individuals at risk for HTLV-III/LAV infection in a methadone program: Preliminary findings. *International Journal of Neuroscience, 32*, 669–676.

Silberstein, C.H., O'Dowd, M.A., Friedland, G.H., Schoenbaum, E.E., Cochrane, K., Hartel, D., and McKegney, F.P. (1991). A four-year decline in neuropsychological function in symptomatic HIV seropositive and seronegative former intravenous drug users. Presented at the VIIth International Conference on AIDS, Florence, Italy (Abst. MB2048).

Stern, Y., Marder, K., Bell, K., Chen, J., Dooneief, G., Goldstein, S., Mindry, D., Richards, M., Sano, M., Williams, J., Gorman, J., Ehrhardt, A., and Mayeux, R. (1991). Multidisciplinary baseline assessment of gay men with and without human immunodeficiency virus infection: III. Neurologic and neuropsychological findings. *Archives of General Psychiatry, 48*, 131–138.

12

HIV, Cognition, and the Basal Ganglia

ALEX MARTIN

During the past decade, a great deal of neuropsychological research has been aimed at characterizing the patterns of cognitive deficit in persons with progressive dementias. One of the central lessons from this body of work concerns the heterogeneity of cognitive dysfunction in dementia. This heterogeneity is manifested at two levels of analysis: a general, interdisease level and a more specific, intradisease level. On the more general level, it is clear that there is no one-to-one mapping between *the clinical state of dementia and a specific pattern of cognitive dysfunction.* Rather, there is now a substantial body of evidence that different types of dementias, as defined by presumed etiology, are associated with different patterns of impaired and preserved cognitive abilities. The landmark studies of Nelson Butters and colleagues at the University of California, San Diego, have firmly established a number of striking and theoretically important differences between the cognitive deficits associated with Alzheimer's disease, on the one hand, and with Huntington's disease (HD), on the other. These contrasting patterns of impairment, in turn, have been instrumental in advancing our knowledge of the relationship between specific cortical and subcortical brain structures and different cognitive processes and memory systems (see Butters et al., 1990, for a recent review). While this point may seem obvious, it was only a few years ago that the idea that Alzheimer's disease and Huntington's disease were associated with distinct patterns of cognitive impairment was seriously challenged (e.g., Mayeux et al., 1983; Whitehouse, 1986).

It has also been well established that there is no one-to-one mapping between a *specific disease or type of dementia and a specific pattern of cognitive dysfunction.* For example, patients with Alzheimer's disease may present with markedly different patterns of cognitive impairment, especially during the earlier stages of the disease process. Studies of these patients have helped to advance our knowledge of the functions associated with specific neocortical regions (see Schwartz, 1990, for recent reviews).

It should be stressed that heterogeneity at the intradisease or disorder level neither supersedes nor negates heterogeneity at the interdisease level. Consideration of the underlying cause of heterogeneity will clarify the reason. The nature of a particular deficit is primarily determined by the location of the pathology. For reasons still unknown, Alzheimer's disease and HD are associated with specific distributions of pathology. Alzheimer's disease largely affects association cortex (parietal, temporal, frontal), medial temporal lobe structures (entorhinal cortex, hippocampus, amygdala), and select subcortical nuclei (locus coeruleus, raphe). In contrast, the neuropathology of HD is largely limited to areas of the basal ganglia (especially caudate and putamen) and to related prefrontal and limbic zones. Thus there is generally little overlap in the brain regions affected by one disorder in comparison to the regions affected by the other. This relative nonoverlap of the regional distribution of pathology is responsible for disease-specific patterns of cognitive dysfunction. However, it is not the case that all of the regions that may be affected by a particular disease are in fact affected in every case. Rather, the brain structures affected by a particular disease should be thought of as being at risk for developing pathology. These at-risk structures impose important disease-specific constraints on the location of pathology in the brains of individuals affected with the disease in question. Within these constraints, individuals may vary with regard to which structures are actually affected and over what time course. This variability is usually most evident during the early stages of a disorder, but it can even be seen at autopsy. Evidence of heterogeneity in Alzheimer's disease has come from detailed case studies. Highly specific patterns of cognitive deficits and related patterns of cortical dysfunction have been revealed by metabolic imaging studies of the brain, comparing one patient to another (see Martin, 1990, for review).

Disease-specific constraints on the location of pathology are responsible for the observed cognitive differences between groups of patients with one disorder (e.g., Alzheimer's disease) in comparison to those with another disorder (e.g., Huntington's disease). Variation within the boundaries of these disease-specific constraints are responsible for individual differences between patients with the same disorder. This intradisease variability is by no means rare. Rather it is commonly seen in association with all neurological diseases, and, as we will see below, serves as a critical starting point for any discussion of cognitive dysfunction in relation to a specific medical condition such as HIV infection.

A Lesson from the Past

From the spring of 1918 to the spring of 1919, of one of the great pandemics of modern times occurred. It has been estimated that nearly half of the world's population was infected with influenza during this period, and by the end of 1919 at least 15 million and perhaps as many as 25 million people died (Bucher, 1987). The flu pandemic of 1918–19 was preceded by the appearance of another infectious disease, also believed to be caused by a virus, that was extremely neurotropic. This pathogen, studied in detail by the famed neuropathologist and clinician Constatin von Economo, produced a constellation of neurological and neuropsychological symptoms that von Economo named *encephalitis lethargica*. From 1916 to 1926, approximately 5 million people were infected. Of these, 2 million died, 1 million recovered fully, and the remaining 2 million were left with various degrees of permanent neurologic deficit. Most common was the development of the parkinsonian syndrome that was described in Oliver Sacks' remarkable book, *Awakenings* (1973).

As Sacks noted, the manifestations of this illness were so varied that it seemed as if "a thousand new diseases had suddenly broken loose." This was true of the cognitive sequelae. Most commonly, however, the mental state of the patients with postencephalitic parkinsonism was characterized by marked slowing of thought (bradyphrenia) (Lishman, 1978). There were also occasional reports of aphasias, agnosias, and apraxias (Merritt, 1979). However, these signs of cortical involvement were apparently quite rare. Much more prominent were a variety of psychiatric disturbances including depression, hypomania, obsessive-compulsive disorder, and impulsive and bizarre behavior (Lishman, 1978). In fact, before von Economo's work, some of these patients were assigned a diagnosis of "epidemic schizophrenia" (Sacks, 1973, p. 13).

The clear association between the development of psychiatric disturbances and the brain pathology of encephalitis lethargica marked a critical point in the development of modern psychiatric thought. As Lishman (1978) noted:

> The thousands of cases available for observation displayed a wealth of psychopathological phenomena which could be clearly ascribed to pathological changes in the brain. This had an important influence on psychiatric thinking at a time when psychodynamic explanations for mental pathology were gaining perhaps too much ground. Certainly it focused attention on the relation between mental symptoms and brain structure in a way which few affections of the nervous system had done before. The sequelae of the disease demonstrated that an organic basis could sometimes exist for "functional" disturbances including tics, psychotic developments, far-reaching disturbances of personality, and particularly compulsions and other disturbances of will. (p. 411).

As stressed by von Economo (1929), the distribution of lesions responsible for these cognitive and behavioral manifestations varied from case to case. Tiny foci of inflammation were seen most prominently in the midbrain, diencephalon, and basal ganglia, although the cerebellum, cortex, and subcortical white matter could also be affected (Merritt, 1979). Nevertheless, inflammation in the basal ganglia and substantia nigra was clearly the most frequent finding. In fact, it was the nearly universal occurrence of pathology in these structures that led von Economo to suggest a common cause for the disorder despite the great variety of neurological and psychiatric symptoms seen (Lishman, 1978).

Given that different patterns of symptoms occurred, it might be expected that diagnostic confusion would be common. While this indeed appeared to be the case, von Economo maintained that a differential diagnosis could be made in the majority of cases. For example, although a schizophrenic-like syndrome could occur, encephalitis lethargica could be readily distinguished by the infected patients' "intellectual integrity, absence of delusions, and the patients' comprehension of their own pathological condition" (von Economo, 1929, p. 136). In this light, the conditions that presented the greatest challenge to von Economo's diagnostic skills are of particular interest. Prominently included by him as most troublesome were tumors of the frontal lobe (von Economo, 1929, p. 96) and "cerebral syphilis," especially when localized in the basal ganglia or substantia nigra (von Economo, 1929, p. 136).

The mention of neurosyphilis may be especially noteworthy. Relatively early in the acquired immunodeficiency syndrome (AIDS) pandemic, parallels were noted between AIDS-associated neurological and psychiatric dysfunction and the "Great Imitator," neurosyphilis (Sabin, 1987). In fact, the list of behavioral, cognitive, and motor symptoms initially offered to characterize the AIDS dementia complex by Price and colleagues was strikingly similar to the list of the most common symptoms of neurosyphilis (compare, e.g., Navia et al., 1986a, and Merritt et al., 1946). It is also of interest to note that although neurosyphilis commonly affected regions of the frontal and temporal lobes, focal presentations could occur with pathology limited to select cortical and/or subcortical regions (Merritt et al., 1946). The syndrome of relatively focal neurosyphilis was described in detail by H. Lissauer and by another prominent neuropathologist with particular interest in focal disease of the cerebral hemispheres, Alois Alzheimer. In fact, it was Alzheimer who suggested that these atypical cases of neurospyhilis be called *Lissauer's dementia paralytica* (Merritt et al., 1946).

Thus, the outbreak of encephalitis lethargica around the time of the great flu pandemic of 1918–19 presented a picture of variable neurological and psychiatric symptoms. Moreover, the disorder seemed to have different consequences, depending on the victim's age: The parkinsonian syndrome was common in adults, psychopathology and personality change were common in children, and generalized mental retardation was most often seen in infants (Lishman, 1978). However, within this picture of variable manifestations, two generalizations stand out with regard to cognitive dysfunction and neuropathology in the adult postencephalitic patient: (1) marked bradyphrenia in the absence of frank aphasic, agnosic, and apraxic symptoms and (2) involvement of certain subcortical regions of the brain, especially the basal ganglia.

HIV Infection and the Basal Ganglia

Evidence for the hypothesis that basal ganglia dysfunction plays a central role in the cognitive and behavioral changes associated with human immunodeficiency virus (HIV) infection of the brain comes from a variety of sources:

1. The regional distribution of neuropathology seen at autopsy (de la Monte et al., 1987; see Sharer, 1992, for recent review).
2. The regional distribution of HIV antigen (Pumarola-Sune et al., 1987; Kure et al., 1990).

3. Regional abnormalities in glucose utilization, as revealed by positron emission tomography (PET) (Rottenberg et al., 1987; van Gorp et al., 1992).

4. Increased sensitivity to the extrapyramidal side effects of neuroleptic treatment (Breitbart et al., 1988; Maj, 1990).

5. The correspondence between the neuropsychological profile of patients with known basal ganglia pathology (e.g., HD) and cognitively impaired, HIV-infected individuals.

All of the data on the regional distribution of pathology in the HIV-infected brain prominently include the basal ganglia. However, HIV-related changes are by no means limited to this region. Rather, as a rule, the neuropathological, immunohistochemical, and neuroimaging data indicate that a wide range of sub-cortical structures are involved. In addition, more recent evidence has demon-strated that cortical tissue, perhaps especially from the frontal region, can also be compromised (Ketzler et al., 1990; Everall et al., 1991; Wiley et al., 1991; Masliah et al., 1992). Nevertheless, the basal ganglia and related structures appear to be the most consistently affected. In this regard, the neuropathological findings are reminiscent of the problem that confronted von Economo regarding a primary site of action for encephalitis lethargica.

Before turning to the clinical manifestations of HIV infection, a final source of evidence relevant to the site of action of HIV should be discussed. Several investigators have proposed that HIV adversely influences brain function by potentiating the release of neurotoxins (see Chapter 17). Despite disagreement over the nature of the purported toxin, there appears to be a consensus among investigators that HIV's adverse effects on brain function are mediated via inter-ruption, and perhaps eventual destruction, of N-methyl-D-aspartate (NMDA) receptors (see Lipton, 1992, for a recent review). These receptors are not found uniformly throughout the brain but rather have a specific distribution, with their highest concentrations in the hippocampus, association cortex (especially frontal cortex), and basal ganglia. In fact, the basal ganglia (in particular, the caudate, putamen, and nucleus accumbens) have a higher concentration of NMDA recep-tors than any other noncortical region (Cotman et al., 1987).

Taken together, the findings from a variety of sources are consistent with the hypothesis that the basal ganglia are a prominent site of action for either the direct or indirect effects of HIV. If so, then it would be expected that the neu-rological and neuropsychological manifestations of HIV infection would be sim-ilar to those commonly seen following structural damage to the basal ganglia and related structures. In other words, with reference to the previous discussion of heterogeneity, one would expect that HIV-infected subjects with central nervous system (CNS) involvement would bear a stronger resemblance to patients with HD than to patients with Alzheimer's dementia.

AIDS and Subcortical Dementia

The pioneer studies by Price and colleagues at the Memorial Sloan-Kettering Cancer Center during the mid-1980s provided the first detailed clinical and neu-ropathological description of an HIV-associated dementia that was not due to opportunistic infection or other secondary manifestations of immune suppression. They termed this syndrome the *AIDS dementia complex* (Navia et al., 1986a,b; see Navia, 1990, for review). Like other neurological conditions we have discussed, the cognitive and behavioral manifestations were quite variable. Nevertheless, the authors maintained that "There was enough uniformity among our patients to define a distinct syndrome resembling in several aspects other disorders that have been classified together as 'subcortical dementias' " (Navia et al., 1986b, p. 523).

The term *subcortical dementia* has been used to group together a number of diverse conditions. These include degenerative disorders (e.g., HD, Parkinson's disease, progressive supranuclear palsy), vascular disorders (e.g., thalamic infarction), metabolic disorders (e.g., Wilson's disease, Binswanger's disease), demyelinating diseases (e.g., multiple sclerosis), and other assorted conditions (e.g., dementia pugilistica, normal pressure hydrocephalus) (Cummings, 1990). It was unfortunate that the distinction between the presentation of patients with these disorders and that of patients with the so-called cortical dementia of Alzheimer's disease was made on anatomical grounds. It is now recognized that, anatomically, this distinction is imprecise. Nevertheless, the conditions classified as subcortical dementias share a number of important similarities with regard to their clinical presentation. Although these features will be described in more detail below, chief among them is a more or less generalized slowing of mentation that occurs in the absence of the syndromes typically associated with cortical damage (i.e., the aphasias, agnosias, and apraxias). It was this clinical presentation, coupled with supportive neuropathological findings, that led Price and colleagues to classify the AIDS dementia Complex as a subcortical dementia (Navia et al., 1986b, p. 523).

As noted by Cummings in a recent review, although the region of brain dysfunction may vary, "The principal structure involved in most subcortical dementias is the striatum" (Cummings, 1990, p. 11). The subcortical dementia that most clearly involves pathology of the striatal region of the basal ganglia (especially the caudate) is HD. Moreover, HD has been the disease most carefully characterized neuropsychologically. Patients with this disorder commonly present with a constellation of deficits that include bradyphrenia (Huber and Paulson, 1987), reduced output on verbal fluency tests (Butters et al., 1986), impaired recall on memory tests (Weingartner et al., 1979), poor performance on tests dependent on egocentric spatial processing (Brouwers et al., 1984; Bylsma et al., 1992), impaired set switching and planning difficulties (Fedio et al., 1979), and impaired acquisition of motor skills (Martone et al., 1984; Heindel et al., 1988, 1989). In contrast, HD patients perform markedly better on tests of recognition memory (Butters et al., 1986), basic language abilities, and extrapersonal visuospatial skills (see Brandt and Butters, 1986; Folstein et al., 1990; and Huber and Shuttleworth, 1990, for recent reviews).

Cognition in HIV Infection: The Walter Reed Study

With this degree of detail in mind, one can ask whether the neuropsychological performance of HIV-infected individuals conforms to the pattern of impaired and preserved cognitive abilities seen in patients with HD. My colleagues and I attempted to address this question in a longitudinal study of individuals in the relatively early stage of infection. Before describing the study, the notion of *early stage* needs to be clarified. As highlighted in a number of chapters in this text, the question of whether cognitive and behavioral changes occur during the early stages of infection has captured considerable attention and remains controversial. From the outset, it should be stressed that *early stage* in this context has almost invariably been defined by whether or not subjects present with constitutional symptoms (e.g., weight loss, persistent fever, and/or diarrhea; judgments usually based on the subject's own report), and not by time since infection, which, in the vast majority of cases, is unknown. Definitions of early stage based on constitutional symptoms, as well as definitions based on immunological parameters such as CD4 lymphocyte cell counts (e.g., the Walter Reed Classification System [WR]; Redfield et al., 1986), presuppose that these markers of disease progression are valid and reliable indicators of the status of the CNS. That is, it has been implicitly assumed that the disease status of the body and the CNS are directly linked and thus highly correlated at all stages of infection. Whether or not this assumption is valid has not been determined. In fact, it is clear that the CNS and bodily disease are not necessarily linked because a substantial proportion of AIDS patients never develop neurological manifestations during the course of their illness (Levy et al., 1985; Price et al., 1988). Conversely, the fact that neurological symptoms, including dementia, have been reported as the first signs of illness (Navia and Price, 1987), and are recognized as a criterion for the diagnosis of AIDS (CDC, 1987), adds further support to the likelihood that constitutional symptoms and peripheral blood CD4 cell count may not be good indicators of the integrity of the CNS.

Our first attempt to explore the presence and nature of cognitive dysfunction in HIV-infected individuals without the complicating factors associated with AIDS utilized a comprehensive neuropsychological test battery. The battery was designed to assess a wide range of functions dependent on the integrity of both cortical and subcortical structures. The battery took approximately 6 hours to complete and was administered according to a fixed schedule during 2-hour sessions on 3 different days (A. Martin et al., 1992).

The HIV+ subject group consisted of 52 active duty military personnel. Because subjects in the relatively early stages of infection as defined by the CD4 count may experience constitutional symptoms, while others with more severe depletion of CD4 cells may not, subjects were classified with regard to both objective measures of immunological status (the WR System) and the presence of one or more constitutional symptoms (CDC, 1986). Using the WR framework, 35 of the subjects (67%) had CD4 counts above 400 cells/mm^3 of blood at initial evaluation (WR stages 1 and 2), with the majority of these individuals having generalized lymphadenopathy ($N = 28$, WR stage 2). The remaining 17 subjects all had CD4 counts <400 cells/mm^3. No subject had an opportunistic infection or a clinical diagnosis of AIDS (WR stage 6). When classified by the presence of constitutional disease independent of CD4 count, 37 (71%) subjects were asymptomatic while the remaining 15 HIV+ individuals had one or more constitutional symptoms. However, in this study the symptomatic subjects were still in the rel-

TABLE 12–1. Percentage of Subjects with Neurobehavioral Complaints

Domain	All HIV+ Subjects (N = 52)	Psychiatric Controls (N = 15)
Mood changes	88	80
Fatigue/concentration	85	53
Sleep	77	73
Sensory changes	69	60
Speech/language	64	40
Headache	60	33
Memory/learning	54	47
Motor	44	27
Visuospatial analysis	33	0
Perceptual recognition	17	7

Source: Based on A. Martin et al. (1992).

Note: Note: A χ^2 analysis indicated that more HIV+ subjects complained of fatigue/concentration difficulties and visuospatial problems than did the psychiatric controls ($p < .05$). All other comparisons were not significant ($p > .05$).

atively early stages, with CD4 counts exceeding 400 cells/mm^3 in 9 of these 15 subjects.

For comparison purposes, we included two HIV− control groups that were matched with the HIV+ group on education and military rank. One group consisted of 18 normal subjects. The other control group consisted of 15 patients meeting established criteria for a psychiatric diagnosis of adjustment disorder (DSM-III-R; American Psychiatric Association, 1987). The combined seronegative (N = 33) and HIV+ groups (N = 52) were closely matched on racial distribution (see A. Martin et al., 1992, for complete details).

The psychiatric control group was included because adjustment disorder is one of the most common psychiatric diagnoses among early-stage, HIV+ individuals (e.g., Maj, 1990), and we were particularly concerned about the effect of mood on neuropsychological performance. Standard clinical interview revealed that suicidal ideation was present in six of these HIV− individuals, with three having recent, documented suicide attempts. These adjustment disorder patients were comparable to the HIV+ group on self-report measures of depression (Beck and Steer, 1987) and anxiety (Spielberger, 1983).

The seronegative adjustment disorder patients and the HIV+ subjects also had similar types of cognitive and motor complaints (see Table 12–1). The main exception was a greater frequency of complaints of fatigue and concentration difficulties, as well as visuospatial problems in the HIV+ subjects in comparison to the psychiatric controls. Although these data may suggest that neurobehavioral complaints by HIV+ subjects primarily reflect mood changes, additional analyses of a larger cohort of subjects suggested that this may not be the case. Rather, we found that HIV+ subjects who complained were also more likely to perform poorly on neuropsychological tests in comparison to HIV+ subjects who did not complain and also in comparison to HIV− psychiatric controls. Thus, although the frequency and type of complaint may be generally similar, these complaints may have a different significance in HIV+ subjects than they do in HIV− controls (Mapou et al., 1993).

Among the findings highlighted in the initial report were that the HIV+ group was significantly slower on tests of simple and choice (go–no go) reaction time (RT) in comparison to both of the HIV− control groups. Approximately 20% of the HIV+ subjects had abnormally slow simple RTs (vs. 9% of the controls), and 33% had abnormally slow choice RTs (vs. 3% of the controls) ("abnormal" was defined as two or more standard deviations [SDs] slower than the mean of the combined group of normal and psychiatric controls).

In contrast, no significant differences were found on standard neuropsychological tests between HIV+ subjects and the combined group of HIV− controls or between the HIV− adjustment disorder and normal control subjects. Analyses of the proportion of subjects in each group with abnormal scores also failed to reveal significant differences.

As we noted in that report, data from the standard measures were included to facilitate comparison with other studies. Moreover, the choice of the specific measures was dictated by the tests that had been used in several large-scale studies that found no differences between early-stage, HIV+ subjects and HIV− controls (Janssen et al., 1989; McArthur et al., 1989). Our intent was to show that whether or not HIV+ subjects perform abnormally may depend, in part, on the type of test employed. We also reported that the HIV+ subjects tended to perform more slowly when the RT tests were repeated 6 months later and that the increased slowing was closely paralleled by increases in cerebrospinal fluid concentrations of a potent endogenous neurotoxin, quinolinic acid. We will return to this topic shortly. We mention this finding here because it played a large role in convincing us that the RT deficit was likely related to CNS dysfunction and not to some confounding variable (A. Martin et al., 1992).

Performance on some of the other measures included in the battery is displayed in Figure 12–1. The figure shows the percentage of HIV+ and HIV− subjects that performed ≥2 SDs below the control group mean. Also indicated are significant group differences based on the t-test or, where appropriate, the Mann-Whitney U Test. There were no significant differences between the normal and psychiatric HIV-controls on either these or any of the other measures in the battery.

RT Tests

Beginning with the studies of Perdices and Cooper (1989) and Wilkie et al. (1990), tasks employing RT as their dependent measure have proven to be among the most sensitive indicators of HIV-related dysfunction (e.g., Levin et al., 1990; Bornstein et al., 1991; A. Martin et al., 1992, 1993a; E. M. Martin et al., 1992; Wilkie et al., 1992). Moreover, several studies, including our own, have reported that significant slowing can be detected prior to the onset of constitutional symptoms (although see Miller et al., 1991, for contrary evidence).

These findings do not, of course, require an explanation based on HIV-produced CNS dysfunction. Subtle slowing of responses when measured with

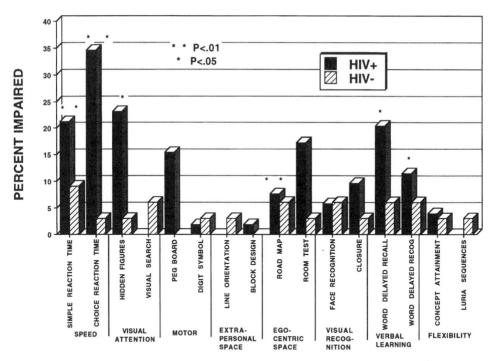

FIGURE 12–1. Percent of subjects in the HIV+ (N = 52) and HIV– (N = 33) groups who performed 2 or more SDs below the control group mean on select neuropsychological measures. Also indicated are significant group differences.

millisecond precision could potentially be due to a variety of sources. These sources could include lack of sleep, drug and alcohol use, depressed mood, history of head injury or psychiatric illness, peripheral neuropathy or injury, or non-CNS effects of the virus that might produce subtle malaise or fatigue. Despite these alternative interpretations, we found the group differences on simple and choice RT compelling for several reasons:

1. In our study, the RT tasks were clearly the most sensitive measures, producing robust group differences at initial evaluation and over repeated testing sessions and capturing the largest percentage of impaired individuals (see Figure 12–1).

2. The HIV+ subjects were significantly slower than equally depressed psychiatric controls.

3. Response speed was significantly correlated with a biological parameter; cerebrospinal fluid concentrations of a known neurotoxin, quinolinic acid (A. Martin et al., 1992, 1993a). (Simple RT has also been found to be significantly correlated with cerebral atrophy in HIV+ subjects as assessed by magnetic resonance imaging; Levin et al., 1990).

4. As will be discussed below, in our study slowing occurred as part of a pattern of impaired and intact abilities consistent with relatively focal involvement of a specific brain region, that is, the basal ganglia (A. Martin et al., 1989a, 1992, 1993a).

Other Measures of Speed, Attention, and Motor Functioning

Although several studies have shown RT differences between relatively early stage HIV+ subjects and appropriate controls, the interpretation of this difference is uncertain. In our study, differences were found on both simple and choice RT and on decision time, as estimated by the differences between the simple and choice conditions (Gottsdanker and Shragg, 1985). In fact, the differences in decision time held when the groups were equated for simple RT by eliminating HIV+ subjects who were abnormally slow on this condition (A. Martin et al., 1989b). This suggested that at least some HIV+ subjects had a true slowing of mentation independent of differences in motor RT.

In addition, however, the data are consistent with one or more deficits in arousal, orienting, sustaining attention, and/or motor processes. Fatigue may have also played a role because the RT tasks took nearly 15 minutes to complete. Given the differences in RT between our HIV+ subjects and controls, and given the prominent role assigned to attention and motor dysfunction in the clinical description of the subcortical dementias, one might expect that differences also would be found on other measures of attention, speeded performance, and motor ability.

In general, however, this was not the case. Additional measures of attention included in our battery were auditory and visual attention span or immediate memory (Wechsler Adult Intelligence Scale-Revised [WAIS-R] Digit Span subtest, Wechsler, 1981; Corsi block span, as described in Milner, 1971), a visual search task, and a hidden figures test. Motor dexterity and coding speed were assessed by the Purdue Pegboard (Vaughn and Costa, 1963) and the WAIS-R Digit Symbol subtest, respectively. Several timed paper-and-pencil tests were also administered. These consisted of the visual search test, a complex maze task, tests of letter, semantic category, and figural fluency (Ekstrom et al., 1976; Benton and Hamsher, 1978), and the Block Design, Object Assembly, and Digit Symbol subtests of the WAIS-R. As a group, the HIV+ subjects tended to perform worse than controls on all of these measures. However, significant group differences were not found using either parametric or nonparametric analyses. Moreover, there were no group differences with regard to the proportion of impaired versus unimpaired scores (with impaired defined as ≥ 2 SDs from the control mean).

While the HIV+ subjects performed well on these tasks, there were two exceptions. First, the HIV+ subjects were impaired on a hidden figures task of visual attention (finding geometric patterns obscured by random lines, t-test, $p < .05$). Second, although the group means were similar, more HIV+ subjects than controls were abnormally slow on the Purdue Pegboard test ($\chi^2 = 5.6$; $p < .05$; see Figure 12–1). Nevertheless, based on the overall pattern of results, one would be forced to conclude that the relatively low-level (with regard to cognitive demands) RT tasks were clearly more sensitive than more traditional measures of attention and motor performance. Although this sensitivity may simply be a reflection of measuring response speed on the millisecond level, additional study is clearly warranted to elucidate the deficit or deficits underlying differences in RT.

Visuospatial Processing

One way of classifying visuospatial processes is with regard to those that rely on extrapersonal versus egocentric frames of reference (e.g., Howard, 1982). *Extrapersonal space* refers to the position of objects within a fixed, external frame of reference and the position of one object relative to another object within this space. Thus, extrapersonal tests rely on judgments of the exact or relative location or orientation of an object in reference to some external frame. Examples of neuropsychological tests that are dependent in part on this ability are constructional tasks (e.g., Rey-Osterrieth Complex Figure, WAIS-R Block Design) and tests of localization and spatial orientation (e.g., Judgment of Line Orientation; Benton et al., 1983). There is a large body of evidence from both human and nonhuman primates indicating that this type of spatial process is critically dependent on the functioning of the parietal lobes (see Desimone and Ungerleider, 1989, for review).

In contrast, *egocentric spatial ability* refers to the analysis of objects in relation to the frame of reference defined by the observer's viewpoint. This ability has not received as much attention in the neuropsychology literature as has extrapersonal spatial skills. However, the available evidence from monkeys (e.g., Pohl, 1973) and humans (e.g., Semmes et al., 1963; Butters et al., 1972) suggests that this ability is dependent on the frontal lobes. In addition, impaired egocentric spatial ability has been found in patients with HD, even though these same patients may have intact or substantially better preserved extrapersonal visuospatial skills (Potegal, 1971; Brouwers et al., 1984; Bylsma et al., 1992). Egocentric spatial dysfunction has also been found in rats with selective lesions of the caudate (Abraham et al., 1983). Thus, the evidence suggests that the basal ganglia and the frontal lobes may play an important role in the performance of egocentric spatial tasks.

Our battery included two measures of egocentric spatial ability. One measure, the Road-Map Test of Directional Sense, was previously used in several of the studies mentioned above. In this test, subjects are required to state whether they would turn left or right to stay on a clearly marked path depicted on a street map (Money, 1976). The other task we employed was a newly devised procedure called the Room Test (A. Martin et al., 1993b). In brief, subjects were shown a drawing of a square with a cross located in the center. Each side of the square was a different color. The subjects were told that the square represented a room with each wall painted a different color. They were asked to imagine themselves positioned on the centrally located cross. They were then read a series of questions, each requiring them to image themselves rotated in a different spatial position in order to achieve the correct answer. For example, subjects were told to "imagine that you have your back to the blue wall; which wall is on your left?"; "imagine that you are lying on your left side with your head towards the red wall; which wall is behind you?"

The HIV+ subjects had difficulty with these egocentric spatial tasks, especially in relation to their performance on tests of extrapersonal spatial functioning (see Figure 12–1). The HIV+ subjects were significantly impaired on the Road-Map Test ($p < .01$); the Mann-Whitney U Test was used because the data were not normally distributed. Differences were also noted on the t-test; ($p < .05$). Although very few individuals performed below the 2-SD cutoff, 21.2% of the HIV+ subjects scored more than 1.5 SDs below the normal mean versus only 6.1% of the controls ($\chi^2 = 3.55$; $p = .06$). On the Room Test, analysis of the group data failed to reveal significant differences. However, 17.3% of the HIV+ subjects versus 3% of the controls performed in the impaired range ($\chi^2 = 3.96$; $p < .05$) (see Figure 12–1). Thus these findings suggested that at least some HIV+ subjects had difficulty with egocentric spatial judgments but not with extrapersonal spatial skills.

Visual Recognition and Identification

Several measures of the ability to recognize and identify visual material were included in the battery to assess the functioning of the posterior temporal lobes. These included tests of face recognition (Benton et al., 1983) and a measure of visual closure that required subjects to name incomplete or fragmented pictures of real objects (items were selected from Ekstrom et al., 1976, and Street, 1931). The HIV+ subjects experienced little difficulty with these tasks (see Figure 12–1) or with a test of object naming (Kaplan et al., 1983; data reported in A. Martin et al., 1992). Thus, taken together with the tests of extrapersonal spatial skills, these findings suggested that posterior parietal and temporal regions were unaffected.

Episodic Memory and Retrieval Processes

Patients with HD often have difficulty recalling recently presented information. It has been argued, however, that this reflects primarily a retrieval problem rather than inability to encode properly or store information (e.g., Butters et al., 1986). This argument is supported by normal or substantially better than would be expected recognition memory for the same material. The reduced output of these patients on tests requiring speeded generation of word lists (verbal fluency tests) is also consistent with a retrieval deficit hypothesis for HD.

As we reported previously (A. Martin et al., 1992), the HIV+ subjects performed well on measures of verbal and nonverbal episodic or declarative memory, as assessed by select subtests from the Wechsler Memory Scale (recall of stories and reproduction of geometric forms; Wechsler and Stone, 1945) and by tests of verbal fluency. These subjects were also tested on a word-list learning test in which 12 items were presented for immediate recall. Five trials of free recall data were collected. Following a delay of 30 minutes, subjects were required to recall the words and to recognize them from among a list that included semantically related, phonemically related, and unrelated foils. The delayed recall data from this test are included in Figure 12–1. In contrast to their normal recall of the more highly organized stories from the Wechsler Memory Scale (at immediate recall and after a 60-minute delay), the HIV+ subjects were impaired on the word-list learning test. More than 20% (vs. 6% of the controls) performed in the abnormal range ($\chi^2 = 3.55$; $p = .06$). As a group, recognition performance was also poorer than control levels, but substantially fewer HIV+ subjects were impaired using the 2-SD cutoff (11.5% of HIV+ subjects vs. 6% for controls).

Overall, these results were rather inconclusive. The HIV+ subjects appeared to perform well on some memory tests and not on others. This inconsistency is reflective of the literature in general, in which some studies have reported learning and memory deficits in early-stage subjects, while others have not (e.g., compare Grant et al., 1987; Wilkie et al., 1990; Stern et al., 1991 to Miller et al., 1990; Selnes et al., 1990; McAllister et al., 1992). Although the word-list learning data suggested that retrieval may be more affected than other components, the good performance by these HIV+ subjects on verbal fluency tasks was not consistent with the retrieval deficit hypothesis. It may be that significant learning and memory deficits do not develop until latter in the illness. Longitudinal study will be needed to determine whether an episodic memory deficit exists and whether this deficit is primarily a problem with retrieval.

Procedural, Motor-Skill Learning

Although the hippocampus and related medial temporal lobe structures are known to play a critical role in episodic or declarative memory, damage to this brain region seems to have little or no effect on the acquisition of procedural knowledge and skills (see Squire and Zola-Morgan, 1991, for a review). In contrast, damage to the basal ganglia has been shown to have detrimental effects on procedural learning (e.g., Butters et al., 1990).

One of the more commonly used measures of procedural learning has been the pursuit rotor learning task. Studies from Nelson Butters' laboratory (Heindel et al., 1988, 1989) have shown that patients with basal ganglia involvement and cognitive dysfunction (HD and Parkinson's disease patients) perform poorly on this task, while amnesic patients and patients with Alzheimer's disease perform as well as their matched controls.

Based on these studies and on the HD-like pattern of cognitive dysfunction that we noted in our HIV+ subjects, we decided to use the pursuit rotor test to assess the acquisition of a novel motor skill. Twenty-nine HIV+ subjects participated in the study. Thirteen had CD4 counts above 400 cells/mm^3 (WR stage 1 or 2), and 25 were without constitutional symptoms. Analysis of the averaged, grouped data failed to indicate a difference. However, similar to HD patients, 24% of the HIV+ subjects (7 of 29, 5 of whom were asymptomatic) showed minimal learning (A. Martin et al., 1993a) (Figure 12–2). Procedural learning, at least when assessed by a motor learning task, seemed to be impaired in some HIV+ subjects.

Working Memory and Processing Capacity

The above findings suggested that memory processes dependent on the functioning of medial temporal lobe structures were generally intact, while those believed to involve the basal ganglia were impaired in a subgroup of HIV+ individuals.

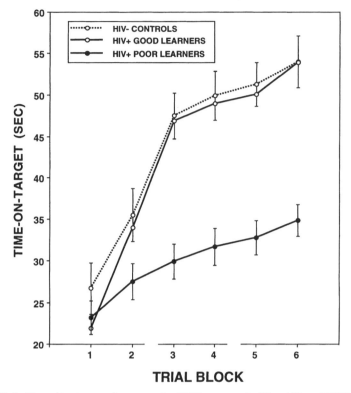

FIGURE 12–2. Pursuit rotor performance by HIV− controls (N = 15) and HIV+ subjects who performed poorly (N = 7) versus those who performed normally (N = 22). The HIV+ poor learners were also significantly slower, and had significantly higher concentrations of CSF QUIN than the HIV+ good learners. Points are mean ± SEM. (From Martin et al., 1993a.)

However, the relatively good performance by the HIV+ subjects on most measures of episodic memory stood in marked contrast to their frequent complaints of learning and concentration difficulties (see Table 12–1). We therefore decided to extend our study of memory processes to components of working memory.

Within the framework proposed by Baddeley, *working memory* refers to a processing system responsible for the temporary storage and manipulation of information (see Baddeley, 1992, for a review). We employed a dual-task paradigm to assess what Baddeley has termed the *central executive*. In his model the central executive is responsible for attentional control and coordination of processing resources and is primarily a function of the frontal lobes. We reasoned that if some HIV+ subjects have limited processing capacity, then a dual-task procedure, which places strong demands on attentional resources, should provide a good means for revealing this difficulty.

The results, however, did not support this prediction. The dual-task manipulation decreased memory span capacity and interfered with a visual detection task to an equal extent in asymptomatic HIV+ subjects ($N = 26$) and HIV− controls ($N = 23$). Interestingly, however, the HIV+ subjects' RTs on the detection task were significantly slower than control levels. This finding added to the evidence that some HIV+ subjects perform abnormally slowly and suggested that the impaired mechanisms or processes underlying this slowing are not involved in working memory (Law et al., in press).

Flexibility, Concept Formation, and Problem Solving

Consistent with the normal performance of the HIV+ subjects on the dual-task, working memory paradigm, the HIV+ subjects performed as well as controls on a number of tasks believed to be sensitive to pathology of the frontal lobes. These included the Wisconsin Card Sorting Test (Grant and Berg, 1948; data presented in A. Martin et al., 1992), the Verbal Concept Attainment Test (Rosen, 1962, as cited in Bornstein and Leason, 1985), and a series of sequential motor and graphomotor tasks requiring production of alternating sequences modeled after procedures developed by Luria (1966) (see Figure 12–1). Other measures that we have employed to evaluate problem-solving ability and mental flexibility include the Tower of London problems (Shallice, 1982), a maze-learning task (Martin and Kampen, 1987), and a measure of the ability to find alternative uses for common objects (Substitute Uses; Ekstrom et al., 1976). The normal performance by our HIV+ subjects on these tasks, as well as on measures of verbal fluency and design fluency, suggested that the frontal lobes may remain relatively intact even in individuals with marked slowing of RT and other indications of CNS involvement.

These results were somewhat surprising given the close anatomical connection between certain basal ganglia structures and the frontal lobes and the difficulty seen in patients with HD on frontal lobe tests. One possibility is that deficits on these measures may not emerge until later in the disease process. In fact, Bornstein, who had previously shown that the Verbal Concept Attainment Test was sensitive to left frontal lobe damage (Bornstein and Leason, 1985), has reported that AIDS patients were more likely to be impaired on this test than were early-stage, HIV+ subjects or controls (Bornstein et al., 1993). A similar pattern of results was reported by Grant et al. (1987, 1992) using another task that has been linked to frontal lobe functioning (Halstead's Category Test). Again, longitudinal evaluation will be needed to confirm this possibility.

Quinolinic Acid and GP-120-Related Neurotoxicity

Although the mechanism by which HIV disrupts neuronal functioning remains to be clarified, there has been mounting evidence that HIV CNS-related effects are mediated via NMDA receptor dysfunction. One possibility is that neuronal dysfunction is mediated directly by the external envelope protein of HIV, gp-120. This hypothesis was tested by Douglas Brenneman and colleagues, who found that low concentrations of gp-120 killed mouse hippocampal neurons in vitro (Brenneman et al., 1988). More recently, Brenneman and colleagues, in collaboration with our Walter Reed group, found that the CSF from 9 of 18 early-stage HIV+ subjects who had participated in our initial neuropsychological investigation was neurotoxic in their mouse hippocampal neuron culture system. Moreover, the CSF neurotoxicity was immunologically and pharmacologically similar to the neurotoxicity that resulted from direct application of gp-120 (e.g., in both cases neuronal death was inhibited by the mouse anti-CD4+ antibody; Buzy et al., 1992).

However, other evidence suggests that gp-120 alone is not sufficient to cause neuronal damage unless it is accompanied by glutamate-related molecules (Lipton, 1992). In a series of studies, Melvyn Heyes of the National Institutes of Mental Health has shown that a glutamate-related endogenous neurotoxin, quinolinic acid (QUIN), is abnormally elevated in the CSF of HIV-infected individuals. CSF QUIN is also elevated in patients with other inflammatory disorders of the CNS but not in patients with noninflammatory CNS conditions, including Alzheimer's disease, HD, schizophrenia, and epilepsy (Heyes et al., 1992b). This excitotoxin is an agonist of the NMDA receptor that mediates its convulsant and neurotoxic effects (Schwarcz et al., 1983). Interestingly, it has been shown that intrastriatal injection of QUIN produces lesions that are highly similar, both neuroanatomically and neurochemically, to the lesions of HD (Schwarcz et al., 1983; Beal et al., 1986; see Bruyn and Stoof, 1990, for a recent review).

Heyes, in collaboration with Richard Price and Bruce Brew of the Memorial Sloan-Kettering Cancer Center and our Walter Reed group, also found that CSF QUIN was significantly related to cognitive impairment. Modest but significant elevations were found in many of our early-stage subjects, and markedly increased concentrations were noted in patients with AIDS dementia (Heyes et al., 1991). More recently, and again in collaboration with Heyes, we have reported that CSF QUIN concentrations can increase over time (6-month test-retest interval) and that this increase is significantly correlated with progressive slowing of RT (A. Martin et al., 1992). We have also found that the HIV+ subjects who performed poorly on the pursuit rotor task also had significantly higher concentrations of CSF QUIN, and were significantly slower, than HIV+ subjects who performed normally on this measure of motor-skill learning (A. Martin et al., 1993a).

The possibility that neurotoxic QUIN may play a critical role in HIV-related CNS dysfunction has been further supported by several additional findings. These include a significant correlation between CSF QUIN and intelligence in HIV+ children and, following antiretroviral treatment, decreased CSF QUIN coupled with improved IQ scores in these infected children (Brouwers et al., 1991; see Heyes et al., 1991, for a similar finding in adult AIDS patients). Abnormally increased CSF QUIN has also been observed in neurologically impaired monkeys infected with the simian immunodeficiency virus (SIV) relative to SIV-infected monkeys without CNS involvement (Heyes et al., 1992a). Finally, as in our adult HIV+ subjects, CSF QUIN was found to be significantly correlated with performance on a motor skill task in SIV-infected monkeys (see Chapter 17).

Based on these and other related findings, the following model is proposed. It is known that QUIN is a normal by-product of the metabolism of the amino acid precursor L-tryptophan via the kynurenine pathway. The first enzyme in this pathway, idolamine 2,3 dioxygenase, is activated by interferon gamma and other cytokines (Heyes et al., 1991). Thus, in response to an infectious agent, the release of gamma interferon may result in abnormally high production of QUIN via activation of the kynurenine pathway. In brain, QUIN may be released from macrophages in response to interferon gamma (Heyes et al., 1992c). The possibility that gp-120 may activate macrophages to secrete QUIN has also been raised (Lipton, 1992).

As mentioned previously, the basal ganglia are rich in NMDA receptors (Cotman et al., 1987) and also have a high concentration of HIV-infected cells (Kure et al., 1990). Therefore, the basal ganglia may be a prominent site of neuronal dysfunction due to HIV-stimulated release of QUIN from macrophages, which would then disrupt functioning in this NMDA receptor-rich region of the brain. The heightened metabolic activity in the basal ganglia seen on PET studies (Rottenberg et al., 1987; van Gorp et al., 1992) may be an indication of QUIN's localized excitotoxic effects. Although speculative in part, such a model illustrates how a generalized inflammatory response may lead to specific disruption of a select region of the brain, which, in turn, could ultimately result in a rather specific pattern of cognitive and behavioral dysfunction.

Final Comment

Our studies of a select group of HIV+-infected individuals suggested a profile of more or less subtle cognitive and motor dysfunction that was broadly consistent with the hypothesis of basal ganglia dysfunction. The findings were strongest for the simple and choice RT tasks, followed by motor skill learning and, to a lesser extent, egocentric spatial ability. Little evidence was obtained in support of deficits in retrieval processes or for impairments on tasks of problem solving, mental flexibility, working memory or other frontal lobe–type functions. Processes dependent on the posterior temporal and parietal cortex were intact. The landscape of impaired and preserved abilities illustrated in Figure 12–1 is thus more similar to the profile that would be expected from patients with HD than from patients with Alzheimer's disease.

However, it should be stressed that the performance of the HIV+ subjects was indistinguishable from that of HIV-controls on the majority of tests that we administered. When deficits were noted, they were found in only approximately 20–33% of the subjects tested. Moreover, it is important to note that none of these HIV+ subjects met diagnostic criteria for dementia (see Chapter 5 for a discussion of diagnostic issues). Dysfunction, when present, was usually mild based on psychometric criteria. Although, from a psychometric standpoint, dysfunction tended to be more severe on the RT tasks for certain individuals (≥ 3 SDs from the control mean), this finding does not necessarily mean that the slowing was clinically significant. In fact, the good performance by many of these same individuals on other tests of speeded performance suggests that the slowing observed on the millisecond level may not be clinically relevant.

On the other hand, as indicated in Table 12–1, the majority of the HIV+

subjects who participated in our studies had many complaints of cognitive and mood changes. Moreover, the subjects themselves often perceived these problems as interfering with their activities of daily living. Whether this was in fact the case cannot be addressed by our data. Studies specifically designed to address this critical but highly complex issue are sorely needed (see Heaton et al., in press, for an excellent example of an approach to this problem).

Our approach has been to formulate and test a highly specific hypothesis. We began with the notion that if cognition and motor functions were disrupted in HIV-infected individuals, then this disruption would be similar to that seen following known damage to the basal ganglia. The study of motor skill learning constituted the most direct test of this hypothesis and generated, in our opinion, the strongest neuropsychological evidence for basal ganglia dysfunction. The significant correlation between motor skill learning, RT, and CSF concentrations of QUIN served to strengthen this conclusion.

Freund and coworkers have taken a similar approach to the study of HIV. These investigators had previously shown that the great majority of patients with HD (95%), as well as a substantial proportion of their at-risk relatives (40%), were abnormally slow on measures of the ability to produce rapid voluntary motor movements (Hefter et al., 1987). When these same tasks were applied to a group of carefully selected HIV+ subjects, a pattern of dysfunction was found that was the same as that seen in patients in the early stages of HD. As in our HIV studies, dysfunction was not related to stage of illness as defined by CDC criteria. The results were particularly noteworthy because subjects with a positive finding on a detailed neurological examination, deficits on standard measures of neuropsychological functioning, or a recent history of headache were excluded. As would be expected, the authors interpreted these data as indicating that the basal ganglia may be HIV's primary site of action and that this could occur relatively early in the disease process (Arendt et al., 1990).

Taken together, the evidence presented in this chapter suggests that a basal ganglia-like pattern of cognitive and motor dysfunction may be evident in a subgroup of HIV+ subjects. Whether other subgroups exist (perhaps subjects who show primarily CNS-related affective changes) remains to be determined. It will also be important to determine the prevalence of these cognitive and motor impairments and their clinical significance both for current real-world functioning and for the eventual development of a frank dementia. Much more work is also needed on the relationship between cognitive and motor dysfunction and specific biological parameters. It is hoped that the evidence presented here will motivate others to generate highly specific and testable hypotheses concerning the neuropsychological consequences of HIV.

Acknowledgment

Special thanks to my colleagues at the Walter Reed Army Medical Center, Andres Salazar, Wendy Law, Robb Mapou, Diane Kampen, Jill Williams, Tina Roller, Michael Coats, Herb Brown, Maria Graves, and Claudia Gomez, and to my colleagues at the National Institutes of Health, Melvyn Heyes, Sanford Markey, and Douglas Brenneman.

This project was supported, in part, by U.S. Army Medical R&D Command Project Grant DAMD17-87-PP-7856. The views of the author do not purport to reflect the position of the Army or the Department of Defense.

References

Abraham, L., Potegal, M., and Miller, S. (1983). Evidence for caudate nucleus involvement in an egocentric spatial task: Return from passive support. *Physiological Psychology, 11*, 11–17.

American Psychiatric Association. (1987). *Diagnostic and Statistical Manual of Mental Disorders.* 3rd ed-rev. Washington, D.C.: American Psychiatric Press, pp. 329–331.

Arendt, G., Hefter, H., Elsing, C., Strohmeyer, G., and Freund, H.-J. (1990). Motor dysfunction in HIV-infected patients without clinically detectable central-nervous deficit. *Journal of Neurology, 237*, 362–368.

Baddeley, A. (1992). Working memory. *Science, 255*, 556–559.

Beal, M.F., Kowall, N.W., Ellison, D.W., Mazurek, M.F., Schwartz, K.J., and Martin, J.B. (1986). Replication of the neurochemical characteristics of Huntington's disease by quinolinic acid. *Nature, 231*, 168–171.

Beck, A.T., and Steer, R.A. (1987). *Beck Depression Inventory.* San Antonio, Tex.: Psychological Corporation.

Benton, A.L., and Hamsher, K.deS. (1978). *Multilingual Aphasia Examination.* Iowa City: University of Iowa.

Benton, A.L., Hamsher, K.deS., Varney, N.R., and Spreen, O. (1983). *Contributions to Neuropsychological Assessment.* New York: Oxford University Press.

Bornstein, R.A., and Leason, M. (1985). Effects of localized lesions on the Verbal Concept Attainment Test. *Journal of Clinical and Experimental Neuropsychology, 7*, 421–429.

Bornstein, R.A., Nasrallah, H.A., Para, M.F., Fass, R.J., Whitacre, C.C., and Rice, R.R. (1991). Rate of CD4 decline and neuropsychological performance in HIV infection. *Archives of Neurology, 48*, 704–707.

Bornstein, R.A., Nasrallah, H.A., Para, M.F., Whitacre, C.C., Rosenberger, P., and Fass, R.J. (1993). Neuropsychological performance in symptomatic and asymptomatic HIV infection. *AIDS, 1*, 519–524.

Brandt, J., and Butters, N. (1986). The neuropsychology of Huntington's disease. *Trends in Neuroscience, 93*, 118–120.

Breitbart, W., Marotta, R.F., and Call, P. (1988). AIDS and neuroleptic malignant syndrome. *Lancet, 2*, 1488–1489.

Brenneman, D.E., Westbrook, G., Fitzgerald, S.P., Ennist, D.L., Elkins, K.L., Ruff, M., and Pert, C.B. (1988). Neuronal cell killing by the envelope protein HIV and its prevention by vasoactive intestinal peptide. *Nature, 335*, 639–642.

Brouwers, P., Cox, C., Martin, A., Chase, T.N., and Fedio, P. (1984). Differential perceptual spatial impairment in Huntington's and Alzheimer's dementia. *Archives of Neurology, 41*, 1073–1076.

Brouwers, P., Pizzo, P., Moss, H., Wolters, P., El-Amin, D., Poplack, D., Markey, S., and Heyes, M. (1991). Abnormalities of the central nervous system (CNS) in children with symptomatic HIV disease: Relation to cerebrospinal fluid (CSF) quinolinic acid. *Proceedings from the Seventh International Conference on AIDS* (Florence, Italy), *2*, 190.

Bruyn, R.P.M., and Stoof, J.C. (1990). The quinolinic acid hypothesis in Huntington's chorea. *Journal of Neurological Sciences, 95*, 29–38.

Bucher, D. (1987). What's bugging you: Closing in on a reliable flu detector. *Thesis, 1*, 10–15.

Butters, N., Heindel, W.C., and Salmon, D.P. (1990). Dissociation of implicit memory in dementia: Neurologic implications. *Bulletin of the Psychonomic Society, 28*, 359–366.

Butters, N., Soeldner, C., and Fedio, P. (1972). Comparison of parietal and frontal lobe spatial deficits in man: Extrapersonal vs. personal (egocentric) space. *Perceptual and Motor Skills, 34*, 27–34.

Butters, N., Wolfe, J., Granholm, E., and Martone, M. (1986). An assessment of verbal recall, recognition, and fluency abilities in patients with Huntington's disease. *Cortex, 22*, 11–32.

Buzy, J., Brenneman, D.E., Pert, C.B., Martin, A., Salazar, A., and Ruff, M.R. (1992). Potent neurotoxic activity in the cerebrospinal fluid of HIV-infected individuals. *Brain Research, 598*, 10–18.

Bylsma, F.W., Brandt, J., and Strauss, M.E. (1992) Personal and extrapersonal orientation in Huntington's disease patients and those at risk. *Cortex, 28*, 113–122.

Centers for Disease Control. (1986). Classification system for human T-lymphotrophic virus type III/lymphadenopathy-associated virus infections. *Annals of Internal Medicine, 105*, 234–237.

Centers for Disease Control. (1987). Revision of the CDC surveillance case definition for acquired immunodeficiency syndrome. *Morbidity and Mortality Weekly Report, 36*, 1S–15S.

Cotman, C.W., Monaghan, D.T., Ottersen, O.P., and Storm-Mathisen, J. (1987). Anatomical organization of excitatory amino acid receptors and their pathways. *Trends in Neuroscience, 7*, 273–280.

Cummings, J.L. (1990). Introduction. In J.L. Cummings, ed., *Subcortical Dementia.* New York: Oxford University Press, pp. 3–16.

de la Monte, S.M., Schooley, R.T., Hirsch, M.S., and Richardson, E.P. (1987). Subacute encephalomyelitis of AIDS and its relation to HTLV-III infection. *Neurology, 37*, 562–569.

Desimone, R., and Ungerleider, L.G. (1989). Neural mechanisms of visual processing in monkeys. In F. Boller and J. Grafman, eds., *Handbook of Neuropsychology*, Vol. 2. The Netherlands: Elsevier, pp. 267–299.

Ekstrom, R.B., French, J.W., Harman, H.H., and Derman, D. (1976). *Manual for the Kit of Factor-Referenced Cognitive Tests.* Princeton, N.J.: Educational Testing Service.

Everall, I., Luthert, P.J., and Lantos, P.L. (1991). Neuronal loss in the frontal cortex in HIV infection. *Lancet, 337*, 1119–1121.

Fedio, P., Cox, C.S., Neophytides, A., Canal-Frederick, G., and Chase, T.N. (1979). Neuropsychological profile of Huntington's disease: Patients and those at risk. In T.N. Chase, N.S. Wexler, and A. Barbeau, eds., *Advances in Neurology*, Vol. 23: *Huntington's Disease.* New York: Raven Press, pp. 239–255.

Folstein, S.E., Brandt, J., and Folstein, M. (1990). Huntington's disease. In J.L. Cummings, ed., *Subcortical Dementia.* New York: Oxford University Press, pp. 87–107.

Gottsdanker, R., and Shragg, P. (1985). Verification of Donders' subtraction method. *Journal of Experimental Psychology: Human Perception and Performance, 11*, 765–776.

Grant, D.A., and Berg, E.A. (1948). A behavioral analysis of degree of reinforcement and ease of shifting to new responses in a Weigl type card sorting problem. *Journal of Experimental Psychology, 38*, 404–411.

Grant, I., Atkinson, J.H., Hesselink, J.R., Kennedy, C.J., Richman, D.D., Spector, S.A., and McCutchan, J. (1987). Evidence for early central nervous system involvement in the acquired immunodeficiency syndrome (AIDS) and other human immunodeficiency virus (HIV) infections. *Annals of Internal Medicine, 107*, 828–836.

Grant, I., Caun, K., Kingsley, D.P.E., Winer, J., Trimble, M.R., and Pinching, A.J. (1992). Neuropsychological and NMR abnormalities in HIV infection: The St. Mary's-Queen Square study. *Neuropsychiatry, Neuropsychology, and Behavioral Neurology, 5*, 185–193.

Heaton, R.K., Velin, R.A., McCutchan, J.A., Gulevich, S.J., Atkinson, H.J., Wallace, M.R., Godfrey, H., Kirson, D.A., and Grant, I. (in press). Neuropsychological impairment in HIV infection: Implications for employment. *Psychosomatic Medicine.*

Hefter, H., Homberg, V., Lange, H.W., and Freund, H.-J. (1987). Impairments of rapid movement in Huntington's disease. *Brain, 110*, 585–612.

Heindel, W.C., Butters, N., and Salmon, D.P. (1988). Impaired learning of a motor skill in patients with Huntington's disease. *Behavioral Neuroscience, 102*, 141–147.

Heindel, W.C., Salmon, D.P., Shults, C.W., Walicke, P.A., and Butters, N. (1989). Neuropsychological evidence for multiple implicit memory systems: A comparison of Alzheimer's, Huntington's, and Parkinson's disease patients. *The Journal of Neuroscience, 9*, 582–587.

Heyes, M., Brew, B.J., Martin, A., Price, R.W., Salazar, A.M., Sidtis, J.J., Yergey, J.A., Mouradian, M.M., Sadler, A.E., Keilp, J., Rubinow, D., and Markey, S.P. (1991). Quinolinic acid in cerebrospinal fluid and serum in HIV infection: Relationship to clinical and neurologic status. *Annals of Neurology, 29*, 202–209.

Heyes, M.P., Jordan, E.K., Lee, K., Saito, K., Frank, J.A., Snoy, P.J., Markey, S.P., and Gravell, M. (1992a). Relationship of neurologic status in macaques infected with the simian immunodeficiency virus to cerebrospinal fluid quinolinic acid and kynurenic acid. *Brain Research, 570*, 237–250.

Heyes, M.P., Saito, K., Crowley, J.S., Davis, L.E., Demitrack, M.A., Der, M., Elia, J., Kruesi, M.J.P., Lackner, A., Larsen, S.A., Lee, K., Leonard, H.L., Markey, S.P., Martin, A., Milstein, S., Mouradian, M.M., Pranzatelli, M.R., Quearry, B.J., Salazar, A., Smith, M., Straus, S.E., Sunderland, T., Swedo, S.E., and Tourtellotte, W.W. (1992b). Quinolinic acid and other neuroactive kynurenines in cerebral and meningeal infections, sepsis, neuropsychiatric disorders and chronic neurodegenerative diseases of man. *Brain, 115*, 1249–1273.

Heyes, M.P., Saito, S.P. (1992c). Human macrophages convert L-tryptophan to neurotoxin quinolinic acid. *Biochemical Journal, 283*, 633–635.

Howard, I.P. (1982). *Human Visual Orientation.* New York: Wiley.

Huber, S.J., and Paulson, G.W. (1987). Memory impairment associated with progression of Huntington's disease. *Cortex, 23*, 275–283.

Huber, S.J., and Shuttleworth, E.C. (1990). Neuropsychological assessment of subcortical dementia. In J.L. Cummings, ed., *Subcortical Dementia.* New York: Oxford University Press, pp. 71–86.

Janssen, R.S., Saykin, A.J., Cannon, L., Campbell, J., Pinsky, P.F., Hessol, N.A., O'Malley, P.M., Lifson, A.R., Doll, L.S., Rutherford, G.W., and Kaplan, J.E. (1989). Neurological and neuropsychological manifestations of HIV-1 infection: Association with AIDS-related complex but not asymptomatic HIV-1 infection. *Annals of Neurology, 26*, 592–600.

Kaplan, E., Goodglass, H., and Weintraub, S. (1983). *Boston Naming Test.* Philadelphia: Lea and Febiger.

Ketzler, S., Weis, S., Haug, H., and Budka, H. (1990). Loss of neurons in the frontal cortex in AIDS brains. *Acta Neuropathologica, 80,* 92–94.

Kure, K., Weidenheim, K.M., Lyman, W.D., and Dickson, D.W. (1990). Morphology and distribution of HIV-1 gp41-positive microglia in subacute AIDS encephalitis. *Neuropathologica, 80,* 393–400.

Law, W.A., Martin, A., Mapou, R.L., Roller, T.L., Salazar, A.M., Temoshok, L., and Rundell, J.R. (in press). An investigation of working memory in individuals with HIV-infection. *Journal of Clinical and Experimental Neuropsychology.*

Levin, H.S., Williams, D.H., Boruncki, M.J., Hillman, G.R., Williams, J.B., Guinto, F.C., Amparo, E.G., Crow, W.N., and Pollard, R.B. (1990). Magnetic resonance imaging and neuropsychological findings in human immunodeficiency virus infection. *Journal of Acquired Immune Deficiency Syndrome, 3,* 752–762.

Levy, R.M., Bredesen, D.E., and Rosenblum, M.L. (1985). Neurological manifestations of the acquired immunodeficiency syndrome (AIDS): Experience at UCSF and review of the literature. *Journal of Neurosurgery, 62,* 475–495.

Lipton, S.A. (1992). Models of neuronal injury in AIDS: Another role for the NMDA receptor? *Trends in Neuroscience, 15,* 75–79.

Lishman, W.A. (1978). *Organic Psychiatry.* London: Blackwell Scientific.

Luria, A.R. (1966). *Higher Cortical Functions in Man.* (B. Haigh, trans.). New York: Basic Books.

Maj, M. (1990). Psychiatric aspects of HIV-1 infection and AIDS. *Psychological Medicine, 20,* 547–563.

Mapou, R.L., Law, W.A., Martin, A., Salazar, A.M., and Rundell, J.R. (1993). Awareness of cognitive and motor difficulties in individuals infected with the human immunodeficiency virus. *Journal of Neuropsychiatry and Clinical Neuroscience, 5,* 86–93.

Martin, A. (1990). Neuropsychology of Alzheimer's disease: The case for subgroups. In M.F. Schwartz, ed., *Modular Deficits in Dementia.* Cambridge, Mass.: MIT Press, pp. 143–176.

Martin, A., Heyes, M.P., Salazar, A.M., Kampen, D.L., Williams, J., Law, W.A., Coats, M.E., and Markey, S.P. (1992). Progressive slowing of reaction time and increasing cerebrospinal fluid concentrations of quinolinic acid in HIV-infected individuals. *Journal of Neuropsychiatry and Clinical Neuroscience, 4,* 270–279.

Martin, A., Heyes, M.P., Salazar, A.M., Law, W.A., and Williams, J. (1993a). Impaired motor-skill learning, slowed reaction time, and elevated cerebrospinal fluid quinolinic acid in a subgroup of HIV-infected individuals. *Neuropsychology, 7,* 149–157.

Martin, A., and Kampen, D.L. (1987). *The Maze Learning Test.* Unpublished test.

Martin, A., Kampen, D., Salazar, A.M., Williams, J., Law, W., and Roller, T. (1989a). Neuropsychological evidence for early involvement of the basal ganglia region in a subgroup of HIV+ individuals. *Abstracts: V International Conference on AIDS.* Montreal: International Developmental Research Centre, p. 463.

Martin, A., Kampen, D., Salazar, A.M., Williams, J., Law, W., Roller, T., and the Walter Reed Retrovirus Research Group. (1989b). Slowed cognitive processing in HIV+ patients in comparison to psychiatric controls. *Abstracts: V International Conference on AIDS.* Montreal; International Developmental Research Centre, p. 210.

Martin, A., Pigott, T.A., Lalonde, F.M., Dalton, I., Dubbert, B., and Murphy, D.L. (1993b). Lack of evidence for Huntington's disease-like cognitive dysfunction in obsessive-compulsive disorder. *Biological Psychiatry, 33,* 345–353.

Martin, E.M., Sorenson, D.J., Robertson, L.C., Edelstein, H.E., and Chirurgi, V.A. (1992).

Spatial attention in HIV-1 infection: A preliminary report. *Journal of Neuropsychiatry and Clinical Neuroscience, 4,* 288–293.

Martone, M., Butters, N., Payne, M., Becker, J.T., and Sax, D.S. (1984). Dissociations between skill learning and verbal recognition memory in amnesia and dementia. *Archives of Neurology, 41,* 965–970.

Masliah, E., Ge, N., Morey, M., DeTeresa, R., Terry, R.D., and Wiley, C.A. (1992). Cortical dendritic pathology in human immunodeficiency virus encephalitis. *Laboratory Investigation, 66,* 285–291.

Mayeux, R., Stern, Y., Rosen, J., and Benson, F. (1983). Is "subcortical dementia" a recognizable clinical entity? *Annals of Neurology, 14,* 278–283.

McAllister, R.H., Herns, M.V., Harrison, M.J.G., Newman, S.P., Connolly, S., Fowler, C.J., Fell, M., Durrance, P., Manji, H., Kendall, B.E., Valentine, A.R., Weller, I.V.D., and Adler, M. (1992). *Journal of Neurology, Neurosurgery, and Psychiatry, 55,* 143–148.

McArthur, J.C., Cohen, B.A., Selnes, O.A., Kumar, A.J., Cooper, K., McArthur, J.H., Soucy, G., Cornblath, D.R., Chmiel, J.S., Wang, M.-C., Starkey, D.L., Ginzburg, H., Ostrow, D.G., Johnson, R.T., Phair, J.P., and Polk, B.F. (1989). Low prevalence of neurological and neuropsychological abnormalities in otherwise healthy HIV-1 infected individuals: Results from the Multicenter AIDS Cohort Study. *Annals of Neurology, 26,* 601–611.

Merritt, H.H. (1979). *A Textbook of Neurology* (6th ed.). Philadelphia: Lea and Febiger.

Merritt, H.H., Adams, R.D., and Solomon, H.C. (1946). *Neurosyphilis.* New York: Oxford University Press.

Miller, E.N., Satz, P., and Visscher, B. (1991). Computerized and conventional neuropsychological assessment of HIV-1-infected homosexual men. *Neurology, 41,* 1608–1616.

Miller, E.N., Selnes, O.A., McArthur, J.C., Satz, P., Becker, J.T., Cohen, B.A., Sheridan, K., Machado, A.M., van Gorp, W.G., and Visscher, B. (1990). Neuropsychological performance in HIV-1-infected homosexual men: The Multicenter AIDS Cohort Study (MACS). *Neurology, 40* 197–203.

Milner, B. (1971). Interhemispheric differences in the localization of psychological processes in man. *British Medical Bulletin, 27,* 272–277.

Money, J. (1976). *A Standardized Road-Map Test of Directional Sense.* San Rafael, Calif.: Academic Therapy Press.

Navia, B.A. (1990). The AIDS dementia complex. In J.L. Cummings, ed., *Subcortical Dementia.* New York: Oxford University Press, pp. 181–198.

Navia, B.A., Cho, E-S., Petito, C.K., and Price, R.W. (1986a). The AIDS dementia complex: II. Neuropathology. *Annals of Neurology, 19,* 525–535.

Navia, B.A., Jordan, B.D., and Price, R.W. (1986b). The AIDS dementia complex: I. Clinical features. *Annals of Neurology, 19,* 517–524.

Navia, B.A., and Price, R.W. (1987). The acquired immunodeficiency syndrome dementia complex as the presenting or sole manifestation of human immunodeficiency virus infection. *Archives of Neurology, 44,* 65–69.

Perdices, M., and Cooper, D.A. (1989). Simple and choice reaction time in patients with human immunodeficiency virus infection. *Annals of Neurology, 25,* 460–467.

Pohl, W. (1973). Dissociation of spatial discrimination deficits following frontal and parietal lesions in monkeys. *Journal of Comparative and Physiological and Psychology, 82,* 227–239.

Potegal, M. (1971). A note on spatial-motor deficits in patients with Huntington's disease: A test of a hypothesis. *Neuropsychologia, 9,* 233–235.

Price, R.W., Brew, B., Sidtis, J., Rosenblum, M., Scheck, A.C., and Cleary, P. (1988). The brain in AIDS: Central nervous system HIV-1 infection and AIDS dementia complex. *Science, 239*, 586–592.

Pumarola-Sune, T., Navia, B.A., Cordon-Cardo, C., Cho, E.-S., and Price, R.W. (1987). HIV antigen in the brains of patients with the AIDS dementia complex. *Annals of Neurology, 21*, 490–496.

Redfield, R.R., Wright, D.C., and Tramont, E.C. (1986). The Walter Reed staging classification for HTLV-III/LAV infection. *New England Journal of Medicine, 314*, 131–132.

Rottenberg, D.A., Moeller, J.R., Strother, S.C., Sidtis, J.J., Navia, B.A., Dhawan, V., Ginos, J.Z., and Price, R.W. (1987). The metabolic pathology of the AIDS dementia complex. *Annals of Neurology, 22*, 700–706.

Sabin, T.D. (1987). AIDS: The new "Great Imitator." *Journal of the American Geriatrics Society, 35*, 467–471.

Sacks, O. (1973). *Awakenings.* New York: Dutton.

Schwarcz, R., Whetsell, W.O., and Mangano, R.E.M. (1983). Quinolinic acid: An endogenous metabolite can produce axon sparing lesions in rat brain. *Science, 219*, 316–318.

Schwartz, M.F., ed. (1990). *Modular Deficits in Dementia.* Cambridge, Mass.: MIT Press.

Selnes, O.A., Miller, E., McArthur, J., Gordon, B., Munoz, A., Sheridan, K., Fox, R., and Saah, A.J. (1990). HIV-1 infection: No evidence of cognitive decline during the asymptomatic stages. *Neurology, 40*, 204–208.

Semmes, J., Weinstein, S., Ghent, L., and Teuber, H.-L. (1963). Correlates of impaired orientation in space. *Brain, 86*, 747–772.

Shallice, T. (1982). Specific impairments of planning. *Philosophical Transactions of the Royal Society of London B, 298*, 199–209.

Sharer, L.R. (1992). Pathology of HIV-1 infection of the central nervous system. *Journal of Neuropathology and Experimental Neurology, 51*, 3–11.

Spielberger, C.D. (1983). *State-Trait Anxiety Inventory.* Palo Alto, Calif.: Consulting Psychologists Press.

Squire, L.S., and Zola-Morgan, S. (1991). The medial temporal lobe memory system. *Science, 253*, 1380–1386.

Stern, Y., Marder, K., Bell, K., Chen, J., Dooneief, G., Goldstein, S., Mindry, D., Richards, M., Sano, M., Williams, J., Gorman, J., Ehrhardt, A., and Mayeaux, R. (1991). Multidisciplinary baseline assessment of homosexual men with and without human immunodeficiency virus infection. III. Neurologic and neuropsychological findings. *Archives of General Psychiatry, 48*, 131–138.

Street, R.F. (1931). *A Gestalt Completion Test.* Contribution to Education, No. 481. New York: Teachers College, Columbia University.

van Gorp, W.G., Mandelkern, M., Gee, M., Hinken, C.H., Stern, C.E., Paz, D., Dixon, W., Evans, G., Flynn, F., Frederick, C.J., Ropchan, J., and Blahd, W. (1992). Cerebral metabolic dysfunction in AIDS: Findings in a sample with and without dementia. *Journal of Neuropsychiatry and Clinical Neurosciences, 4*, 280–287.

Vaughn, H.G., Jr., and Costa, L.D. (1963). Performance of patients with lateralized cerebral lesions. II. Sensory and motor tests. *Journal of Mental Diseases, 134*, 237–243.

von Economo, C. (1929). *Encephalitis Lethargica: Its Consequences and Treatment* (trans. K.O. Newman, 1931.) London: Oxford University Press.

Wechsler, D. (1981). *Wechsler Adult Intelligence Scale-Revised Manual.* New York: Psychological Corporation.

Wechsler, D., and Stone, C.P. (1945). *Wechsler Memory Scale.* New York: Psychological Corporation.

Weingartner, H., Caine, E.D., and Ebert, M.H. (1979). Encoding processes, learning, and recall in Huntington's disease. In T.N. Chase, N.S. Wexler, and A. Barbeau, eds., *Advances in Neurology,* Vol. 23: *Huntington's Disease.* New York: Raven Press, pp. 215–226.

Whitehouse, P.J. (1986). The concept of subcortical dementia: Another look. *Annals of Neurology, 19,* 1–6.

Wiley, C.A., Masliah, E., Morey, M., Lemere, C., DeTeresa, R., Grafe, M., Hansen, L., and Terry, R. (1991). Neocortical damage during HIV infection. *Annals of Neurology, 29,* 651–657.

Wilkie, F.L., Eisdorfer, C., Morgan, R., Loewenstein, D.A., and Szapocznik, J. (1990). Cognition in early human immunodeficiency virus infection. *Archives of Neurology, 47* 433–440.

Wilkie, F.L., Morgan, R., Fletcher, M.A., Blaney, N., Baum, M., Komaroff, E., Szapocznik, J., and Eisdorfer, C. (1992). Cognition and immune function in HIV-1 infection. *AIDS, 6,* 977–981.

13

Neuroimaging in HIV Infection: Neuropsychological and Pathological Correlation

THOMAS A. KENT, BENJAMIN B. GELMAN,
KAREN CASPER, HANS A. LANGSJOEN,
HARVEY S. LEVIN, and GILBERT R. HILLMAN

Although early reports of cognitive deficits in asymptomatic HIV patients (Grant et al., 1987) have not been confirmed in all studies (Janssen et al., 1989; McArthur et al., 1989b), it is clear that a significant number of patients suffer from a dementing process secondary to the HIV infection, not solely as a result of opportunistic infection (Rosenblum, 1990). The neurological impairment has cognitive, motor, and psychiatric dimensions. This chapter will deal only with brain involvement, though spinal cord disease is briefly mentioned. The pathogenesis of neurological impairment will be reviewed from the standpoint of what can be seen on brain imaging and what this might mean for various theories about the causes of brain dysfunction and improvement seen after anti–human immunodeficiency virus (HIV) therapy.

HIV-Asociactd Motor/Cognitive Complex

The neurological impairment seen with HIV infection has been noted since early in the HIV epidemic. It was not unusual for patients, especially pediatric patients, to present initially with neurological impairment. With the current practice of starting anti-HIV therapy (e.g., zidovudine) early, initial presentation with neurological complications seems somewhat rarer, but these complications remain a serious problem as the disease progresses.

The impairments most often described in association with HIV infection include what are considered subcortical dementing signs. These signs include psychomotor retardation, apathy, diminished concentration, and problems with sequential tasks (motor perseveration). Other motor problems include ataxia and dyspraxia. Later, probably also due to spinal cord involvement, weakness and bowel and bladder incontinence occur. Psychiatric illness (especially mania) may occur (Maj, 1990). Recent studies and our own preliminary data have shown that attention, information-processing rate, and memory are particularly sensitive to impairment in patients with HIV (Perdices and Cooper 1989; Wilkie et al., 1990).

The relationship between stage of HIV infection and neurological impairment remains obscure. Early studies suggested that asymptomatic, HIV-infected individuals show cognitive impairment. Most later studies could not reproduce this finding. The use of different comparison groups has been suggested to explain these discrepancies since HIV− subjects of the same psychosocial background also seem to demonstrate some impairment. Many studies have found impairment in Centers for Disease Control (CDC) stage IV, which is corroborated by the neuroimaging studies described below.

Anti-HIV therapy can improve cognitive performance (Schmitt et al., 1988; Hollweg et al., 1991). Improvement after zidovudine therapy can be seen after 4 months, although the duration of improvement is not yet known. Because the mechanism of neurological impairment is not known, the mechanism of improvement is equally unclear. Reducing the viral burden is probably a necessary component for cognitive improvement. It is not yet clear if the magnitude of infection (viral numbers) (Egan, 1991) or the development of resistant strains may correlate with brain damage.

Pathology of Neurological Involvement

Examination of the central nervous system (CNS) at autopsy has revealed a wide spectrum of neuropathological abnormalities in acquired immunodeficiency syndrome (AIDS) patients, and many lesions are presumed to be closely associated with infection of the CNS by HIV-1. Patients with AIDS-associated dementia are, in general, more likely to have these abnormalities at autopsy, but the clinicopathological correlations is not clear-cut in many cases (Price et al., 1988; Budka et al., 1991). Specific neuropathological abnormalities can occur with very different frequencies and in varied combinations at autopsy (Gelman et al., 1992; Gelman and Guinto, 1992). Individual abnormalities may be weakly correlated with each other or with the functional status of the patient. Thus, putative HIV-1-related CNS anomalies need to be investigated more critically to elucidate the cause of CNS dysfunction associated with HIV-1 infection.

HIV-1 is widely believed to enter the CNS within infected cells of the monocyte-macrophage system (Price et al., 1988; Budka et al., 1991). Multinucleated cells infected with HIV-1 are considered a hallmark of infection (Price et al., 1988; Budka et al., 1991), but they are detected only in a minority of AIDS patients at autopsy (less than 25% in our series; see Gelman et al., 1992; Gelman and Guinto, 1992). Immunohistology of HIV-1 antigens does not consistently establish the presence of this virus in the CNS of AIDS patients at autopsy (Budka, 1990), and its presence is not routinely documented in most neuropathological examinations. Microglial nodules are a nonspecific inflammatory reaction in the CNS (subacute encephalitis), usually in response to viral infection. It seems very likely that their presence in the brains of patients with AIDS is a response to HIV-1 infection because HIV-1 antigens are sometimes localized immunohistochemically to microglial cells. However, the insidious presence of other pathogens, particularly cytomegalovirus, is always difficult to rule out. White matter degeneration with glial scarring (progressive diffuse leukoencephalopathy) is observed commonly in AIDS patients; disturbances of brain white matter staining frequently are very subtle, and outright degeneration of the myelin with an astroglial reaction is not always evident. This has led to the suggestion that a disturbance in the blood-brain barrier causes at least part of the "pallor" that is evident in stained white matter and may lead to the destruction of myelin (Smith et al., 1990). Because HIV-1 does not display any apparent tropism of myelin-forming oligodendrocytes, the cause of the white matter disturbances remains unknown. Abnormalities related to nerve cell structure have been recognized, most severely as a polioencephalopathy (Budka et al., 1991) and more subtly as a disturbance of the dendritic morphology of Golgi-stained cortical neurons (Masliah et al., 1992). The apparent lack of HIV-1 tropism for neurons makes these abnormalities difficult to explain in terms of a direct attack associated with a productive viral infection. Vacuolar degeneration of spinal cord white matter tracts is observed in at least 25% of AIDS patients in most reports (Petito et al., 1985; Gelman and Guinto, 1992). The histopathological features are not specific for AIDS, and no convincing evidence for a consistent relationship to HIV-1 infection in spinal white matter is available. The myelopathy resembles subacute combined degeneration associated with vitamin B_{12} disturbances, but there is no apparent connection to vitamin B_{12} in AIDS patients. It seems likely that this lesion results from a metabolic and/or immunological imbalance in AIDS patients (Budka et al., 1991). We have been impressed that signs of spinal tract degeneration remain unrecognized clinically in a substantial proportion of our patients, in part because inanition serves to obscure it.

The lack of a clear-cut anatomical connection between productive HIV-1 infection and neurodegeneration presents a challenging problem. At present, the mechanism whereby HIV-1 infection of the CNS produces all these neuropathological phenomena is a matter of speculation. The gp-120 protein itself may be neurotoxic, possibly by increasing intracellular calcium (Lipton, 1991). A popular hypothesis is that HIV-1-infected macrophages and microglial cells produce toxic quantities of catabolic secretory products (cytokines) that mediate the degenerative changes in the CNS milieux (Giulian et al., 1990). In vitro evidence supporting this concept has been presented, but direct evidence in HIV-infected CNS tissue has not yet appeared. The fact that brain atrophy in patients with AIDS is symmetrical seems to support the concept of a toxic or metabolic disturbance (Gelman and Guinto, 1992). Brain wasting can be reliably evaluated in patients using brain imaging, but the clinical and pathological significance of atrophy still is not obvious (Gelman and Guinto, 1992). Severity of cerebral atrophy does not have a strong correlation with any single microscopic change, and the specific cellular structures that are damaged as the brain atrophies have not been defined clearly. A diffuse proliferation of microglial cells is one anomaly that is linked to brain wasting (Gelman, 1993). If these microglia are infected with HIV-1, then a relationship to the viral burden in the CNS is possible. In general, the clinico-pathological correlation in patients with HIV-1 disease of the CNS remains obscure. Elucidating the pathophysiology and strict application of Koch's postulates are major challenges for the future.

Neuropsychological Findings in HIV Infection

The onset of neuropsychological dysfunction in HIV+ patients is a subject of controversy, beyond the scope of this discussion, primarily related to selection criteria and choice of control populations (reviewed in Stern, 1991).

Specific neuropsychological tasks that reflect this cognitive impairment, employed in our research and other studies, include simple and choice reaction time; the paced auditory serial addition test (PASAT) (Gronwall and Wrightson, 1974); the selective reminding test (Buschke and Fuld, 1974); the Wisconsin Card Sorting Test (WCST) (Grant and Berg, 1948); Trail Making B (Army Industrial Battery, 1944); Verbal Fluency; and the Positive Symptom Distress Index of the Symptom Checklist-90R. The PASAT measures information processing speed, as reflected by the efficiency of adding successively presented single-digit numbers. The PASAT has been found to be sensitive to the stage of disease (Grant et al., 1987), and we have found that speed of information processing declines in patients with HIV disease (Levin et al., 1990). The selective reminding test is a test of recall of 12 unrelated words and is suggested to reflect left temporal lobe function. Wilkie et al. (1990) have recently shown that the selective reminding test is sensitive to memory deficit in HIV disease that had not progressed to AIDS. The WCST is a test of concept formation and shifting response set that is particularly sensitive to frontal lobe disease. We used a computer-administered version in our study. Trail Making B measures the time required to trace a path connecting scattered circles in alternating numeric and alphabetic sequences. Verbal Fluency evaluates the patient's capacity to generate words beginning with a designated letter within a 1-minute time limit, repeated for three letters. This brief procedure, which requires 5 minutes to administer, is highly sensitive to left frontal dysfunction (Benton, 1968). Schmitt et al. (1988) found that the Positive Symptom Distress Index of the Symptom Checklist-90R (Derogatis and Towson, 1977), a summary measure of this mood/affect questionnaire, was sensitive to the effect of zidovudine azidothymidine, (AZT) in AIDS patients.

Recent consensus conferences (Adams and Heaton, 1990) emphasize the need to control for extraneous factors that may influence performance on neuropsychological testing, including uniform administration of tests, and issues related to the selection of subjects, such as substance abuse and prior neurological injury.

Neuroimaging Studies in HIV

Many of the same issues that bias neuropsychological testing also influence neuropathological and neuroimaging studies. Functional neuroimaging tests such as position emission tomography (PET), single photon emission computed tomography (SPECT), and perhaps magnetic resonance spectroscopy would likely be sensitive to the emotional state of the subject, whereas structural studies, such as x-ray computed tomography (CT) or magnetic resonance imaging (MRI), would be influenced by prior brain injury. These factors are emphasized by McAllister et al. (1992), who found MRI lesions in 53% of his psychosocial matched HIV− controls.

Nevertheless, brain abnormalities have been frequently demonstrated by neuroimaging studies of patients with the HIV-associated motor/cognitive complex, formerly known as the *AIDS dementia complex (ADC)* (Price et al., 1988), including atrophy on CT, white matter lesions and atrophy on MRI, and abnormal metabolism on PET and SPECT (Jarvik et al., 1988; Olsen et al., 1988; Post et al., 1988; Brunetti et al., 1989; Jakobsen et al., 1989).

MRI may be particularly sensitive to anatomical abnormalities in ADC (Olsen et al., 1988; Maini et al., 1989), although abnormalities have not been observed in all patients with cognitive impairment (Miller, 1990). As discussed above, psychosocial-matched, HIV− controls may demonstrate some of these abnormalities. To address some of these confounding variables, the neuroimaging literature will be reviewed by discussing neuroimaging studies in symptomatic subjects separately from asymptomatic subjects.

Symptomatic HIV+ Subjects

Using a semiautomated computer analysis method developed by us to determine the cerebrospinal fluid (CSF)/intracranial volume (ICV) ratio on T_2-weighted MRI images, we have studied groups of patients with CDC stages II–IV disease compared to a group of age- and education-matched control subjects. Stage IV patients had a larger CSF/ICV ratio (implying atrophy) than normal controls ($\chi^2(1) = 6.94$, $p < .01$) and a trend emerged for higher CSF volume in lymphadenopathy patients than controls ($\chi^2(1) = 2.73$, $p < .09$). Significant overall group differences were obtained ($\chi^2(3) = 8.11$, $p < .05$; Wilcoxon rank sums). A larger CSF/ICV ratio was inversely correlated with motor speed, measured by reaction time (Levin et al., 1990).

Others have also found an association with features of neuropsychological impairment and structural brain abnormalities. For example, using MRI, Post et al. (1991) noted ventricular enlargement and cortical atrophy in symptomatic subjects more often than in asymptomatic ones. Lesions observed on MRI included multiple small, high-intensity lesions in a bilateral and subcortical distribution or patchy confluence that increased and became more diffuse with progression of dementia. Additional pathological analysis revealed subcortical gray and posterior fossa lesions not observed on CT or MRI, suggesting a lack of sensitivity to some abnormalities. Measuring ventricular brain ratio (VBR) and cortical sulci, Moeller and Backmund (1990) concluded that an increased VBR was found only in those suffering from AIDS dementia, implicating subcortical structures. Marotta and Perry (1989) concluded that MRI is sensitive to parenchymal changes, but only severe parenchymal changes correlated with decreased mental status.

In children, Wiley et al. (1990) found that white matter gliosis predominated over gray matter changes. In their cohort, some children's neuropsychological deficits progressed. More gliosis was found in those children, again supporting a general association between MRI abnormalities and cognitive function.

Regional vulnerability to atrophy is becoming increasingly recognized. In a relatively large study, Jernigan (see Egan, 1991) found ventricular enlargement and atrophy in the diencephalic regions, the medial temporal lobes, and frontal, uncal, and temporo-occipital regions, thus confirming reports of gray matter as well as white matter changes in HIV. A large Finnish study (Raininko et al., 1992) also found a correlation between HIV stage and brain atrophy. In a non-automated study using transaxial CT and ultra-low field MRI scans in 101 subjects at various stages of the disease (with a psychosocial matched control group), atrophy was visible in 31% of asymptomatic HIV+ subjects, increasing to 70% in AIDS patients. Atrophy was primarily infratentorial at early stages, becoming supratentorial and diffuse as the clinical stage progressed. High-intensity lesions were visible less often. A few cases came to autopsy: lesions considered typical for HIV encephalopathy (e.g., multinucleated giant cells, microglial nodules, and diffuse myelin loss) were found to explain the lesions seen, but as reported by others, histological abnormalities occurred that were not visible by imaging. Atrophy was most prominent in the temporal lobes, followed by the parietal and frontal lobes. Posterior fossa atrophy and ventricular and sulcal space enlargements were also observed. Many of these findings were consistent with a recent neuroimaging-pathological correlation study (Gelman and Guinto, 1992) performed at the University of Texas Medical Branch that found a good correlation between atrophy seen by CT scan and at autopsy. CSF space was most expanded in the frontal and temporal lobes, and the ventricular space was more enlarged than the sulcal space. To see if microscopic changes could explain this atrophy, the relationship of the atrophy to HIV-associated histopathological changes was examined. Only a weak correlation with atrophy was found, indicating that atrophy could occur independently of any specific histopathological abnormality.

In addition to atrophy, a consistent vulnerability of subcortical structures, particularly the basal ganglia, has been noted in PET (Rottenberg et al., 1987), CT, and MRI (Abbruzzese et al., 1990; Kodama et al., 1991).

Asymptomatic Subjects

As in neuropsychological studies, less robust results have emerged from these studies. McAllister et al. (1992) noted a higher incidence of abnormal MRI scans (widened sulci, enlarged ventricles, focal hyperintense lesions) in his seronegative control group, with roughly equal performance on neuropsychological testing. The results of qualitative analyses of MRI scans have been considered normal in asymptomatic, seropositive subjects in many (McArthur et al., 1989b) but not all (Coats et al., 1989) studies. Notably, completely automated MRI image analysis has not been applied in the study of HIV subjects. It is possible that abnormalities may be seen despite a qualitatively normal appearance. Given the findings of abnormal CSF in asymptomatic, seropositive subjects (reviewed in Grant and Atkinson, 1990), such a finding would not be surprising.

Functional Imaging Studies

PET and SPECT are promising tests to use in following the course of HIV and the brain (LaFrance et al., 1988; Kramer and Sanger, 1990). Most functional imaging studies have been performed in symptomatic subjects, with the goal of assessing whether they would be useful as diagnostic tools in neurological HIV involvement. Hence, it is not surprising that abnormalities have been found in most of these studies. No extensive pathological correlations have been performed, but enough has been done to allow us to reach some conclusions. It is noteworthy that, as in structural studies, investigators have not been uniform with regard to which behavioral assessments were correlated with imaging abnormalities.

In a pioneering PET study, Rottenberg et al. (1987) found prominent subcortical abnormalities. Performance on the Grooved Pegboard Test correlated with subcortical metabolism, while cortical metabolic abnormalities correlated with verbal fluency and performance on the Trail Making B test. White matter rates did not correlate with neuropsychological performance. There is a resemblance between these findings and the correlation between CSF spaces and specific neuropsychometric tasks seen by Levin et al. (reviewed above). Pohl et al. (1988) found focal deficits by SPECT that explained focal neurological signs. Ajmani et al. (1991) found focal temporal and frontal defects. The number of defects increased with the severity of dementia and correlated with CD4 counts. Similarly, Kuni et al. (1991) demonstrated a correlation between decreased ^{123}I inosine-5'-monophosphate (IMP) uptake and dementia in AIDS patients.

Remarkably similar to the structural imaging findings of Raininko et al. (1992) and Kramer and Sanger (1990), functional abnormalities were found in subcortical regions early in HIV infection, followed by cortical and then diffuse disturbances.

Using a recently developed technique for assessing functional neural loss with MR spectroscopy, Menon et al. (1990), found a reduction in N-acetyl aspartate levels in areas that appeared normal on routine structural MRI scans, again suggesting that not all functional abnormalities are visible on conventional MRI scans. The cause of the functional abnormalities is not yet known, and whether they would also be reflected in SPECT or PET scans has not been studied.

Treatment Reversal

AZT may ameliorate HIV-induced cognitive dysfunction (Schmitt et al., 1988). In addition, qualitative improvement on neuroimaging has been noted, including reduced atrophy on CT (Matthes et al., 1988), disappearance of white matter hyperintensities on MRI (Olsen et al., 1988), and a more "homogeneous" metabolic pattern on PET (Yarchoan et al., 1988; Brunetti et al., 1989). It is conceivable that in cases in which MRI scans appear qualitatively normal or have not changed after treatment, quantitative analysis might reveal alterations. DeCarli et al. (1991), using CT, noted a reduced VBR after treatment and cognitive improvement. Although the magnitude of improvement was not correlated with the change in VBR, the author recognized the desirability of obtaining regional measures of brain volumes and the need for quantitative studies for detailed correlations. In terms of functional studies, Brunetti et al. (1989) found that functional imaging demonstrated a response to treatment with normalization of metabolic abnormalities. Unfortunately, patients progress while on anti-HIV therapy [Day et al., 1992]. It is possible that progression may also be reflected by neuroimaging. Children appear particularly sensitive to neurological involvement in AIDS, accompanied by significant atrophy. AZT therapy reverses the atrophy (DeCarli et al., 1991), manifested especially by an increase in VBR. Potential mechanisms and artifacts to explain the reversal have been extensively discussed.

Quantitative Studies of Reversal

To study the neuroanatomical substrate of the cognitive decline in HIV disease, we have developed methods to determine the volumes of gray and white matter and to make a quantitative determination of white matter disease based on an analysis of abnormally bright regions in T_2-weighted images.

Image analysis tools could potentially yield objective and rapid characterization of brain abnormalities on MRI and measure the effects of drug treatment on brain tissue that are also reflected by neuropsychological testing. Moreover, with the growing use of metabolic imaging techniques, such as SPECT and PET, and their apparent sensitivity in preliminary studies in detecting abnormalities in ADC (Pohl et al., 1988; Brunetti et al., 1989), availability of quantitative anatomical imaging data may also be useful in comparing the relationship between structural abnormalities and brain metabolic patterns. Although metabolic abnormalities may parallel neuropsychological deficits, quantitative MRI analysis may provide information on the anatomical substrate of the reversible deficits. Although possible (McArthur et al., 1989a), it will likely be difficult to obtain neuropathological information on reversible deficits with postmortem studies because this stage of disease is early, not preterminal. It is possible that quantitative MRI can provide a means for noninvasive, safe, quantitative testing of the effectiveness of AIDS treatment. Although in preliminary work there is a correlation between MRI indices and neuropsychological impairment (Jakobsen et al., 1989; Levin et al., 1990), should such a relationship and a correlation with the effects of AZT not be confirmed, this information would be equally useful in suggesting that MRI does not reflect the processes that underlie the neuropsychological deficits. This question has not yet been studied quantitatively.

Our current methods allow determination of gray and white matter volumes,

A

B

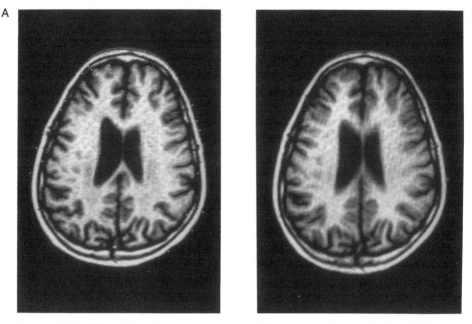

FIGURE 13–1. T2-weighted inversion recovery MR images before and after AZT treatment. Atrophy, primarily of the cortical gray matter, is apparent on the baseline MRI (Figure 13–1A; December, 1988). At follow up (Figure 13–1B; April, 1989), an increase in gray matter is observed.

intracranial volume (Hillman et al., 1991), and a comparison of the statistical distribution of pixel intensities before and after treatment. We have applied these analyses to the MRI of an ADC patient before and after AZT treatment. In a 25-year-old male HIV+ homosexual who had no evidence of opportunistic infection or malignancy, whose complaints consisted of memory difficulties, slowed thinking, calculation problems, and psychiatric disturbance, initial MRI demonstrated confluent white matter high-intensity lesions and brain atrophy (Figures 13–1a and 13–2a). Neuropsychological testing revealed deficits in information processing speed, concept formation, verbal memory, and visual reproductive memory (Table 13–1). Treatment with AZT resulted in a dramatic improvement in neuropsychological performance (Table 13–1). Moreover, improvement in brain appearance was observed on repeat MRI: less atrophy was apparent, and the white matter appeared nearly normal (Figures 13–1b and 13–2b).

New information was obtained by applying quantitative analytical techniques. An estimate was made of the pathological portion of the white matter. These lesions were identified as a high-intensity "shoulder" on the intensity histogram of white matter pixels (Figure 13–3). These bright pixels converted to normal intensity after treatment, and the posttreatment brain resembled that of a normal control. The difference between the histogram pre- and posttreatment reflects the area of white matter lesions that normalized.

Analysis of gray and white matter volumes showed that the reduction in

A

B

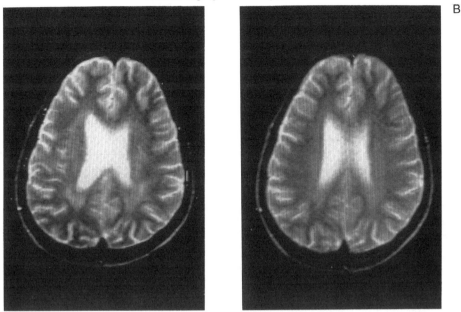

FIGURE 13–2. T2-weighted MR images before and after AZT treatment. The white matter demonstrates widespread diffuse hyperintensities at the start of AZT treatment (Figure 13–2A). At follow up (Figure 13–2B), the appearance of the white matter has normalized.

brain atrophy was a result of both increased gray matter volume and decreased white matter volume, and an increased gray/white matter ratio was found (1.03 at baseline, 1.36 five months later, and 1.26 several months later). Autopsy correlation is being performed.

These findings may be assessed in light of current hypotheses regarding the pathophysiology of ADC and the mechanism of AZT's beneficial effects. In agreement with our findings, studies suggest that AZT can improve mental function (Schmitt et al., 1988) in some subjects. White matter lesions on MRI are nonspecific with respect to pathogenesis and seem to be reversible. Demyelination and treatment-associated remyelination may occur. A recent postmortem study of early ADC (McArthur et al., 1989c) found astrocytosis without the characteristic microglial invasion, microvacuolation, and multinucleate giant cells seen in advanced cases (Elder and Sever, 1988; Rosenblum, 1990). Anecdotal reports in the literature have described improvement (Olsen et al., 1988) or no change (Brunetti et al., 1989) in white matter lesions coincident with improved mental function after treatment with AZT. Therefore, it is possible that these changes are not critical to the neuropsychological benefits of AZT. It is also possible that ADC is a heterogeneous disorder with respect to etiology (Rosenblum, 1990), with different mechanisms that might be manifested in different ways on neuroimaging studies.

TABLE 13–1. Neuropsychological Test Results for Patient K.L. and Normative Data

	HIV + Patient (K.L.)			Normal Controls (n = 8; Mean/S.D.)
	11-17-88	1-2-89	8-17-89	
Verbal memory				
CLTR	2	27	33	32.5/11.1
Recall	4	10	10	8.5/2.8
Visual Memory				
Correct	6	10	9	7.8/1.2
Errors	7	0	1	2.8/1.7
PASAT				
Oprates[a]	.30	.53	.50	.35/.05
WCST				
Errors	84	30	9	26.6/15.3
Reaction time (msec)				
Simple	928	492	472	571.7/122.3
Choice	1073	788	679	746.2/78.6

[a]Oprate refers to the rate of processing, which is given by (number of correct additions × interdigit interval)/number of possible additions. The interval could range from 2.4 to 1.2 seconds, and the number of total possible additions is 49.

In early studies, gray matter generally appeared more benign than white matter on postmortem studies (Price et al., 1988; Rosenblum, 1990). Recent reports have suggested neuronal loss in the cortex in AIDS. Consistent with this finding, we found changes in the volume of this compartment. Gray matter volume has not been studied quantitatively in MRI reports in AIDS. Apparent reversal of gray matter atrophy after treatment suggests three possibilities. Neuronal loss may not be a significant factor in certain patients early in illness, at the reversible stage. Increased gray matter volume may be due to alterations in processes and sprouting. Dendritic changes, a potentially reversible phenomenon, have been reported in postmortem studies. Improvement in neuropsychological function and increased gray matter volume may take place by normalization of cellular processes (e.g., dendrites) or by alteration in the extracellular matrix as the viral burden is reduced. Increased extracellular water or protein synthesis in general may also occur in some conditions (DeCarli et al., 1991).

Although reversal of brain atrophy may seem surprising, there is evidence of this phenomenon in alcoholics after abstinence (Schroth et al., 1988). The atrophy in alcoholism is predominantly of white matter (de la Monte, 1988), but whether this reversal is due to changes in gray or white matter volume has not yet been studied in alcoholism or other diseases.

In the future, we expect to obtain information regarding which MRI indices correlate with the effects of AZT on cognitive function. The indices may be useful as a quantitative basis for comparing the effectiveness of AIDS therapies. If the abnormal properties of the brain image can be measured quantitatively, repeatably, and conveniently, and if these abnormal properties are correlated with abnormal brain function, image analysis may be a valuable tool in the development and testing of new AIDS treatments.

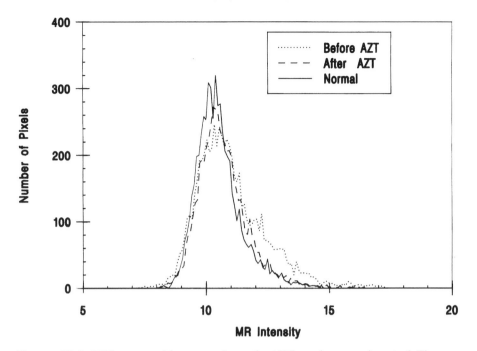

FIGURE 13–3. White matter histograms for patient K.L. and a normal control. The number of pixels (Y axis) was plotted for a given pixel intensity (X axis) in the white matter in a transverse T2-weighted slice above the level of the caudate. The dotted line represents the intensity histogram prior to AZT treatment. A shoulder is visible at 11.8, which represents high intensity white matter lesions. The dashed line represents the histogram derived from a matching slice approximately 5 months after beginning AZT. As can be seen, the shoulder at high intensity values disappeared after treatment, and resembles the histogram taken from a matching slice from a normal control subject (solid line). The difference between the before and after AZT histograms represents the area of white matter whose intensity changed after treatment.

Acknowledgment

This work was supported in part by NIMH RO3 MH49552-01. Dr. Richard B. Polland assisted with the care of this patient.

References

Abbruzzese, G., Rizzo, F., Dall-Agata, D., Morandi, N., and Favale, E. (1990). Generalized dystonia with bilateral striatal computer-tomographic lucencies in a patient with human immunodeficiency virus infection. *European Neurology, 30,* 271–273.

Adams, K.M., and Heaton, R.K. (1990). Statement concerning the NIMH neuropsychological battery. *Journal of Clinical and Experimental Neuropsychology, 12,* 960–962.

Ajmani, A., Habte-Gabr, E., Zarr, M., Jayabalan, V., and Dandala, S. (1991). Cerebral blood flow SPECT with TC-99m exametazine correlates in AIDS dementia complex stages. A preliminary report. *Clinical Nuclear Medicine, 16*, 656–659.

Army Industrial Test Battery. (1944). *Manual of Directions and Scoring.* Washington, D.C.: War Department, Adjutant General's Office.

Benton, A.L. (1968). Differential behavioral effects in frontal lobe disease. *Neuropsychologica, 6*, 53–60.

Brunetti, A., Berg, G., DiChiro, G., Cohen, R.M., Yarchoan, R., Pizzo, P.A., Broder, S., Eddy, J., Fulham, M.J., Finn, R.D., and Larson, S.N. (1989). Reversal of brain metabolic abnormalities following treatment of AIDS dementia complex with 3'-azido-2',3'-dideoxythymidine: A PET-FDG study. *Journal of Nuclear Medicine, 30*, 581–590.

Budka, H. (1990). Human immunodeficiency virus (HIV) envelope and core proteins in CNS tissues of patients with the acquired immune deficiency syndrome (AIDS). *Acta Neuropathologica (Berlin), 79*, 611–619.

Budka, H., Wiley, C.A., Kleihues, P., Artigas, J., Asbury, A.K., Cho, E.-S., Cornblath, D.R., Dal Canto, M.C., DeGirolami, U., and Dickson, D. (1991). HIV-associated disease of the nervous system: Review of nomenclature and proposal for neuropathology-based terminology. *Brain Pathology, 1*, 143–152.

Buschke, H., and Fuld, P.A. (1974). Evaluating storage, retention, and retrieval in disordered memory and learning. *Neurology, 24*, 1019–1025.

Coats, M., Salazar, D.M., and Martin, A. (1989). Neurological findings in early HIV infection. Paper presented at the Fifth International Conference on AIDS, Montreal, Canada, June 7.

Day, J., Grant, I., Atkinson, J.H., Brysk, L., McCutchan, J.A., Hesselink, J.R., Spector, S.A., and Richman, D.D. (1992). Incidence of AIDS Dementia in a two year follow-up of AIDS and ARC patients on an initial phase II AZT placebo-controlled study: San Diego cohort. *Journal of Neuropsychiatry and Clinical Neurosciences, 4*, 15–20.

DeCarli, C., Fugate, L., Falloon, J., Eddy, J., Katz, D.A., Friedland, R.P., Rapoport, S.I., Brouwers, P., and Pizzo, P.A. (1991). Brain growth and cognitive improvement in children with human immunodeficiency virus–induced encephalopathy after 6 months of continuous infusion zidovudine therapy. *Journal of Acquired Immune Deficiency Syndromes, 4*, 585–592.

de la Monte, S.M. (1988). Disproportionate atrophy of cerebral white matter in chronic alcoholics. *Archives of Neurology, 45*, 990–992.

Derogatis, L.R., and Towson, M.D. (1977). *SCL-90R (revised) Version Manual I.* Baltimore: Clinical Psychometric Research.

Egan, V. (1991). Neurological and neuropsychological complications of HIV infection. Conference Report, Monterey, CA, June 16–19, 1990. *Postgraduate Medical Journal, 67*, 3078.

Elder, G.A., and Sever, J.L. (1988). Neurologic disorder associated with AIDS retroviral infection. *Reviews of Infectious Diseases, 10*, 286–302.

Gelman, B.B. (1993). Diffuse microgliosis associated with cerebral atrophy in the acquired immunodeficiency syndrome. *Annals of Neurology, 34*, 65–70.

Gelman, B.B., and Guinto, F.C., Jr. (1992). Morphometry, histopathology, and tomography of cerebral atrophy in the acquired immunodeficiency syndrome. *Annals of Neurology, 32*, 31–40.

Gelman, B.B., Rodriguez-Wolf, M.G., Wen, J., Kumar, S., Campbell, G.R., and Herzog, N. (1992). Siderotic cerebral macrophages in the acquired immunodeficiency syndrome. *Archives of Pathology and Laboratory Medicine, 116*, 509–516.

Giulian, D., Vaca, K., and Noonan, C.A. (1990). Secretion of neurotoxins by mononuclear phagocytes infected with HIV-1, *Science, 250*, 1593–1596.

Grant, I., and Atkinson, J.H. (1990). The evolution of neurobehavioral complications of HIV infection. *Psychological Medicine, 20*, 747–754.

Grant, I., Atkinson, J.H., Hesselink, J.R., Kennedy, C.J., Richman, D.D., Spector, S.A., and McCutchan, J.A. (1987). Evidence for early central nervous system involvement in the acquired immunodeficiency syndrome and other human immunodeficiency virus infections. *Annals of Internal Medicine, 107*, 828–836.

Grant, D.A., and Berg, E.A., (1948). A behavioral analysis of degree of reinforcement and ease of shifting to new responses in a Weigl-type card-sorting problem. *Journal of Experimental Psychology, 38*, 404–411.

Gronwall, D., and Wrightson, P. (1974). Recovery after minor head injury [letter]. *Lancet 2*, 1452.

Hillman, G.R., Kent, T.A., Kaye, A., Brunder, D.G., and Tagare, H. (1991). Measurement of brain compartment volumes in MR using voxel composition calculations. *Journal of Computer Assisted Tomography, 15*, 640–646.

Hollweg, M., Riedel, R.R., Groebel, F.D., Schick, U., and Naber, D. (1991). Remarkable improvement of neuropsychiatric symptoms in HIV-infected patients after AZT therapy. *Klinische Wochenschrift (Berlin), 69*, 409–412.

Jakobsen, J., Gyldensted, C., Brun, B., Bruhn, P., Helweg-Larsen, S., and Arlien-Soborg, P. (1989). Cerebral ventricular enlargement relates to neuropsychological measures in unselected AIDS patients. *Acta Neurologica Scandinavica, 79*, 59–62.

Janssen, R.S., Saykin, A.J., Cannon, L., Campbell, J., Pinsky, P.F., Hessol, N.A., O'Malley, P.M., Lifson, A.R., Doll, L.S., Rutherford, G.W., and Kaplan, J.E. (1989). Neurological and neuropsychological manifestations of HIV-1 infection: Association with AIDS-related complex but not asymptomatic HIV-1 infection. *Annals of Neurology, 26*, 592–601.

Jarvik, J.G., Hesselink, J.R., Kennedy, C., Teschke, R., Wiley, C., Spector, S., Richman, D., and McCutchan, J.A. (1988). Acquired immunodeficiency syndrome magnetic resonance patterns of brain involvement with pathologic correlation. *Archives of Neurology, 45*, 731–736.

Kodama, T., Numaguchi, U., Gellad, F.E., and Sadato, N. (1991). High signal intensity of both putamina in patients with HIV infection. *Neuroradiology, 33*, 362–363.

Kramer, E.L., and Sanger, J.J. (1990). Brain imaging in acquired immunodeficiency syndrome dementia complex. *Seminars in Nuclear Medicine, 20*, 353–363.

Kuni, C.C., Rhame, F.S., Meier, M.J., Foehse, M.C., Loewenson, R.B., Lee, B.C.P., Boudreau, R.J., and duCret, R.P. (1991). Quantitative I-123 IMP brain SPECT and neuropsychological testing in AIDS dementia. *Clinical Nuclear Medicine, 16*, 174–177.

LaFrance, N.D., Pearlson, A.D., and Schaerf, F.W. (1988). I-123 IMP-SPECT in HIV-related dementia. *Advances in Functional Neuroimaging, 1*, 9–15.

Levin, H.S., Williams, D.H., Borucki, M.J., Hillman, G.R., Williams, J.B., Guinto, F.C., Jr., Amparo, E.G., Crow, W.N., and Pollard, R.B. (1990). Magnetic resonance imaging and neuropsychological findings in human immunodeficiency virus infection. *Journal of Acquired Immune Deficiency Syndromes, 3*, 757–762.

Lipton, S.A. (1991). Calcium channel antagonists and human immunodeficiency virus coat protein–mediated neuronal injury. *Annals of Neurology, 30*, 110–114.

Maini, C.L., Pigorini, F., Pau, F.M., Tatsch, K., Schielke, E., Einhaupl, K.M., Bauer, M., Markl, A.E., and Kirsch, C.M. (1989). ^{99m}Tc-HMPAO-SPECT in patients with HIV-infection: A comparison with neurological, CT, and MRI findings. *European Journal of Nuclear Medicine, 15*, 418 (abst.).

Maj, M. (1990). Psychiatric aspects of HIV-1 infection and AIDS. *Psychological Medicine,* *20,* 547–563.

Marotta, R., and Perry, S. (1989). Early neuropsychological dysfunction caused by human immunodeficiency virus. *Journal of Neuropsychiatry and Clinical Neuroscience, 1,* 225–235.

Masliah, E., Ge, N., Morey, M., DeTeresa, R., Terry, R.D., and Wiley, C.A. (1992). Cortical dendritic pathology in human immunodeficiency virus encephalitis. *Laboratory Investigation, 66,* 285–291.

Matthes, J., Walder, L.A., Watson, J.G., and Bird, A.G. (1988). AIDS encephalopathy with response to treatment. *Archives of Diseases in Childhood, 63,* 545–547.

McAllister, R.H., Herns, M.V., Harrison, M.J., Newman, S.P., Connolly, S., Fowler, C.J., Fell, M., Durrance, P., Manji, H., Kendall, B.E., Valentine, A.R., Weller, I.V.D., and Adler, M. (1992). Neurological and neuropsychological performance in HIV seropositive men without symptoms. *Journal of Neurology, Neurosurgery and Psychiatry, 55,* 143–148.

McArthur, J.C., Becker, P.S., Parisi, J., Trapp, B., Selnes, O.A., Cornblath, D.R., Balakrishnan, J., Griffin, J.W., and Price, D. (1989a). Neuropathological changes in early HIV-1 dementia. *Annals of Neurology, 26,* 681–684.

McArthur, J.C., Cohen, B.A., Selnes, O.A., Kumar, A.J., Cooper, K., McArthur, J.H., Soucy, G., Cornblath, D.R., Chmiel, J.S., Wang, M.C., Starkey, D.L., Ginzburg, H., Ostrow, D.G., Johnson, R.T., Phair, J.P., and Polk, B.F. (1989b). Low prevalence of neurological and neuropsychological abnormalities in otherwise healthy HIV-1-infected individuals: Results from the Multicenter AIDS Cohort Study. *Annals of Neurology, 26,* 601–611.

Menon, D.K., Bardouin, C.J., Tomlinson, D., and Hoyle, C. (1990). Proton MR spectroscopy and imaging of the brain in AIDS: Evidence of neuronal loss in regions that appear normal with imaging. *Journal of Computer Assisted Tomography, 14,* 882–885.

Miller, R.F. (1990). Nuclear medicine and AIDS. *European Journal of Nuclear Medicine, 16,* 103–118.

Moeller, A.A., and Backmund, H.C. (1990). Ventricle brain ratio in the clinical course of HIV infection. *Acta Neurologica Scandinavica, 81,* 512–515.

Olsen, W.L., Longo, F.M., Mills, C.M., and Norman, D. (1988). White matter disease in AIDS: Findings at MR imaging. *Radiology, 169,* 445–448.

Perdices, M., and Cooper, D.A. (1989). Simple and choice reaction time in patients with human immunodeficiency virus infection. *Annals of Neurology, 25,* 460–467.

Petito, C.K., Navia, B.A., Cho, E.-S., Jordan, B.D., George, D.C., and Price, R.W. (1985). Vacuolar myelopathy pathologically resembling subacute combined degeneration in patients with the acquired immunodeficiency syndrome. *New England Journal of Medicine, 312,* 874–879.

Pohl, P., Vogl, G., Fill, H., Rossler, H., Zangerle, R., and Gerstenbrand, F. (1988). Single photon emission computed tomography in AIDS dementia complex. *Journal of Nuclear Medicine, 29,* 1382–1386.

Post, M.J., Berger, J.R., and Quencer, R.M. (1991). Asymptomatic and neurologically symptomatic HIV-seropositive individuals: Prospective evaluation with cranial MR imaging. *Radiology, 178,* 131–139.

Post, M.J., Tate, L.G., Quencer, R.M., Hensley, G.T., Berger, J.R., Sheremata, W.A., and Maul, G. (1988). CT, MR, and pathology in HIV encephalitis and meningitis. *American Journal of Roentgenology, 151,* 373–380.

Price, R.W., Brew, B., Sidtis, J., Rosenblum, M., Scheck, A.C., and Cleary, P. (1988). The brain in AIDS: Central nervous system HIV-1 infection and AIDS dementia complex. *Science, 239*, 586–592.

Raininko, R., Elovaara, I., Virta, A., Valanne, L., Haltia, M., and Valle, S.L. (1992). Radiological study of the brain at various stages of the human immunodeficiency virus infection: Early development of brain atrophy. *Neuroradiology, 34*, 190–196.

Rosenblum, M.K. (1990). Infection of the central nervous system by the human immunodeficiency virus type 1. Morphology and relation to syndromes of progressive encephalopathy and myelopathy in patients with AIDS. *Pathology Annual, 25* (Pt. 1), 117–169.

Rottenberg, D.A., Moeller, J.R., Strother, S.C., Sidtis, J.J., Navia, B.A., Dhawan, V., Ginos, J.A., and Price, R.W. (1987). The metabolic pathology of the AIDS dementia complex. *Annals of Neurology, 22*, 700–706.

Schmitt, F.A., Bigley, J.W., Mckinnis, R., Logue, P.E., Evans, R.W., and Drucker, J.L. (1988). Neuropsychological outcome of zidovudine treatment of patients with AIDS and AIDS-related complex. *New England Journal of Medicine, 319*, 1573–1578.

Schroth, G., Naegele, T., Klose, U., Mann, K., and Petersen, D. (1988). Reversible brain shrinkage in abstinent alcoholics, measured by MRI. *Neuroradiology, 30*, 385–389.

Smith, T.W., DeGirolami, U., Henin, D., Bolgert, F., and Hauw, J.D. (1990). Human immunodeficiency virus (HIV) leukoencephalopathy and the microcirculation. *Journal of Neuropathology and Experimental Neurology, 49*, 357–370.

Stern, Y. (1991). The impact of human immunodeficiency virus on cognitive function. *Annals of the New York Academy of Sciences, 640*, 219–223.

Wiley, C.A., Belman, A.L., Dickson, D.W., Rubinstein, A., and Nelson, J.A. (1990). Human immunodeficiency virus within the brains of children with AIDS. *Clinical Neuropathology, 9*, 1–6.

Wilkie, F.L., Eisdorfer, C., Morgan, R., Loewenstein, D.A., and Szapocznik, J. (1990). Cognition in early human immunodeficiency virus infection. *Archives of Neurology, 47*, 433–440.

Yarchoan, R., Thomas, R.V., Grafman, J., Wichman, A., Dalakas, M., McAtee, N., Berg, G., Fischl, M., Perno, C.F., Klecker, R.W., Buchbinder, A., Tay, S., Larsen, S.M., Myers, C.E., and Broder, S. (1988). Long-term administration of 3'-azido-2',3'-dideoxythymidine to patients with AIDS-related neurological disease. *Annals of Neurology, 23*(Suppl.), S82–S87.

14

Neuropsychological Response to Antiretroviral Therapy in HIV Infection

FREDERICK A. SCHMITT, LESLEY R. DICKSON,
and PIM BROUWERS

Neurological and neuropsychological symptoms have been reported as frequent complications of HIV infection in adults and children by a number of authors (e.g., Ammann, 1985; Shaw et al., 1985; Grant et al., 1987; Belman, 1990; Maj, 1990). Generally, central nervous system (CNS) involvement with human immunodeficiency virus (HIV) infection has included opportunistic infections of the CNS as well as diffuse brain atrophy (Navia et al., 1986b). Price and colleagues (1988) have estimated that roughly 40% of adults with acquired immunodeficiency syndrome (AIDS) suffer some type of CNS dysfunction. In some patients, neurological signs appear as the first symptoms of HIV infection, often before the systemic opportunistic infections and cancers associated with AIDS are seen (e.g., Navia and Price, 1987). In children with symptomatic HIV infection, encephalopathy has been estimated to occur in 50–90% of these cases. Pediatric CNS manifestations of HIV infection reflect general and diffuse neurodevelopmental abnormalities including developmental delays, loss of acquired skills and developmental milestones, plus significant declines and/or impairment on psychometric measures (e.g., Epstein et al., 1985, 1987; see also Chapter 16).

The mechanisms involved in HIV infection of the brain are not clearly understood at present even though HIV is associated with CNS and immunological disease (Grant and Heaton, 1990). Direct infection of the CNS by HIV (e.g., Pumarola-Sune et al., 1987) may account for the neuropsychological dysfunction seen with HIV infection. Further support for CNS infection can be found in data showing encephalopathy (Epstein et al., 1985, 1987) and acute meningitis concurrent with HIV antibodies (Hollander and Levy, 1987) in CSF. Further, virus has been cultured from the CSF in infected but asymptomatic individuals (Resnick et al., 1985) and in patients with AIDS dementia complex (Pumarola-Sune et al., 1987). Finally, Navia et al. (1986a), Petito et al. (1986), and Gray et al. (1988) have presented autopsy data that show postmortem brain abnormalities in patients with AIDS. Although the presence of HIV in the CNS has been documented by these studies (70–90% of autopsies are abnormal; Petito, 1988), the mechanisms of HIV's effects on the CNS and the resultant changes in cognitive and day-to-day functioning are unclear (Price et al., 1988). Correlations between CNS lesions (on magnetic resonance imaging [MRI]) and neuropsychological performance appear to be limited (Saykin et al., 1988; Dooneief et al., 1992), although there is evidence of structural changes (e.g., Everall et al., 1991), hypoperfusion (Schielke et al., 1990), and changes in regional metabolic activity (Rottenberg et al., 1987). Several studies have suggested that HIV may damage the CNS through associated neurotoxins that might be secreted by infected mononuclear phagocytes (Giulian et al., 1990) or through alterations in metabolism resulting in increased levels of excitotoxins such as quinolinic acid (Heyes et al, 1989, 1990). If HIV-associated cognitive impairments are related to viral or host-mediated factors (e.g., Weber et al., 1990; Gorman et al., 1991) rather than to structural damage alone, a positive CNS response to antiretroviral treatments or treatments targeting neurotoxic processes might be expected.

Given that neuropsychological sequelae are associated with HIV infection of the CNS, assessment of brain functioning is an important marker of disease progression, as well as a measure of treatment efficacy for antiretrovial agents. To date, several pediatric and adult clinical trials of antiretroviral treatment have incorporated neuropsychological measures as outcome parameters. After a brief discussion of medical issues related to HIV infection and measurement of the CNS response to treatment, this chapter will primarily review studies of zidovudine (ZDV; azidothymidine, AZT) in adult and pediatric patients with HIV infection. Other antiretroviral agents will be briefly reviewed, followed by recommendations for neuropsychological evaluations in different patient populations.

Medical Complications of HIV Infection

It is well known that HIV infection is a multistage, multisystem illness with numerous manifestations that frequently overlap, and these conditions may significantly affect the cognitive functioning of an infected individual (Markowitz and Perry, 1990). The viral infection itself can cause a multiplicity of symptoms, and its destruction of the immune system results in systemic problems including opportunistic infections and malignancies. Thus, sorting out individual symptoms and determining a treatable etiology can be extremely complicated. Further, studies involving neuropsychological assessments need to consider the effect of systemic illness on the brain in addition to the primary CNS pathology (Beckett, 1990).

HIV infection in adults is presently divided into four stages (CDC, 1987), with initial infection described as flu-like, including fevers, fatigue, and a meningitis-like presentation. This stage is followed by a mainly asymptomatic period of seropositivity in which it is sometimes possible to demonstrate cognitive changes in individuals, suggesting that the virus has begun to invade the CNS (Grant et al., 1987). The third stage of generalized lymphadenopathy is followed by the development of constitutional symptoms including fever, weight loss, anemia, decreasing T4 lymphocyte counts, fatigue, and chronic diarrhea.

The fourth stage of infection is usually heralded by the appearance of an opportunistic infection or one of the secondary cancers. It may also be diagnosed by the appearance of a significant neurological disease such as dementia (e.g., Sidtis and Price, 1990), neuropathy, or myelopathy (e.g., McArthur, 1987). Frequently the patient with HIV has more than one infection at the same time. A malignancy and infections may coexist or a CNS infection and primary viral CNS involvement may be present at the same time. These neurological conditions can further complicate the picture of cognitive dysfunction. This fourth stage of infection may closely resemble a depression, and a "pseudodementia" picture may appear in some patients. Malnutrition and its attendant vitamin and mineral deficiencies may become problematic during this stage, further influencing CNS functioning, as indexed by neuropsychological tests (e.g., Kieburtz et al., 1991). Some of the more common coexisting conditions that must be considered by the treating physician and the evaluating neuropsychologist will be described briefly.

The most frequent opportunistic infection is *Pneumocystis carinii* pneumonia (Markowitz and Perry, 1990). Beginning as a mild respiratory syndrome, it can progress rapidly to high fever, weight loss, and severe respiratory distress. This may be accompanied by significant hypoxia (Leoung, 1989) and therefore mental impairment. Another frequent systemic condition is a chronic diarrhea that can be caused by several organisms, including *Cryptosporidium, Giardia, Mycobacterium avium intracellulare* (MAI), cytomegalovirus (CMV), and *Salmonella* (Friedman, 1989; Markowitz and Perry, 1990). This diarrhea can result in significant weight loss, malnutrition, and, in severe cases, dehydration and electrolyte abnormalities, with a resultant encephalopathic presentation. Organ failure can also cause an encephalopathic picture, with both renal and hepatic disease having been described in patients with AIDS (Friedman, 1989; Schoenfeld, 1991). These syndromes are frequently due to infections such as MAI, CMV, *Cryptococcus,* or HIV itself. Finally, the anorexia of the illness and the pain from oral infections such as *Candida* (Friedman, 1989) can lead to vitamin, mineral, and protein/calorie deficiencies, which may cause a chronic dementia or other organic mental syndromes.

Opportunistic infections of the brain are frequent causes of neurological and cognitive difficulties. *Toxoplasma gondii* can cause an encephalitis with symptoms of headache, fever, delirium, or coma, or it can result in focal problems such as seizures and mental status changes from a mass lesion (Markowitz and Perry, 1990). *Cryptococcus* is a fungus that presents as a slowly progressive meningitis or encephalitis with headache, personality changes, memory loss, and confusion. Other CNS infections that must be considered in HIV-infected individuals with mental status changes are CMV, herpes zoster virus, herpes simplex virus, and syphilis.

HIV-related malignancies are also occasionally causes of neuropsychological difficulties. While Kaposi's sarcoma was the cancer first diagnosed in relation to AIDS, it rarely causes CNS problems. However, it is extremely disfiguring and can cause significant psychological problems. Further, Kaposi's sarcoma can invade internal organs, causing respiratory distress and gastrointestinal dysfunction (Markowitz and Perry, 1990) and thus contributing to an encephalopathic picture. HIV-infected patients are at increased risk of developing a non-Hodgkin's lymphoma, which usually presents as a primary lymphoma of the brain (Beckett, 1990). Symptoms associated with CNS lymphoma include confusion or cognitive impairment, in addition to headaches, seizures, aphasia, incontinence, and other neurological problems. In addition to malignancies, patients with HIV seem to be at increased risk of cerebrovascular disease, primarily strokes. Pathological explanations include opportunistic infections, thromboembolism, and damaged endothelial linings of blood vessels (Beckett, 1990).

In summary, HIV infection causes multiple medical problems that include the viral infection itself, direct CNS involvement, opportunistic infections, malignancies, and cerebrovascular disease. These conditions are often accompanied by additional medical problems such as nutritional abnormalities, organ failure, anemia, and electrolyte disturbances. All of these conditions, in isolation and in combination, can result in a patient presentation that includes cognitive dysfunction and behavioral abnormalities suggesting a neuropsychiatric illness. Therefore, it is incumbent on the treatment team to search diligently for more than one explanation of the cognitive symptoms and to use treatment approaches that address multiple etiologies at any one time. (The physiological alterations associated with HIV infection can be treated with various regimens.) As these abnormalities can impair brain functioning, medical interventions might provide cognitive benefit in addition to improving the systemic medical condition.

Current Medical Therapies

Treatment of HIV infection and the accompanying secondary medical problems can cause significant and frequently unrecognized neuropsychological problems. Many pharmacological agents have side effects that can cause a florid delirium or more subtle problems that should be considered during neuropsychological evaluations.

Medications used to treat patients with HIV infection are often limited by their toxic side effects (e.g., Richman et al., 1987). ZDV treatment, for example, is notable for its suppression of the bone marrow and a resulting anemia that can compromise oxygenation of the CNS. Treatment with ZDV has been reported to cause or contribute to fatigue, depressive symptoms, confusion, and an acute meningoencephalitis (Crowe et al., 1990). Drugs used to treat opportunistic infections can also lead to significant changes in mentation. These compounds include amphotericin B for *Cryptococcus,* trimethoprim-sulfamethoxazole and dapsone for *Pneumocystis,* acyclovir for herpes, isoniazid for *Mycobacterium,* and ketoconazole for *Candida.* CNS complications associated with these compounds include confusion, delirium, hallucination, paranoia, and depression (Drugs That

Cause Psychiatric Symptoms, 1989; Crowe et al., 1990). Interferon, which is used for HIV infection or Kaposi's sarcoma, has also been reported to be associated with changes in cognitive functioning (Drugs That Cause Psychiatric Symptoms, 1989; Crowe et al., 1990).

Patients with HIV infection frequently develop psychiatric complications that require pharmacological management, and some will have used recreational drugs. The anticholinergic effects of neuroleptics and tricyclic antidepressants used to treat psychiatric problems can cause neuropsychiatric difficulties such as memory dysfunction and confusion. Similarly, medications used for symptoms of anxiety such as the benzodiazepines, narcotics for symptoms of pain, and non-steroidal anti-inflammatory agents have been described as causing problems with concentration, confusion, and symptoms of depression (Drugs That Cause Psychiatric Symptoms, 1989). These same pharmacological agents, as well as cocaine and other street drugs, may be used surreptitiously by patients and should always (in conjunction with premorbid ability) be considered as possible causes of neuropsychological problems (Wilkins et al., 1990). Alternatively, stimulants such as methylphenidate or dextroamphetamine, used to treat depression, may actually ameliorate some cognitive problems experienced by patients with HIV infection (Fernandez and Levy, 1990).

Neuropsychological Outcomes of ZDV Treatment in Adults

Since HIV is a viral infection, the primary method of treatment will involve therapeutic agents that demonstrate antiviral activity and compounds that might restore normal immune system functioning. Historically, ZDV showed effective inhibition of HIV replication in vitro (Mitsuya et al., 1985) and was therefore used in several in vivo clinical trials.

The first report of the antiviral and cognitive benefit of ZDV treatment was published by Yarchoan and colleagues (1987). This study involved five patients with AIDS-related neurological dysfunction who received oral ZDV. These patients essentially met cognitive criteria for HIV-associated cognitive and motor impairment (three with AIDS dementia complex) and received 250 mg of ZDV orally every 4 hours. The case reports on these patients demonstrated changes in regional glucose metabolism on position emission tomography (PET), improved amplitude and conduction velocity on nerve conduction studies, and improved muscle strength on neurological examination. Neuropsychological measures also reflected improved functioning on Trail Making B, on the Digit Symbol test, on verbal recall from the Wechsler Memory Test, and on the Purdue Pegboard Test. A subsequent extension of this study (Yarchoan et al., 1988b) showed that six of the seven patients improved on neurological and neuropsychological measures while on ZDV. Further, three of the six patients who improved with ZDV maintained this improvement in functioning for 5–18 months after starting ZDV therapy.

In February 1986, a large-scale multicenter, double-blind, placebo-controlled trial of ZDV began for more than 200 patients with advanced AIDS-related complex (ARC) and early AIDS. Treatment with ZDV showed decreased mortality and reduced frequency of opportunistic infections over the 8–24 weeks of the study; interim survival analyses showed 19 deaths in the placebo group in contrast to 1 death in the ZDV group, while the occurrence of opportunistic infections was roughly double in the placebo group (Fischl et al., 1987). Treatment was accompanied by an increased risk of bone marrow toxicity, however (Richman et al., 1987). Neuropsychological measures were included in this clinical trial to document potential CNS toxicity as a result of treatment (Schmitt et al., 1988). Overall, patients receiving ZDV in comparison to placebo showed improved performance on neuropsychological measures of attention, verbal memory, visuospatial scanning, and symptomatic distress, similar to those reported by Yarchoan et al. (1987).

Studies of neuropsychological performance in patients with HIV infection, however, have documented varying degrees and types of cognitive impairment at different stages of HIV disease (e.g., Grant et al., 1987; Janssen et al., 1988; Goethe et al., 1989). While it is generally accepted that the existence of neuropsychological dysfunction is more common in increasingly symptomatic patients (ARC and AIDS; Grant et al., 1987; Janssen et al., 1989; McArthur et al., 1989; Selnes et al., 1990), different assessment, statistical, and clinical methods can be used to define performance deficits. This use of an objective index of neuropsychological dysfunction is a critical issue for treatment research. If reversal of CNS impairments is to be used as an index of treatment efficacy, only patients with demonstrable neurological and neuropsychological dysfunction might be studied. In contrast to such an interventive approach, treatment might be designed to be preventive (e.g., Volberding et al., 1990). If prevention of brain impairment is the goal of treatment, then patients might be evaluated for the development of impairment (or subtle changes in mentation).

When patients demonstrate symptoms of AIDS dementia complex (ADC; Price and Brew, 1988; Sidtis and Price, 1990) or AIDS-associated cognitive and motor impairment (Working Group, AAN Task Force, 1991), both the preventive and ameliorative effects of treatment should be considered. Further, since patients with advanced disease were included in the double-blind study of ZDV, a reanalysis of the treatment response of neuropsychologically impaired AIDS and advanced AIDS-related complex patients seemed to be an important undertaking. As the neuropsychological data from the ZDV trial included two pretreatment assessments, we were able to estimate the degree of cognitive impairment in patients enrolled in this clinical trial. In addition to documenting initial rates of impairment, these criteria could be used to investigate the effects of ZDV on impaired AIDS and ARC participants in contrast to possibly progressive cognitive dysfunction in the control or placebo group (Schmitt et al., 1988).

Two pretreatment evaluations were completed for the 281 patients enrolled in the ZDV trial. In reviewing the abnormalities seen on the neuropsychological tests (Ruff 2 and 7, Finger Oscillation, Selective Reminding, Digit Span, Trailmaking, Symbol Digit), we used a criterion similar to that reported by Grant et al. (1987), in which patients were considered to be "possibly impaired" if they scored at least 1 SD below a normative mean test score on at least two out of nine screening measures at two separate test sessions. Additionally, patients were considered to be "probably impaired" if they showed a deficit of 2 SD or more

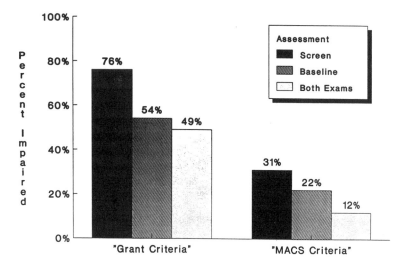

FIGURE 14–1. Impairment rates for AIDS and advanced ARC patients enrolled in the double-blind placebo-controlled trial of zidovudine. Rates are calculated using two sets of criteria for single examinations (screening and baseline) and for stability of impairment on both screening and baseline examinations.

on any individual test. These estimates are considerably more conservative than those of Grant et al., as they were based on patients who were classified as "abnormal" on both the screening and baseline assessments approximately 1 week later (Figure 14–1). An alternative criterion of impairment from the Multicenter AIDS Cohort Study (MACS; Miller et al., 1990) is also included for comparison. Impairment in the MACS study is based on two cognitive tests that are at least 2 SD below a normative mean.

Practice or learning effects due to exposure to the neuropsychological procedures were seen on most of the tests. Therefore, patients who showed abnormalities on only one assessment (screening or baseline) were excluded from the estimate of impairment. As these data clearly demonstrate (see Figure 14–1), estimates for the prevalence of impairment in patients with HIV infection were influenced by the criteria and number of assessments used to define impairment for this population. By requiring impairment to remain stable over two assessments or by increasing the degree of impairment required on these tests, the rates of impairment dropped roughly 20–30% in our population.

Results of ZDV treatment on neuropsychological functions reported in the original outcome paper were analyzed for changes from baseline for all patients enrolled in the study. By applying the criteria discussed above (at least two tests at 1 SD below a standardized mean and/or one or more tests at 2 SD below a

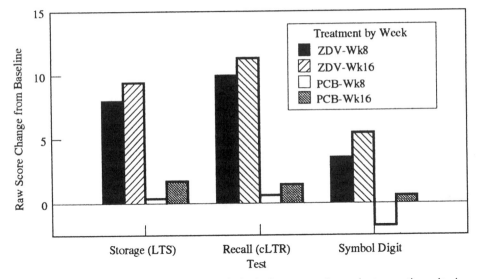

FIGURE 14–2. Mean change on neuropsychological measures for patients meeting criteria for impairment (at least one or more test(s) at 2 SD or two or more tests at least 1 SD below normative mean) as a result of zidovudine treatment over four months. All between group comparisons (ZDV = zidovudine; PCB = placebo) of treatment differences were significant ($p < .001$) with the exception of long-term storage (LTS) at week 16 ($p < .08$) using the Wilcoxon Rank Sum Test for treatment differences.

standardized mean for both baseline and screening exams), the treatment response focused on potentially encephalopathic patients. The results of treatment for the patients in our study who met this impairment criterion prior to beginning treatment are summarized in Figures 14–2 and 14–3. The data for weeks 8 and 16 of the study show consistent treatment effects across the cognitive measures. Once again, patients receiving ZDV showed improvement as a result of treatment, while patients in the placebo arm of the study showed stability or decline in performance. Not surprisingly, the change seen in these patients with pretreatment neuropsychological dysfunction is larger than that reported for the overall group (Schmitt et al., 1988).

Neuropsychological Outcomes of ZDV Treatment in Children

The neuropsychological data from the first study of ZDV therapy for pediatric HIV infection have been reported in detail elsewhere (Pizzo et al. 1988; Brouwers et al., 1990). Several important points need to be emphasized about the differences between the adult and pediatric trials, however. The pediatric study by Pizzo and colleagues at the National Cancer Institute (NCI) differed from the adult multicenter trial not only in the patient population studied but also in terms of drug delivery and neurobehavioral measures. Children in the NCI study

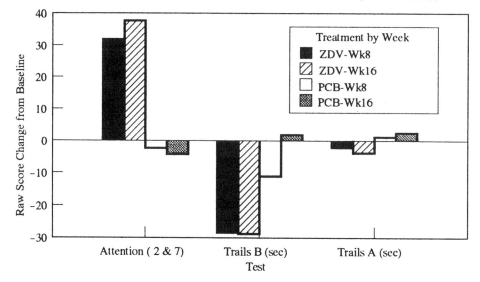

FIGURE 14–3. Mean change on neuropsychological measures for patients meeting criteria for impairment (at least one or more test(s) at 2 SD or two or more tests at least 1 SD below normative mean) as a result of zidovudine treatment over 4 months. All between group comparisons of treatment differences (ZDV = zidovudine; PCB = placebo) were significant ($p < .001$) with the exception of Trails A at week 8 ($p < .10$) and week 16 ($p < .03$), and Trails B for week 8 ($p < .03$) using the Wilcoxon Rank Sum Test for treatment differences.

received ZDV via continuous intravenous infusion primarily in an attempt to circumvent the short half-life of ZDV reported in adults (Klecker et al., 1987) but also in an attempt to maintain higher serum and cerebrospinal fluid levels of the drug. Four different doses of ZDV (0.5, 0.9, 1.4, and 1.8 mg/kg/hr) were used with at least three children at each dose level. Of the 21 symptomatic (Centers for Disease Control [CDC] class P2) children in the study (median age, 4.8 years), 14 required blood transfusions related to bone marrow suppression with resulting low levels of hemoglobin, but neutropenia occurred in the majority of the patients at the highest two doses of ZDV. Four of the original 21 patients died during the 6 months of therapy.

Neurobehavioral measures were available for 13 children in the NCI study after 6 months of infusion. Eight of these 13 children were encephalopathic before treatment was initiated. Significant intellectual gains made by these children, however, were not different from the gains seen in their nonencephalopathic cohorts. Age-appropriate measures of intellectual functioning (e.g., Bayley, McCarthy, Wechsler Intelligence Scale for Children-Revised [WISC-R]). demonstrated a mean gain in IQ of 15.3 points, with only one of the 13 children showing a decline at the 6-month assessment point. These gains in intellectual ability clearly exceeded any change attributable to possible practice on these measures. Additional measures showed improved gait and social interactions, as well as correlations with regional cerebral glucose metabolism on PET. Changes on measures of brain atrophy by computed tomography (CT) scans have also been reported for children receiving ZDV (DeCarli et al., 1991). Finally, there was a significant correlation between the number of opportunistic infections and improvement in verbal IQ for continuous-infusion ZDV patients (Brouwers et al., 1990). In addition, extended follow-up on three patients and on a parallel cohort receiving oral intermittent ZDV for at least 12 months showed a significantly larger improvement with continuous-infusion ZDV (15 vs. 4 IQ points) after 6 months and maintenance of the original gains in IQ but no further significant improvements (Brouwers et al., 1990).

A more recently complete phase II multicenter study of oral ZDV in children (McKinney et al., 1991) did not demonstrate the dramatic gains in intellectual functioning that were seen in the continuous-infusion study. Oral ZDV (180 mg per square meter of body surface area) was given to 88 children every 6 hours for at least 24 weeks. By week 24, improvement was seen in weight gain, serum and cerebrospinal fluid p24 antigen levels, and CD4+ lymphocyte counts over the first 12 weeks of treatment. Toxicity was evident, however, with 61% of the children experiencing hematological toxicity during the study.

Given an age range of 4 months to 11 years, cognitive functioning was evaluated in 55 children with age-appropriate intelligence tests (Bayley Scales, McCarthy, WISC-R). Overall, an average improvement of roughly 4 to 5 points was observed. This improvement is similar to the gains reported by Brouwers et al. (1990) in their phase 1 study of oral ZDV. Of interest is that in the McKinney et al. (1991) study, statistically significant improvement was seen only in the group of children assessed with the Bayley Scales (i.e., the youngest). This observation of differential improvement in the youngest patients of their sample, may, however, be biased due to baseline floor effects (15 of 25 patients had a median score of 50, which is the lowest score possible) and extreme variability in change scores (from −29 to +51). An analysis of raw scores from the Bayley Scales might have provided a clearer picture of treatment efficacy for these children.

Other Antiretroviral Treatments

Several other promising antiretroviral agents are currently being studied as potential treatments for HIV infection (e.g., Perno et al., 1988; Yarchoan et al., 1988a, 1989; Merigan et al., 1989; Zurlo and Lane, 1990). Two of these compounds are the dideoxynucleoside analogs dideoxyinosine (ddI) and dideoxycytidine (ddC), which are being investigated in clinical trials with neuropsychological measures incorporated into the protocols. For example, phase I data on ddI (Yarchoan et al., 1990) suggest that adult patients with AIDS or ARC who show cognitive impairment may benefit from treatment with regard to cognitive functioning. As the large-scale adult trials are still in progress, the neuropsychological data for these two treatments are not yet available. However, several studies involving pediatric HIV patients receiving ddI or ddC have reported general benefits from these compounds.

Data from a phase I–II trial of ddI in children with HIV infection (CDC class P-2) have provided some intriguing findings regarding their biological and neuropsychological response to treatment. Butler and colleagues (1991) have recently reported on 43 children receiving various oral doses (60, 120, 180, 360, or 540 mg/m²) of ddI for 24 weeks. Over the 6-month study period, eight children dropped out, one child was withdrawn due to continued disease progression despite treatment, and six children died. These children ranged in age from 3 months to 18 years; 16 had prior treatment with ZDV. Of the 27 patients with detectable p24 antigen levels at baseline, treatment resulted in a significant reduction in the mean serum antigen level (272 pg/ml at baseline to 77 pg/ml at week 24). Of the 34 children available for study after 6 months of therapy, age-appropriate measures of IQ showed no statistically significant change from baseline. However, plasma absorption over time of ddI, available for a subgroup of these patients, showed significant correlations with declines in serum p24 antigen levels and with changes on intelligence tests, suggesting that variability in drug bioavailability may have accounted for the variability in neuropsychological response and the lack of an overall effect.

Another recent pediatric HIV study reporting assessment of intellectual functions involved treatment with ddC (Pizzo et al., 1990). This pilot study involved 15 children between the ages of 6 months and 13 years who met criteria for CDC class P-2 or symptomatic HIV infection. This study was designed to provide oral doses of ddC every 6 hours for 8 weeks followed by an alternating schedule of 1 week of ddC and 3 weeks of ZDV. After the initial 8 weeks of ddC therapy, positive results of treatment were found for several disease markers, including weight gain, decreased lymphadenopathy, improved CD4 levels, and improved CD4/CD8 ratios for a number of children. A slight decline in functioning was noted, however, on formal assessment with a set of age-appropriate neuropsychological tests after treatment with ddC alone. This trend was reversed with the introduction of the ZDV/ddC alternating schedule, and after 24 weeks, patients had once again reached baseline levels of functioning (this V-shaped response pattern was significant at the .05 level). These findings may reflect the inability of ddC or its active metabolites, compared to ZDV, to cross the blood-brain barrier in sufficient concentrations to affect HIV replication within the CNS. Data from the AIDS Clinical Trials Group (ACTG) in persons with advanced HIV disease (ACTG 106 and ACTG 114 protocols) have shown that ddC in combination with ZDV results in an increase in CD4 counts. Since the data showed higher CD4 counts with combination therapy in contrast to ZDV monotherapy, ddC was approved by the Food and Drug Administration for use in conjunction with ZDV (Cotton and Friedland, 1992).

Conclusions

The data from these pediatric and adult trials of antiretroviral treatment are encouraging. Characteristic changes in brain metabolism and neuropsychological performance have been reliably described for patients with HIV infection (Rottenberg et al., 1987; Van Gorp et al., 1992). As such, these early studies of changes in cognitive performance in pediatric and adult cases of symptomatic HIV infection support the hypothesis that HIV-associated neurobehavioral abnormalities are reversible to some extent with ZDV and other agents. The data showing change in regional brain glucose metabolism with antiretroviral therapy (Yarchoan et al., 1987) suggest that treatment may improve brain functioning by potentially altering the excitotoxic effects possibly associated with HIV (e.g., Giulian et al., 1990). Several investigations are underway to evaluate the effectiveness of lower doses of ZDV in order to evaluate efficacy and possibly reduce toxicity (e.g., Collier et al., 1990).

On an individual level, the pediatric (and, to some extent, adult) data for each of the treatments reviewed above show remarkable improvements in neuropsychological function. These changes appear to be much greater than those due to any possible practice effect, although some patients have shown no change or have shown decline. This large degree of variability in response to antiretroviral agents indicates the need to search for possibly patient subgroups and prognostic factors associated with this potentially differential treatment response.

Future clinical trials of antiretroviral agents will most likely lack placebo or untreated control groups. Most treatment studies from now on, particularly in symptomatic patients, will be equivalence or historical trials (Brouwers and Mohr, 1991). The object of the equivalence studies will be to show that a new treatment is at least as good as ZDV, the current standard, in a two-arm study. Historical trials, on the other hand, will use currently obtained data from a one-arm study and then compare these data with previously obtained data. These approaches require a careful evaluation of the data actually available.

Even with the data showing neuropsychological benefits of antiretroviral therapy, a standardized consensus for defining neuropsychological impairment will be required, not only for making accurate estimates of cognitive impairment in HIV-infected individuals but also for determining an individual's response to pharmacological intervention. Another important methodological and conceptual issue involves the purpose of neuropsychological measures in treatment research. If one wishes to evaluate a compound for its ability to prevent the cognitive deterioration potentially associated with disease progression, and objective definition of a clinically significant change will be required. For example, an asymptomatic but seropositive person may show high levels of neuropsychological test performance as a result of high premorbid levels of functioning. However, even though test data are within normal limits, the individual may still have HIV-associated cognitive dysfunction that may progress without treatment but stabilize (and possibly improve) with therapy. Such a trial to prevent the negative effects of HIV on the CNS might require a large population for study, along with a relatively long study duration with several repeated assessments. In contrast to the patient without obvious cognitive dysfunction is the one with HIV-associated impairment. Here dysfunction can be established prior to initiating therapy, and treatment response can be evaluated in terms of how much function(s) return to either the normal range or approximate premorbid estimates of ability. This type of study would enroll patients with some indication of HIV effects on the CNS, and the duration of the study can be relatively short, as one would expect a rapid and readily observable treatment response. Therefore, it is important that the goal of treatment and the patient's CNS status prior to receiving treatment be carefully delineated. Further, careful investigation of patient response based on premorbid CNS deficits is required to assess for potentially toxic effects of treatment and for practice effects on cognitive tests in addition to CNS improvement.

Other conceptual issues associated with the neuropsychological investigation of HIV-related CNS dysfunction and treatment involve the nature of the measures used to evaluate performance. Many approaches are available for assessing CNS functioning. One approach has been presented by a National Institute of Mental Health (NIMH) work group (Butters et al., 1990), and several other suggested test batteries has been reviewed (e.g., Adams et al., 1991; Stern et al., 1991). While evaluating treatment response to antiretrovirals, test selection and analyses should be guided primarily by the design of the intervention study, as well as by the target population. Ideally, using a comprehensive assessment to establish baseline levels of functioning and posttreatment performance, accompanied by a more limited set of repeated measures for use during the treatment phase, would be an optimal approach (e.g., Brouwers and Mohr, 1991; see also Chapters 7 and 8). Decisions about test selection will also be influenced by the treatment goals, whether preventive or interventive, and by the degree of dysfunction seen in the patient population. Finally, it is important to note that true placebo-controlled trials may no longer be possible, as promising compounds may be compared to already available treatments such as ZDV or used in some combination with ZDV. Therefore, neuropsychological measures would be used to evaluate patients' response to changes in treatment, as well as the overall outcome of a treatment approach. Many of these issues are apparent in the studies reviewed in this chapter and have been discussed in greater detail in presentations from the NIMH work groups (Adams et al., 1991; Stern et al., 1991).

Even though the mechanisms of CNS-related impairment due to HIV infection are still unclear, it is possible that improvement due to treatment is partially accounted for by improved health due to antiretroviral effects or other supportive medical interventions. Data from the placebo-controlled trial of ZDV suggest that the amount of improvement seen in cognitive scores is much larger than the change see in patients' self-ratings of improvement in physical symptoms (Schmitt et al., 1988). Cognitive benefit from antiretroviral drugs may be associated with the compounds' ability to enter the CNS as opposed to systemic availability. The CNS availability of certain compounds may be dose- and delivery-dependent, so that combination trials of antiretrovirals may result in high systemic concentrations but not adequate CNS levels of compounds that can cross the blood-brain barrier. The data reviewed above also highlight an important issue regarding antiretroviral treatment for CNS impairment. In the studies using antiretroviral therapy for HIV infection, a number of patients showed no response to treatment, while others showed continued progression of symptoms despite therapy. Therefore, an issue related to CNS availability of a given compound is whether or not such a compound by itself is sufficient to reverse the effects of HIV on the CNS. Given the data on excitatory neurotoxins associated with HIV infection, it is quite possible that therapy might combine an antiretroviral compound for anti-HIV effects with compounds designed to counteract neurodegenerative processes. Overall, the data reviewed above suggest that neuropsychological assessment is a reliable surrogate marker for HIV effects on the CNS. Therefore, depending on the nature of the study, neuropsychological measures should be included when evaluating the potential effects of antiretroviral agents in an effort to measure cognitive functioning. The use of neuropsychological outome measures therefore supplements biological markers such as mortality and vital titers. By adding these additional efficacy measures, treatments can be evaluated not only for their biological impact, but also for their impact on patients' quality of life.

Acknowledgment

The authors thank Dr. David Lamb and Ms. Henriette Holder for their assistance with the manuscript. This work was supported by a grant from Roche Pharmaceuticals and by National Institute on Aging (NIA) Grant 2P50AG05144-07.

References

Adams, K.M., Butters, N., Becker, J., Boccellari, A., Brouwers, P., Campbell, A., Chelune, G., Heaton, R.K., Martin, A., Pequegnat, W., Schmitt, F., Stern, Y., and Wilkie, F. (1991). Methodological and neuropsychological assessment issues of HIV-1 infected adults (abst). *Journal of Clinical and Experimental Neuropsychology, 13*, 97.

Ammann, A.J. (1985). The acquired immunodeficiency syndrome in infants and children. *Annals of Internal Medicine, 103*, 734–737.

Beckett, A. (1990). The neurobiology of human immunodeficiency virus infection. In A. Tasman, S.M. Goldfinger, and C.A. Kaufmann, eds., *Review of Psychiatry.* Washington, D.C.: APA Press, pp. 593–613.

Belman, A.L. (1990). AIDS and pediatric neurology. *Pediatric Neurology, 8*, 571–603.

Brouwers, P., and Mohr, E. (1991). Design of clinical trials. In E. Mohr and P. Brouwers, eds., *Handbook of Clinical Trails: The Neurobehavioral Approach.* Amsterdam, The Netherlands: Swets and Zeitlinger, Lisse, pp. 45–65.

Brouwers, P., Moss, H., Wolters, P., Eddy, J., Balis, F., Poplack, D.G., and Pizzo, P.A. (1990). Effect of continuous-infusion zidovudine therapy on neuropsychologic functioning in children with symptomatic human immunodeficiency virus infection. *Journal of Pediatrics, 117*, 980–985.

Butler, K.M., Husson, R.N., Balis, F.M., Brouwers, P., Eddy, J., El-Amin, D., Gress, J., Hawkins, M., Jarosinski, P., Moss, H., Poplack, D., Santacroce, S., Venzon, D., Wiener, L., Wolters, P., and Pizzo, P. (1991). Dideoxyinosine in children with symptomatic human immunodeficiency virus infection. *New England Journal of Medicine, 324*, 137–144.

Butters, N., Grant, I., Haxby, J., Judd, L.L., Martin, A., McClelland, J., Pequegnat, W., Schachter, D., and Stover, E. (1990). Assessment of AIDS-related cognitive change: Recommendations of the NIMH Workgroup on neuropsychological assessment approaches. *Journal of Clinical and Experimental Neuropsychology, 12*, 963–978.

Centers for Disease Control. (1987). Antibody to human immunodeficiency virus in female prostitutes. *Morbidity and Mortality Weekly Report, 36*, 157–161.

Collier, A.C., Bozzette, S., Coombs, R.W., Causey, D., Schoenfeld, D.A., Spector, S., Pettinelli, C., Davies, G., Richman, D., Leedon, J., Kidd, P., and Corey, L. (1990).

A pilot study of low-dose zidovudine in human immunodeficiency virus infection. *New England Journal of Medicine, 323*, 1015–1021.

Cotton, D.J., and Friedland, G.H. (eds.) (1992). *AIDS Clinical Care*, Vol. 4, No. 8. Waltham, Mass.: Massachusetts Medical Society, 68.

Crowe, S.M., McGrath, M.S., and Volberding, P. (1990). Anti-HIV drug therapy. *AIDS Clinical Care, 2*, 17–20.

DeCarli, C., Fugate, L., Falloon, J., Eddy, J., Katz, D.A., Friedland, R.P., Rapoport, S.I., Brouwers, P., and Pizzo, P.A. (1991). Brain growth and cognitive improvement in children with human immunodeficiency virus–induced encephalopathy after six months of continuous infusion zidovudine therapy. *Journal of Acquired Immune Deficiency Syndromes, 4*, 585–592.

Dooneief, G., Bello, J., Todak, G., Mun, I.K., Marder, K., Malouf, R., Gorman, J., Hilal, S., Stern, Y., and Mayeux, R. (1992). A prospective controlled study of magnetic resonance imaging of the brain in gay men and parenteral drug users with human immunodeficiency virus infection. *Archives of Neurology, 49*, 38–43.

Drugs That Cause Psychiatric Symptoms. (1989). *The Medicine Letter, 31*, 113–118. (No author. Senior editor Mark Abramowicz).

Epstein, L.G., Goudsmitt, L., Paul, D., Morrison, S.H., Connor, E.M., Oleske, J.M., and Holland, B. (1987). Expression of human immunodeficiency virus in cerebrospinal fluid of children with progressive encephalopathy. *Annals of Neurology, 21*, 397–401.

Epstein, L.G., Sharer, L. R., Joshi, V.V., Fojas, M.M., Koenigsberger, M.R., and Oleske, J.M. (1985). Progressive encephalopathy in children with acquired immune deficiency syndrome. *Annals of Neurology, 17*, 488–496.

Everall, I.P., Luthert, P.J., and Lantos, P.L. (1991). Neuronal loss in the frontal cortex in HIV infection. *Lancet, 337*, 1119–1121.

Fernandez, F., and Levy, J.K. (1990). Psychiatric diagnosis and pharmacotherapy of patients with HIV infection. In A. Tasman, S.M. Goldfinger, and C.D. Kaufmann, eds., *Review of Psychiatry*. Washington, D.C.: American Psychiatric Association Press, pp. 614–630.

Fischl, M.A., Richman, D.D., Grieco, M.H., Gottlieb, M., Volberding, P., Laskin, O., Leedom, J., Groopman, J., Mildvan, D., Schooley, R., Jackson, G., Durack, D., King, D., and the AZT Collaborative Working Group. (1987). The efficacy of azidothymidine (AZT) in the treatment of patients with AIDS and AIDS-related complex: A double-blind, placebo-controlled trial. *New England Journal of Medicine, 317*, 185–191.

Friedman, S.L. (1989). Gastrointestinal symptoms in AIDS. *AIDS Clinical Care, 1*, 17–20.

Giulian, D., Vaca, K., and Noonan, C.A. (1990). Secretion of neurotoxins by mononuclear phagocytes infected with HIV-1. *Science, 250*, 1593–1596.

Goethe, K.E., Mitchell, J.E., Marshall, D.W., Brey, R.L., Cahill, W.T., Leger, G.D., Hoy, L.J., and Boswell, R.N. (1989). Neuropsychological and neurological function of human immunodeficiency virus seropositive asymptomatic individuals. *Archives of Neurology, 46*, 129–133.

Gorman, J.M., Ketzner, R., Cooper, T., Goetz, R.R., Langomasino, I., Navacenko, H., Williams, J.B., Stern, Y., Mayeux, R., and Ehrhardt, A.A. (1991). Glucocorticoid level and neuropsychiatric symptoms in homosexual men with HIV infection. *American Journal of Psychiatry, 148*, 41–45.

Grant, I., Atkinson, J.H., Hesselink, J.R., Kennedy, C.J., Richman, D.D., Spector, S.A., and McCutchan, J.A. (1987). Evidence for early central nervous system involvement in the acquired immunodeficiency syndrome (AIDS) and other human immunodeficiency virus (HIV) infections. *Annals of Internal Medicine, 107,* 828–836.

Grant, I., and Heaton, R.K. (1990). Human immunodeficiency virus-type 1 (HIV-1) and the brain. *Journal of Consulting and Clinical Psychology, 58,* 22–30.

Gray, F., Gherardi, R., and Scaravilli, F. (1988). The neuropathology of the acquired immune deficiency syndrome (AIDS). A review. *Brain, 111,* 245–266.

Heyes, M.P., Mefford, I.N., Quearry, B.J., Dedhia, M., and Lackner, A. (1990). Increased ratio of quinolinic acid to kynurenic acid in cerebrospinal fluid of D retrovirus–infected rhesus macaques: Relationship to clinical and viral status. *Annals of Neurology, 27,* 666–675.

Heyes, M.P., Rubinow, D., Lane, C., and Markey, S.P. (1989). Cerebrospinal fluid quinolinic acid concentrations are increased in acquired immune deficiency syndrome. *Annals of Neurology, 26,* 275–277.

Hollander, H., and Levy, J.A. (1987). Neurologic abnormalities and recovery of human immunodeficiency virus from cerebrospinal fluid. *Annals of Internal Medicine, 106,* 692–696.

Janssen, R.S., Saykin, A.J., Cannon, L., Campbell, J., Pinsky, P., Hessol, N., O'Malley, P., Lifson, A., Doll, L., Rutherford, G.W., and Kaplan, J.E. (1989). Neurologic and neuropsychological manifestations of HIV-1 infection: Association with AIDS-related complex but no asymptomatic HIV-1 infection. *Annals of Neurology, 26,* 592–600.

Janssen, R.S., Saykin, A.J., Kaplan, J.E., Spira, T., Pinsky, P., Sprehn, G., Hoffman, J., Mayer, W., and Schonberger, L. (1988). Neurological complications of human immunodeficiency virus infection in patients with lymphadenopathy syndrome. *Annals of Neurology, 23,* 49–55.

Kieburtz, K.D., Giang, D.W., Schiffer, R.B., and Vakil, N. (1991). Abnormal vitamin B_{12} metabolism in human immunodeficiency virus infection. *Archives of Neurology, 48,* 312–314.

Klecker, R.W., Collins, J.M., Yarchoan, R., Thomas, R., Jenkins, J.F., Broder, S., and Myers, C.E. (1987). Plasma and cerebrospinal fluid pharmacokinetics of 3'-azido-3'-deoxythymidine: A novel pyrimidine analog with potential application for the treatment of patients with AIDS and related diseases. *Clinical Pharmacological Therapy, 41,* 407–412.

Leoung, G.S. (1989). *Pneumocystis carinii* pneumonia, Part I: Clinical presentation, diagnosis and treatment. *AIDS Clinical Care, 1,* 9–12.

Maj, M. (1990). Organic mental disorders in HIV-1 infection. *AIDS, 4,* 831–840.

Markowitz, J.C., and Perry, S.W. (1990). AIDS: A medical overview for psychiatrists. In A. Tasman, S.M. Goldfinger, and C.A. Kaufmann, eds., *Review of Psychiatry.* Washington, D.C.: American Psychiatric Association Press, pp. 574–592.

McArthur, J.C. (1987). Neurologic manifestations of AIDS. *Medicine, 66,* 407–437.

McArthur, J.C., Cohen, B.A., Selnes, O.A., Kumar, A.J., Cooper, K., McArthur, J., Soucy, G., Cornblath, D.R., Chmiel, J.S., Wang, M., Starkey, D.L., Ginzburg, H., Ostrow, D.G., Johnson, R.T., Phair, J.P., and Polk, B.F. (1989). Low prevalence of neurological and neuropsychological abnormalities in otherwise healthy HIV-1 infected individuals: Results from the Multicenter AIDS Cohort Study. *Annals of Neurology, 26,* 601–611.

McKinney, R.E., Maha, M.A., Connor, E.M., Feinberg, J., Scott, G.B., Wulfsohn, M., McIntosh, K., Borkowsky, W., Modlin, J.F., Weintrub, P., O'Donnell, K., Gelber, R.D., Rogers, G.K., Lehrman, S.N., Wilfert, C.M., and the Protocol 043 Study Group. (1991). A multicenter trial of oral zidovudine in children with advanced human immunodeficiency virus disease. *New England Journal of Medicine, 324*, 1018–1025.

Merigan, T.C., Skowron, G., Bozzette, S.A., Richman, D., Uttamchandani, R., Fischl, M., Schooley, R., Hirsch, M., Soo, W., and Pettinelli, C. (1989). Circulating p24 antigen levels and response to dideoxycytidine in human immunodeficiency virus (HIV) infection. A phase I and II study. *Annals of Internal Medicine, 10*, 189–194.

Miller, E.N., Selnes, O.A., McArthur, J.C., Satz, P., Becker, B.A., Cohen, B.A., Sheridan, K., Machado, A.M., Van Gorp, W.G., and Visscher, B. (1990). Neuropsychological performance in HIV-1 infected homosexual men: The Multicenter AIDS Cohort Study (MACS). *Neurology, 40*, 197–203.

Mitsuya, H., Weinhold, K.J., Furman, P.A., St. Clair, M.H., Lehrman, S.N., Gallo, R.C., Bolognesi, D., Barry, D.W., and Broder, S. (1985). 3'-Azido-3'-deoxythymidine (BW A 509U): An antiviral agent that inhibits the infectivity and cytopathic effect of human T-lymphotropic virus type III/lymphadenopathy-associated virus in vitro. *Proceedings of the National Academy of Science, 82*, 7096–7100.

Navia, B.A., Jordan, B.D., and Price, R.W. (1986a). The AIDS dementia complex: I. Clinical features. *Annals of Neurology, 19*, 517–524.

Navia, B.A., Petito, C.K., Gold, J.W., Cho, E.-S., Jordan, B.D., and Price, R.W. (1986b). Cerebral toxoplasmosis complicating the acquired immune deficiency syndrome: Clinical and neuropathological findings in 27 patients. *Annals of Neurology, 19*, 224–238.

Navia, B.A., and Price, R.W. (1987). The acquired immunodeficiency syndrome dementia complex as the presenting or sole manifestation of human immunodeficiency virus infection. *Archives of Neurology, 44*, 65–69.

Perno, C.F., Yarchoan, R., Cooney, D., Hartman, N.R., Gartner, S., Popovic, M., Hao, Z., Gerrard, T.L., Wilson, Y.A., Johns, D.G., and Boder, S. (1988). Inhibition of human immunodeficiency virus (HIV-1-HTLV-III$_{Ba-L}$) replication in fresh and human peripheral blood monocytes/macrophages by azidothymidine and related 2'3'-dideoxynucleosides. *Journal of Experimental Medicine, 168*, 1111–1125.

Petito, C.K. (1988). Review of central nervous system pathology in human immunodeficiency virus infection. *Annals of Neurology, 23*, S54–S57.

Petito, C.K., Cho, E.S., Lemann, W., Navia, B.A., and Price, R.W. (1986). Neuropathology of acquired immunodeficiency syndrome (AIDS): An autopsy review. *Journal of Neuropathology and Experimental Neurology, 45*, 635–646.

Pizzo, P.A., Butler, K., Balis, F., Brouwers, E., Hawkins, M., Eddy, J., Einloth, M., Falloon, J., Husson, R., Jarosinski, P., Meer, J., Moss, H., Poplack, D.G., Santacroce, S., Wiener, L., and Wolters, P. (1990). Dideoxycytidine alone and in an alternating schedule with zidovudine in children with symptomatic human immunodeficiency virus infection. *Journal of Pediatrics, 117*, 799–808.

Pizzo, P.A., Eddy, J. Falloon, J., Balis, F., Murphy, R., Moss, H., Wolters, P., Brouwers, P., Jarosinski, P., Rubin, M., Broder, S., Yarchoan, R., Burnetti, A., Maha, M., Nusinoff-Lehrman, S., and Poplack, D. (1988). Effect of continuous infusion of zidovudine (AZT) in children with symptomatic HIV infection. *New England Journal of Medicine, 319*, 889–896.

Price, R.W., and Brew, B.J. (1988). The AIDS dementia complex. *Journal of Infectious Diseases, 158*, 1079–1083.

Price, R.W., Brew, B., Sidtis, J., Rosenblum, M., Scheck, A.C., and Cleary, P. (1988). The brain in AIDS: Central nervous system HIV-1 infection and AIDS dementia complex. *Science, 239*, 586–592.

Pumarola-Sune, T., Navia, B.A., Cordon-Cardo, C., Cho, E., and Price, R.W. (1987). HIV antigen in the brains of patients with the AIDS dementia complex. *Annals of Neurology*, 21, 490–496.

Resnick, L., DiMarzio-Veronese, F., Schupbach, J., Tourtellotte, W.W., Ho, D.D., Muller, F., Shapshak, P., Vogt, M., Groopman, J.E., Markham, P.D., and Gallo, R.C. (1985). Intra-blood brain-barrier synthesis of HTLV-III-specific IgG in patients with neurologic symptoms associated with AIDS or AIDS-related complex. *New England Journal of Medicine, 313*, 1498–1504.

Richman, D.D., Fischl, M.A., Grieco, M.H., Gottlieb, M.S., Volberding, P.A., Laskin, O.L., Leedom, J.M., Groopman, J.E., Mildvan, D., Hirch, M.S., Jackson, G.G., Durack, D.T., Nusinoff-Lehrman, S., and the AZT Collaborative Working Group. (1987). The toxicity of azidothymidine (AZT) in the treatment of patients with AIDS and AIDS-related complex: A double-blind, placebo-controlled trial. *New England Journal of Medicine, 317*, 192–197.

Rottenberg, D.A., Moeller, J.R., Strother, S.C., Sidtis, J.J., Navia, B.A., Dhawan, V., Ginos, J.Z., and Price R.W. (1987). The metabolic pathology of the AIDS dementia complex. *Annals of Neurology, 22*, 700–706.

Saykin, A.J., Janssen, R.S., Sprehn, G.C., Kaplan, J.E., Spira, T.J., and Weller, P. (1988). Neuropsychological dysfunction in HIV-infection: Characterization in a lymphadenopathy cohort. *International Journal of Clinical Neuropsychology, 10*, 81–95.

Schielke, E., Tatsch, K., Pfister, H.W., Trenkwalder, C., Leinsinger, G., Kirsch, C.M., Matuschke, A., and Einhaupl, K.M. (1990). Reduced cerebral blood flow in early stages of human immunodeficiency virus infection. *Archives of Neurology, 47*, 1342–1345.

Schmitt, F.A., Bigley, J.W., McKinnis, R., Logue, P.E., Evans, R.W., Deucker, J.L., and the AZT Collaborative Working Group. (1988). Neuropsychological outcome of zidovudine (AZT) treatment of patients with AIDS and AIDS-related complex. *New England Journal of Medicine, 319*, 1573–1578.

Schoenfeld, P. (1991). HIV infection and renal disease. *AIDS Clinical Care, 3*, 9–11.

Selnes, O.A., Miller, E., McArthur, J., Gordon, B., Munoz, A., Sheridan, K., Fox, R., Saah, A.J., and the Multicenter AIDS Cohort Study (1990). HIV-1 infection: No evidence of cognitive decline during the asymptomatic stages. *Neurology, 40*, 204–208.

Shaw, G.M., Harper, M.E., Hahn, B.H., Epstein, L.G., Gajdusek, D.C., Price, R.W., Navia, B.A., Petito, C.K., O'Hara, C.J., Groopman, J.E., Cho, E., Oleske, J.M., Wong-Staal, F., and Gallo, R.C. (1985). HTLV-III infection in brains of children and adults with AIDS encephalopathy. *Science, 227*, 177–182.

Sidtis, J.J., and Price, R.W. (1990). Early HIV-1 infection and the AIDS dementia complex. *Neurology, 40*, 323–326.

Stern, Y., Adams, K.M., Butters, N., Becker, J.T., Boccellari, A., Brouwers, P., Campbell, A., Chellune, G., Heaton, R.A., Martin, A., Pequegnat, W., Schmitt, F., and Wilkie, F. (1991). Assessment of AIDS-related cognitive changes: Recommendations of the NIMH workgroup on neuropsychological assessment approaches. Paper presented at the Nineteenth Annual International Neuropsychological Society Meeting. San Antonio, Texas.

Van Gorp, W.G., Mandelkern, M., Gee, M., Hinkin, C.H., Stern, C.E., Paz, D., Dixon, W., Evans, G., Flynn, F., Frederick, C.J., Ropchan, J., and Blahd, W. (1992). Cerebral metabolic dysfunction in AIDS: Findings in a sample with and without dementia. *Journal of Neuropsychiatry and Clinical Neurosciences, 4*, 280–287.

Volberding, P.A., Lagakos, S.W., Koch, M.A., Pettinelli, C., Myers, M.W., Booth, D.K., Balfour, H.H., Reichman, R.C., Bartlett, J.A., and Hirsch, M.S. (1990). Zidovudine in asymptomatic human immunodeficiency virus infection: A controlled trial in persons with fewer than 500 CD4-positive cells per cubic millimeter. *New England Journal of Medicine, 322*, 941–949.

Weber, R., Ledergerber, B., Opravil, M., Siegenthaler, W., and Luthy, R. (1990). Progression of HIV infection in misusers of injected drugs who stop injecting or follow a program of maintenance treatment with methadone. *British Medical Journal, 301*, 1362–1365.

Wilkins, J.W., Robertson, K.R., van der Horst, C., Robertson, W.T., Fryer, J.G., and Hall, C.D. (1990). The importance of confounding factors in the evaluation of neuropsychological changes in patients infected with human immunodeficiency virus. *Journal of Acquired Immune Deficiency Syndromes, 3*, 938–942.

Working Group of the American Academy of Neurology AIDS Task Force. (1991). Nomenclature and research case definitions for neurologic manifestations of human immunodeficiency virus-type 1 (HIV-1) infection. *Neurology, 41*, 778–785.

Yarchoan, R., Berg, G., Brouwers, P., Fischl, M.A., Spitzer, A.R., Wichman, A., Grafman, J., Thomas, R.V., Safai, B., Brunetti, A., Perno, C.F., Schmidt, R.J., Larson, S.M., Myers, C.E., and Broder, S. (1987). Response of human immunodeficiency-virus-associated neurological disease to 3′-azido-3′-deoxythymidine. *Lancet, 1*, 132–135.

Yarchoan, R., Mitsuya, H., and Broder, S. (1989). Clinical and basic advances in the antiretroviral therapy of human immunodeficiency virus infection. *American Journal of Medicine, 87*, 191–200.

Yarchoan, R., Perno, C.F., Thomas, R.V., Klecker, R.W., Allain, J.P., Wills, R.J., McAtee, N., Fischl, M.A., Dubinsky, R., McNeely, M.C., Mitsuya, H., Pluda, J.M., Lawley, T.J., Leuther, M., Safai, B., Collins, J.M., Myers, C.E., and Broder, S. (1988a). Phase I studies of 2′,3′-dideoxycytidine in severe human immunodeficiency virus infection as a single agent and alternating with zidovudine (AZT). *Lancet, 1*, 76–81.

Yarchoan, R., Pluda, J.M., Thomas, R.V., Mitsuya, H., Brouwers, P., Wyvill, K.M., Hartman, N., Johns, D.G., and Broder, S. (1990). Long-term toxicity/activity profile of 2′,3′-dideoxyinosine in AIDS or AIDS-related complex. *Lancet, 1*, 526–529.

Yarchoan, R., Thomas, R.V., Grafman, J., Wichman, A., Dalakas, M., McAtee, N., Berg, G., Fischl, M., Perno, C.F., Klecker, R.W., Buchbinder, A., Tay, S., Larson, S.M., Myers, C.E., and Broder, S. (1988b). Long-term administration of 3′-azido-2′,3′-dideoxythymidine to patients with AIDS-related neurological disease. *Annals of Neurology, 23*, S82–S87.

Zurlo, J.J., and Lane, H.C. (1990). The role of antiretroviral therapy in living long and living well. *Maryland Medical Journal, 39*, 161–165.

15

The Use of Methylphenidate in HIV Patients: A Clinical Perspective

FRANCISCO FERNANDEZ, JOEL K. LEVY,
and PEDRO RUIZ

There has been a long-standing controversy regarding the use of amphetamines and other psychostimulants in the treatment of patients experiencing depressive disorders and other psychiatric disorders (Wittenborn, 1981). To date, the superiority of psychostimulants over placebo for the treatment of depression has not been sufficiently documented (Mattes, 1985; Warneke, 1990). The use of psychostimulants as antidepressants was thought to be moot issue after the introduction of effective antidepressants. Even if psychostimulants were demonstrated to be as effective as the polycyclic antidepressants now available, the potential for tolerance, habituation, and abuse is thought to be so great as to rule them out as an acceptable alternative to the antidepressants. Due to this factor, federal controls have now confined the primary use of psychostimulants to the treatment of attention deficit disorder in children and adults, hyperkinetic disorder in children, narcolepsy, and as a limited treatment for refractory obesity. The concern for habituation and abuse has even led to a change in the nomenclature of this class of compounds to distance the medical use from illicit activities. The term now being used for these compounds in such academic activities as computer literature searches is *analeptics*. Nonetheless, there are ways to make effective use of the psychostimulant properties of certain amphetamines and related substances as adjuvants to standard pharmacotherapy for depression and pain management.

Although the psychostimulants have not been demonstrated to provide, on their own, a substantial or sustained antidepressant effect, they may be helpful in a supplementary standard antidepressant therapy for the treatment of apathetic states and secondary depression in the medically ill or elderly. In this fashion, they can be effectively prescribed at lower doses for these populations and, to the uninitiated in stimulant pharmacotherapy, their potential for abuse as well as other toxicities becomes acceptably limited.

Chiarello and Cole (1987) have reviewed the role of psychostimulants in general psychiatry, concluding that their judicious use may be helpful in the treatment of several adult psychiatric syndromes in medically ill patients. Evidence is presently accumulating on the contribution of the psychostimulants as adjuvant therapy for abnormal mood states in the medically ill (Kaufmann et al., 1982, 1984a,b; Woods et al., 1986; Satel and Nelson, 1989; Massand et al., 1991), geriatric depressive disorders (Pickett et al., 1990), poststroke depression (Lingham et al., 1988), depression after closed head injury (Evans et al., 1987) or neurodegenerative disease (Lahmeyer, 1982; Goodnick and Gershon, 1984; Cantello et al., 1989), and the neuropsychiatric conditions associated with advanced, symptomatic acquired immunodeficiency syndrome (AIDS) or AIDS-related complex (ARC) (Fernandez and Levy, 1990). The available literature supports the adjuvant psychopharmacological role of the psychostimulants in the treatment of human immunodeficiency virus (HIV)-related depression (Fernandez et al., 1988a,b; Holmes et al., 1989; Fernandez and Levy, 1991) and cognitive impairment (Fernandez et al., 1988a; Angrist et al., 1992; White et al., 1992).

Psychopharmacology

General Overview

Amphetamine compounds are phenylisopropylamines with central nervous system (CNS) properties (Glennon, 1987). Amphetamines have wide-ranging behavioral effects, such as anorexia, euphoria, locomotor activity, and psychotomimetic effects (Tesar, 1982). Behavioral effects are rapidly achieved (usually in 1–3 hours) because they are easily absorbed and readily cross the blood-brain barrier. Their mechanism of action involves a direct neuronal release of dopamine and norepinephrine, along with the reuptake blockade of other catecholamines (Biel and Bopp, 1978). The half-life of the commercially available amphetamines ranges from 6 to 18 hours, the d-isomer being several times more biologically active than the l-isomer. They may also have a weak monoamine oxidase inhibitory effect (Biel and Bopp, 1978).

Methylphenidate has a structure and pharmacological effects similar to those of the amphetamines. The mechanism of action, side effects, and toxicities are also similar to those of the amphetamines. Methylphenidate is rapidly absorbed, with peak plasma levels being achieved within 2 hours. It has a shorter duration of action than the amphetamines, with an elimination half-life of 2–6 hours (Tesar, 1982). It is almost exclusively excreted in the urine.

Magnesium pemoline is a milder CNS stimulant with a different structure than the amphetamines and methylphenidate. Its mechanism of action is presumed to be secondary to the augmentation of catecholaminergic transmission, particularly by release of dopamine at receptor sites (Everett, 1980). Magnesium pemoline is not a controlled compound because its side effects and potential for abuse are alleged to be minimal in comparison to those of other amphetamines. Its use is limited to hyperkinetic syndrome in children. This compound has not received wide use, to our knowledge, for antidepressant activity in the medically ill. This may be because of its potential for adverse effects in an already metabolically compromised patient, with risks including hepatic dysfunction and, rarely, aplastic anemia and dyskinesias. Recently, however, it has been reported to be useful clinically as a sublingual medication in individuals with limited gastrointestinal access or poor absorption from the gut (Breitbart and Mermelstein, 1992).

Medical/Legal Issues

As mentioned above, the medical use of the psychostimulants has been limited by their abuse potential. A stigma has been attached to these compounds, creating much resistance to any consideration of their use. This controversy continues to cloud the analysis of the therapeutic potential of amphetamines in psychiatry (Editorial, 1982; Hackett, 1982; Warneke, 1990). In the United States, many states have enacted legislation banning amphetamine production or use altogether, even for Food and Drug Administration (FDA)-approved indications. Seemingly prompted by the excesses of the drug culture of the 1960s and the often theoretically unjustified use of these compounds for various conditions, a backlash occurred. Addiction to these agents is always possible in any individual; therefore, some believe that total unavailability is the only way to rule out abuse.

This blanket condemnation is unfortunate because the few controlled clinical investigations done have found them to be both safe and effective, and sometimes unique in their benefit when appropriately prescribed. In addition to the limited uses approved by the FDA, clinical investigations have determined their usefulness in childhood nocturnal enuresis, postencephalitic parkinsonism, and as analgesic adjuvants (Bouckoms, 1981; Tesar, 1982). Neurasthenia-fatigue syndromes, hiccups, and some forms of myoclonic seizures have also responded to psychostimulant treatment (Tesar, 1982).

As noted earlier, the role of psychostimulants in consultation-liaison psychiatry with medically ill patients who are apathetic, withdrawn, or depressed has long been established. The clinical response is rapid and usually devoid of significant treatment-related side effects. Many of these patients also suffer from cognitive impairments, and an additional benefit, perhaps related to dopamine activation, is that quantitative and qualitative improvements in cognitive function have been found (Fernandez et al., 1988a; Fernandez and Levy, 1990; Angrist et al., 1992; White et al., 1992). Because of these two effects, mood enhancement and cognitive regulation, psychostimulants were logically considered as a therapeutic strategy for depressed human immunodeficiency virus (HIV) patients and, specifically, for HIV patients with cognitive impairment.

Psychostimulant Treatment of Depression, Cognitive Impairment, and Organic Mental Disorders in HIV Disease

The Role of Dopamine in HIV Encephalopathy

Maccario and Scharre (1987), in discussing a case of psychosis in an HIV patient, cited Hollander et al. (1985) as developing a hypothesis about dopamine dysregulation in HIV-CNS infection. The hypothesis suggests that HIV has a special affinity for dopaminergic or catecholaminergic systems in its neurotropism, although it can attack all parts of the central and peripheral nervous systems. The hypothesis is supported by certain clinical observations. Cases of sudden-onset schizophreniform psychosis in HIV-infected patients who do not have AIDS or prior histories of thought disorders have emerged in the literature (Perry and Jacobsen, 1986; Beckett et al., 1987; Jones et al., 1987). When these episodes were treated with neuroleptics, parkinsonian symptoms replaced the psychosis. When the movement disorders were treated with anticholinergics, the parkinsonism symptoms resolved but hallucinations resumed. This swing from one extreme to the other seemed to implicate dopaminergic instability. Such instability was also suggested by the emergence of motor dysfunction in other HIV patients taking antiemetics (Edelstein and Knight, 1987). Movement disorders involving the extrapyramidal system have also been reported de novo, without the etiology being traced to treatment-related effects, and these seem to implicate basal ganglia involvement in HIV disease (Nath et al., 1987). Price and colleagues observed that HIV viral protein was most prevalent in the white matter and basal ganglia of patients with neurological manifestations of the AIDS dementia complex (Navia et al., 1986). Experimentally, it has also been demonstrated by autoradiographic labeling that the CD4 antigen/HIV receptor is present in animal limbic structures (Hill et al., 1987). At the neurochemical level, some data indicate reduced cerebrospinal fluid (CSF) dopamine and its metabolite, homovanillic acid (HVA), in samples taken from HIV-infected persons (Britton et al., 1989; Tourtellotte et al., 1989).

Cognitive slowing and verbal memory dysfunction, fatigue, and mood disturbance, with sparing of higher-level abstract reasoning, have suggested a subcortical process in HIV disease. These symptoms appear to respond favorably to analeptic treatment, specifically methylphenidate and dextroamphetamine (Fernandez et al., 1988a; Fernandez and Levy, 1990). From our previous studies (Fernandez et al., 1988b), both ARC and AIDS patients had improvement in cognitive processing speed and long-term verbal memory function after methylphenidate treatment that was substantially significant. Improvement was also demonstrated in patients with concomitant affective or other psychiatric symptoms when treated with the psychostimulant (Fernandez et al., 1988a,b; Holmes et al., 1989; Fernandez and Levy, 1990, 1991). Based on this experience with analeptics, we will focus on our clinical experience with 150 consecutive HIV patients with various psychiatric diagnoses treated open label with methylphenidate.

Methods

All patients were recruited from an indigent outpatient clinic designated solely for the management of AIDS. They had already been diagnosed with either AIDS or ARC, according to accepted criteria, and were referred to us for a psychiatric evaluation by their primary care physicians for clinically demonstrable signs and symptoms of depressed mood. All patients were evaluated by psychiatric physicians using the DSM-III-R criteria for mood disorders. Original psychiatric diagnoses made by the psychiatric consultants based on these criteria were confirmed and retained. Diagnoses were thus made based on clinical observational material, and no psychometric instruments were employed otherwise to characterize or quantify the disorders. Using guidelines developed by the Massachusetts General Hospital Consultation-Liaison Service for psychostimulant treatment in depressed, medically ill patients (Table 15–1), methylphenidate was prescribed in this open-label trial for various mood disorders (Murray and Schochet, in press). Forty-five patients were already receiving pharmacotherapy with various antidepressants. The demographic characteristics of the patients can be found in Table 15–2, and their psychiatric diagnoses (along with their response to treatment with methylphenidate) are indicated in Table 15–3. By convention, patients with a previous history of stimulant or intravenous drug abuse, epilepsy, head trauma, secondary CNS disease, cardiac arrhythmias, or hypertension were considered as having relative contraindications to psychostimulant treatment and thus were not administered these medications. Patients were also excluded from consideration for this treatment if they had been hospitalized in the previous 3 months or if they scored below 60% on the Karnofsky Performance Status Scale. Hematological and immunological indices were recorded from each patient's medical records and matched temporally with neurobehavioral test results (see below). These blood markers were accepted if the laboratory tests had been

TABLE 15–1.   Clinical Guidelines for Use of Psychostimulants in Depressed HIV
               Patients

---

1. There is no history of psychostimulant abuse or intravenous drug use.[a]

2. The patient needs a quick-acting, mobilizing agent.[a]

3. Clinically, the patient has failure to thrive or fails to sustain nutrition.[a]

4. The primary diagnosis, whether dementia and/or depression, is unclear.[a]

5. Clinically, there is more apathy than depression.[a]

6. The patient is known to be intolerant of the treatment-related side effects of standard antidepressants.[a]

7. The patient has cognitive impairment regardless of the underlying affective state.

8. The patient suffers from fatigue and has two or more constitutional symptoms of advanced HIV-1 infection.

9. There is evidence of depressive encephalopathy secondary to treatment effects for either HIV-1 infection or other systemic complications.

10. There is a syndrome of neurasthenia-fatigue from treatment with immunorestorative agents.

---

[a]Adapted, in part, from Murray and Schochet (in press) with permission.

TABLE 15–2. Characteristics of the Patients Receiving Methylphenidate

Characteristics		Number	(%)
Total		150	(100)
Sex			
Male		18	(79)
Female		32	(21)
Age			
15–19		3	(2)
20–29		69	(46)
30–39		51	(34)
40–49		27	(18)
Prior psychiatric history of depression		44	(29)
Prior psychiatric treatment[a]		59	(39)
Amitriptyline	9		
Protriptyline	3		
Imipramine	5		
Desipramine	8		
Amoxapine	2		
Trazodone	6		
Doxepin	6		
Nortriptyline	12		
Fluoxetine	8		
Performance status[b]			
90		44	(30)
80		65	(43)
70		23	(15)
60		18	(12)

[a]Some patients had more than one course of treatment.

[b]Based on the Karnofsky Performance Status Scale.

performed within 2 weeks of the neurobehavioral test. Eighty patients (53%) met this criterion, and this subsample's laboratory values (along with the results of neurobehavioral testing) are indicated in Table 15–4.

The 80 patients were evaluated with a mini-neuropsychological screen that included the Mini-Mental State Examination (MMSE), Verbal Selective Reminding Test (VSRT), and Trail Making Test, Parts A and B (TMT-A and TMT-B, respectively) (Fernandez et al., 1988a). These neuropsychological variables were transformed to deviation IQ-type scores (see Table 15–4).

Treatment

The regimen for all patients involved initiating treatment with methylphenidate, 5 mg orally on a twice daily schedule (typically at 8:00 A.M. and noon). Doses were subsequently adjusted by increments of 5–10 mg per dose after an observation period of 2–3 days. When doses were increased to three times per day, they were typically given at 7:00 A.M., 10:00 A.M., and 1:00 P.M. The adjustments

TABLE 15–3. Methylphenidate Trials and Response

	Major Depression[a] (N = 48)	Adjustment Disorder with Depressed Mood[a] (N = 32)	Dementia + Depressed Mood (N = 26)	Dementia (N = 12)	Organic Affective (N = 21)	Organic Personality (N = 9)	Amnestic Syndrome (N = 2)	Total (%) (N = 150)
Marked	20	12	16	1	12	1		62 (41%)
Moderate	15	11	6	4	5	6		47 (31%)
Minimal	10	6	2	6	2	1	1	29 (19%)
None	3	3	2	1	2		1	12 (9%)

[a]Diffuse cognitive deficits were present and were greater than those expected from the primary psychiatric diagnosis alone.

were based either on the patient's clinical response or on the presence of side effects, and doses of methylphenidate were increased to a maximum of 60 mg daily by the second week of treatment. The dose increase for each patient was individualized on the basis of his or her response to treatment.

Generally, the dosage required for remission of depressive symptoms was maintained for a week, after which a progressive decrease over 2 weeks was attempted. If at any point during dose reduction recurrent depressive, behavioral, or cognitive symptoms were detected, the dosage was reset at the preceding level and maintained for another 2 weeks.

Throughout this open-treatment study, patients were evaluated weekly for the first 3 weeks, every 2 weeks during the next 2 months, and then at 3-month intervals for 1 year. Blood pressure, pulse, and temperature were recorded at

TABLE 15–4. Neuropsychological and Immunological Markers: Group Values (N = 80)

	ARC (n = 39) (Mean ± SD)	AIDS (n = 41) (mean ± SD)	t-Test ([+]p ≤ .05)
Trail Making Test[a]			
A	69.32 ± 32.04	45.05 ± 82.08	1.570 (ns)
B	63.31 ± 39.12	28.40 ± 108.34	1.721 (ns)
Verbal Selective Reminding Test[a]			
Long-term storage	72.14 ± 26.51	69.62 ± 19.41	0.289 (ns)
Consistent long-term retrieval	65.34 ± 14.04	59.11 ± 21.87	0.882 (ns)
Mini-Mental State Examination	28.05 ± 1.76	27.71 ± 1.93	0.645 (ns)
White blood cell count ($\times 10^3$ cells)	4.24 ± 1.86	3.9 ± 4.32	0.333 (ns)
Total T-cell count (cells/mm³)	1158.86 ± 882.41	593.88 ± 469.24	2.788 (+)
T4 cell (cells/mm³)	269.95 ± 172.15	102.19 ± 111.10	4.651 (+)
Helper/suppressor ratio	0.3025 ± 0.2101	0.1689 ± 0.1643	2.600 (+)

[a]Scores have been age-corrected, z-transformed, and converted to standard scores, with an overall mean of 100 and an SD of 15.

each clinic visit. Laboratory studies were done routinely by the patient's primary physician in the clinic, and an electrocardiogram was obtained only for patients who showed changes in vital signs: specifically, peak systolic pressures of ≥180 mm Hg or sustained systolic pressures of ≥170 mm Hg; peak diastolic pressures of ≥120 mm Hg or sustained diastolic pressures of ≥110 mm Hg; and/or peak seated, resting pulse rates of 150 beats/minute or sustained rates of 125 beats/minute.

Evaluation of the Response to Treatment

The Clinical Global Improvement Scale (CGIS: Guy, 1976) was used to rate improvement in the patient's psychiatric disorders. This subjective rating system classified the patients' clinical response to treatment into four categories. The patient was considered to be *completely improved* if symptoms totally disappeared with the psychostimulant methylphenidate. Partial remission of symptoms was divided into two categories: *Moderately improved* patients showed marked improvement in several areas but did not achieve a complete remission, and *minimally improved* patients had a definite but slight rise in mood or energy accompanied by corresponding changes in such symptoms as ambulation, appetite, concentration and attention, spontaneity, shortened latency of response, and the like. Patients having no change or worsening of symptoms were classified as showing *no improvement.* All methylphenidate-treated patients were considered evaluable for their treatment response. The frequencies of patients in the different diagnostic categories were tabulated by the CGIS classification. The frequencies were also combined across diagnostic categories and tabulated. Chi-square analysis was applied with an alpha level of 0.05.

Results

Of the 150 patients initally referred, 81 had ARC and 69 had AIDS. Hematological and immunological indices, as well as the neuropsychological markers available on 80 subjects (nARC = 39; nAIDS = 41), are shown in Table 15–4.

The response to pharmacotherapy with methylphenidate in patients with HIV disease is shown in Table 15–3. In the 150 treatment courses, the range of daily doses was from 10 to 60 mg, with a mean of 25 mg. The duration of treatment ranged from 1 week to 18 weeks, with a mean of 12 weeks.

Of the 150 patients treated with methylphenidate, 138 (91%) had some notable clinical improvement, of whom 62 (41%) had had a complete remission of symptoms. Seventy-six patients (50%) had a partial remission, 47 (31%) of whom had a moderate response and 29 (19%) a minimal response. Chi-square analysis indicated a significant response across all diagnostic categories (χ^2 = 37.68; $p <$ .05). The incidence of objective responses (i.e., either complete or partial) did not appear to vary with the clinical diagnosis of the patient, age, prior diagnosis of depression, prior treatment, or Karnofsky performance status. The median duration of response, as measured from the time of treatment, was 28 weeks for

TABLE 15–5. Psychostimulant Response and Neuropsychological Markers

	Patients with ARC		
Neuropsychological Marker *(N = 6)*	*Drug Free* *(Mean ± SD)*	*Posttreatment* *(Mean ± SD)*	*t-Test*
Trail Making Test			
A	43.04 ± 47.71	77.77 ± 43.89	−2.691[a]
B	33.37 ± 48.29	91.26 ± 29.65	−3.501[a]
Mini-Mental State Examination	28.17 ± 0.98	29.00 ± 0.89	−2.712[a]
Verbal Selective Reminding Test *(N = 3)*			
Long-term storage	91.86 ± 9.00	111.03 ± 10.47	−10.148[a]
Consistent long-term retrieval	73.10 ± 10.03	98.02 ± 306	−5.649[a]
	Patients with AIDS		
Neuropsychological Marker *(N = 10)*	*Drug Free* *(Mean ± SD)*	*Posttreatment* *(Mean ± SD)*	*t-Test*
Trail Making Test			
A	48.56 ± 92.68	86.16 ± 31.50	−1.810[b]
B	63.16 ± 57.76	94.68 ± 20.94	−2.340[a]

Note: All raw scores are converted to standard scores (by *z*-transformation, with a mean of 100 and an SD of 15), except for Mini-Mental State Examination scores, which are in raw score form.

[a]*p* < .05.

[b]Not significant (p > .05).

Source: Portions adapted from Fernandez et al. (1988a). Reproduced by permission.

the patients with a complete remission and 16 weeks for those with a partial remission. The treatment courses of the 138 patients who initially had a therapeutic response revealed that nearly 80% had recurrent symptoms. All of the 44 patients with a previous history of depression had recurrence and were openly treated with standard antidepressant therapy. We have recently begun retreating 66 of the 106 depressive patients without a past psychiatric history of depression with methylphenidate whose symptoms have recurred to determine whether further treatment can prolong the duration of the therapeutic benefit. In all but two of the patients, retreatment has thus far induced a remission.

With regard to cognitive functioning, treatment with methylphenidate normalized rote verbal memory and cognitive sequencing rate in a subset of patients treated (Fernandez et al., 1988a). In both AIDS and ARC patients, a significant improvement in standardized test scores on rote, verbal long-term memory retrieval, and alphanumeric graphomotor sequencing rate tasks was demonstrated. These scores not only showed statistically significant improvement from severe impairment, but also, as a group, reached the average range of functioning, based on comparison with published norms for these instruments (Table 15–5; Fernandez et al., 1988a).

The adverse effects associated with methylphenidate treatment are listed in

TABLE 15–6. Number of Patients with Side Effects During Treatment
with Methylphenidate ($N = 18$)[a]

Side Effects	Number
Hypertension	10
Tachycardia	8
Confusion	6
Nervousness/irritability	5
Agitation	2
Insomnia	2

[a]More than one adverse effect/patient.

Table 15–6. Virtually all these effects were associated with methylphenidate administration, in accordance with previous studies, demonstrating that methylphenidate itself was associated with only minor side effects. Of the 18 patients (12%) experiencing toxic effects, 10 demonstrated transient alterations of blood pressure (i.e., systolic blood pressure ≥ 180 mm Hg and/or diastolic blood pressure ≥ 105 mm Hg) and pulse (peak resting heart rate ≥ 150 beats/minute). The resulting hypertension and tachycardia were never of sufficient magnitude to require intervention. Neither phenomenon appeared with reintroduction of the agent. Five patients experienced increased nervousness and irritability, and two experienced both agitation and insomnia. Confusion occurred in half of the patients with dementia. All side effects remitted with either dose reduction or discontinuation. No evidence of long-term adverse sequelae was noted. The development of side effects did not appear to impair the therapeutic efficacy of retreatment with a lower dose. No anorexia or weight loss due to treatment with methylphenidate were observed, and appetite actually improved in many patients treated with methylphenidate by their subjective reports.

Discussion

This chapter reviews the use of analeptics in persons with symptomatic HIV disease and presents our experience with the administration of 150 courses of methylphenidate to HIV patients with various psychiatric diagnoses. We observed objective responses to pharmacotherapy in 138 (91%) patients receiving methylphenidate, 62 of whom (41%) achieved a complete remission. In our experience, the administration of methylphenidate alone is capable of producing remission of depressive signs and symptoms from diverse etiologies. The therapeutic effects of methylphenidate in other medically ill patients have been described, and our preliminary experience with HIV patients has indicated that this drug may also have specific beneficial neurocognitive effects (Fernandez et al., 1988a). The maximum dose that could be tolerated by HIV patients was 60 mg daily (in two or three divided doses). By contrast with cancer patients, in whom higher doses of methylphenidate can be used (Fernandez et al., 1987), we have observed a significant increase in the incidence of side effects in HIV patients at higher doses. It is possible that the difference in maximum dosage that can be tolerated in HIV patients reflects a greater sensitivity to CNS stimulation with these agents.

Patients who were refractory to treatment with antidepressants also appeared to benefit from treatment with methylphenidate. Previously, we suggested that the depression in ARC and AIDS patients might be a prodrome of organic mental disorders, including the AIDS dementia complex that is prevalent in this population (Fernandez et al., 1988a; Fernandez and Levy, 1990). However, this speculation awaits confirmation. Nevertheless, it is noteworthy that diffuse cognitive deficits were present even in those patients who had seemingly functional psychiatric diagnoses.

Due to the frequent finding of depressive symptoms in this patient population (Atkinson et al., 1988), the pseudodementia syndrome of depression is often considered in the differential diagnosis of cognitive impairment of HIV patients. This syndrome has, as common features, poor verbal memory, psychomotor retardation, awareness of cognitive deficits, and the psychological and vegetative signs of depression (Cummings and Benson, 1983). However, pseudodementia is described as having a rapid onset. Additionally, pseudodementia patients usually respond to neuropsychological testing with quick discontinuation of cognitively taxing tasks or tend to answer "I don't know." Thus, they demonstrate cognitive impairment *without effort,* as opposed to the demented patient's unsuccessful but concerted effort, or even struggle, with cognitive tasks.

HIV patients with neurological involvement may indeed demonstrate vegetative signs of depression, including sleep disturbance (Norman et al., 1990), psychomotor retardation, and apathy, all of which might be characterized as "pseudodepression" of HIV encephalopathy. Our hypothesis is that, in many cases, the constellation of symptoms appearing as an affective disorder that arises within HIV disease is a pseudodepression and that treatment with standard antidepressant agents may not only be ineffective, but may also further compromise brain function by causing anticholinergic effects ranging from a mild cognitive inefficiency to a fully developed delirium.

Treatment with methylphenidate in our patients was clearly associated with low morbidity. A major side effect in this group appeared to be transient hypertension associated with the administration of the drug. It should be emphasized that changes in blood pressure and pulse were self-limiting and that the patients became tolerant to this effect without loss of therapeutic efficacy. Other side effects associated with the administration of methylphenidate, even when severe, were transient and resolved promptly after reducing or discontinuing the drug. The development of these side effects did not preempt retreatment at a lower dose, which then usually resulted in a significant therapeutic response. The patients in this report did not experience any reduction in appetite. In fact, subjective appetite improvement was the general rule.

Major problems remain that must be overcome if treatment with methylphenidate is to be widely used in HIV spectrum disorders. Well-designed clinical studies to replicate and extend these findings from open studies on the therapeutic effect of methylphenidate, both qualitatively and quantitatively, are urgently needed. These studies need to include further investigation of dose modifications and treatment schedules and the use of reinstituted treatment in relapsing patients; they must also address the concerns of tolerance, habituation, and abuse. Use in demented and encephalopathic patients who were substance abusers or who may be on methadone maintenance is a sensitive and unresearched issue. While these agents may potentially provide some relief for affective and cognitive dysfunction, the possibility of dependency may outweigh these benefits. Inpatient studies may help delineate the value of psychostimulants in such patients.

Like any other innovative treatment, psychostimulant therapy in HIV disease will need further refinement before general clinical use is possible. Immunological studies to assess the effects of these agents on the immune systems of HIV patients need to be carefully examined. It is important to assess whether methylphenidate treatment may compromise these patients' immune competence, as has been reported for some tricyclic antidepressants (Miller et al., 1986; Eisen et al., 1989). Until this occurs, methylphenidate treatment should continue to be considered as an innovative approach to be applied carefully, in clinical settings, and only in selected patients for whom no other effective therapy is available or in whom standard therapy has failed or has had incomplete results. Methylphenidate has also been used successfully in patients with the AIDS dementia complex, organic personality disorders, and organic affective disorders, with marked improvement in both affective and cognitive disturbances (Fernandez et al., 1988a,b; Holmes et al., 1989; Fernandez and Levy, 1990; Angrist et al., 1992; White et al., 1992). In these patients, psychostimulant treatment can be continued for several weeks or even months as a quality-of-life measure for those who are disabled by the cognitive and mood disturbances associated with this malignant disorder.

Conclusion

Recognizing and managing the depression that often accompanies HIV infection is vital. Psychopharmacological interventions have much therapeutic potential for depressed HIV patients, and a careful trial of antidepressants is warranted. Our experience with the psychostimulants, specifically methylphenidate, is highlighted by the quick remission of the affective, behavioral, and cognitive dysfunction, with a few significant treatment-related side effects. We found methylphenidate to be effective in the treatment of HIV-related depression from various etiologies even for those patients in whom standard antidepressant therapy had failed.

References

Angrist, B., D'Hollosy, M., Sanfilipo, M., Satriano, J., Diamond, P.G., Simberoff, M., and Weinreb, H. (1992). Central nervous system stimulants as symptomatic treatments for AIDS-related neuropsychiatric impairment. *Journal of Clinical Psychopharmacology, 12,* 268–272.

Atkinson, J.H., Grant, I., Kennedy, C.J., Richman, D.D., Spector, S.A., and McCutchan, J.A. (1988). Prevalence of psychiatric disorders among men infected with human immunodeficiency virus. *Archives of General Psychiatry, 45*, 859–864.

Beckett, A., Summergrad, P., Manschrek, T., Vitagliano, H., Henderson, M., Buttolph, M.L., and Jenike, M. (1987). Symptomatic HIV infection of the CNS in a patient without clinical evidence of immune deficiency. *American Journal of Psychiatry, 144*, 1342–1347.

Biel, J.H., and Bopp, B.A. (1978). Amphetamines: Structure–activity relationships. In L. Iverson, S. Iverson, and S. Snyder, eds., *Handbook of Psychopharmacology*, Vol. II. New York: Plenum Press, pp. 1–39.

Bouckoms, A.J. (1981). Analgesic adjuvants: The role of psychotropics, anticonvulsants and prostaglandin inhibitors. *Drug Therapy, 6*, 41–48.

Breitbart, W., and Mermelstein, H. (1992). Pemoline: An alternative psychostimulant for the management of depressive disorders in cancer patients. *Psychosomatics, 33*, 352–356.

Britton, C.B., Cote, L., and Alsteil, L. (1989). Cerebrospinal fluid biogenic amine metabolites in patients with AIDS. *Neurology, 39*(Suppl. 1), 380.

Cantello, R., Muggia, M., Gilli, M., Delsidime, M., Chiardo-Cutin, I., Riccio, A., and Mutani, R. (1989). Major depression in Parkinson's disease and the mood response to intravenous methylphenidate: Possible role of the hedonic dopamine synapse. *Journal of Neurology, Neurosurgery, and Psychiatry, 52*, 724–731.

Chiarello, R.J., and Cole, J. (1987). The use of psychostimulants in general psychiatry. *Archives of General Psychiatry, 44*, 286–295.

Cummings, J.L., and Benson, D.F. (1983). *Dementia: A Clinical Approach*. Boston: Butterworths, pp. 237–248.

Edelstein, H., and Knight, R.T. (1987). Severe Parkinsonism in two AIDS patients taking prochlorperazine [letter]. *Lancet, 2*, 341–342.

Editorial. (1982). Amphetamines, depression and psychiatrists. *Journal of Clinical Psychiatry, 43*, 390.

Eisen, J.N., Irwin, J., Quay, J., and Livnat, S. (1989). The effect of antidepressants on immune function in mice. *Biological Psychiatry, 26*, 805–817.

Evans, R.W., Gualtieri, C.T., and Patterson, D. (1987) Treatment of chronic closed head injury with psychostimulant drugs: A controlled case study and an appropriate evaluation procedure. *Journal of Nervous and Mental Disorders, 175*, 106–110.

Everett, G. (1980). Pemoline: A specific long acting dopamimetic drug. In G. Gessa, ed., *Apomorphine and Other Dopaminomimetics*, Vol. 1. New York: Raven Press, pp. 261–263.

Fernandez, F., Adams, F., Holmes, V.F., Levy, J.K., and Neidhart, M. (1987). Methylphenidate for depressive disorders in cancer patients. *Psychosomatics, 28*, 455–461.

Fernandez, F., Adams, F., Levy, J.K., Holmes, V., Neidhart, M., and Mansell, P.W.A. (1988a). Cognitive impairment due to AIDS-related complex and its response to psychostimulants. *Psychosomatics, 29*, 38–46.

Fernandez, F., and Levy, J.K. (1990). Adjuvant treatment of HIV dementia with psychostimulants. In D.G. Ostrow, ed., *Behavioral Aspects of AIDS*. New York: Plenum Publishing, pp. 279–286.

Fernandez, F., and Levy, J.K. (1991). Psychopharmacotherapy of psychiatric syndromes in asymptomatic and symptomatic HIV infection. *Psychiatric Medicine, 9*(3), 294–377.

Fernandez, F., Levy, J.K., and Galizzi, H. (1988b). Response to HIV-related depression to psychostimulants: Case reports. *Hospital and Community Psychiatry, 39*, 628–631.

Glennon, R.A. (1987). Psychoactive phenylisopropylamines. In H.Y. Meltzer, ed., *Psychopharmacology: The Third Generation of Progress*. New York: Raven Press, pp. 1627–1633.

Goodnick, P., and Gershon S. (1984). Chemotherapy of cognitive disorders in geriatric subjects. *Journal of Clinical Psychiatry, 45*, 196–209.

Guy W. (1976). *ECDEU Assessment Manual for Psychopharmacology*. Publication No. 76-338. Washington, D.C.: U.S. Department of Health, Education and Welfare.

Hackett, T.P. (1982). Amphetamines, depression and psychiatrists [letter]. *Journal of Clinical Psychiatry, 43*, 390.

Hill, J.M., Farrar, W.L., and Pert, C.B. (1987). Autoradiographic localization of T4 antigen, the HIV receptor, in human brain. *International Journal of Neuroscience, 32*, 687–693.

Hollander, H., Golden, J., Mendelson, T., and Cortland, D. (1985). Extrapyramidal symptoms in AIDS patients given low-dose metoclopramide or chlorpromazine [letter]. *Lancet, 2*, 1186.

Holmes, V.F., Fernandez, F., and Levy, J.K. (1989). Psychostimulant response in ARC/AIDS patients. *Journal of Clinical Psychiatry, 50*, 5–8.

Jones, G.H., Kelly, C.L., and Davies, J.A. (1987). HIV and onset of schizophrenia. *Lancet, 1*, 982.

Kaufmann, M.W., Cassem, N.H., Murray, G.B., and Jenike, M. (1984a). Use of psychostimulants in medically ill patients with neurological disease and major depression. *Canadian Journal of Psychiatry, 29*, 46–49.

Kaufmann, M.W., Cassem, N., Murray, G., and MacDonald, D. (1984b). The use of methylphenidate in depressed patients after cardiac surgery. *Journal of Clinical Psychiatry, 45*, 82–84.

Kaufmann, M.W., Murray, G.B., and Cassem, N.H. (1982). Use of psychostimulants in medically ill depressed patients. *Psychosomatics, 23*, 817–819.

Lahmeyer, H.W. (1982). Frontal lobe meningioma and depression. *Journal of Clinical Psychiatry, 43*, 254–255.

Lingham, V.R., Lazarus, L.W., Groves, L., and Oh, S.H. (1988). Methylphenidate in treating post-stroke depression. *Journal of Clinical Psychiatry, 49*, 151–153.

Maccario, M., and Scharre, D.W. (1987). HIV and acute onset of psychosis. *Lancet, 2*, 342.

Massand, P., Pickett, P., and Murray, G.B. (1991). Psychostimulants for secondary depression in medical illness. *Psychosomatics, 32*, 203–208.

Mattes, J.A. (1985). Methylphenidate in mild depression: A double-blind controlled trial. *Journal of Clinical Psychiatry, 46*, 525–527.

Miller, A.H., Asnis, G.H., Van Praag, H.M., and Norin, A.J. (1986). Influence of desmethyl imipramine on natural killer cell activity. *Psychiatry Research, 19*, 9–15.

Murray, G.B., and Schochet, R.B. (in press). The use of psychostimulants in medical and surgical patients. *International Journal of Psychiatry and Medicine*.

Nath, A., Jankovic, J., and Pettigrew, C. (1987). Movement disorders and AIDS. *Neurology, 37*, 37–41.

Navia, B.A., Cho, E.S., Petito, C.K., and Price, R.W. (1986). The AIDS dementia complex. II. Neuropathology. *Annals of Neurology, 19*, 525–535.

Norman, S.E., Chediak, A.D., Kiel, M., and Cohn, M.A. (1990). Sleep disturbances in HIV-infected homosexual men. *AIDS, 4*, 775–781.

Perry, S. and Jacobsen, P. (1986). Neuropsychiatric manifestations of AIDS-spectrum disorders. *Hospital and Community Psychiatry, 37*, 135–142.

Pickett, P., Masand, P., and Murray, G.B. (1990). Psychostimulant treatment of geriatric depressive disorders secondary to medical illness. *Journal of Geriatric Psychiatry and Neurology, 3*, 146–151.

Satel, S.L., and Nelson, J.C. (1989). Stimulants in the treatment of depression: A critical overview. *Journal of Clinical Psychiatry, 50,* 241–249.

Tesar, G.E. (1982). The role of stimulants in general medicine. *Drug Therapy, 3,* 186–196.

Tourtellotte, W.W., Syndulko, K., Singer, E.J., Fahy-Chandon, B., Singer, P., Resnick, L., and Shapshak, P. (1989). Cerebrospinal fluid and neuro-performance findings in HIV-1 infected individuals with and without neurological deficits. Preliminary findings of a prospective study. Presented in Proceedings of the First Satellite Conference on Neurological and Neuropsychological Complications of HIV Infection, Quebec City, Canada, May.

Warneke, L. (1990). Psychostimulants in psychiatry. *Canadian Journal of Psychiatry, 35,* 3–10.

White, J.C., Christensen, J.F., and Singer, C.M. (1992). Methylphenidate as a treatment for depression in acquired immunodeficiency syndrome: An *n*-of-1 trial. *Journal of Clinical Psychiatry, 53,* 153–156.

Wittenborn, J.R. (1981). Antidepressant use of amphetamines and other psychostimulants. *Modern Problems in Pharmacopsychiatry, 18,* 178–195.

Woods, S., Tesar, G., Murray, G., and Cassem, N. (1986). Psychostimulant treatment of depressive disorders secondary to medical illness. *Journal of Clinical Psychiatry, 47,* 12–15.

16

Developmental Deficits and Behavioral Change in Pediatric AIDS

PIM BROUWERS, HOWARD MOSS,
PAM WOLTERS, and FREDERICK A. SCHMITT

Infection with human immunodeficiency virus (HIV) is rapidly becoming a major source of morbidity and mortality in infants and children. As of October 1, 1993, the Centers for Disease Control (CDC) had received reports of 4906 cases of AIDS in children in the United States, and several thousand more are believed to be infected (CDC, 1993). These infants and children are at very high risk for developing severely disabling neurological and neuropsychological abnormalities. In adults, it is important to distinguish the encephalopathy caused by HIV from that which is secondary to opportunistic infections. In children, however, opportunistic infections (e.g., cryptococcal meningitis, toxoplasmosis) and lymphoma of the central nervous system (CNS) are rather uncommon. Therefore, the predominant causes of behavioral deficits appear to be related directly to the effects of HIV infection on the CNS (Epstein et al., 1987; Brouwers et al., 1990a).

It is difficult to determine the extent and character of HIV-associated neuropsychological deficits and behavioral change in children. There is a clinical impression of marked interindividual differences in CNS abnormalities among HIV-infected children, even among patient subgroups with comparable (HIV) disease factors (e.g., similar stages of the disease, CD4/p24 counts, number and type of opportunistic infections). Furthermore, a number of medical and environmental conditions (e.g., prematurity, poverty and deprivation, CNS effects associated with other previous illness) may contribute to, resemble, or be confounded with HIV-related CNS manifestations. Investigations are needed to differentiate patterns of altered cognitive development and/or behavioral deficits associated with HIV infection from profiles associated with the confounding factors related to independent medical and environmental variables.

This chapter reviews the effect of HIV infection on the development of the CNS in infants and children. First, the epidemiology and characteristics of the pediatric AIDS population are described, illustrating the impact and magnitude of this disease. The pathogenesis of HIV in the CNS is discussed next. The central section of the chapter deals with the neuropsychological and behavioral manifestations of HIV disease. In the final section, considerations of neuropsychological testing, methodological issues of longitudinal follow-up, and novel assessment procedures for evaluating the neurodevelopmental functioning of infants and children with HIV infection are illustrated.

Background and Epidemiology

The earliest pediatric cases of acquired immunodeficiency syndrome (AIDS) were reported to the CDC in 1982, approximately 18 months after the first case report in adults (Rogers et al., 1987). It is important to note that only cases with AIDS are reported to the CDC, and their numbers thus represent just a proportion of the total number of children infected with HIV who will eventually develop AIDS. Although pediatric AIDS cases account for only about 2% of the reported AIDS cases, the number of infected infants and children, particularly those with vertically acquired HIV, is expected to continue to rise as more and more women of childbearing age become infected (Rubinstein and Bernstein, 1986; Rogers et al., 1987; Scott et al., 1989). In fact, 1.5 per 1000 women giving birth in the United States in 1989 were HIV+ (Gwinn et al., 1991). Based on a 30% transmission rate, Gwinn estimates that approximately 1800 infants will acquire the infection from HIV-infected mothers over a 1-year period. Pediatric cases are concentrated in metropolitan areas and in the most populated states along the East and West coasts. HIV-infected children are becoming, however, more prevalent in other states, smaller cities, and rural areas all over the United States (Rogers et al., 1987; CDC, 1993; Oxtoby, 1990).

Infants and children under 13 years of age acquire the infection predominantly from an HIV+ mother (vertical transmission occurs in 85% of the cases). Transfusion of blood (8%) or blood products for treatment of hemophilia (5%) account for the remaining determined cases. The mother's infection in over 70% of the vertically infected children is associated with intravenous drug abuse either by herself or by her sexual partner. The remaining children were born to mothers infected through blood transfusions or heterosexual contact with a male whose infection was associated with hemophilia, transfusions, or bisexual practice (Rogers et al., 1987; Curran et al., 1988).

Evidence suggests that a mother can transmit HIV to her child by three possible routes: in utero by transplacental passage throughout gestation (Sprecher et al. [1986] have documented the presence of HIV-1 in a fetus of 15 weeks), during the intrapartum period through exposure to maternal blood or other fluids, or, more rarely, through breast feeding (Friedland and Klein, 1987;

Rogers, 1989). It is not yet determined, however, at what stage of pregnancy vertical transmission of HIV is most likely to occur.

Estimated rates of HIV transmission from mother to child vary widely but seem lower than first estimated and may be dependent on the disease status of the mother. Earlier studies estimated transmission rates ranging from 35% to as high as 65% (Scott et al., 1985; Rubinstein and Bernstein, 1986), while more recent studies have estimated transmission rates as low as 13% when most mothers were symptom-free (European Collaborative Study, 1991). Risk factors associated with vertical transmission have also been investigated; however, the evidence is inconclusive. Some studies have not found an association between the mother's preterm clinical status or mode of delivery and vertical transmission rate (European Collaborative Study, 1988; Goedert et al., 1989). Others have suggested that the risk of infection is higher in infants born to mothers who have symptoms of AIDS during pregnancy (Mok et al., 1987). The cumulative evidence currently suggests that the vertical transmission rate is approximately 30% (Rogers et al., 1987; Italian Multicentre Study, 1988; European Collaborative Study, 1988; Blanche et al., 1989; Goedert et al., 1989; Ryder et al., 1989; Andiman et al., 1990).

The latency period between infection and the first signs of HIV disease in vertically infected children varies widely, ranging from those who become symptomatic as soon as a few months after birth to others who do not show symptoms until 7–10 years later (Rogers et al., 1987). The interval from infection to the onset of symptoms, on the average, tends to be longer in children who acquired the virus by transfusion, and it is also longer in adults than in children (Medley et al., 1987; Rogers et al., 1987).

Several studies have indicated a bimodal distribution in the latency to onset of symptomatic HIV disease, and in the course of the illness among vertically infected children, suggesting the presence of two distinct subgroups (Auger et al., 1988; Scott et al., 1989; Blanche et al., 1990; DePaula et al., 1991). Auger et al. (1988) estimate that one subgroup has an onset of symptoms at a median age of 4.1 months and a shorter survival time compared to the second subgroup, which develops symptoms at a median age of 6.1 years. The median age of patients belonging to the second distribution probably will become even older, as more patients are likely to be identified with longer symptom-free survival. In a French study of vertically infected children by Blanche et al. (1990), one-third of the 94 pediatric patients studied had an early onset and severe progression of disease, exhibiting opportunistic infections and encephalopathy before 12 months; this pattern was associated with an earlier death. The other group of patients had a later onset of symptoms, without either opportunistic infections or encephalopathy in the first year, and are still alive at age 5 years. Age of occurrence of symptomatic infection, therefore, is an important prognostic factor for progression of disease and survival time and may be predictive of encephalopathy or developmental delay. In addition, the occurrence of opportunistic infections and/or severe encephalopathy within the first year of life is associated with an earlier death (Blanche et al., 1990).

The reason for this variability in the onset of symptomatic infection and length of survival is not yet understood, but genetic factors or perhaps different strains of the virus may influence the rate of disease progression (Pizzo and Wilfert, 1990). It is also not yet known whether the timing of infection during gestation may affect the clinical course of the disease.

Heterogeneity of the Pediatric AIDS Population

Pediatric AIDS patients form a heterogeneous group that can be divided into different subgroups based on social and environmental background, personal characteristics, and preexisting, non-HIV medical and current disease parameters. These factors may color and confound the evaluation of possible HIV-associated deficits in behavioral, neuropsychological, and neurological development. In addition, the age of the child, which also varies with the above factors, may determine some of the behavioral consequences of HIV infection.

There is a historical basis for the differences in mean age among the various pediatric AIDS subgroups defined above. Since the blood supply has been essentially safe from the early spring of 1985, the youngest children born in the United States who acquired HIV through blood product or coagulation factor transfusion are now at least 8 years of age. Indeed, the majority of children with HIV disease older than 9 as of late 1993 will have been infected through the transfer of blood products. Most of these patients will be males, due to the higher likelihood for males to have medical conditions that require blood products. Vertical infection is less likely in the group between 9 and 13 and is almost nonexistent in patients 14 years of age and older. Indeed, the vertically infected children who have survived to middle childhood (8–13 years) are a select group. These children may have lived this long either because they have a less virulent form of the virus and/or they are more resilient hosts. In summary, children older than 9 years of age will tend to have transfusion-acquired HIV disease and be male, while children 8 years and younger will have vertically acquired HIV.

Extraneous medical factors that could influence psychological functioning in patients with vertical infection and be confounded with HIV-related CNS effects include the adverse effect of in utero exposure to drugs for infants whose mothers have a history of drug abuse. Heroin (Naeye et al., 1973), cocaine (MacGregor et al., 1987; Chasnoff et al., 1989), and alcohol (Iosub et al., 1981; Day et al., 1989) use have all been associated with detrimental effects (Fulroth et al., 1989) on the newborn. In addition, the quality of prenatal care and the increased incidence and degree of prematurity may impact on the child's early development.

Patients with transfusion-acquired HIV may be affected by potentially adverse CNS sequelae from the medical conditions that required the transfusion that led to the infection. For example, late adverse effects of premature birth (Spreen et al., 1984), cardiac surgery (Terplan, 1973), and some forms of childhood cancer (Poplack and Brouwers, 1985) have all been reported. It may sometimes be difficult to distinguish between these late effects and the more acute CNS manifestations of HIV. The contributions of these confounding variables to neuropsychological abnormalities are often difficult to assess quantitatively and independently.

With regard to environmental factors, children infected through transfusion tend to come more often from intact, stable families with better economic and social support systems than the majority of vertically infected children. In addition, these families often have had to cope with chronic, potentially life-threatening medical illness before (hemophilia, cancer, major surgery, etc.) and may have developed strategies, defenses, and attitudes for dealing with the stress and uncertainties associated with such conditions.

Vertically infected children have parent(s) who are also infected with HIV. Because parental infection is often associated with specific high-risk behaviors, vertically infected children are more likely to be in unstable, nonsupportive family situations. Frequently one will encounter single parents, multiple substance abuse, low socioeconomic status, and prostitution in the families of vertically infected children. In addition, the disease in the parent(s) may also have progressed, so that they are less able to care optimally for their children. In more extreme cases, the child may have been placed in an institution or shifted among various foster or adoptive homes. The largely negative influences of the impoverished home environment, and the effects of other adverse conditions on psychosocial adjustment, mental growth, and development, have been well documented (Capron and Duyme, 1989) and certainly could confound and exacerbate the effects of HIV.

Neuropathology

Evidence suggests that CNS dysfunction observed in AIDS patients may be caused by direct infection of the brain by HIV (Epstein et al., 1986, 1987; Ho et al., 1987; Falloon et al., 1989). HIV has been isolated in the brains and cerebrospinal fluid (CSF) of both infected children (Epstein et al., 1987) and adults (Ho et al., 1985; Levy et al., 1985) with neurological symptoms. The pathogenesis of the neurological abnormalities, however, remains largely unclear. Infection of neurons and glia (except microglia) within the CNS by HIV seems to occur to only a very small extent. Therefore it has been hypothesized that the neuronal dysfunction seen in symptomatic HIV disease is due to an indirect mechanism, including the presence of either host- or viral-mediated toxins within the CNS.

Neuropathological Findings

Postmortem microscopic examinations of the brains and spinal cords of children with symptomatic HIV disease may reveal mineralizations, diffuse white matter astrocytosis, and inflammatory infiltrates (Sharer et al., 1986; Belman et al., 1988; Epstein et al., 1988; Dickson et al., 1989).

Mineralization in the walls of small blood vessels (calcific vasculopathy) is most often found in the basal ganglia and sometimes the centrum semiovale. Calcific deposits are also seen in the walls of larger vessels, including arteries (Belman et al., 1986, 1988; Sharer et al., 1986), frequently without appreciable inflammatory CNS disease.

Diffuse or more discrete pallor of myelin in the deep cerebral white matter, the latter often associated with inflammatory foci, has been observed with staining (Sharer et al., 1986; Epstein et al., 1988; Dickson et al., 1989). These myelin stains in children, however, are less reliable due to ongoing myelination, particularly in infants below age 3 (Sharer et al., 1986; Dickson et al., 1989).

An inflammatory response characterized by perivascular mononuclear inflammatory cell infiltrates, microglial nodules, and multinucleated giant cells has also been noted (Sharer et al., 1985; Belman et al., 1988; Epstein et al., 1988; Pang et al., 1990). Viral particles and/or HIV antigen have been demonstrated within multinucleated cells, monocytes, and cells resembling intrinsic microglia (Epstein et al., 1985; Koenig et al., 1986; Wiley et al., 1986; Michaels et al., 1988). Pathological changes have also been seen in the spinal cords of children, including corticospinal tract degeneration, inflammatory infiltrates, and, uncommonly, vacuolar myelopathy (Sharer et al., 1990).

Measures Associated with CNS Neuronal Function

Clinical investigations in both adults and children have identified a number of agents that seem to be associated with the presence and/or severity of neurological/developmental abnormalities. In children, Tardieu et al. (1989) reported correlations between CSF p24 antigen and neurological abnormalities. Mintz (1989) showed a relation between serum but not CSF tumor necrosis factor alpha (TNFα) and neurological function. Surtees et al. (1990) found abnormalities in methyl-group metabolism and neopterin in the CSF of children with encephalopathy. Brouwers et al. (1993) showed a relation between degree of encephalopathy and CSF levels of quinolinic acid (QUIN). In adults, abnormalities in CSF neopterin (Brew et al., 1990), serum TNFα (Grimaldi et al., 1991) and β-2-microglobulin (Brew et al., 1989) are also reported and related to neurological status. Furthermore, increased CSF levels of QUIN were observed, particularly in patients with AIDS dementia complex (Heyes et al., 1989, 1991). Apart from TNFα and QUIN (an excitotoxin that in large concentrations may act as a convulsant [Schwarc et al., 1983], the other markers (neopterin, β-2-microglobulin) may not have potentially causative involvement in CNS changes.

Neuroimaging Findings

Computed tomography (CT) head scans show variable degrees of cerebral atrophy, with ventricular enlargement and widening of sulci, decreased attenuation in the white matter that may be progressive (Belman et al., 1985, 1986, 1988; Epstein et al., 1985, 1986), as well as bilateral symmetrical calcification of the basal ganglia and frontal white matter (DeCarli et al., 1993) (Figure 16–1). Quantitative CT brain scan analysis (DeCarli et al., 1991) indicates abnormalities in the ventricular area and ventricular brain area ratio of children with symptomatic HIV disease that improve with azidothymidine (AZT) therapy. Magnetic resonance imaging (MRI) reveals atrophy and may show increased signal intensity in the basal ganglia and/or the white matter (Belman et al., 1986; Epstein et al.,

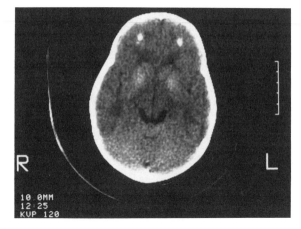

FIGURE 16–1. Computed tomography (CT) head scan of a 23 month old child with vertically acquired symptomatic HIV infection. The CT scan clearly shows bilateral mineralizations (calcifications) in the basal ganglia as well as in the periventricular white matter of the frontal lobes. The child was functioning in the "borderline" range of cognitive ability and exhibited specific deficits in expressive language and gross motor skills.

1986) on T_2-weighted images. However, Tardieu et al. (1991) suggest that the white matter abnormalities visualized with MRI in these children may have little prognostic value and do not seem to correlate with current clinical status. The use of positron emission tomography (PET) was reported in one child with HIV-1 infection, an 11-year-old hemophiliac boy being treated on a phase I study of AZT (Pizzo et al., 1988). PET scans of this child showed diffused cortical hypometabolism and focal areas of markedly reduced metabolism in the right frontal and right superior temporal cortices prior to treatment. Posttreatment scans revealed considerable improvement, with only mild abnormalities remaining in the left frontal cortex and associated improvements in neuropsychological function.

Secondary Neurological Complications

Neurological complications secondary to immune deficiency, including neoplasm, stroke, and CNS infections, although infrequent, may develop in children with HIV-1 infection. These complications are usually associated with the onset of focal neurological deficits, seizures, or abrupt changes in mental status and can easily be distinguished from the more insidious decline or lack of further development of cognitive, behavioral, and motor functions characteristic of HIV-1 encephalopathy.

The most common cause of CNS mass lesions in children over 1 year of age with HIV-1 infection is primary CNS lymphoma (Epstein et al., 1988). The basal ganglia and periventricular areas seem most frequently involved, and there are often multiple lesions. Strokes that often seem to occur in association with thrombocytopenia have also been reported, but their true incidence is unknown (Belman et al., 1988; Park et al., 1988; Frank et al., 1989). Opportunistic infections of the CNS (such as toxoplasmosis and papovavirus infection) are uncommon in HIV-1 infected children (Sharer et al., 1986; Epstein et al., 1988), but serious bacterial infections including sepsis and meningitis have been reported, sometimes resulting in sensorineural hearing loss (Belman et al., 1985, 1988; Epstein et al., 1988). Cytomegalovirus (CMV) encephalitis has also been documented but is very infrequent. Disseminated CMV infection has been seen at autopsy in many children, but morphologically recognizable cytomegalic inclusions in the brain are rare (Dickson et al., 1989).

In summary, given the metabolic, neuroradiological, and neuropathological data, it may be hypothesized that HIV infection in the CNS affects functioning by modulating neurophysiological processes that may eventually result in cell death. The available evidence suggests that viral factors may determine neuroinvasiveness but that host factors may be largely responsible for the neuropathological and clinical findings associated with encephalopathy (Brouwers et al., 1990a). The rather global character of the pediatric CNS impairments would suggest that a "free floating" compound may be involved. A possible candidate, as discussed earlier, is QUIN, which may play a role in HIV-related neurological disease (Heyes et al., 1991).

Neuropsychology

As stated earlier, it is not yet clear if, when, and how the CNS of infants and children becomes infected with HIV. CNS infection may also vary with subsets of patients and by itself does not necessarily mean that there will be clinical manifestations of the HIV infection (Tardieu et al., 1989).

In general, a number of subgroups with different patterns of cognitive functioning have been observed in infants and children with symptomatic HIV disease. At least three general pediatric groups can be identified (see also Table 1 of the report of the Working Group of the American Academy of Neurology AIDS Task Force on Nomenclature and research case definitions for neurological manifestations of HIV infection [1991]: those with encephalopathy, those with neuropsychological impairment, and those with apparently normal neuropsychological functioning.

Encephalopathy

In children with encephalopathy, neurological changes associated with HIV-1 infection include impaired cranial growth resulting in acquired microcephaly, cerebral atrophy, enlargement of the ventricles, and calcification in the basal ganglia. Clinically, extrapyramidal and cerebellar signs, delays or regression in motor and language development, and deterioration in cognitive abilities have been described, particularly in children younger than age 5 (Belman et al., 1985, 1988; Epstein et al., 1985, 1986; Ultmann et al., 1985, 1987; Falloon et al., 1989).

Heterogeneity in patterns of development have, however, been notable. The most severe form is *progressive subacute encephalopathy,* which is characterized by a gradual but progressive deterioration in motor, language, and adaptive functions. The infant or young child frequently loses previously acquired milestones. Progression of neurological symptoms may be accompanied by progressive apathy or increased hyperactivity, increased emotional lability (Belman, 1990), loss of interest in the environment and in school performance, and decreased gestures and vocalizations (Belman et al., 1988). A characteristic facial appearance has been described (Belman et al., 1988). The child has an alert, wide-eyed expression with a paucity of spontaneous facial movements. Level of psychological functioning is in general pervasively and globally impaired (Brouwers et al., 1992).

Many encephalopathic children have an episodic course. Periods of progressive encephalopathy with deterioration are interrupted by variable periods of relative neurological stability (Belman et al., 1988), sometimes alternating in a stepwise fashion (Epstein et al., 1986). In others, neurological deterioration is uninterrupted and rapid (over a period of a few months) (Belman et al., 1985, 1988; Epstein et al., 1985, 1986).

A more frequent and possibly less severe form of encephalopathy is the *plateau course.* Infants and young children gain little or no further developmental skills over time, but no loss of milestones or previously acquired abilities is observed. New milestones are either not acquired or the rate of acquisition is markedly slow, deviating not only from the norm but also from the child's previous rate of progress (Diamond et al., 1987; Ultmann et al., 1987; Belman et al., 1989). IQ scores decline, and the mental developmental age stays essentially the same. Motor deficits are common during this phase but their progression and severity may vary, with potentially significant divergence from concurrent cognitive development (Belman et al., 1985; Pizzo et al., 1988). As HIV disease advances, patients with the plateau course may have further neurological deterioration (Epstein et al., 1986, 1988; Belman et al., 1988, 1989). During both progressive subacute and plateau phases, however, longitudinal measurement of head circumference shows poor brain growth, with loss of percentile rank (Epstein et al., 1986; Belman et al., 1988).

Children with *static encephalopathy* continue to acquire skills and abilities at rates consistent with their impaired initial level of functioning, though still below their pre-illness expected rate (Belman et al., 1985; Epstein et al., 1986). That is, their functioning may be lowered because of HIV CNS infection, but there is no progressive decline. Initial levels of functioning may vary from the moderate to mild range of mental retardation to the low average range, and these levels remain relatively stable over time (Ultmann et al., 1985; Epstein et al., 1986; Belman et al., 1988). A large percentage of these patients also have varying degrees of motor involvement.

The cause of static encephalopathy and the relationship to CNS HIV infection remain uncertain. Interpretation has to take into consideration confounding risk factors that accompany but are not directly related to HIV infection (Ultmann et al., 1985, 1987; Epstein et al., 1986; Belman et al., 1988).

Neuropsychological Impairments

As with the encephalopathic patterns, studies report heterogeneity in cognitive deficits associated with HIV in children without a diagnosis of encephalopathy. Children with symptomatic HIV disease may function within the normal range, but some show more accentuated profiles between impaired and preserved cognitive abilities. Selective weaknesses or impairments in perceptual motor functioning (Epstein et al., 1986), gait and motor coordination (Diamond et al., 1987), attentional functioning (Brouwers et al., 1989; Hittleman et al., 1991), and expressive language (Belman et al., 1985; Wolters et al., 1989) have been described. However, individual studies of neuropsychological functioning have in general focused on different specific abilities and described deficits, but few investigations have conducted within-study comparisons of the different abilities.

Two domains of cognitive function appear the most susceptible to the effects of CNS HIV infection in children: attentional processes and expressive behavior.

1. Attention difficulties have been widely recognized in pediatric and adult patients with HIV disease. In children, attention deficits may be documented as a relative weaknesses on the "freedom from distractability" subscales of IQ tests (Brouwers et al., 1989; Figure 16–2) and on behavioral assessment (Moss et al., in press; Hittleman et al., 1991). In adults, attentional deficits are one of the observed hallmarks of AIDS dementia complex (ADC) (Price et al., 1988). With children, however, it is not clear whether attentional problems are directly attributable to HIV. Other etiologies are possible, including those related to medical and psychosocial factors (discussed in detail in the section on "Indirect Effects"). In addition, the base rate of attention disorders for this age group is relatively high in the general population. In a cluster analysis using the Wechsler Intelligence Scale for Children Revised (WICS-R) subtests of children with symptomatic HIV disease, one subgroup (representing 21% of the cases) was identified that was almost exclusively responsible for the appearance of an overall attention deficit effect (Brouwers et al., 1992). A similar group of comparable size (25%) was also identified in a matched group of children in remission from acute lymphoblastic leukemia (ALL). Whether this attention deficit pattern is directly associated with HIV infection or with a chronic illness (i.e., ALL) remains to be further investigated.

2. Expressive functioning across several modalities of behavior, including the expression of language, motor abilities, social skills, and affect, appears to be differentially affected in a number of pediatric HIV patients. Loss of speech, regression in motor function, delayed socially adaptive skills, and flat affect have been observed in children with advanced HIV-related CNS disease (Ultmann et al., 1985, 1987; Epstein et al., 1986; Belman et al., 1988; Moss et al., in press; Wolters et al., in press; Hittleman et al., 1990, 1991). Following are the areas of expressive behavior most commonly affected by HIV infection in children.

LANGUAGE.   Speech and language abilities frequently become impaired in children with symptomatic HIV disease. Some children who were speaking in full sentences are observed to regress to using single words, their articulation

Mean (sem) WISC-R Scaled Subtest Scores

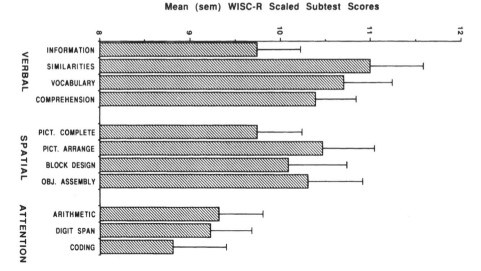

FIGURE 16–2. Overall subtest profile on the WISC-R for school-age children with symptomatic HIV-1 disease showing the relative weakness on subjects that are critically dependent on intact attentional functioning. (From Brouwers et al., 1989.)

becomes slurred, and their speech is labored. During this decline in expressive language, the children's receptive language is often retained or is less impaired than their expressive skills. Infants may exhibit a delay in developing expressive language, but again, they often appear to have near-age-appropriate receptive verbal skills.

Early natural history studies reported developmental abnormalities in the language functioning of some children with HIV infection (Ultmann et al., 1985, 1987; Epstein, et al., 1986; Belman et al., 1988); however, specific language dysfunction in pediatric AIDS is not well documented. Inconsistencies in the findings are common, probably because different HIV-infected pediatric populations were studied (i.e., transfusion vs. vertical infection; impoverished vs. stable environment) and a variety of different assessment techniques were used, including clinical observations (Belman et al., 1985), developmental histories (Epstein et al., 1985; Ultmann et al., 1987; Belman et al., 1988), parent report measures (Wolters et al., in press), developmental and language screening tests (Epstein et al., 1985; Ultmann et al., 1985, 1987; Belman et al., 1988), general intelligence tests (Epstein et al., 1986; Ultmann et al., 1987; Nozyce et al., 1989), and comprehensive language tests (McCardle et al., 1991). Despite these differences, a similar conclusion was reached by several investigators (Epstein et al., 1986; Wolters et al., in press; McCardle et al., 1991): deficits in expressive language were more common and more severe than delays in receptive language (Figure 16–3).

MOTOR SKILLS.   In infants and children with symptomatic HIV infection, motor skills are frequently one of the first and often the most severely affected areas of functioning (Hittleman et al., 1991). Infants tend to exhibit a delay in overall

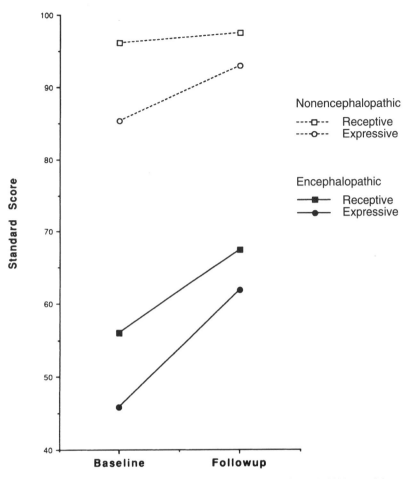

FIGURE 16–3. The receptive and expressive language functioning of children with symptomatic HIV infection were assessed before and after six months of AZT treatment using the Vineland Adaptive Behavior Scales in a structured interview with the child's primary caregiver (From Wolters et al., in press). Before treatment, expressive language was significantly lower than receptive language in the encephalopathic and non-encephalopathic children. After six months of AZT, results indicated significant gains in overall language skills. (See the section on Neuropsychological impairments: Expressive functioning.)

motor development and abnormalities in muscle tone. Preschool or older school-age children are more likely to develop impairments in lower extremity motor skills, such as disturbances in balance and gait, and in some cases they may lose the ability to walk. Reports of abnormalities in motor functioning have been consistent and in general are based on developmental histories, parent report, clinical observations, and/or standard tests of motor development (Belman et al., 1985, 1988; Epstein et al., 1985, 1986; Ultmann et al., 1985, 1987; Hittleman et al., 1990, 1991). Neurological examination of motor function may reveal generalized muscle weakness, axial hypotonia, hyperreflexia in the lower extremities;

spastic diperesis; spastic quadriparesis, often with rigidity and pseudobulbar palsy; and pyramidal tract signs in the most severely affected children with progressive encephalopathy (Belman et al., 1985, 1988; Epstein et al., 1985; Ultmann et al., 1985, 1987).

SOCIAL ADAPTIVE SKILLS AND AFFECT. HIV-infected children may also exhibit impaired social skills and affect (Ultman et al., 1987; Belman et al., 1988; Moss et al., in press; Wolters et al., in press). Some children become withdrawn and apathetic, and have difficulty expressing their feelings and emotions both verbally and nonverbally. In extreme cases, some children display autistic-like characteristics; for example, they are unresponsive to social interaction, do not exhibit facial expressions, and cannot be comforted or soothed (Moss et al., 1989) (see also the section on "Behavioral Manifestations").

Finally, these observations of disruptions in expressive behavior may be further supported by the data from a study evaluating the effects of continuous-infusion AZT therapy in children (Pizzo et al., 1988; Brouwers, et al., 1990b). Premorbid data were available for several transfusion-infected children who showed significant declines in IQ scores prior to receiving therapy as a consequence of progressive HIV infection (mean of -19 IQ points over an average of 52 months). Remarkably, however, after 6 months of intravenous AZT treatment, their IQs recovered rapidly to levels very similar to those prior to the diagnosis of AIDS. This would suggest that these transfusion-infected patients must have been acquiring new skills and abilities, possibly through latent learning, at a rate almost commensurate with that of their healthy peers. HIV infection in these children may, therefore, interfere primarily with the retrieval and expression of knowledge rather than impeding the acquisition and underlying maturation of abilities and skills.

Apparently Normal Functioning

A number of HIV-positive children are unimpaired on neuropsychological evaluation. Their neurological exams are also unremarkable, despite the fact that they may have had opportunistic or chronic bacterial infections. However, subtle effects of HIV on the CNS have been observed in a number of such older children (Pizzo et al., 1988); subjective changes in psychomotor speed, fatigue, and mood were reported by parents and caregivers. Furthermore, some patients whose baseline functioning was in the average range ($85 < FIQ < 115$) nevertheless showed significant improvements with AZT therapy that were comparable in magnitude to the change seen in the encephalopathic group (Brouwers et al., 1990b).

On the other hand, treatment-related improvement in functioning may be unlikely in a sample of patients who show no evidence of CNS compromise. In a study evaluating the benefits of didanosine (ddI) (Butler et al., 1991), patients who scored more than one standard deviation above the mean for their age (FIQ > 115) and who did not have any documented evidence of decline in their functioning were analyzed separately from the rest of the sample (FIQ < 115). Over the 6- and 12-month follow-up periods, the level of performance of these patients basically remained unchanged (Wolters et al., 1991). These longitudinal data suggest that these patients (FIQ > 115) did not experience measurable effects of HIV infection on the CNS and for this reason did not show CNS benefits of antiretroviral therapy. The inclusion of such a high-functioning subgroup of patients has to be considered carefully in studies evaluating the potentially beneficial effect of anti-retroviral agents on CNS dysfunction. Not excluding these patients would negatively bias the study and dilute the magnitude of the statistical effect in subgroups who are compromised and who do show benefit from treatment (see also Chapter 14). They are, however, a crucial population in which to assess the possible prophylactic protection against the development of HIV-associated encephalopathy.

Natural History of CNS Disease

Studies evaluating the natural history of HIV infection provide compelling evidence that CNS dysfunction may occur in a large percentage of HIV-infected infants and children (Ultmann et al., 1985, 1987; Barnes 1986; Epstein et al., 1986, 1987, 1988; Rubinstein and Bernstein, 1986; Belman et al., 1988) as well as in adults (Navia et al., 1986; Grant and Heaton, 1990). The degree and course of HIV-related encephalopathy in children appear to vary (Epstein et al., 1986; Rogers et al., 1987; Belman et al., 1988). Although behavioral abnormalities and encephalopathy have been reported as the first and sometimes the only signs of HIV infection (Scott et al., 1989), neurological and neuropsychological defects are more likely to occur in the later stages of the infection, when the children have symptomatic HIV disease. It has been hypothesized that the rate of CNS disease progression may be associated with differences in the timing and route of HIV transmission and possibly influenced by confounding environmental and medical factors (Brouwers et al., 1990a).

It has not yet been conclusively documented whether subtle deficits are also present in older, asymptomatic pediatric patients, as has been observed in asymptomatic adult patients (Grant et al., 1987; Ollo et al., 1990; Stern et al., 1990; Wilkie et al., 1990). Cohen et al. (1991) studied 15 children between 4 and 8 years old infected with HIV through blood transfusion, of whom 67% were asymptomatic. The neuropsychological performance of these patients was compared to that of a matched group of 33 children who had also received blood transfusions associated with prematurity but who were not infected with HIV. The two groups did not differ in overall intelligence, but small differences were found in school achievement, motor speed, visual scanning, and cognitive flexibility. These changes were statistically significant, with the HIV+ children functioning below the level of the control group.

Incidence

HIV-related encephalopathy was originally estimated to occur in as many as 50–90% of children with symptomatic HIV infection (Barnes 1986; Epstein et al., 1986, 1987; Belman et al., 1988). These estimates may have been upwardly biased, however, as they were drawn from samples in which children had more severely progressive disease. In European studies the incidence varied between 9% and 20%, but since these investigations did not have very long follow-up periods, this rate may be an underestimate (Mok et al., 1987; European Collaborative Study, 1988; Blanche et al., 1989). On the basis of recent studies at the National Cancer Institute (e.g., Butler et al., 1991) of a broad sample of children with HIV disease prior to treatment, we would estimate that currently 35–40% of all symptomatic pediatric, HIV-infected patients may exhibit HIV-associated encephalopathy. The incidence of encephalopathy is greater in infants and young children and in patients in whom the disease has progressed further. Some degree of neurological and neuropsychologic impairment is probably found in the majority of symptomatic, HIV-1-infected children (Belman et al., 1985, 1988; Epstein et al., 1985, 1986; Ultmann et al., 1985, 1987). The likelihood of frank encephalopathy as a first or only sign is, however, relatively low but occurs most frequently in young children and infants. Twelve percent of perinatally infected children with symptomatic HIV-1 infection have encephalopathy reported as their first manifestation (Scott et al., 1989). In some children with vertically acquired HIV infection, however, signs of CNS impairment do not manifest until many years later (Moss et al., 1991). Static encephalopathy, as evidenced by nonprogressive cognitive and/or motor deficits, has been observed in approximately 25% of symptomatic children (Ultmann et al., 1985, 1987).

Behavioral Manifestations

The psychological impact of HIV infection on the child and adolescent is often enormous. Salient effects may be direct, such as HIV-associated CNS manifestations, or indirect, such as psychological reactions to myriad illness-related stressful experiences.

Direct Effects

Direct effects of HIV on the CNS and its cognitive and motor manifestations are well documented in children, adolescents, and adults, as discussed previously. The clinical presentation of CNS disease, however, is somewhat different in the various age groups. For example, encephalopathy tends to occur more frequently and earlier in the disease process in younger, vertically infected children and often results in more severe impairments. It is less common and usually less severe in older children, adolescents, and adults.

Children with progressive HIV encephalopathy often exhibit a variety of behavioral symptoms, personality changes, and psychiatric syndromes (Belman et al., 1985, 1988; Ultmann et al., 1985; Moss et al., 1989). They tend to show significant maladaptive behaviors similar to those observed in autism, such as flattened affect, lack of social responsiveness, muteness, withdrawal, and minimal interest in the outside world. Children with less severe forms of encephalopathy (plateau or static) or mild neuropsychological impairments may display behaviors that resemble symptoms of depression, such as fatigue, lethargy, and lack of interest in participating in some activities. A continuum in the severity of encephalopathy may explain these different degrees of behavioral impairment. Occasionally, older children with progressive encephalopathy may exhibit unusual personality changes during the end stage of their disease, including agitated behavior, mood swings, extreme impulsiveness, verbal outbursts, flights of association, and even hallucinations. The incidence of the extreme behavioral symptoms observed in encephalopathic children, as described above, appears to be less frequent than a few years ago, probably due to earlier and more widespread treatment with antiretroviral agents (Portegies et al., 1989). Even so, their occurrence indicates severe progression of the infection and often predicts end-stage disease.

Indirect Effects

The indirect psychological consequences of HIV infection are qualitatively different for adults and children and, furthermore, vary with the child's age and the types of psychosocial issues that are salient for their respective developmental stages. The behavioral reactions to HIV infection arise from stresses that can be classified into three primary categories based on their source: (1) *medical stressors* are medical procedures and hospitalizations, recurring interfering medical symptoms, loss of abilities, pain, and discomfort; (2) *psychological stressors* are secrecy, fear of ostracism or death; guilt, uncertainties, inhibition of sexual activity (adolescents); and the need to alter future perspectives; and (3) *social stressors* are ostracism by the school, community, and extended family and underachievement due to absenteeism. Some of these stressors are omnipresent, whereas others are transient or modulated by prevailing medical and psychosocial conditions and by the developmental status of the child. Younger children are more sensitive to issues regarding separation and physical injury. They also may lack the cognitive framework for organizing, understanding, and coping with the extreme variation in feelings of well-being and with the invasive, restrictive, and traumatizing effects of medical procedures. The child from 6 to 12 years of age is more likely to be concerned with how the disease affects peer relations and social acceptance. The adolescent is more preoccupied with the consequences of the disease for the development and expression of independence, sexual behavior, and investing in the future. Deficits in physical growth are also common among HIV-infected children (Pizzo et al., 1990) and may lead to a poor self-concept, particularly among school-age children and adolescents.

Hyperactivity and attentional difficulties may represent one indirect behavioral reaction to such stressors. Preliminary studies have shown improvements in general adaptive behavior with AZT therapy, but hyperactivity seemed unaffected by the treatment (Moss et al., in press). Many of the children who exhibit hyperactivity and attentional difficulties in the hospital setting also exhibit learning and behavior problems in school, and some have been held back one or two grades. This is the case even for some children with above-average to superior IQs. It is not yet clear whether hyperactivity and attention deficits are directly associated with HIV infection. The etiology of these symptoms in HIV-infected children is difficult to determine because of the number of plausible alternative explanations for their occurrence, related to both their medical and psychosocial histories. In addition, the base rate of these behavioral disorders is relatively high in the general population for early school-age children.

Despite the many stressors, older children who are relatively symptom free show few outward signs of adjustment difficulties, at least in coping with their illness. There is a tendency to be private and not want to talk about their illness, even with parents. Instead, they seem to prefer and are able to focus effectively on their typical everyday activities. Many of these children seem remarkably resilient, are active, exhibit appropriate positive and negative affect, are outgoing, and engage in the usual social interactions with peers and adults. This is not to say that they may not be preoccupied and privately dealing with aspects of their illness and feel great tension. However, as a group, they seem to have their feelings, personal relations, and everyday activities under control, want to continue with their lives, and are usually able to cope effectively (Bose et al., in press).

Treatment

A number of studies have shown improvements in neuropsychological function and even reversibility of deficits associated with HIV disease after antiretroviral therapy with a number of agents (AZT, ddC, ddI) that block HIV replication by their action on the enzyme reverse transcriptase (see also Chapter 14). Significant neuropsychological improvements have been found with continuous intravenous infusion of AZT in children (Pizzo et al., 1988). The magnitude of these changes could not be explained by practice effects, changes in environment, or general improvement in the physical state of the patient (Pizzo et al., 1989; Brouwers, et al., 1990b). In addition, concurrent improvement in ventricular area and ventricular brain area ratio was demonstrated with quantitative CT brain scan analysis (DeCarli et al., 1991). Less dramatic improvements in neuropsychological function have also been reported with oral AZT on an intermittent schedule in adults (Schmitt et al., 1988) and in children (McKinney et al., 1991), as well as with ddC (Pizzo et al., 1990) and ddI (Wolters et al., 1990, 1991; Butler et al., 1991).

On an individual basis, with each of the antiretroviral treatment modalities (AZT, ddC, ddI), some patients have shown remarkable improvements in neuropsychological functioning, while others have remained stable and some have continued to decline (Pizzo and Wilfert, 1990; Butler et al., 1991). This large degree of variability in neuropsychological response indicates the importance of standardized and valid assessment, as well as the need to search for prognostic factors and possible patient subgroups with differential responses to these agents.

Psychological Assessment of Children with AIDS

Various approaches to the assessment of pediatric HIV patients have recently been described (Brouwers et al., 1990a; Watkins et al., 1991) and will not be a main focus of this chapter. Besides showing cognitive deficits of varying degrees of severity, children with AIDS may exhibit behavioral problems, physical impairments, and medical complications that may require novel approaches or modification of common psychological testing procedures and novel data analysis (Fletcher et al., 1991).

Modifications or Changes in Testing Procedures

LEVEL OF DEVELOPMENT.   A number of pediatric AIDS patients present with encephalopathy and function at a developmental level significantly below their chronological age. These children are frequently unable to respond to many of the items on age-appropriate tests. Therefore, tests more suited to their developmental level rather than their age level need to be administered. Under such circumstances, normative tables cannot be used for determining standard scores, so developmental levels should be based on extrapolation estimates (e.g., ratio rather than deviation IQs).

IMPAIRMENTS.   Some children may have impairments (motor problems; sensory deficits in the auditory, tactile, or visual modality; muteness or diminished expressive language) that limit their ability to respond to items on tests. For these children, specific instruments designed to assess cognitive functioning without relying on verbal, motor, or visual responses should be utilized. The use of these special tests will help to ensure that the child's physical problems do not interfere with the evaluation of his or her mental abilities. Other children may be bilingual or not experienced in the English language at all. In the assessment of such children, the examiner must have the knowledge and skill to select and administer the most appropriate test to meet the needs of each patient.

UNUSUAL BEHAVIOR FACTORS AND HIGH OR LOW ENERGY LEVELS.   Many HIV-infected children exhibit unmodulated activity levels, short attention spans, and uncooperative and resistant behaviors that may make the evaluation process difficult. It is imperative that the examiner have skills in behavior management techniques and experience in testing behaviorally difficult children. Pediatric AIDS patients are sometimes easily fatigued, become irritable and/or inattentive, and may require short breaks or several testing sessions to complete their assessment. Some children are frightened of the hospital setting and may need initial play time with the examiner before testing begins. Moreover, as more children are becoming infected prenatally with HIV, resulting in AIDS at earlier ages, the importance and need for highly qualified examiners with the necessary skills to evaluate such young children and infants become even greater. This requires not only full knowledge of a variety of scales to best measure areas of behavioral, social, affective, and cognitive functioning, but also clinical skills in managing behaviorally difficult children.

Novel Procedures in the Assessment of Children with AIDS

There is a solid armamentarium of psychometric instruments for measuring cognitive, motor, and language functioning in this population. However, appropriate and systematic procedures for measuring social, emotional, and personality changes that are often profound in symptomatic pediatric HIV patients are lacking.

Two new methods have been developed at the Pediatric Branch of the National Cancer Institute (NCI) to characterize systematically those behavioral and affective changes that appear to be a direct effect of HIV on the CNS. One procedure consists of a Q-sort behavioral rating methodology. The other consists of collecting and rating standard behavior samples from videotaped semistructured age-appropriate interaction situations between the examiner and the child. The two procedures are summarized below.

NCI CHILD Q-SORT RATINGS.   Some children with HIV-associated encephalopathy may exhibit extreme and deviant emotional, social, and behavioral patterns. These behaviors tend to resemble symptoms that characterize certain childhood psychiatric disorders (e.g., childhood autisms, attention deficit disorder with or without hyperactivity, and childhood depression). Symptoms that are observed include vacant staring, flattened affect, lethargy, lack of social interest, poor attention and concentration, decreased motor activity, or excitable, impulsive behavior. More subtle expressions or milder forms of these symptoms have also been observed. In some instances, the behaviors may gradually progress or be transformed abruptly into more aberrant behavior.

A rating system was thus developed to evaluate these behavioral, emotional, and interpersonal characteristics of children with HIV infection. Symptoms were selected from DSM-III classifications (Wicks-Nelson and Israel, 1984; APA, 1987) of the above-listed disorders that were behaviorally relevant for this patient population and that were likely to occur in the settings where we would be observing the children. Additional items reflecting appropriate adaptive behavior were also included so that raters had the latitude to classify patients as normal when appropriate. A Q-sort rating procedure (Block, 1971) was developed, using a total of 49 items devised from these descriptions. The Q-sort format, a forced-choice approach, was selected because it minimizes rater response bias and allows for reliable within- as well as between-subject comparisons of these behaviors. The derived scores can reflect normal adaptive behavior or mild to severe maladaptive behavior patterns.

In a preliminary study (Moss et al., 1989), staff members and parents rated 29 pediatric AIDS patients (approximate mean age of 5 years, 6 months) at baseline and again after 6 months of AZT treatment. Item analysis and factor analysis resulted in five robust scales: (1) autism, (2) depression, (3) hyperactivity and attentional problems, (4) irritability, (5) adaptive behavior. Patients who were classified as encephalopathic on independent criteria had significantly higher ratings than the nonencephalopathic patients on the autism and depression factors prior to treatment. These elevated scores dropped significantly after 6 months of AZT therapy, at which point these patients no longer differed from the nonencephalopathic patients. The two patient groups did not differ significantly on the irritability or hyperactivity factors either before or after treatment (Figure 16–4). The parental ratings yielded findings parallel to those of the staff but to a less pronounced degree.

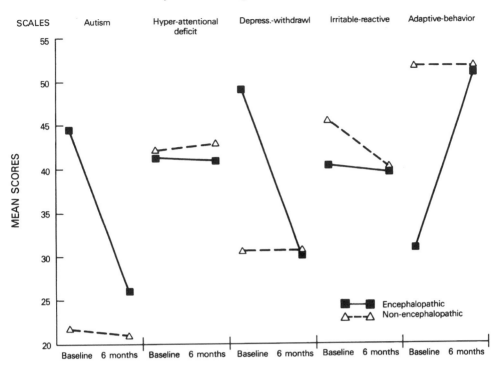

FIGURE 16–4. The social and emotional behavior of children with symptomatic HIV infection was assessed with a Q-sort procedure. Significant change from baseline was seen for the encephalopathic patients after 6 months of AZT treatment on the Autism and the Depression-Withdrawal scales, and a reciprocal improvement on the adaptive behavior scale. No differences in baseline ratings or in therapy-related change was seen between encephalopathic and non-encephalopathic patients on the Hyperactivity-Attentional deficit and Irritable-Reactive scales. (From Moss et al., 1989.)

THE VIDEOTAPE PROCEDURE.   The videotape procedure was developed for the same reasons as the Q-sort technique: to create a methodology that is sensitive and relevant to aberrant behavioral patterns observed among pediatric patients with symptomatic HIV disease and that can be used to quantify objectively aspects of these behaviors.

The videotape procedure consists of 20- to 30-minute sessions in which the child is engaged by an examiner in a series of structured tasks developed to elicit specific classes of behavior. The children are videotaped and evaluated before and after 6 months of antiretroviral therapy. Different tasks are used according to the child's age and level of functioning (Moss and Wolters, 1988). The following five domains are evaluated: (1) goal-directed behavior, (2) interpersonal-social behavior, (3) affective behavior, (4) sensorimotor behavior, and (5) communication skills.

A series of 15 variables are used to rate behaviors on a 7-point scale pertaining to each of these five domains. Examples of the variables to be rated are (1) persistence, (2) impulsivity, (3) positive social behavior, (4) speech and language, and (5) motor skills.

The videotaped procedure offers a number of scientific and practical benefits:

1. *Standardization of observational data:* A standard set of events and stimuli are used to obtain comparable behavioral samples across children and at different stages of treatment.

2. *Objectivity of evaluation:* The use of videotapes makes it possible for behaviors to be evaluated objectively by individuals who are unfamiliar and thus "blind" regarding the children and their health and treatment status.

3. *Reliability of evaluations:* Two or more individuals can rate the videotapes independently in order to establish interrater reliability.

4. *The creation of a permanent record:* The videotapes provide a reservoir of behavioral data that can be restudied and reanalyzed as new hypotheses emerge.

5. *Communication:* The impact of encephalopathy can be so pervasive and complex that efforts to describe verbally or classify systematically discrete elements do not communicate the global and profound changes that take place. Viewing the tapes or edited versions thereof can be useful for education and communication purposes.

Summary and Conclusion

Future of HIV-1 Infection in Children

Existing data indicate that the incidence of HIV-1 infection in children will continue to rise. Advances in the development of therapy will proceed along a number of different avenues. New anti-HIV (antiretroviral) agents, either alone or in combination with other drugs, will help to slow down the rate of progression of the disease. In addition, new prophylactic interventions will reduce the incidence and severity of infections. The combination of these treatment approaches will lead to longer survival. For these long-term survivors, a number of issues need to be addressed.

First, it is not clear whether the CNS may become a sanctuary for HIV-1, either because of virus-related factors (i.e., HIV may be dormant and undetected in cells within the CNS, different from the rest of the body) or because therapeutic agents may not cross the blood-brain barrier in sufficient amounts to stop viral growth and replication completely in the CNS. Neuropsychologically, this could result in a greater incidence of HIV-related CNS manifestations.

Second, the psychological problems experienced by these children may become exacerbated since they will live for prolonged periods with the stressors that were previously described. The continuous and extended effect of HIV-related stress on personality development in children is still unclear (Post et al., 1988).

Third, the increasing number of vertically infected long-term survivors may change the mean age of the pediatric HIV population so that a larger segment of it will consist of school-age and adolescent children. This will put new and increased demands on a number of social and educational systems, in addition to those associated with the currently younger population. School and educational resources will be taxed since a majority of these children may require special educational attention due to common HIV-related neuropsychological impairments. Social service departments may also see an increase in their case loads, as a larger proportion of these children may lose one or both parents to the disease. In general, the clinical approach to these children should be multidisciplinary, including professionals from the medical (pediatrics, neurology, infectious diseases, psychiatry), behavioral, educational, and rehabilitative fields.

Future Research

As stated earlier, little is known about the underlying pathogenesis and natural history of the neuropsychological impairments associated with HIV and their behavioral consequences. Research activities could emphasize the discovery of prognostic factors and the identification of possible subgroups. One such subgroup that demands further study includes children with vertically acquired HIV who are of school age and/or older and are still largely asymptomatic. Factors contributing to their medical and behavioral resilience may allow further insights into the progression of and resistance to the disease and provide guidelines for possible future interventions.

A second area of continued research is the possible direct and indirect effects of antiretroviral treatment on CNS function, particularly in pediatric AIDS. It is not yet clear how antiretroviral agents work within the CNS to produce improvements in neuropsychological function. It is therefore important to determine the extent to which improvements in neuropsychological function reflect the anti-HIV activity of a compound within the CNS or the action of the agent on other organ systems that may indirectly effect cognitive function. In addition, studies of the direct effects of antiretroviral agents on neurotoxins (such as QUIN and TNFα) that are associated with HIV-related encephalopathy are needed.

Another area of treatment research is the investigation of CNS-specific issues such as drug penetration and protection of the CNS against the negative effects of infection. Finally, further data and analysis are needed to determine whether neuropsychological function, particularly change therein, is an appropriate predictor of the further natural history and survival of the patient. The firm ascertainment of such a relation would clearly establish neuropsychological function as a surrogate marker for drug effectiveness.

Neuropsychological abnormalities are more frequent in pediatric HIV patients than in adults and are likely to have more long-term effects on functioning. Therefore, by studying these children, an opportunity exists not only to better understand how HIV disease compromises the CNS, but also to improve significantly the quality of life of all HIV patients by applying what is learned from these investigations to pharmaceutical and behavioral interventions.

Acknowledgments

We wish to thank Dr. Philip Pizzo and the members of the HIV Team, Pediatric Branch, NCI as well as the children for their support. Debra El-Amin and Renee Smith provided assistance with the neurobehavioral assessments and Gene Tassone with computer problems and analysis.

References

American Psychiatric Association. (1987). *Diagnostic and Statistical Manual of Mental Disorders* (3rd ed.-revised). Washington, D.C.: American Psychiatric Association Press.

Andiman, W., Simpson, B., Olson, B., Dember, L., Silva, T., and Miller, G. (1990). Rate of transmission of human immunodeficiency virus type 1 infection from mother to child and short-term outcome of neonatal infection. *American Journal of Diseases of Children, 144*, 758–766.

Auger, I., Thomas, P., De Gruttola, V., Morse, D., Moore, D., Williams, R., Truman, B., and Lawrence, C.E. (1988). Incubation periods for paediatric AIDS patients. *Nature, 336*, 575–577.

Barnes, D.M. (1986). Brain function decline in children with AIDS. *Science, 232*, 1196.

Belman, A.L. (1990). AIDS and pediatric neurology. *Neurology Clinics, 8*, 571–603.

Belman, A.L., Diamond, G., Dickson, D., Horoupian, D., Liena, J., Lantos, G., and Rubinstein, A. (1988). Pediatric acquired immunodeficiency syndrome. *American Journal of Diseases of Children, 142*, 29–35.

Belman, A., Diamond, G., Park, Y., Nozyce, M., Douglas, C., Cabot, T., Bernstein, L., and Rubinstein, A. (1989). Perinatal HIV infection: A prospective longitudinal study of the initial CNS signs. *Neurology, 39*(Suppl. 1), 278–279 (abst.).

Belman, A.L., Lantos, G., Horoupian, D., Novick, B.E., Ultmann, M.H., Dickson, D.W., and Rubinstein, A. (1986). AIDS: Calcification of the basal ganglia in infants and children. *Neurology, 36*, 1192–1199.

Belman, A.L., Ultmann, M.H., Horoupian, D., Novick, B., Spiro, A.J., Rubinstein, A., Kurtzberg, D., and Cone-Wesson, B. (1985). Neurological complications in infants and children with acquired immune deficiency syndrome. *Annals of Neurology, 18*, 560–566.

Blanche, S., Rouzioux, C., Moscato, M.L., Veber, F., Mayaux, M.J., Jacomet, C., Tricoire, J., Deville, A., Vial, M., Firtion, G., De Crepy, A., Douard, D., Robin, M., Courpotin, C., Ciraru-Vigneron, N., Le Deist, F., and Griscelli, C. (1989). A prospective study of infants born to women seropositive for human immunodeficiency virus type 1: HIV Infection in Newborns French Collaborative Study Group. *New England Journal of Medicine, 320*, 1643–1648.

Blanche, S., Tardieu, M., Duliege, A., Rouzioux, C., Le Deist, F., Fukunaga, K., Caniglia, M., Jacomet, C., Messiah, A., and Griscelli, C. (1990). Longitudinal study of 94 symptomatic infants with perinatally acquired human immunodeficiency virus infection. *American Journal of Diseases of Children, 144*, 1210–1215.

Block, J. (1971). *Lives Through Time*. Berkeley, Calif.: Bancroft Books.

Brew, B., Bhalla, R., Fleisher, M., Paul, M., Khan, A., Schwartz, M.K., and Price, R.W. (1989). Cerebrospinal fluid beta-2-microglobulin in patients infected with human immunodeficiency virus. *Neurology, 39*, 830–834.

Brew, B., Bhalla, R., Paul, M., Gallardo, H., McArthur, J., Schwarta, M., and Price, R. (1990). Cerebrospinal fluid neopterin in human immunodeficiency virus type-1 infection. *Annals of Neurology, 28*, 556–560.

Brouwers, P., Belman, A.L., and Epstein, L.G. (1990a). Central nervous system involvement: Manifestations and evaluation. In P.A. Pizzo and K.M. Wilfert, eds., *Pediatric AIDS: The Challenge of HIV Infection in Infants, Children, and Adolescents*. Baltimore: Williams and Wilkins, pp. 318–335.

Brouwers, P., Moss, H., Wolters, P., Eddy, J., Balis, F., Poplack, D., and Pizzo, P. (1990b). Effect of continuous-infusion zidovudine therapy on neuropsychologic functioning in children with symptomatic human immunodeficiency virus infection. *Journal of Pediatrics, 117*, 980–985.

Brouwers, P., Moss, H., Wolters, P., Eddy, J., and Pizzo, P. (1989). Neuropsychological profile of children with symptomatic HIV infection prior to antiretroviral therapy. *Proceedings from the V International Conference on AIDS, 1*, 316 (abst.).

Brouwers, P., Moss, H., Wolters, P., el-Amin, D., Tassone, E., and Pizzo, P. (1992). Neurobehavioral typology of school-age children with symptomatic HIV disease. *Journal of Clinical and Experimental Neuropsychology, 14*, 113 (abst.).

Brouwers, P., Heyes, M., Moss, H., Wolters, P., Poplack, D., Markey, S., and Pizzo, P. (1993). Quinolinic acid in the cerebrospinal fluid of children with symptomatic HIV-1 disease: relationships to clinical status and therapeutic response. *The Journal of Infectious Diseases, 168*, 1380–1386.

Bose, S., Moss, H., Brouwers, P., Lorion, R., and Pizzo, P. (in press). Psychological adjustment of HIV-infected school age children. *Journal of Developmental and Behavioral Pediatrics*.

Butler, K.M., Husson, R.N., Balis, F.M., Brouwers, P., Eddy, J., el-Amin, D., Gress, J., Hawkins, M., Jarosinski, P., Moss, H., Poplack, D., Santacroce, S., Venzon, D., Wiener, L., Wolters, P., and Pizzo, P.A. (1991). Dideoxyinosine (ddI) in symptomatic HIV-infected children: A phase I–II study. *New England Journal of Medicine, 324*, 137–144.

Capron, C., and Duyme, M. (1989). Assessment of effects of socio-economic status on IQ in a full cross-fostering study. *Nature, 340*, 552–554.

Centers for Disease Control. (1989). First 100,000 cases of acquired immunodeficiency syndrome—United States. *Morbidity and Mortality Weekly Report, 38*, 561–563.

Centers for Disease Control and Prevention (1993). *HIV/AIDS Surveillance Report, 5*, 1–19.

Chasnoff, I., Griffith, D., MacGregor, S., Dirkes, K., and Burns, K. (1989). Temporal patterns of cocaine use during pregnancy. *Journal of the American Medical Association, 261*, 1741–1744.

Cohen, S., Mundy, T., Karrassik, B., Lieb, L., Ludwig, D., and Ward, J. (1991). Neuropsychological functioning in human immunodeficiency virus type 1 seropositive children infected through neonatal blood transfusion. *Pediatrics, 88*, 58–68.

Curran, J., Jaffe, H., Hardy, A., Morgan, W., Selik, R., and Dondero, T. (1988). Epidemiology of HIV infection and AIDS in the United States. *Science, 239*, 610–616.

Day, N., Jasperse, D., Richardson, G., Robles, N., Sambamoorthi, U., Taylor, P., Scher, M., Stoffer, D., and Cornelius, M. (1989). Prenatal exposure to alcohol: Effect on infant growth and morphologic characteristics. *Pediatrics, 84*, 536–541.

DeCarli, C., Civitello, L.A., Brouwers, P., and Pizzo, P.A. (1993). The prevalence of Computed Axial Tomographic abnormalities of the cerebrum in 100 consecutive children symptomatic with the HIV. *Annals of Neurology, 34*, 198–205.

DeCarli, C., Fugate, L., Falloon, J., Eddy, J., Katz, D.A., Friedland, R.P., Rapoport, S.I., Brouwers, P., and Pizzo, P.A. (1991). Brain growth and cognitive improvement in children with human immune deficiency virus–induced encephalopathy after six months of continuous infusion azidothymidine therapy. *Journal of Acquired Immune Deficiency Syndromes, 4*, 585–592.

DePaula, M., Queiroz, W., Llan, Y., Rodreguez Taveras, C., Janini, M., and Soraggi, N. (1991). Pediatric AIDS: Differentials in survival. *Proceedings of the VII International Conference on AIDS, 2*, 190 (abst.).

Diamond, G.W., Kaufman, J., Belman, A.L., Cohen, L., Cohen, H.J., and Rubinstein, A. (1987). Characterization of cognitive functioning in a subgroup of children with congenital HIV infection. *Archives of Clinical Neuropsychology, 2*, 245–256.

Dickson, D.W., Belman, A.L., Park, Y.D., Wiley, C., Horoupian, D.S., Llena, J., Kure, K., Lyman, W.D., Morecki, R., and Mitsudo, S. (1989). Central nervous system pathology in pediatric AIDS: An autopsy study. *Acta Pathologica, Microbiologica, et Immunologica Scandinavica (Suppl), 8,* 40–57.

Epstein, L.G., Sharer, L.R., and Goudsmit, J. (1988). Neurological and neuropathological features of human immunodeficiency virus infection in children. *Annals of Neurology, 23*(Suppl.), S19–S23.

Epstein, L.G., Goudsmit, J., Paul, D.S., Morrison, S.H., Connor, E.M., Oleske, J.M., and Holland, B. (1987). Expression of human immunodeficiency virus in cerebrospinal fluid of children with progressive encephalopathy. *Annals of Neurology, 21,* 397–401.

Epstein, L.G., Sharer, L.R., Joshi, V.V., Fojas, M.M., Koenigsberger, M.R., and Oleske, J.M. (1985). Progressive encephalopathy in children with acquired immune deficiency syndrome. *Annals of Neurology, 17,* 488–496.

Epstein, L.G., Sharer, L.R., Oleske, J.M., Connor, E.M., Goudsmit, J., Bagdon, L., Robert-Guroff, M., and Koenigsberger, M.R. (1986). Neurologic manifestations of human immunodeficiency virus infection in children. *Pediatrics, 78,* 678–687.

European Collaborative Study. (1988). Mother-to-child transmission of HIV infection. *Lancet, 2,* 1039–1042.

European Collaborative Study. (1991). Children born to women with HIV-1 infection: Natural history and risk of transmission. *Lancet, 337,* 253–260.

Falloon, J., Eddy, J., Wiener, L., and Pizzo, P.A. (1989). Human immunodeficiency virus infection in children. *Journal of Pediatrics, 114,* 1–30.

Fletcher, J., Francis, D., Pequegnat, W., Raudenbush, S., Bornstein, M., Schmitt, F., Brouwers, P., and Stover, E. (1991). Neurobehavioral outcomes in diseases of childhood: Individual change models for pediatric human immunodeficiency viruses. *American Psychologist, 46,* 1267–1277.

Frank, Y., Lim, W., and Kahn, E. (1989). Multiple ischemic infarcts in children with AIDS, varicella zoster infection and cerebral vasculitis. *Pediatric Neurology, 5,* 64–67.

Friedland, G., and Klein, R. (1987). Transmission of the human immunodeficiency virus. *New England Journal of Medicine, 317,* 1125–1135.

Fulroth, R., Phillips, B., and Durand, D. (1989). Perinatal outcome of infants exposed to cocaine and/or heroin in utero. *American Journal of Diseases in Children, 143,* 905–910.

Goedert, J., Mendez, H., Drummond, J., Robert-Guroff, M., Minkoff, H., Holman, S., Stevens, R., and Rubinstein, A. (1989). Mother to infant transmission of human immunodeficiency virus type 1: Association with prematurity or low anti-gp 120. *Lancet, 2,* 1351–1354.

Grant, I., Atkinson, J.H., Hesselink, J.R., Kennedy, C.J., Richman, D.D., Spector, S.A., and McCutchan, J.A. (1987). Evidence for early central nervous system involvement in the acquired immunodeficiency syndrome (AIDS) and other human immunodeficiency virus infections. *Annals of Internal Medicine, 107,* 828–836.

Grant, I., and Heaton, R. (1990). Human immunodeficiency virus-type 1 (HIV-1) and the brain. *Journal of Consulting and Clinical Psychology, 58,* 22–30.

Grimaldi, L., Martino, G., Franciotta, D.R.B., Castagna, A., Pristerla, R., and Lazzarin, A. (1991). Elevated alpha-tumor necrosis factor levels in spinal fluid from HIV-1 infected patients with central nervous system involvement. *Annals of Neurology, 29,* 21–25.

Gwinn, M., Pappaioanou, M., George J., Hannon, W., Wasser, S., Redus, M., Hoff, R., Grady, G., Willoughby, A., Novello, A., Petersen, L., Dondero, T., and Curran, J. (1991). Prevalence of HIV infection in childbearing women in the United States. *Journal of the American Medical Association, 265,* 1074–1078.

Heyes, M., Brew, B., Martin, A., Price, R., Salazar, A., Sidtis, J., Yergey, J., Mouradian, M., Sadler, A., Keilp, J., Rubinow, D., and Markey, S. (1991). Quinolinic acid in cerebrospinal fluid and serum in HIV-1 infection: Relationship to clinical and neurological status. *Annals of Neurology, 29*, 202–209.

Heyes, M., Rubinow, D., Lane, C., and Markey, S. (1989). Cerebrospinal fluid quinolinic acid concentrations in acquired immune deficiency syndrome. *Annals of Neurology, 26*, 275–277.

Hittleman, J., Willoughby, A., Mendez, H., Nelson, N., Gong, J., Holman, S., Muez, L., Goedert, J., and Landesman, S. (1990). Neurodevelopmental outcome of perinatally-acquired HIV infection on the first 15 months of life. *Proceedings from the VI International Conference on AIDS, 3*, 130 (abst.).

Hittleman, J., Willoughby, A., Mendez, H., Nelson, N., Gong, J., Mendez, H., Holman, S., Muez, L., Goedert, J., and Landesman, S. (1991). Neurodevelopmental outcome of perinatally-acquired HIV infection on the first 24 months of life. *Proceedings from the VII International Conference on AIDS, 1*, 65 (abst.).

Ho, D., Pommerantz, R., and Kaplan, J. (1987). Pathogenesis of infection with human immunodeficiency virus. *New England Journal of Medicine, 317*, 278–286.

Ho, D.D., Rota, T.R., Schooley, R.T., Kaplan, J.C., Allan, J.D., Groopman, J.E., Resnick, L., Felsenstein, D., Andrews, C.A., and Hirsch, M.S. (1985). Isolation of HTLV-III from cerebrospinal fluid and neural tissues of patients with neurologic syndromes related to the acquired immunodeficiency syndrome. *New England Journal of Medicine, 313*, 1493–1497.

Iosub, S., Fuchs, M., Bingol, N., and Gromisch, D. (1981). Fetal alcohol syndrome revisited. *Pediatrics, 68*, 475–479.

Italian Multicentre Study. (1988). Epidemiology, clinical features, and prognostic factors of paediatric HIV infection. *Lancet, 2*, 1043–1045.

Koenig, S., Gendelman, H.E., Orenstein, J., Dal Canto, M.C., Pezeshkpour, G.H., Yungbluth, M., Janotta, F., Aksamit, A., Martin, M.A., and Fauci, A.S. (1986). Detection of AIDS virus in macrophages in brain tissue from AIDS patients with encephalopathy. *Science, 233*, 1089–1093.

Levy, J.A., Hollander, H., Shimabukuro, J., Mills, J., and Kaminsky, L. (1985). Isolation of AIDS-associated retroviruses from cerebrospinal fluid and brain of patients with neurological symptoms. *Lancet, 2*, 586–588.

MacGregor, S., Keith, L., Chasnoff, I., Rosner, M., Chisum, G., Shaw, P., and Minoque, J. (1987). Cocaine use during pregnancy: Adverse perinatal outcome. *American Journal of Obstetrics and Gynecology, 157*, 686–690.

McCardle, P., Nannis, E., Smith, R., and Fischer, G. (1991). Patterns of perinatal HIV-related language deficit. *Proceedings from the VII International Conference on AIDS, 2*, 187 (abst.).

McKinney, R.E., Jr., Maha, M.A., Connor, E.M., Feinberg, J., Scott, G.B., Wulfsohn, M., McIntosh, K., Borkowsky, W., Modlin, J.F., Weintrub, P., O'Donnell, K., Gelber, R.D., Rogers, G.K., Lehrman, S.N., and Wilfert, C.M. (1991). A multicenter trial of oral zidovudine in children with advanced human immunodeficiency virus disease. *New England Journal of Medicine, 324*, 1018–1025.

Medley, A., Anderson, R., Cox, D., and Billard, L. (1987). Incubation period of AIDS in patients infected via blood transfusion. *Nature, 328*, 719–721.

Michaels, J., Sharer, L., and Epstein, L. (1988). Human immunodeficiency virus type 1 (HIV-1) infection of the nervous system: A review. *Immunodeficiency Reviews, 1*, 71–104.

Mintz, M. (1989). Elevated serum levels of tumor necrosis factor are associated with progressive encephalopathy in children with acquired immunodeficiency syndrome. *American Journal of Diseases of Children, 143*, 771–774.

Mok, J., Rossi, A., Ades, A., Giaquinto, C., Grosch-Worner, I., and Peckman C. (1987). Infants born to mothers seropositive for human immunodeficiency virus. *Lancet 1*, 1164–1168.

Moss, H., Brouwers, P., Wolters, P., el-Amin, D., Butler, K., and Pizzo, P. (1991). Gender differences in neuropsychological vulnerability of children with vertically-acquired HIV infection. *Proceedings of the VII International Conference on AIDS, 1*, 185 (abst.).

Moss, H.A., Brouwers, P., Wolters, P.L., Wiener, L., Hersh, S.P., and Pizzo, P.A. (in press). The development of a Q sort behavior rating procedure for pediatric HIV patients. *Journal of Pediatric Psychology.*

Moss, H., and Wolters, P. (1988). *The NIH Pediatric Behavioral Videotape Procedures.* Unpublished manuscript.

Moss, H., Wolters, P., Eddy, J., Weiner, L., and Pizzo, P. (1989). The effects of encephalopathy on the social and emotional behavior of pediatric AIDS patients. *Proceedings of the V International Conference on AIDS, 1*, 328 (abst.).

Naeye, R., Blanc, W., Leblanc, W., and Khatamee, M. (1973). Fetal complications of maternal heroin addiction: Abnormal growth, infections, and episodes of stress. *Journal of Pediatrics, 83*, 1055–1061.

Navia, B., Jordan, B., and Price, R. (1986). The AIDS dementia complex: I. Clinical features. *Annals of Neurology, 19*, 517–524.

Nozyce, M., Diamond, G., Belman, A., Cabot, T., Douglas, C., Hopkins, K., Cohen, H., Rubinstein, A., and Willoughby, A. (1989). Neurodevelopmental impairments during infancy in offspring of IVDA and HIV seropositive mothers. *Pediatric Research, 25*, 359A.

Ollo, C., Johnson, R., and Grafman, J. (1990). Signs of cognitive change in HIV disease: An event-related brain potential study. *Neurology, 41*, 209–215.

Oxtoby, M. (1990). Epidemiology of pediatric AIDS in the United States. In P. Kozlowski, D. Wnider, P. Vietze, and H. Wisniewski, eds. *Brain in Pediatric AIDS.* Basel: Karger, pp. 1–8.

Pang, S., Koyanagi, Y., Miles, S., Wiley, C., Vinters, H., and Chen, I. (1990). High levels of unintegrated HIV-1 DNA in brain tissue of AIDS dementia patients. *Nature, 343*, 85–89.

Park, Y., Belman, A., Dickson, D., Llena, J., Josephina, F., Lantos, G., Diamond, G., Bernstein, L., and Rubinstein, A. (1988). Stroke in pediatric AIDS. *Annals of Neurology, 24*, 279 (abst.).

Pizzo, P., Brouwers, P., and Poplack, D. (1989). Intravenous infusion of zidovudine (AZT) in children with HIV infection. *New England Journal of Medicine, 320*, 805–806.

Pizzo, P., Butler, K., Balis, F., Brouwers, E., Hawkins, M., Eddy, J., Einloth, M., Falloon, J., Husson, R., Jarosinski, P., Meer, J., Moss, H., Poplack, D., Santacroce, S., Wiener, L., and Wolters, P. (1990). Dideoxycytidine alone and in an alternating schedule with zidovudine in children with symptomatic human immunodeficiency virus infection. *Journal of Pediatrics, 117*, 799–808.

Pizzo, P., Eddy, J., Falloon, J., Balis, F., Murphy, R., Moss, H., Wolters, P., Brouwers, P., Jarosinski, P., Rubin, M., Broder, S., Yarchoan, R., Brunetti, A., Maha, M., Nusinoff-Lehrman, S., and Poplack D. (1988). Effect of continuous intravenous infusion of zidovudine (AZT) in children with symptomatic HIV infection. *New England Journal of Medicine, 319*, 889–896.

Pizzo, P., and Wilfert, C. (1990). Treatment considerations for children with HIV infection. In P. Pizzo and C. Wilfert, eds., *Pediatric AIDS: The Challenge of HIV Infection in Infants, Children, and Adolescents.* Baltimore: Williams and Wilkins, pp. 478–494.

Poplack, D., and Brouwers, P. (1985). Adverse sequelae of central nervous system therapy. *Clinics of Oncology, 4,* 263–285.

Portegies, P., DeGans, J., Lange, J.M., Derix, M.M., Speelman, H., Bakker, M., Danner, S.A., and Goudsmit, J. (1989). Declining incidence of AIDS dementia complex after introduction of zidovidine treatment. *British Medical Journal, 299,* 819–821.

Post, R., Weiss, S., and Pert, A. (1988). Implications of behavioral sensitization and kindling for stress-induced behavioral change. In G. Chrousos, D. Loriaux, and P. Gold, eds., *Mechanisms of Physical and Emotional Stress.* New York: Plenum Press, pp. 441–463.

Price, R., Brew, B., Siditis, J., Rosenblum, M., Scheck, A., and Cleary, P. (1988). The brain in AIDS: Central nervous system HIV-1 infection and AIDS dementia complex. *Science, 239,* 586–592.

Rogers, M. (1989). Modes, rates, and risk factors for perinatal transmission of HIV. *Proceedings of the V International Conference on AIDS, 1,* 199 (Abstract #T.B.O. 19).

Rogers, M.F., Thomas, P.A., Starcher, E.T., Noa, M.C., Bush, T.J., and Jaffe, H.W. (1987). Acquired immunodeficiency syndrome in children: Report of the Center for Disease Control National Surveillance, 1982 to 1985. *Pediatrics, 79,* 1008–1014.

Rubinstein, A., and Bernstein, L. (1986). The epidemiology of pediatric acquired immunodeficiency syndrome. *Clinical Immunology and Immunopathology, 40,* 115–121.

Ryder, R.W., Wato, N., Hassig, S.E., Behets, F., Rayfield, M., Eklungola, B., Nelson, A.M., Mulenda, U., Francis, H., Mwandabalirwa, K., Davachi, F., Rogers, M., Nzilambi, N., Greenberg, A., Mann, J., Quinn, T.C., Piot, P., and Curran, J.W. (1989). Perinatal transmission of the human immunodeficiency virus type 1 to infants of seropositive women in Zaire. *New England Journal of Medicine, 320,* 1639–1642.

Schmitt, F., Bigley, J., McKinnis, R., Logue, P., Evans, R., Drucker, J., and the AZT Collaboration Group. (1988). Neuropsychological outcome of zidovudine (AZT) treatment of patients with AIDS and AIDS-related complex. *New England Journal of Medicine, 319,* 1573–1578.

Schwarc, R., Whetsell, W., and Mangano, R. (1983). Quinolinic acid: An endogenous metabolite can produce axon sparing lesions in rat brain. *Science, 219,* 316–318.

Scott, G.B., Fischl, M., Klimas, N., Fletcher, M., Dickinson, G., and Parks, W. (1985). Mothers of infants with acquired immunodeficiency syndrome: Outcome of subsequent pregnancies. *Proceedings of the International Conference on AIDS, 1,* 21 (abst.).

Scott, G.B., Hutto, C., Makuch, R.W., Mastrucci, M.T., O'Connor, T., Mitchell, C.D., Trapido, E.J., and Parks, W.P. (1989). Survival in children with perinatally acquired human immunodeficiency virus type 1 infection. *New England Journal of Medicine, 321,* 1791–1796.

Sharer, L., Cho, E.S., and Epstein, L.G. (1985). Multinucleated giant cells and HTLV-111 in AIDS encephalopathy. *Human Pathology, 16,* 760.

Sharer, L.R., Dowling, P., Michaels, J., Cook, S., Menonna, J., Blumberg, B., and Epstein, L. (1990). Spinal cord disease in children with HIV-1 infection: A combined biological and neuropathological study. *Neuropathology of Applied Neurobiology, 16,* 317–331.

Sharer, L.R., Epstein, L.G., Cho, E., Joshi, V.V., Meyenhofer, M.F., Rankin, L.F., and Petito, C.K. (1986). Pathologic features of AIDS encephalopathy in children: Evidence for LAV/HTLV-III infection of brain. *Human Pathology, 17,* 271–284.

Sprecher, S., Soumenkoff, G., Puissant, F., and Degueldre, M. (1986). Vertical transmission of HIV in 15-week fetus [letter]. *Lancet, 2,* 288–289.

Spreen, O., Tupper, D., Risser, A., Tuokko, H., and Edgell, D. (1984). *Human Developmental Neuropsychology.* New York: Oxford University Press.

Stern, Y., Marder, K., Bell, K., Chen, J., Dooneief, G., Goldstein, S., Mindry, D., Richards,

M., Sano, M., Williams, J., Gorman, J., Ehrhardt, A., and Mayeux, R. (1990). Multidisciplinary baseline assessment of homosexual men with and without human immunodeficiency virus infection. *Archives of General Psychiatry, 48,* 131–138.

Surtees, R., Hyland, K., and Smith, I. (1990). Central nervous system methyl-group metabolism in children with neurologic complications of HIV infection. *Lancet, 335,* 619–621.

Tardieu, M. (1991). Brain imaging in pediatric HIV infection. In A. Belman and A.M. Laverda, chairs, *Pediatric HIV-1 Infection: Neurological and Neuropsychological Aspects.* Symposium conducted at the meeting of the Neuroscience of HIV Infection: Basic and Clinical Frontiers, Padova, Italy, June.

Tardieu, M., Blanche, S., Duliege, A., Rouzioux, C., and Griscelli, C. (1989). Neurologic involvement and prognostic factors after materno-fetal infection. *Proceedings of the V International Conference on AIDS, 1,* 194 (abst.).

Terplan, J. (1973). Patterns of brain damage in infants and children with congenital heart disease: Association with catherization and surgical procedures. *American Journal of Diseases of Children, 125,* 175–185.

Ultmann, M.H., Belman, A.L., Ruff, H.A., Novick, B.E., Cone-Wesson, B., Cohen, J.J., and Rubinstein, A. (1985). Developmental abnormalities in infants and children with acquired immune deficiency syndrome (AIDS) and AIDS-related complex. *Developmental Medicine and Child Neurology, 27,* 563–571.

Ultmann, M.H., Diamond, G.W., Ruff, H.A., Belman, A.L., Novick, B.E., Rubinstein, A., and Cohen, H.J. (1987). Developmental abnormalities in children with acquired immunodeficiency syndrome (AIDS): A follow up study. *International Journal of Neuroscience, 32,* 661–667.

Watkins, J.M., Brouwers, P., and Huntzinger, R. (1992). Neuropsychological assessment. In M.L. Stuber, ed., *Children and AIDS.* Washington, D.C.: American Psychiatric Press, pp. 119–146.

Wicks-Nelson, R., and Israel, A. (1984). *Behavioral Disorders of Childhood.* Englewood Cliffs, N.J.: Prentice-Hall.

Wiley, C., Schrier, R., Nelson, J., Lampert, P., and Oldstone, M. (1986). Cellular localization of human immunodeficiency virus infection within the brains of acquired immunodeficiency syndrome patients. *Proceedings of the National Academy of Science, U.S.A., 83,* 7089–7093.

Wilkie, F., Eisdorder, C., Morgan, R., Loewenstein, D., and Szapocznik. (1990). Cognition in early human immunodeficiency virus infection. *Archives of Neurology, 47,* 433–440.

Wolters, P., Brouwers, P., Moss, H., el-Amin, D., Eddy, J., Butler, K., Husson, R., and Pizzo, P. (1990). The effect of 2'3' dideoxyinosine (ddI) on the cognitive functioning of infants and children with symptomatic HIV infection. *Proceedings of the VI International Conference on AIDS, 3,* 130 (abst.).

Wolters, P., Brouwers, P., Moss, H., el-Amin, D., Gress, J., Butler, L., and Pizzo, P. (1991). The effect of dideoxyinosine on the cognitive functioning of children with HIV infection after 6 and 12 months of treatment. *Proceedings from the VII International Conference on AIDS, 2,* 194 (abst.).

Wolters, P., Brouwers, P., Moss, H., and Pizzo, P. (in press). Adaptive behavior of children with symptomatic HIV infection before and after Zidovudine therapy. *Journal of Pediatric Psychology.*

Working Group of the American Academy of Neurology AIDS Task Force. (1991). Nomenclature and research case definitions for neurologic manifestations of human immunodeficiency virus-type 1 infection. *Neurology, 41,* 778–785.

17

Motor and Cognitive Functioning in Nonhuman Primates Infected with Simian Immunodeficiency Virus

Lee E. Eiden, Elisabeth A. Murray,
and Dianne M. Rausch

Neurological syndromes caused by opportunistic infections of the central nervous system (CNS), CNS neoplasms, and cerebrovascular disease are complications of acquired immunodeficiency syndrome (AIDS) (Snider et al., 1983; Koppel et al., 1985; Levy et al., 1985; Berger et al., 1987). In addition, 30–50% of adults and more than 60% of children with AIDS exhibit signs of CNS dysfunction independent of opportunistic infection, neoplasia, or systemic metabolic disturbances (Navia et al., 1986b; Belman et al., 1988). The latter kind of CNS impairment, with human immunodeficiency virus (HIV) infection as the only known cause, may range from subtle to profound and includes psychomotor slowing, cognitive impairment, and behavioral withdrawal (Epstein et al., 1986, 1988; Navia et al., 1986a,b; Belman et al., 1988; Price et al., 1988; Ho et al., 1989; Grant and Heaton, 1990). These signs have been collectively referred to as *AIDS dementia complex* (Navia et al., 1986a,b). The severity of the AIDS dementia complex may be rated according to a four-stage classification system (Price and Brew, 1988; Price and Sidtis, 1990). More recently, the term *HIV-associated motor/cognitive complex* has been adopted to include both mild and severe motor, cognitive, and affective components of HIV disease (WHO, 1990; Janssen et al., 1991).

CNS manifestations of HIV infection are a devastating aspect of AIDS, significantly impairing the quality of lives already circumscribed by the diagnosis of a fatal disease and increasing the difficulty of caring for such individuals (Price et al., 1988). In pediatric AIDS in particular, CNS disease appears also to be

TABLE 17–1. Major Questions Concerning the Mechanisms and Causation of Neuro-AIDS That Can Be Addressed in a Primate Animal Model System

---

1. Virus entry and replication in the brain.
   * Is brain infection dependent on host factors, viral factors, or both?
   * In what form does the virus exist in brain throughout the course of disease?
   ** Rhesus macaques can be inoculated with a single isolate and a known titer of virus, with a clearly defined time of inoculation.
   ** The CNS can be examined for the presence of viral DNA, viral RNA, and viral protein sequentially throughout the course of disease.

2. Host versus viral components of motor/cognitive impairment.
   * Is the proportion of individuals cognitively or motorically affected by immunodeficiency virus infection determined epidemiologically, by the virus subtype infection, or by host factors including penetration of virus infection to bone marrow, brain, lung, and so on?
   ** Experimental infection of the nonhuman primate host allows viral inoculum (viral subtype and route of inoculation) to be controlled as an independent variable.
   ** Lymphotropic and macrophagetropic clones of SIV that are nonneuroinvasive and encephalitogenic, respectively, can be compared for motor/cognitive sequelae after inoculation.

3. Correlation of psychomotor functioning and neurochemical and immune status of brain.
   * Does immune activation (major histocompatibility complex expression, cytokine production) occur early in immunodeficiency virus infection or is it a consequence of end-stage viral insult in the already immunodeficient host?
   * Are neurochemical changes driven by early immune activation or latent infection of the brain or by late-stage, perhaps metabolic alterations in the brain of the already immunodeficient host?
   ** Direct examination of brain tissue following the onset of psychomotor impairment but prior to end-stage disease can be examined systematically only in primates experimentally infected with SIV.

4. Causative mechanisms of CNS dysfunction.
   * Do viral protein products, endogenous neurotoxins, or endogenous cytokine immunotoxins produced in the virally infected brain produce CNS dysfunction and organic dysfunction?
   ** Motor and cognitive performance, as well as neuropathology, can be compared in SIV-infected animals and noninfected animals in which neurotoxins, immunotoxins, or viral protein products are administered intracerebroventricularly in the absence of virus.

---

prognostic of a more rapid course of immune disease (Epstein et al., 1986). Thus, the progression of immune and CNS diseases may be linked, and the natural course of AIDS may frequently involve the brain as a target organ.

In this chapter we will use the term neuro-AIDS to discuss three critical and possibly overlapping modes of interaction that may occur between the brain and immunodeficiency virus: (1) progressive encephalopathy and other motor/cognitive (i.e., functional) deficits that result from direct viral infection of the brain or indirectly from alteration of the blood-brain barrier or changes in the immune status of the brain; (2) infection of the host brain as a potential reservoir providing viral protection from immune surveillance during clinical latency and later generation of cytopathogenic viral quasi-species preceding the development of

AIDS; and (3) activation of the hypothalamo-pituitary adrenal (HPA) axis, directly by brain infection or indirectly through peripheral cytokine production. Increased cortisol levels due to altered function of the HPA axis may lead to aberrant modulation of cellular and humoral immune responses, further affecting the course of viral disease.

Investigators have linked the clinical course of immune disease to immunopathological changes in the immune system by examining peripheral lymphoid cells easily obtained from patients at all stages of disease. Establishing a link between progressive neuropathological changes in the brain and clinically observable motor and cognitive deficits is obviously far more challenging. Cells of the HIV-infected brain, unlike peripheral blood lymphoid cells, are not routinely accessible to biochemical or virological examination during life. It is not clear whether sampling of the cerebrospinal fluid (CSF) compartment reflects viral infection of choroid plexus, brain parenchyma, or both. The neuropathological status of the brain at autopsy may manifest predominantly end-stage effects of disease rather than a record of viral insult to the brain during the course of disease. Indeed, the poor correlation between the extent and severity of virus-induced brain lesions at autopsy and neurocognitive functioning throughout the course of AIDS in humans suggests that more subtle structural or even neurochemical alterations in the brain may underlie HIV-associated motor/cognitive impairment (Wiley et al., 1991). Thus, a full understanding of the role of the CNS in HIV disease and the molecular mechanisms of HIV-induced motor/cognitive dysfunction may require extensive employment of animal models of lentivirus infection to complement basic clinical and pathological observations in humans. Animal models for infection of the CNS by HIV, and for HIV-associated motor/cognitive complex, can be used to test directly the neuropathogenic potential of molecules implicated as causative agents in CNS viral disease and to determine the efficacy of therapeutic agents to prevent or ameliorate neuro-AIDS.

In this chapter, we describe the simian immunodeficiency virus (SIV)-infected rhesus macaque as a model for HIV-associated motor/cognitive complex and explore the usefulness of this model for testing current hypotheses about the pathobiology of immunodeficiency virus-related CNS disease (Table 17–1).

SIV Immune Disease in Rhesus Macaques

SIVs include those isolated from African green monkeys, mandrils, chimpanzees, and sooty mangabeys in the wild (SIV_{agm}, SIV_{mnd}, SIV_{cpz} and SIV_{smm}, respectively) and from pig-tailed, stump-tailed, and rhesus macaques in captivity (SIV_{mne}, SIV_{stm}, and SIV_{mac}, respectively) (Desrosiers, 1990). Only SIV_{mac} and SIV_{smm} will be discussed here since these have been the most extensively studied SIVs. SIV_{smm}, like SIV_{mac}, is approximately 43% identical to HIV-1 and 72% identical to HIV-2 at the amino acid level, and it encodes proteins corresponding to the major structural and regulatory gene products of the human viruses (Chakrabarti et al., 1987; Franchini et al., 1987). SIV shares with HIV-1 and HIV-2 a tropism for cells of the lymphoid and monocytoid lineages that express the CD4 cell surface antigen, which functions as the primary primate lentivirus receptor

(Kannagi et al., 1985; Watanabe et al., 1989). Following inoculation into rhesus macaques, SIV_{mac} and SIV_{smm} cause disease strikingly similar to human AIDS (Baskin et al., 1988; Simon et al., 1992). SIV inoculation in the rhesus macaque, like HIV infection in humans, results in an initial viral antigenemia and a host antiviral immune response, including production of antiviral antibodies (Kannagi et al., 1986; Zhang et al., 1988). SIV is found in both lymphoid and monocytoid cells in infected macaques in vivo, as is HIV in humans (Koenig et al., 1986; Wyand et al., 1989). Virus can be consistently cultured from peripheral blood during the course of disease, although the virus titer, as in human AIDS, is sometimes dramatically decreased in the terminal stages of disease. SIV infection in the rhesus macaque is also accompanied by a gradual decrease in CD4-positive cells in the peripheral blood (Baskin et al., 1988; Zhang et al., 1988; Hirsch et al., 1991; Kestler et al., 1991). This decrease is often less dramatic than the CD4 cell depletion observed in human AIDS, perhaps because normal rhesus CD4 cell counts are significantly higher than normal CD4 cell counts in humans. Nevertheless, SIV infection causes immune dysfunction manifested in persistent generalized lymphadenopathy and decreased humoral and cell-mediated immune responses to recall antigens early in the course of disease, as well as lymphoid atrophy later in the course of disease (Desrosiers, 1990; L.N. Martin, personal communication). Finally, SIV inoculation into rhesus macaques results in AIDS: wasting, diarrhea, gut and lung syncytial disease, susceptibility to opportunistic infections including cytomegalovirus (CMV), adenovirus, and *Pneumocystis carinii* pneumonia (PCP), and in some cases lymphoma (Baskin et al., 1988; Desrosiers, 1990; Simon et al., 1992). The average survival time postinoculation for both SIV_{mac} and SIV_{smm} is 0.5–2 years (Letvin et al., 1985; Baskin et al., 1988; Desrosiers, 1990). In rhesus macaques necropsied following death due to SIV disease, viral DNA and RNA have been found in peripheral organs rich in macrophage and lymphoid cells, including the spleen, lung, and gastrointestinal tract, and in the brain (Hirsch et al., 1991; Lackner et al., 1991). The pathobiology of SIV infection of the rhesus host thus remarkably parallels that of HIV infection of the human host, but with a compressed disease course relative to human AIDS, which has a clinical latency period that may extend over a decade or more.

SIV Infection of the CNS in Rhesus Macaques

Not surprisingly, SIV_{smm} ($SIV_{smm/Delta}$), as well as some strains of SIV_{mac}, are neurotropic in the rhesus macaque in vivo (Baskin et al., 1988). SIV infection of the brain appears to be an early event in the disease process. There is evidence of viral RNA and antigen in the brain as early as a few weeks following intravenous inoculation with virus (Chakrabarti et al., 1991; Hurtrel et al., 1991; Sharer et al., 1991). A similar inference, based on necessarily limited data, has been drawn for HIV infection of the CNS in humans (Ho et al., 1985; McArthur et al., 1989; Gray et al., 1992). SIV_{smm} encephalitis has been compared in detail to HIV-1 encephalitis in the juvenile host (Sharer et al., 1988). More extensive leptomeningeal perivascular inflammation and leptomeningeal giant cell formation, as well as karyorrhexis and necrosis in giant cell formations in brain parenchyma, are distinguishing features of SIV compared to HIV encephalitis (Sharer et al., 1988). This may be a fundamental difference between SIV and HIV infection or simply a reflection of a more compressed disease course in macaques, in which early postinfection CNS events perhaps resolved at the time of death in humans are unresolved in SIV-infected macaques. The giant multinucleated cells of macrophage origin found in brain parenchyma are, however, a prominent feature of both SIV and HIV CNS infection. In both human and rhesus lentivirus-infected brain, giant cells may apparently be derived from macrophage as well as microglial cells and are primarily perivascular (Koenig et al., 1986; Sharer et al., 1988).

The basic similarities between SIV infection of the primate brain and HIV infection of the human brain, however, beg the question of whether or not SIV infection of the primate brain causes a motor/cognitive disease similar to AIDS dementia complex. While the brain is certainly infected in the SIV-inoculated rhesus monkey, it has been difficult to acquire evidence suggesting a specific disease such as AIDS dementia complex or primate immunodeficiency virus–associated motor/cognitive impairment. A CNS neurological syndrome has been observed in SIV-infected rhesus macaques, including gait disturbances, ataxia, and lethargy (Heyes et al., 1992), although it is not clear if these animals also exhibited secondary neuropathies and/or metabolic dementia excluded from the original definition of human AIDS dementia complex (Navia et al., 1986b).

We have characterized motor and cognitive performance in SIV-infected rhesus macaques to determine whether this primate lentiviral disease fulfills an important criterion for similarity to human AIDS, that is, both a viral encephalitis and virus-associated motor/cognitive impairment. If so, the relationships between immune and neurocognitive AIDS disease courses, the occurrence of specific alterations in brain immuno- and neurochemistry following infection, and the effects of these alterations on normal brain function can be experimentally examined.

Motor and Cognitive Impairment in the SIV-Infected Rhesus Macaque

The rhesus macaque is capable of exhibiting complex behaviors in the functional domains known to be affected in humans with AIDS. Tests that have been used to demonstrate motor/cognitive impairment in SIV-infected rhesus macaques are shown in Figure 17–1. These tasks were chosen for two major reasons. First, performance on them is known to depend, at least in part, on specific cortical and subcortical neural substrates (see Figure 17–1 and references therein). Certain lesions of the basal ganglia can specifically perturb visual discrimination learning without affecting either recency or recognition memory, and certain cortical and limbic lesions cause decrements in performance based on recency/recognition memory without affecting visual discrimination learning. Thus, differential impairments in performing these tasks could serve to identify regions of the brain (e.g., subcortical vs. cortical) affected by virus infection. Second, while performance on recognition versus visual discrimination tasks can be selec-

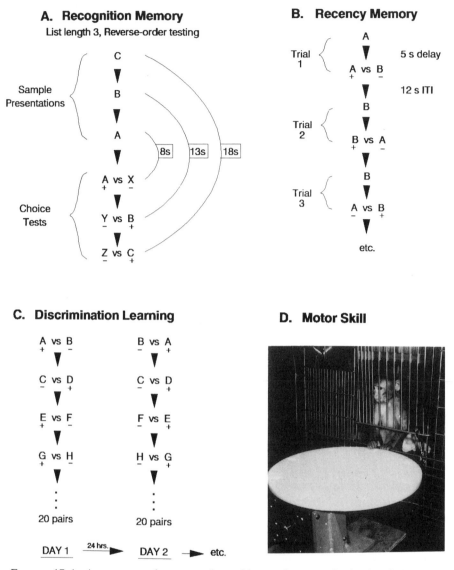

FIGURE 17–1. Assessment of motor and cognitive performance in the SIV-infected juvenile rhesus macaque.

A. *Recognition Memory.* This task required the animal to identify the correct trial-unique stimulus from a pair of stimuli by touching the correct symbol. The correct symbol is defined as that symbol in the pair previously viewed in the absence of the accompanying (incorrect) symbol. A trial consists in individual presentation of three symbols on the screen approximately 3 seconds apart, followed by the presentation of the same three symbols in reverse order, each accompanied by a novel (incorrect) stimulus. Thus, C, B, and A, and the pairs A-X, B-Y, and C-Z are presented in order, and correct identification of A, B, and C from the paired sequence is rewarded in each case. The degree of difficulty for each choice increases with increased time between sample presentation and choice test, which allows a range of scores for performance evaluation.

tively spared following the development of brain lesions that cause performance decrements in the other task, each task appears to require the integrity of multiple cortical (recognition memory) and/or subcortical (visual discrimination learning) areas or stations. Therefore, a diffuse global or regional insult to the CNS, within either cortical or subcortical areas, that might result in psychomotor slowing, as observed in AIDS dementia complex, would be expected to affect performance on these tasks as well. Obviously, even anatomically discrete, virally induced CNS damage might translate into functional deficits differently than mechanical lesions within the same brain structures. Determining the inflammatory and neurochemical pathways leading from CNS viral infection to functional impairment is perhaps the most compelling reason to establish an SIV model of AIDS dementia complex.

In an initial study, eight juvenile rhesus macaques were productively infected with $SIV_{smm/B670}$ ($SIV_{smm/Delta}$) following training to criterion on the tasks described in Figure 17–1. These animals demonstrated a range of performance deficits in motor skill, visual discrimination, and delayed matching-to-sample tasks when tested over an 11-month period (Murray et al., 1992). The first observation of motor or cognitive deficits always preceded overt signs of disease by several weeks to months. Decreased performance occurred without significant alteration in the overall frequency of responding to test stimuli for any of the

---

B. *Recency Memory.* In this task, the animal sees a single stimulus, and then sees the same stimulus paired with a second stimulus. The same two symbols are used repeatedly, so that the animal must remember which of the two familiar images was seen most recently, and choose it each time in order to receive a food reward. In this test there is a 5-second delay between sample presentation and choice test, and a 12-second inter-trial interval. *Performance decrements specific to recognition and recency memory tasks relative to visual discrimination tasks (see below) can occur following periallocortical and limbic lesions* (Malamut et al., 1984; Gaffan and Murray, 1992).

C. *Discrimination Learning.* This task consists in identification of the correct symbol from each of 20 pairs of symbols. The 20 pairs are presented for choice only once each day. The correct symbol in each pair is fixed arbitrarily prior to testing and remains correct throughout sequential presentations of the 20 pairs of symbols. Correct responses are initially random (i.e., ~10/20) and progress to 16–20 correct as the animals learns the correct (i.e., rewarding) responses over the course of presentation of the twenty pairs of symbols daily for 20 days (5 days/week for 1 month). *Performance decrements specific to this task relative to recognition and recency memory tasks can occur following lesions of certain portions of the basal ganglia* (Wang et al., 1990; Gaffan and Murray, 1992).

D. *Motor Skill.* This task consists in food reward retrieval from a rotating wheel, and increases in difficulty as the speed of the wheel is progressively increased. Performance is quantitated according to the highest wheel speed at which the animal can successfully retrieve food fifty percent of the time. *Performance decrements involving motor skill in the absence of performance impairment in other tasks may reflect lesions or dysfunction of the basal ganglia* (Heindel et al., 1989).

TABLE 17–2. Summary of Motor/Cognitive Deficits in SIV-Infected Juvenile Rhesus Macaques

Early Deficits	Motor+	RM+	VD+	Cause of Death
M011	+(8)	−	+(5)	Scheduled (>10)
M014	+(4)	−	−	Wasting (8)
M023	+(4)	−	+(2)	Seizure (8)
M025	−	+(4)	+(2)	Pneumonia (10)
Late Deficits	Motor	RM	VD	Cause of Death
M007	+(10)	−	−	Wasting (>10)
M008	+(10)	−	−	Scheduled (>10)
M030	+(10)	−	−	Scheduled (>10)
M031	+(10)	−	−	Scheduled (>10)

A total of 15 monkeys were divided into two groups, one consisting of 5 animals and the other 10, that were matched for their final preinoculation performance levels in recognition memory and motor skill. The group of 5 were sham inoculated, and the group of 10 were given 10 RID_{50} of $SIV_{smm/B670}$ intravenously. Performance was tested over a 10-block (45-week) period. Numbers in parentheses show blocks in which deficits were first noted or animals were sacrificed. Of the 10 animals inoculated with SIV, 2 (M010, M019; not shown) were not productively infected (virus rescue negative throughout the study) and did not exhibit motor, cognitive, or other clinical or pathological abnormalities.

[+]Motor = motor skill; RM = recency memory; VD = visual discrimination. See descriptions in text accompanying Figure 17–1.

Source: Adapted from Murray et al. (1992).

tasks, indicating that motivation to perform each task was unaltered by the disease process. Home cage behavior (locomotion, play, exploration, social contact, grooming, stereotypies) of infected and noninfected animals was indistinguishable throughout the study, demonstrating that the impairments in motor and cognitive performance observed were due to viral effects on the brain per se, rather than to general lethargy induced by systemic disease.

Three of eight infected macaques exhibited cognitive deficits, and five additional animals exhibited impairment in a motor skill task, following inoculation with the neurotropic $SIV_{smm/B670}$ isolate. Monkeys could be divided into two groups, consisting of those animals with early (<8 months) onset of motor/cognitive deficits and those with late (≥10 months) onset of motor deficits (Table 17–2). Early appearance of cognitive or motor deficits presaged a more rapid immune disease course following SIV infection. Thus, 75% of the animals exhibiting early deficits succumbed to disease during the course of the study compared to only 25% of the animals exhibiting late deficits (Table 17–2). Decreased performance on motor skill and visual discrimination learning tasks was the most frequently observed impairment in this study. Only one animal manifested a profound impairment in the delayed matching-to-sample task. These results are consistent with the notion that primate immunodeficiency virus–associated CNS impairment is more similar to "subcortical" human dementias, such as those associated with Parkinson's and Huntington's diseases, than to "cortical" human dementias such as Alzheimer's disease (Cummings and Benson, 1984; Heindel et al., 1989).

In a second study, seven juvenile animals were inoculated with SIV prior to any behavioral training so that the effect of SIV infection on rate of acquisition of recognition memory task performance could be determined. Three monkeys demonstrated a decreased rate of learning (increased number of trials and errors to attain performance criterion relative to uninfected controls) on the recognition memory task. Two of these animals were the only subjects in the study to succumb to disease within the first 6 months after inoculation (D.M. Rausch et al., unpublished observations), confirming the concordance between rapid disease course and functional involvement of the CNS in SIV disease reported earlier (Murray et al., 1992). These preliminary results suggest that impaired ability to *learn* a recognition memory task may be a more frequent manifestation of SIV disease than impaired ability to *perform* this task. Additional studies comparing learning with performance on motor and cognitive tasks may help elucidate whether CNS impairment in adult and pediatric AIDS is fundamentally similar despite varied manifestations of CNS dysfunction.

In both studies described above, the rhesus monkeys were all inoculated with an identical isolate of SIV, yet only a proportion of each cohort of SIV-infected animals exhibited profound motor or cognitive impairments. This is reminiscent of the variable penetrance of AIDS dementia complex in the human HIV–infected population. Variability in host factors predisposing to CNS dysfunction on infection, rather than the epidemiology of nonneuropathogenic versus neuropathogenic HIV-1 virus strains, may explain the incidence of HIV-associated motor/cognitive complex in humans.

A correlation appears to exist between severity of cognitive impairment and survival time after inoculation in SIV-infected rhesus macaques, as reported for progressive encephalopathy and disease course in pediatric AIDS (Epstein et al., 1986). Minimal evidence of virally induced neuropathology in some SIV-infected macaques with profound and early cognitive dysfunction is also consistent with the neuropathology of AIDS dementia complex, in which attendant neuropathology was reported to be relatively mild in several cases of profound dementia (Navia et al., 1986a). For this reason, potential indirect effects of viral infection, including autoimmune activation within the brain and subsequent neurochemical alterations leading to functional impairment, must be considered and evaluated in both human and nonhuman primate immunodeficiency virus disease.

Neurochemical Correlates of SIV-Induced Motor/Cognitive Impairment

Changes in brain immunochemistry, cytochemistry, and neurochemistry can be correlated temporally and anatomically with CNS dysfunction in the SIV-infected rhesus macaque. The rhesus brain is similar to that of humans not only neuroanatomically but immunologically as well. For example, the monkey brain, like the human but unlike the rodent brain, expresses significant levels of the mRNA encoding the CD4 antigen (Maddon et al., 1986; Crocker et al., 1987; Gorman et al., 1987; Lonberg et al., 1988; Erickson et al., 1991; Erickson et al., unpublished observations). Thus, the causes of dysfunction in complex behavior after lenti-virus infection of the rhesus macaque are likely to be qualitatively similar, cyto-chemically, immunochemically, and neurochemically, to HIV encephalitis and AIDS dementia complex in humans. In this regard, reactive astrocytosis (increased staining of fibrous astrocytes for glial fibrillary acidic protein [GFAP]) has been observed in cerebrocortical gray matter of rhesus macaques with motor and cognitive impairments at time of sacrifice, even in brain regions apparently spared from extensive SIV-induced lesions, including perivascular inflammation, microglial nodules, and lymphocytic infiltration (Eiden et al., 1992). Increased GFAP immunoreactivity has also been reported in the cerebrocortical gray mat-ter of HIV-infected individuals and correlated with white matter encephalopathy (Ciardi et al., 1990). CSF concentrations of the endogenous excitotoxic quinolinic acid, shown to be produced in HIV-infected human macrophages, have been reported to be elevated in both HIV-infected humans and SIV-infected rhesus macaques (Heyes et al., 1991, 1992; Brew et al., 1992). Recently, we have noted a correlation between increased CSF levels of quinolinic acid and development of motor impairment in monkeys infected with SIV and followed throughout the course of disease (Rausch et al., in press), consistent with the reported correlation between increasing CSF quinolinic acid and decreased motor performance in HIV-infected individuals (Martin et al., 1992, 1993).

The regional rather than focal up-regulation of GFAP following SIV infec-tion suggests that the local effects of SIV infection may be transmitted at a dis-tance via soluble factors or widespread changes in the blood-brain barrier caused by rather discrete viral lesions. Indeed, changes in expression of the mRNA encoding preprosomatostatin (preproSOM) have been observed in CNS tissue from SIV-infected macaques (A. da Cunha et al., unpublished observations) in some but not all regions of frontal and parietal cortex examined. Future exper-iments will need to address the concordance of GFAP and preproSOM mRNA changes in specific brain regions of SIV-infected animals to determine if a cor-relation in the expression of these markers for the glial and neuronal compart-ments exists and, if so, if dysregulation in specific brain regions correlates with specific motor and/or cognitive deficits in SIV-infected macaques.

Testing Hypotheses About Neuro-AIDS in the SIV-Infected Rhesus Macaque

Desrosiers (1992) has pointed out that current SIV research has begun a transi-tion period from efforts spent "developing the model" to its application toward breaking new ground in AIDS research. With the development of the model of SIV-associated motor/cognitive impairment, this process has now also been com-pleted, and attention must turn to definitively answering long-standing questions about the role of the brain in, and effects on the brain of, primate immunodefi-ciency virus infection. Some critical areas for SIV neuro-AIDS research are con-sidered below.

Both HIV and SIV exist in lymphocytetropic and monocytetropic forms, that is, distinct viral isolates that replicate preferentially in CD4-positive helper T cells or in cells of monocyte/macrophage lineage, including microglial cells of the brain (Price et al., 1988; Desrosiers, 1990). Cloned lymphotropic and macrophagetropic SIV isolates have allowed direct testing in vivo of the relative roles of lympho- and macrophagetropic virus in disease pathogenesis. Desrosiers and coworkers (1991) concluded, on the basis of such experiments, that macrophage tropism is required for SIV encephalitis and SIV-associated pneumonia but is not required for development of immunodeficiency. The availability of cloned virus isolates and the definition of their pathogenic behavior in vivo will be a significant step in determining the relationship between macrophage tropism and brain infection and between viral tropism and motor/cognitive impairment. From such data, the requirement or lack thereof for a direct neurotropic mechanism for AIDS dementia complex can be determined. If lymphotropic viruses can cause both immune and CNS dysfunction without causing encephalitis, for example, the hypothesis that HIV and SIV cause motor and cognitive impairment by immune-mediated perturbation of blood-brain barrier function, with direct viral infection of the brain incidental to this process, would need to be considered. A second question concerns the role of the brain in affecting the course of immune disease. Is brain infection an obligate component of AIDS itself, at least in some HIV-infected individuals, or is neuro-AIDS independent of HIV infection of the immune system and immune disease? Infection in vivo with cloned lymphotropic and macrophagetropic SIV isolates, followed by rescue and characterization of virus from central and peripheral tissue compartments, should clarify this issue as well (Sharma et al., 1992). The demonstration of AIDS without SIV encephalitis in rhesus macaques inoculated with "lymphocytetropic" virus (see above) suggests that macrophage tropism and brain infection are not required for the generation of immune disease. However, "macrophagetropic" or at least non-lymphocytopathic HIV is the form of the human virus most commonly rescued from peripheral blood of AIDS patients prior to end-stage AIDS (Tersmette et al., 1989; Groenink et al., 1991; Schuitemaker et al., 1991), and therefore the form of the virus most likely to be commonly transmitted from one individual to another. Thus, in addition to infected blood monocytes, the brain or lung may function as an "organ of passage" during the natural course of disease for the generation of lymphotropic/cytopathic variants that are directly responsible for T-cell depletion and immunodeficiency. The need to study the CNS and immune disease course in the rhesus macaque following administration of cloned SIV isolates with the tropism, and by the routes of infection, most commonly found in AIDS patients is obvious.

Determining the route of viral entry into the CNS is critical to understanding neuro-AIDS. Systematic study of this question is limited almost solely to animal models for human AIDS, although some data do exist for HIV from the study of brains obtained from HIV-infected individuals following suicide or accidental death. (McArthur et al., 1989; Gray et al., 1992). In addition, evidence for latent infection of the brain via HIV-1 infection of the astrocyte compartment has recently been obtained, although whether this is in fact an early or a late event in the disease process is not yet known (C. Tornatore et al., B. Blumberg, et al., in preparation; personal communication). In situ hybridization, histochemical, and sequential virus rescue studies designed to answer these questions in SIV-infected macaques have only recently been reported (Chakrabarti et al., 1991; Hurtrel et al., 1991; Sharer et al., 1991), in part because methods of requisite sensitivity for detecting low levels of viral DNA, RNA, and protein have only recently become available. Initial work does, however, suggest early viral entry into the CNS. More detailed study of the early changes in CNS neurochemistry and function accompanying viral entry can now be carried out. In particular, detection of latent infection of cellular compartments within the brain not detectable by conventional methods should now be possible using in situ polymerase chain reaction (ISPCR).

The HPA axis is a major regulatory component linking nervous and immune system functions that has not been systematically examined in human AIDS or neuro-AIDS. In part this is because absolute levels of adrenocorticotropic hormone and cortisol, or even assessment of HPA axis function, against a background of progressive immune deficiency disease are unlikely to provide a comprehensive picture of the involvement of the HPA axis in HIV disease without extensive longitudinal study (Membreno et al., 1987; Merenich et al., 1990; Oberfield et al, 1990; Villette et al., 1990). Increased bioassayable interleukin (IL)-1 levels in rodent brain following central administration of the HIV envelope glycoprotein gp120 has been reported (Sundar et al., 1991), and IL-1-positive cells have been reported to be increased in the brains of HIV-positives examined at autopsy (Tyor et al., 1992). Central and peripheral administration of IL-1 leads to activation of the HPA axis and to subsequent effects on cellular and humoral immune function, as well as potential direct effects on neurotransmitter expression in the brain itself (Berkenbosch et al., 1987; Sapolsky et al., 1987; Sternberg et al., 1989; Scarborough, 1990; Saperstein et al., 1992). Longitudinal examination of the HPA axis in the SIV-infected rhesus macaque throughout the course of acquired immunodeficiency disease may yield important information about the role of neurogenic and immune stress and viral infection on the reciprocal regulation of the brain and the immune system at this neuroendocrine locus. Activation of corticotropin-releasing factor (CRF) neurons in the CNS by cytokine administration also, at least in rodents, causes immune suppression independent of the HPA axis (Saperstein et al., 1992). Intracerebroventricular administration of CRF in rodents causes reduction in natural killer (NK) cell activity that is blocked by chlorisondamine, a ganglionic blocking drug that interrupts signal transmission from the brain to target organs via the sympathetic nervous system (SNS) (Irwin et al., 1990). These data suggest a second link (the SNS) between CNS activation by cytokine up-regulation and peripheral immune function that may be operative in HIV infection and should be explored in the SIV-infected nonhuman primate.

Finally, exacerbation or generation of motor/cognitive deficits by direct CNS administration of agents thought to be precipitating or causal factors in AIDS dementia complex is a particular challenge for SIV experimentation in the nonhuman primate. The list of potential candidates for mediation of CNS dysfunction includes direct neurotoxicity by viral antigens such as the HIV large envelope glycoprotein gp120 (Brenneman et al., 1988; Dreyer et al., 1990), quinolinic acid produced by inflammatory cells within the CNS (Heyes et al., 1992) or protein factors elaborated by HIV-infected macrophages (Pulliam et al., 1990), autoimmune damage to the CNS precipitated by viral antigen mimicry (Yamada et al., 1991), and neurochemical dysregulation induced by cytokine elaboration within the infected CNS (Tyor et al., 1992). These hypotheses can be directly tested in the rhesus macaque model, assuming that some notion can be obtained of how much of each putative substance must be present in what regions of the brain, and for how long, before functional consequences are apparent. Measurement of alterations in CNS neurochemistry consequent to SIV infection in the rhesus macaque CNS should provide not only insight into the pathogenesis of motor/ cognitive impairment, but also neurochemical markers for efficiently determining the relative merit of these disparate hypotheses. In particular, up-regulation of mRNA encoding the neuropeptides somatostatin and cholecystokinin has been observed following damage to the blood-brain barrier in rodents (Olenik and Meyer, 1990). Since mechanical damage to the brain, like SIV infection, results in activation of astroglia in both gray and white matter (Hozumi et al., 1990; Chakrabarti et al., 1991; Hurtrel et al., 1991; Eiden et al., 1992), a link between SIV infection and dysregulation of neuropeptide neurotransmitter systems in the macaque CNS may be worthy of examination.

Concluding Remarks

Fundamental questions about human neuro-AIDS can be addressed experimentally in the SIV-infected rhesus macaque (Table 17–1). In addition to examining mechanisms of viral neuropathogenesis and directly testing the potentially causal role of molecules implicated in CNS dysfunction, the SIV-infected rhesus macaque will play a crucial role in attempts to determine the efficacy of therapeutic agents with the potential to prevent or ameliorate neuro-AIDS.

The presence or absence of cofactors in both human and nonhuman primate AIDS and neuro-AIDS also requires continual reassessment. Nonhuman primates may harbor endogenous viruses whose expression in the immunodeficient state contributes to CNS dysfunction. Cofactors such as drugs of abuse and malnutrition can and should be systematically examined in the SIV-infected macaque. The effect of route of infection, both cellular and anatomical, on disease course and outcome, and the types of cell involved in both viral transmission and reception in the CNS, are currently being examined in the rhesus macaque infected with SIV. Immunologically, the observation that SIV causes immunodeficiency without profound CD4 cell loss may be considered either a limitation of the SIV model or a feature that can be exploited to learn if there is a critical role for specific T-cell subpopulations whose loss precipitates the human immunodeficiency syndrome prior to the profound total CD4-positive T-cell loss that could be a concomitant rather than a cause of end-stage AIDS in humans.

The relationship between the role of the brain as a viral reservoir during HIV disease and the effect of viral infection, central or peripheral, on brain function remains unclear. It is crucial to understand neuro-AIDS from both of these perspectives, especially because advances in prolongation of life with non-CNS-directed antiviral therapies could be accompanied by increases in the incidence of CNS complications of HIV infection. Data from behavioral studies involving SIV-infected rhesus macaques indicate that the involvement of the brain in viral disease in monkeys, as manifested in motor/cognitive deficits, as in humans, presages a poor prognosis for survival. At the same time, motor deficits and, in some cases, cognitive deficits in rhesus macaques do not seem to require extensive or even histochemically detectable, virally induced brain lesions. Widespread astrocytic activation, on the other hand, is a hallmark of SIV infection of the brain. Elevation of quinolinic acid appears to be a late phenomenon, but changes in quinolinic acid in the CSF may not reflect the time course of changes in quinolinic acid levels in the brain. Altered expression of neuropeptide neurotransmitters in the CNS infected with SIV may correlate with the pattern of infection of the CNS, but the functional effects of these alterations may be restricted to a few critical sites within the brain. To understand the relationship between lentivirus infection, alteration in brain neurochemistry, and changes in motor or cognitive function, it will be necessary to know when and how immunodeficiency viruses enter the brain, the nucleic acid and the protein forms of the virus that are expressed once there, and the neurochemical changes triggered by the presence of virus in the CNS, in an anatomically detailed fashion. Experimental study of the SIV-infected rhesus macaque can critically contribute to resolving this and other issues in neuro-AIDS which depend on biochemical and histochemical access to the brain immediately following viral infection and throughout the course of immunological and neurological disease.

Acknowledgments

The work described from the authors' laboratories were carried out in collaboration with Drs. Anna da Cunha, Melvyn Heyes, Judit Lendvay, Donatus Nohr, Sabina Rhem, Leroy Sharer, Jerrold Ward, and Eberhard Weihe, and with the invaluable assistance of Mssrs. Russell Byrum and David Huddleston. We thank Drs. Ben Blumberg, Len Kapcala, Alex Martin, Eugene Major, Lou Martin, Michael Murphey-Corb, Philip Pizzo, and Ljubisa Vitkovic for valuable discussions and for sharing unpublished data. Citation of the literature herein is of necessity representative rather than comprehensive. We acknowledge the contributions of those cited directly and through citation of comprehensive reviews.

References

Baskin, G.B., Murphey-Corb, M., Watson, E.A., and Martin, L.N. (1988). Necropsy findings in rhesus monkeys experimentally infected with cultured simian immunodeficiency virus (SIV)/Delta. *Veterinary Pathology, 25*, 456–467.

Belman, A.L., Diamond, G., Dickson, D., Horoupian, D., Ilena, J., Lantos, G., and Rubinstein, A. (1988). Pediatric acquired immunodeficiency syndrome. Neurologic syndromes. *American Journal of Diseases of Children, 142* 29–35.

Berger, J.R., Moskowitz, L., Fischl, M., and Kelley, R.E. (1987). Neurologic disease as the presenting manifestation of acquired immunodeficiency syndrome. *Southern Medical Journal, 80*, 683–686.

Berkenbosch, F., van Oers, J., del Rey, A., Tilders, F., and Besedovsky, H. (1987). Corticotropin-releasing factor-producing neurons in the rat activated by interleukin-1. *Science, 238*, 524–526.

Blumberg, B. et al. (1993). Personal communication.

Brenneman, D.E., Westerbrook, G.L., Fitzgerald, S.P., Ennis, D.L., Elkins, K.L., Ruff, M.R., and Pert, C.B. (1988). Neuronal cell killing by the envelope protein of HIV and its prevention by vasoactive intestinal peptide. *Nature, 335*, 639–642.

Brew, B.J., Corbeil, J., Pemberton, L., Heyes, M., Evans, L., Penny, R., and Cooper, D.A. (1992). Quinolinic acid and the pathogenesis of AIDS dementia. *Neuroscience of HIV infection: Basic and clinical frontiers* (meeting proceedings). Amsterdam: p. 53.

Chakrabarti, L., Guyader, M., Alizon, M., Daniel, M.D., Desrosiers, R.C., Tiollais, P., and Sonigo, P. (1987). Sequence of simian immunodeficiency virus from macaque and its relationship to other human and simian retroviruses. *Nature, 328*, 543–547.

Chakrabarti, L., Hurtrel, M., Maire, M.-A., Vazeux, R., Dormont, D., Montagnier, L., and Hurtrel, B. (1991). Early viral replication in the brain of SIV-infected rhesus monkeys. *American Journal of Pathology, 139*, 1273–1280.

Ciardi, A., Sinclair, E., Scaravilli, F., Harcourt-Webster, N.J., and Lucas, S. (1990). The involvement of the cerebral cortex in human immunodeficiency virus encephalopathy: A morphological and immunohistochemical study. *Acta Neuropathologica, 81*, 51–59.

Crocker, P.R., Jefferies, W.A., Clark, S.J., Chung, L.P., and Gordon, S. (1987). Species heterogeneity in macrophage expression of the CD4 antigen. *Journal of Experimental Medicine, 166*, 613–618.

Cummings, J.L., and Benson, D.F. (1984). Subcortical dementia. Review of an emerging concept. *Archives of Neurology, 41*, 874–879.

Desrosiers, R.C. (1990). The simian immunodeficiency viruses. *Annual Review of Immunology, 8*, 557–578.

Desrosiers, R.C. (1992). Introduction. Special issue dedicated to SIV. *AIDS Research and Human Retroviruses, 8*, 325.

Desrosiers, R.C., Hansen-Moosa, A., Mori, K., Bouvier, D.P., King, N.W., Daniel, M.D., and Ringler, D.J. (1991). Macrophage-tropic variants of SIV are associated with specific AIDS-related lesions but are not essential for the development of AIDS. *American Journal of Pathology, 139*, 29–35.

Dreyer, E.B., Kaiser, P.K., Offermann, J.T., and Lipton, S.A. (1990). HIV-1 coat protein neurotoxicity prevented by calcium channel antagonists. *Science, 248*, 364–367.

Eiden, L., Rausch, D., Lendvay, J., Sharer, L., Weihe, E., Nohr, D., and Murray, E. (1992). Motor and cognitive impairments in SIV-infected rhesus macaques. *Proceedings of the VIII International Conference on AIDS/III STD World Congress,* Amsterdam, *2*, A83.

Epstein, L.G., Sharer, L.R., and Goudsmit, J. (1988). Neurological and neuropathological features of human immunodeficiency virus infection in children. *Annals of Neurology, 23*, S19–S23.

Epstein, L.G., Sharer, L.R., Oleske, J.M., Connor, E.M., Goudsmit, J., Bagdon, L., Robert-Guroff, M., and Koenigsberger, M.R. (1986). Neurologic manifestations of human immunodeficiency virus infection in children. *Pediatrics, 78*, 678–687.

Erickson, J.D., Trojanowski, J.Q., and Eiden, L.E. (1991). Regional distribution and partial molecular characterization of CD4-related mRNA in human brain and peripheral tissues. *Molecular Brain Research, 10*, 23–31.

Franchini, G., Gurgo, C., Guo, H.-G., Gallo, R.C., Collalti, E., Fargnoli, K.A., Hall, L.F., Wong-Staal, F., and Reitz, M.S.J. (1987). Sequence of simian immunodeficiency virus and its relationship to the human immunodeficiency viruses. *Nature, 328*, 539–543.

Gaffan, D., and Murray, E.A. (1992). Monkeys *(Macaca fascicularis)* with rhinal cortex ablations succeed in object discrimination learning despite 24-hr intertrial intervals and fail at matching to sample despite double sample presentations. *Behavioral Neuroscience, 106*, 30–38.

Gorman, S.D., Tourvieille, B., and Parnes, J.R. (1987). Structure of the mouse gene encoding CD4 and an unusual transcript in brain. *Proceedings of the National Academy of Science USA, 84*, 7644–7648.

Grant, I., and Heaton, R.K. (1990). Human immunodeficiency virus-type 1 (HIV-1) and the brain. *Journal of Consulting and Clinical Psychology, 48*, 22–30.

Gray, F., Lescs, M.-C., Keohane, C., Paraire, F., Marc, B., Durigon, M., and Gherardi, R. (1992). Early brain changes in HIV infection: neuropathological study of 11 HIV seropositive, non-AIDS cases. *Journal of Neuropathology and Experimental Neurology, 51*, 177–185.

Groenink, M., Fouchier, R.A.M., de Goede, R E.Y., de Wolf, F., Gruters, R.A., Cuypers, H.T.M., Huisman, H.G., and Tersmette, M. (1991). Phenotypic heterogeneity in a panel of infectious molecular human immunodeficiency virus type 1 clones derived from a single individual. *Journal of Virology, 65*, 1968–1975.

Heindel, W.C., Salmon, D.P., Shults, C.W., Walicke, P.A., and Butters, N. (1989). Neuropsychological evidence for multiple implicit memory systems: a comparison of Alzheimer's, Huntington's, and Parkinson's disease patients. *Journal of Neuroscience, 9*, 582–587.

Heyes, M., Brew, B.J., Martin, A., Price, R.W., Salazar, A.M., Sidtis, J.J., Yergey, J.A., Mouradian, M.M., Sadler, A.E., Keilp, J., Rubinow, D., and Markey, S.P. (1991). Quinolinic acid in cerebrospinal fluid and serum in HIV infection: Relationship to clinical and neurologic status. *Annals of Neurology, 29*, 202–209.

Heyes, M.P., Jordan, E.K., Lee, K., Saito, K., Frank, J.A., Snoy, P.J., Markey, S.P., and Gravell, M. (1992). Relationship of neurologic status in macaques infected with the simian immunodeficiency virus to cerebrospinal fluid quinolinic acid and kynurenic acid. *Brain Research, 570*, 237–250.

Hirsch, V.M., Zack, P.M., Vogel, A.P., and Johnson, P.R. (1991). Simian immunodeficiency virus infection of macaques: end-stage disease is characterized by widespread distribution of proviral DNA in tissues. *Journal of Infectious Disease, 163*, 976–988.

Ho, D.D., Bredesen, D.E., Vinters, H.V., and Daar, E.S. (1989). The acquired immunodeficiency syndrome (AIDS) dementia complex. *Annals of Internal Medicine, 111*, 400–410.

Ho, D.D., Rota, T.R., Schooley, R.T., Kaplan, J.C., Allan, J.D., Groopman, J.E., Resnick, L., Felsenstein, D., Andrews, C.A., and Hirsch, M.S. (1985). Isolation of HTLV-III from cerebrospinal fluid and neural tissues of patients with neurologic syndromes related to the acquired immunodeficiency syndrome. *New England Journal of Medicine, 313*, 1493–1497.

Hozumi, I., Chiu, F.-C., and Norton, W.T. (1990). Biochemical and immunocytochemical changes in glial fibrillary acidic protein after stab wounds. *Brain Research, 524*, 64–71.

Hurtrel, B., Chakrabarti, L., Hurtrel, M., Maire, M.A., Dormont, D., and Montagnier, L. (1991). Early SIV encephalopathy. *Journal of Medical Primatology, 20*, 159–166.

Irwin, M., Vale, W., and Rivier, C. (1990). Central corticotropin-releasing factor mediates the suppressive effect of stress on natural killer cytotoxicity. *Endocrinology, 126,* 2837–2844.

Janssen, R.S., Cornblath, D.R., Epstein, L.G., Foa, R.P., McArthur, J.C., Price, R.W., Asbury, A.K., Beckett, A., Benson, D.F., Bridge, T.P., Leventhal, C.M., Satz, P., Saykin, A.J., Sidtis, J.J., and Tross, S. (1991). Nomenclature and research case definitions for neurological manifestations of human immunodeficiency virus type-1 (HIV-1) infection. Report of a Working Group of the American Academy of Neurology AIDS Task Force. *Neurology, 41,* 778–785.

Kannagi, M., Kiyotaki, M., Desrosiers, R.C., Reimann, K.A., King, N.W., Waldron, L.M., and Letvin, N.L. (1986). Humoral immune responses to T cell tropic retrovirus simian T lymphotropic virus type III in monkeys with experimentally induced acquired immune deficiency-like syndrome. *Journal of Clinical Investigation, 78,* 1229–1236.

Kannagi, M., Yetz, J.M., and Letvin, N. (1985). In vitro growth characteristics of simian T-lymphotropic virus type III. *Proceedings of the National Academy of Science USA, 82,* 7053–7057.

Kestler, H.W.I., Ringler, D.J., Mori, K., Panicali, D.L., Sehgal, P.K., Daniel, M.D., and Desrosiers, R.C. (1991). Importance of the *nef* gene for maintenance of high virus loads and for development of AIDS. *Cell, 65,* 651–662.

Koenig, S., Gendelman, H.E., Orenstein, J.M., Canto, M.C.D., Pezeshkpour, G.H., Hung-bluth, M., Janotta, F., Aksamit, A., Martin, M.A., and Fauci, A.S. (1986). Detection of AIDS virus in macrophages in brain tissue from AIDS patients with encephalopathy. *Science, 233,* 1089–1093.

Koppel, B.S., Wormser, G.P., Tuchman, A.J., Maayan, S., Hewlett, D., Jr., and Daras, M. (1985). Central nervous system involvement in patients with acquired immunodeficiency syndrome (AIDS). *Acta Neurologica Scandinavica, 71,* 337–353.

Lackner, A.A., Smith, M.O., Munn, R.J., Martfeld, D.J., Gardner, M.B., Marx, P.A., and Dandekar, S. (1991). Localization of simian immunodeficiency virus in the central nervous system of rhesus monkeys. *American Journal of Pathology, 139,* 609–621.

Letvin, N.L., Daniel, M.D., Sehgal, P.K., Desrosiers, R.C., Hunt, R.D., Waldron, L.M., MacKey, J.J., Schmidt, D.K., Chalifoux, L.V., and King, N.W. (1985). Induction of AIDS-like disease in macaque monkeys with T-cell tropic retrovirus STLV-III. *Science, 230,* 71–73.

Levy, R.M., Bredesen, D.E., and Rosenblum, M.L. (1985). Neurological manifestations of the acquired immunodeficiency syndrome (AIDS). Experience at UCSF and reviews of the literature. *Journal of Neurosurgery, 62,* 475–495.

Lonberg, N., Gettner, S.N., Lacy, E., and Littman, D.R. (1988). Mouse brain CD4 transcripts encode only the COOH-terminal half of the protein. *Molecular and Cellular Biology, 8,* 2224–2228.

Maddon, P., Dalgleish, A.G., McDougal, J.S., Clapham, P.R., Weiss, R.A., and Axel, R. (1986). The T4 gene encodes the AIDS virus receptor and is expressed in the immune system and the brain. *Cell, 47,* 333–348.

Malamut, B.L., Saunders, R.C., and Mishkin, M. (1984). Monkeys with combined amygdalo-hippocampal lesions succeed in object discrimination learning despite 24-hour intertrial intervals. *Behavioral Neuroscience, 98,* 759–769.

Martin, A., Heyes, M.P., Salazar, A.M., Kampen, M.S., Williams, J., Law, W.A., Coats, M.E., and Markey, S.P. (1992). Progressive slowing of reaction time and increasing cerebrospinal fluid concentrations of quinolinic acid in HIV-infected individuals. *Journal of Neuropsychiatry and Clinical Neuroscience, 4,* 270–279.

Martin, A., Heyes, M.P., Salazar, A.M., Law, W.A., and Williams, J. (1993). Impaired motor-skill learning, slowed reaction time, and elevated cerebrospinal fluid quinolinic acid in a subgroup of HIV-infected individuals. *Neuropsychology, 7,* 149–157.

McArthur, J.C., Becker, P.S., Parisi, J.E., Trapp, B., Selnes, O.A., Cornblath, D.R., Balakrishnan, J., Griffin, J.W., and Price, D. (1989). Neuropathological changes in early HIV-1 dementia. *Annals of Neurology, 26,* 681–684.

Membreno, L., Irony, I., Dere, W., Klein, R., Biglieri, E.G., and Cobb, E. (1987). Adrenocortical function in acquired immunodeficiency syndrome. *Journal of Clinical Endocrinology and Metabolism, 65,* 482–487.

Merenich, J.A., McDermott, M.T., Asp, A.A., Harrison, S.M., and Kidd, G.S. (1990). Evidence of endocrine involvement early in the course of human immunodeficiency virus infection. *Journal of Clinical Endocrinology and Metabolism, 70,* 566–571.

Murray, E.A., Rausch, D.M., Lendvay, J., Sharer, L.R., and Eiden, L.E. (1992). Cognitive and motor impairments associated with SIV infection in rhesus monkeys. *Science, 255,* 1246–1249.

Navia, B.A., Cho, E.-S., Petito, C.K., and Price, R.W. (1986a). The AIDS dementia complex: II. Neuropathology. *Annals of Neurology, 19,* 525–535.

Navia, B.A., Jordan, B.D., and Price, R.W. (1986b). The AIDS dementia complex. I. Clinical features. *Annals of Neurology, 19,* 517–524.

Oberfield, S.E., Kairam, R., Bakshi, S., Bamji, M., Bhushan, V., Mayes, D., and Levine, L.S. (1990). Steroid response to adrenocorticotropin stimulation in children with human immunodeficiency virus infection. *Journal of Clinical Endocrinology and Metabolism, 70,* 578–581.

Olenik, C., and Meyer, D.K. (1990). Effect of partial removal of frontal or parietal bone on concentrations of mRNAs coding for preprocholecystokinin and preprosomatostatin in rat neocortex. *Neuropeptides, 15,* 115–121.

Price, R.W., and Brew, B.J. (1988). The AIDS dementia complex. *Journal of Infectious Diseases, 158,* 1079–1083.

Price, R.W., Brew, B., Sidtis, J., Rosenblum, M., Scheck, A.C., and Cleary, P. (1988). The brain in AIDS: central nervous system HIV-1 infection and AIDS dementia complex. *Science, 239,* 586–592.

Price, R.W., and Sidtis, J.J. (1990). Early HIV infection and the AIDS dementia complex. *Neurology, 40,* 323–326.

Pulliam, L., Herndier, B.G., Tang, N.M., and McGrath, M.S. (1990). Human immunodeficiency virus-infected macrophages produce soluble factors that cause histological and neurochemical alterations in cultured human brains. *Journal of Clinical Investigation, 87,* 503–512.

Rausch, D.M., Heyes, M.P., Murray, E.A., Lendvay, J., Sharer, L.R., Ward, J.M., Rehm, S., Nohr, D., Weihe, E., and Eiden, L.E. (in press). Cytopathologic and neurochemical correlations of progression to motor/cognitive impairment in SIV-infected rhesus monekys. *Journal of Neuropathology and Experimental Neurology.*

Saperstein, A., Brand, H., Audhya, T., Nabriski, D., Hutchinson, B., Rosenzweig, S., and Hollander, C.S. (1992). Interleukin 1β mediates stress-induced immunosuppression via corticotropin-releasing factor. *Endocrinology, 130,* 152–158.

Sapolsky, R., Rivier, C., Yamamoto, G., Plotsky, P., and Vale, W. (1987). Interleukin-1 stimulates the secretion of hypothalamic corticotropin-releasing factor. *Science, 238,* 522–524.

Scarborough, D.E. (1990). Somatostatin regulation by cytokines. *Metabolism, 39,* 108–111.

Schuitemaker, H., Kootstra, N.A., de Goede, R.E.Y., de Wolf, F., Miedema, F., and Tersmette, M. (1991). Monocytotropic human immunodeficiency virus type 1 (HIV-1) variants detectable in all stages of HIV-1 infection lack T-cell line tropism and syncytium-inducing ability in primary T-cell culture. *Journal of Virology, 65*, 356–363.

Sharer, L.R., Baskin, G.B., Cho, E., Murphey-Corb, M., Blumberg, B.M., and Epstein, L.G. (1988). Comparison of simian immunodeficiency virus and human immunodeficiency virus encephalitides in the immature host. *Annals of Neurology, 23*(Suppl), S108–S112.

Sharer, L.R., Michaels, J., Murphey-Corb, M., Hu, F.-S., Kuebler, D.J., Martin, L.N., and Baskin, G.B. (1991). Serial pathogenesis study of SIV brain infection. *Journal of Medical Primatology, 20*, 211–217.

Sharma, D.P., Zink, M.C., Anderson, M., Adams, R., Clements, J.E., Joag, S.V., and Narayan, O. (1992). Derivation of neurotropic simian immunodeficiency virus from exclusively lymphocytetropic parental virus; pathogenesis of infection in macaques. *Journal of Virology, 66*, 3550–3556.

Simon, M.A., Chalifoux, L.V., and Ringler, D.J. (1992). Pathologic features of SIV-induced disease and the association of macrophage infection with disease evolution. *AIDS Research and Human Retroviruses, 8*, 327–337.

Snider, W.D., Simpson, D.M., Nielsen, S., Gold, J.W.M., Metroka, C.E., and Posner, J.B. (1983). Neurological complications of acquired immunodeficiency syndrome. Analysis of 50 patients. *Annals of Neurology, 14*, 403–418.

Sternberg, E.M., Hill, J.M., Chrousos, G.P., Kamilaris, T., Listwak, S.J., Gold, P.W., and Wilder, R.L. (1989). Inflammatory mediator-induced hypothalamic-pituitary-adrenal axis activation is defective in streptococcal cell wall arthritis-susceptible Lewis rats. *Proceedings of the National Academy of Science USA, 86*, 2374–2378.

Sundar, S.K., Cierpial, M.A., Kamaraju, L.S., Long, S., Hsieh, S., Lorenz, C., Aaron, M., Ritchie, J.C., and Weiss, J.M. (1991). Human immunodeficiency virus glycoprotein (gp120) infused into rat brain induces interleukin 1 to elevate pituitary-adrenal activity and decrease peripheral cellular immune responses. *Proceedings of the National Academy of Science USA, 88*, 11246–11250.

Tersmette, M., Gruters, R.A., de Wolf, F., de Goede, R.E.Y., Lange, J.M.A., Schellekens, P.T.A., Goudsmit, J., Huisman, H.G., and Miedema, F. (1989). Evidence for a role of virulent human immunodeficiency virus (HIV) variants in the pathogenesis of acquired immunodeficiency syndrome: Studies on sequential HIV isolates. *Journal of Virology, 63*, 2118–2125.

Tornatore, C., Chandra, R., and Major, E.O. (1993). Personal communication.

Tyor, W.R., Glass, J.D., Griffin, J.W., Becker, P.S., McArthur, J.C., Bezman, L., and Griffin, D.E. (1992). Cytokine expression in the brain during the acquired immunodeficiency syndrome. *Annals of Neurology, 31*, 349–360.

Villette, J.M., Bourin, P., Doinel, C., Mansour, I., Fiet, J., Boudou, P., Dreux, C., Roue, R., Debord, M., and Levi, F. (1990). Circadian variations in plasma levels of hypophyseal, adrenocortical and testicular hormones in men infected with human immunodeficiency virus. *Journal of Clinical Endocrinology and Metabolism, 70*, 572–577.

Wang, J., Aigner, T., and Mishkin, M. (1990). Effects of neostriatal lesions on visual habit formation in rhesus monkeys. *Society of Neuroscience Abstracts, 16*, 617.

Watanabe, M., Reimann, K.A., DeLong, P.A., Liu, T., Fisher, R.A., and Letvin, N.L. (1989). Effect of recombinant soluble CD4 in rhesus monkeys infected with simian immunodeficiency virus of macaques. *Nature, 337*, 267–270.

World Health Organization. (1990). World Health Organization consultation on the neuropsychiatric aspects of HIV-1 infection. Geneva, January, 11–13. *AIDS, 4*, 935–936.

Wiley, C.A., Masliah, E., Morey, M., Lemere, C., DeTeresa, R., Grafe, M., Hansen, L., and Terry, R. (1991). Neocortical damage during HIV infection. *Annals of Neurology, 29*, 651–657.

Wyand, M.S., Ringler, D.J., Naidu, Y., Mattmuller, M., Chalifoux, L.V., Sehgal, P.K., Daniel, M.D., Desrosiers, R.C., and King, N.W. (1989). Cellular localization of simian immunodeficiency virus in lymphoid tissues. II. *In situ* hybridization. *American Journal of Pathology, 134*, 385–393.

Yamada, M., Zurbriggen, A., Oldstone, M.B.A., and Fujinami, R.S. (1991). Common immunologic determinant between human immunodeficiency virus type 1 gp41 and astrocytes. *Journal of Virology, 65*, 1370–1375.

Zhang, J.-Y., Martin, L.N., Watson, E.A., Montelaro, R.C., West, M., Epstein, L., and Murphey-Corb, M. (1988). Simian immunodeficiency virus/Delta-induced immunodeficiency disease in rhesus monkeys: relation of antibody response and antigenemia. *Journal of Infectious Diseases, 158*, 1277–1286.

Epilogue: Neuropsychological Investigations: The Challenge of HIV

ALEX MARTIN and IGOR GRANT

Our main goal for this volume was to provide an overview of current knowledge and thinking about the neuropsychological consequences of human immunodeficiency virus (HIV) infection. Given the fast-paced, dynamic nature of HIV research, the task has been a challenging one. The chapters in Part I reviewed medical, immunological, neurological, and neuroradiological information. These chapters thus provided a framework for the discussions of neuropsychological issues and findings presented in Part II. As might be expected from a survey of a rapidly evolving field, the contributors to the second section of the book raised more questions than they were able to answer. Thus, it should not be surprising that a central theme of the book is that progress in understanding the neuropsychological consequences of HIV infection will depend on coming to grips with a number of thorny conceptual problems and methodological issues.

Why has this been the case? At first, the task of describing the natural history of HIV-related neurocognitive change seemed straightforward. After all, many neuropsychology researchers had been engaged in the study of cognitive dysfunction during the early stages of Alzheimer's disease, which can be complicated by considerable diagnostic uncertainty. With HIV infection, however, the situation promised to be quite different. Here we had a definite biological marker (HIV serostatus) and thus would know with certainty who was at risk for CNS pathology and who was not. Moreover, what seemed to be valid markers of disease progression had already been identified. All that remained was to determine how many HIV+ subjects were impaired, what kinds of tasks they were having difficulty with, and how the picture would change as a function of treatment and/or disease progression.

Of course, things did not turn out to be quite so simple. Rather, the neuropsychology of HIV presented, and continues to present, a formidable challenge to our research capability, ingenuity, and creativity. To begin with, it was apparent from the outset that HIV-infected individuals might perform poorly on neuropsychological measures for a variety of reasons. Some of these reasons could be attributed to generalized, nonspecific effects of disease such as fatigue, malaise, or simply "not feeling well." Other problems could stem from the psychosocial consequences of knowing that one was infected with this deadly virus. Reactions of depression and anxiety would be perfectly understandable but nonetheless an unwelcome complication for test score interpretation. Whether significant mood changes would occur, and whether they would have an adverse impact on test performance, was not known.

In addition, researchers had to confront the possibility that certain segments of the infected population may be more likely than the general population to have histories of preinfection risk factors such as psychiatric illness (Atkinson et al., 1988), learning disabilities, head injury, and drug or alcohol abuse (Marder et al., 1992). How do we control for the influence of these confounding variables? If we simply excluded subjects, might we run the risk of creating a study population that bore little resemblance to those actually infected? Could these subject variables actually predispose certain individuals to develop HIV-related central nervous system (CNS) dysfunction or make such dysfunction more detectable by lowering the threshold for impairment?

Recent evidence suggests that the largest group of infected individuals in the United States (i.e., homosexual men) may have brain-related biological differences in comparison to the heterosexual population (e.g., Le Vay, 1991). Do homosexual subjects, for whatever reason, have brains that differ in important ways from the brains of subjects from whom our knowledge of functional brain organization has been derived? If so, would neuropathology or neuronal dysfunction produce unique and unexpected patterns of impairment? Clearly, special control groups would be needed. But, who should be included, and how many groups would be necessary?

One solution to the problem of disease-related factors (including both the systemic factors listed above and CNS factors such as the development of brain tumors and opportunistic infections) would be to study only early-stage, medically asymptomatic patients. An additional rationale for focusing on this group was provided by societal concerns. If millions of people are infected and this infection could occur in the brain, then we need to know whether cognitive dysfunction occurs in otherwise outwardly healthy individuals. And, perhaps most important, we need to know whether this dysfunction is clinically significant. However, if the number of cognitively impaired individuals increases as the disease progresses, then focusing on early stages of infection would be expected to decrease the likelihood of finding impaired subjects. Moreover, one would also expect that the extent of impairment, if any, would be more subtle in early-stage patients than in those with more advanced illness or acquired immunodeficiency syndrome (AIDS). Thus, we were confronted with a signal detection problem. Could subtle degrees of impairment be detected? If so, what types of evidence would be needed to attribute this dysfunction to HIV rather than to myriad other possible causes?

The ability to detect dysfunction is dependent, of course, on the sensitivity and reliability of the tests employed. But exactly what types of tests should be used? And how would we know whether they were sufficiently sensitive to the types of problems that may be associated with this disease? This problem might be particularly acute when the study design called for the assessment of hundreds of subjects. Such studies often cannot afford the time and personnel required for a lengthy evaluation. As a result, investigators might be forced to make do with a best-guess estimate of tests to form a screening instrument with unproved sensitivity.

Perhaps the ideal approach would be to begin with a large battery of measures, including well-standardized neuropsychological instruments and experimental procedures, that would assess a wide range of functions and abilities. But this mega-battery approach is not without its own set of problems. How, for example, do we define impairment? If, on the one hand, we rely on a single global index, we may run the risk of being unable to detect dysfunction because one or more abnormal scores may be overwhelmed by a majority of normal scores. If, on the other hand, we treat each measure separately, we run a strong risk of committing a type I error. How does the likelihood of finding an abnormal score change as a function of the number of tests employed, the correlation between the tests, and the cutoff established for each test? How does the criterion for establishing impairment on a particular measure change as a function of repeated testings?

These and other potential problems highlighted the need to obtain concurrent biological data that could provide external validation for any observed behavioral and/or cognitive dysfunction. After all, it is one thing to demonstrate that some HIV+ individuals have abnormally slowed response times and quite another to show that this slowing is significantly related to the degree of brain atrophy on magnetic resonance imaging (Levin et al., 1990) or concentrations of a neurotoxin in cerebrospinal fluid (Martin et al., 1992, 1993). Additional measures are clearly needed, but what should they be? Because we are dealing with a disease that attacks the immune system, it seemed reasonable to focus on immunological parameters (e.g., CD4 cell counts or percentages; CD4/CD8 cell ratio). Most studies, however, have failed to find a relationship between these parameters and neuropsychological functioning. In fact, the usefulness of the CD4 count as an indicator of the stage of disease or degree of illness is now being questioned (Cohen, 1992). Perhaps a better approach would be to concentrate on neurological measures (e.g., brain imaging, electrophysiological, or cerebrospinal fluid parameters), yet the results to date have been rather inconclusive.

Finally, perhaps more than any other disorder in recent history, HIV has forced us to pay particular attention to the interpretation and implications of our findings. Because of the social stigma surrounding HIV-infected individuals, special care must be taken to ensure that findings are not misinterpreted. This consideration has forced us to come to grips with the differing meanings of *impairment*. Poor performance on certain measures might have great significance for localizing abnormal functioning in the brain but no clinical significance, while poor performance on other measures may indicate impairments that strongly and adversely affect real-world behavior. The neuropsychology of HIV has motivated us to think seriously about the distinctions between clinically insignificant but

TABLE E–1. HIV-1 Associated Cognitive Disorders

As Defined by Grant and Atkinson	*As Proposed by the AAN Working Group*
HIV-1-Associated Neurocognitive Disorders **A. HIV-1-Associated Dementia (HAD)**	*HIV-1-Associated Cognitive/Motor Complex* **A. Probable[a] HIV-1-Associated Dementia Complex**
1. *Marked acquired impairment in cognitive functioning,* involving at least two ability domains (e.g., memory, attention); typically the impairment is in multiple domains, especially in learning of new information, slowed information processing, and defective attention/concentration. The cognitive impairment can be ascertained by history, mental status examination, or neuropsychological testing.	1. *Acquired abnormality in at least two of the following cognitive abilities* (present for at least 1 month): attention/concentration; speed of information processing; abstraction/reasoning; visuospatial skills; memory/learning; speech/language. *Cognitive dysfunction causes impairment in work or activities of daily living.*
2. The cognitive impairment produces *marked interference with day-to-day functioning* (work, home life, social activities).	2. *At least one of the following:* a. Acquired abnormality in motor functioning. b. Decline in motivation or emotional control or change in social behavior.
3. The marked cognitive impairment has been present for at least 1 month.	3. Absence of clouding of consciousness during a period long enough to establish presence of #1.
4. The pattern of cognitive impairment *does not meet criteria for delirium* (e.g., clouding of consciousness is not a prominent feature); or, if delirium is present, criteria for dementia need to have been met on a prior examination when delirium was not present.	4. Absence of another cause of the above cognitive, motor, or behavioral symptoms or signs (e.g., active CNS opportunistic infection or malignancy, psychiatric disorders, substance abuse).
5. There is *no evidence of another, pre-existing etiology* that could explain the dementia (e.g., other CNS infection, CNS neoplasm, cerebrovascular disease, preexisting neurological disease, or severe substance abuse compatible with CNS disorder).	
B. HIV-1-Associated Mild Neurocognitive Disorder (MND)	**B. Probable[a] HIV-1-Associated Minor Cognitive/Motor Disorder**

1. Acquired impairment in cognitive functioning, involving at least two ability domains, documented by performance of at least 0.5 standard deviations below age-education-appropriate norms on standardized neuropsychological tests. The neuropsychological assessment must survey at least the following abilities: verbal/language; attention/speeded processing; abstraction; memory (learning, recall); complex perceptual-motor performance; motor skills.	1. Acquired cognitive/motor/behavior abnormalities (must have both a and b):
	a. At least two of the following symptoms present for at least 1 month, verified by a reliable history:
	  i. impaired attention or concentration
	  ii. mental slowing
	  iii. impaired memory
	  iv. slowed movements
	  v. incoordination
	b. Acquired cognitive/motor abnormality verified by clinical neurologic examination or neuropsychological testing.

TABLE E–1. (continued)

As Defined by Grant and Atkinson	As Proposed by the AAN Working Group

2. The cognitive impairment produces at least mild interference in daily functioning (at least one of the following):
  a. Self-report of reduced mental acuity, inefficiency in work, homemaking, or social functioning.
  b. Observation by knowledgeable others that the individual has undergone at least mild decline in mental acuity, with resultant inefficiency in work, homemaking, or social functioning.
	2. Cognitive/motor/behavioral abnormality causes mild impairment of work or activities of daily living (objectively verifiable or by report of a key informant).

3. The cognitive impairment has been present for at least 1 month.	3. Does not meet criteria for HIV-1-associated dementia complex or HIV-1-associated myelopathy.
4. Does not meet criteria for delirium or dementia	4. Absence of another cause of the above cognitive/motor/behavioral abnormality (e.g., active CNS opportunistic infection or malignancy, psychiatric disorders, substance abuse).
5. There is no evidence of another preexisting cause for the MND.[b]	

[a] The designation *probable* is used when criteria are met, there is no other likely cause, and data are complete. The designation *possible* is used if another potential etiology is present whose contribution is unclear, or where a dual diagnosis is possible, or when the evaluation is not complete.

[b] If the individual with suspected MND also satisfies criteria for a *major depressive episode* or *substance dependence*, the diagnosis of MND should be deferred to a subsequent examination conducted at a time when the major depression has remitted or at least 1 month has elapsed following termination of dependent-substance use.

Note: This table also appears in Grant, I., and Atkinson, J. H. (in press).

theoretically meaningful dysfunction, clinically significant focal deficits, and dementia. It has also highlighted the need for systematic study of the relationship between deficits on neuropsychological tests and real-world functioning.

These are a sampling of the types of problems confronted by the investigators who have contributed chapters to this book. Although their efforts have been specifically directed to the study of HIV, the lessons they have learned should have wide applicability to a host of methodological issues concerning the early detection of abnormality, longitudinal assessment, and the determination of clinical significance.

Where does the field stand at present? The first wave of research, which was dominated by questions concerning the presence and prevalence of neuropsychological dysfunction in otherwise asymptomatic HIV+ individuals, has run its course. In our view, the currently available evidence suggests that there is a subgroup of subjects in the relatively early stages of infection (perhaps 15–20% of persons at CDC stages II–III) who experience mild neurocognitive disorder despite the fact that their medical disease is not very far advanced. We acknowledge, however, that this is not a universally held view. In contrast, there is little question that persons at CDC stage IV are at substantially increased risk of mild neurocognitive disorder, with rates of 25–40% regularly reported. The prevalence of HIV-associated dementia is much less, perhaps 5–15%. It should be noted, however, that these estimates may apply only to Western societies. In regions of the world where antiretroviral treatments are unavailable, and where nutritional deprivation and other diseases can alter the clinical picture, the rates may be substantially higher. An important direction for future clinical research will be to develop culturally relevant neuropsychological test batteries that can be applied in developing countries.

The actual pathogenesis of HIV brain disease remains poorly understood. However, in view of the fact that neurons appear to be rarely infected, a "bystander effect" is strongly suspected. This means that neurons may reside in a "toxic" metabolic/neuromodulator environment as a result of abnormal products being generated by infected cells nearby. If this is so, it should be possible to modify the course of brain disease associated with HIV through treatments aimed either at blocking virus replication itself or at interfering with the effects of these by-products. Preliminary data from neuropsychological and brain-imaging studies indicate that there may indeed by reversibility with azidothymidine (AZT) treatment (see Chapter 14). Researchers are starting to explore the roles of other treatments such as $CD4^+$ receptor blockers (e.g., peptide T) or calcium channel blockers (e.g., nimodipine). Future research will determine whether mild neurocognitive disorder inevitably progresses to a more severe stage in persons who live long enough, or whether a static, fluctuating, or improving course can be identified in some persons.

Although there may be disagreement about the prevalence and clinical significance of early-stage, HIV-related cognitive impairment, there is a clear consensus that neurocognitive disorder is an important and sometimes disabling complication of HIV infection. As a final note, we would like to stress that to advance clinical care and to improve communication among researchers, it will be important to differentiate clearly two levels of cognitive dysfunction. Diagnosis of the more severe form, *HIV-associated dementia (HAD)*, should be reserved for those individuals who have multiple cognitive deficits of sufficient severity to interfere with their day-to-day functioning (see Chapter 5). Such a designation would be compatible with DSM-III-R and the proposed terminology of the American Association of Neurology (AAN) Task Group recommendations (see Chapter 3). The criteria for HAD in use at the San Diego HNRC are presented in the Table E–1.

The label *mild neurocognitive disorder* should be reserved for those individuals who experience subtle cognitive deficits in two or more areas but in whom the severity of such deficits is insufficient to interfere markedly with ordinary life function. The San Diego HNRC criteria for MND are also presented in Table E–1. These criteria are conceptually similar to the AAN Work Group's recommendations (see Chapter 3) but may be more reliable since they employ neuropsychological test results.

References

Atkinson, J.H., Grant, I., Kennedy, C.J., Richman, D.D., Spector, S.A., and McCutchan, J.A. (1988). Prevalence of psychiatric disorders among men infected with the human immunodeficiency virus. *Archives of General Psychiatry, 45*, 859–864.

Cohen, J. (1992). Searching for markers on the AIDS trail. *Science, 258*, 388–390.

Grant, I., and Atkinson, J.H. (in press). Psychobiology of HIV Infection. In H.I. Kaplan and B.J. Sadock, eds., *Comprehensive Textbook of Psychiatry/VI.* Baltimore: Williams and Wilkins.

Le Vay, S. (1991). A difference in hypothalamic structure between heterosexual and homosexual men. *Science, 253*, 1034–1037.

Levin, H.S., Williams, D.H., Boruncki, M.J., Hillman, G.R., Williams, J.B., Guinto, F.C., Amparo, E.G., Crow, W.N., and Pollard, R.B. (1990). Magnetic resonance imaging and neuropsychological findings in human immunodeficiency virus infection. *Journal of Acquired Immune Deficiency Syndromes, 3*, 752–762.

Marder, K., Stern, Y., Malouf, R., Tang, M., Bell, K., Dooneief, G., El Sadr, W., Goldstein, S., Gorman, J., Richards, M., Sano, M., Sorrell, S., Todak, G., Williams, J., Ehrhardt, A., and Mayeux, R. (1992). Neurological and neuropsychological manifestations of HIV infection in intravenous drug users without AIDS: Relationship to head injury. *Archives of Neurology, 49*, 1169–1175.

Martin, A., Heyes, M.P., Salazar, A.M., Kampen, D.L., Williams, J., Law, W.A., Coats, M.E., and Markey, S.P. (1992). Progressive slowing of reaction time and increasing cerebrospinal fluid concentrations of quinolinic acid in HIV-infected individuals. *Journal of Neuropsychiatry and Clinical Neuroscience, 4*, 270–279.

Martin, A., Heyes, M.P., Salazar, A.M., Law, W.A., and Williams, J. (1993). Impaired motor-skill learning, slowed reaction time, and elevated cerebrospinal fluid quinolinic acid in a subgroup of HIV-infected individuals. *Neuropsychology, 7*, 149–157.

Index

Italic letter *f* indicates a figure. Italic letter *t* denotes a table.